Voluntary Arrangements

Voluntary Arrangements

Edward Bailey MA, LLB (Cantab)

One of Her Majesty's Circuit Judges

LexisNexis™ UK

Members of the LexisNexis Group worldwide

United Kingdom	LexisNexis UK, a Division of Reed Elsevier (UK) Ltd, Halsbury House, 35 Chancery Lane, LONDON, WC2A 1EL, and 4 Hill Street, EDINBURGH EH2 3JZ
Argentina	LexisNexis Argentina, BUENOS AIRES
Australia	LexisNexis Butterworths, CHATSWOOD, New South Wales
Austria	LexisNexis Verlag ARD Orac GmbH & Co KG, VIENNA
Canada	LexisNexis Butterworths, MARKHAM, Ontario
Chile	LexisNexis Chile Ltda, SANTIAGO DE CHILE
Czech Republic	Nakladatelství Orac sro, PRAGUE
France	Editions du Juris-Classeur SA, PARIS
Germany	LexisNexis Deutschland GmbH, FRANKFURT, MUNSTER
Hong Kong	LexisNexis Butterworths, HONG KONG
Hungary	HVG-Orac, BUDAPEST
India	LexisNexis Butterworths, NEW DELHI
Ireland	Butterworths (Ireland) Ltd, DUBLIN
Italy	Giuffrè Editore, MILAN
Malaysia	Malayan Law Journal Sdn Bhd, KUALA LUMPUR
New Zealand	LexisNexis Butterworths, WELLINGTON
Poland	Wydawnictwo Prawnicze LexisNexis, WARSAW
Singapore	LexisNexis Butterworths, SINGAPORE
South Africa	LexisNexis Butterworths, DURBAN
Switzerland	Stämpfli Verlag AG, BERNE
USA	LexisNexis, DAYTON, Ohio

A CIP Catalogue record for this book is available from the British Library.

ISBN 0 406 94600 0

Typeset by Doyle & Co, Colchester.

Printed by Cromwell Press, Trowbridge, Wilts.

Foreword

The law of voluntary arrangements for individuals has for a long time been the Rip van Winkle of the legal world. However, after seventy-two years asleep, it awoke to new activity in the Insolvency Act 1986. At the same time, equivalent provisions for companies were enacted for the first time. Since then, the law of voluntary arrangements has been the focus of much attention by lawyers, economists and politicians. Various amendments to the new statutory schemes have been made. During the same period, the EC Bankruptcy Convention, which was first conceived in the 1960s, slowly evolved into the EC Regulation on Insolvency Proceedings. This Regulation took effect in 2002 and it is principally concerned with jurisdiction and recognition. In sum, the law of voluntary arrangements has in recent years undergone great change.

The reform of the law relating to voluntary arrangements has been influenced by the modern approach of reducing the creditor orientation of our insolvency law and of seeking to enhance debt recovery through the rescue and rehabilitation of debtors, whether individual or corporate. At the same time there has been a major shift in policy to enable parties to bring about voluntary arrangements without the intervention of the court. This places a substantial onus on professional advisers to an insolvent party. The courts will expect all professional advisers to discharge their obligations in full compliance with the law and their professional responsibilities. The loosening of judicial control on voluntary arrangements is not a signal for cutting corners or ignoring procedural safeguards for the benefit of creditors. It is a cause for heightened awareness of the law and of the need for compliance with professional standards.

Like any legislation, the new law is not written as a narrative exposition of the subject with examples and illustrations. It simply records the changes in the law in as precise a manner as possible. Accordingly, there is a need for a book that explains the complex statutory scheme in straightforward terms. That is what this book so ably does. It is aimed at practitioners. If the reader is concerned with such questions as whether an interim order protecting an individual debtor while an arrangement is prepared can be made or extended, or how a company wishing to propose a company voluntary arrangement can obtain a moratorium under the new provisions of the Insolvency Act 2000, what companies are eligible to obtain such a moratorium and what the effect of such a moratorium is, or whether, in the case of individuals, there should be an after-acquired assets clause dealing with insurance policies in the event of the debtor's death, and so on, this book will provide the answers in a comprehensive and uncluttered way. It animates a complicated and technical subject with practical insight.

I congratulate the author for writing this book so promptly after the enactment of the Enterprise Act 2002, and the publishers on the clear manner in which the text is presented.

The Rt Hon Lady Justice Arden DBE

The Royal Courts of Justice
Strand
London WC2A 2LL

Preface

With approved arrangements exceeding 7,000 a year the Individual Voluntary Arrangement has proved to be one of the big successes of the 1986 Insolvency legislation. The IVA is of course of primary interest to the debtors, who keep out of bankruptcy, and the creditors who, usually, receive a higher dividend that they would if the debtor became insolvent. It is also of interest to the managers of the administration of civil justice. For with greater confidence in insolvency practitioners than generally existed before 1986 the IVA procedure has moved on from the formal structure envisaged in the Insolvency Act 1986. The insolvency practitioner rather than the court manages the procedure from the initial proposal to the decision of the creditors' meeting. The court is left with what is essentially a monitoring rôle.

The government has declared a resolve to promote a 'rescue culture' in the economy which extends to corporate as well as individual business failures. The manisfestation of this resolve is the Insolvency Act 2000, which came into force on 1 January 2003, and the Enterprise Act 2002, yet to be implemented. The Company Voluntary Arrangement has not had the success of its individual counterpart. Approvals of CVAs have been running at a little over 500 a year. And while the difference in the implications of the death of the debtor in each case are likely always to result in more IVAs than CVAs, it is the aim of the Insolvency Act 2000 to increase the numbers of the latter. The introduction of the moratorium, a procedure which builds on the practice in IVA and which requires no direct court involvement, should begin the furtherance of this aim. The amendments to the law of administration and administrative receiverships introduced in the Enterprise Act 2002 should carry it further.

The voluntary arrangement also extends to partnerships, and although in many cases the interlocking IVA/CVA will be the preferred route where the members of a partnership face insolvency the PVA will in appropriate cases be an important option for such a partnership.

The aim of this book is to give the reader, whether legal practitioner or insolvency practitioner, a comprehensive guide to all the law of voluntary arrangements in a succinct but readable style. Thanks to the immediacy of law reporting on the web I have been able to include in the text a number of decisions of the Court of Appeal and the Chancery Division which have yet to find their way into the law reports. The appendices include all the relevant statutory materials, with precedents for proposals, the R3 standard conditions of arrangement, fast becoming the first choice for practitioners, and procedural tables cross referenced to the text.

I would like to thank my publishers for their support and speed of production.

I have endeavoured to state the law as at 1 March 2003. I have however included in the text (suitably noted) the amendments which are to be introduced to the voluntary arrangement regime by the Enterprise Act 2002.

EB

London

March 2003

Contents

Appendices

Table of statutes

Table of statutory instruments

Table of European legislation

Table of cases

A

B

C

D

E

F

G

S

T

V

W

X

Chapter 1

Introduction

1.1 Historical background. The concept of the voluntary arrangement was introduced by the Insolvency Act 1986 ('IA 1986') following the recommendations of the Review Committee on Insolvency Law and Practice[1]. The aim was to introduce procedures for both individuals and companies whereby a debtor facing financial difficulties could enter into binding arrangements with creditors which would obviate the need for formal insolvency. The procedures which were then available for making such arrangements were largely ineffective. For individuals there were the provisions of the Deeds of Arrangement Act 1914. A variety of arrangements might be entered into between the individual debtor and his creditors which required registration with the Department of Trade and Industry to be valid[2]. The essential weakness of such deeds is that they cannot bind non-assenting creditors who remain free to petition for the debtor's bankruptcy. Indeed, under the law prior to the coming into force of IA 1986 any creditor of the individual debtor could rely on the making of a deed of arrangement as an act of bankruptcy on which to base his petition. The Deeds of Arrangement Act 1914 was therefore seldom used. It still remains in force, however[3]. For companies, procedures existed under the Companies Acts by which a corporate debtor could enter into binding arrangements with its creditors, but they were not suitable in cases where arrangements had to be put in place with some speed in an attempt to rescue a company facing formal insolvency[4].

1 The Review Committee on Insolvency Law and Practice (Cmnd 8558), whose report, ('the Cork Report') was published in June 1982. The relevant discussion in the Cork Report is at paras 400–430.

2 For Deeds of Arrangement generally see: Berry, Bailey and Schaw Miller *Personal Insolvency* (3rd edn) ch 31.

3 There are currently 12 deeds of arrangement.

4 The options under CA 1985 are:

(1) A compromise or arrangements under CA 1985, ss 425–427 under which a compromise or arrangement between the company and its creditors or any class of creditors might be reached or scheme of reconstruction of any company or companies, or the amalgamation of any two companies might be effected. The proposed scheme under these provisions has to be approved by a majority in number representing three-fourths in value of the creditors or class of creditors or members or class of members attending the meeting, and the scheme thus approved must then obtain the sanction of the court.

(2) A reconstruction under CA 1985, s 582, now replaced by IA 1986, s 110 whereby the liquidator of a company which is proposed to be, or is being, wound up voluntarily may transfer the whole or any part of the company's undertaking. These provisions related only to solvent companies under CA 1985, but have now been extended to

creditors' voluntary liquidations by IA 1986. In the case of a members' winding-up the liquidator must obtain the sanction of a special resolution and in a creditors' winding-up the sanction of the liquidation committee or the court.

(3) An arrangement under CA 1985, s 601 between a company about to be, or in the course of being, wound up and its creditors. Such an arrangement requires an extraordinary resolution to bind the company and to bind the creditors the agreement of three-fourths both in number and value. It is further open to any creditor or contributory to appeal to the court against the arrangement within three weeks of its completion.

None of these options were in common use at the time of the Cork Report, and indeed the s 601 arrangement was described as a 'dead letter'.

1.2 The statutory scheme. The essential element of a voluntary arrangement is the creditors' meeting. The debtor makes a proposal to the creditors who consider its terms, sometimes agreeing modifications with the debtor, and who then vote on the proposal in accordance with the rules. Where the debtor is a company it is the directors who make the proposal which is put to meetings of both creditors and the company. If different results are obtained from these meetings the decision of the creditors prevails. Essentially, provided that (1) at least 75% of the creditors by value approve the proposal and (2) the proposal is not opposed by more than 50% of the creditors who are not associates[1] of the debtor, then the voluntary arrangement is approved[2]. Once approved the voluntary arrangement binds all the creditors of the debtor entitled to vote at the creditors' meeting as from the time of the meeting, whether they voted in favour of the proposal and whether they attended the meeting or not. Since 1 January 2003 even creditors who were unaware of the proposal and the holding of the creditors' meeting are bound by the voluntary arrangement once it has been approved at the creditors' meeting[3].

The legal analysis of the approved arrangement is that there is a consensual agreement between the debtor and all the creditors entitled to vote at the creditors' meeting; all these creditors are treated as consenting parties to the arrangement under the statutory hypothesis[4] whichever way they voted, if at all, and whatever their attitude to the voluntary arrangement[5]. As all creditors are treated as having consented to the voluntary arrangement questions as to the consequences of the arrangement on the rights of creditors and third parties are to be determined on a proper construction of the terms of the arrangement[6].

Time is often of the essence in the establishment of a voluntary arrangement. A debtor who needs to make an arrangement with his creditors will usually have to act with expedition. IA 1986 affords protection to the debtor from legal process and execution while the proposal is formulated and put to the creditors. This is by way of moratorium for the corporate debtor and interim order for the individual debtor. But this protection is available only for a short time. The procedure cannot be used, or misused, to stay the hands of creditors for any lengthy period. Equally important is the time available to creditors to challenge an approved arrangement. All parties bound by a voluntary arrangement need to know where they stand as soon as possible, free from the uncertainty which results from there being a right to challenge the arrangement in court. Once a voluntary arrangement is approved the chairman of the creditors' meeting has four days to report to the court[7]. Any application to challenge the approval of the arrangement or the conduct of the creditors' meeting which approved it must be brought within 28 days of this report to the court. This time period cannot be extended in CVAs. There is power to extend the 28-day period in IVAs but it is sparingly used[8]. To protect creditors who were not given notice of the meeting such a creditor has 28 days to challenge the voluntary arrangement from the date on which he became aware of it[9]. It follows that to the extent that there may be one or more creditors who were not given notice of the meeting the parties to the arrangement cannot be certain that it will continue undisturbed once 28 days after the chairman's report to the court has passed. This is unavoidable, but the existence of such creditors should rarely be encountered in practice.

1 For the definition of 'associate' see IA 1986, s 435, Appendix 1.
2 See para 6.10 below.
3 IA 1986, s 5(2) (CVA without moratorium), Sch A1, para 37(2) (CVA with moratorium), s 260(2) (IVA), as amended by IA 2000, see para 9.1 below.
4 Imposed by IA 1986, ss 5(2), Sch A1, paras 37(2), 260(2)
5 See *Johnson v Davies* [1999] Ch 117 at 138, CA, approved in *Raja v Rubin and Goodman* [2000] Ch 274, CA. As both these cases pre-date the changes introduced by IA 2000, the principle is there framed in terms that there is a consensual agreement between the debtor and all the creditors who *had notice of and* were entitled to vote at the meeting. The words in italics now need to be deleted.
6 See paras 9.1, 9.2 below.
7 IR 1986, r 1.24(2) (CVA), r 5.22(3) (IVA) – the report to the court must be made whatever the outcome of the creditors' meeting.
8 See para 7.8 below.
9 IA 1986, s 6(3) (CVA without moratorium), Sch A1, para 38(3) (CVA with moratorium), s 262(3)(b) (IVA).

1.3 Extension of voluntary arrangements to partnerships. Since 1 December 1994, when the Insolvent Partnerships Order 1994 came into force, voluntary arrangements have been extended to partnerships. This is achieved by treating the partnership as if it were a limited liability company, thereby bringing partnerships within the statutory provisions governing CVAs. The introduction of the moratorium in CVAs has been extended to PVAs by virtue of the Insolvent Partnerships (Amendment) (No 2) Order 2002. A PVA will cover the joint debts and assets of the partnership; it will not be concerned with the debts and assets of individual partners. It seems unrealistic to suppose that there will be many if any creditors who will be prepared to accept a composition of their joint debts in a PVA without pursuing their claims against the members of the partnership severally. However, it remains open to an individual or corporate partner to propose an IVA or CVA either by himself, or as one of a group of partners, or all the partners acting together proposing a series of interlocking IVAs/CVAs. Such interlocking arrangements may be made alongside a PVA.

For the purposes of this work, express reference to PVAs will be made only where essential; all references to CVAs will apply to partnerships except where stated[1]. In CVAs the directors are responsible for making the proposal and for providing information to the nominee, both by way of the statement of affairs and in responding to requests for specific further information. The directors may also continue the company's business during a moratorium and, as officers of the company, may be required to attend the creditors' meeting. Quite how any particular partnership conducts its affairs and so meets the obligations which fall on company directors will depend on the partnership deed or other agreement between the members of the partnership. In many instances partnerships have officers who equate to officers of a company. Although it is unlikely that the partnership deed will contain express reference to the manner in which the partnership should act in the event of a proposal for and implementation of a PVA, the clauses governing the management of the partnership's affairs will ordinarily be sufficiently widely drawn to meet any situation arising in PVAs. In the absence of sufficient specific provision in the partnership deed the provisions of the Partnership Act 1890 will apply[2].

1 And see Chapter 13, which deals with partnership voluntary arrangements.
2 See Partnership Act 1890, s 24(8) and para 13.6 below.

1.4 The changes introduced by the Insolvency Act 2000. The Insolvency Act 2000 ('IA 2000'), which came into force on 1 January 2003, introduces a number of changes to the voluntary arrangement regime. Two of these changes will have an immediate impact of significance; two more may prove to be of significance in years to come; the remainder may be seen to be more technical in nature. The first change of immediate significance is the introduction of the CVA moratorium[1]. The absence in IA 1986 as originally enacted of the equivalent in CVAs of the IVA interim order, an order which gives the debtor temporary protection from his creditors while a proposal for a voluntary arrangement is formulated and put to creditors, may be explained by the fact that it was thought CVAs could be prepared and implemented under the protection of an Administration Order. This has indeed happened, but on a much more limited scale than had been hoped. The prime difficulty has been the attitude of the banks, as debenture holders. Quite understandably, the banks have preferred to appoint an administrative receiver to take control of the company's affairs as soon as the position is reached where a company may be considering a CVA. This is a 'problem' with which the government has taken a firm line in the Enterprise Act 2002. Within the more limited confines of the CVA moratorium the matter is dealt with by providing that no administrative receiver may be appointed while a moratorium is in force[2]. A moratorium is available only to small companies[3]. It is obtained without formal application to the court; the directors simply file the necessary documentation in court and the moratorium takes effect[4]. The directors may then continue the company's trading, but are monitored in doing so by the nominee subject to a right of challenge to the court on the part of any person affected by the moratorium. In enacting the necessary legislation Parliament decided to place all the statutory provisions relating to a CVA where a moratorium is obtained in one place, separate from the provisions governing a CVA without a moratorium, even where precisely the same provisions apply. CVAs without a moratorium continue to comprise IA 1986, Pt I. The provisions governing CVAs where a moratorium is or has been in force are to be found in IA 1986, Sch A1[5]. This separation is largely carried through in IR 1986[6], chapter 9 being devoted to the rules applying where a moratorium is or has been in force[7].

The second change of immediate significance is the amendment of the 1986 law, applicable in all cases or CVA or IVA, so that every creditor of the debtor who would have been entitled to vote at the creditors' meeting had he been given notice of it is bound by a voluntary arrangement once approved whether or not he did in fact have notice of the meeting. Previously, only creditors who did in fact have notice of the creditors' meeting were bound to the voluntary arrangement if approved. The change strengthens the voluntary arrangement regime preventing such creditors from petitioning for liquidation or bankruptcy. The position of a creditor who discovers that he is bound to a voluntary arrangement of which he had no knowledge is protected in two ways. First, he has 28 days from the date on which he became aware of the creditors' meeting to apply to the court to challenge that approval. This short time period within which a challenge application may be brought[8] is consistent with the period within which any creditor may bring a challenge after the creditors' meeting[9]. The creditor who discovers late that he is bound by a voluntary arrangement, and his lawyers, will have to move quickly from a standing start to mount a challenge. It may well be that many applications will be issued solely for protective purposes. The second protection afforded the creditor who had no notice of the creditors' meeting, and who discovers the position too late to participate in the voluntary arrangement, is the right to the payment of the dividend to which he would have been entitled had he had notice of the meeting[10]. In cases where the debtor, particularly a corporate debtor, has become formally insolvent this may be a very illusory protection indeed. Deliberate omission of creditors from the statement of affairs is not unknown. In suitable cases it is to be hoped that the courts will develop ways in which the creditor may make a personal recovery from the directors of corporate debtors.

The two changes introduced by IA 2000 which may prove to be of significance in years to come. First, the extension of the right to act as nominee or supervisor beyond the ranks of licensed insolvency practitioners to members of other bodies approved by the Secretary of State expressly for the purpose of acting in relation to voluntary arrangements. The idea is that voluntary arrangements, in particular CVAs where a moratorium is in force, may be handled by business rescue specialists. It is indeed encouraging to think that the government's hopes for a 'rescue culture' will be realised; reality may be rather different. The second change which may take several years to have an impact is the extension of criminal liability in connection with voluntary arrangements. It is idle to deny that voluntary arrangements have not attracted their fair share of fraudulent or dubious behaviour. The arrival of the moratorium will increase the scope for criminal conduct. The amendments introduced by IA 2000 widen the scope of criminal liability and impose on nominees and supervisors the duty to report directors of corporate debtors or individual debtors who appear to have committed any offence in connection with a moratorium or a voluntary arrangement.

The remaining changes introduced by IA 2000 are the following. (1) In CVAs it is no longer necessary for both the creditors' and the company meeting to reach the same decision on a proposed CVA. If the meetings should reach different decisions, the decision of the creditors' meeting prevails subject to the right of a member to apply to the court. The court may order the company meeting's decision to take effect or make such other order as it thinks fit[11]. (2) Both in CVAs (with or without moratorium) and IVAs the nominee is now required in his report to the court to express his opinion that the proposal has a 'reasonable prospect of being approved and implemented' before it may go forward to a creditors' (and company) meeting[12]. This amendment effectively imports the requirement developed by the court that the nominee should be satisfied that there was a 'real prospect' of approval and implementation before he reports to the court that the proposal should go before the creditors[13]. (3) A proposal for an IVA may now proceed without the need for an interim order. This procedure may be used in any case, but is best suited to proposals made by bankrupts seeking to get out of bankruptcy[14]. (4) Where in IVA an interim order is in force, or an application for an interim order is pending, distress may not be levied on the debtor's goods nor may a right of forfeiture by peaceful re-entry be exercised without the leave of the court[15].

1 See generally Chapter 3.
2 IA 1986, Sch A1, para 12(1)(e).
3 See para 3.1 below.
4 This approach takes advantage of the experience gained with IVAs: see para 4.1 below. Note that in order to restrict abuses of the moratorium procedure a moratorium cannot be obtained within 12 months of an earlier moratorium which did not lead to the approval and successful implementation of a CVA: IA 1986, Sch A1, para 4(1)(f).

5 This necessitates a double reference in the footnotes when dealing with common provisions.
6 As amended by the Insolvency (Amendment) Rules 2002.
7 However, as the provisions of many rules applying to CVAs without moratorium are applied by direct reference in chapter 9 it appears that the rules committee lost enthusiasm for the (wholly unnecessary) task of maintaining separation between the statutory provisions relating to CVAs without a moratorium and CVAs with a moratorium.
8 Which may be extended in IVA but not CVA: see para 7.8 below.
9 A creditor who had notice of the meeting is in a better position not only because he is aware beforehand of the proposal but also because his 28 days begins not on the date of the meeting but on the date on which the chairman reports the result of the meeting to the court (see para 6.15 below), which may be up to four days later.
10 See para 9.1 below.
11 See para 6.3 below.
12 See IA 1986, s 2(2)(a) (CVA without moratorium), Sch A1, para 6(2)(a) (CVA with moratorium), s 256(1)(a) (IVA).
13 See para 4.6 below.
14 See para 2.7 below.
15 See IA 1986, ss 252(2), 254(1) and para 2.5 below.

1.5 Transitional arrangements on implementation of IA 2000 changes. The amendments introduced by IA 2000 came into effect on 1 January 2003 for all voluntary arrangements which had not then commenced the formal process of seeking approval from the creditors and, in CVA, the company. Transitional provisions are contained in IA 2000 (Commencement No 3 and Transitional Provisions) Order 2002[1]. There are four distinct cases to consider:

1. Where a proposal is made by the directors of a company they are required to give the intended nominee written notice of their proposal accompanied by a copy of the proposal[2]. The approval process commences when the intended nominee endorses a copy of the director's notice to the effect that it has been received by him on a specified date[3]. Where the date of that endorsement is before 1 January 2003 the proposal must continue under the law previously in force.
2. Where a proposal is made by a liquidator or administrator who is acting as nominee the approval process commences when he sends out a notice summoning a creditors' and company meeting[4]. Where that notice has been sent out before 1 January 2003 the proposal continues under the law previously in force.
3. Where a proposal is made by a liquidator or administrator ('office-holder') who is not acting as nominee the approval process commences when the intended nominee endorses a copy of the written notice of proposal served on him by the office-holder[5]. Where the date of that endorsement is before 1 January 2003 the proposal continues under the law previously in force.
4. Where a proposal is made by an individual debtor he is required to give the intended nominee written notice of his proposal accompanied by a copy of the proposal[6]. The approval process commences when the intended nominee endorses a copy of the debtor's notice to the effect that it has been received by him on a specified date[7]. Where the date of that endorsement is before 1 January 2003 the proposal continues under the law previously in force.

Similar provisions apply in PVAs. It is the date on which the nominee endorses the notice of the proposal, or in the case of a proposal by an office-holder who is also the nominee, the date on which he sends out a notice summoning meetings of creditors and the members of the partnership which determines whether the proposal continues under the law previously in force[8].

1 SI 2002/2711: see art 3 for CVA, art 4 for IVA.
2 IR 1986, r 1.4(1)(2), see para 4.3 below.
3 IR 1986, r 1.4(3).
4 IR 1986, r 1.11, see para 5.3 below.
5 IR 1986, r 1.12, see para 5.2 below.
6 IR 1986, r 5.4(1)(2), see para 4.3 below.
7 IR 1986, r 5.4(3).
8 The Insolvent Partnerships (Amendment) (No 2) Order 2002, SI 2002/2708, art 11.

1.6 Advantages and disadvantages of CVA. Voluntary arrangements by a debtor company offer both the company and its creditors great flexibility in putting in place a binding arrangement which can be closely tailored to the company's particular situation. Arrangements may not be approved which seek to affect the rights of a secured creditor to enforce his security or interfere with the rights of a preferential creditor without the express agreement of the creditor concerned[1], but subject to these qualifications there is no statutory restriction on the type of arrangements which may be approved by the creditors and the company. In addition to flexibility the CVA can offer cost advantages over other insolvency procedures both in the setting up and the implementation of the procedure. Where the company is responsible for realising its assets subject to the arrangement the insolvency practitioner's costs of realisation may be avoided or reduced. Department of Trade and Industry fees will not be incurred. The proceeds of realisation may be held with institutions paying higher rates of interest than the Insolvency Services Account[2]. The arrangement may be so arranged as to avoid capital gains tax. There may, however, be tax disadvantages in an arrangement[3]. Where the arrangements involve a formal release of part of the company's debts the company is deemed to receive trading income to an equivalent amount, and the creditor may not necessarily obtain a corresponding corporation tax deduction. Bad debt relief has been available to all creditors since 1990[4]. Further disadvantages for creditors may arise from the fact that the provisions of IA 1986 relating to the adjustment of prior transactions will not apply in a CVA, neither may claims be made against directors or other officers of the company for wrongful trading or misfeasance.

A voluntary arrangement may expressly or by necessary implication regulate the rights inter se of a creditor or the company and of third parties liable for the same debt, but if this is to be the case the intention to regulate such rights must be made plain on the face of the proposal[5], and notice of the meeting given to those affected so that they may make representations[6].

The strengthening of the CVA regime by the introduction of the IA 2000 amendments forms part the government's strategy to promote a rescue culture in the troubled areas of the economy. One of the key aims of the Enterprise Act 2002 is to simplify the company administration procedure available under IA 1986 and to shift the balance from administrative receivership to administration. With the emphasis on rescue and rehabilitation the CVA may gain a new lease of life, particularly as the Enterprise Act 2002 abolishes the Crown's preferential rights to recover unpaid taxes[7]. Many companies in financial difficulties have significant unpaid tax bills. It is not possible to conclude a CVA which interferes with the rights of preferential creditors without their consent[8]. A significant restriction in the size of preferential debts may now make viable CVAs which had no prospect of success before the implementation of the Enterprise Act 2002[9].

1 See IA 1986, s 4(3)(4) (CVA without moratorium), Sch A1, para 31(4)–(6) (CVA with moratorium).

2 It is, however, the stated aim of the government through the Enterprise Act 2002 to simplify fees and reform the Insolvency Services Account so as to increase the interest payable on funds in this account.
3 Taxation aspects of IA 1986 are outside the scope of this work. The Institute of Chartered Accountants have issued a technical release (TR 799) entitled 'Tax Aspects of the Insolvency Act 1986' which deals with items of importance to practitioners and is available free of charge.
4 Ie since the coming into force of the Finance Act 1990, s 11; see now Value Added Tax Act 1994, s 36.
5 See *Burford Midland Properties Ltd v Marley Extrusions Ltd* [1995] 1 BCLC 102.
6 *March Estates plc v Gunmark* [1996] 2 BCLC 1 at 6, and see *Johnson v Davies* [1999] Ch 117, CA; *R A Securities Ltd v Merchantile Credit Co Ltd* [1994] 2 BCLC 721.
7 Enterprise Act 2002, s 251.
8 IA 1986, s 4(4) (CVA without moratorium), Sch A1, para 31(5)(6) (CVA with moratorium).
9 This is expected to be in Summer 2003.

1.7 The nature of voluntary arrangements: compositions or schemes of arrangement. IA 1986 provides that a CVA or IVA may comprise either a composition with creditors or a scheme of arrangement[1]. An arrangement can, and not infrequently does, involve both a composition and a scheme of arrangement. There is no distinction under IA 1986 between compositions and schemes either as to procedure or effect of approval. Where a composition or scheme is approved in accordance with the provisions of the statute it is legally binding on all creditors of the debtor by virtue of IA 1986[2]. IA 1986 does not impose the arrangement directly on a dissenting creditor. He is bound to the arrangement by virtue of a statutory hypothesis which requires him to be treated as though he had consented to it[3]. Voluntary arrangements are to be treated as, and have the same consequences as, consensual deeds of arrangement. The same consequences therefore follow as if the dissenting creditor had agreed to be bound by the arrangement[4].

A proposal for a voluntary arrangement by a debtor constitutes an offer to all the creditors as a class, and does not comprise an offer to each creditor individually[5].

A 'composition' is an agreement between the debtor and his creditors whereby the compounding creditors agree with the debtor and between themselves to accept from the debtor payment of less than the respective amounts due to them in full satisfaction of the whole of their claim[6]. Outside statutory provision the consideration which would support the agreement by each creditor to accept part payment as a discharge of the whole debt is the mutual agreement of the other creditors to do likewise[7]. It is essential, however, that a money payment is made or some other consideration is provided by the debtor. Accordingly, a proposal which provides for a nil dividend to unsecured creditors (a dividend being payable to secured creditors) is not capable of being a composition[8].

A 'scheme of arrangement' may take any form acceptable to the parties[9]. The usual method is an assignment by the debtor of his property or a specified part of his property to a trustee (the supervisor) for realisation and distribution of the proceeds of sale amongst the creditors rateably or in such proportions as they agree. The trusts under which the supervisor holds the debtor's property will be agreed by the creditors and specified in the deed of assignment. Such deeds have in the past appointed a committee of inspection to control the trustee's administration of the estate. Such provision is not necessary with an arrangement under IA 1986, as the court may control the supervisor on the application of any creditor, the debtor or other person dissatisfied by any act, omission or decision of the supervisor[10]. Other forms of scheme of arrangement involve a moratorium, often coupled with the payment of a dividend at the end of the moratorium period. However, a moratorium by itself may comprise a valid scheme of arrangement[11].

It is interesting to note that many of the standard forms of arrangement in use do not actually spell out the consequences of the composition or scheme on the creditors' debts. Where there is a composition the debts will be compromised and no longer exist in their original form. But with a scheme of arrangement it may be necessary in the absence of express provision for the court to imply a term that creditors bound by the arrangement may not take any steps to enforce their debts against the debtor while the debtor is complying, or has complied, with his obligations under the scheme[12].

1 IA 1986, s 1(1) (all CVAs), s 253(1) (IVA).
2 IA 1986, s 5(2) (CVA without moratorium), Sch A1, para 37(2) (CVA with moratorium), s 260(2) (IVA).
3 *Johnson v Davies* [1999] Ch 117; *Raja v Rubin and Goodman* [2000] Ch 274.
4 So where, as in *Johnson v Davies*, the issue whether a co-debtor was discharged by the arrangement fell to be determined by construction of the terms of the arrangement. In the event the terms of the arrangement in that case did not have the effect of releasing co-debtors who remained liable to the creditor on the joint debt.
5 *Re A Debtor (No 2389 of 1989)* [1991] Ch 326.
6 See eg *Irish Land Commission v Grant* (1884) 10 App Cas 14 at 30; and see *Re Griffith* (1886) 3 Morr 111 at 116, per Cave J: 'Where the debtor makes over his assets to be administered by a trustee there is no doubt that that is a scheme. Where the debtor keeps his assets and undertakes to pay over the creditors a certain sum, that is a composition.'
7 *Good v Cheesman* (1831) 2 B & Ad 328; *Boyd v Hind* (1857) 1 H & N 938; and see *West Yorkshire Darracq Agency Ltd v Coleridge* [1911] 2 KB 326 and *Snelling v John G Snelling* [1973] QB 87.
8 *IRC v Adam & Partners Ltd* [2001] 1 BCLC 222, CA, overruling the judge on this point, reported at [1999] 2 BCLC 730.
9 And see the comments of Lightman J in *March Estates v Gunmark Ltd* [1996] 2 BCLC 1 at 5. Although (at 5b) the learned judge states that 'a scheme of arrangement (a scheme) is plainly something different from a composition and involves something less than the release or discharge of creditors' debts, eg a moratorium', a scheme may involve something *more* than release or discharge. The learned judge states (at 5e): 'A scheme does not, or does not necessarily, involve any compromise or release.' There was no compromise or release in the case before him, but schemes have been implemented involving both a moratorium and the release and discharge of debts.
10 IA 1986, s 7(3) (CVA without moratorium), Sch A1, para 39(3)(4) (CVA with moratorium); s 263(3) (IVA).
11 See, eg, *IRC v Adam* [2001] 1 BCLC 222, CA, where the proposal anticipated no payment of dividend to unsecured creditors during a three-year period during which it was thought that the bank as secured creditor would receive a better return. The proposal also provided that if the creditors received distributions these were to be accepted in full and final settlement of all sums due from the debtor at the start of the voluntary arrangement. If, however, no distributions were made the creditors were entitled to assert such contractual rights as they had at the end of the moratorium period.
12 See *Johnson v Davies* [1999] Ch 117 at 128F; note that the precise ambit of the implied term may well depend upon the precise terms of the individual scheme.

1.8 Involvement of third parties. There is no limit to the potential flexibility of a scheme of arrangement which may be tailored to suit the circumstances of the individual debtor. It may comprise no more than a short term moratorium on the enforcement of the creditor's debts, perhaps coupled with the payment of dividends during the period of the moratorium[1], or it may require the active involvement of a third party who is prepared to give assistance to the debtor on certain terms. The involvement of third parties is envisaged by IR 1986[2], but there is no statutory mechanism whereby a third party may incur rights and obligations under the arrangement. Neither is there any provision restrictive of such participation. In

Australia it has been held that someone other than the debtor or his creditors may become a party to a scheme of arrangement[3], and there is no obvious reason why this approach should not be followed in England. Certainly, if the scheme depends upon monetary contributions or other benefits being supplied by a third party it is important that the party in question is bound to the creditors either by joining the scheme or by entering into a contract with the nominee which the supervisor may then enforce on behalf of the creditors. Thus, for example, where a third party agrees to provide one or more payments if an arrangement is carried into effect the nominee should ensure that there is an enforceable contract with the third party for the benefit of the arrangement. Furthermore, it would be advisable for the nominee to ensure that the third party binds himself to the relevant proposal, conditional upon its acceptance by the creditors, before it is voted on in creditors' meeting. A voluntary arrangement may expressly or by necessary implication regulate the rights inter se of a creditor of a debtor and of third parties liable for the same debt[4], and there is no obvious reason why the third party should not become a party to the arrangement if, exceptionally, the third party, the debtor and the creditors wish this to be so.

It may also be noted that the statutory sanction for default in connection with an IVA, namely the making of a bankruptcy order against the debtor, arises only where the debtor himself fails to honour his obligations[5]. In cases where the involvement of a third party is essential to the arrangement, therefore, the nominee and the creditors should consider what sanction if any there should be on the debtor in the event that the third party defaults on his obligations. The more usual practice is so to draft the terms of the arrangement that there is an obligation on the debtor to ensure that the benefits due from the third party do accrue to the arrangement. The debtor will therefore be in default if the third party fails to honour his commitment to the arrangement leaving the creditors free to petition for the debtor's bankruptcy.

1 See eg the CVA in *March Estates plc v Gunmark Ltd* [1996] 2 BCLC 1.
2 See IR 1986, r 1.3(2)(b)(j) (all CVAs), r 5.3(2)(b)(j) (IVA).
3 See *Re Glendale Land Development Ltd* (1982) 1 ACLC 540, NSW S Ct.
4 *Johnson v Davies* [1999] Ch 117, CA; *March Estates plc v Gunmark* [1996] 2 BCLC 1 at 6d; *Burford Midland Properties Ltd v Marley Extrusions Ltd* [1995] 1 BCLC 102.
5 IA 1986, ss 264(1)(c), 276(1)(a), (c).

1.9 Drafting the terms of the voluntary arrangement. See generally Appendix 4. is particularly important that arrangements are drawn so as to cope so far as possible with the possibility that circumstances may change. The relevant provisions of IA 1986[1] take the arrangement through to its initial implementation, but make no provision to enable the supervisor, debtor or creditors to return to the court to obtain directions for a further creditors' meeting to consider a new proposal in the event that the circumstances in which the arrangement is being implemented are rather different to those envisaged at the creditors' meeting[2]. Even the most honest debtor and careful nominee may not foresee how matters will turn out. Assets may realise less than envisaged, estimates of tax claims may be proved wrong and unforeseen costs may arise. Provided that the information given to creditors at the meeting was not misleading there is little a disgruntled creditor may do should he receive a lower dividend than expected through changing circumstances. He is precluded by the fact of the arrangements from obtaining a winding-up or bankruptcy order against the debtor. Alternatively, the supervisor may find that he can more beneficially administer the assets which the debtor has made available under the arrangements if he is able to adopt a different course to that allowed in the scheme approved by creditors. It will usually be advisable therefore for the proposal to include a provision enabling the details of the arrangement to be varied if the supervisor considers this appropriate with the consent of three quarters of the creditors at a further meeting called for this purpose[3]. In the absence of a variation provision the arrangement may be amended only with the approval of all the creditors[4] or by proposing a new (varied) arrangement and carrying it through all its stages to a creditors' meeting. Until the implementation of the amendments introduced by IA 2000 there was an effective 12-month delay on seeking amendment to an approved IVA through the full voluntary arrangement procedure. This was because an IVA could only be approved after the grant of an interim order, and IA 1986, mindful of the interference of such an order with creditors' legal rights, prohibits the grant of a further interim order within 12 months of an earlier interim order[5]. A similar prohibition exists on the eligibility of a company for a moratorium[6]. As it is now possible for an IVA to be made without first obtaining an interim order[7] there is no longer a 12-month bar to the making of a new arrangement varying an existing IVA. In both IVAs and CVAs, therefore, a variation to an existing voluntary arrangement may be secured by means of a new proposal at any time provided no interim order or moratorium is obtained, and at any time after the arrangement has been in force for 12 months with an interim order or moratorium. This is a very cumbersome way, however, to make a variation to an existing arrangement.

The terms of the arrangement will usually require the debtor to make available any 'windfall' to the creditors to increase the dividend, and unless expressly excluded this will include any bequests received by the debtor. In *Re Abram* [8] the debtor had been disinherited by his mother but made an application for reasonable provision out of his mother's estate[9]. It was a term of his IVA that any capital sum received from the mother's estate should be paid to the creditors. The court held that as the 1975 Act made provision for 'maintenance' it was inappropriate that a capital sum should be paid out to creditors. It ordered that a portion of the estate should be settled on the sum on protective trusts with a life interest determinable on attempted alienation or bankruptcy when it would be replaced with a discretionary trust in favour of the son and his immediate family.

1 Ie ss 1–7 (CVA without moratorium), Sch A1 (CVA with moratorium), ss 252–263 (IVA).
2 Under IA 1986, s 7(3) (CVA without moratorium), Sch A1, para 39(3), (4) (CVA with moratorium), or s 263(3) (IVA) the debtor, the creditors or any other person dissatisfied by any act, omission or decision of the supervisor may apply to the court to reverse or modify that decision or for directions: see paras 10.4, 10.5 below. However, an application under these provisions could not be a vehicle to alter the terms of the voluntary arrangement as approved by the creditors.
3 As to varying a voluntary arrangement, see paras 10.6, 10.7 below.
4 See *Raja v Rubin and Goodman* [2000] Ch 274, see para 10.7 below.
5 IA 1986, s 255(1)(c).
6 IA 1986, Sch A1, para 4(1)(f).
7 IA 1986, s 256A.
8 [1997] BPIR 1.
9 Under the Inheritance (Provision for Family and Dependants) Act 1975.

1.10 When an individual may seek an IVA. To make a proposal for an IVA a debtor must be either an undischarged bankrupt, or be able to petition for his own bankruptcy. As originally enacted, IA 1986 permits an IVA only after an interim order has been made, providing that an interim order may be applied for only by an undischarged bankrupt or a debtor who 'on the day of the making of the application [for an interim order] was able to petition for his own bankruptcy'[1]. As amended by IA 2000, it is now possible for a debtor to make a proposal for an IVA without an interim order first being made[2]. The debtor then simply instructs a practitioner prepared to act as nominee[3], and the nominee submits a report to the court if he is 'of the opinion that the debtor is an undischarged bankrupt or is able to petition for his own bankruptcy'[4].

A debtor may present a petition for his own bankruptcy only on the ground that he is unable to pay his debts[5]. An inability to pay debts is determined on a liquidity basis – that is, whether the debtor is able to pay his debts as they fall due, irrespective of whether he is insolvent on a balance-sheet basis, namely a comparison of his assets and his liabilities[6].

1 IA 1986, s 255(1)(b).
2 IA 1986, s 256A (introduced by IA 2000, Sch 3, para 7).
3 See para 1.12 below.
4 IA 1986, s 256A(3).
5 IA 1986, s 272.
6 *Re Coney (a bankrupt)* [1998] BPIR 333.

1.11 Those who may propose a CVA. Where the company is not in administration or liquidation its directors[1] make the proposal for a voluntary arrangement[2]. The proposal is made *to* the company not *by* the company. Accordingly, as the directors are not here acting on behalf of the company it would appear that they will not be bound to follow those articles of association of the company which govern the exercise by the directors of the powers of the company. The authority to make a proposal is given by the Act to 'the directors' not 'any director'. It would appear therefore that to be valid the proposal should be made by all the directors, but it may well be acceptable that the directors act by majority vote. It may be noted that the statement of affairs of the company[3] need only be certified by two directors or by the secretary and one director other than the secretary[4].

No one else may propose an arrangement except where an administration order is in force against the company or the company is being wound up. In these cases any proposal must be made by the administrator or liquidator as the case may be[5]. There is no restriction in IA 1986 on a proposal being made by a provisional liquidator. A provisional liquidator is appointed to carry out such functions as the court may confer on him[6] and his powers may be limited by the court in the order appointing him[7]. He will need specific authority from the court to make a proposal and act either as nominee or supervisor for the arrangements. There may be cases where a receiver considers voluntary arrangements to be an appropriate course for the company to adopt, but he will have to arrange for the directors to make the proposal in their name.

A specific offence is committed by any officer[8] if he makes any false representation or fraudulently does or omits to do anything for the purpose of obtaining the approval of the company's members or creditors to a proposal for a voluntary arrangement[9]. A person guilty of this offence is liable to imprisonment or a fine, or both[10]. An agreement between a debtor and a creditor whereby the debtor agrees to pay to the creditor a sum additional to that to which the creditor is entitled under a compromise or scheme is fraudulent and unenforceable by the creditor[11].

1 'Director' is defined by IA 1986, s 251 as including any person occupying the position of director by whatever name called.
2 IA 1986, s 1(1).

3 See para 4.5 below (where there is no moratorium). For the rules governing a statement of affairs required to obtain a moratorium, see para 3.4 below.
4 IR 1986, r 1.5(4).
5 IA 1986, s 1(3).
6 IA 1986, s 135(4).
7 IA 1986, s 135(5).
8 'Officer' includes a shadow director (IA 1986, s 6A(3)), a 'shadow director' being a person in accordance with whose directions or instructions the directors of the company are accustomed to act: IA 1986, s 251. A person is not deemed a shadow director by reason only that the directors act on advice given by him in a professional capacity. It is not clear why this offence is restricted to officers of the company.
9 IA 1986, s 6A. Prior to 1 January 2003 an offence might be committed under IR 1986, r 1.30 (now repealed) by any past or present officer. IA 1986, s 6A widens the offence, but does include past officers.
10 IA 1986, s 6A(4). It is an offence under the Theft Act 1968, s 19, punishable by seven years' imprisonment, for an officer of a company with intent to deceive members or creditors of the company about its affairs to publish or concur in publishing a written statement or account which to his knowledge is or maybe misleading, false or deceptive in a material particular.
11 *Mallalieu v Hodgson* (1851) 16 QB 689.

1.12 Nominee. A debtor, whether a company, partnership, or an individual, cannot proceed to an IVA on his own. The assistance of an authorised practitioner, styled for these purposes as 'the nominee', is required. He must report to the court, and thus to the creditors, on the merits of the proposal. This practitioner must either be an insolvency practitioner[1] or a person who has been authorised to act as a nominee or supervisor of voluntary arrangement[2]. IA 2000[3] introduced the possibility that a nominee or supervisor need not need not be a qualified insolvency practitioner provided he is a member of a body recognised by the Secretary of State for the express purpose of acting in relation to voluntary arrangements[4]. Any person so authorised to act as a nominee or supervisor may be referred to in IR 1986 as an 'authorised person'[5]. The aim is to encourage individuals who have business rescue experience rather than accountancy experience to assist debtors or small companies in financial difficulties and keep them out of insolvency[6]. There will, however, be very few IVAs where it will be of interest to a business rescue practitioner to act as a nominee or supervisor. The primary purpose of authorising such practitioners to act in voluntary arrangements is to utilise their skills in company voluntary arrangements under the new moratorium procedure[7].

Where the proposal is approved by the creditors, the nominee, now called the 'supervisor', implements the composition or scheme subject to the control of the court. IA 1986[8] provides that the supervisor should act 'either as trustee or otherwise' no other capacity being specified. There is no restriction on the powers the supervisor may have under an arrangement, but there are no statutory powers afforded the supervisor in the carrying out of the arrangement. The court may exercise control over the supervisor in his implementation of the arrangement, and in doing so may make any order it thinks fit with respect to any act, omission or decision of the supervisor[9].

1 Licensed for the purposes of IA 1986, s 389, and see the Insolvency Practitioners (Recognised Professional Bodies) Order 1986, SI 1986/1764, and the Insolvency Practitioners Regulations 1990, SI 1990/439.
2 Under IA 1986, s 389A, introduced by IA 2000, s 4.
3 IA 2000, s 4.
4 Under IA 1986, s 389A, inserted by IA 2000, s 4(4). Security will be required for the proper performance of the nominee/supervisor's functions, IA 1986, s 389A(2)(b), which may be exercised in respect of CVAs, PVAs or IVAs.

5 IR 1986, r 13.9(3).
6 In winding up the debate on the second reading of the Insolvency Bill on 4 April 2000, Lord McIntosh of Haringey stated with respect to the recognition of a relevant body: 'We are certainly not in a hurry to introduce it. We shall not introduce it until there is a body which recognises business rescue skills and is prepared to impose them, and we should not recognise anybody as a nominee or a supervisor unless he had agreed to abide the rules of such a body.'
7 IA 1986, Sch A1, introduced by IA 2000.
8 IA 1986, s 1(2) (CVA), s 253(2) (IVA).
9 See para 10.4 below.

1.13 Voluntary arrangements and the Human Rights Act 1998. The Human Rights Act 1998 ('HRA 1998') is unlikely to have much impact on voluntary arrangements. In giving effect to 'convention rights' under the European Convention on Human Rights, HRA 1998 operates in two ways. First, in its interpretative effect on primary and secondary legislation: all such legislation must now be interpreted in a way which is compatible with the convention rights incorporated into English law by HRA 1998. It is improbable that any part of voluntary arrangement legislation will be found to be incompatible. Secondly, HRA 1998 provides a right of action to victims of acts of public authorities which are unlawful because they contravene a convention right. There is no comprehensive definition of public authority in HRA 1998. All courts are public authorities, as is any person who exercises functions of a public nature while exercising those public functions.

Within the field of insolvency official receivers, liquidators and trustees in bankruptcy are all public authorities for the purposes of HRA 1998. All exercise functions of a public nature under the provisions of IA 1986 and they also carry out court functions delegated to them under IA 1986. All their functions are of a public nature. The nominee performs a rôle which is almost entirely public in nature. He will be acting privately when advising a debtor on a proposal for a voluntary arrangement, but in obtaining an interim order, reporting to the court on the proposal, summoning and presiding over the creditors' meeting, and reporting the decision of the meeting to the court the nominee will be acting as a public authority. So too will the nominee who acts for a company with the benefit of a moratorium in monitoring the company's affairs. The moratorium interferes significantly with the rights of creditors of the company. The nominee is responsible that the moratorium, coming into force as it does simply by the lodging of specified documents in court, is properly obtained and continued through to the holding of the creditors' meeting.

The supervisor of an individual voluntary arrangement is in a rather different position. Essentially, the supervisor acts in a private capacity when administering the arrangement whether it be a composition or a scheme of arrangement. Voluntary arrangements are to be treated as, and have the same consequences as, consensual deeds of arrangement. Creditors either consent to be bound to the arrangement or are bound to it by virtue of a statutory hypothesis which requires dissenting creditors to be treated as though they had consented to the arrangement[1]. It follows that in supervising the arrangement the supervisor is not exercising a public function. The supervisor is, however, subject to the control of the court[2]. Were the court to give the supervisor directions in relation to any particular matter arising under the voluntary arrangement, it would appear that the supervisor would be acting as a public authority in carrying out those directions.

In *King v Anthony*[3] the Court of Appeal stated with respect to individual voluntary arrangements that of IA 1986, Pt VIII comprised a self-contained scheme including express powers in the court to give appropriate directions if complaint is made to the court of the conduct of the supervisor. The court took the view that since IA 1986 provided an effective means of enforcing the duty of a supervisor, this indicated that parliament intended that matters arising in connection with this duty should be enforceable by application under IA 1986 and not by private right of action[4]. To the extent that the supervisor or nominee is carrying out public functions, as outlined above, it is doubtful that this decision now applies to prevent private actions against an insolvency practitioner for breach of a convention right.

The right to a fair and public hearing within a reasonable time for the determination of civil rights and obligations afforded by Article 6 of the European Convention on Human Rights will naturally apply to any disputes arising in connection with voluntary arrangements. Detailed consideration of the rights afforded by Article 6 is outside the scope of this work. Two points are made. First, the rights afforded by Article 6 arise only where there is a *determination* of a civil right. It is not sufficient that a civil right may be breached. There must be a dispute (or 'contestation') and the proceedings are only covered by Article 6 where the result of that contestation is decisive of a civil right[5]. A contestation may relate to the existence of a civil right and or to the scope or enjoyment of that right, provided that it is of a genuine and serious nature[6]. Secondly, where a citizen's complaint is against a decision of a public authority whose decisions may be challenged in court, as is case with the decisions of nominees and supervisors exercising their public functions, judicial proceedings on a challenge may cure breaches of Article 6 by the public authority. Before complaining of a breach by the nominee or supervisor the complainant should exercise his right of challenge to the court. 'No violation of the Convention may be found if the proceedings before the public authority are subject to subsequent control by a judicial body that has full jurisdiction and does provide the guarantees of Article 6(1)'[7].

1 *Johnson v Davies* [1999] Ch 117; *Raja v Rubin and Goodman* [2000] Ch 274.
2 IA 1986, s 263(3), (4).
3 [1999] BPIR 73.
4 See [1999] BPIR 73 at 78–79.
5 *Ringeisen v Austria* (1971) 1 EHRR 455 (para 9).
6 *Bentham v Netherlands* (1982) 5 EHRR 533, (1985) 8 EHRR 1.
7 *Albert and Le Compte v Belgium* (1982) 5 EHRR 533, (1983) Series A No 58, para 29: 'providing the guarantees of the Article 6(1)' imports considerations of fairness and adequacy, and see *Fischer v Austria* (1995) 20 EHRR 340.

1.14 The impact of the EC Regulation. On 31 May 2002, Council Regulation (EC) 1346/2000 on Insolvency Proceedings came into effect throughout the EU, except in Denmark. It is not a harmonisation instrument. It controls the exercise of the jurisdiction to commence insolvency proceedings in respect of EU debtors, and provides uniform rules for the choice of law. Voluntary arrangements under IA 1986 are included among the insolvency procedures subject to the EC Regulation. The scheme of the Regulation is to ensure primacy for insolvency proceedings opened in the debtor's state, that is the member state in which the debtor has his 'centre of main interests'. These proceedings are termed 'main proceedings'. Insolvency proceedings against the debtor in other member states are 'secondary proceedings', although if they are commenced before the main proceedings are opened they are termed 'territorial proceedings' and must be restricted in effect to those assets of the debtor which are situated in the state in which the territorial proceedings are opened. Once main proceedings have been opened against the debtor the liquidator[1] in those proceedings may involve himself in secondary proceedings. He may seek a stay on the realisation of assets[2], propose a rescue plan or composition in those proceedings[3], or apply for a voluntary arrangement to be converted into formal insolvency[4]. The EC Regulation contains provisions relating to the lodgment of claims which will apply to voluntary arrangements, although couched in terms more appropriate for formal insolvency[5].

The impact of the EC Regulation on voluntary arrangements generally will be minimal. Overwhelmingly, proposals will be made by debtors who have their 'centre of main interests' in England and Wales and the proceedings on the proposal will be main proceedings. Nominees must, however, be aware of the EC Regulation and the meaning of main and territorial proceedings[6] both for the preparation of the proposal and in reporting to the court.

In all proposals for voluntary arrangements it must be stated 'whether the EC Regulation will apply and if so, whether the proceedings will be main proceedings or territorial proceedings'[7]. Strictly, the EC Regulation always applies. The rule presumably requires the proposal to state whether issues may arise under the Regulation, in other words does the debtor have a 'centre of main interests' in another EU state and, possibly, does the debtor has an 'establishment' in another EU state in respect of which territorial proceedings have been commenced to which the proposal will be main proceedings. A voluntary arrangement cannot constitute secondary proceedings, ie proceedings running concurrently with main proceedings in the state where the debtor has his 'centre of main interests', because Article 3(3) provides that such proceedings must be winding-up proceedings. There is a quasi exception, namely where the liquidator in the main proceedings wishes to end the secondary proceedings by proposing a voluntary arrangement by way of rescue plan or composition[8]. If a proposal is put to creditors on this basis it is plainly important that it explains what has happened in the main proceedings and any other secondary proceedings that might have been opened in other member states.

When the chairman of the creditors', and any company, meeting reports to the court he must include a statement whether, in his opinion, the EC Regulation applies to the voluntary arrangement, and if so, whether the proceedings are main proceedings or territorial proceedings. The statement will usually be in the affirmative, see above, and in almost every case will be that the proceedings are main proceedings.

1 A term used to encompass all office-holders including the supervisor of a voluntary arrangement.
2 EC Regulation, Art 33.
3 EC Regulation, Art 34 provided the secondary law allows it. A liquidator in foreign main proceedings could propose a voluntary arrangement in England and Wales. There is no express provision for this in IR 1986, but presumably he would proceed as would an office-holder in the debtor's English insolvency.
4 EC Regulation, Art 37, see para 14.7 below.
5 See para 14.6 below.
6 As to which see paras 14.2 and 14.3 below.
7 IR 1986, r 1.3(2)(q) (all CVAs), r 5.3(2)(r) (IVA).
8 Under his powers given by EC Regulation, Art 34(1).

1.15 The changes to be introduced by the Enterprise Act 2002. In the field of insolvency the Enterprise Act 2002 ('EA 2002') is concerned primarily with the revision of the law relating to company administration, the restriction of the use of administrative receivership, and the abolition of the Crown's preferential status as a creditor so as to improve unsecured creditors' prospects of recovery against insolvent estates. The loss of preferential status for crown debts will have its impact on voluntary arrangements, not least because the Inland Revenue and Customs and Excise are often substantial creditors. There are a number of other provisions of EA 2002 which will have an impact on the law relating to voluntary arrangements either immediately or where powers given by EA 2002 are exercised by the Secretary of State in secondary legislation:

1. any provision of IA 1986, including the law relating to voluntary arrangements, may be extended to companies incorporated outside Great Britain[1];
2. the law relating to voluntary arrangements may be extended to an Industrial or Provident Society or a Friendly Society whether registered or unregistered[2];
3. on the approval of an IVA proposed by an undischarged bankrupt either the bankrupt or the official receiver may apply for the bankruptcy order to be annulled[3];
4. a new 'fast-track' procedure for an IVA is introduced for debtors who are undischarged bankrupts[4];
5. the official receiver is authorised to act as nominee or supervisor in relation to an IVA made by an undischarged bankrupt[5].

These last two changes are part of the government's drive to reduce the number and length of bankruptcies. Under the fast track scheme for post-bankruptcy IVAs a proposal is agreed between the bankrupt and the official receiver and filed with the court. There is no meeting of creditors. In its place the official receiver will circulated the proposal to all creditors and invite them to vote on it in correspondence on a 'take it or leave it' basis. A 75% majority is still required for the voluntary arrangement to be approved. The official receiver will be the nominee and, it may be anticipated, in most cases will be the supervisor. The creditors will, however, be able to appoint a private sector insolvency practitioner if they prefer. The attraction of the official receiver acting as nominee and supervisor is cost. The aim in allowing the official receiver to act as nominee and supervisor in any post-bankruptcy IVA, whether fast track or not, is encourage creditors to accept such IVAs where a relatively simple IVA may be put in place at low cost administered by the official receiver.

1 EA 2002, s 254.
2 EA 2002, s 255.
3 IA 1986, s 261, as amended by EA 2002, s 264 and Sch 22.
4 IA 1986, s 263A-263G inserted by EA 2002, s 264 and Sch 22.
5 IA 1986, s 389B, inserted by EA 2002, s 264 and Sch 22.

1.16 Co-operation between insolvency courts. With voluntary arrangements involving cross-border issues assistance may be given between courts under the provisions of IA 1986, s 426(4). This provides that: 'The courts having jurisdiction in relation to insolvency law in any part of the United Kingdom shall assist the courts having the corresponding jurisdiction in any other part of the United Kingdom or any relevant country or territory.' A relevant country or territory is (a) any of the Channel Islands or the Isle of Man, or (b) any country or territory designated by the Secretary of State by order made by statutory instrument[1]. It should be noted that the duty of assistance exists only as between courts. A foreign trustee, assignee or other office-holder will have therefore to obtain a letter of request from the appropriate court in his country before assistance may be had from the English court; he may not make an application direct to the English court. The Federal Court of Australia has held that it is for the recipient court to determine the extent of its own jurisdiction to aid a requesting court, and it would be undesirable for the requesting court to seek to do so when considering an application for the issue of letters of request[2].

IA 1986 provides that a request made to a court in any part of the United Kingdom by a court in any other part of the United Kingdom or in a relevant country or territory constitutes authority for the court to which the request is made to apply, in relation to any matters specified in the request, the insolvency law which is applicable by either court in relation to comparable matters falling within its jurisdiction[3]. 'Insolvency Law' is defined by reference to specific statutory provisions with respect to the several parts of the United Kingdom[4], and in relation to any relevant country or territory is defined as 'so much of the law of that country or territory as corresponds to provisions falling within any of the [laws of the relevant part of the United Kingdom]'[5].

Accordingly, when a request for assistance is made by a foreign court, the English court has a choice whether to apply English or the relevant foreign law. If foreign law is chosen the provisions of English law which would have applied, and by which the 'comparable' provisions of the foreign law will have been ascertained, cease to have any further relevance to the application[6]. The provisions of the foreign law should be applied by reference to the general principles applicable in the foreign jurisdiction:

> 'I do not consider that it is possible to divorce from a provision of insolvency law, as defined, which confers jurisdiction on the court of the relevant country the principles and practice by which that jurisdiction is exercised by the court ... Were it otherwise s 426 would be deprived of much of its effect, for the choice of the law of the requesting court would be circumscribed by limitations to be found in the corresponding provisions of the insolvency law of England.'[7]

When considering a request from a foreign court the English court should have in mind the implications of comity. It is evident that one of the objects of IA 1986, s 426 is to provide for some form of reciprocal assistance for insolvencies with an international dimension. Once the English court has elected to apply foreign law it should not stigmatise either the substantive law or the exercise by the requesting court of its jurisdiction as oppressive and so refuse the request, bearing in mind that the Secretary of State has determined in his discretion to designate the relevant country or territory for the purposes of the section[8].

The English court has a discretion whether or not to give assistance to the foreign court, and if so what assistance it provides, notwithstanding the words 'shall assist' in IA 1986, s 426(4)[9]. In exercising its discretion whether or not to render assistance the fact of the foreign court's request is no more than a factor, albeit a weighty one, particularly where it is plain that the foreign court has given judicial consideration to the issuing of the letter of request and has concluded that it is just and convenient to do so[10]. While a request might be refused because to comply with it would be oppressive under English law, account must be had of all the facts and circumstances of the case, including the procedure adopted by the foreign court in relation to the application of the provisions of law in question[11], and (where appropriate) the proposed manner in which the foreign court will act on the assistance provided[12]. While, therefore, it remains open to the English court to refuse assistance on the ground that the order sought would be oppressive in English law, this will only rarely be a ground on which the court will act.

It will be rare for assistance to be sought in voluntary arrangement cases, but this jurisdiction has been used to assist the High Court of the Isle of Man, where voluntary arrangements are unknown, to place two Isle of Man companies into CVA by extending the provisions of IA 1986, Pt I and the relevant rules in IR 1986 to those companies[13]. Each of the companies had carried on business in England and therefore had a close connection with England, although neither was registered as an overseas company.

1 IA 1986, s 426(11); The Co-operation of Insolvency Courts (Designation of Relevant Countries and Territories) Orders 1986, 1996, and 1998 have designated the following countries or territories: Anguilla, Australia, The Bahamas, Bermuda, Botswana, Brunei Darussalam, Canada, Cayman Islands, Falkland Islands, Gibraltar, Hong Kong, Republic of Ireland, Malaysia, Montserrat, New Zealand, South Africa, St Helena, Turks and Caicos Islands, Tuvalu, Virgin Islands.

2 *Re Clunies-Ross* (1988) [2000] BPIR 714.

3 IA 1986, s 426(5); the court is required to have regard 'in particular' to the rules of private international law in exercising its discretion which law to apply. In *Slinn v Official Receiver and liquidator of Seagull Manufacturing Co Ltd* (1991) [2000] BPIR 847 the Court of Aldernay applied English insolvency law when requested to act in aid of and be auxiliary to the High Court in England for the purposes of holding a private examination of former directors and for ordering the production of the company's books of account and financial records still in the custody or control of those directors.

4 In relation to England and Wales: IA 1986 and the Company Directors Disqualification Act 1986, ss 6–10, 12, 15, 19(c) and 20 with IA 1986, s 426(10)(a), Sch 1. In *Hughes v Hannover Rückversicherungs-Aktiengesellschaft* [1997] 1 BCLC 497 the Court of Appeal stressed that these provisions are what the words 'insolvency law' mean not what they include, see at 516d.

5 IA 1986, s 426(10).

6 *Re Southern Equities Corpn Ltd, England v Smith* [2000] 2 BCLC 21 at 63, CA.

7 Per Morritt LJ in *Re Southern Equities Corpn Ltd* [2000] 2 BCLC 21 at 63; in this case the application was for an examination under IA 1986, s 236 (cf IA 1986, s 366 in bankruptcy) by a liquidator in South Australia pursuant to a request by the Supreme Court of South Australia. At first instance the court, following *Re J N Taylor Finance Pty Ltd* [1999] 2 BCLC 256, refused the request because the proposed examination was of a partner of a firm of accountants against which the liquidator had already commenced proceedings. In these circumstances an English court would refuse an application to examine under IA 1986, s 236. In South Australia the courts would permit an examination in such circumstances, but subject to strict control. Thus the examination must be for information only. It may not be a dress rehearsal for cross examination nor an exercise in attacking the credibility of a potential witness.

8 *Re Southern Equities Corpn Ltd, England v Smith* [2000] 2 BCLC 21 at 64, 66, CA.

9 *Hughes v Hannover Rücckversicherungs-Aktiengesellschaft* [1997] 1 BCLC 497; *Re Southern Equities Corpn Ltd, England v Smith* [2000] 2 BCLC 21 at 66, CA.

10 See *Hughes v Hannover Ruckversicherungs-Aktiengesellschaft* [1997] 1 BCLC 497 at 518.

11 *Re Southern Equities Corpn Ltd, England v Smith* [2000] 2 BCLC 21 at 66, CA.

12 In *Re Southern Equities Corpn Ltd, England v Smith* [2000] 2 BCLC 21 at 67 it was stated to be of significance that the proposal was that the examination requested would be carried out in England by a master of the Supreme Court of South Australia who was both familiar with the affairs of the company in liquidation and also very experienced in the supervision of examinations under the Australian Companies Code.

13 *Re Television Trade Rentals Ltd, Re TTR Ltd* [2002] EWHC 211 (Ch) [2002] BCC 807, [2002] All ER (D) 259 (Feb).

Chapter 2

IVA: with or without interim order

2.1 Interim order. An interim order protects the debtor from all proceedings and execution while his proposal is prepared and put before his creditors. IA 1986 as originally enacted required every debtor, even a bankrupt debtor, who wished to make a proposal to his creditors for a voluntary arrangement[1] to apply first to the court for an interim order[2]. Following the implementation of IA 2000 it is possible for a debtor, as an alternative, to make a proposal for an IVA without the protection of an interim order[3]. It is envisaged that the interim order will remain the preferred route for a substantial majority of creditors; certainly for those creditors who have not been made bankrupt. Where a debtor is bankrupt he may of course have accrued further debts since the commencement of his bankruptcy, but in most cases he is unlikely to need the protection from creditors that the interim order provides. Further changes will come with the implementation of EA 2002. The aim of these further changes is to seek to encourage undischarged bankrupts to propose for IVA by the introduction of a new 'fast-track' procedure. Under the fast-track procedure the official receiver will be able to put a proposal to creditors for approval or rejection by post, without the need for an interim order or any involvement of the court[4].

While an application for an interim order is pending no right of forfeiture by peaceable re-entry of premises let to the debtor may be exercised without leave of the court[5], and the court has a discretionary power to stay any action, execution or other legal process[6] against the debtor or his property[7]. This power is exercisable by the bankruptcy court[8] or by any other court in which proceedings against the debtor are pending and covers the levying of distress on the debtor's property or its subsequent sale[9]. Either court may stay the proceedings or allow them to continue on such terms as the court considers fit[10]. Similar powers in the court to protect the assets of insolvent companies are intended to be exercised widely to enable the proper implementation of insolvency principles[11], and the court should similarly protect the assets of debtors proposing to enter into IVAs under the provisions of IA 1986.

1 Ie a composition in satisfaction of his debts or a scheme of arrangement of his affairs.
2 IA 1986, s 253(1). The interim order was an essential prerequisite of an IVA: *Fletcher v Vooght* [2000] BPIR 435, where the court concluded that on the wording of the legislation a 'report to the court' in a case where no interim order has been made cannot be a report under IA 1986, s 256 and cannot lead to a creditors' meeting being summoned

under IA 1986, s 257 nor, therefore, to a voluntary arrangement with binding force under IA 1986, s 260.

3 IA 1986, s 256A, introduced by IA 2000, Sch 3, para 7.

4 See para 2.9 below.

5 IA 1986, s 254(1).

6 See *Re Smith (A Bankrupt), ex p Braintree District Council* [1990] 2 AC 215, where the House of Lords held that the equivalent provision in bankruptcy proceedings covered a warrant of committal for non-payment of rates in magistrates' court proceedings.

7 IA 1986, s 254(1).

8 IA 1986, s 254(1). If an application for a stay is made to a court other than that in which the proceedings are pending, it is necessary to adduce proof that the application for an interim order has been made. IA 1986 does not specify any form of proof. Ideally this will be by a sealed copy of the application formally produced by affidavit or witness statement.

9 IA 1986, s 254(2).

10 IA 1986, s 254(2).

11 See *Re Paramount Airways Ltd, Bristol Airport plc v Powdrill* [1990] Ch 744, CA.

2.2 Applicant for interim order. An application for an interim order may be made personally by a debtor, or where the debtor is an undischarged bankrupt, by the debtor, the trustee of his estate or the official receiver[1]. A debtor who wishes to enter into an IVA with his creditors must formulate a proposal for a composition or scheme of arrangement[2]. The proposal must provide for a qualified practitioner[3] to act in relation to the IVA either as trustee or otherwise for the purpose of supervising its implementation[4].

IA 1986 and IR 1986 proceed upon the basis that the debtor himself applies for the interim order and makes the proposal, which he then delivers to the intended nominee who, if he agrees to act, endorses the written notice of the proposal to this effect[5]. In practice the debtor will usually engage an insolvency practitioner to prepare the proposal for him and this will be done before the application is made for an interim order. The practical effect is that the nominee can present both the proposal and his report upon it[6] when applying for the interim order, and the court can make a 'concertina order' under which both an interim order and an order for a meeting of the creditors are made with the effective period of the interim order extended beyond the date of the creditors' meeting. This cuts out one stage of what is envisaged by IA 1986 to be a two-stage procedure. In suitable cases a concertina order may be made without the attendance of any party[7].

An application for an interim order may not be made while a bankruptcy petition presented by the debtor is pending where the court has decided to appoint an insolvency practitioner to prepare a report on the feasibility of the debtor entering into a voluntary arrangement. In that event the court may if appropriate proceed to make an interim order without there being a formal application by the debtor[8].

An application for an interim order may not be made where the proposal which the debtor intends to make to his creditors involves realisable property which is the subject of a restraint order under s 41 of the Proceeds of Crime Act 2002[9].

1 IA 1986, s 253(3). An application may not be made by a debtor who is an undischarged bankrupt unless he has given notice of the proposal he intends to make to his creditors to the official receiver and any trustee who has been appointed to this estate: IA 1986, s 253(4).

2 IA 1986, s 253. The rules effectively require the proposal to be in writing as IR 1986, r 5.4(2) provides that the debtor must give his intended nominee written notice of his proposal, this notice 'accompanied by a copy of the proposal' to be delivered to the nominee or to a person.

3 The supervisor may be a qualified insolvency practitioner or an authorised practitioner under the provisions of IA 1986, s 389A: see para 1.12 above.

4 IA 1986, s 253(2).
5 See IR 1986, r 5.4(3).
6 See para 4.7 below.
7 *Practice Direction Insolvency Proceedings* para 16.1(3). See Appendix 6.
8 IA 1986, ss 253(5) and 273(2).
9 *Re M (restraint order)* [1992] QB 377 at 382; previously Drug Trafficking Offences Act 1986, s 8.

2.3 Procedure on application for interim order. A debtor who is not bankrupt should present an originating application[1] for an interim order to a court in which the debtor would be entitled to present his own petition in bankruptcy[2]. The general rule is that a bankruptcy petition is to be presented to the county court for the insolvency district in which the debtor has resided or carried on business for the longest period during the six months immediately before the presentation of the petition[3]. Should the debtor's place of business be situated in a different insolvency district from his place of residence, it is the place of business which is decisive[4]. If the debtor has carried on business in more than one insolvency district, the correct court is that for the insolvency district in which the debtor's principle place of business is situated or has been for the longest period during the six months immediately before presentation of the petition[5]. The High Court is the insolvency court for the London insolvency district, and it is to the High Court that petitions should be presented where the debtor is not resident in England or Wales[6]. In the case of an undischarged bankrupt the application should be made to the court having the conduct of the bankruptcy[7].

The application must be accompanied by an affidavit[8] dealing with the following matters:

(a) the reasons for making the application;
(b) particulars of any execution or other legal process which, to the debtor's knowledge, has been commenced against him;
(c) that he is an undischarged bankrupt or is able to petition for his own bankruptcy, as appropriate;
(d) that no previous application for an interim order has been made by or in respect of the debtor in the period of 12 months ending with the date of the affidavit; and
(e) naming the nominee under the proposal, and stating that he is qualified to act as an insolvency practitioner in relation to the debtor and is willing to act[9] in relation to the proposal[10].

On receiving the application and affidavit the court fixes a venue[11] for the hearing[12]. The applicant must give at least two days' notice[13] of the hearing (i) to the nominee who has agreed to act, and (ii) to any creditor who to the debtor's knowledge has presented a bankruptcy petition against him, or, where the application is made by or on behalf of an undischarged bankrupt, to whoever of the bankrupt, his trustee or the official receiver is not the applicant[14]. Any person to whom notice has been given may appear or be represented at the hearing of the application[15].

In suitable cases the bankruptcy registrar or district judge will make a 14-day interim order with the application adjourned 14 days for consideration of the nominee's report without the attendance or the parties[16]. The papers must be in order and the nominee's signed consent to act must include a waiver of notice of the application or a consent by the nominee to the making of an interim order without attendance[17].

In deciding whether to make an interim order the court is required to take into account any representations made by or on behalf of any person who is entitled to notice of the hearing[18]. In particular, where the application relates to an undischarged bankrupt the court must consider any representations made as to the exercise of the court's power[19] (a) to make provision in the interim order for the conduct of the bankruptcy and the administration of the estate during the period for which the interim order is in force, and (b) to include in such provision a stay of the bankruptcy proceedings or the modification of any provision in IA 1986 or IR 1986 in their application to the debtor's bankruptcy[20]. This potentially wide discretion in the court to modify provisions of IA 1986 or IR 1986 may only be exercised where the court is satisfied that the modification proposed is unlikely to result in any significant diminution in, or in the value of, the debtor's estate for the purposes of the bankruptcy[21].

Where a High Court judge allows an appeal against a refusal by a district judge to make an interim order, the matter can be dealt with by the judge who may make an interim order in the High Court to save incurring further costs on a remission back to the county court[22].

1 Ie in Form 7.1: see IR 1986, r 7.2(1), Sch 4.
2 IR 1986, r 5.8(1): see IR 1986, r 6.40. The application must contain sufficient information to establish that it is brought in the appropriate court: IR 1986, r 5.8(2).
3 IR 1986, r 6.9(2).
4 IR 1986, r 6.9(3).
5 IR 1986, r 6.9(4).
6 IR 1986, r 6.9(1).
7 IR 1986, r 5.8(3), which provides that the application must be filed with the bankruptcy proceedings.
8 Following the provisions of IA 1986, s 253(3) where the application is made by or in respect of an undischarged bankrupt the affidavit may presumably be sworn by the debtor, the trustee of his estate or the official receiver. Where the debtor has not been adjudicated bankrupt he should swear the affidavit.
9 A copy of the notice to the intended nominee under IR 1986, r 5.4 (see para 4.3 below) endorsed to the effect that he agrees to act, together with a copy of the debtor's proposal given to the nominee under r 5.4, must be exhibited to the affidavit: IR 1986, r 5.7(2). In some courts proof of the nominee's certification is required.
10 IR 1986, r 5.7(1).
11 Under the Insolvency Rules 'venue' means not only the place but also the time and date for the hearing: IR 1986, r 13.6.
12 IR 1986, r 5.7(3).
13 The provisions of CPR, r 2.8 (time) apply, and accordingly Saturdays, Sundays, Bank Holidays, Christmas Day and Good Friday are excluded from the computation of time where the specified period is five days or less, IR 1986, r 12.9.
14 IR 1986, r 5.7(4).
15 IR 1986, r 5.9(1).
16 See *Practice Direction Insolvency Proceedings* para 16.1(1): see Appendix 6.
17 An interim order made without a hearing under the Practice Direction may be combined with a standard order made on consideration of the nominee's report to the court, see para 2.2 above: a 'concertina' order.
18 IR 1986, r 5.9(2).
19 Under IA 1986, s 255(3), (4).
20 IR 1986, r 5.9(2).
21 IA 1986, s 255(5).
22 *Knowles v Coutts & Co* [1998] BPIR 96.

2.4 The making of an interim order. On the hearing of the application the court may make an interim order if it considers that it would be appropriate to do so for the purpose of facilitating consideration and implementation of the debtor's proposals for a voluntary arrangement[1], provided that it is satisfied that:

(a) the debtor intends to make a proposal for an IVA;
(b) on the day of the making of the application the debtor was an undischarged bankrupt or was able to petition for his own bankruptcy[2];
(c) no previous application has been made by the debtor for an interim order during the 12 months preceding the date of the application[3]; and
(d) the nominee under the debtor's proposal is authorised[4] and is willing to act in relation to the proposal[5].

There is no statutory guidance as to when it will be 'appropriate' for the court to make an interim order. As envisaged by IA 1986 the debtor is at this stage of the procedure asking for an interim order preparatory to the nominee considering its details and reporting back to the court[6]. It is likely to be very difficult for the court to reach any firm conclusion as to the bona fides of the proposal or the practicability of the proposal's terms. In practice, however, most proposals will have been prepared by or with the assistance of the nominee and this will usually give the court confidence to grant an interim order to allow the proposal to proceed.

The court has a full discretion in all the circumstances of the case to make or decline to make an interim order[7]. The court should be satisfied that the proposal is one which can be described as 'serious and viable'[8] being careful not to allow applications for interim orders simply to become a means of postponing the making of a bankruptcy order in circumstances where there is no apparent likelihood of benefit to the creditors from such postponement[9]. If the court concludes that there is no reasonable prospect of the proposal being complied with were it to be approved an interim order should be refused[10]. While a small return to the creditors from the proposed arrangement is a factor the court may take into consideration it is not by itself a proper reason for refusing to make an interim order; that is matter for the creditors to consider[11].

In considering all the circumstances of the case the court is entitled to take into account the debtor's previous conduct and litigation history; where the debtor showed a propensity for relentless and misconceived litigation and the court concluded that an IVA was unlikely to proceed in good faith or lead to finality between the debtor and his creditors an interim order could properly be refused[12]. The court may also take into account the size of the nominee's fee and, in exceptional cases, the remuneration which it is proposed should be paid to the supervisor if the proposal is approved. The level of remuneration might affect the validity of the proposal; it will (almost invariably) take priority over distributions to creditors and will thus both reduce the amount of any dividend and postpone the time of payment[13]. Whether or not the level of remuneration may affect the viability of the proposal the court may refuse an interim order on the ground that the remuneration in itself is excessive, particularly in respect of payments to the nominee over which there can be no direct control by the creditors[14]. However, the court should only intervene by refusing to allow the proposal to proceed in a plain case of overcharging, and only after affording the nominee the opportunity to justify his proposed remuneration[15]. It is understandable that the court should adopt this approach, and there will be many instances of individual debtors requiring a measure of protection from insolvency practitioners on the question of fees. On this basis it may well be justifiable that a different practice develops in IVA than in CVA, where it may well be that company directors are better able where necessary to bargain with insolvency practitioners. In CVA the court has no real opportunity to intervene as it does in IVA where an interim order is sought. Where a moratorium is in force the necessary documents are lodged[16] and the proposal proceeds to the creditors' and company meetings, unless a challenge is made by a creditor, without the involvement of the court. Where there is no moratorium a favourable report to the court by the nominee[17] is followed by the summoning of meetings to consider the proposal 'unless the court otherwise directs'[18]. At this stage the court could intervene to direct that no meetings should take place unless the terms of the nominee's remuneration are revised. It is not the general practice of the courts, however, to give a proposed company voluntary arrangement the degree of scrutiny required for this purpose.

Where the debtor is an undischarged bankrupt the court may include provisions in the interim order regulating the conduct of the bankruptcy and the administration of the estate while the order is in force[19]. Such provisions may stay proceedings in the bankruptcy or modify any provision in IA 1986 or IR 1986 relating to the bankruptcy[20] provided that the court is satisfied that no significant diminution in, or in the value of, the debtor's estate will result[21].

Where an interim order is made the court must send at least two sealed copies of the order to the applicant who must then (i) serve one of the copies on the nominee under the proposal[22], and (ii) give notice forthwith of the making of the order to any person who was given notice of the hearing[23] but was not present or represented at it[24].

On making an interim order the court must fix a time and place for consideration of the nominee's report[25], unless the report has been filed on the making or hearing of the application for an interim order[26]. The consideration of the nominee's report must take place within the 14-day life of the interim order[27], though where the nominee is granted an extension of time for filing his report[28] the court should order a corresponding extension to the period for which the interim order has effect unless there appear to be good reasons against doing so[29]. An interim order may not be made retrospectively so as to validate an otherwise invalid voluntary arrangement[30].

1 IA 1986, s 255(2).

2 The only ground on which a debtor may present his own petition is that he is unable to pay his debts, ie pay his debts as they fall due: *Re Coney (a bankrupt)* [1998] BPIR 333. The requirement that a debtor must be either an undischarged bankrupt or able to present his own petition is clear. It follows that a discharged bankrupt cannot enter into an IVA as a means of paying her creditors in full when it transpires that because of a significant increase in property values the assets in her estate become worth rather more than was at first thought to be the case: see *Wright v Official Receiver* [2001] BPIR 196, a decision of the Medway County Court district judge. It is surprising that an interim order was ever made in this case, but it does perhaps demonstrate that interim orders are readily obtained. A discharged bankrupt will be able to propose an IVA only in respect of (a) debts which are not released on his discharge, as to which see IR 1986, r 12.3(2), (2A), or (b) post bankruptcy debts.

3 The fact that a proposal was not properly formulated and there was no nominee (the insolvency practitioner having refused to act further) did not prevent it being an application for an interim order on which the court made a decision to dismiss. Accordingly, when an application was made a month later with a different proposal and a new nominee it failed under the 12-month rule: *Hurst v Bennett (No 2)* [2001] EWCA Civ 1398, [2002] BPIR 102.

4 See para 1.12 above.

5 IA 1986, s 255(1).

6 See para 4.7 below.

7 See *Hook v Jewson Ltd* [1997] BPIR 100 at 104–105, where Scott V-C rejected the suggestion that the court had only a limited discretion to refuse an application for an interim order.

8 *Cooper v Fearnley, Re a Debtor (No 3 of 1994)* [1997] BPIR 20 at 21. When the nominee reports to the court as to the holding of a creditors' meeting he must now express an opinion whether or not the proposals have a reasonable prospect of being approved and implemented: IA 1986, s 256(1)(a), as amended by IA 2000: see para 4.6 below.

9 *Hook v Jewson Ltd* [1997] 1 BCLC 664 at 669; [1997] BPIR 100.

10 *Re a Debtor (No 140 of 1995)* [1996] 2 BCLC 429, where the court refered to a 'realistic' prospect of acceptance. The amendments to IA 1986, s 256(1)(a) introduced by IA 2000 now require 'reasonable' prospect of acceptance and implementation: there should be no difference in practice.
11 *Knowles v Coutts & Co* [1998] BPIR 96.
12 *Hurst v Kroll Buchler Phillips Ltd* [2002] All ER (D) 41 (Dec), Ch D, 4 December 2002.
13 In *Hook v Jewson* [1997] BPIR 100 an important factor in the court's refusal of an interim order was the fact that payment to the creditors would be postponed by some four years. In *Re O'Sullivan* [2001] BPIR 534 the court suggested that a postponement of dividend by 18 months would be insufficient to justify a refusal of an interim order. It is important to note, however, that the creditors may propose a modification of the voluntary arrangement terms as to payment before agreeing to approve them. It is for the creditors rather than the court to make judgments as to the supervisor's (as opposed to the nominee's) remuneration.
14 *Re O'Sullivan* [2001] BPIR 534 at 538, where the court rejected the argument that the amount of the remuneration to be paid to nominee or supervisor was a matter for the debtor and creditors alone and beyond the scope of any proper intervention by the court in the exercise of its discretion whether to make an interim order.
15 *Re O'Sullivan* [2001] BPIR 534. The district judge had taken the view that for a relatively simple IVA the nominee's fee of £2,500 was excessive; he was not prepared to allow more than £1,000. The High Court judge deferred to his experience.
16 See para 3.3 below.
17 Under IA 1986, s 2: see para 4.7 below.
18 IA 1986, s 3(1).
19 IA 1986, s 255(3).
20 Ie any provision in the 'second group of parts' IA 1986, ss 252–385.
21 IA 1986, s 255(4), (5).
22 IR 1986, r 5.10(1). For the form of interim order, see IR 1986, Sch 4, Form 5.2, and see Appendix 4.14.
23 Under IR 1986, r 5.7(4): see para 2.3 above.
24 IR 1986, r 5.10(2).
25 IR 1986, r 5.9(3).
26 See para 2.3 above.
27 See IA 1986, s 255(6) and para 2.6 below.
28 Under IA 1986, s 256(4) and see para 2.6 below.
29 IR 1986, r 5.9(4). Note that the court may direct that the interim order should continue for such further period as it may specify where the debtor applies for the replacement of the nominee on the ground that he has failed to submit his report: see IA 1986, s 256(3).
30 *Fletcher v Vooght* [2000] BPIR 435.

2.5 Effect of interim order. The interim order has the effect of preventing a bankruptcy petition being presented or proceeded with against the debtor[1], neither may any other proceedings or execution or other legal process[2] be commenced or continued against the person or property of the debtor without the leave of the court[3]. This means that secured creditors require the leave of the court to commence or continue proceedings to enforce their security. For example, a bank would need leave before seeking an order for possession and sale of property charged as security for a debt. In the normal course of events a secured creditor will be granted the leave he requires, but he should not neglect to obtain it before enforcing his security. Retrospective leave can be given, even after the expiry of the limitation period[4]. However, leave is mandatory and if not obtained, and in the absence of an application for retrospective leave, the security will be set aside[5]. Any court may give leave, not just the court making the interim order[6].

A secured creditor will not need leave to appoint a receiver under a charge or a statutory power because such an appointment does not involve any court process. An interim order does not preclude the appointment of a receiver by the court under the Proceeds of Crime Act 2002, s 41(7)[7], nor does it prevent the enforcement either of a fine for a criminal offence or a criminal compensation order[8].

The courts have interpreted 'execution or other legal process' as meaning a process of a judicial, adjudicative or quasi-judicative nature[9]. As a result both the levying of distress[10] and peaceable re-entry under the forfeiture clause of a lease[11] were permitted despite an interim order. These decisions were reversed by IA 2000, and now a landlord requires the leave of the court before he can either levy distress or exercise a right of re-entry[12].

Any court in which proceedings are pending against an individual may, on proof that an application has been made for an interim order in respect of that individual, either stay the proceedings or allow them to continue on such terms as it thinks fit[13]. The interim order has a short initial life. It ceases to have effect at the end of 14 days beginning with the day after the order is made[14]. The period for which the interim order has effect may, however, be extended by the court on the application of the nominee[15] in order to give the nominee more time to prepare his report to the court[16].

Within the period during which the interim order is valid the nominee must submit a report to the court stating whether, in his opinion, a meeting of the debtor's creditors should be summoned to consider the debtor's proposal, and if so the date, time and place where the meeting should take place[17].

1 IA 1986, s 252(2)(a).
2 Which will include the bankruptcy administration itself where the applicant for an interim order is a bankrupt.
3 IA 1986, s 252(2)(b).
4 *Re Saunders (a bankrupt)* [1997] Ch 60 approved by implication in *Clarke v Coutts & Co* [2002] BPIR 916, CA: see paras 44, 45.
5 *Clarke v Coutts & Co* [2002] BPIR 916, CA; a charging order nisi is not a completed execution and therefore leave is required to make the order absolute if the debtor chargor obtains an interim order after charging order nisi.
6 *Clarke v Coutts & Co* [2002] BPIR 916, CA: see para 50.
7 *Re M (restraint order)* [1992] QB 377. The Proceeds of Crime Act 2002 replaces the Drug Trafficking Offences Act 1986, which was in force in 1992.
8 *R v Barnet Justices, ex p Phillipou* [1997] BPIR 134.
9 See *Smith (a bankrupt) v Braintree District Council* [1990] 2 AC 215, HL; *Re Paramount Airways Ltd; Bristol Airport plc v Powdrill* [1990] BCC 130; *Exchange Travel Agency Ltd v Triton Property Trusty plc* [1991] BCC 341; *Re Olympia and York Canary Wharf Ltd* [1993] BCC 154.
10 *McMullen & Sons Ltd v Cerrone* [1994] BCC 25, where, however, the court noted that distress was precluded without leave of the court in company administration: IA 1986, s 11(3).
11 *Re a Debtor (No 13A of 1994)* [1996] BPIR 43, but see *Re Naeem* [1990] 1 WLR 48 at 50E.
12 IA 1986, s 252(2)(aa) (peaceable re-entry); IA 1986, s 252(2)(b) (distress), as amended by IA 2000, Sch 3, para 2.
13 IA 1986, s 254(2).
14 IA 1986, s 255(6), where the interim order is made after the presentation of a debtor's petition for bankruptcy the court has power to determine the length of its validity: IA 1986, s 274(4).
15 See para 2.6 below.
16 IA 1986, s 256(4): for the nominee's report to the court see para 4.7 below.
17 IA 1986, s 256(1). The court must fix a date for the consideration of the nominee's report when making the interim order: IR 1986, r 5.9(3). The nominee's report must be delivered to the court not less than two days before the interim order ceases to have effect: IR 1986, r 5.11(1).

2.6 Duration of interim order. Unless extended an interim order ceases to have effect at the end of a period of 14 days beginning with the day after it is made[1]. Should the nominee fail to submit a report to the court[2], the debtor may apply to the court for a direction that the interim order shall continue, or if it has ceased to have effect shall be renewed, for such period as the court may specify in the direction[3]. On the application of the nominee, the court may extend the period for which the interim order has effect so as to enable the nominee to have more time to prepare his report[4].

If satisfied on receiving the nominee's report that a meeting of the debtor's creditors should be summoned to consider the debtor's proposal, the court should then extend the period for which the interim order has effect for such further period as is necessary for the purpose of enabling the debtor's proposal to be considered by his creditors[5].

In practice interim orders are often extended to enable the nominee either to obtain further instructions or to discuss amendments to the proposal with major creditors. Fourteen days is a short time in which to consider the debtor's proposals and formulate an effective proposal for a voluntary arrangement. Additionally, interim orders are extended because it does not prove possible to hold the creditors' meeting on the date anticipated, not least because the proposal has to be amended by the nominee in the light of further information received from the debtor or creditors. A further difficulty which is not infrequently encountered is that major creditors will be represented at the creditors' meeting by junior staff who do not have the authority to vote on any significant amendment to the proposal which may be raised during the course of the meeting. When considering applications to extend the interim order the court should consider whether there remains a sufficient likelihood that arrangements will be approved by the creditors to justify the continuance of an order which restricts creditors' legal rights and remedies against the debtor. Where there is evidence that the meeting will not approve the proposal, and in particular where creditors holding 25% in value of the debtor's debts adamantly oppose it, the court should not continue the interim order even if directions have been given for the holding of a creditors' meeting which has not yet taken place[6].

An interim order which is in force immediately before the end of the period of 28 days beginning with the day on which the decision of the creditors meeting was reported to the court[7] ceases to have effect at the end of that period[8], unless the court continues or renews the order in the course of an application to challenge the decision of the creditors' meeting[9]. Where the creditors' meeting has declined to approve the debtor's proposal the court may discharge any interim order then in force[10].

The court may discharge an interim order if it is satisfied, on the application of the nominee, that the debtor has failed to comply with his obligation[11] to submit to the nominee a proposal and statement of affairs or that for any other reason it would be inappropriate for a meeting of the debtor's creditors to be summoned to consider the debtor's proposal[12].

1 IA 1986, s 255(6).
2 IA 1986, s 256(3). As to the obligation of the nominee to submit a report, see para 4.7 below.
3 IA 1986, s 256(3).
4 IA 1986, s 256(4).
5 IA 1986, s 256(5); the court extends the interim order by direction.
6 *Re Cove (a debtor)* [1990] 1 All ER 949.
7 See para 6.15 below.
8 IA 1986, s 260(4).
9 Under IA 1986, s 262. See IA 1986, s 260(4) and Chapter 7 below.
10 IA 1986, s 259(2).
11 Under IA 1986, s 256(2).
12 IA 1986, s 256(6).

2.7 Proceeding without interim order. By an amendment introduced by IA 2000 a debtor, whether or not he is an undischarged bankrupt, may propose a voluntary arrangement without an interim order first being in place[1]. This is plainly appropriate where a proposal is being made by an undischarged bankrupt. It may also be useful in the rare case where a debtor who has a voluntary arrangement in place wishes to amend the terms of the arrangement and has no procedure available to him to do so within the terms of the arrangement[2]. Before bankruptcy an interim order will not be necessary where the debtor has only a few creditors who are prepared to stay their hands pending a proposal for a voluntary arrangement. A debtor who is an undischarged bankrupt must first give notice of his proposal to the official receiver and his trustee, if one has been appointed, before he may proceed[3].

The statutory scheme[4] envisages the debtor providing the nominee with a document setting out the terms of his proposed voluntary arrangement together with a statement of affairs containing the prescribed information[5]. Provided the nominee is satisfied that the debtor is either an undischarged bankrupt or is able to petition for his own bankruptcy, he has 14 days after receiving the debtor's documentation to submit a report to the court stating his opinion whether the proposed arrangement has a reasonable prospect of being approved and implemented, whether a meeting of creditors should be summoned, and the date, time and place of the creditors' meeting if this is being proposed[6]. The court is not to consider the report unless an application is made under IA 1986 or IR 1986 in respect of the debtor's proposal[7]. It is therefore accepted by IR 1986 that no useful purpose is served by the court considering the nominee's report as a matter of course; the court is to assume that all is well unless and until an application is made by a creditor or a debtor in respect of any aspect of the procedure or the proposal itself. With his report the nominee must deliver to the court (a) a copy of the debtor's proposal (with any amendments authorised by the nominee[8]), (b) a copy or summary of any statement of affairs provided by the debtor and (c) a copy of the nominee's consent to act[9]. If the nominee expresses the opinion that the debtor's proposal has a reasonable prospect of being approved and implemented, and that a meeting of the debtors creditors should be summoned, his report must annex his comments on the proposal[10]. If his opinion is against the proposal proceeding he must give reasons[11]. These documents must also be sent to the official receiver and any trustee in cases where the debtor is an undischarged bankrupt[12], and where he is not a bankrupt the documents must be sent to any person who has presented a bankruptcy petition[13]. Where the debtor is an undischarged bankrupt the nominee's report must be filed in the court having the conduct of the bankruptcy proceedings and must be filed with those proceedings[14]. In all other cases the nominee files his report in the court in which the debtor would be entitled to present his own bankruptcy petition[15]. Any creditor of the debtor is entitled to inspect the file, at all reasonable times on any business day[16].

1 IA 1986, s 256A(1).
2 As an interim order may not be made within 12 months of a previous application for an interim order (IA 1986, s 255(1)(c)) it was not previously possible for a new voluntary arrangement to vary an existing arrangement to be made in the first 12 months of that arrangement.
3 IA 1986, s 256A(1)(b); notice has to be given of the proposal not merely the intention to propose.
4 IA 1986, s 256A(2).
5 See paras 4.4–4.6 below.
6 IA 1986, s 256A(3); the court may allow a longer period than 14 days for the nominee to submit his report on the nominee's own application: IA 1986, s 256A(5) and also IR 1986, r 5.14(1).
7 IR 1986, r 5.14(1).

8 IR 1986, r 5.3(3) permits amendments at any time up to the delivery of the nominee's report to the court with the written consent of the nominee.
9 IR 1986, r 5.14(2); with these documents must be served two copies of Form 5.5 listing the various documents delivered by the nominee together with a statement that no interim order is to be made. On receipt of the report and Form 5.5 the court is to endorse one copy with the date of filing in court and return it to the nominee: IR 1986, r 5.14(4).
10 IR 1986, r 5.14(3).
11 IR 1986, r 5.14(3).
12 IR 1986, r 5.14(6).
13 IR 1986, r 5.14(7).
14 IR 1986, r 5.15(3).
15 Under IR 1986, r 6.40, see para 2.3 above, IR 1986, r 5.15(1). The report must contain sufficient information to establish that it is filed in the appropriate court: IR 1986, r 5.15(2).
16 IR 1986, r 5.14(5); express provision is made by r 5.14(8) that the service of the report under IA 1986, s 256A constitutes an insolvency proceeding for the purpose of the rules requiring the court to keep records of insolvency proceedings (IR 1986, r 7.27) with a file opened and maintained for each case in which all documents relating to the relevant proceedings are to be placed: IR 1986, r 7.30.

2.8 Applications to the court where no interim order; replacement of nominee. Any application in relation to any matter relating to a voluntary arrangement or a proposal for a voluntary arrangement where there is no interim order is to be made to the court in which the nominee's report was filed[1].

The court may replace the nominee with another practitioner authorised to act in relation to a voluntary arrangement either on the application of the debtor where the nominee has failed to submit his report or has died, or on the application of the nominee or the debtor where it is impracticable or in appropriate for the nominee to continue acting on behalf of the debtor[2]. A debtor who wishes to apply for the nominee to be replaced must give at least seven days' notice of his application to the nominee[3]. A nominee must also give seven days' notice of any application he wishes to make to be replaced by the court[4]. Before any order is made replacing a nominee there must be filed in court a statement from the replacement indicating his consent to act as nominee[5].

1 IR 1986, r 5.16(1); as to this court see para 2.7 and para 2.3 above.
2 IA 1986, s 256A(4).
3 IR 1986, r 5.16(2).
4 IR 1986, r 5.16(3).
5 IR 1986, r 5.16(4).

2.9 Fast-track procedure for undischarged bankrupt. This procedure is introduced by EA 2002 in order to encourage the greater use of IVAs and reduce the number of debtors in bankruptcy. It is available only to undischarged bankrupts where the official receiver is the proposed nominee and there is no application for an interim order[1], and any IVA which may be approved is restricted to bankruptcy creditors[2]. Once the fast-track procedure is underway, however, it will be possible for a bankrupt with post-bankruptcy debts to make a further proposal to his post-bankruptcy creditors under the protection of an interim order[3]. The fast-track scheme is that a proposal will be agreed between the bankrupt and the official receiver. It is then filed with the court. No meeting of creditors will be called and it will not be possible to modify the proposal. The official receiver will simply send out the details of the proposal to the creditors on a 'take it or leave it' basis, and the creditors will either agree to or disagree with the proposal by correspondence. A 75% majority in value of the creditors will still be required for acceptance. If the proposed IVA is approved, the official receiver will notify the court which can then annul the bankruptcy order.

Apart from the variations noted above the statutory provisions for a fast-track voluntary arrangement follow much the same format as for any other IVA. It is envisaged that the debtor will submit to the official receiver a document setting out the terms of the proposed voluntary arrangement together with a statement of affairs[4]. If the official receiver considers that the proposal has a reasonable prospect of being approved and implemented, he may make arrangements for inviting the creditors to decide whether to approve it[5]. For these purposes the 'creditors' are restricted to bankruptcy debt creditors where the official receiver is aware of both the creditor's claim and his address[6]. In practice a proposal for a fast-track IVA will usually be instigated by the official receiver who, having undertaken a preliminary investigation of a new bankruptcy, decides that the case is of sufficient simplicity to warrant a fast-track IVA and avoid the full investigation of the bankrupt's affairs which should ordinarily be undertaken in bankruptcy.

The official receiver, in making arrangements for inviting creditors to consider the proposal, must ensure that each creditor receives both a copy of the proposal and also information as to the criteria by reference to which the official receiver will determine whether the creditors approve or reject the voluntary arrangement[7]. The official receiver may not include an opportunity for modifications to the proposal to be suggested or made[8], although there would seem to be no reason why the official receiver should not raise the possibility and or terms of a proposed fast-track IVA with the major creditors in advance of agreeing a proposal with the bankrupt. This would make sense particularly where the creditors concerned are banks or Crown creditors who are familiar with voluntary arrangements and may well be in a position to make useful suggestions as to how an acceptable fast-track proposal might be formulated.

Once a bankrupt has submitted a proposal and statement of affairs to the official receiver with a view to proposing a fast-track voluntary arrangement, he may not apply for an interim order in respect of his non-bankruptcy debts until the official receiver has made arrangements for approval of the fast-track voluntary arrangement or informed the debtor that he does not intend to make such arrangements. This may be because he does not consider that there is a reasonable prospect of approval and implementation or because he declines to act[9]. It follows that once the official receiver has put in train the procedure for obtaining the creditors' votes on the fast-track proposal the bankrupt may apply for an interim order under which he may make a proposal for an IVA to his post-bankruptcy creditors.

As soon as reasonably practical after taking the views of creditors the official receiver must report the result to the court[10]. If the proposal is approved the voluntary arrangement takes effect as does any other IVA[11]. After the period for challenging the IVA has passed[12] the court annuls the bankruptcy order and, if appropriate, gives directions as to the conduct of the bankruptcy and for facilitating the IVA[13]. The provisions of IA 1986 applying to the implementation of an IVA[14], a challenge to the approval of a proposal[15], and as to criminal offences which may be committed in connection with an IVA[16], apply also to a fast-track IVA.

1 IA 1986, s 263A; note that a bankruptcy order has no effect on debts arising after the date on which it is made, so that this procedure (which applied only to bankruptcy creditors) may be difficult to utilise in the relatively rare cases where the bankrupt continues to trade and incur debts shortly after becoming bankrupt.

2 IA 1986, s 263B(3).

3 See IA 1986, s 263B(5).
4 IA 1986, s 263B(1).
5 IA 1986, s 263B(2).
6 IA 1986, s 263B(3).
7 IA 1986, s 263B(4)(a)(b); on the face of it this seems a rather convoluted way of stating that the official receiver has to inform creditors of the voting provisions of IR 1986, r 5.23 (essentially 75% majority in value where 50% of the non-associate and non-secured vote do not vote against the proposal, but see para 6.11 below). However, it is to be hoped that the official receiver will explain why he considers a fast-track IVA is appropriate and why a full investigation of the bankrupt's affairs is not necessary.
8 IA 1986, s 263B(4)(c).
9 IA 1986, s 263B(5).
10 IA 1986, s 263C.
11 IA 1986, s 263D(1)(2): see para 9.1 below.
12 IA 1986, s 263F(3), ie 28 days from the date on which the official receiver reports the result of the creditors' vote to the court, and see para 7.8 below.
13 IA 1986, s 263D(3), (4), (5).
14 Ie IA 1986, s 263, see Chapter 10 below; IA 1986, applied by IA 1986, s 263E.
15 See IA 1986, s 263F, which is in the same terms as IA 1986, s 262, see Chapter 7 below, save that the official receiver is included among the persons who may make a challenge application: IA 1986, s 263F(2)(d).
16 Ie IA 1986, s 262A and s 262B, applied by IA 1986, s 263G.

Chapter 3

The CVA moratorium: procedure to creditors' meeting

3.1 Company eligible for moratorium. The introduction of the moratorium regime is part of the government's efforts to encourage a rescue culture in the economy. It is hoped that a greater awareness of the availability of CVAs, with a moratorium period covering the preparatory stage, will encourage small companies in financial difficulty to put together a rescue plan for the benefit of creditors and, ultimately, employees and the economy generally. The moratorium gives the company's management a short time, initially 28 days, during which they can put together a proposal to place before the creditors as a whole without pressure from any particular creditor. In preparing the proposal the company's management will have the assistance of an insolvency practitioner or, in due course, an expert in company rescue[1] who will act as nominee. It will be an important task of the nominee to monitor the company's affairs during the moratorium period for the protection of creditors. A moratorium is optional[2], but while it will still be possible for a company to propose and enter a voluntary arrangement without a moratorium first being in place, it is anticipated that the moratorium route will be that followed by an overwhelming majority of companies which enter into voluntary arrangements. It should be noted that when a moratorium is or has been in force the entire procedure applicable to the CVA is governed by IA 1986, Sch A1 in place of IA 1986, Pt I. These latter provisions will continue to govern company voluntary arrangements for which no moratorium is obtained[3].

Where the company is a financial services company regulated by the Financial Services Authority, the Authority is able to oversee and influence a voluntary arrangement proposed and entered into by the company. The Financial Services Authority must be summoned to and is entitled to participate in (but not vote at) any creditors' meeting of a regulated company, and is entitled to be heard on any application made to the court with respect to a proposed or approved voluntary arrangement of a regulated company[4].

A moratorium is obtained simply by filing specified documents with the court[5]; there is no need for a formal application or court hearing. Questions of eligibility are determined as on that date, the 'date of filing'. A company is eligible for a moratorium if it meets two or more of the three conditions specified in CA 1985[6] for being a small company and it is not excluded from eligibility[7]. The specified conditions[8], are:

1. Turnover: not more than £2.8m.
2. Balance sheet total: not more than £1.4m.
3. Number of employees: not more than 50.

A company's balance sheet total, as defined[9], comprises the aggregate of the amounts shown on the balance sheet for called up share capital not paid, fixed assets[10], current assets[11], and prepayments and accrued income. These qualifying conditions must be met either (a) in the year ending with the date of filing[12], or (b) in the financial year of the company which ended last before the date of filing[13]. A company's financial year is to be determined in accordance with the provisions of CA 1985[14]. The number of employees means the average number of persons employed by the company in the year determined on a monthly basis[15].

An insolvent partnership whose members wish to propose a PVA may also obtain a moratorium. The equivalent qualifying conditions apply; turnover of not more than £2.8m, assets of not more than £1.4m, and no more than 50 employees[16]. These qualifying conditions may be met either in the year ending with the date of filing or in the last tax year of the insolvent partnership to end before the date of filing[17]. The total of turnover is the amount which is, or would be, entered as turnover in the partnership's tax return[18]. The total of assets is the amount that is or would be entered in the partnership's statement of affairs if prepared for the relevant period[19], and the number of employees is the average number of persons employed in the relevant period[20].

1 IA 1986, s 389A permits the Secretary of State to allow persons who are not insolvency practitioners to act as nominees on the basis that such persons will be rescue experts: see para 1.12 above.
2 IA 1986, s 1A(1).
3 IA 1986, s 1A(2).
4 See IA 1986, Sch A1, para 44.
5 IA 1986, Sch A1, paras 1, 7 and see para 3.3 below.
6 See CA 1985, s 247(3).
7 IA 1986, Sch A1, paras 2(1), 3.
8 Which may be modified by the Secretary of State by regulations: IA 1986, Sch A1, para 5.
9 In CA 1985, s 247(5), incorporated by IA 1986, Sch A1, para 3(3).
10 Which comprise intangible assets, tangible assets and investments: see CA 1985 Sch 4, Pt I, section B.
11 Which comprise stocks, debtors and investments: see CA 1985, Sch 4, Pt I, s B.
12 Ie of the specified documents with the court in order to obtain the moratorium: IA 1986, Sch A1, paras 1, 7 and see para 3.3 below.
13 IA 1986, Sch A1, para 3(1).
14 See CA 1985, s 223, which provides that a company's financial year is determined by reference to its accounting reference periods. If any such reference period is less than a year a proportionate adjustment should be made to the turnover and or balance sheet total figures to ascertain whether or not the company qualifies as a 'small company': CA 1985, s 247(4), incorporated by IA 1986, Sch A1, para 3(3).
15 CA 1985, s 247(6), incorporated by IA 1986, Sch A1, para 3(3). The figure is to be determined by ascertaining the number of persons employed under contracts of service by the company in each month, whether the employment lasts throughout the month or not, arriving at a total for the relevant financial year which is then divided by the number of months in that financial year.
16 IA 1986, Sch A1, para 3(3), as modified by IPO 2002.
17 IA 1986, Sch A1, para 3(1), as modified by IPO 2002.
18 Where the period covered by the qualifying conditions is not an exact year the turnover shall be proportionately adjusted: IA 1986, Sch A1, para 3(5), as modified by IPO 2002.
19 When the partnership is relying on the figures from the last tax year ending before the date of filing this will be a notional statement of affairs. Note that the statement of affairs which has to be served to obtain a moratorium (see para 3.4 below) must be up to date.
20 IA 1986, Sch A1, para 3(4), as modified by IPO 2002; for the manner of calculation see n 14 above.

3.2 Exclusion from eligibility. There are six categories of company which are excluded from eligibility for a moratorium:

1. The first category is a holding company where the group[1] of which it is the holding company does not qualify as a small or medium sized group[2] judged in respect of the last financial year of the company to end before the date of filing, or rather what would be the date of filing[3].
2. The second category of exclusions involves banks, insurance companies, and companies or partnerships operating in the financial markets. These are excluded from eligibility because they are subject to special insolvency regimes designed to protect depositors, policyholders and customers[4].
3. The third category of exclusion involves companies or partnerships in respect of which insolvency procedures are already in place, or where a moratorium has been obtained in the previous 12 months without a voluntary arrangement being approved or, an arrangement having been approved, it then ending prematurely. This is to reduce the risk of improper use of the moratorium procedure. Accordingly, a company is excluded from being eligible for a moratorium if, on the date of filing:
   (a) an administration order is in force in relation to the company;
   (b) the company is being wound up;
   (c) there is an administrative receiver[5] of the company;
   (d) a voluntary arrangement has effect in relation to the company;
   (e) there is a provisional liquidator of the company;
   (f) a moratorium has been in force for the company at any time during the period of 12 months ending with the date of filing and –
      (i) no voluntary arrangement had effect at the time at which the moratorium came to an end, or
      (ii) a voluntary arrangement which had effect at any time in that period has come to an end prematurely, or
   (g) a voluntary arrangement entered into by the company in pursuance of a proposal made by an administrator or liquidator of the company[6] has come to an end prematurely and, during the period of 12 months ending with the date of filing, the court has made an order[7] staying all proceedings in the winding up or discharging the administration order[8].

   A company remains eligible for a moratorium where, by reason of a winding-up order made after the date of filing, it is to be treated as being wound up on that date[9].

   The same restrictions apply to an insolvent partnership as listed above. In addition an insolvent partnership may not obtain a moratorium where an order has been made on an 'Article 11 petition', that is a joint petition presented under IPO 1994, Art 11 for the bankruptcy of all the individual members of a partnership, there being no corporate or limited partners in the partnership[10].
4. The fourth category of company excluded from eligibility for a moratorium is a company which is a party to a capital market arrangement under which a party has incurred, or was expected to incur on the making of the agreement, a debt of least £10m under the arrangement, and the arrangement involves the issue of a capital market[11].
5. The fifth category of excluded company is a project company of a public-private partnership project which includes step-in rights[12].
6. The sixth category of excluded company is a company which, on the date of filing, has incurred a liability under an agreement of £10m or more[13].

The liability may be present or future, certain or contingent and includes liabilities to be paid wholly or in part in foreign currency[14]. Where the liability is a contingent liability under or by virtue of a guarantee, indemnity or security provided on behalf of another person, the amount of that liability is the full amount of the liability in relation to which the guarantee, indemnity or security is provided[15].

1 'Group' means a parent undertaking and its subsidiary undertakings: CA 1985, s 262, applicable by virtue of IA 1986, Sch A1, para 2(5).
2 By virtue of CA 1985, s 249, the qualifications for a small group are: (1) aggregate turnover not more than £2.8m net (or £3.36m gross); (2) aggregate balance sheet total not more than £1.4m net (or £1.68m gross); (3) aggregate number of employees not more than 50. The qualifications for a medium-sized group are: (1) aggregate turnover not more than £11.2m net (or £13.44m gross); (2) aggregate balance sheet total not more than £5.6m net (or £6.72m gross); (3) aggregate number of employees not more than 250, applicable by virtue of IA 1986, Sch A1, para 2(5).
3 IA 1986, Sch A1, para 2(4).
4 IA 1986, Sch A1, para 2(2)(3).
5 Or agricultural receiver in the case of a partnership.
6 Ie under IA 1986, s 1(3).
7 Under IA 1986, s 5(3)(a).
8 IA 1986, Sch A1, para 4(1).
9 IA 1986, Sch A1, para 4(2).
10 IA 1986, Sch A1, para 4(1), as modified by IPO 2002.
11 IA 1986, Sch A1, para 4A. A capital market arrangement and capital market investment is defined in IA 1986, Sch A1, paras 4D, 4E and 4F, and the £10m debt may be incurred at any time during the life of the capital market arrangement and may be expressed wholly or in part in a foreign currency: IA 1986, Sch A1, para 4G. These provisions do not apply to insolvent partnerships, IA 1986, s 1A(4), as modified by IPO 2002.
12 IA 1986, Sch A1, para 4B. Project company is defined in para 4H, a public-private partnership project in para 4I, and step-in rights in para 4J.
13 IA 1986, Sch A1, para 4C(1).
14 IA 1986, Sch A1, para 4C(3); the sterling equivalent is to be calculated as at the time when the liability is incurred: IA 1986, Sch A1, para 4C(3)(b).
15 IA 1986, Sch A1, para 4C(2).

3.3 Obtaining a moratorium. Experience with interim orders in IVAs has shown that insolvency practitioners have more than simply given advice on proposals; they have taken control of the process leading to the creditors' meeting. In consequence it is rare that the court holds formal hearings to make the interim order, consider the nominee's report, extend the interim order and direct that a creditors' meeting be summoned. Where there is no pending petition for bankruptcy all such orders may now be made without the parties' attendance on the filing of the required documents[1]. This practice is now adopted and extended with the CVA moratorium. A moratorium is obtained simply by the directors of the company filing specified documents in court[2]. There are five documents which have to be filed with the court in order to obtain a moratorium[3]:

1. the terms of the proposed voluntary arrangement;
2. a statement of the company's affairs containing the prescribed information and particulars of its creditors and of its debts and other liabilities and of its assets;
3. a statement that the company is eligible for a moratorium;
4. a statement from the nominee that he has given his consent to act; and
5. the nominee's statement.

Each of the statements 2 to 5 above, except the particulars of the company's creditors, debts, liabilities and assets, must be in the prescribed form[4]. The

Secretary of State is given power to modify this documentary requirement by regulation[5].

As with other voluntary arrangements the directors of the debtor company will have been in detailed discussion with the insolvency practitioner[6] who is intended to be the nominee before any decision is made to make a proposal for a CVA and to do so under the protection of a moratorium. The intended nominee will advise the directors as to and assist in the preparation of the necessary documents and no proposal will proceed unless the nominee feels able to support it for the purpose of the nominee's statement. There is no reason why the nominee should not file the documents in court on behalf of the directors, and in practice the nominee will in most cases undertake all dealings with the court after obtaining the necessary authority from the company's directors.

The formal scheme of IA 1986 is that the directors of the debtor company prepare the proposal[7]. The proposal is submitted to the nominee who considers it and then, in a formal document in prescribed form[8] submitted by the nominee to the directors, the nominee indicates his opinion whether or not:

(a) the proposed voluntary arrangement has a reasonable prospect of being both approved and implemented;
(b) the company is likely to have sufficient funds available to it during the proposed moratorium; and
(c) meetings of the company and its creditors should be summoned to consider the proposed voluntary arrangement.

Provided they obtain the written consent of the nominee, the directors may amend the proposal at any time before the nominee submits his nominee's statement to them[9]. Documents delivered by the directors to the nominee must be delivered to the nominee personally or to a person expressly authorised to take delivery of documents on his behalf[10]. The nominee is given 28 days within which to consider the proposal and submit his nominee's statement to the directors[11]. The nominee's statement must have annexed to it (a) his comments on the proposal, unless he expresses a negative opinion as to either the proposal's prospects of success or whether the company is likely to have sufficient funds to enable it to carry on its business during the period of the moratorium in which event he must give his reasons for that opinion, and (b) where he is willing to act as nominee a statement of his consent to act[12].

Plainly it would be inappropriate for the directors to sit on a nominee's statement supporting a proposed arrangement and moratorium; circumstances may change. Accordingly, the directors are given just three working days from receipt of the nominee's statement to file the necessary documents for the moratorium in court[13].

Two further documents should be filed with the moratorium documents[14]. First, any statement of reasons given by the nominee when allowing the directors to prepare the company's statement of affairs to a date earlier than two weeks before the date on which the proposal was delivered to the nominee[15]. Second, the nominee's comments on the proposal[16].

1 See *Practice Direction: Insolvency Proceedings* para 16, Appendix 6.
2 IA 1986, Sch A1, para 7(1), which specifies both the documents to be filed and that they are to be filed at court by the directors.
3 IA 1986, Sch A1, para 7(1).
4 IA 1986, Sch A1, para 7(2). See Appendix 5.1.
5 IA 1986, Sch A1, para 7(4); not in PVA where modifications are made by the Lord Chancellor with the concurrence of the Secretary of State: IA 1986, s 420.

6 Or, when sanctioned, other authorised person: see para 1.12 above.
7 IA 1986, Sch A1, para 6(1) and IR 1986, r 1.35(1)(a).
8 Form 1.5: see Appendix 5.
9 IR 1986, r 1.35(2).
10 IR 1986, r 1.36(1); on receiving the documents the nominee must immediately acknowledge their receipt to the directors, specifying the date on which they were received: IR 1986, r 1.36(2).
11 IR 1986, r 1.38(1).
12 IR 1986, r 1.38(2).
13 IR 1986, r 1.39(1); the moratorium documents must be delivered to court together with four copies of a schedule listing them: IR 1986, r 1.39(1). The schedule may be in Form 1.9, see Appendix 5. These copies are endorsed by the court with the date on which they were filed in court, and three copies of the schedule duly endorsed and sealed by the court are then returned to the person who filed the documents: IR 1986, r 1.39(3).
14 IR 1986, r 1.39(2).
15 IR 1986, r 1.37(3) and see para 3.4 below.
16 IR 1986, r 1.38(2) and see text to n 12 above.

3.4 The moratorium documents. Five separate documents are required to be filed at court to obtain a moratorium and one or two further documents may have to be served with the moratorium documents[1].

1. *The terms of the proposed voluntary arrangement.* This document is usually called 'the proposal'. IR 1986 require the proposal to provide a short explanation why, in the directors' opinion, a voluntary arrangement is desirable giving reasons why the company's creditors may be expected to concur with the proposed arrangement and must state, or deal with, the various matters specified in the Rules[2]. There are 17 heads of matter to be dealt with in the proposal. The detail required for an effective voluntary arrangement will be beyond most company directors and the terms will usually be prepared by the intended nominee. Those terms which relate specifically to the particular arrangement are usually prepared with some care. As for the remaining terms, there are a number of standard forms of voluntary arrangement in general circulation. It is not unknown for these to be imported into proposals without any thought being given to their appropriateness to the particular case. The reader is referred to the observations made in relation to the drafting of voluntary arrangements in Appendix 4 below. The attitude of the Inland Revenue and Customs & Excise to the proposal is usually of great importance to its prospects of approval. This is for three reasons. First, the Revenue and Customs will usually be preferential creditors at least as to part of their debt. Their preferential rights may not be altered without their consent[3]. Secondly, they are often substantial creditors. Thirdly, their position as tax authorities usually gives them a good deal of background information on the debtor and its business affairs, certainly more than is available to the average creditor. Even after the abolition of Crown preference[4], the Revenue and Customs will frequently be important creditors. For comment on the approach to voluntary arrangements which will be adopted by the Revenue and Customs see para 4.12 below.
2. *Statement of affairs.* The same details are required for a statement of affairs when a moratorium is obtained as when a CVA proceeds without a moratorium[5]. The particulars which IR 1986 specify have to be included in the statement of affairs all take up matters which have to be in the proposal. Indeed, IR 1986, r 1.37(2) provides that the statement of affairs is 'to supplement or amplify, so far as is necessary for clarifying the state of

the company's affairs [the particulars] already given in the directors' proposal'. The statement of affairs needs to be up to date. It must be prepared to a date not earlier than two weeks before the date on which the proposal is delivered to the nominee[6]. The nominee may, however, allow an extension of this two-week period to the nearest practicable date not earlier than two months before the date of delivery of the proposal; if he does so the nominee must give a written statement of his reasons to the directors[7]. The use in the rules of the word 'practicable' indicates that it is for reasons of practicality, and those alone, that a nominee may extend the period. The statement of affairs must be in the prescribed form[8], and must be certified as correct, to the best of their knowledge and belief, by two or more directors of the company or by the company secretary and at least one (other) director[9].

3. *Statement that company is eligible for a moratorium.* A company is eligible for a moratorium if it meets two or more of the conditions specified in CA 1985 for being a small company, and is not excluded from eligibility[10]. The three specified conditions are turnover not more than £2.8m, balance sheet total not more than £1.4m and not more than 50 employees. IA 1986[11] requires only a statement of eligibility[12], and the prescribed form simply states that the company (1) meets the requirements for eligibility and (2) is not excluded from being eligible. It is not therefore required that the statement identifies which of the three specified conditions are met or what the relevant figures are for turnover, balance sheet total or number of employees.

4. *Statement from nominee that he has given his consent to act.* This statement must be given in the prescribed form[13]. This form (in common with the other prescribed forms) is as straightforward a form as might be devised. It requires the nominee to give his name, address and qualification.

5. *The nominee's statement.* Under the formal requirements of the Act[14] this statement is prepared by the nominee after receiving details of the proposal and the prescribed information from the directors. In practice the nominee will in most cases have been in discussion with the directors as to the possibility of preparing a suitable proposal, and on the assumption that the directors accept his advice on a proposal which may be put to creditors the nominee will be able to complete the requisite prescribed form for the nominee's statement along with the proposal[15]. The nominee's statement must indicate whether or not, in his opinion:
   (a) the proposed voluntary arrangement has a reasonable prospect of being approved and implemented[16];
   (b) the company is likely to have sufficient funds available to it during the proposed moratorium to enable it to carry on its business; and
   (c) meetings of the company and its creditors should be summoned to consider the proposed voluntary arrangement[17].

The nominee is entitled to rely on the information submitted to him by the directors when forming the opinions expressed in the nominee's statement unless he has reason to doubt its accuracy[18]. If he requires more information for the purpose of preparing his statement, the nominee is entitled to require the directors to provide it[19]. The business for which the company must be likely to have sufficient funds is the business which the company proposes to carry on during the moratorium, whatever activities it may have carried out previously[20]. The directors may have to curtail the company's activities in order to ensure that it may trade throughout the moratorium, and if the nominee's opinion as to the sufficiency of funds is based on a restriction of trading activity this should be made clear in the nominee's statement. In many cases the company will be dependent on its bankers for any continued trading. The nominee will have to secure the bank's agreement to maintain facilities over to the date proposed for a creditors' meeting.

1 See para 3.3 above.
2 IR 1986, r 1.35(2); see para 4.4 below and Appendix 2. The proposal must also state the address to which notice of the nominee's consent to act, the nominee's statement and the nominee's comments on the proposal are to be sent: IR 1986, r 1.35(1)(c).
3 IA 1986, Sch A1, para 31(5).
4 Crown preference is abolished by EA 2002, s 251 when it comes into force.
5 IR 1986, r 1.39(4) and see para 4.5 below.
6 IR 1986, r 1.37(3). For the delivery of the proposal to the nominee, see para 3.3 above.
7 IR 1986, r 1.37(3).
8 IA 1986, Sch A1, para 7(2), Form 1.6 (see Appendix 5) which requires the makers of the statement to set out the details referred to in IR 1986, rr 1.37(2) and 1.39(4) without requiring these to be in any particular format.
9 IR 1986, r 1.37(4).
10 See para 3.2 above.
11 IA 1986, Sch A1, para 7(1)(c).
12 The statement must be in the prescribed form, IA 1986, Sch A1, para 7(2): see Form 1.7.
13 IA 1986, Sch A1, para 7(2): see Form 1.8.
14 IA 1986, Sch A1 para 6
15 That the statement must be in the prescribed form, see IA 1986, Sch A1, para 7(2). For the Form see 1.5
16 See para 4.6 below.
17 IA 1986, Sch A1, para 6(2)(a), (b), (c).
18 IA 1986, Sch A1, para 6(3).
19 IA 1986, Sch A1, para 6(1)(c).
20 IA 1986, Sch A1, para 6(4).

3.5 Duration of moratorium. The moratorium comes into force when the specified documents are filed with the court[1]. The moratorium ends[2]:

(a) at the end of the day on which the creditors' and company meetings[3] are first held, or, if the meetings are held on different days, the later of those days, subject to any extension of the moratorium[4];
(b) if either of the creditors' or company meetings has not met before the end of the period of 28 days beginning with the day on which the moratorium comes into force, the moratorium ends at the end of the day on which those meetings were to be held (or, if those meetings were summoned to be held on different days, the later of those days), unless the moratorium is extended[5];
(c) if the nominee fails to summon either meeting within the period of 28 days of the moratorium coming into force, the moratorium ends at the end of the last day of that period[6];
(d) if the moratorium is extended (or further extended) it ends at the end of the day to which it is extended (or further extended)[7].

A moratorium may, however, come to a premature end if the nominee withdraws his consent to act[8], or the court so orders on an application to challenge the actions of the nominee or directors[9], or either or both of the creditors' and company meetings decides to end the moratorium[10]. If the moratorium is still in existence when the proposed voluntary arrangement is approved it ends at the end of the day on which it receives the necessary approval[11].

1 IA 1986, Sch A1, para 8(1). This date is referred to as 'the beginning of the moratorium'.
2 IA 1986, Sch A1, para 8(2)–(4). The 28-day period may be increased or reduced by order of the Secretary of State (para 8(8)), except in PVAs, where such modifications are by

order of the Lord Chancellor with the concurrence of the Secretary of State: IA 1986, s 420.
3 Ie the meetings summoned under IA 1986, Sch A1, para 29(1) (see para 3.16 below). The 'end' of the day is not defined. It should be taken literally.
4 IA 1986, Sch A1, para 8(2); it may be extended under para 32: see para 3.16 below.
5 IA 1986, Sch A1, para 8(3).
6 IA 1986, Sch A1, para 8(4).
7 IA 1986, Sch A1, para 8(5). It may be extended or further extended under para 32: see para 3.16 below.
8 See para 3.11 below.
9 See paras 3.12 and 3.15 below.
10 IA 1986, Sch A1, para 8(6).
11 IA 1986, Sch A1, para 8(7).

3.6 Notification and advertisement of moratorium. As soon as the moratorium comes into force the directors must give notice to the nominee[1], and the nominee must then immediately advertise the start of the moratorium and give notice to the registrar of companies, the company and any petitioning creditor of the company of whose claim he is aware[2]. A 'petitioning creditor' means a creditor by whom a winding-up petition has been presented before the beginning of the moratorium, and whose petition has not been dismissed or withdrawn[3]. It is anticipated that in all but rare cases the nominee will have been involved in the preparation of the moratorium documents, and in their filing at court. He will therefore be well aware that the documents have been filed and the moratorium has commenced. The formal scheme of IA 1986, however, is that the directors file the documents at court in order to obtain the moratorium. It is therefore necessary that the nominee receives notice of filing and this is achieved by the requirement that the directors serve two copies of the schedule of documents duly endorsed with the date of filing and sealed by the court[4] on the nominee as soon as it is received from the court[5]. Immediately he has received the copies of the schedule of documents the nominee is required to advertise the moratorium coming into force in the *Gazette* and in such newspaper as he thinks most appropriate for ensuring that the moratorium comes to the notice of the company's creditors[6]. The nominee must also notify the registrar of companies, the company and any petitioning creditor of the company of whose claim he is aware that the moratorium has come into force and the date on which it came into force[7]. Additionally, to protect the company's assets, the nominee must also give notice of the moratorium to any sheriff or other officer who to his knowledge is charged with an execution or other legal process against the company or its property and to any person who, to his knowledge, has distrained against the company or its property[8].

The end of the moratorium must also be advertised by the nominee, immediately on it coming to an end, with notice to the court, the registrar of companies, the company and any creditor of the company of whose claim the nominee is aware[9]. An advertisement of the end of the moratorium must give the date on which it ended and be placed in the *Gazette* and in a newspaper considered by the nominee to be appropriate for ensuring notice to the company's creditors[10].

1 IA 1986, Sch A1, para 9(1). The directors commit an offence if they fail to comply with this requirement without reasonable excuse: para 9(2).
2 IA 1986, Sch A1, para 10(1). The nominee commits an offence if he fails to comply with this requirement without reasonable excuse: para 10(3).
3 IA 1986, Sch A1, para 10(2).
4 See para 3.3 above.
5 IR 1986, r 1.40(1). The third copy of the schedule is served on the company.
6 IR 1986, r 1.40(2) and Form 1.10. Only one advertisement need be placed in the *Gazette* and the relevant newspaper.

7 IR 1986, r 1.40(3) and Form 1.11.
8 IR 1986, r 1.40(4).
9 IA 1986, Sch A1, para 11(1) and IR 1986, r 1.42(2), which provides that the notice must state the date on which the moratorium came to an end. The rules provide forms which may be used for these notices; Form 1.14 for the registrar of companies and Form 1.15 for the court. The nominee commits an offence if he fails to comply with this requirement without reasonable excuse: para 11(2).
10 IR 1986, r 1.42(1). For the form of notice, see Form 1.10.

3.7 Effect of moratorium on creditors. During the period for which a moratorium is in force for a company:

(a) no petition may be presented for the winding up of the company;
(b) no meeting of the company may be called or requisitioned except with the consent of the nominee or the leave of the court and subject (where the court gives leave) to such terms as the court may impose;
(c) no resolution may be passed or order made for the winding up of the company;
(d) no petition for an administration order in relation to the company may be presented;
(e) no administrative receiver of the company may be appointed;
(f) no landlord or other person to whom rent is payable may exercise any right of forfeiture by peaceable re-entry in relation to premises let to the company in respect of a failure by the company to comply with any term or condition of its tenancy of such premises, except with the leave of the court and subject to such terms as the court may impose,
(g) no other steps may be taken to enforce any security over the company's property, or to repossess goods in the company's possession under any hire-purchase agreement, except with the leave of the court and subject to such terms as the court may impose; and
(h) no other proceedings and no execution or other legal process may be commenced or continued, and no distress may be levied, against the company or its property except with the leave of the court and subject to such terms as the court may impose[1].

The coming into force of a moratorium also has the effect of disapplying the provisions of IA 1986, s 127 which invalidate any disposal of company property or transfer of its shares after the presentation of a winding-up petition. Where a petition, other than an excepted petition[2], for the winding up of the company has been presented before the beginning of the moratorium, dispositions of property or transfer of shares or alteration in status of the company's members may be validly made during the time when the moratorium is in force[3] or at any time before the end of the 28-day period commencing with the day on which each of the reports of the meetings has been made to the court, that is the period within which a challenge may be made to the decision of the meetings[4]. These restrictions on proceedings and enforcement are the essence of the moratorium and are self-explanatory. It will be a rare case where the court gives leave for proceedings or enforcement to be pursued.

Additionally, any security granted by the company at a time when a moratorium is in force may only be enforced if, at that time, there were reasonable grounds for believing that it would benefit the company[5]. The aim of this provision is to make it possible for the directors to borrow money on security to assist the company in the business it is pursuing during the moratorium, while preventing pressure being applied by existing creditors. It will nevertheless act as a discouragement to many lenders, who will in any event be reluctant to lend money to a company which is in financial difficulties. The fact that the company is subject to a moratorium must be notified to any person from whom the company obtains credit in excess of £250[6].

The nominee is given the power to require public utilities to provide essential services to the company during the moratorium[7].

Floating charges. IA 1986 also seeks to protect companies both from provisions in floating charges designed to crystallise the charge in the event of a moratorium, and also from notice being given under the terms of a floating charge to crystallise or restrict the disposition of property[8]. Any provision in an instrument creating a floating charge is void if it provides that the obtaining a moratorium, or the doing of anything with a view to obtaining a moratorium (including any preliminary decision or investigation) should constitute an event causing the floating charge to crystallise or a ground for the appointment of a receiver[9]. If at any time that a moratorium is in force the conditions exist under the terms of a floating charge for the holder of the charge to give notice either to crystallise the charge or to restrict the disposal of any property of the company, notice may not be given until after the moratorium has come to an end[10]. It is not open to the holder of the charge to seek the leave of the court either to crystallise the charge or impose any restriction on the disposal of company property[11].

1 IA 1986, Sch A1, para 12(1).
2 Ie a petition presented by the Secretary of State under IA 1986, s 124A on the grounds that it is in the public interest to wind up a company which has been the subject of an investigation, or to help an overseas regulatory authority or a banking or financial services company; or petitions presented under the Financial Services Act 1986, s 72(1)(b), or under the Banking Act 1987, s 92(1)(b), or the Financial Services and Markets Act 2000, s 367(3)(b); such petitions are excepted by virtue of IA 1986, Sch A1, para 12(4), (5).
3 IA 1986, Sch A1, para 12(2).
4 IA 1986, Sch A1, paras 12(2), 37(5)(a), but not during the time taken for any appeal: see para 37(5)(b).
5 IA 1986, Sch A1, para 14.
6 See IA 1986, Sch A1, para 17(1).
7 IA 1986, s 233(1)(ba), as amended by IA 2000 and see para 10.10 below.
8 Note that on the implementation of EA 2002, s 250 there will be a general prohibition on the appointment of an administrative receiver, subject to a few quite limited exceptions: see IA 1986, ss 72A–72H (when in force).
9 IA 1986, Sch A1, para 43(1). 'Receiver' includes a manager and a person who is appointed both receiver and manager: para 43(2).
10 IA 1986, Sch A1, para 13(1)–(4).
11 IA 1986, Sch A1, para 13(5).

3.8 Effect of moratorium on the company. The aim of the legislation is to leave the directors in charge of the company albeit subject to the monitoring of the nominee, and, it is hoped, with his assistance in rescuing the company. There is also a measure of protection afforded the company's creditors. Disposals of property and payments are restricted[1]. And although it is permitted to carry on business, the company must be open about its position. Accordingly, every invoice, order for goods or business letter which is either issued by or on behalf of the company, and on or in which the company's name appears, must also contain the nominee's name and a statement that the moratorium is in force for the company[2]. Neither may the company may obtain credit to the extent of £250[3] or more from a person who has not been informed that a moratorium is in force in relation to the company[4]. Obtaining credit includes both (a) obtaining goods which are bailed to the company under a hire-purchase agreement, or agreed to be sold to the company under a conditional sale agreement, and (b) where the company is paid in advance (whether in money or otherwise) for the supply of goods or services[5].

In addition, the company may not enter into a market contract, or give a transfer order within the meaning of the settlement finality regulations[6] or grant either a market charge or a collateral security charge under those regulations during the continuance of the moratorium[7].

1 See para 3.9 below.
2 IA 1986, Sch A1, para 16(1). The company and any officer who, without reasonable excuse, authorised or permits any default in complying with this requirement is guilty of an offence: para 16(2)(3). An insolvent partnership, as opposed to its officers, cannot be guilty of an offence: IA 1986, s 1A(5), as modified by IPO 2002.
3 This sum may be increased or reduced by order of the Secretary of State under IA 1986, s 417A.
4 IA 1986, Sch A1, para 17(1), where the company obtains credit in contravention of this provision (a) the company, and (b) any officer of the company who knowingly and wilfully authorised or permitted the contravention, are guilty of an offence: para 17(3). An insolvent partnership, as opposed to its officers, cannot be guilty of an offence: IA 1986, s 1A(5), as modified by IPO 2002.
5 IA 1986, Sch A1, para 17(2).
6 Ie the Financial Markets and Insolvency (Settlement Finality) Regulations 1999, SI 1999/2979: see IA 1986, Sch A1, para 1.
7 IA 1986, Sch A1, para 23. Such a transaction is not void and remains enforceable against the company (para 23(2)), but the company and its responsible officer will be criminally liable. An insolvent partnership, as opposed to its officers, cannot be guilty of an offence: IA 1986, s 1A(5), as modified by IPO 2002.

3.9 Disposals and payments by company during moratorium. The company is permitted to carry on business during the period of the moratorium, but it may not dispose of assets and or make payments which may prejudice the creditors. No disposal of property belonging to the company may take place other than in the ordinary way of the company's business[1], and no payment in respect of any debt or other liability of the company in existence before the beginning of the moratorium may be made unless (a) there are reasonable grounds for believing that the disposal will benefit the company, and (b) the disposal is approved by the moratorium committee[2] or, where there is no such committee, by the nominee[3]. The restriction on making payments does not, however, apply to a payment which is required to discharge a liability arising on a disposal of property which is subject to a security or a hire-purchase agreement where the holder of the security or the court agrees[4].

Where the company owns property which is subject to a security, or goods are in the possession of the company under a hire-purchase agreement, the company may dispose of the property as if it were not subject to the security or all the rights of the owner were vested in the company if the holder of the security or the owner of the goods consents, or the court gives leave[5]. Such a disposal is not to be to the prejudice of the holder of a security which, as created, was a floating charge. The holder of such a security has the same priority in respect of any property of the company directly or indirectly representing the property disposed of as he would have had in respect of the property subject to the security[6].

An application for leave will be by originating application, unless there are pending proceedings when an ordinary application may be used[7]. Speed is likely to be essential and such urgency as there is should be made clear to the court in which the application is issued. On receiving a date from the court the company must immediately give notice to the holder of the relevant security or the owner of the hire-purchase agreement as appropriate[8]. The evidence in support should make clear the benefit the company expects to accrue from the disposal. It should also detail the precise sum due under the charge or owed under the hire-purchase agreement and the amount expect to be obtained on the disposal, giving reasons as necessary.

If the leave of the court is given to a disposal of property subject to a charge or goods held under a hire-purchase agreement, it must be a condition of leave that (a) the net proceeds of the disposal, and (b) where those proceeds are less than such amount as may be agreed, or determined by the court, to be the net amount which would be realised on a sale of the property or goods in the open market by a willing vendor, the company must pay such sums as may be required to make good the deficiency toward the discharge of the sums secured by the security or payable under the hire-purchase agreement[9]. Should there be two or more securities on the property, the sums realised on the disposal or the sums agreed or determined to represent the balance of an open market value are to be applied toward the discharge of the relevant securities in the order of their priorities[10].

Where the court gives leave for a disposal of secured property or goods held under a hire-purchase agreement, the directors must immediately give notice of the order to the holder of the security or the owner of the goods the subject of the hire-purchase agreement[11]. Within 14 days of leave being given, the directors must send an office copy of the order giving leave to the registrar of companies[12].

An offence is committed by the company which disposes property or goods without the necessary consent or leave of the court and by any officer of the company who without reasonable excuse authorises or permits such a disposal[13].

1 IA 1986, Sch A1, para 18(2).
2 Ie the committee established under IA 1986, Sch A1, para 35(1): see para 3.15 below.
3 IA 1986, Sch A1, para 18(1), para 19(1). If the company does makes a prohibited disposal or payment, (a) the company, and (b) any officer of the company who authorised or permitted the disposal or payment without reasonable excuse, is guilty of an offence: IA 1986, Sch A1, para 18(3), para 19(3). An insolvent partnership, as opposed to its officers, cannot be guilty of either offence: IA 1986, s 1A(5), as modified by IPO 2002.
4 IA 1986, Sch A1, para 19(2); as to such disposal see following text.
5 IA 1986, Sch A1, para 20(1)–(3).
6 IA 1986, Sch A1, para 20(4).
7 IR 1986, r 7.1, Form 7.1 (originating application), Form 7.2 (ordinary application): see Appendix 4.
8 IR 1986, r 1.43(1), (2).
9 IA 1986, Sch A1, para 20(5), (6).
10 IA 1986, Sch A1, para 20(7).
11 IR 1986, r 1.43(3). The court sends two sealed copies of the order to the company, one of which must be sent to the chargee or hire-purchase owner: r 1.43(4).
12 IA 1986, Sch A1, para 20(8). Failure to comply without reasonable excuse is an offence: para 20(9).
13 IA 1986, Sch A1, para 22. An insolvent partnership, as opposed to its officers, cannot be guilty of an offence, IA 1986: s 1A(5), as modified by IPO 2002.

3.10 Monitoring the company's activities by nominee. During the moratorium, the nominee is required to monitor the company's affairs for the purpose of forming an opinion as to whether:

(a) the proposed voluntary arrangement or, if he has received notice of any proposed modifications, the proposed arrangement with those modifications, has a reasonable prospect of being approved and implemented, and

(b) the company is likely to have sufficient funds available to it during the remainder of the moratorium to enable it to continue to carry on its business[1].

This provision is designed to alleviate any concerns creditors may have as to the conduct of the company's business by the directors under the protection of the moratorium. In order to assist him in complying with his obligation to monitor the company's affairs the nominee is entitled to require the directors to provide him with any information necessary for the purpose[2]. In forming his opinion the nominee is entitled to rely on the information provided to him by the directors unless he has reason to doubt its accuracy[3].

1 IA 1986, Sch A1, para 24(1). The business is that which the company proposes to carry on during the remainder of the moratorium: para 24(4).
2 IA 1986, Sch A1, para 24(2).
3 IA 1986, Sch A1, para 24(3).

3.11 Withdrawal by nominee of consent to act. A withdrawal of the nominee's consent to act on behalf of the company for its moratorium acts both as a protection for creditors against a moratorium continuing after it is apparent that there is no longer a real prospect of a voluntary arrangement being put in place and as the sanction available to the nominee who finds that the company's directors are being unco-operative. Once the nominee has withdrawn his consent to act, the moratorium automatically comes to an end[1]. The nominee must withdraw his consent to act if, at any time during a moratorium:

(a) he forms the opinion that –
 (i) the proposed voluntary arrangement or, if he has received notice of proposed modifications[2], the proposed arrangement with those modifications no longer has a reasonable prospect of being approved or implemented; or
 (ii) the company will not have sufficient funds available to it during the remainder of the moratorium to enable it to continue to carry on its business[3];
(b) he becomes aware that, on the date of filing[4], the company was not eligible for a moratorium; or
(c) the directors fail to comply with their duty[5] to provide information to the nominee to enable him to carry out his monitoring obligations[6].

The nominee may only withdraw his consent to act on one of the above grounds[7]. Accordingly, he may not use the threat of withdrawing consent for ulterior motives. On withdrawing his consent to act the nominee must notify the court, the registrar of companies, the company and any creditor of the company of whose claim he is aware both of the fact of his withdrawal and the reason for it[8].

1 IA 1986, Sch A1, para 25(4).
2 Ie under IA 1986, Sch A1, para 31(7).
3 Ie the business as the company proposes to carry it on during the remainder of the moratorium, IA 1986, Sch A1, para 25(3).
4 Ie the date on which the relevant documents are filed in court: see para 3.3 above.
5 Under para 24(2): see para 3.10 above.
6 IA 1986, Sch A1, para 25(2).
7 IA 1986, Sch A1, para 25(1).
8 IA 1986, Sch A1, para 23(5); IR 1986, r 1.44. Notice to the registrar of companies is in Form 1.16 and to the court in Form 1.17. If the nominee without reasonable excuse fails to give the required notices he is liable to a fine: IA 1986, Sch A1, para 25(6).

3.12 Challenge to nominee. Any creditor, director or member of the company, or any other person affected by a moratorium, who is dissatisfied[1] by any act, omission or decision of the nominee during the moratorium, may make an application to the court[2]. Such an application may be made during the moratorium or after it has ended[3]. The applicant must give seven days' notice of his application to the nominee[4]. The court has power on hearing the application to:

(a) confirm, reverse or modify any act or decision of the nominee;
(b) give him directions; or
(c) make such other order as it thinks fit[5].

There court is expressly given the power to make an order which brings the moratorium to an end, and if such an order is made the court may make such consequential provision as the court thinks fit[6].

For a consideration of the basis on which the court may interfere with the acts of the nominee during the moratorium, see paras 10.4 and 10.5 below considering the similar question in relation to the court interfering with the acts, omissions or decisions of the supervisor in the implementation of a voluntary arrangement. The relationship between the nominee and the directors during a moratorium and the relationship between the supervisor and the directors during the implementation of a voluntary arrangement may not be precisely the same, depending always on the precise terms of a voluntary arrangement as it applies to the supervisor's rôle during the voluntary arrangement. Nevertheless, similar considerations will apply when the court has to decide whether or not to accede to any application that might be made by a dissatisfied applicant, and if so what order should be made.

1 As to 'person dissatisfied', see para 10.4 below.
2 IA 1986, Sch A1, para 26(1); the challenge will be by originating application: see Appendix 4.11.
3 IA 1986, Sch A1, para 26(2).
4 IR 1986, r 1.47.
5 IA 1986, Sch A1, para 26(3).
6 IA 1986, Sch A1, para 26(4).

3.13 Liability of nominee. The nominee is given no statutory protection with respect to the performance of his duties in connection with the moratorium. A nominee must be aware that he may be called to account if his acts or any failure to act causes loss to the company, and that creditors in addition to the company have the right to make an application to recover that loss. Any creditor of the company may apply to the court for relief where there are reasonable grounds for believing both that (a) as a result of any act, omission or decision of the nominee during the moratorium, the company has suffered loss, but (b) the company does not intend to pursue any claim it may have against the nominee[1]. Such an application may be made during the moratorium or after it has ended[2]. At least seven days' notice of the application must be given by the applicant to the nominee[3]. As in the case of IA 1986, Pt VIII, it may be seen that IA 1986, Sch A1 comprises a self-contained scheme including express powers in the court to give appropriate directions if complaint is made about the conduct of the nominee in the course of a moratorium. Accordingly, any dissatisfaction with the nominee must be raised with the court by application under IA 1986, Sch A1, para 26 and is not enforceable by private right of action[4].

This provision provides a summary remedy to any dissatisfied person who wishes to complain about any act, omission or decision of the nominee. It would also enable an applicant whether creditor third party or member to seek an order requiring the nominee to make good any loss occasioned by the company or to the applicant alone or as one of a distinct class. As to the question generally of liability on the part of the nominee, see para 4.17 below.

On the making of an application by a creditor the court may:

(a) order the company to pursue any claim against the nominee;
(b) authorise any creditor to pursue such a claim in the name of the company; or
(c) make such other order with respect to such a claim as it thinks fit,

unless the court is satisfied that the act, omission or decision of the nominee was in all the circumstances reasonable[5]. The court's order may (among other things): (i) impose conditions on any authority given to pursue a claim; (ii) direct the company to assist in the pursuit of a claim; (iii) make directions with respect to the distribution of anything received as a result of the pursuit of a claim; or (iv) bring the moratorium to an end with such consequential provision as the court thinks fit[6]. On hearing any application brought against the nominee the court is required to have regard to the interests of the members and creditors of the company generally[7].

1 IA 1986, Sch A1, para 27(1).
2 IA 1986, Sch A1, para 27(2).
3 IR 1986, r 1.47.
4 *King v Anthony* [1998] 2 BCLC 517.
5 IA 1986, Sch A1, para 27(3).
6 IA 1986, Sch A1, para 27(4).
7 IA 1986, Sch A1, para 27(5).

3.14 Replacement of nominee by court. The court may direct that the nominee be replaced by another person qualified to act as an insolvency practitioner, or authorised to act as nominee, in relation to the voluntary arrangement either:

(a) on an application made by the directors in a case where the nominee has failed to comply with any duty imposed on him by IA 1986[1] or has died; or
(b) on an application made by the directors or the nominee in a case where it is impracticable or inappropriate for the nominee to continue to act as nominee for the company's moratorium[2].

The applicant, whether the directors or the nominee, must give not less than seven days' notice of the application to whoever is the respondent[3]. Time is likely to be of the essence. The evidence in support should be full and served with the application.

Before any person is appointed as a replacement nominee he must first submit to the court a statement indicating his consent to act[4]. On appointment the replacement nominee must immediately give notice to the registrar of companies, the court (unless he was appointed by the court) and the person who he has replaced as nominee[5].

1 Ie IA 1986, Sch A1. As to when the court will treat the nominee as being in breach of a duty which involves the exercise of discretion, see para 10.5 below in the context of the court's control of a supervisor's implementation of the voluntary arrangement.
2 IA 1986, Sch A1, para 28(1).
3 IR 1986, r 1.45(1), (2).
4 IA 1986, Sch A1, para 28(2); IR 1986, r 1.45(3), which imposes the same requirement as para 28(2) although differently worded. The statement must be filed at court.
5 IR 1986, r 1.46; see Forms 1.18, 1.19.

3.15 Challenge to directors' actions. Either a creditor or a member of the company[1] may apply to the court to complain about the acts or omissions of the company's directors during a moratorium on the ground that the company's affairs, business and property are being or have been managed by the directors in a manner which is unfairly prejudicial to the interests of its creditors or members generally, or of some part of its creditors or members. The complaint may relate to the conduct of the company's affairs generally or by made in respect of any actual or proposed act or omission of the directors[2]. Where the complaint relates to the interests of part only of the company's creditors or members the applicant must belong to the affected class; the class may indeed comprise only the applicant himself[3]. An application may be made during the moratorium or after its conclusion[4].

The court is given a wide discretion on the on the petitioner's application and may: (i) make such order as it thinks fit for giving relief in respect of the complaint; (ii) adjourn the hearing conditionally or unconditionally; or (iii) make an interim order or any other order that it thinks fit[5]. In particular, the court is authorised[6] to:

(a) regulate the management by the directors of the company's affairs, business and property during the remainder of the moratorium;
(b) require the directors to refrain from doing or continuing an act complained of by the petitioner, or to do an act which the petitioner has complained they have omitted to do;
(c) require the summoning of a meeting of creditors or company for the purpose of considering such matters as the court may direct;
(d) bring the moratorium to an end and make such consequential provision as the court thinks fit.

It will be seen that it is envisaged from these specific examples of orders that might be made that the court might become concerned in the overall management, or at least management strategy of the company. The examples do not include the making of orders against the directors or any individual director requiring compensation to be paid to creditors who have suffered loss through their actions or omissions. However, the width of the relief available to the court is clearly wide enough for such an order to be made in appropriate cases. In considering applications against company directors personally the court will have to undertake a balancing exercise between legitimate attempts by the directors to rescue the company's business and the interests of existing creditors in receiving the maximum return on their debts and other claims. It is possible that authorities on wrongful trading may provide assistance in individual cases[7], but for directors trading in a moratorium IA 1986 itself provides a framework within which such trading should take place[8]. If they stay within this framework, and act in good faith to rescue the company's position, the directors should be free from court interference and certainly any order against them personally. In making an order the court is required to have regard to the need to safeguard the interests of persons who have dealt with the company in good faith and for value[9].

1 Except where the company is in administration or liquidation in pursuance of a petition presented before the moratorium came into force. In such cases only the administrator or liquidator may make an application.
2 IA 1986, Sch A1, para 40(1), (2).
3 IA 1986, Sch A1, para 40(2).
4 IA 1986, Sch A1, para 40(3).
5 IA 1986, Sch A1, para 40(4).
6 IA 1986, Sch A1, para 40(5).
7 See Bailey, Groves and Smith *Corporate Insolvency* (2nd edn) paras 16.17–16.37.
8 Sch A1, paras 12–23; paras 3.7–3.11 above.
9 IA 1986, Sch A1, para 40(6).

3.16 Summoning of meetings; extension of moratorium. While the moratorium is in force the nominee is required to summon meetings of the company and its creditors to consider the proposal for a voluntary arrangement[1]. Notice of the creditors' meeting must be given to every creditor of whose claim the nominee is aware[2]. Experience shows that creditors not infrequently raise concerns and queries at the creditors' meeting which cannot immediately be dealt with by the nominee or propose amendments to the original proposal which require further consideration and notification to those creditors who have not attended the meeting but are voting by proxy. The creditors'/company meetings[3] may vote to adjourn, or further adjourn, consideration of the proposal[4], and the creditors'/company meetings[5] may at the same time resolve to extend, or further extend, the moratorium and to do so either with or without conditions[6]. No extension, including any further extension, may, however, extend the moratorium to a date later than two months[7] after the day on which the meetings of creditors and company are held, or the later of those meetings if they are held on different days[8]. Before any decision is taken on a proposal to extend the moratorium the nominee is required to inform the meeting: (i) what he has done in order to comply with his duty to monitor the moratorium[9] and the cost of his actions for the company; (ii) what he intends to do to continue to comply with that duty if the moratorium is extended (or further extended); and (iii) the expected cost of his actions for the company[10]. In the event that the nominee intends to incur cost in conducting further monitoring duties during the remainder of the moratorium the creditors'/company meetings[11] must resolve whether or not to approve the expected cost[12]. If the decision is against approval of the expected cost of the nominee's intended actions, the moratorium comes to an end[13]. It is always open to the creditors'/company meetings to resolve to bring an extended moratorium to an end before the expiry of the period of extension[14]. If a decision is made to extend, or further extend, the moratorium the nominee must notify the registrar of companies and the court, specifying the new expiry date of the moratorium[15].

Paragraph 36 decision. Each of these various decisions – ie any decision (1) to extend or further extend the moratorium, (2) to approve the expected cost of the nominee's intended actions if further cost is to be incurred during any period of extension to the moratorium, or (3) to bring the moratorium to an end before its date of expiry – is, together with a decision (4) to establish a moratorium committee[16], or (5) to approve the voluntary arrangement[17], a 'paragraph 36' decision. That is a decision which takes effect if approved by both the creditors' and company meetings, or by the creditors' meeting where its decision differs from that of the company meeting, or where the court orders that a decision taken by the company meeting should have effect notwithstanding an absence of support or even a contrary decision by the creditors' meeting. The effect of IA 1986, Sch A1, para 36[18], is to give the creditors' meeting precedence over the company meeting in the event that there is a divergence of view as to any significant decision relating to a voluntary arrangement, including in particular the approval of the arrangement itself. But where the two meetings reach different decisions it is open to any member of the company to apply to the court, and on such an application the court may order that the company meeting decision should have effect rather than that of the creditors, or make any other order which is considered appropriate[19]. In the ordinary case the effect of a voluntary arrangement will impinge rather more on the rights of the creditors than those of the members. Accordingly, the power of the court to override the creditors' views must be seen as very much a safeguard available only in the extremely rare case where the creditors may be seen to be acting perversely to the detriment of the rights of the members.

When imposing conditions on an extension, or further extension, of a moratorium the creditors' and company meetings may replace the nominee with another person appropriately qualified[20] to act in relation to the voluntary arrangement. Such a decision cannot, however, be taken without notice. Not only does IA 1986 require the replacement nominee to submit a statement to the court indicating his consent to act[21], but the replacement nominee must then immediately assume the duties imposed on the nominee of informing the meeting what he intends to do to comply with the nominee's monitoring duty during the remainder of the moratorium and the expected cost to the company of his proposed actions, preparatory to the meeting voting on whether or not to approve the expected cost[22].

1 IA 1986, Sch A1, paras 29, 31 and see para 6.3 below.
2 IA 1986, Sch A1, para 29(2).
3 This is one of the decisions which take effect if it is taken (a) by both the creditors' and company meetings, or (b) the creditors' meeting alone, or (c) the company meeting alone if the court so orders (a 'paragraph 36' decision): see IA 1986, Sch A1, para 36.
4 IA 1986, Sch A1, para 30.
5 This is a 'paragraph 36' decision.
6 IA 1986, Sch A1, para 32(1).
7 This period of time may be increased or reduced by order by the Secretary of State: IA 1986, Sch A1, para 32(7). This does not apply in PVAs, where alterations are ordered by the Lord Chancellor with the concurrence of the Secretary of State: IA 1986, s 420.
8 IA 1986, Sch A1, para 32(2).
9 Ie under IA 1986, Sch A1, para 24: see para 3.10 above.
10 IA 1986, Sch A1, para 32(3).
11 This is a 'paragraph 36' decision.
12 IA 1986, Sch A1, para 32(4).
13 IA 1986, Sch A1, para 32(5).
14 IA 1986, Sch A1, para 32(6); this is a 'paragraph 36' decision.
15 IA 1986, Sch A1, para 34(1); IR 1986, r 1.41(1); see Forms 1.12 and 1.13 for forms of notice; in CVAs (but not of course in PVAs) in the event that the decision takes effect as a result of the court ordering that the company meeting should have effect despite a contrary decision of the creditors' meeting, the nominee is required to send an office copy of the court order to the registrar of companies: IA 1986, Sch A1, para 34(2). Failure by the nominee without reasonable excuse to give the required notices is punishable by a fine: para 34(3).
16 See para 3.17 below.
17 See para 6.13 below.
18 And IA 1986, s 4A (also inserted by IA 2000) in respect of a voluntary arrangement which is not preceded by a moratorium.
19 IA 1986, Sch A1, para 36(3), (5) (see also IA 1986, s 4A(3), (4)); IR 1986, r 1.41(2). The nominee must immediately send the registrar of companies an office copy of any order extending or further extending the moratorium.
20 See para 1.12 above.
21 IA 1986, Sch A1, para 33(2).
22 IA 1986, Sch A1, para 33(3). Failure to approve the cost automatically brings the moratorium to an end: IA 1986, Sch A1, para 32(5).

3.17 Moratorium committee. A creditors' or company meeting which resolves that the moratorium should be extended, or further extended, may, with the consent of the nominee, resolve that a committee be established to exercise such functions as are conferred on it by the meeting[1]. A resolution to establish a moratorium committee is a 'paragraph 36' decision, that is it takes effect if approved by both the creditors' and company meetings, or by the creditors' meeting alone where the decision of that meeting differs from that of the company meeting, or the court orders that the decision to establish a moratorium committee taken by the company meeting should have effect notwithstanding an absence of support or even a contrary decision by the creditors[2]. The meeting or meetings which authorise the establishment of the committee must, however, first approve an estimate of the expenses to be incurred by the committee in the exercise of its proposed functions[3]. Provided the expenses incurred by the committee do not exceed the estimate they are to be reimbursed by the nominee[4]. The ability to establish a moratorium committee will provide the creditors or the members of the company with a mechanism to keep a check on, or even take over, functions which are the responsibility of the nominee. It is likely to be a rare case where the creditors feel the need for a moratorium committee, and even rarer in the case of the members. The committee cannot, however, be used as a vehicle to investigate the affairs of the company during the course of a moratorium which has run its course, for the committee automatically ceases to exist when the moratorium comes to an end[5].

1 IA 1986, Sch A1, para 35(1).
2 IA 1986, Sch A1, para 36(1)–(5).
3 IA 1986, Sch A1, para 35(2).
4 IA 1986, Sch A1, para 35(3).
5 IA 1986, Sch A1, para 35(4).

Chapter 4

CVA (without moratorium) and IVA: from proposal to creditors' meeting

4.1 The procedure through to the creditors' meeting. We have now had over 16 years' experience of voluntary arrangements[1] and it is no criticism of the framers of the original legislation that practice has shown that the procedures laid down in the 1986 legislation were unnecessarily formal. The scheme envisaged by this legislation is that the debtor, by himself when an individual and by the directors when a company, would prepare a proposal. An individual debtor would himself apply to the court for an interim order. The proposal would then be passed to the intended nominee. The nominee would consider it against a statement of affairs provided by the debtor and would, if he thought appropriate, seek further information from the debtor. With all the information in hand the nominee would then make a report to the court stating whether or not in his opinion a meeting of creditors, and the company in CVA, should be summoned to consider the proposal. At this point an individual debtor's interim order would be about to expire, and the court would hold a hearing to consider the nominee's report and decide whether to extend the interim hearing. In cases where the nominee had expressed an opinion in favour of the proposal being considered by the creditors, and the company in CVA, notices would then be sent to those entitled to attend and the meeting(s) would take place as suggested by the nominee.

For a procedure where time is usually of the essence this is unnecessarily cumbersome, and where money is scarce, unnecessarily expensive. Furthermore, it has the unrealistic starting point that a debtor, whether individual or corporate, will be able to formulate a proposal which both complies with the rules and is likely to meet the expectations of creditors. In practice the first step any debtor will take is to seek the advice of an insolvency practitioner as to whether or not a voluntary arrangement is a realistic proposition. By the time an insolvency practitioner is in a position to give confident advice he will have a sufficient knowledge of the debtor's affairs to formulate a proposal, at least in draft, and except in unusual cases it will be sensible to complete the proposal before taking any further steps. Accordingly, when an application for an interim order is made it is almost invariably made by an insolvency practitioner who has already prepared, or almost prepared, the proposal and neither in CVA nor IVA is there any real need for a formal report to the court. The nominee's report to the court[2] is a good discipline; the report is available to any interested party[3] but only rarely is it an important document for creditors deciding how to vote at the creditors' meeting. Under the amendments introduced by IA 2000 the report to the court is used to require the nominee to state publicly that he is of the opinion that the proposed voluntary arrangement has a reasonable prospect of being approved and implemented[4]. There is, however, no compelling reason why the court should take time to consider the report in a formal hearing even in IVA when the need for extension of the interim order arises[5]. Indeed, the court is unlikely to be in any position to give informed consideration to the report without requiring a great deal of information from the nominee and spending an appreciable amount of time on the report, time which can be better spent on other matters. The best assurance for the court that the proposal for voluntary arrangement is being properly pursued, and that an interim order should be extended in IVA, is in the fact that it is being handled by an insolvency practitioner whose licence to practice is at risk if he does not conduct himself properly[6].

It is not surprising, therefore, that practice has run ahead of the legislation. In IVA the *Practice Direction*[7] provides that in the absence of a bankruptcy order or pending petition the court will 'normally be prepared to make orders . . . without the attendance of either party' which take the procedure through to the meeting of creditors, and indeed to a final order after the chairman of the meeting has reported its decision to the court. An IVA may therefore be put in place without any formal court hearing. If a creditor considers that the proposal for a voluntary arrangement is improper, or merely a device to delay inevitable insolvency, he may issue a petition for winding up or bankruptcy and bring his complaint to the court. In CVA there is no statutory requirement for a court hearing where an Administrator or Liquidator is the nominee. CVAs outside formal insolvency have been relatively rare. There is no provision in the rule comparable to IR 1986, r 5.13, which anticipates a court hearing before the before the proposal is put before creditors. If the nominee submits a favourable report to the court he proceeds to summon the meetings as proposed 'unless the court otherwise directs'[8]. There is therefore no need for a formal rule of practice to be introduced to avoid the parties' attendance on the nominee's report to the court; this is the practice envisaged by IA 1986.

In introducing the CVA moratorium, Parliament accepted the practice as it has developed in IVA. As has been seen above, a moratorium requires no court hearing. It is obtained by filing the appropriate documents in court[9] and the nominee's report to the court is replaced by the nominee's statement. Creditors, the company and any third party affected by the moratorium are protected by imposing a duty on the nominee to monitor the activities of the company in moratorium[10] and by giving any creditor, director or member of the company, or any such third party the right to challenge in court any act, omission or decision of the nominee[11]. It is perhaps unfortunate that Parliament did not take the opportunity afforded by IA 2000 or EA 2002 to bring the legislation for voluntary arrangements more into line with practice. This chapter covers all the relevant provisions of IA 1986 and IR 1986, but in practice the overwhelming majority of voluntary arrangements will follow the more informal practice outlined above.

1 IA 1986 and IR 1986 first came into effect on 29 December 1986.
2 Required by IA 1986, s 2(2) (CVA), s 256(1) (IVA with interim order), s 256A(2) (IVA without interim order).

3 IR 1986, r 1.7(3) (CVA), r 5.10(4) (IVA): the report is put on the court file and any creditor, or director or shareholder of a corporate debtor may inspect the file 'at all reasonable times on any business day'.
4 IA 1986, s 2(2)(a) (CVA without moratorium), s 256(2)(a) (IVA).
5 In CVA there is no express provision for the court to consider the nominee's report; in IVA IR 1986, r 5.12 provides for a hearing with notice to be given to any creditor who has presented a bankruptcy petition against the debtor.
6 In many instances the insolvency practitioner will be known personally by the district judge or registrar at the court in which the voluntary arrangement is proceeding.
7 Ie *Practice Direction: Insolvency Proceedings* para 16: see Appendix 6.
8 IA 1986, s 3(1).
9 See para 3.3 above.
10 IA 1986, Sch A1, para 24: see para 3.19 above.
11 IA 1986, Sch A1, para 26: see para 3.12 above.

4.2 The preparation of the proposal. The scheme envisaged by IA 1986 and IR 1986 is that the individual debtor or the directors of a corporate debtor prepare 'a document setting out the terms of the proposed voluntary arrangement'[1] or 'proposal'[2] which is passed to the intended nominee and on which the nominee then makes his report to the court[3]. This proposal may be amended at any time up to the delivery of the nominee's report to the court, with the agreement in writing of the nominee[4]. The directors of a corporate debtor who wish to have the protection of a moratorium are also required to submit a document setting out the terms of the proposed voluntary arrangement to the nominee for him to prepare his nominee's statement[5]. The detail required for the proposal demands both time and legal knowledge, and thus in practice the proposal will almost invariably be prepared by the insolvency practitioner who it is intended should act as nominee[6].

1 The wording of IA 1986, s 2(3) (CVA without moratorium), s 256(2) (IVA with interim order), s 256A(2) (IVA without interim order).
2 The wording of IR 1986, r 1.2 (CVA without moratorium), r 5.2 (IVA).
3 For the duty to report to the court under IA 1986, s 4(6) (CVA), s 256(1) (IVA with interim order), s 256A(2) (IVA without interim order), see para 4.7 below.
4 IR 1986, r 1.3(3) (CVA without moratorium), r 5.3(3) (IVA).
5 IA 1986, Sch A1, para 6: see para 3.2 above.
6 If and when the Secretary of State implements IA 2000 amendment which permits members of business rescue bodies to act as nominees and supervisors it will be interesting to see how this aspect of their work will be managed.

4.3 Notice to nominee. The formal requirement of IR 1986 is that written notice of the proposal must be given to the intended nominee by delivery of such notice, together with a copy of the proposal, either to the nominee himself or his authorised agent for the purpose[1]. If the intended nominee agrees to act he must endorse a copy of the notice to the effect that it has been received by him on a specified date, and return a copy of the endorsed notice to the directors of the corporate debtor or the individual debtor at the address specified in the notice for that purpose[2]. The nominee of a corporate debtor making a proposal for a CVA without a moratorium has 28 days to submit his report to the court from the date on which he endorses the copy notice served on him[3]. In practice the nominee will have helped prepare the proposal, and will be ready to report to the court. Where the debtor is an undischarged bankrupt, the notice he is required to give the official receiver and any trustee of his estate[4] must contain the name and address of the insolvency practitioner who has agreed to act as his nominee[5].

1 IR 1986, r 1.4(1), (2) (CVA without moratorium), r 5.4(1), (2) (IVA).
2 IR 1986, r 1.4(3), (4) (CVA without moratorium), r 5.4(3), (4) (IVA).
3 IR 1986, r 1.4(3). The period of 28 days is prescribed by IA 1986, s 2(2).

4 Under IA 1986, s 253(4).
5 IR 1986, r 5.4(5).

4.4 The contents of the proposal. The proposal must:

(a) provide a short explanation why in the debtor's or directors' opinion, a voluntary arrangement is desirable, and give reasons why the creditors may be expected to concur with such an arrangement[1];

(b) state, or deal with, the various matters specified in the Rules. There are 17 heads of matters to be dealt with, the same for both CVA and IVA[2].

The desirability of the arrangement will often be indicated by a comparison of the dividends to be received under the arrangement with the dividends which might be anticipated in liquidation or bankruptcy[3]. An effective voluntary arrangement will usually require a wider range of matters to be covered that the 17 heads of matters which must be dealt with in order to comply with the Rules. In practice the terms which relate specifically to the particular arrangement are usually prepared with some care. As for the remaining terms there are a number of standard forms of voluntary arrangement in general circulation. It is not unknown for these to be imported into proposals without any thought being given to their appropriateness to the particular case. The reader is referred to the observations made in relation to the drafting of voluntary arrangements in Appendix 4 below.

First and foremost, the proposal must identify the debtor's assets and liabilities specifying the extent to which assets have been charged. An estimate of the value of each asset must be given, and if any particular asset is to be excluded from the voluntary arrangement that fact must be specifically stated. The nature and amount of the debtor's liabilities must be stated together with an explanation as to how it is proposed that these liabilities will be dealt with under the arrangement. The proposal must identify any preferential creditors[4] and associates[5] and state how their debts are to be dealt with. It must state whether to the directors' or individual debtor's knowledge there are circumstances giving rise to the possibility of claims to set aside transactions as being at an undervalue, or preferences or extortionate credit transactions[6], and whether and if so how it is proposed to indemnify the company's assets or debtor's estate, either wholly or in part, in respect of such claims. These provisions are aimed at ensuring that creditors are informed as to their position should the debtor enter liquidation or become bankrupt, or, in the case of a proposal by an undischarged bankrupt, should the bankruptcy continue[7]. In so far as the creditors may be looking to provision being made to maximise the assets available to them under the arrangement, the difficulty arises that the jurisdiction of the court to set aside transactions at an undervalue or preferences only arises in formal insolvency[8]. The directors or the individual debtor, with the assistance of the nominee, may be prepared to assess the prospects of a successful application to the court to set aside such transactions in the event of formal insolvency. It has to be recognised, however, that it will not be in the debtor's interests to suggest that applications made after formal insolvency may increase the assets available to creditors. In all but rare cases effective indemnification of the debtor's assets for the purposes of a voluntary arrangement in respect of perceived undervalue transactions or preferences will require the co-operation of the relevant third party which may not be forthcoming.

The directors or individual debtor must also state whether or not guarantees are being offered for the purposes of the arrangement by third parties, and in the case of CVA by the directors. An explanation must be given as to how the corporate or individual debtor's business will be conducted the course of the arrangement. The proposed duration of the voluntary arrangement must be given. The proposed supervisor of the arrangement, usually the nominee, must be identified with an explanation of his functions under the arrangement and details of his proposed remuneration.

In preparing his proposal the directors or individual debtor must not only be honest but should take care to put all relevant facts before the creditors[9]. The duty of the proposer under IR 1986 to give details of assets, charges and liabilities is qualified by the phrase 'so far as within the [proposer's] immediate knowledge'. Accordingly, painstaking research into old matters need not be undertaken, but the proposer cannot avoid checking matters readily available to him in documentary material. The directors or individual debtor should bear in mind that the making of any false representation or the commission of any other fraud for the purpose of obtaining the approval of his creditors to a proposal for an arrangement is a criminal offence[10]. An agreement between a debtor and a creditor behind the arrangement whereby the debtor agrees to pay to the creditor a sum additional to that to which the creditor is entitled under the arrangement is fraudulent and unenforceable by the creditor[11]. The information provided by the debtor must be complete in all material particulars[12] and the obligation to provide such particulars to all the creditors continues up to the date of and during the meeting of the creditors itself[13].

1 IR 1986, r 1.3(1) (CVA with or without moratorium: note that in a moratorium r 1.35(1) applies rules 1.3(1)(2)), r 5.3(1) (IVA).
2 IR 1986, r 1.3(2) (CVA with or without moratorium), r 5.3(2) (IVA), see Appendix 2.
3 Ideally this comparison will be shown in schedule form with all appropriate calculations.
4 IR 1986, r 1.3(2), r 5.3(2), para (c)(i), as defined by IA 1986, s 386. Note that EA 2002, s 251 abolishes crown preference leaving employee's remuneration (as limited under IA 1986, Sch 6)' occupational pension scheme contributions, and ECSC levies as the only remaining preferential debts.
5 IR 1986, r 1.3(2), r 5.3(2), para (c)(ii), as defined by IA 1986, s 435 in CVA a 'connected person', IA 1986, s 249: see Appendix 1.
6 IR 1986, r 1.3(2), r 5.3(2), para (c)(iii). In a proposal for CVA the possibility of a claim to set aside a floating charge under IA 1986, s 245 must be included.
7 In cases where the debtor is an undischarged bankrupt the interim order may not make provision relaxing or removing any of the requirements of IA 1986 or IR 1986 in relation to bankruptcy unless the court is satisfied that any particular provision relaxed or removed is unlikely to result in any significant diminution in, or in the value of, the debtor's estate for the purposes of the bankruptcy: IA 1986, s 255(5).
8 See IA 1986, ss 238–241 (liquidation), ss 339 –342C (bankruptcy).
9 *Re a Debtor (No 2389 of 1989)* [1991] 2 WLR 578 at 586.
10 IA 1986, s 6A (CVA), s 262A (IVA) (as inserted by IA 2000, Schs 2 and 3). These provisions extend the criminal offence previously contained in IR 1986, r 1.30(1) (CVA), r 5.30(1) (IVA). A person guilty of an offence under either provision is liable to imprisonment or a fine or both. It has been customary to include a statement signed by the directors or individual debtor setting out IR 1986, r 1.30 or r 5.30, as appropriate, or stating that the rule has been brought to the proposer's attention. This statement should now refer to IA 1986, s 6A or s 262A as appropriate.
11 *Mallalieu v Hodgson* (1851) 16 QB 689.
12 A particular, or its omission, is material if, objectively assessed, it would be likely to have made a material difference to the way in which the creditors would have considered and assessed the terms of the proposed IVA: *Cadbury Schweppes plc v Somji* [2001] 1 WLR 615, para 25, CA.
13 *Cadbury Schweppes plc v Somji* [2001] 1 WLR 615, para 43, CA.

4.5 Information to nominee; statement of affairs. In addition to the document setting out the terms of the arrangement[1] the directors of the corporate debtor in CVA or the individual debtor in IVA are required[2] to submit to the nominee a statement of affairs containing the following prescribed particulars of the debtor's creditors, debts, other liabilities, assets and other information[3]:

(a) a list of assets, divided into such categories as are appropriate for easy identification, with estimated values assigned to each category;
(b) in the case of any property on which a claim against the debtor is wholly or partly secured, particulars of the claim and its amount, and of how and when the security was created;
(c) the names and addresses of the debtor's preferential creditors with the amounts of their respective claims;
(d) the names and addresses of the debtor's unsecured creditors, with the amounts of their respective claims;
(e) particulars of any debts owed by or to the debtor to or by persons or companies who are associates of the debtor;
(f) such other particulars, if any, as the nominee may in writing required to be furnished for the purposes of making his report to the court on the debtor's proposal.

For a corporate debtor the names and addresses of the company's members, with details of their respective shareholdings must also be given.

All these above particulars relate to matters which are required to be in the proposal. The purpose of the statement of affairs is to 'supplement or amplify, so far as is necessary for clarifying the state of the [debtor's] affairs the particulars already given in the proposal'[5]. IR 1986 do not prescribe forms to be used for the debtor's statement of affairs in CVA or IVA as is the case in liquidation (Form 4.17) or bankruptcy (Form 6.33), but there would appear to be no good reason why these forms should not be used, if convenient, provided all the prescribed particulars, set out above, are included[6].

The statement of affairs must be made up to a date not earlier than two weeks before the date on which the debtor gives notice of the proposal to the intended nominee, though the nominee may allow an extension of that period to the nearest practicable date (not earlier than two months before the date of notice) and if he does so he must give his reasons in his report to the court on the debtor's proposal[7]. The use in the rules of the word 'practicable' indicates that it is for reasons of practicality, and those alone, that a nominee may extend the period.

A debtor who is an undischarged bankrupt and who has already delivered a statement of affairs[8] need not deliver a further one unless required to do so by the nominee in order to supplement or amplify the earlier one[9]. The directors of a corporate debtor or an individual debtor who is not an undischarged bankrupt have seven days after delivery of the proposal to the nominee to deliver the statement of affairs, or such longer period as the nominee shall allow[10].

If it appears to the nominee that he cannot properly prepare his report on the basis of the details given in the debtor's proposal and statement of affairs, he may call on the directors or individual debtor to provide him with further information[11] and allow him access to the debtor's accounts and records[12]. The nominee may also call on an individual debtor to inform him whether the debtor has been concerned with the affairs of any company, wherever incorporated, which has become insolvent or whether the debtor has previously been adjudged bankrupt or entered into an arrangement with his creditors[13]. With a corporate debtor the nominee may also call on the directors to inform him, with respect to any person who is, or has at any time within the previous two years[14] been a director or officer of the company, whether and in what circumstances (without limit in time) that person (a) has been concerned in the affairs of any other company wherever incorporated which has become insolvent, or (b) has himself been adjudged bankrupt or entered into an arrangement with his creditors[15].

1 The 'document setting out the terms of the proposed voluntary arrangement' IA 1986, s 2(3) (CVA without moratorium), s 256(2) (IVA) s 256A(2) (IVA without interim order) is called 'the proposal' in IR 1986; and see para 4.4 above
2 IA 1986, s 2(3) (CVA without moratorium) s 256(2) (IVA with interim order), s 256A (IVA without interim order)
3 The particulars which are to be contained in the statement of affairs are prescribed by IR 1986, r 1.5(2) (CVA without moratorium), r 5.3(3) (IVA). The statement must be certified as correct to the best of his knowledge and belief by the individual debtor, r 5.3(5), or by two or more directors or a director and the company secretary of a corporate debtor, IR 1986, r 1.5(4) (CVA without moratorium).
4 See IA 1986, Sch 6. Note that crown preference is abolished by EA 2002, s 251 leaving as preferential debts only outstanding employee's remuneration (limited to four months' pay and a statutory maximum), sums owed by way of contribution to an occupational pension scheme and, theoretically, outstanding levies on coal and steel production under the ECSC treaty.
5 IR 1986, r 1.5(2) (CVA without moratorium), r 5.5(3) (IVA).
6 See para 4.4 above.
7 IR 1986, r 1.5(3) (CVA without moratorium), r 5.5(4) (IVA).
8 Under IA 1986, s 272 (debtor's petition) or s 288 (creditor's petition).
9 IR 1986, r 1.5(1) (CVA without moratorium), r 5.5(1) (IVA); there no limit to the extension of time permitted under this rule.
10 IR 1986, r 1.5(1) (CVA), r 5.5(2) (IVA).
11 IR 1986, r 1.6(1) (CVA), r 5.6(1) (IVA) which give the nominee extremely wide authority to call for: (a) further and better particulars as to the circumstances in which, and the reasons why, the debtor is insolvent or is threatened with insolvency; (b) particulars of any previous proposals the debtor may have made for voluntary arrangements; and (c) further information with respect to the debtors affairs which the nominee thinks necessary for the purposes of his report.
12 IR 1986, r 1.6(3) (CVA), r 5.6(3) (IVA).
13 IR 1986, r 5.6(2) (IVA).
14 That is the two years immediately preceding the date of 'the notice under r 1.4', presumably the date on which the nominee endorses the copy notice of the directors' proposal which serve on him under this rule: see para 4.3 above.
15 IR 1986, r 1.6(2) (CVA without moratorium).

4.6 Investigation by nominee. While the nominee has wide powers to investigate the debtor's proposals and statement of affairs, there is no duty on him to do so imposed by statute. Undoubtedly nominees can find themselves in a difficult position. They have to prepare or consider a debtor's proposal in a relatively short time. They have to do so with no real prospect of being paid to carry out any detailed investigation of the full extent of the debtor's assets or liabilities, or check whether any of the debts disclosed on the statement of affairs are in fact shams in the names of confederates who the debtor can count on to vote in favour of the proposal, and who will then improperly take a share of the assets made available to creditors under the arrangements if approved[1].

Difficult though an independent investigation may be, the nominee is nevertheless in the position of an officer of the court and, subject to the limitations of his position, must be satisfied that the proposal is properly carried forward and that the statement of affairs may be relied on by creditors. He must do more than simply act as a post-box, accepting without query what he is told by the corporate debtor's directors or the individual debtor[2]. It is fundamental to the intended operation of voluntary arrangements that what the creditors vote on is not the debtor's raw material but a proposal that has survived scrutiny and to that extent at least has commended itself to an independent professional practitioner[3] as being proper to put before the creditors[4]. The nominee's duty is to report his *opinion*[5] as to whether the proposals have a reasonable prospect of being approved and implemented, and whether a meeting of creditors[6] should be summoned[7]. In *Greystoke v Hamilton-Smith*[8] Lindsay J considered what is to be expected of a nominee before he reaches a conclusion whether or not a meeting should be summoned to consider a proposed voluntary arrangement within the context of an IVA but equally applicable to a CVA. He concluded that, at least in those cases where the fullness or candour of the debtor's information has properly come into question, the nominee must take such steps as are in all the circumstances reasonable to satisfy himself on three counts:

(1) that the debtor's true position as to assets and liabilities does not appear to him in any material respect to differ substantially from that which it is to be represented to the creditors to be;
(2) that the debtor's proposal as put to the creditors' meeting has a real prospect[9] of being implemented in the way it is to be represented it will be. A measure of modification to proposals is possible under IA 1986, s 258[10] so this question is to be approached broadly;
(3) that the information that the nominee has provides a basis such that (within the broad limits inescapably applicable to what have to be the speedy and robust functions of admitting or rejecting claims to vote and agreeing values for voting purposes) no already manifest yet unavoidable prospective unfairness in relation to those functions is present[11].

The court considered whether there should be a fourth count, namely that the proposed arrangement must appear to offer a reasonable prospect of a better recovery for the creditors, in financial terms, than would bankruptcy (or liquidation). While noting that this would almost invariably be a highly relevant consideration, this was not seen as a necessary condition[12].

It is particularly important that nominees should ensure that if further information does come to light the details are circulated to all creditors, and in particular those who have given him as chairman of the meeting proxy votes in favour of the proposal without being aware of such further information[13]. Creditors at the meeting who find that the details of the statement of affairs or proposal are revised after the nominee's report to the court are well advised to check the date of any proxy votes held by the chairman in favour of the proposal and object to the proposal being put to the vote until the creditors who have given proxies which antedate the revisions have been fully appraised of all developments.

1 Furthermore, having prepared the proposal the nominee can face the risk of having the role of supervisor taken from him by another insolvency practitioner acting in conjunction with one or more of the substantial creditors.
2 See the Dept. of Trade *Guidance Notes to Insolvency Practitioners* of March 1995 quoted by Lindsay J. in *Greystoke v Hamilton-Smith* [1997] BPIR 24 at 27.
3 See para 1.12.
4 See *Greystoke v Hamilton-Smith* [1997] BPIR 24 at 29B.
5 stressed by the Insolvency Service's 'Dear IP' letter millennium edition, chapter 24(1) (Appendix 7) which continues 'The clear implication is that as nominee you will consider the proposal, and make such enquiries as you consider necessary to satisfy yourself that the proposal ought to be put to creditors'.
6 And, in the case of a corporate debtor, a meeting of the company's members.
7 As laid down in IA 1986, s 2(2) (CVA without moratorium), s 256(1) (IVA with interim order), s 256A(3) (IVA without interim order). The requirement of an opinion as to the proposed arrangement having a reasonable prospect of being approved and implemented was introduced by IA 2000.

8 [1997] BPIR 24.
9 With the amendments introduced by IA 2000 this is now, by statute, a 'reasonable prospect', see IA 1986, s 2(2)(a) (CVA), s 256(1)(a) (IVA). There is no difference in substance, it is suggested, between a 'real prospect' and a 'reasonable prospect'.
10 Or IA 1986, s 4 (CVA) .
11 The Society of Insolvency Practitioners have advised members that if a nominee cannot satisfy himself that these three conditions are met but still wishes to recommend that a meeting be held, he should explain in his comments to the court the basis on which he is making the recommendation and qualify his comments so that the fact that the three conditions are not met is 'conspicuously' brought to the court's attention, see Statement of Insolvency Practice 3, November 1997. The nominee must now explain how it is that he is able to hold the opinion required of him by IA 1986, s 2(2)(a) (CVA), s 256(1)(a) (IVA) that there is a reasonable prospect of approval and implementation.
12 The point was made that Parliament could so easily have specified as a necessary condition something analogous to IA 1986, s 8(3)(d) (administration orders) ('a more advantageous realisation of the company's assets that would be effected on a winding up') that it must be taken to have decided against such a provision. Note that IA 1986, s 8 is repealed by EA 2002, s 248 and replaced by the provisions of EA 2002, Sch 18, ie IA 1986, Sch B1.
13 See *Cadbury Schweppes v Somji* [2001] 1 WLR 615, para 43.

4.7 Nominee's report to the court. The purpose of the nominee's report is to state whether, in the nominee's opinion (a) the voluntary arrangement being proposed has a reasonable prospect of being approved and implemented[1], (b) whether a meeting of the debtor's creditors (and in CVA a meeting of the company) should be summoned to consider the debtor's proposal and, if a meeting should be summoned, when and where the creditors' meeting (and the company meeting) should be[2]. The statutory scheme is that the nominee should deliver his report to the court together with a copy of the proposal and any statement of affairs provided by the debtor to the court not less than two days before the interim order ceases to have effect in IVA and within 28 days of the nominee receiving notice of the proposal in CVA[3]. In practice a CVA proposal or the application for an interim order in IVA is frequently made on the basis of a report which has already been prepared. If the nominee expresses an opinion that a creditors' meeting should be summoned to consider the proposals his report should have annexed to it his comments on the proposal, and if he expresses an adverse opinion he must give his reasons[4]. The court endorses the report with the date on which it is filed and any creditor is entitled to inspect the file[5]. In IVA the documents which are delivered to the court together with a copy of the nominee's report and any comments he has made upon it must also be sent by the nominee to any person who has presented a bankruptcy petition against the debtor[6], or, where the debtor is an undischarged bankrupt, to the official receiver and any trustee in bankruptcy[7]. In CVA the nominee must send a copy of his report and any comments to the company[8].

As noted in para 4.1 above, the court rarely holds a hearing to consider the nominee's report. Nevertheless, as was pointed out by the court in *Fletcher v Vooght*[9], the terms in which IA 1986 has been drafted make the nominee's report a pre-requisite to the valid summoning of the creditors', and in CVA the company, meeting. On receiving the report, the court may consider it inappropriate to proceed further with the proposal in its existing form. It may then (it is hoped only after holding a hearing at which its concerns are raised with the nominee and, where necessary, the proposer) direct that meetings should not be held[10].

1 IA 1986, s 2(2)(a) (CVA without moratorium), s 256(1)(a) (IVA with interim order), s 256A (3) (IVA without interim order), this requirement being added by IA 2000.
2 IA 1986, s 2(2)(aa)(b) (CVA without moratorium), s 256(1)(aa)(b) (IVA with interim order), s 256A(3)(b)(c) (IVA without interim order).

3 IA 1986 s 2(2) (CVA without moratorium), IR 1986, r 5.11(1)(2) (IVA). With the report to the court is to be delivered a copy of the proposal incorporating any amendments authorised by the nominee under IR 1986, r 1.3(3) (CVA) r 5.3(3) (IVA); a summary of the statement of affairs may be provided rather than the full statement if the nominee prefers.
4 IR 1986, r 1.7(2) (CVA without moratorium), r 5.11(3) (IVA).
5 IR 1986, r 1.7(3) (CVA without moratorium), r 5.11(4)(5) (IVA) inspection may be at all reasonable times on any business day, r 1.7(3), r 5.11(5).
6 IR 1986, r 5.11(7).
7 IR 1986, r 5.11(6).
8 IR 1986, r 1.7(4).
9 [2000] BPIR 435. In this case, through an error, no interim order had been made. However, the IVA proceeded as if it had been made, both to approval and implementation for some three years before the debtor was in breach of its requirements and the error was noted. The court held that in the absence of an interim order there could not be a valid report to the court because of the wording of IA 1986, s 256(1), 'where an interim order has been made ... the nominee ... shall submit a report to the court'. As there had been no valid report to the court, there could be no valid creditors' meeting and therefore no valid IVA. When the error was discovered the IVA had to be declared invalid although it had been partly executed. Since 1 January 2003 a report may be made to the court without an interim order being made: IA 1986, s 256A. There must, however, be a report to the court.
10 See IA 1986, s 3(1) (CVA without moratorium), s 257(1) (IVA).

4.8 Content of nominee's report. The nominee should take care to ensure that his report is one which is as thorough as it can be on the information available to him, and taking into account his powers to seek further information from the debtor[1]. There is no specific duty imposed on the nominee in IA 1986 or IR 1986 in relation to the preparation of the report. Insolvency practitioners have, however, been rightly criticised for providing short and uninformative reports appearing simply to rubber stamp the proposal which they themselves have helped to formulate. Severe criticism of the nominee for a 'deplorably low quality' report was made by the court in *Re a Debtor (No 222 of 1990), ex p Bank of Ireland*[2], but it is fair to say that standards have rarely, if ever, fallen to this standard in more recent times.

The Insolvency Service of the Department of Trade and Industry (DTI), in stressing that nominees should exercise their professional judgment when considering proposals and making their reports to the court, have expressed the view[3] that, at the least, the following questions should be considered in relation to each and every arrangement:

1. Is it feasible?
2. Is it fair to creditors?
3. Is it fair to the debtor?
4. Is it an acceptable alternative to bankruptcy?
5. Is it fit to be considered by the creditors?

There is plainly a good degree of overlap with these questions, but they serve to remind the nominee that 'any old' arrangement which can be put together to stave off bankruptcy or liquidation is not necessarily in the debtor's interests, and no arrangement should be put before the creditors that does not have a reasonable prospect of acceptance by the creditors or of working in practice. It is now indeed a statutory requirement that the nominee express his opinion in his report to the court that the proposed voluntary arrangement has a reasonable prospect of being approved and implemented before a creditors' (and company) meeting is summoned[4].

In November 1997 the Association of Business Rescue Professionals[5] (Technical Committee) revised its Guidance Notes[6] to nominees for the preparation of their reports to the court with regard to proposed voluntary arrangements, stating that the matters upon which the nominee will wish to comment, although varying from case to case should include:

(a) the extent to which the nominee has investigated the debtor's circumstances;
(b) the basis upon which assets have been valued;
(c) the extent to which the nominee considers that reliance can be placed upon the debtor's estimate of the liabilities to be included in the voluntary arrangement;
(d) information on the attitude adopted by the debtor with particular reference to instances of failure to co-operate with the nominee;
(e) the result of any discussions between the nominee and secured creditors or other interested parties upon whose co-operation the performance of the voluntary arrangement will depend;
(f) information on the attitude of any major unsecured creditor which may affect the approval of the arrangement by creditors;
(g) details of any previous history of failures in which the debtor has been involved in so far as they are known to the nominee;
(h) an estimate of the result for the creditors if the voluntary arrangement is approved, explaining why it is more beneficial for creditors than any alternative insolvency proceeding;
(i) the likely effect of the proposal's rejection by the creditors;
(j) details of any claims which have come to his attention which might be capable of being pursued by a trustee in bankruptcy if one were appointed.
(k) where the conditions set out in *Greystoke v Hamilton-Smith*[7] have not been met, the basis on which the nominee is recommending that a meeting be held.

The nominee must now explain how it is that he is able to hold the opinion required of him by statute that there is a reasonable prospect of approval and implementation[8].

1 See para 4.4 above. As IR 1986, r 1.6(3) (CVA without moratorium), r 5.6(3) (IVA) require the debtor to give the nominee access to his accounts and records in order that the nominee may prepare his report to the court. The implication, therefore, is that the nominee will be expected to have examined the debtor's financial records before reporting to the court.
2 [1992] BCLC 137 at 140.
3 See 'Dear IP' letter, millennium edition, ch 24 voluntary arrangements, see Appendix 7.
4 IA 1986, s 2(2)(a) (CVA), s 256(1)(a) (IVA).
5 Then called the Society of Practitioners in Insolvency.
6 Reproduced by kind permission of the Association of Business Rescue Professionals.
7 [1996] 2 BCLC 429, [1997] BPIR 24: see para 4.6 above.
8 IA 1986, s 2(2)(a) (CVA), s 256(1)(a) (IVA).

4.9 Replacement of nominee. As the procedure for a voluntary arrangement (other than for a corporate debtor in moratorium) requires the nominee to report to the court, the debtor will be unable to proceed if the nominee fails to make such a report for whatever reason. In the event that the nominee does fail to report to the court, due to his death or for any other reason, an application may be made to the court by the person intending to make the proposal[1] for a direction that the nominee be replaced by another person qualified to act as an insolvency practitioner or authorised to act as nominee in relation to the voluntary arrangement[2]. Where a nominee finds that it is impracticable or inappropriate to continue to act for the debtor he or the debtor may apply to the court for a replacement nominee to be appointed[3].

In an IVA with an interim order it will usually be necessary to seek a direction that the interim order shall continue or be renewed for a further period[4]. The debtor is required to give the nominee at least seven days' notice of the application to replace him as nominee[5]. Accordingly, if the debtor is not to wait for the interim order to expire, with the serious consequences that such expiry may entail, and if he is not in a position to give notice at least five days before the last date allowed by the rules to the nominee to submit his report, which is unlikely, the debtor should on making his application to replace the nominee apply immediately to the court for the continuation of the interim order pending the hearing of his application.

1 Ie any one or more of the directors of a corporate debtor or the individual debtor.
2 IA 1986, s 2(4)(a) (CVA without moratorium), s 256(3)(a) (IVA with interim order), s 256A(4)(a) (IVA without interim order). For a person other than a qualified insolvency practitioner authorised to act as nominee, see para 1.12 above
3 IA 1986, s 2(4)(b) (CVA without moratorium), s 256(3)(b) (IVA with interim order), s 256A(4)(b) (IVA without interim order).
4 IA 1986, s 256(3A).
5 IR 1986, r 5.11.

4.10 The court's consideration of the nominee's report in IVA. For the reasons given in para 4.1 above, the court rarely holds a hearing to consider the nominee's report[1]. Nevertheless, in IVA, though not in CVA, IR 1986 envisage a court hearing to consider the nominee's report as a matter of course[2].

At any hearing by the court to consider the nominee's report any of the persons who were given notice of the application for an interim order[3] may appear or be represented[4]. This includes any creditor petitioning for bankruptcy[5], who may presumably request the court to direct that a creditors' meeting should not be held despite the nominee's opinion to the contrary. In practice, where an application is made for an interim order or for the consideration of a nominee's report where a petition has been issued, the application is usually stood over to the date fixed for the hearing of the petition to be heard immediately before the hearing of the petition.

Where a creditor appears at the court's consideration of a nominee's report which expresses the opinion that a meeting should be held, he will have to show that more than 25% in value of the debtor's creditors are implacably opposed to the proposal[6], or that the proposal has no reasonable prospect of being approved and implemented[7] if he is successfully to oppose a direction that a creditors' meeting be held to consider the proposal. Provided that the proposal appears to have a reasonable prospect of success it will only be in exceptional circumstances that the court will prevent the creditors' meeting considering the proposal. Whatever doubts the court may have as to its eventual approval by the creditors, it is the creditors who are concerned with the payment or compromise of their debts; without a compelling reason to the contrary, the clear scheme of the Act is to leave the decision on the proposal with them[8]. The court should, however, delay the holding of a creditors' meeting in the event that a creditor is able to establish that the debtor has not been completely frank with his nominee as to the extent of his liabilities or assets, or that the nominee has not taken proper steps to verify the accuracy of the debtor's statement of affairs. In this event it would be inappropriate if not futile to proceed to the creditors' meeting until the nominee has had an opportunity to consider any deficiencies in the debtor's statement of affairs and amend the proposal accordingly.

If, having considered the nominee's report, the court is satisfied that the proposal should be put before the creditors' meeting it will direct that the interim order be extended for such further period as it may specify for the purpose of enabling the creditors' meeting to be held[9].

Where there is no bankruptcy order in existence, and so far as is known, no pending petition for the debtor's bankruptcy, the court will normally be prepared to make a 'standard order' on consideration of the nominee's report without the need for the parties' attendance[10]. The standard order extends the interim order to a date seven weeks after the date of the proposed meeting, directing the meeting to be summoned and adjourning to a date about three weeks after the meeting. Before this order will be made the nominee's report must be delivered to the court and the date proposed for the creditors' meeting must be not less than 14, or more than 28 days, after the date of the order[11].

1 A hearing will be necessary, however, in IVA where there is a pending bankruptcy petition against the debtor see *Practice Direction: Insolvency Proceedings* para 16.1, Appendix 6.
2 IR 1986, r 5.13. It is essential that there be a report to the court and a hearing if required, see *Fletcher v Vooght* [2000] BPIR 435: see para 4.7 above.
3 See IR 1986, r 5.7(4), para 2.3 above, ie the nominee, any creditor who to the debtor's knowledge has presented a bankruptcy petition, or in applications by undischarged bankrupts, the trustee or official receiver.
4 IR 1986, r 5.13(1).
5 IR 1986, r 5.7(4).
6 See eg *Re a Debtor (No 83 of 1988)* [1990] 1 WLR 708; note the court should always be aware that creditors may change their minds, and that at the creditors' meeting the debtor or other creditors will have an opportunity to persuade dissentients to alter their position; and see *Kent Carpets Ltd v Symes* [1996] BPIR 169.
7 The nominee must express the opinion that the voluntary arrangement has this reasonable prospect: IA 1986, s 256(1), as amended by IA 2000. Previously, the court had developed a 'serious and viable' test: see *Cooper v Fearnley, Re a Debtor (No 103 of 1994)* [1997] BPIR 20 and *Greystoke v Hamilton-Smith* [1997] BPIR 24.
8 Both IA 1986, s 257(1) and IR 1986, r 5.17 proceed upon the basis that the nominee's opinion in favour of a creditors' meeting will be acted upon. IR 1986, r 5.13(2) applies IR 1986, r 5.10 to any 'order' made by the court at the hearing, ie two sealed copies of the order are sent by the court to the applicant one of which is to be served on the nominee. Notice of any order made, which includes a direction that the meeting should not be held or should be held at a time and place other than that proposed by the nominee, must be given to anyone given notice of the hearing but who was not present or represented at it.
9 IA 1986, s 256(5), usually 49 days, see Appendix 9.5, step 19.
10 *Practice Direction Insolvency Proceedings* para 16.1(2): see Appendix 6.
11 This order may be made in conjunction with an interim order made without the parties' attendance (see para 2.2 above) ie a 'concertina' order.

4.11 Presentation of petition for insolvency before creditors' meeting is held. The court will not make an order for winding up or bankruptcy where it is satisfied that the debtor will be able to come to terms with the creditors such that there will be no debt to support the petition. The aim of insolvency law is to treat all ordinary creditors alike. It would plainly be inappropriate were one or more creditors with debts amounting to less than 25% of the debtor's total liabilities able to thwart a voluntary arrangement by presenting a petition for winding up or bankruptcy[1]. Were a petition for winding up or bankruptcy to be presented while the debtor was preparing to put proposals for a voluntary arrangement before the creditors the court might readily stay proceedings on the petition until after the meeting(s) of creditors (and the company) had considered the proposals. Indeed, in an appropriate case the court may review and set aside a winding-up or bankruptcy order so as to enable the debtor to propose a voluntary arrangement[2]. However, before granting a stay the court would have to be satisfied not only that there was a reasonable prospect of the voluntary arrangement being approved and implemented but that it was in all the circumstances a proper case in which to refuse a winding-up or bankruptcy order[3].

1 And see para 4.10 above.
2 See eg *Re Dollar Land (Feltham) Ltd* [1995] BCC 740.
3 *Re Piccadilly Property Management Ltd* [1999] 2 BCLC 145, where the court refused to rescind a winding up order even though it was apparent that a CVA would be supported by a creditor with more than 75% of the vote. A previous CVA had failed and the operation of the company required investigation.

4.12 Inland Revenue and Customs & Excise. Prior to the implementation of EA 2002[1] both the Revenue and Customs & Excise will usually be preferential creditors at least as to a part of their debt[2]. In common with other preferential rights these Crown preferential rights may not be altered in the arrangement without the consent of the holder of the debt. Accordingly, the view taken by the Revenue and Customs & Excise whether or not to approve the CVA or IVA has often been decisive to the success of the proposal. Even as ordinary creditors (and both will sometimes defer at least part of their preferential claim, see below), the Revenue and Customs & Excise will frequently be influential at the creditors' meeting, in part because their debt is often sizeable and in part because both are likely to have more information on the debtor than will other creditors.

Since 1 April 2001 the Revenue and Customs & Excise have operated a joint single unit to handle voluntary arrangements, called the Voluntary Arrangements Service (VAS). VAS has pledged itself to assist in the development of a rescue culture by supporting businesses which are seen to be viable but experiencing temporary financial difficulties. More importantly, VAS is prepared to discuss proposals with nominees or the proposer in an effort to arrive at a proposal which is acceptable and can be supported at the creditors' meeting[3]. To assist practitioners VAS has published a leaflet explaining how it approaches proposals for voluntary arrangements[4]. Understandably, nominees are expected to do their job properly. VAS looks to nominees to confirm to creditors (a) the proposer's true position as to assets and liabilities, (b) that the open market value of assets is not materially different from that in the proposal, (c) that the value being placed upon liabilities is not materially different from that in the proposal, and (d) that the proposal has a real prospect of being implemented. VAS will also compare its knowledge of the debtor's financial position with that in the proposal, raising any difficulties. It will also review projected income and expenditure to ensure that all expenditure is reasonable and necessary and that unacceptable expenditure is eliminated, and require that achievable provision is made for payment of statutory liabilities as they fall due within the lifetime of the arrangement. If this is done conscientiously in all cases where the debtor is in trade or business VAS will be performing a useful service not simply for the Crown but for the other creditors. VAS will discuss relevant matters with the other creditors. It will, of course, hold confidential material on the debtor, but VAS has indicated that they will divulge such material to the nominee if it influenced their decision on voting on the proposal. To this end, VAS requests that proposals sent to it are accompanied by the proposer's signed authority to disclose to the nominee or supervisor information held in Revenue or Customs files.

Modifications. VAS expects the 'optimum offer' to be put forward to creditors after due provision for necessary business expenses including all statutory liabilities as they fall due. If it appears that the offer may be improved this will be discussed and if the proposal is not improved voluntarily VAS is likely to insist that modifications designed to improve the return to creditors are approved before it agrees to support the proposal. It will also put forward technical amendments where these are considered necessary.

Deferment of part of preferential claim. VAS indicates that deferment may be agreed but only where all PAYE/NIC/VAT returns (and any other Customs returns) are produced in good time before the meeting of creditors, a predetermined amount of the preferential debt is to be paid before any dividend is paid to non-preferential creditors, the whole of the Revenue/Customs debt is admitted for voting purposes and constitutes less than 75% (or a lesser pre agreed percentage) of votes cast at the creditors' meeting, and in VAS' view supporting the proposal with a deferment of part of the preferential claim will provide a better return on the existing debt than rejection of the proposal. VAS further makes clear that there will be no deferment where the Revenue/Customs debt exceeds 75% of the debts shown in the proposal, or where the VAS claims exceed 75% of the votes cast at the creditors' meeting, or where VAS concludes that there is such support for a proposed arrangement that there is no commercial justification for agreeing to any deferment.

Opposition to the proposal. VAS will not support a proposal unless satisfied that there has been full and honest disclosure of: (a) a detailed business cash flow forecast; (b) all professional valuations; (c) business assets and liabilities; and in the case of individual debtors; (d) a statement of personal assets and liabilities; and (e) a statement of the proposer's current personal income and expenditure and a projection for the period of the proposed arrangement. Where the information shows that the return offered in the proposal may be improved upon this will be discussed. VAS also makes clear that there may be overriding reasons why it considers that it has no choice but to vote against the proposal. So far as confidentiality allows, it will inform the nominee of the reasons. Examples given are: (i) a history of deliberate default or evasion of statutory liabilities; (ii) proposers who do not work with VAS and the nominee to allay reasonable concerns about the proposal; (iii) debtors who have operated a policy of withholding payment of money due to the crown; (iv) evidence of contrived insolvency of any business or company controlled by persons in common or in which the proposer has had an interest.

While no specific reference is made in the VAS guidance leaflet to outstanding accounts and returns, where the nominee finds that the debtor's outstanding tax liabilities are uncertain he will usually have to agree outstanding accounts and assessments if VAS (the Revenue) are not to oppose the proposed arrangement. A nominee who is not an accountant should normally seek the assistance of the debtor's accountants. The nominee must also bear in mind that realising assets of the debtor for an arrangement may attract capital gains tax. As this liability will arise after the approval of the arrangement the nominee should consider whether VAS may be persuaded to agree in advance to this liability coming within the terms of the arrangement and be both postponed and subject to any composition alongside other Crown liabilities and liabilities to other creditors generally. Other taxation implications may well result from the implementation of an arrangement, particularly as regards reliefs where the debtor continues to trade, and should not be overlooked by the nominee[5]. Once the arrangement has been approved any liability for corporation or income tax on subsequent profits or earnings will remain with the debtor, and this future liability should be taken into account when formulating the proposal. Future PAYE liabilities in respect of employees will also remain the debtor's liability, although VAS may require the proposal to contain provisions designed to ensure that such liabilities are met, if necessary through the intervention of the supervisor.

In the case of VAT the nominee will almost certainly have to ensure that all outstanding VAT returns are completed within a relatively short period following the creditors' meeting if the support of VAS (Customs & Excise) is to be secured. The debtor's registration for VAT will not be affected by his becoming bound to an arrangement, and the debtor rather than the supervisor will be responsible for VAT on any continuing trading even where this trading forms an integral part of the arrangement. The nominee should, however, check in each case with the relevant Customs & Excise office what provisions, if any, may be required to be inserted in the proposal with regard to maintaining proper VAT records and paying VAT as it accrues due. On the realisation of assets the supervisor rather than the debtor will usually find himself responsible for accounting for any VAT which arises.

Bad debt relief is available to any creditor involved in a voluntary arrangement where he has written off the whole or any part of the consideration for the relevant supply in his accounts as a bad debt, and a period of six months has elapsed, beginning with the date of supply[6]. VAT becomes due at the time of supply[7] and therefore VAT due on supplies which have taken place by the date of the creditors' meeting will comprise a debt covered by the arrangement even if the debtor was not then liable to account for the VAT[8].

Debtors should note that entering into voluntary arrangements does not automatically result in de-registration for VAT. A formal request to be de-registered must be made otherwise on resumption of trading even below the registration threshold the debtor will be liable to pay VAT on his receipts[9].

1 Crown preference is abolished by EA 2002, s 251. It is anticipated that this part of the Act will be implemented in summer 2003.
2 IA 1986, Sch 6. For the 'relevant date' for the purposes of determining the amount of the preferential debt see IA 1986, s 387(2) (CVA), s 387(5)(6) (IVA).
3 The address is Voluntary Arrangements Service, Durrington Bridge House, Barrington Road, Worthing, West Sussex, BN12 4SE. Nominees are urged to send proposals direct to this address as soon as possible, quoting clearly the NIC number(s), PAYE/Tax reference(s) and VAT registration number.
4 Guidance leaflet CWL5.
5 Taxation aspects of the IVA are outside the scope of this work. The Institute of Chartered Accountants have issued a technical release (TR 799) entitled 'Tax aspects of the Insolvency Act 1986' which deals with items of importance to practitioners. It is available free of charge.
6 Value Added Tax Act 1994, s 36.
7 Value Added Tax Act 1994, s 1(2).
8 *Re KG Hoare* [1997] BPIR 683.
9 *Patrick Bedford v Customs and Excise Comrs (No 17085 of 2001)* (8 February 2001, unreported). De-registration cannot be retrospective.

4.13 The debtor's wife. Where an individual debtor is married the nominee must take care to consider the position of the debtor's wife[1] under the proposal. It has to be borne in mind that the financial problems which have resulted in the debtor having to propose an IVA could have precipitated or be consequent upon matrimonial problems giving rise to the possibility of matrimonial proceedings. It may be noted that although an order made in matrimonial proceedings is not a debt provable in bankruptcy[2], the definition of debt for the purposes of presenting a bankruptcy petition[3] is wide enough to include debts arising from matrimonial orders. Accordingly, a wife may petition for her husband's bankruptcy based on his failure to pay sums due under a matrimonial order, even though the wife may not then prove in the consequent bankruptcy[4]. The bankruptcy of the husband will not preclude the making of a lump sum or property adjustment order against him[5] although no such orders may be made against assets which have become vested in the trustee[6].

Where the wife is a creditor of the debtor (other than by order in matrimonial proceedings) the nominee should take into account that as a creditor in her husband's bankruptcy the wife is postponed to all other debts and interest on those debts[7]. In an IVA her debts should similarly be postponed.

Where the debtor's wife is standing by him, she may wish to help promote the arrangement by enabling the realisation of jointly owned assets. There will doubtless be pressure on her to co-operate with the nominee so as to avoid the stigma of a bankruptcy order falling on her husband. It is important that the nominee assures himself that any assertions by the debtor as to his wife's willingness to help and perhaps sacrifice her interest in jointly owned assets may properly be relied upon. In most cases the debtor's wife should be advised to seek independent legal advice. The nominee must bear in mind that the wife may be in a position to prevent an arrangement proceeding if she has not in fact agreed to her interest in jointly held assets being realised, whether or not for the benefit of the scheme. Even where her agreement has been obtained, the nominee should be aware that an agreement obtained by misrepresentation or undue influence may be set aside. The case law relating to the wife's execution of bank guarantees or charges should be noted[8]. In particular, if the nominee arranges or even allows the debtor to obtain his wife's consent to the realisation of her assets or her vacating the matrimonial home the husband is likely to be treated by the court as the nominee's agent for this purpose[9]. In this event the nominee would be liable for any fraudulent misrepresentation or undue influence practiced on his wife by the debtor and could find that an essential ingredient of the arrangement was set aside by reason of deceit or pressure applied to his wife by the debtor of which the nominee was completely unaware.

1 For convenience it is here assumed that the debtor is a husband. In the interests of correctness it is noted that the principles are the same where the debtor is a wife.
2 IR 1986, r 12.3(2).
3 See IA 1986, s 382(1).
4 See eg *Russell v Russell* [1998] BPIR 259, where the court stressed that as a matter of discretion a bankruptcy order would not usually be made. In that case, however, it was considered that there were special circumstances justifying the making of a bankruptcy order, namely the husband's failure to give full disclosure of his financial position in the family proceedings, his failure to pay the wife's costs of those proceedings (which was a provable debt in the bankruptcy), and his failure to pay costs to another creditor. See also *Re a Debtor, JP v a Debtor* [1999] BPIR 206.
5 *Hellyer v Hellyer* [1997] BPIR 8; *Re X (a bankrupt)* [1996] BPIR 494.
6 *Hellyer v Hellyer* [1997] BPIR 85; *McGladdery v McGladdery* [1999] 2 FLR 1102.
7 IA 1986, s 329.
8 See *Royal Bank of Scotland plc v Etridge (No 2)* [2001] UKHL 44, [2002] 2 AC 773; *Barclays Bank v O'Brien* [1994] 1 AC 180; *Barclays Bank v Boulter* [1997] 2 All ER 1002; *National Westminster Bank v Morgan* [1985] AC 686; *Bank of Baroda v Shah* [1988] 3 All ER 24; *Bank of Credit and Commerce International v Aboody* [1990] 1 QB 923.
9 See *Barclays Bank v O'Brien* [1994] 1 AC 180; and *King's North Trust v Bell* [1986] 1 WLR 119.

4.14 Matrimonial proceedings. Where the debtor's wife is not standing by the debtor the nominee may well face the prospect of an order made in matrimonial proceedings depleting the debtor's assets. The proposal for an IVA will not restrict the exercise of the discretion of the matrimonial court to make lump sum or periodical awards in favour of the wife, though the nominee should take steps to ensure that a matrimonial court before which a wife's application is pending is fully appraised of the husband's liabilities and the terms of the proposal for IVA. The making of an interim order will operate as a stay in respect of any matrimonial proceedings which affect the debtor's property, although the leave of the court to continue such proceedings will readily be given[1].

Any obligation of the debtor to his wife in consequence of an order in family or domestic proceedings is not a debt provable in a bankruptcy and is not therefore a debt which is postponed to the debts held by preferential and ordinary creditors[2]. The effect of this rule may be to disadvantage the wife. For while she is not bound to accept a dividend in her husband's bankruptcy, her husband's assets will pass to his trustee and will be distributed to the proving creditors ahead of the wife's claim; in effect she will rank behind them all[3]. The suggestion that in consequence IR 1986, r 12.3(2)(a) was ultra vires was rejected by the Court of Appeal in *Woodley v Woodley (No 2)*[4]. In many of the standard conditions incorporated into a proposal for an IVA there is express provision to the effect that any creditor whose claim falls within IR 1986, r 12.3(2) will not be bound by the arrangement or entitled to vote in connection with or prove in the arrangement. In such a case it follows that in respect of a liability owed to her under a matrimonial order the wife is not a 'creditor'[5] and so will not be eligible to challenge the meeting's decision[6] on the grounds of unfair prejudice should she consider that the IVA adversely affects her interests. However, where there is no express exclusion of the wife as a creditor entitled to prove and vote in respect of the proposal, she is a creditor so entitled and she will be bound by the arrangement[7]. Furthermore, where the proposal expressly provided for the (former) wife, who had a lump sum order in her favour, to receive a dividend and she proved in and voted on the proposal it was held that she was a creditor bound by the IVA, the standard condition to the contrary being impliedly excluded by the express terms of the proposal[8].

While the wife (or former wife) may be a creditor bound by the arrangement she is in a special position, for her matrimonial debt is not released on the discharge of a bankrupt. This distinguishes her position from that of the creditors generally, and to the extent that she is compelled by the terms of an arrangement to accept a dividend in satisfaction of the matrimonial debt her right to enforce her matrimonial debt irrespective of bankruptcy is overridden. This may result in unfair prejudice entitling her to mount a successful challenge to an approval of an IVA[9]. Equally, other creditors may be prejudiced if a wife with no right to prove in the bankruptcy is able either to frustrate a voluntary arrangement against the creditors' wishes or use her voting rights to force them to accept an arrangement which would otherwise be rejected[10]. It is essential, therefore, that the special position of the wife or former wife who has obtained an order in matrimonial proceedings in her favour is recognised. If the wife is not simply excluded from the IVA, as will usually be the case, the nominee must consider how her position is to be safeguarded. At the least it will probably be necessary expressly to provide that the wife's debt will not be compromised by a dividend less than 100p in the £, even though she will not received more than other creditors before all the dividends due under the arrangement have been paid. Depending upon the exact circumstances an IVA which provides for the postponement in the payment of the wife's debt may not be unfairly prejudicial towards her.

The wife may be able to prevent the debtor parting with his assets for an IVA or have disposals of assets set aside under the provisions of the Matrimonial Causes

Act 1973[11]. Where proceedings for financial relief are brought by his wife against the debtor the court may restrain any proposed disposition or dealing with property ('disposition') where it is satisfied that the debtor is acting with the intention of defeating the claim for financial relief. The court may also set aside any completed disposition if satisfied that (a) the disposition was made with the intention of defeating the wife's claim and (b) if the order is made financial relief (which otherwise would not be granted) or different financial relief would be granted to the wife[12]. The wife must establish the necessary intention on the part of the debtor to defeat her claim. However, where any disposition took place within three years of the wife's application for financial relief there is a statutory presumption that the debtor had the intention of defeating the wife's claim unless the contrary is shown[13]. The nominee must therefore be aware that where the debtor proposes to dispose of or assign the bulk of his assets for the benefit of the IVA there is a risk that the debtor's wife may seek to have the disposition set aside. The fact that the debtor is concerned to avoid bankruptcy and is making the disposition for this purpose may well be sufficient to satisfy the court that the relevant disposition was not made with the requisite intention, even against the presumption in favour of the intention during the three years following the disposition. But it will be a question of fact in each case.

Where the disposition is made for valuable consideration to the supervisor or other trustee on behalf of the IVA who acted in good faith and without notice of any intention on the part of the debtor to defeat the wife's claim, it cannot be set aside by the court[14]. A lack of good faith for these purposes amounts to something akin to fraud and should at the very least involve a lack of honesty[15].

1 IA 1986, s 252(2)(b)
2 IR 1986, r 12.3(2)(a) which defines domestic and family proceedings by reference to the Magistrates' Courts Act 1980 and the Matrimonial and Family Proceedings Act 1984.
3 'She would receive the crumbs from her husband's table left unconsumed by his other creditors', per Sir Donald Nicholls V-C in *Re Mordant, Mordant v Halls* [1996] BPIR 302 at 307.
4 [1994] 1 WLR 1167.
5 For the purposes of the 'second group of parts' of IA 1986 (which include IVAs) creditor is defined in IA 1986, s 383 by reference to 'bankruptcy debts': 'Creditor, *in relation to a bankrupt*, means a person to whom any of the bankruptcy debts is owed'. Sums due to the wife under a matrimonial order are not such debts: IR 1986, r 12.3(2). But where the debtor husband is not a bankrupt it may be objected that this definition does not apply.
6 Under IA 1986, s 262: see para 7.1 below.
7 *Re Bradley-Hole (a bankrupt)* [1995] 2 BCLC 163.
8 *Re a Debtor; JP v a Debtor* [1999] BPIR 206.
9 See *Re a Debtor; JP v a Debtor* [1999] BPIR 206 at 219.
10 See *Re a Debtor; JP v a Debtor* [1999] BPIR 206.
11 Section 37.
12 Matrimonial Causes Act 1973, s 37(2).
13 Matrimonial Causes Act 1973, s 37(5).
14 Matrimonial Causes Act 1973, s 37(4).
15 *Whittingham v Whittingham* [1979] Fam 9.

4.15 The matrimonial home. In preparing the proposal the nominee will usually have to consider the matrimonial home. In most cases it will constitute the debtor's largest single asset, but one in which his wife may well have an interest. When considering the matrimonial home the nominee should first ascertain whether the debtor's wife has a legal or beneficial interest in the property, and the extent of any beneficial interest. Even if she has no beneficial interest in the property the wife will have rights of occupation in the matrimonial home, and these may affect the supervisor's ability to realise the home as an asset for the

IVA[1]. In the majority of cases the creditors will wish to be assured before approving a proposed IVA that all the assets which would be readily realised in a bankruptcy will be brought into account to fund the IVA. The nominee will therefore have to have regard to the bankruptcy provisions relating to the realisation of the matrimonial home[2]. The debtor's spouse, having taken independent advice, may wish to encourage the creditors to vote for the IVA by contributing her share or part of her share of the beneficial interest to the IVA, waiving her rights of exoneration[3], or agreeing to vacate the home to enable an earlier sale than might be possible in the event of her husband's bankruptcy bearing in mind the 12 months she is given under IA 1986 before the interest of the husband's creditors outweigh her interests[4]. The nominee should have in mind that giving up the matrimonial home may be emotionally very difficult and should ensure that a clear agreement to vacate the property and authorise a sale is reached, after independent advice for the spouse, before the proposal is put to the creditors. It may become necessary to institute proceedings for possession and sale[5], and it will assist the eventual supervisor if the proposal includes the debtor's agreement to proceedings being brought in his name for this purpose. Where the supervisor holds what was the debtor's interest in the matrimonial home on behalf of the creditors he will be able to bring proceedings under the Trusts of Land and Appointment of Trustees Act 1996, s 14 in his own name[6]. If, however, the terms of the IVA provide simply for the realisation of the home and other assets by the debtor with the proceeds being paid to the supervisor, it will not be possible for the supervisor to bring proceedings in his own name, as he will have no proprietary interest in the property[7].

The debtor and his wife should also be advised to consult the local housing authority at an early stage if they have no other accommodation available, and the nominee should be ready to explain to the housing authority that there is no real alternative to the debtor and his wife to giving their agreement to vacate the property. This is to reduce the risk that the debtor and his wife are treated as having made themselves intentionally homeless, thus adversely affecting their right to be re-housed by the local authority.

1 Family Law Act 1996, s 30 which defines a spouse's 'matrimonial homes rights' as:
'(a) if in occupation, a right not to be evicted or excluded from the dwelling-house or any part of it by the other spouse except with the leave of the court given by an order under [Family Law Act 1996], s 33;
(b) if not in occupation, a right with the leave of the court so given to enter into and occupy the dwelling-house.'

2 In this regard the amendments to IA 1986 which are introduced by EA 2002, s 261 should be noted.

3 See *Re Pittortou* [1985] 1 WLR 58 at 61, and see generally Berry, Bailey and Schaw Miller *Personal Insolvency* (3rd edn, 2001) para 18.29ff.

4 IA 1986, s 336(5).

5 Under the Trusts of Land and Appointment of Trustees Act 1996, s 14 (replacing the Law of Property Act 1925, s 30).

6 Cf *Re a Debtor, ex p Trustee v Solomon* [1967] Ch 573 and *Re McCarthy, ex p Trustee v McCarthy* [1975] 1 WLR 807, CA, cases where the trustee in bankruptcy was held to be a 'person interested' for the purposes of the Trusts of Land and Appointment of Trustees Act 1996, s 14 (replacing the Law of Property Act 1925, s 30(1)) and *Levermore v Levermore* [1979] 1 WLR 1277, where a receiver appointed by way of equitable execution was able to bring proceedings.

7 See *Re No 39 Carr Lane, Acomb, Stevens v Hutchinson* [1953] Ch 299.

4.16 Foreign assets and liabilities. No distinction is drawn between the debtor's assets and liabilities within and outside the jurisdiction. Assets held abroad must be disclosed together with an estimate of their value and details of any charges on such assets[1]. Equally, details of any foreign liabilities must be included in the proposal together with details of how it is proposed that such liabilities are to be met, modified, postponed or otherwise dealt with under the arrangement[2]. There is no express requirement in IR 1986 that the proposal explain how assets are to be realised. Unless foreign assets are to be excluded from the voluntary arrangement, however, it is sensible that the proposal addresses the realisation of foreign assets, both as to cost and time, and in the absence of such information a creditor should seek it. Obtaining the information may often itself take some time; if foreign assets form a significant part of the estate issues as to realisation should be raised early.

A particular point of difficulty may be the existence of so-called 'bankruptcy havens' where local rules provide that assets situated within the foreign jurisdiction must first be realised to meet local tax liabilities and even local creditors before the assets or their proceeds may be utilised to meet claims of creditors outside the local jurisdiction. This is one of the matters dealt with by the EU Regulation, but there remain many jurisdictions, with a number in the USA, which operate a rigid policy in this respect.

Foreign creditors have to be given notice of the creditors' meeting and be sent a form of proxy, as with any creditor[3]. They will be bound by the voluntary arrangement, at least in England. Enforcement abroad, especially where the creditor has voted against the proposal may be another matter. It is still the law that the UK courts will not enforce claims by foreign revenue authorities[4], although in the case of member states of the EU[5], claims of the tax authorities and social security authorities must now be admitted[6]. It would in any event be inappropriate to extend it so as to prevent foreign revenue claims being the subject of a voluntary arrangement. For it is of the essence of voluntary arrangements that there is a consensual agreement between the debtor and the creditors. The court does not enforce the claim when imposing the statutory hypothesis that all creditors are bound irrespective of whether and if so how they voted.

1 IR 1986, r 1.3(2)(a)(i) (all CVAs), r 5.3(2)(a)(i) (IVA).
2 IR 1986, r 1.3(2)(c) (all CVAs), r 5.3(2)(c) (IVA).
3 Creditors who are habitually resident, domiciled or have a registered office in another EU member state are entitled to information as to lodging claims, and in particular any time limits applying, and may lodge their claim in their own state's official language: see para 14.6 below.
4 *Government of India v Taylor* [1955] AC 491, HL. This principle is ripe for review.
5 Other than Denmark, which is exempt from the EC Regulation.
6 EC Regulation, Art 39.

4.17 Liability of nominee in relation to the proposal. As has been noted, although the scheme envisaged by IA 1986 is for the proposal to be prepared by the debtor or the directors of a corporate debtor, and then submitted to the nominee, in practice the proposal will almost invariably be prepared by the insolvency practitioner who it is intended should act as nominee; on rare occasions it is prepared by the debtor's solicitor, even more rarely by the debtor or directors themselves. In the usual case reliance will be placed by the debtor or directors on the insolvency practitioner's expertise in advising on and drafting the proposal. The insolvency practitioner will be well aware of this reliance. When the proposal is being considered by the creditors some will take their own advice from solicitors or insolvency practitioners; others will rely on the expertise of the insolvency practitioner chosen by the debtor or directors, ie the nominee. He may be aware of such reliance. It is in the nature of life, and certainly of affairs arising in the context of insolvency, that things will from time to time go wrong and that persons suffering loss, actual or perceived, will wish to claim damages for asserted professional negligence. The question arises whether, under general principles, there is the necessary conjunction of purpose, reliance, proximity of relationship, policy and loss for a claim successfully to be mounted against the insolvency practitioner concerned[1]. It appears that few claims against insolvency practitioners have been brought, an indication perhaps of the difficulties inherent in mounting such claims. This paragraph looks at the liability of the insolvency practitioner not only as nominee but throughout his involvement with the voluntary arrangement.

It is convenient to classify the duties performed by an insolvency practitioner under four heads:

1. advising on the nature and form of proposal and, when asked to do so, drafting the proposal;
2. acting as nominee up to the holding of the creditors' meeting;
3. acting as chairman of the creditors' (and any company) meeting and reporting the result of the meeting(s) to the court;
4. acting as supervisor of the approved voluntary arrangement.

When considering heads (2)–(4) above it is important to note that the insolvency practitioner as nominee or supervisor will be undertaking a public rôle, one in which he acts as an officer of the court performing the statutory duties imposed on him by IA 1986 and IR 1986. In this connection any claimant wishing to pursue a private right of action must establish that such a right arises under the statute for breach of statutory duty. The law in this area may be taken from the speech of Lord Browne-Wilkinson in *X (minors) v Bedfordshire County Council*[2]. There is no general rule for ascertaining whether a statute confers a private right of action for breach of a statutory duty. However, where the statute provides its own means of enforcing a duty, that will normally indicate that the statutory right was intended to be enforceable by those means and not by private right of action[3]. Further, although a common law duty of care may co-exist with a statutory duty no such duty will be imposed which is inconsistent with a statutory duty nor where its imposition would enable a claimant by private right of action to circumvent the statutory means of enforcing the statutory obligations.

In *King v Anthony*[4] the Court of Appeal considered an application to strike out pleadings as showing no cause of action. The plaintiff insolvency practitioner [IP] was asked by the debtors, a farming couple, to prepare proposals for IVA[5] and in due course these proposals were approved by the creditors' meeting. Subsequently, the defendants, who were creditors bound by the IVAs, reached a separate agreement with IP to accept certain farm equipment in settlement of their claims, and they also agreed to pay a specified sum for crops then growing at the debtors' farm. On being sued for this sum the defendants served a counterclaim asserting breaches of duty on the part of IP, as nominee, (a) properly and fully to consider the debtors' financial affairs, (b) to avoid an uncritical endorsement of any proposals put to him by the debtors, (c) ensure that his comments on the proposal were the product of an independent professional judgment, and (d) as chairman of the creditors' meeting and a supervisor to exercise an independent professional judgment and not to act merely as agent for the debtors[6]. The counterclaim also included a claim arising under the separate agreement to pay for growing crops asserting a breach of duty to exercise good husbandry which is of no immediate interest. The Court of Appeal held that IA 1986, Pt VIII[7] comprised a self-contained statutory scheme which included express power in the court to give appropriate directions if complaint was made of the conduct of the supervisor. As there was an effective statutory means of enforcing the duty of a supervisor[8] this indicated that the statutory right was intended to be enforceable by the statutory means and not by private right of action. The court therefore dismissed the appeal against the striking out of the counterclaim.

It may be noted that although the judgment of Brooke LJ[9] deals expressly only with the claim against IP as supervisor this was only part of the pleaded claim. Indeed although the pleading included the assertion that IP owed a duty of care as supervisor and that his breaches of duty included a breach of his duty as supervisor, this seems to be more the product of all embracing pleading than careful analysis of the facts. The claim essentially complained of IP's acts and omissions as nominee. The pleading appears not to have differentiated between IP's rôle as an insolvency practitioner advising the debtor and drafting the proposal, and his rôle as nominee. Accordingly, no claim was pursued that he owed the debtor a duty as an insolvency practitioner independent of his rôle as nominee, chairman and supervisor. In the event counsel conceded that the right of challenge afforded by IA 1986, s 262[10] was effective to bar any claim the defendants might have against IP in his capacity as nominee or as chairman of the creditors' meeting[11]. Accordingly, only the claim for breach of duty of supervisor remained to be dealt with by the Court of Appeal. The judgment of the Court of Appeal as to the claim against IP as supervisor must surely apply equally to the claim against IP as nominee and chairman of the meeting.

That counsel's concession that no private law duty to the debtor arose on the part of an insolvency practitioner when acting as nominee and chairman of the creditors' meeting was rightly made was accepted in *Prosser v Castle Sanderson and Geoffrey Martin & Co*[12]. The claim in this case arose on very narrow facts, namely whether the chairman of the creditors meeting, as an insolvency practitioner rather than as nominee, owed a duty of care to the debtor during a short adjournment of the creditors' meeting to advise the debtor that he might seek a longer adjournment of the meeting in order to formulate a more attractive proposal to creditors who were showing hostility toward the existing proposal at the creditors' meeting. It was common ground that the insolvency practitioner had owed the debtor a duty of care both in contract and tort when advising on the formulation of the proposal[13]. At first instance the court held that it would not be fair just and reasonable to impose a duty of care on the insolvency practitioner in respect of 'an opinion which could be regarded as constituting advice to the debtor' given in the course of a five-minute break in the middle of a creditors' meeting. The Court of Appeal disagreed:

> 'I agree that the courts should be careful not to impose duties upon nominees or chairmen of creditors' meetings when they are acting in that capacity. However, to my mind [the insolvency practitioner] was not acting in that capacity during the discussion with [the debtor] and [the solicitor] during the short adjournment. He was acting in precisely the same capacity as he had when he gave advice in the period before the meeting.' [14]

In the event the claim failed on issues of causation[15].

In *Pitt v Mond*[16], an IVA case, the court concluded (it being conceded by counsel) that the insolvency practitioner owed a tortious duty of care[17] to the individual debtor to act as would a reasonably competent insolvency practitioner practising at the relevant time in drafting the proposal (if asked to do so) and on advising on the proposals[18]. The court noted that this duty had to be 'moderated' by the fact that the nominee owed duties both to the debtor and to the creditors, so it could not extend to a duty to advise one how to get the better of the other. The duty to advise continues until the close of the creditors' meeting, but does not continue once the nominee becomes supervisor. At this stage only public duties are owed to the creditors, and any complaint about his rôle as supervisor has to be made to the court under the statutory procedure[19].

Underlying the debtors' complaint in *Pitt v Mond* was the concern that the nominee had failed to take steps within the proposal to protect the debtors from the fall in property values which followed the approval of their proposals in 1990. The court considered the extent of the nominee's duty when dealing with freehold property and its valuation. It concluded that the nominee was under no duty proactively to carry out a detailed investigation of the debtors' assets position, nor seek a valuation as a matter of course. The nominee was, however, required to be properly sceptical of information provided to him by the debtor[20], and if such information seemed unreliable he should investigate it as far as the constraints of time and cash permitted. If the nominee remained doubtful after such investigation as he could carry out he should openly express such doubts. In considering the facts of *Pitt v Mond* it is important to keep in mind that the debtors' statements of affairs disclosed a surplus of £900,000 based on property valuations obtained by and other information provided by the debtors. In essence the proposal was for a one year moratorium and payment of 100p in the £. The fall in property prices, coupled with generous valuations in the proposals, made this quite unachievable. Against this background it is not surprising that the court rejected the debtors' criticisms that the proposal involved a scheme of arrangement which contained no provision binding secured creditors as regards their shortfalls and no provision that such distributions as the unsecured creditors received should be in full and final settlement of their claims. Had the proposal been intended to comprise a composition rather than a moratorium scheme of arrangement then there would be no question that the absence of such provisions would have been negligent. The claim failed on the court's finding that the insolvency practitioner concerned could not be held to have owed the debtors a duty to foresee the collapse of the property market.

In CVA the distinction arises that the directors, as directors in their own right and not on behalf of the company, engage the insolvency practitioner who becomes the nominee to advise on and assist draft the proposal which is then made to the creditors and to the company. A duty in contract and tort will be owed by the insolvency practitioner to the directors in circumstances where breach is more likely to cause loss to the company than to the directors personally. However, as the insolvency practitioner well knows, the proposal is for the benefit of the company and is put to the company as well as to the creditors for consideration in their respective meetings. Accordingly, there should be no difficulty in the court finding that the insolvency practitioner owes a duty to the company (in tort) in addition to his duty to the directors which in most cases will be coterminous with that owed to the directors.

The following conclusions may be drawn:

1. When advising on the nature and form of proposal and, when asked to do so, drafting the proposal. The insolvency practitioner will owe the individual debtor or directors of a corporate debtor a duty both in contract and in tort, and the corporate debtor in tort alone, to exercise such care as

would a reasonably competent insolvency practitioner practising at the relevant time. The duty continues until the creditors have finally voted on the proposal. Only in very exceptional circumstances might the insolvency practitioner owe a duty in tort to a creditor of the debtor. There would have to be a special reason why a duty should be owed to particular creditor as opposed to all the creditors in respect of whom the insolvency practitioner will be acting in his statutory capacity as nominee. Even then the creditor would have to overcome the objection that he would only suffer loss if, to his detriment, the proposal was approved in circumstances where he was unable to sustain a challenge to the approved arrangement. It is difficult to postulate such circumstances.

2. Acting as nominee up to the holding of the creditors' meeting. The courts have accepted that no duty of care giving rise to a private right of action is owed by the nominee to the debtor or the creditors, but the point has yet to be argued. It may be noted that there is no general right of challenge to the court in respect of acts or omissions of the nominee before the holding of the creditors' (and company) meeting(s). In the case of a CVA moratorium there is a right on the part of any creditor, director or member of the company or any other person affected by a moratorium who is dissatisfied by any act, omission or decision of the nominee during the moratorium to apply to the court[21]. Plainly that will be the only route available to a potential claimant against the nominee in a moratorium. In CVAs with no moratorium and in IVA, however, no right to complain to the court exists in respect of acts omissions or decisions of the nominee[22]. It is conceivable, though rare, that the circumstance will arise, that carelessness on the part of the nominee in considering the proposal or the statement of affairs or in respect of seeking further information may give rise to loss on the part of one or more creditors which cannot be remedied by a challenge to the arrangements or even, perhaps, when arrangements are rejected in circumstances where they should never have proceeded to a creditors' meeting. In such circumstances, there being no statutory remedy, a private right of action may possibly lie in tort against the nominee.
3. Acting as chairman of the creditors' (and any company) meeting and reporting the result of the meeting(s) to the court. Any complaint as to the conduct of the chairman may be pursued under IR 1986 where appropriate[23] or otherwise under IA 1986[24]. There is no scope for a private right of action.
4. Acting as supervisor of the approved voluntary arrangement. Any complaint as to the conduct of the supervisor must be pursued under IA 1986[25]. There is no scope for a private right of action.

There may exist the possibility that a nominee or supervisor might be liable to creditors in respect of negligent misrepresentations when under a duty not to make representations[26].

Where an application is made to the court in respect of any act, omission or decision of a nominee during a moratorium or a supervisor during the implementation of an approved voluntary arrangement the court is given a complete discretion as to the order it may make[27]. It will be open, therefore, for any particular applicant to show that he has suffered loss for which an compensatory order should be made. The court will, however, be considering the matter in the context of the moratorium or voluntary arrangement as a whole. It may be noted that the statutory provisions enabling a dissatisfied applicant to complain about an act, omission or decision of a nominee in the course of moratorium, state expressly that in hearing that application the court must have regard to the interests of the members and creditors of the company generally[28]. The absence of this provision from other parts of the voluntary arrangement legislation is not significant; it is of the essence of voluntary arrangements as with other insolvency procedures that all creditors, and all members, are treated equally. The court has more restrictive powers when considering a complaint against the chairman as to entitlement to vote or against the nominee or chairman in respect of an approval or rejection of a proposal by the creditors. It is difficult, however, to conceive of circumstances where the powers available to the court, namely the revocation or suspension of any approval of the proposal or a direction that a further meeting be held to consider either the original or a revised proposal, will not be sufficient to do justice in any particular case.

1 It is outside the scope of this text to consider the proper formulation of the test for a duty of care to arise where no physical damage is suffered. Readers will be aware of the relevant decisions from *Hedley Bryne & Co v Heller & Partners* [1964] AC 465 through *Caparo Industries plc v Dickman* [1990] 2 AC 605 and beyond.

2 [1995] 2 AC 633 at 730–771; all the remaining members of the judicial committee concurred in the reasoning.

3 [1995] 2 AC 633 at 731.

4 [1998] 2 BCLC 517.

5 Presumably interlocking IVAs for the husband and wife.

6 The pleading drew heavily on well-known comments of Harman J in *Re a Debtor (No 222 of 1990), ex p Bank of Ireland (No 2)* [1993] BCLC 233.

7 Which governs IVAs; the decision is equally applicable to IA 1986, Pt I, which governs CVAs.

8 Ie by application under IA 1986, s 263(3) (IVA), s 7(3) (CVA without moratorium), IA 1986, Sch A1, para 39(3) (CVA with moratorium).

9 With whom both the other members of the court agreed.

10 In IVA, IA 1986, s 6 (CVA without moratorium), Sch A1, para 38 (CVA with moratorium).

11 [1998] 2 BCLC 517 at 523.

12 [2002] EWCA Civ 1140, [2002] All ER (D) 507 (Jul).

13 There was an initial proposal drafted by the debtor's solicitor (also a defendant to the proceedings and in respect of whom it was conceded that he owed a duty of care both in contract and tort throughout his work for the debtor) which was then amended with the assistance of the insolvency practitioner who had by then commenced his work as nominee under the initial proposal.

14 At para 66, per Clarke LJ, with whom both the other members of the court agreed.

15 The court applying principles derived from *Allied Maples Group Ltd v Simmons & Simmons* [1995] 1 WLR 1602. The judgment of Clarke LJ, from para 74 onwards, provides a helpful discussion on the proper approach to a claim for damages where the claimant's claim has to take into account the actions third parties as well as the claimant would have taken had matters proceeded differently at an adjourned creditors' meeting.

16 [2001] BPIR 624.

17 As a duty in tort was conceded there was, on the facts, no need for the court to consider a contractual duty. The judge observed at 642C: 'Because of the nature of a LIP's (licensed insolvency practitioner) peculiar position there are likely to be problems if the liability is formulated in contract.' That may be so, but it is not obvious what those problems are, and the Court of Appeal in *Prosser v Castle Sanderson and Geoffrey Martin & Co* [2002] EWCA Civ 1140, [2002] All ER (D) 507 (Jul) had no difficulty with the duty being in contract. There is after all always a contract except in the very rare case where an insolvency practitioner agrees to act gratuitously.

18 Ie under the '*Hedley Byrne*' principle, the court relying specifically on *Midland Bank Trust Co Ltd v Hett Stubbs & Kemp* [1979] Ch 384: see [2001] BPIR 624 at 645. The court was considering in January 2001 a proposal put to creditors in December 1990 and it was acknowledged that professional standards had changed markedly in the intervening ten years.

19 Ie under IA 1986, s 263(3) (IVA); s 7(3) (CVA without moratorium); Sch A1, para 38(3) (CVA with moratorium): see para 10.4 below; *King v Anthony* [1998] 2 BCLC 517. The passage of the judgment 'How far does the duty extend' at 642 does not clearly distinguish

between the activities of the insolvency practitioner as adviser to the debtor and as nominee, and might be thought to extend the duty owed as covering acts or omissions as nominee. There is no statement, however, that duties are owed as nominee; if there had been it would not have been correct.

20 *Greystoke v Hamilton-Smith* [1996] 2 BCLC 429.

21 IA 1986, Sch A1, para 26: see para 3.12 above.

22 It may be open to a creditor to apply to the court to resist the extension of an interim order on any hearing following the submission of the report to the court for the summoning of a creditors' meeting under IA 1986, s 256(1): see para 4.7 above.

23 See para 6.8 below.

24 See para 7.1 below.

25 See para 10.4 below.

26 See *Heritage Joinery v Krasner* [1999] BPIR 683.

27 See para 3.11 above and para 10.4 below.

28 See IA 1986, Sch A1, para 27, and in particular para 27(5).

Chapter 5

Preparation of proposal by office-holder or undischarged bankrupt

5.1 Proposal for CVA by administrator or liquidator. It is open to the administrator or liquidator of a company in administration or liquidation to make a proposal for a CVA[1]. With the company in formal insolvency there will be no need for a moratorium; a company in administration or liquidation is in any event expressly excluded from eligibility for a moratorium[2]. The aim will be to enable the company to survive its insolvency and resume trading with the consent of its creditors who will become creditors in the CVA. The administrator or liquidator (styled in IR 1986, 'the responsible insolvency practitioner'[3]) wishing to propose a scheme of voluntary arrangements may either act as the nominee himself or appoint another insolvency practitioner to act as nominee for the proposal. Where he is acting as nominee himself, the responsible insolvency practitioner should prepare a proposal which specifies all the matters that are required to be included by the directors in a proposal by them[4] together with 'such other matters (if any) as the insolvency practitioner considers appropriate for ensuring that members and creditors of the company are enabled to reach an informed decision on the proposal'[5]. If the proposal is made in respect of a company in administration, it must also include the names and addresses of the company's preferential creditors[6] with the amount of their respective claims[7]. Notice of the proposal is to be given to the official receiver where it is made in respect of a company in compulsory liquidation[8].

1 IA 1986, s 1(3).
2 IA 1986, Sch A1, para 4(1).
3 See IR 1986, r 1.1(3).
4 See para 4.4 above and IR 1986, r 1.3: see Appendix 1.
5 IR 1986, r 1.10(1).
6 As defined in IA 1986, s 386.
7 IR 1986, r 1.10(1)(a).
8 IR 1986, r 1.10(2).

5.2 Preparation of proposal for CVA by nominee who is not the responsible insolvency practitioner. The company's responsible insolvency practitioner may prefer to have the proposal and any resulting CVA handled by a specialist in voluntary arrangements. Where another practitioner acts as nominee for the company in administration or liquidation, IR 1986[1] make specific provision for the procedure to be followed in the preparation of the proposal and giving notice to the nominee. This procedure substantially follows that for a proposal initiated by the directors:

1. the responsible insolvency practitioner gives notice to the intended nominee and prepares his proposal for a voluntary arrangement in the same manner as is required of directors[2];
2. the content of the proposal is to be the same as a proposal by directors together with 'such other matters, if any, as the responsible insolvency practitioner considers appropriate for ensuring that members and creditors of the company are enabled to reach an informed decision on the proposal', and, in the case of a company in administration, the names and addresses of the company's preferential creditors[3] with the amounts of their respective claims[4];
3. the responsible insolvency practitioner must provide the nominee with a statement of affairs[5] and the nominee is entitled to call on the responsible insolvency practitioner to provide additional information should he require it to enable him to prepare his report to the court[6];
4. the nominee submits his report to the court[7], and meetings of creditors and members are summoned if in the opinion of the nominee the proposal should be put before the company and its creditors[8].

Where the company is being compulsorily wound up, the responsible insolvency practitioner must send a copy of the proposal to the official receiver, accompanied by the name and address of the practitioner who has agreed to act as nominee[9].

1 IR 1986, r 1.12.
2 IR 1986, r 1.12(1), (2) and see para 4.4 above.
3 As defined in IA 1986, s 386.
4 IR 1986, r 1.12(3).
5 IR 1986, r 1.12(5).
6 IR 1986, r 1.12(4), which applies IR 1986, r 1.6: see para 4.5 above.
7 Complying with IR 1986, r 1.7: see para 4.7 above.
8 IR 1986, r 1.12(7).
9 IR 1986, r 1.12(7).

5.3 Summoning CVA meetings where office-holder is nominee. A responsible insolvency practitioner acting as nominee does not have to submit a report to the court. Having prepared his proposal he proceeds to summon meetings of the company and its creditors to consider the proposal for such a time, date and place as he thinks fit[1]. At least 14 days' notice[2] of the meetings must be given (i) to all the creditors specified in the company's statement of affairs[3] and to any other creditors of whom the insolvency practitioner is aware; and (ii) to all persons who are to the best of the insolvency practitioner's belief members of the company[4]. Each notice must:

(a) explain to the creditors that the arrangements can only be approved by a three-quarters majority, and the circumstances in which a creditor's vote may be left out of account[5] or a resolution may be invalid[6]; and
(b) be accompanied by copies of the responsible insolvency practitioner's proposal and the statement of affairs, or if the practitioner thinks fit a summary of the statement of affairs which must include a list of creditors and the amount of their debts[7].

1 IA 1986, s 3(2).
2 With every notice there must be a form of proxy, IR 1986, r 1.13(4), which is to be in IR 1986, Sch 4, Form 8.1.
3 See para 4.5 above.
4 IR 1986, r 1.11(1).
5 Under IR 1986, r 1.19(3) and see para 6.9 below.
6 Under IR 1986, r 1.19(4), see para 6.9 below.
7 IR 1986, r 1.11(2).

5.4 Proposal for PVA by article 11 trustee. A proposal may be made on behalf of an insolvency partnership by an administrator or liquidator where an administration order is in force or the partnership is being wound up as an unregistered company, and also by the trustee of the partnership where an order has been made under the Insolvent Partnerships Order 1994, SI 1994/2421, art 11[1]. This is an order made on the joint bankruptcy petitions of all the members of a partnership, all being individuals. An art 11 petition may not be presented where there are corporate or limited partners. The sole ground on which an art 11 petition may be presented is that the partnership is unable to pay its debts[2], and the petition must be accompanied by statements of affairs of each member and the partnership in the prescribed forms[3]. A single trustee is then appointed to administer the various members' estates and he will be able to assess the appropriateness of a proposal for a PVA (and, probably, interlocking IVAs alongside the PVA). He may act as nominee himself[4], or he may appoint another qualified practitioner to act as nominee[5]. Where the art 11 trustee acts as nominee he may proceed to summon meetings of creditors and the members of the partnership to consider the proposal without reporting to the court[6].

1 IA 1986, s 1(a), as modified by IPO 2002.
2 IA 1986, s 272(1), as modified by IPO 1994, Sch 9, para 5.
3 IA 1986, s 272(2), as modified by IPO 1994, Sch 7, para 5 and see IPO 1994, Sch 9, Forms 17 and 18 for the prescribed forms for the members' and partnership's statement of affairs.
4 See para 5.1 above.
5 See para 5.2 above.
6 IA 1986, s 3(2), as modified by IPO 2002.

5.5 Proposal for IVA by undischarged bankrupt. In contrast to the position in a CVA or a PVA, a trustee in bankruptcy may not make a proposal for an IVA; that is a matter for the individual debtor himself. Should an undischarged bankrupt wish to propose an IVA he himself, his trustee in bankruptcy or the official receiver may make an application for an interim order[1], should it be thought advisable to obtain such an order[2]. An interim order may be required when the bankrupt has incurred post-bankruptcy debts and the post-bankruptcy creditors are threatening proceedings.

Notice of the application must be given to whichever of the three (debtor, official receiver, trustee in bankruptcy) is not the applicant for the interim order[3], and the court hearing the application may include in any interim order directions as to the conduct of the bankruptcy or the administration of the estate while the order remains in force[4]. The undischarged bankrupt makes his proposal as would any other debtor[5], although he need not prepare a statement of affairs if he has already delivered one in the bankruptcy unless expressly required to do so by the nominee for the purpose of supplementing or amplifying the existing statement[6]. If there has been post-bankruptcy trading a further statement of affairs is likely to be necessary. There is no need for the bankrupt's nominee to be the trustee in bankruptcy; there may indeed be a dispute between the bankrupt, supported by his nominee, and the trustee in bankruptcy as the appropriateness of a proposal going forward to the creditors. It will be important for an undischarged bankrupt that his proposal includes creditors whose debts have arisen since the date of the bankruptcy order. This is achieved through IA 1986, s 257(3), which provides that the creditors of an undischarged bankrupt to be summoned to the creditors' meeting include both the bankruptcy debt creditors and 'every person who would be such a creditor if the bankruptcy had commenced on the day on which notice of the meeting is given'.

Once a bankrupt debtor has been discharged it is no longer possible for the debtor to seek an IVA in respect of his bankruptcy debts[7]; he may of course propose for an IVA in respect of debts arising after the commencement of his bankruptcy or indeed for debts which are not provable in the bankruptcy and from which the debtor is not released on his discharge[8]. It may seem surprising that any debtor should wish to propose for an IVA in respect of debts from which he has been discharged by his bankruptcy. However, the recovery of the housing market from its low point in the early 1990s gave rise to a number of problematic cases where trustees who had long since finished actively administering the estate but had not held final meetings or sought their release discovered that matrimonial homes which had negative equity at the date of the bankruptcy had risen in value far faster than the loans to which they had been charged. Whatever routes may be available to the discharged bankrupt debtor in such circumstances, an IVA is not one of them[9].

It is the case that significant numbers of debtors made bankrupt in the early 1990s discovered years later, long after their discharge, the harsh reality of the law which automatically transfers the bankrupt's property to the trustee and leaves it with him even if he takes no steps to realise it. Long after the bankrupt and the creditors thought it was all over the trustee discovered that the bankrupt's home had increased in value faster than the mortgage debt. The trustee was then in a position to realise the asset. Provisions designed to prevent this happening in the future were introduced by EA 2002, s 261. From the implementation of these provisions, by IA 1986, s 283A any interest in the bankrupt's sole or principal residence automatically re-vests in the bankrupt after three years from the date of the bankruptcy if the trustee has not within that period applied for an order to realise the asset for the estate. Additionally, a new provision, IA 1986, s 313A, provides that any application to realise a 'low value home', that is an interest of the bankrupt in his sole or principal residence the value of which is less than a prescribed amount, shall be dismissed by the court.

1 IA 1986, s 253(3).
2 Note that since the implementation of the amendments introduced by IA 2000, it is not essential to obtain an interim order before proceeding with a proposal for an IVA, see IA 1986, s 256A.
3 IR 1986, r 5.5(4)(a).
4 IA 1986, s 255(3).
5 See para 4.4 above.
6 IR 1986, r 5.8(1).
7 Under IA 1986 as originally enacted, an IVA could only be sought after obtaining an interim order, and such an order could only be obtained by an undischarged bankrupt or a debtor who was able to petition for his own bankruptcy. The only ground on which a debtor may petition for his own bankruptcy is that he is unable to pay his debts. Once debts have been discharged under IA 1986, s 281 they are no longer debts. Under IA 1986, as amended by IA 2000, it is no longer necessary to obtain an interim order. However, an IVA cannot proceed without the nominee first reporting to the court, and by IA 1986, s 256A(3) the nominee may only report to the court if he is of the opinion that

the debtor is an undischarged bankrupt or is able to petition for his own bankruptcy. An IVA may be sought where there are debts accruing after the bankruptcy, but the original (bankruptcy) 'creditors' cannot become parties to the IVA under the provisions of IA 1986, s 260(2).

8 See IA 1986, s 281 and IR 1986, r 12.3(2), which specifies the debts not provable in a bankruptcy.

9 For an example in the law reports, see *Wright v Official Receiver* [2001] BPIR 196.

Chapter 6

Consideration of the proposal

6.1 The creditors' meeting. The creditors' meeting is the centre-piece of the voluntary arrangement procedure. The statutory scheme is that in open meeting, with all relevant information before them, the creditors decide whether or not to accept the debtor's proposals for a voluntary arrangement or, in effect, put the debtor into liquidation or bankruptcy. In many cases the reality is rather different. Many creditors have neither the time nor the will to consider the detail of a proposed arrangement, investigate the completeness of the debtor's information and form a considered view as to the appropriateness of the proposals. In revising the criminal offence of fraud in connection with a voluntary arrangement[1] and in imposing an obligation on the nominee or supervisor to report criminal conduct to the Secretary of State[2], Parliament has acknowledged that improper advantage has been taken by many debtors of the availability of statutory voluntary arrangements. Few insolvency offences reach the criminal courts, however, and without more careful monitoring of voluntary arrangements it seems unlikely that these new provisions will result in any significant improvement in conduct on the part of those debtors who are prepared to 'play the system' and those insolvency practitioners who acquiesce in such behaviour by their clients.

In CVA the proposal is also put before a meeting of the company for approval or rejection. In the event of a disagreement between the meetings the decision of the creditors' meeting will take priority, subject to any order of the court[3].

The creditors' meeting, and in CVA the company meeting, will be under the control of the chairman who will be the nominee[4] unless he is unable to attend. In this event the nominee may nominate another person to chair the meeting in his place, provided that person is authorised to act in relation to the voluntary arrangement or is an employee of the nominee or his firm who is experienced in insolvency matters[5].

1 Previously, IR 1986, r 1.30 (CVA), r 5.30 (IVA), now IA 1986, s 6A (CVA without moratorium), Sch A1, paras 41, 42 (CVA with moratorium), s 262A (IVA): see Chapter 8 below.
2 IA 1986, s 7A(2) (CVA), s 262B (IVA): see Chapter 8 below.
3 See para 6.13 below.
4 IR 1986, r 1.14(1) (CVA with or without moratorium), r 5.19(1) (IVA): note that IR 1986, r 1.14, 1.16 (unnecessarily) specify that in CVA the 'convener' chairs the meeting, the convener being either the nominee appointed by the directors, or, where the company is in liquidation or administration, the nominee appointed by the responsible

insolvency practitioner (see para 5.2 above) or the responsible insolvency practitioner himself where he acts as nominee: IR 1986, r 5.15(1) (IVA).
5 IR 1986, r 1.14(2) (all CVAs), r 5.19(2) (IVA).

6.2 Summoning meeting of IVA creditors. On receiving the nominee's report the court considers whether a meeting of the debtor's creditors should be summoned to consider the debtor's proposal, and if satisfied that a creditors' meeting should be called the court must direct that the interim order should be extended for such further period as may be necessary for the debtor's proposals to be considered[1]. While the court is given a discretion in the matter it will be a rare case where the court does not follow the nominee's recommendation that a meeting be held. Both IA 1986[2] and IR 1986[3] proceed upon the assumption that the nominee's opinion in the matter will be followed. Where there are no complications it is possible for the court to make an order carrying the procedure forward to the holding of the creditors' meeting without the need for hearing. Provided the nominee's report has been delivered to the court, complies with the Act and the rules[4], and proposes a date for the creditors' meeting which complies with the rules, a 'standard order' may be made on consideration of the nominee's report. This order extends the interim order to a date seven weeks after the date of the proposed meeting, directs the meeting to be summoned and adjourns the application to the court to a date about three weeks after the meeting, and may be made without attendance of any party[5].

The creditors' meeting will be held at the time date and place proposed by the nominee unless the court directs otherwise[6]. This meeting must be held not less than 14 days from that on which the nominee's report is filed in court nor more than 28 days after the date on which the report is considered by the court[7]. It is essential that the nominee summons the meeting in accordance with his report to the court. On a true construction of IA 1986, s 257(1), approval is only effective at a meeting held in accordance with the terms of the interim order[8].

The nominee must summon every creditor of the debtor of whose existence he is aware[9], giving at least 14 days notice of the meeting[10]. The notice given to the creditors must (1) explain the rules governing the majorities required to approve the IVA[11], and (2) be accompanied by (a) a copy of the proposal, (b) the debtor's statement of affairs or a summary of it (at the nominee's discretion), and (c) the nominee's comments on the proposal[12]. It is plainly important that once the meeting has been convened the venue should not be changed without giving all creditors reasonable notice of the change[13].

The nominee is to act as chairman of the meeting[14], but should he be unable to attend he may nominate another person to act as chairman in his place provided that person is either an insolvency practitioner or is an employee of the nominee's firm who is experienced in insolvency matters[15].

1 IA 1986, s 256(5).
2 IA 1986, s 257(1).
3 IR 1986, r 5.17(1).
4 Ie IA 1986, s 256(1) and IR 1986, r 5.11(2), (3).
5 See *Practice Direction : Insolvency Proceedings* para 16.1(2), see Appendix 6. IR 1986, r 5.17(1) requires the meeting to be held not less than 14 days from that on which the nominee's report is filed in court nor more than 28 days from that on which the report is considered by the court.
6 IA 1986, s 257(1). In fixing the venue for the creditors' meeting, the nominee must have regard to the convenience of creditors (IR 1986, r 5.18(1)) and must summon the meeting to start between 10.00 and 16.00 hours on a business day: r 5.18(2).

7 IR 1986, r 5.17(1).

8 *Re N (a debtor)* [2002] BPIR 1024. The meeting was held on 11 July at 3.30 pm and not on 12 June at noon. This discrepancy was picked up when it was noted that the report to the court was not in proper form as it failed to deal with the EC Regulation on insolvency. The court considered that the chairman should apply under IA 1986, s 262 to revoke the IVA and seek a further meeting of creditors, bearing all the cost personally.

9 Ie all creditors of whom the nominee is aware whether or not they have been listed in the debtor's statement of affairs: IR 1986, r 5.17(2). It should be noted that IA 1986, s 257(2) specifies that the nominee needs to be aware both of the creditor's claim and of his address. In the case of a debtor who is an undischarged bankrupt creditors who must be given notice include (a) every person who is a creditor of the bankrupt in respect of a bankruptcy debt, and (b) every person who would be a creditor in respect of a bankruptcy debt if the bankruptcy had commenced on the day on which notice of the meeting is given: IA 1986, s 257(3).

10 IR 1986, r 5.17(2).

11 Ie the provisions of IR 1986, r 5.23(1), (3), (4).

12 IR 1986, r 5.17(3).

13 Cf *Re High Spirits Cellars Pty Ltd* (1988) 6 ACLC 644, NSW S Ct, where a scheme of arrangement was set aside after approval at a meeting held at a changed time not notified to a number of creditors whose addresses were not traced even though their votes would not have altered the outcome. In England this case would probably have been differently decided, since to form the basis of a successful challenge the irregularity must be material, ie the number of missing votes may have altered the outcome: see eg *Doorbar v Alltime Securities Ltd* [1996] 1 BCLC 487; *Re a Debtor (No 259 of 1990)* [1992] 1 WLR 226 at 229; *Cadbury Schweppes v Somji* [2001] 1 WLR 615, para 25.

14 IR 1986, r 5.19(1); as chairman of the meeting the nominee may cast proxy votes but may not use such votes to increase or reduce the amount of the remuneration or expenses of the nominee or the supervisor of the proposed arrangement unless the proxy specifically directs him to vote that way: IR 1986, r 5.20. Should the chairman use a proxy vote contrary to this rule, it does not count towards any requisite majority as defined in IR 1986, r 5.23(1) or (2), r 5.23(6).

15 IR 1986, r 5.19(2); for 'experience in insolvency matters' note the provisions of Insolvency Practitioners Regulations 1990, SI 1990/439, regs 5–8. These lay down the experience required of an applicant for authorisation as an insolvency practitioner. Presumably less experience will be required of the employee who stands in for the nominee who is unable to attend the creditors' meeting.

6.3 Summoning CVA meetings of creditors and the company. In CVA the nominee summons both a meeting of creditors and also a meeting of the company, that is the members whether holders of shares or any other interest in the company[1]. This reflects the fact that the statutory scheme is for the directors to propose a voluntary arrangement for the company as directors and not on behalf of the company. Accordingly, the members of the company are given an opportunity to express their approval or disapproval of the directors' proposals. As IA 1986 was enacted originally, a CVA required the approval of both the creditors' meeting and the company meeting by their respective majorities[2]. As amended by IA 2000, a CVA may be approved by the creditors' meeting alone[3] or, by order of the court, by the company meeting alone. This follows from the fact that if the decision taken by the creditors' meeting differs from that taken by the company meeting, a member of the company may apply to the court[4]. On the member's application the court may order that the decision of the company meeting should have effect instead of the decision of the creditors' meeting or make such other order as it thinks fit[5]. Accordingly, the court may reverse the creditors' approval of the CVA or impose the CVA on creditors despite their rejection of the proposal. It will take very exceptional circumstances for a court to reverse the decision of the creditors' meeting and impose a CVA. In cases where a member is able to demonstrate impropriety as between the creditors and the company the court may be persuaded to set aside the creditors' decision and order further meetings to take place.

Where the court does make an order on an application by a member of the company following different decisions by the creditors' and company meetings, the applicant must serve sealed copies of the order on the supervisor and the directors of the company[6], and an office copy on the registrar of companies[7]. After receiving a copy of the order the supervisor, if one is in post, or the directors if there is no supervisor must give notice of the order to everyone who was sent notice of the creditors' or company meetings and anyone else who is affected by the order[8].

Having reported his opinion to the court that meetings of the creditors and the company should be held, the nominee is required to send notice of the creditors' meetings to all the creditors specified in the statement of affairs and any other creditor of whom he is otherwise aware. In CVA the nominee must give notice of the company meeting to all persons who are, to the best of his belief, members of the company[9]. At least 14 days' notice of the meetings must be given[10]. The date on which the meetings are to be held must be not less than 14 nor more than 28 days from the date on which the nominee's report is filed in court where there is no moratorium or from the date on which the nominee summons the meetings where a moratorium is in force[11]. Each notice sent to a creditor or member must explain the rules relating to the majorities required in the creditors' meeting to approve the proposal[12], and with each notice must be sent (a) a copy of the directors' proposal, (b) a copy of the statement of affairs or, if the nominee thinks fit a summary to include a list of creditors and the amount of their debts, and (c) the nominee's comments on the proposal[13]. When deciding upon the venue for the meetings, the convener is to have regard primarily to the convenience of the creditors[14]. The meetings must commence between 10.00 and 16.00 hours on a business day[15]. They may be held on the same day or on different days provided that they are not more than seven days apart, but with the creditors' meeting fixed for an earlier time than that of the company meeting[16]. If the chairman of the meetings thinks fit he may arrange for the meetings to be held together[17]. Every notice summoning a meeting must be accompanied by a form of proxy[18].

1 See IR 1986, r 1.18(3).
2 See paras 6.10, 6.11 below (essentially three-quarters for creditors, simple majority for the company meeting, but with certain creditors' votes left out of account in the creditors' vote and the need for more than 50% of creditors not associated with the company to vote for any approval).
3 IA 1986, s 4A(2) (CVA without moratorium), Sch A1, para 36(2) (CVA with moratorium).
4 IA 1986, s 4A(3) (CVA without moratorium), Sch A1, para 36(3) (CVA with moratorium).
5 IA 1986, s 4A(6) (CVA without moratorium), Sch A1, para 36(5) (CVA with moratorium). Where the applicant is a member of a regulated company (as defined in IA 1986, Sch A1, para 44) the Financial Services Authority is entitled to be heard on the application: IA 1986, s 4A(5), Sch A1, para 44(10).
6 IR 1986, r 1.22A(1), (2); this rule applies to CVAs where a moratorium is in force by virtue of IR 1986, r 1.54(2). Service on the directors may be effected by serving a single copy on the company at its registered office: IR 1986, r 1.22A(3).
7 IR 1986, r 1.22A(5) (all CVAs); this office copy must be delivered within seven days.
8 IR 1986, r 1.22A(4) (all CVAs).
9 IR 1986, r 1.9(2) (CVA without moratorium), r 1.48(2) (CVA with moratorium).
10 IR 1986, r 1.9(2) (CVA without moratorium), r 1.48(2) (CVA with moratorium).
11 IR 1986, r 1.9(1) (CVA without moratorium), r 1.48(1) (CVA with moratorium).
12 Ie the effect of IR 1986, r 1.19(1), (3), (4) (CVA without moratorium), r 1.52(1), (4), (5) (CVA with moratorium): see para 6.10 below.
13 IR 1986, r 1.9(3) (CVA without moratorium), r 1.48(4) (CVA with moratorium).
14 IR 1986, r 1.13(1) (all CVAs; r 1.13 applies where a moratorium is in force by virtue of r 1.48(5)).
15 IR 1986, r 1.13(2) (all CVAs).
16 IR 1986, r 1.13(3) (all CVAs); this rule was amended by the Insolvency (Amendment) (No 2) Rules 2002, SI 2002/2712. Previously it was a requirement that the meetings were

held on the same day and in the same place. Although there can now be up to seven days between the meetings the aim where possible should be to have the company meeting immediately following the creditors' meeting or to hold both meetings together.
17 IR 1986, r 1.21(1) (CVA without moratorium), r 1.53(2) (CVA with moratorium).
18 IR 1986, r 1.13(5) (all CVAs).

6.4 Attendance of company officers in CVA. The directors of a company proposing a voluntary arrangement have the right to 14 days' notice from the convener of the meetings[1]. They, together with any officer of the company or former director, may, however, be excluded from all or any part of the meetings if the chairman thinks fit[2]. Should he consider that their presence is required at the meetings, the convener may require the attendance of any person who is an officer of the company or who has been a director or officer of it at any time in the two years immediately preceding the date of the notice[3].

In PVA the wording of this rule, under which the convener may require the attendance of officers or persons 'having been directors or officers of [the company]' means that any person who has been an officer or member of the partnership at any time in the immediately preceding two years may be required to attend either the creditors' meeting or the meeting of the members of the insolvent partnership[4].

1 IR 1986, r 1.16(1)(a) (all CVAs; r 1.16 applies where a moratorium is in force by virtue of r 1.48(5)).
2 IR 1986, r 1.16(2) (all CVAs); this applies whether or not notice of the meeting has been given to the person excluded.
3 IR 1986, r 1.16(1)(b) (all CVAs).
4 See IA 1986, s 1A(7)(a), as added by IPO 2002, which provides that reference to directors of a company shall be construed as a reference to the members of a partnership. Note IR 1986 applies to PVAs by virtue of IPO 1994, art 18, Sch 10. Although the rules of construction set out in IA 1986, s 1A(7) do not specifically apply to IR 1986, it is anticipated that they will be applied where necessary to the provisions of IR 1986.

6.5 Power of the meeting(s) to modify the proposal. It is open to the creditors' meeting, and in CVA the company meeting, to modify the proposal under consideration. In practice modifications are often made with creditors pressing for more advantageous terms. The meeting(s) may therefore approve the proposal with modifications, but:

(a) in IVA the debtor must consent to each modification[1];
(b) no modification may be approved which has the effect of causing the proposal to cease to be a composition or scheme of arrangement[2];
(c) no proposal or modification may be approved which affects the right of a secured creditor of the debtor to enforce his security unless that creditor concurs with the relevant provision[3];
(d) no proposal or modification may be approved which prejudices the rights of a preferential creditor[4] whether by interfering with his right to priority in payment or by paying him a smaller proportion of his debt than that paid in respect of another preferential debt, except with the concurrence of the preferential creditor involved[5].

A modification may be approved which has the effect of replacing the nominee with another insolvency practitioner or practitioner authorised to act as nominee qualified to act in relation to the voluntary arrangement[6], provided the replacement signifies his consent in person at the meeting or in writing produced to the chairman of the meeting[7]. It is permissible for there to be more than one practitioner (whether qualified insolvency practitioner or other authorised person) responsible for implementing the approved arrangements[8]. Subject to the above there are no further statutory provisions qualifying the meetings' power to modify the proposed arrangement.

It is suggested that the power to modify is just that and cannot be extended to changing the proposal so radically that it becomes in effect a different proposal. Not only is this a matter of interpretation of 'modification' but there is the practical consideration that all creditors and members will have received a copy of the proposal and have determined whether or not to attend the meeting or given proxy votes on their assessment of the proposal in its original form. Although the necessary majorities may be obtained for a radically altered proposal from those creditors and members attending their respective meetings the presence of other creditors or members at the meetings who voted by proxy may have given a different result.

1 IA 1986, s 258(2). There is no similar requirement in CVA for the directors to approve modifications. This is because any modification to the CVA introduced by the creditors has to be approved by the company meeting and once so approved the necessary consensual agreement between company and creditors has been reached. The statutory requirement in IVA is clear and mandatory. An IVA cannot be valid if the debtor has not approved the modifications for there is no consensual agreement between him and his creditors. In *Reid v Hamblin* [2001] BPIR 929 (Milton Keynes County Court) a nomineee (who subsequently lost his licence) wrote to the debtors after the creditors' meeting, which no creditor had attended and at which the nominee used a proxy vote without informing the creditor concerned that modifications had been required by the bank (a major creditor), stating 'I am pleased to confirm that your IVAs have been approved by your creditors, subject to you formally consenting to the 4 modifications [sought by the bank]'. Documents for signature were enclosed which the debtors would not sign. The debtors then made payments apparently under the impression that the original proposal was in force. In due course the IVA was held to be a nullity and an order made for payments made under it to be returned. If nothing else the reporting of this case serves as a useful reminder of quite how bad things can be in the hands of a minority of insolvency practitioners.
2 IA 1986, s 4(2) (CVA without moratorium), Sch A1, para 31(3) (CVA with moratorium), s 258(3) (IVA).
3 IA 1986, s 4(3) (CVA without moratorium), Sch A1, para 31(4) (CVA with moratorium), s 258(4) (IVA).
4 'Preferential debt' is defined as in IA 1986, s 386 and 'preferential creditor' is to be construed accordingly: IA 1986, s 4(7) (CVA without moratorium), Sch A1, para 31(8) (CVA with moratorium), s 258(7) (IVA). Note that Crown preference is abolished by EA 2002, s 251.
5 IA 1986, s 4(4) (CVA without moratorium), Sch A1, para 31(5) (CVA with moratorium), s 258(5) (IVA).
6 IA 1986, s 4(2) (CVA without moratorium), Sch A1, para 31(2) (CVA with moratorium), s 258(3) (IVA). With voluntary arrangements involving substantial debtors it is not unknown for a major creditor to agree to vote for the proposal only on the basis that an insolvency practitioner of his choice replaces the nominee.
7 IR 1986, r 1.22(3) (all CVAs – r 1.22 applies where a moratorium is in force by virtue of r 1.54(2)), r 5.20(2) (IVA).
8 See the provisions of IR 1986, r 1.22(1) (all CVAs), r 5.25(1) (IVA): see Appendix 2.

6.6 Entitlement to vote at creditors' meeting. A creditor's entitlement to vote at the creditors' meeting is a critical consideration for it is on this entitlement that the question whether or not he is bound to the voluntary arrangement if approved is determined. In understanding the relevant statutory provisions it is necessary to follow their history. As originally drawn IA 1986[1] provided that an approved voluntary arrangement bound 'every person who in accordance with the rules had notice of, and was entitled to vote at, the [creditors'] meeting (whether or not he was present or represented at the meeting) as if he were a party to the voluntary arrangement'. This might be seen as imposing two requirements for a person to be bound to the voluntary arrangement as a creditor. First notice in accordance with the rules and secondly entitlement *as a creditor* to vote. IR 1986 made provision for notice to be given to the creditors; the nominee was required to give notice 'to all creditors specified in the debtor's statement of affairs, and any other creditors of whom [the nominee] is otherwise aware'[2]. Neither IA 1986 nor IR 1986, however, made any provision as to what might be seen as the second requirement for a creditor to be bound to the voluntary arrangement, namely that of being a creditor of the debtor. Thus despite the wording of IA 1986 quoted above IR 1986 treated the requirement to be bound to a voluntary arrangement as a single composite requirement, and provided that 'every creditor who was given notice of the creditors' meeting is entitled to vote at the meeting or any adjournment of it'[3].

The amendment introduced by IA 2000 to tackle the problem of the 'omitted creditor'[4] adopted an approach consistent with IR 1986 in treating the requirement for being bound to the voluntary arrangement as a single composite requirement. It was unable, therefore, to adopt the simple expedient of removing the requirement of receipt of notice and restrict the binding to an approved voluntary arrangement to creditors of the debtor as at the date of the meeting. Rather, IA 1986, as amended[5], binds as a party to the approved arrangement 'every person who in accordance with the rules (i) was entitled to vote at the meeting (whether or not he was present or represented at it)[6], or (ii) would have been so entitled if he had had notice of it'. Entitlement to vote at the creditors' meeting remains, therefore, a question of receipt of notice of the meeting even though ultimately receipt of notice is irrelevant to the question of being bound to the approved arrangement.

Every creditor who has been given notice of the creditors' meeting may vote at the meeting or any adjournment of it[7]. Additionally, any creditor who was not given notice of the meeting but who learns of it and attends may also vote, provided he can satisfy the chairman that he is indeed a creditor[8]. The important question when is a person a creditor, and what is the value of his debt for the purposes of voting, is considered in the following paragraph.

Secured creditors. A secured creditor may vote in respect of any unsecured balance of his debt. The standard terms of many voluntary arrangements incorporate the provisions of IR 1986[9] as to valuation, sale and revaluation of a creditor's security. Where these rules apply, and indeed unless there is express provision to the contrary in the terms of the arrangement, a secured creditor is not debarred from revaluing his security after a dividend has been declared and paid or even after the arrangement has come to an end. The secured creditor is not, therefore, bound by his original valuation. He may realise his security for what it is worth at the time of realisation notwithstanding the fact that he has claimed and received dividends on the basis of a lower valuation[10]. If a secured creditor does vote for the arrangement in respect of the secured portion of his debt he impliedly, if not expressly, surrenders his rights as a secured creditor[11].

1 Section 5(2) (CVA), s 260(2) (IVA).
2 IR 1986, r 1.9(2)(a) (CVA), r 5.13(2), now r 5.17(2), (IVA).
3 IR 1986, r 1.17(1) (CVA), r 5.17(1), now r 5.21(1), (IVA).
4 That is a debtor who was not given notice of the meeting and was therefore not bound to any approved arrangement: see para 1.4 above.
5 Section 5(2)(b) (CVA without moratorium), Sch A1 para 37(2) (CVA with moratorium), s 260(2)(b) (IVA).
6 Entitlement still being dependent on notice.
7 IR 1986, r 1.17(1) (CVA without moratorium), r 1.49 (CVA with moratorium), r 5.21(1) (IVA).

8 *Re a Debtor (No 400 IO of 1996)* [1997] 2 BCLC 144, [1997] BPIR 431. Rimer J at 153 held that the wording of IR 1986, r 5.21(1) (the same as r 1.17(1)) meant 'every creditor who was given notice of the creditors' meeting by the nominee', but that, nevertheless, all the debtor's creditors were entitled to attend and vote at the creditors' meeting regardless of whether they learnt of the meeting from the nominee or some other source. Note also that IR 1986, r 5.23(3)(a) (IVA) (r 1.19(3)(a) (CVA)) envisages that written notice of the creditor's claim may be given to the chairman or convener of the meeting at the creditors' meeting as well as before it. See also *Beverley Group plc v McClure* [1995] BCC 751 at 759.

9 IR 1986, rr 4.95–4.99 (liquidation), rr 6.115–6.119 (bankruptcy).

10 *Khan v Mortgage Express* [2000] BPIR 473.

11 *Khan v Permayer* [2001] BPIR 95. Once the creditor had accepted the dividends due under the voluntary arrangement the (secured) debt became discharged. The security here was a second charge on a lease which at the time of the proposal was worth less than the sum secured by the first charge.

6.7 Creditors of the debtor: The rôle of the chairman. At the creditors' meeting votes are calculated in accordance with the amount of the creditor's debt as at the date of the meeting[1], except where a moratorium is in force in which case the debt is calculated as at the date of the beginning of the moratorium[2]. Whether a person is a creditor and if so the amount of his debt will be an important consideration at the creditors' meeting. There is no provision in either IA 1986 or IR 1986 which defines 'creditor' specifically for the purposes of a voluntary arrangement. For IVA there are statutory definitions[3] for both 'debt' and 'liability' which would give a wide interpretation to 'creditor': debt and liability includes 'debts or liabilities which are present or future, certain or contingent, or in respect of an amount which is fixed or liquidated or is capable of being ascertained by fixed rules or as a matter of opinion'. The same definition appears in IR 1986[4] with respect to any reference to a debt or liability in winding up. There is a clear indication that a similarly wide interpretation to creditor is intended in CVA. The provisions of the rules relating to voting rights[5] cover a creditor with a 'debt for an unliquidated amount' or any 'debt whose value is not ascertained'. While accepting that it was possible for the word 'creditor' to include only those with present and enforceable claims the court in *Re Cancol*[6] rejected this construction as applying in a CVA and held that a landlord entitled to a future payment under an existing valid instrument was a creditor.

A 'contingent claim' or 'contingent liability' is not a term of art and its precise meaning will depend on its context. Although a contingent liability has been defined as a liability which depends for its existence upon an event which may or may not happen[7], a CVA is a commercial contract which should be construed in a practical fashion[8]. Accordingly, where the debtor's liability to pay a creditor was technically contingent on the creditor raising invoices, as the creditor had an immediate or vested or unrestricted right to raise invoices on outstanding instalments under a contract the court refused to construe these debts as contingent liabilities[9].

The chairman has the task of adjudicating on any disputes as to the right of anyone claiming to be a creditor to vote, and as to the value of the votes which may be cast by any particular creditor. The chairman has a complete discretion as to whether he admits or rejects a creditor's claim or any part of it for the purpose of that creditor's entitlement to vote[10].

Where there is a dispute as to whether any person is in fact a creditor of the debtor it should only be in the clearest of cases that the chairman decides not to treat the person in question as a creditor and so omit him from the list of creditors to whom notice of the meeting is sent. It is to be noted that IR 1986 governing voting rights at the meeting provide that if the chairman of the creditors' meeting is in doubt whether a creditor's claim should be admitted or rejected he should mark it as objected to and allow the creditor to vote, subject to his vote subsequently being declared invalid if an objection is taken to court[11]. There is therefore, in effect, a presumption that a person claiming to be a creditor is entitled to vote, although the chairman will plainly have a discretion to ignore claims which are clearly invalid, and in appropriate cases he may seek legal advice[12]. The assertion of a set-off of doubtful validity which, if good, would have extinguished the claim, is no justification for the nominee's omission to give the relevant creditor notice of the meeting[13].

It is incumbent on a creditor who wishes to vote in respect of his debt to state to the best of his ability the total amount that he states is owing to him, and, if the value of his debt or of some part of it is not ascertained, to state that fact and to supply the chairman of the creditors' meeting with as much information as is available to enable the chairman to put an estimated minimum value on the debt[14].

Unliquidated and unascertained debts. Entitlement to vote is dependent upon being a creditor with a debt of certain value for voting purposes. IR 1986 provides that an unliquidated or unascertained debt must be valued at £1, unless the chairman 'agrees' to put a higher value on it[15]. This 'agreement' required by the rules is merely the preparedness of the chairman to estimate a minimum value; there is no need for the chairman to reach an agreement with the creditor as to the proper minimum value for the debt[16]. The chairman may estimate the minimum value of a debt at the meeting itself; there is no need for him to notify the creditor of the value that he will put on the debt before the meeting, although it is plainly good practice that he should do so if possible[17]. Neither need the creditor be in agreement with the chairman; he may be bound by a valuation of his debt of which he is unaware[18]. The fact that the debtor has a counterclaim against the creditor or has objected to the quantum of the creditor's claim does not render the debt in question either unliquidated or unascertained for the purposes of voting[19].

Not infrequently the chairman of a creditors' meeting faces difficult decisions in the calculation of unliquidated and contingent claims. Following amendment to the rules, from 1 January 2003, it is now provided that in the absence of a higher value put on such debts by the chairman they should be given a value of £1 for voting purposes[20]. While this amendment to the rules ensures that the creditor is bound to any approved arrangement, the need for careful consideration by the chairman of the value of such a debt remains, particularly where it is clear that the value put on the debt may affect the outcome of the vote at the creditors' meeting. It is open to a creditor to apply to the court to alter the outcome of the vote whichever way it goes on the basis that the chairman was wrong not to put a higher, or indeed a lower, value on any unliquidated or unascertained debt. In *Re Cranley Mansions Ltd*[21] the chairman put a value of £1 on an uncertain counterclaim estimated at £900,000 and costs. The court considered the valuation to be deeply suspect[22], but found it impossible to say that the chairman ought to have valued the claim at some other, much higher figure. In valuing a debt arising under a continuing contract as at the date of the meeting the chairman may have to take into account the possibility that either the debtor or the creditor may act in breach of contract at some later date. In *Re Millwall Football Club and Athletic Co (1985) plc*[23] the debtor, a company, entered voluntary arrangements after it had been the subject of an administration order. The holders of all debts incurred before the date of the administration order ('the record date') were to be paid a small dividend under the CVA. Following their appointment the administrators had dismissed various employees including the respondent. After voting for the CVA he then claimed that he was not bound by the arrangements because his claim for premature termination of his contract of employment arose on his dismissal after the record date. The court rejected his claim holding that it was based on a liability incurred by the debtor before the record date. The debtor's liability to make payments to its employee under his contract of employment was one which was in existence at the record date and it was one which was destined to give rise in the future to the damages claim. Although the events which gave rise to the claim had not happened at the record date when they did happen they were founded on an obligation or liability incurred before the record date. The debtor's liability could properly be characterised as a future, prospective or contingent liability before the relevant date. This decision, understandable in its context[24], and straightforward to assess because the events giving rise to the liability occurred before the making of the CVA could give rise to extremely difficult questions of valuation if taken to its logical extremes. In *Lombard North Central plc v Brook*[25] the proof submitted by the applicant in respect of lease purchase agreements with the debtor company included both arrears and a specific sum by way of agreed damages payable in the event of termination of the agreement. The court held that the chairman had been wrong to admit the proof only as to the arrears. The term in the agreement for the payment of agreed damages was not a penalty. It represented a contractual obligation to pay a certain sum on the happening of a specified event and was, therefore, properly included in the applicant's proof. A litigant in ongoing proceedings against the debtor where no order for costs has been made may not vote in respect of potential liability to costs on the part of the debtor[26].

Perhaps the most frequently encountered situation in which the chairman has to put a minimum value on the debtor's future liabilities is in the case of future rent for leasehold property. An important factor to be taken into account in such an assessment will be the state of the property market and thus the value of the landlord's right to forfeit the tenancy and re-let the premises. In two reported decisions[27] the court has accepted the chairman's assessment of one year's rent to cover all future rent liabilities, and it is understood that this is an approach adopted by several chairmen where no other assessment is plainly more appropriate in the circumstances.

There is a right of appeal against any decision of the chairman as to the rights of any one claiming to be entitled to vote[28].

1 IR 1986, r 1.17(2) (CVA), r 5.21(2) (IVA); but where a corporate debtor is in liquidation or administration, or an individual debtor is bankrupt, the calculation of votes is as at the date of the relevant insolvency order, rr 1.17(2), 5.21(2).
2 IR 1986, r 1.49(2); any amount paid after that date must be deducted.
3 See IA 1986, s 382(3).
4 IR 1986, r 13.12(3).
5 See IR 1986, r 1.17(3) and see para 6.10 below.
6 [1996] 1 BCLC 100 at 110.
7 See *Winter v IRC* [1963] AC 235 at 253, per Lord Guest, a case where there was a divergence of view in the House of Lords as to whether there had to be an existing underlying obligation. The majority considered that this was too narrow a view. Either the liability itself or payment due under it might arise on the happening of a future event. See also *Glenister v Rowe* [2000] Ch 76, where the Court of Appeal considered *Winter v IRC* and other authorities in point.
8 *Re Brelec Installations* [2001] BPIR 210 at 218D–G; *County Bookshops Ltd v Grove* [2002] EWHC 1160 (Ch), [2002] BPIR 772, para 35.

9 *County Bookshops v Grove* [2002] BPIR 772, paras 47, 49.
10 IR 1986, r 1.17A(1) (CVA without moratorium), r 1.50(1) (CVA with moratorium), (IVA), r 5.22(1) (IVA).
11 IR 1986, r 1.17A(4) (CVA without moratorium), r 1.50(4) (CVA with moratorium), (IVA), r 5.22(4) (IVA), and see *National Westminster Bank v Scher* [1998] BPIR 224. But see *Re Cranley Mansions Ltd* [1994] 1 WLR 1610 at 1625C. The chairman should make a reasonable attempt to value the claim, perhaps with legal assistance if time permits, before he allows doubt to take over and passes the task to the courts.
12 The court *Re Cranley Mansions Ltd* [1994] 1 WLR 1610 concluded that the chairman had made no real attempt to value the claim or even to arrive at a minimum value for the claim. He merely put a value of £1 on what the creditor asserted was a claim for over £900,000. In the circumstances the court found the £1 valuation 'deeply suspect'. It is suggested that the chairman should make a reasonable attempt to value the claim, perhaps with legal assistance if time permits, before he allows doubt to take over, places a nominal value on the claim and, in effect, and passes the task to the court with the inevitable delay and cost that entails. The rules (IR 1986, r 1.17(3), r 1.49(3), r 5.21(3)) now provide that an unliquidated or unascertained debt be valued at £1 'unless the chairman agrees to put a higher value on it'. That is not, however, an excuse for a chairman to leave a debt at £1 because a proper valuation is not straightforward, especially where the creditor is understood to be hostile to the proposal.
13 *Re a Debtor (No 400 IO of 1966)* [1997] 2 BCLC 144.
14 *Re KG Hoare* [1997] BPIR 683 at 695. The deputy judge continued: 'Just as it does not lie in the mouth of a creditor who stays away to say that the chairman has not agreed to minimum value for his debt and that he is therefore not bound by the IVA, so in my judgment it does not lie in the mouth of a creditor who has put a figure on his debt, albeit one that he says is subject to verification and possible amendment at a later date, to claim later that he is owed some other debt which he has not included in the figure he has stated and in respect of which he has not voted, and that he is therefore not bound in respect of that other debt.'
15 IR 1986, r 1.17(3) (CVA without moratorium), r 1.49(3) (CVA with moratorium), r 5.21(3) (IVA).
16 *Doorbar v Alltime Securities Ltd* [1996] 1 WLR 456 at 465C (overruling *Re Cranley Mansions Ltd* [1994] 1 WLR 1610); see also *Beverley Group plc v McClue* [1995] 2 BCLC 407 and 417–418, and *Re Cancol Ltd* [1996] 1 BCLC 100. This avoids the unsatisfactory situation which would arise if a creditor refused to reach any sensible agreement with the chairman in order not to be bound to the arrangement.
17 *Re Cancol Ltd.* [1996] 1 BCLC 100; also reported as *Cazaly Irving Holdings v Cancol Ltd* [1996] BPIR 252, where the creditor had corresponded with the chairman before the meeting but did not attend the meeting itself.
18 See *Beverley Group plc v McClue* [1995] 2 BCLC 407, where the company proposing the arrangement had put an estimated value on the creditor's unliquidated claim but the creditor, who knew about the meeting, did not attend on the ground that he had not received formal notice. The court held that as the creditor knew about the meeting and that notice had been duly sent to, albeit not apparently received by, the creditor was bound by the arrangement.
19 *Re a Debtor (No 222 of 1990), ex p Bank of Ireland* [1992] BCLC 137.
20 IR 1986, r 1.17(3) (CVA without moratorium), r 1.49(3) (CVA with moratorium), r 5.21(3) (IVA); the £1 value is 'for the purposes of voting (but not otherwise)' and so the creditor will not be prejudiced by the valuation on the payment of dividends.
21 [1994] 1 WLR 1610.
22 Had any valuation above £1,722 been ascribed to the debt the creditor could have prevented approval of the arrangement. Note that the decision in this case turned on the holding that it was necessary under the rules for the chairman to reach agreement with the creditor as to the value of the debt, a view overruled by the Court of Appeal in *Doorbar v Alltime Securities Ltd* [1996] 1 WLR 456.
23 [1999] BCC 455.
24 The company had a strong secondary argument in estoppel, as the court found.
25 [1999] BPIR 701.
26 *Re Wisepark Ltd* [1994] BCC 221.
27 *Doorbar v Alltime Securities Ltd* [1996] 1 WLR 456 (7½ years to run). *Re Sweatfield Ltd* [1997] BCC 744 (7 years to run to break clause).
28 IR 1986, r 1.17A(3) (CVA without moratorium), r 1.50(3) (CVA with moratorium), r 5.22(3) (IVA): see para 6.8 below.

6.8 Appeal from chairman's decision on entitlement to vote. The chairman's decision on a creditor's entitlement to vote at the creditors' meeting is subject to appeal to the court by any creditor or the debtor[1]. The chairman should reject claims that are clearly bad, admit those which are clearly good and admit claims which are doubtful on the basis that the votes are cast marked as objected to, to assist any party dissatisfied with the outcome to appeal to the court[2]. A decision of the chairman as to entitlement to vote may also result in an irregularity on which the meeting's decision may be challenged if it is material, that is if the votes involved would have altered the outcome of the vote. Both the chairman's decision and the meeting's decision may be the subject of one appeal[3]. Any application to the court by way of appeal against the chairman's decision must be made within the period of 28 days from the day on which the chairman makes his report to the court[4], although this 28-day time limit may be extended under the court's general discretionary power to disregard time limits[5]. Where the creditors' approval of voluntary arrangements was successfully challenged by creditors on the ground that a supporting creditor ought not to have voted, the court allowed the debtor to challenge out of time the entitlement to vote of an approving creditor[6]. In exercising the discretion to extend the time limits the court relied on the guidelines suggested in *CM Van Stillevolt BV v EL Carriers Inc*[7], the relevant factors being:

1. length of delay;
2. reasons for delay;
3. the apparent merits of the underlying application;
4. the prejudice to each side other than the inevitable prejudice inherent in re-opening the matter.

At the hearing of the appeal the court will have to decide the merits of the dispute over the debt, and in so doing will not be confined to such evidence as was before the chairman of the meeting. The court is entitled to consider whatever evidence the parties to the appeal decide to put before the court[8]. The court does not, however, have to try fully what might be a complex claim. Rather it should come to a conclusion whether, on balance, the claim of the creditor has been established and, if so, in what amount[9].

On appeal the court may reverse or vary the chairman's decision, or declare a vote to be invalid, but only if the court considers the matter is such as to give rise to unfair prejudice or a material irregularity[10]. It has been said that the test for unfair prejudice or material irregularity on an appeal against the chairman's decision on an entitlement to vote is the same as on a challenge to the decision of the creditors' meeting[11]. This must, however, be seen in the respective contexts of these appeals. An appeal against a chairman's decision on entitlement to vote is just that. It is the decision on voting which must give rise to the unfair prejudice. It is only on an appeal against the meeting's decision that the court will consider whether the terms of the arrangement itself give rise to unfair prejudice. It follows that an appeal solely under IR 1986 will be restricted to a complaint as to the chairman's decision to allow or disallow a vote[12], and where a creditor also wishes to complain about other decisions of the chairman and their implication on the fairness of the arrangement as a whole it will be necessary to couple the appeal under IR 1986, r 1.17 (CVA), r 5.17 (IVA) with an appeal under IA 1986, s 6 or Sch A1, para 38 (CVA), s 262 (IVA).

On upholding an appeal the court may order another meeting to be summoned, or make such order as it thinks just[13]. The chairman may not be personally liable for any costs incurred by any person in respect of an appeal against his decision as to a creditor's right to vote[14], but he is not necessarily protected against an order for costs if there are successful appeals both against his decision on voting and against the meeting's decision on the basis that there was a material irregularity at the meeting by reason of the chairman's decision on a creditor's entitlement to vote[15].

If a creditors' claim is not admitted for voting purposes by the chairman of the meeting the creditor will not be bound by the voluntary arrangement. The creditor cannot later be compelled to participate in the voluntary arrangement when it is shown that his claim has been wrongly rejected. Where, however, the debtor was a company in administration as well as CVA it was open to the court to order that the creditor should rank pari passu with the CVA creditors. He should neither be adversely affected by the approval of the CVA nor should he be able to seek an advantage over the CVA creditors by enforcing the entirety of his claim[16].

1 IR 1986, r 1.17A(3) (CVA without moratorium), r 1.50(3) (CVA with moratorium), r 5.22(3) (IVA).

2 IR 1986, r 1.17A(4) (CVA without moratorium), r 1.50(4) (CVA with moratorium), (IVA), r 5.22(4) (IVA); and see *Re a Debtor (No 222 of 1990), ex p Bank of Ireland* [1992] BCLC 137; *National Westminster Bank v Scher* [1998] BPIR 224, but note *Re Cranley Mansions Ltd* [1994] 1 WLR 1610 and *Doorbar v Alltime Securities* [1996] 1 WLR 456, and see para 6.7 above.

3 See eg *Ex p Bank of Ireland* [1992] BCLC 137. As to challenge of the meeting's decision to approve the voluntary arrangement, see para 7.1 below.

4 IR 1986, r 1.17A(6) (CVA without moratorium), r 1.50(6) (CVA with moratorium), (IVA), r 5.22(6) (IVA). The chairman reports to the court under IA 1986, s 4(6) (CVA), Sch A1, para 30(3) (CVA with moratorium), s 259(1) (IVA), see para 6.13 below. It may be noted that any challenge of whatever nature to any decision of the creditor's meeting must be brought within 28 days: see para 7.8 below.

5 In IVA under IA 1986, s 376, and in either IVA or CVA under the rules. In CVA a problem arises. In *Re Bournemouth and Boscombe Athletic Football Club Co Ltd* [1998] BPIR 183 there was an application to extend time to challenge an approved CVA. The court made the point that the wording of IA 1986, s 6(3) (which is followed in IR 1986, r 1.17A(6)) 'An application ... shall not be made after the end of the period of 28 days' has the effect of imposing a limitation period. The rules (then importing RSC now importing CPR) contain a general power to extend time limits, see also IR 1986, r 12.9(2), which imports CPR rule 3.1(2)(a) into IR 1986 'so as to enable the court to extend or shorten the time for compliance with anything required or authorised to be done by the rules'. The court held that this power in the rules could not override what was in effect a limitation period in the statute. It would appear that it would be permissible for the court to extend the time for appealing a chairman's decision on voting for this is an appeal under the rules not the statute. If the result of the chairman's decision is that the voluntary arrangement is not approved an appeal might be mounted, although the court will be slow to allow an appeal out of time, see para 7.8 below. But if the result of the chairman's decision on voting is that a CVA is approved an appeal against the chairman's decision in circumstances where an appeal may not be brought to challenge the CVA itself would be a worthless exercise.

6 *Tager v Westpac Banking Corpn* [1997] BPIR 543, Judge Weeks QC.

7 [1983] 1 WLR 207, CA, per Griffiths LJ.

8 *Re a Company (No 4539 of 1993)* [1995] 1 BCLC 459 (a decision on the equivalent wording in IR 1986, r 4.70 – liquidation); *National Westminster Bank v Scher* [1998] BPIR 224.

9 *Re a Company (No 4539 of 1993)* [1995] 1 BCLC 459.

10 IR 1986, r 1.17A(5) (CVA without moratorium), r 1.50(5) (CVA with moratorium), (IVA), r 5.22(5) (IVA).

11 *Re Sweatfield Ltd* [1998] BPIR 276; as to the meaning of unfair prejudice or material irregularity see paras 7.3, 7.6 below.

12 Which will include a decision on a proxy.

13 IR 1986, r 1.17A(5) (CVA without moratorium), r 1.50(5) (CVA with moratorium), (IVA), r 5.22(5) (IVA).

14 IR 1986, r 1.17A(7) (CVA without moratorium), r 1.50(7) (CVA with moratorium), (IVA), r 5.22(7) (IVA).

15 *Ex p Bank of Ireland* [1992] BCLC 137, and as to costs *Ex p Bank of Ireland (No 2)* [1993] BCLC 233.
16 *Re TBL Realisations; Oakley-Smith v Greenberg* [2002] EWCA Civ 1217, [2002] All ER (D) 36 (Aug).

6.9 Conduct of the creditors' meeting. The nominee[1] takes the chair at the creditors' meeting and, in CVA, the company meeting or at any combined meeting[2]. If for any reason the convener is unable to attend he may nominate as chairman in his place either another insolvency practitioner qualified to act or an authorised person in relation to the debtor or an employee of the convener or his firm who is experienced in insolvency matters[3]. The chairman has overall control of the meeting.

IA 1986 expressly provides that the creditors' meeting must be conducted in accordance with IR 1986[4]. The first task of the chairman will usually be to determine who is entitled to vote and in what amounts. The chairman, as nominee, will normally explain the reasons for the proposal and why it has been formulated in the manner which is being put to the creditors. The debtor, or its officers where the debtor is a company, should usually be present to answer questions from the creditors where these cannot properly be dealt with by the nominee or his representative. Any modifications to or amendments of the proposal put forward by creditors will need to be debated and even where acceptable to the debtor may require voting on by the creditors. Once the proposal is in its final form the chairman may proceed to putting it to the vote, subject to the need to adjourn should there be significant alterations to the proposal which ought to be put before creditors who have not attended the meeting.

Casting a vote. A creditor must have a debt of certain value, if necessary estimated by the chairman, and must attend the meeting in person or by proxy to cast his vote[5].

Proxy voting. In practice many votes are cast by proxy[6]. Provided that the form of proxy is with the chairman before the vote is taken it is validly lodged for voting purposes even if it was not presented before the meeting started[7]. A creditor is free to withdraw a proxy and replace it with a new one at any time before the vote is taken[8]. A proxy which is sent by fax is valid for voting purposes[9]. Inevitably, proxies are given before the meeting, often some time before the meeting. The creditor concerned will therefore have given his proxy without knowledge of any information which is given to the meeting or which becomes available shortly before the meeting. Where new information of significance becomes available the nominee, or chairman of the creditors' meeting if this is someone other than the nominee, should consider whether he ought to adjourn the meeting and report the new information to all creditors including those for whom he holds proxies, even if this means that he may have to obtain an extension of the interim order or an extension of time of moratorium to hold the meeting[10]. This is unlikely to be necessary where the debtor, perhaps under pressure from the creditors at the meeting, has improved the proposal from the creditors' point of view. There have been cases, however, where the chairman has used proxy votes to support a proposal where the dividend forecast to the creditors has been reduced. To use proxy votes in such a situation may well amount to a material irregularity leaving the approval of the voluntary arrangements open to challenge[11].

Remuneration and expenses of nominee or supervisor. The chairman of the creditors' meeting may not use any proxy held by him to increase or reduce the amount of the remuneration or expenses of the nominee or the supervisor of the proposed arrangement without specific authorisation by the proxy[12]. If he does so the vote does not count towards any majority on such a resolution[13].

Quorum. The meeting is competent to act if a quorum of at least one creditor entitled to vote is present in person or by proxy[14]. The chairman must delay the start of the meeting from its appointed time by at least 15 minutes where there is a quorum comprised of the chairman alone (ie a chairman with a proxy) or the chairman and one other person and the chairman is aware that there are other persons entitled to vote[15].

Adjournment of meeting. The chairman may adjourn a creditors' meeting from time to time, and he must do so if the meeting resolves to adjourn[16]. It is assumed that in fixing the time and place of the adjourned meeting the chairman must comply with the provisions of the rules governing the summoning of the initial meeting[17]. The final adjournment may not be to a date later than 14 days after the original day on which the meeting is held[18]. The chairman may, however, apply to the court for an extension of time, either before or after the 14 days has expired, under the general power vested in the court to extend time limits[19]. Should a proposal fail to obtain the agreement of creditors on the final adjournment it is deemed to be rejected[20].

Calculation of votes. Votes are calculated according to the amount of the creditor's debt as at the date of the meeting or, in the case of an arrangement proposed by a company in administration or liquidation or an undischarged bankrupt, the amount of the debt as at the date of the relevant insolvency order[21].

Votes to be left out of account. A creditor's vote is to be left out of account where, in respect of any claim or part of a claim:

(a) Written notice of the claim was not given either at the meeting or before it, to the chairman or convener of the meeting.
(b) The claim or part of a claim is secured[22].
(c) The claim is in respect of a debt wholly or partly on, or secured by, a current bill of exchange or promissory note. However, where the creditor is willing to treat the liability to him on the bill or note of every person who is liable on it antecedently to the debtor, and against whom a bankruptcy order or winding up order has not been made, as a security in his hands, and having estimated the value of this security, deduct it from his claim, the balance may be voted and the vote taken into account[23].

The chairman determines whether a vote should be left out of account under one of these heads[24]. It should be noted that creditors whose votes are left out of account are nevertheless creditors entitled to vote at the meeting, and will therefore be bound by the arrangement should it be approved.

Recording of votes. The chairman must take care to record how each creditor votes on each resolution taken at the meeting for he is required to include this information in his report to the court[25]. It follows that creditors' votes cannot be confidential.

Voting subject to objection. If in doubt whether to admit or reject a claim, or leave a vote out of account[26], the chairman should mark it as objected to and allow the creditor to vote subject to the vote being subsequently declared invalid if the objection to the claim is sustained[27].

Appeal from Chairman's decision. Any creditor may appeal to the court against the chairman's decision on a creditor's entitlement to vote or on any value he puts on an unliquidated or unascertained debt[28], or any decision made by him whether or not to leave a vote out of account, see above, or to declare a resolution invalid[29].

Time for appeal. No appeal may be made to the court against the chairman's decision after the end of the period of 28 days from the first day on which each of the chairman's report[30] is submitted to the court[31]. This time period may be extended under the court's general power to extend time limits[32].

Where chairman's decision is reversed. If on appeal the court reverses or varies the chairman's decision, or declares a creditor's vote invalid, the court may order another meeting to be summoned, or make such other order as it thinks just[33]. Before making such an order, however, the court must first be satisfied that the matter is such as to give rise to unfair prejudice or a material irregularity[34].

Liability of chairman. See para 4.17 above.

Costs of appeal. The chairman may not be made personally liable for any costs incurred by any person in respect of an appeal against his decisions on voting rights, leaving votes out of account or the validity of resolutions[35].

1 In CVA 'the convener' ie the nominee appointed by the directors, or, where the corporate debtor is in liquidation or administration, the nominee appointed by the responsible insolvency practitioner or the responsible insolvency practitioner himself when he acts as nominee.
2 IR 1986, r 1.14(1) (all CVAs); r 1.14 applies where a moratorium is in force by virtue of r 1.48(5), r 5.19(1) (IVA): see para 6.3 above.
3 IR 1986, r 1.14(2) (all CVAs), r 5.19(2) (IVA).
4 IA 1986, s 4(5) (CVA without moratorium), Sch A1, para 30(1) (CVA where a moratorium is in force); IA 1986, s 258(6) (IVA), expressly provide that the meeting shall be conducted in accordance with the rules. The relevant rules are IR 1986, rr 1.13–1.21 (CVA; rr 1.48–1.53 where a moratorium is in force) or IR 1986, rr 5.17–5.24 (IVA).
5 *Beverley Group plc v McClue* [1995] 2 BCLC 407.
6 A form of proxy must be sent out with every notice summoning the creditors' meeting, IR 1986, r 1.13(4) (all CVAs), r 5.18(3) (IVA).
7 *Re Philip Alexander Securities & Futures Ltd.* [1999] 1 BCLC 124 (company administration) and *Re a Company (No 4539 of 1993)* [1995] BCC 116 (liquidation).
8 *Re Cardona* [1997] BPIR 604 where the terms of the proxy were altered between the first and the adjourned meeting.
9 *Re a Debtor (No 2021 of 1995), ex p IRC* [1996] 2 All E R 345 also reported at *IRC v Conbeer and White* [1996] BPIR 398.
10 *Cadbury Schweppes plc v Somji* [2001] 1 WLR 615 at 626, para 25; in all bankruptcy matters an extension of time may be obtained under IA 1986, s 376 either before or after the original period of time has expired. In CVA reliance must be had to IR 1986, r 12.9(2) which imports CPR r 3.1(2)(a) into IR 1986 and enabling the court to extend (or shorten) the time for compliance with anything required or authorised to be done by the rules.
11 See para 7.6 below.
12 Which will be contrary to IR 1986, r 1.15 (all CVAs), r 5.20 (IVA).
13 IR 1986, r 1.19(6) (CVA without moratorium), r 1.52(7) (CVA with moratorium), r 5.23(6) (IVA).
14 IR 1986, r 12.4A; this rule governs any meeting in 'insolvency proceedings' which by IR 1986, r 13.7 means any proceedings under IA 1986 or IR 1986. Although it is arguable on the precise wording of the rule that a creditor may not attend by his authorised representative it is anticipated that the court will hold that such a representative fulfills the requirement of the rule.
15 IR 1986, r 12.4A(4).
16 IR 1986, r 1.21(2) (CVA without moratorium), r 1.53(3) (CVA with moratorium), r 5.24(1) (IVA). In CVA the chairman may hold the creditors' and company meetings together: r 1.21(1), r 1.53(3).
17 Ie in accordance with IR 1986, r 1.13 (all CVAs), r 5.18 (IVA) which provide that: (1) the nominee must 'have regard ['primarily' in CVA] to the convenience of creditors' when fixing the venue; (2) the meeting must be summoned to commence between 10.00 and 16.00 hours on a business day. Presumably it will not be necessary for the chairman to send a further form of proxy which is required when summoning the initial meeting.

18 IR 1986, r 1.21(3) (CVA without moratorium), r 1.53(3) (CVA with moratorium), r 5.24(3) (IVA). Such adjournment may take place even if the requisite majority has not been obtained after a vote, and indeed if the meeting resolves to adjourn the chairman must abide by this decision, r 1.21(2), r 1.53(2) (CVA), r 5.24(2) (IVA). Notice of any adjournment which follows a failed vote to approve the proposal must be given to the court, IR 1986, r 1.21(4) (CVA – but only where the proposal has been made by the directors), r 5.24(4) (IVA).

19 IA 1986, s 376 (IVA only). For CVA see IR 1986, r 12.9(2) which imports CPR, r 3.1(2)(a) into IR 1986 'so as to enable the court to extend or shorten the time for compliance with anything required or authorised to be done by the rules'. Either under IA 1986, s 376 or IR 1986, r 12.9(2) and CPR r 3.1(2), an application to extend time may be made after the time limit in question has expired.

20 IR 1986, r 1.21(5) (CVA without moratorium), r 1.53(5) (CVA with moratorium), r 5.24(5) (IVA).

21 IR 1986, r 1.17(2) (CVA without moratorium), r 1.49(2) (CVA with moratorium), r 5.21(2) (IVA).

22 Where part only of a creditor's claim is secured only the secured part is to be discounted for the purpose of voting: *Calor Gas Ltd v Piercy* [1994] BCC 69.

23 IR 1986, r 1.19(3) (CVA without moratorium), r 1.52(4) (CVA with moratorium), r 5.23(3) (IVA); with respect to sub-r (c) it is provided in the rule that the estimating of the value of the security provided by antecedent holders of the bill or promissory note is for the purpose of entitlement to vote only and not in respect of any distribution under the arrangement.

24 IR 1986, r 1.19(5)(a) (CVA without moratorium), r 1.52(6)(a) (CVA with moratorium), r 5.23(5)(a) (IVA).

25 IR 1986, r 1.24(2)(c) (all CVAs by virtue of r 1.54(2) where a moratorium is in force), r 5.27(2)(c) (IVA).

26 IR 1986, r 1.19(7) (CVA without moratorium), r 1.52(8) (CVA with moratorium), r 5.23(7) (IVA) provide that the provisions of IR 1986, r 1.17A (CVA without moratorium), r 1.50 (CVA with moratorium), r 5.22 (IVA) which grant and govern an appeal against the chairman's decision on entitlement to vote apply equally in relation to an appeal against the chairman's decision on whether a vote is to be left out of account or on whether a person is an associate of the debtor.

27 IR 1986, r 1.17A(4) (CVA without moratorium), r 1.50(4) (CVA with moratorium), r 5.22(4) (IVA), and see *Re a Debtor (No 222 of 1990), ex p Bank of Ireland* [1992] BCLC 137; *National Westminster Bank v Scher* [1998] BPIR 224. But note *Re Cranley Mansions Ltd* [1994] 1 WLR 1610: the chairman should make a reasonable attempt to value the claim, perhaps with legal assistance if time permits, before he allows doubt to take over and passes the task to the courts.

28 IR 1986, r 1.17A(3) (CVA without moratorium), r 1.50(3) (CVA with moratorium), r 5.22(3) (IVA).

29 IR 1986, r 1.19(7) (CVA without moratorium), r 1.52(8) (CVA with moratorium), r 5.23(7) (IVA).

30 The chairman is required by IA 1986, s 4(6) (CVA), Sch A1, para 30(3) (CVA with moratorium), s 259(1) (IVA) to report to the court at the conclusion of the creditors' meeting.

31 IR 1986, r 1.17A(6) (CVA without moratorium), r 1.50(6) (CVA with moratorium), r 5.22(6) (IVA). The scheme of the legislation is to restrict all appeals to this 28-day period but it is open to the court to extend the time for appealing: see para 7.8 below.

32 See para 6.8, n 5 above.

33 IR 1986, r 1.17A(5) (CVA without moratorium), r 1.50(5) (CVA with moratorium), r 5.22(5) (IVA).

34 IR 1986, r 1.17A(5) (CVA without moratorium), r 1.50(5) (CVA with moratorium), r 5.22(5) (IVA); as to unfair prejudice and material irregularity see paras 7.3 and 7.6 below.

35 IR 1986, r 1.17A(7) (CVA without moratorium), r 1.50(7) (CVA with moratorium), r 5.22(7) (IVA), and as to leaving votes out of account or the validity of resolutions, r 1.19(7) (CVA), r 1.52(8) (moratorium in force), r 5.23(7) (IVA) which apply r 1.17A(7), r 1.50(7) or r 5.22(9) to an appeal against a chairman's decision as to leaving a vote out of account.

6.10 Creditors' meeting: required majorities. In making provision for the majority required to approve the proposal for voluntary arrangement, the rules are concerned to ensure that minority creditors should not be forced into an acceptance by majority creditors who are closely associated in some way with the debtor[1].

Accordingly, in order to secure approval the voluntary arrangements must pass what is in effect a two-stage process. First, any resolution to approve the proposal or any modification of the proposal must pass with a majority in excess of three-quarters in value of the creditors present in person (or by representative) or by proxy and voting on the resolution[2]. Secondly, notwithstanding the obtaining of this three-quarters majority, the resolution is nevertheless invalid if those voting against it include more than half in value of the creditors, counting only those:

(a) to whom notice of the meeting was sent;
(b) whose votes are not to be left out of account (see para 6.9 above); and
(c) who are not connected persons or associates[3] of the debtor, to the best of the chairman's belief[4].

It is for the chairman to decide whether a person is a connected person to a corporate debtor or an associate of an individual debtor[5], subject to an appeal to the court[6].

It is understandable that the rules should be concerned to protect minorities against decisions of majorities comprised substantially of creditors who are associated with the debtor. It is perhaps less clear why importance should be attached to the fact of notice of the meeting being sent. In practical terms the nominee will be heavily dependant on the debtor giving full information regarding the identity of his creditors when determining who should be given notice of the meeting. Where the debtor has failed to inform the nominee of the existence of a creditor and that creditor does somehow manage to learn of the meeting and attend, it might be thought that his vote should be given every prominence[7]. It should be noted that, following the amendments to IA 1986 introduced by IA 2000, a creditor who did not receive notice of the meeting but who would have been entitled to vote had he been given notice of the meeting will be bound by the voluntary arrangement should it be approved[8]. A creditor who is not given notice of the meeting will be entitled to challenge the meeting's decision provided he does so within 28 days of his learning of the meeting[9]. A creditor who finds himself bound to an arrangement of which he did not receive notice is entitled to receive from the debtor the dividend he would have received had he been part of the arrangement, even after the arrangement has ceased to have any effect, provided that the arrangement did not come to an end prematurely[10].

In order to carry any resolution proposed at the creditors' meeting other than one to approve or modify the proposal a majority in excess of one-half in value of the creditors present in person or by proxy and voting on the resolution is required[11]. Any resolution which amends any essential term of the proposed composition or scheme of arrangement will be a resolution to modify the proposal for the purposes of deciding whether a one-half or three-quarters majority is required. In order to determine whether any particular resolution is one which modifies the proposal regard may be had to the matters which must be dealt with in the proposal under IR 1986, r 1.3(2)[12]. As it is mandatory that these various matters should be stated or otherwise dealt with in the proposal, it is hard to resist the conclusion that alteration of any these matters constitutes a modification of the proposal for the purpose of determining the majority required to pass the relevant resolution.

1 That is IR 1986, r 1.19(1)(4) (CVA without moratorium), r 1.52(1)(5) (CVA with moratorium), r 5.23(1)(4) (IVA).

2 IR 1986, r 1.19(1) (CVA without moratorium), r 1.52(1) (CVA with moratorium), r 5.23(1) (IVA).

3 For 'connected person' and 'associate', see IA 1986, ss 249, 435 set out in Appendix 1.
4 IR 1986, r 1.19(4) (CVA without moratorium), r 1.52(5) (CVA with moratorium), r 5.23(4) (IVA).
5 IR 1986, r 1.19(5)(b) (CVA without moratorium), r 1.52(6)(a) (CVA with moratorium), r 5.23(5)(b) (IVA), and for these purposes the chairman is entitled to rely on the information provided by the debtor's statement of affairs and on any further information given to the nominee: see para 4.5 above.
6 IR 1986, r 1.19(7) (CVA without moratorium), r 1.52(8) (CVA with moratorium), r 5.23(7) (IVA), applying the provisions of IR 1986, rr 1.17A, 1.50, 5.22 to decisions by the chairman as to whether a person is connected to or an associate of the debtor.
7 It is possible that the court will deem that a creditor who attends the meeting had notice of it for these purposes.
8 IA 1986, s 5(2)(b) (CVA no moratorium), Sch A1, para 37(2) (moratorium in force), s 260(2)(b).
9 IA 1986, s 6(3)(b) (CVA no moratorium), Sch A1, para 38(3) (moratorium in force), s 262(3)(b) (IVA).
10 IA 1986, s 5(2A) (CVA no moratorium), Sch A1, para 37(2) (moratorium in force), s 260(2A) (IVA).
11 IR 1986, r 1.19(2) (CVA without moratorium), r 1.52(2) (CVA with moratorium), r 5.23(2) (IVA).
12 See para 4.4 above, and Appendix 2.

6.11 CVA company meeting: voting rights and majorities. A company meeting is quorate if at least two members entitled to vote are present in person or by proxy[1]. The basic rule is that members of the company vote at their meeting in accordance with the rights attaching to their shares or other interest held in the company as a member in accordance with the articles[2]. A member with shares carrying no voting rights may not vote at the company meeting[3]. It follows that a member of the company with no voting rights may not challenge any decision approving the voluntary arrangement.

There is no specific provision in IR 1986 as to the resolution of any dispute as to a member's entitlement to vote. In the first instance any such dispute will be a matter for the chairman of the meeting. If a member is dissatisfied with a ruling from the chairman he may challenge the decision of the company meeting on the ground of material irregularity[4] or, if there is time to do so during an adjournment of the meeting, he may seek an interim declaration of his entitlement from the court[5].

In order to carry any resolution at the company meeting, subject to any express provision made in the articles, a majority is required in excess of one-half in value of the members present in person or by proxy and voting on the resolution, the value of members being determined by reference to the number of votes conferred by the company's articles[6]. As in the case of the creditors' meeting, the vote of the chairman with any proxy not specifically authorising him to vote on a resolution relating to the remuneration or expenses of the nominee or supervisor of the proposed arrangement does not count towards any majority for such resolution[7].

1 IR 1986, r 12.4A(2). This rule governs any meeting in 'insolvency proceedings' which by r 13.7 means any proceedings under IA 1986 or IR 1986. The chairman must delay the start of the meeting by at least 15 minutes where there is a quorum comprised of the chairman alone or the chairman and one other person and the chairman is aware that there are one or more other persons entitled to vote: IR 1986, r 12.4A(4).
2 IR 1986, r 1.18(1)(3) (all CVAs by virtue of r 1.51 where a moratorium is in force). References to a person's shares include any other interest which he may have as a member of the company: IR 1986, r 1.18(3).
3 IR 1986, r 1.18(2) which previously permitted a member without voting rights to vote at the company meeting (though without his vote counting towards any majority) has now been removed from the rules.

4 See paras 7.1, 7.6 below.
5 Under CPR Pt 25.1, incorporated into the Insolvency Rules by IR 1986, r 7.51.
6 IR 1986, r 1.20(1) (all CVAs by virtue of r 1.53(1) which applies IR 1986, r 1.20 where a moratorium is in force).
7 IR 1986, r 1.20(3) (all CVAs).

6.12 Secured creditors. The scheme of IA 1986 is to leave any secured creditor outside the arrangement free to enforce his security as he is able, unless he is prepared to join the arrangement despite any interference with his rights over his security that this may entail. Accordingly, any vote which a secured creditor may cast at the creditors' meeting is to be left out of account to the extent that it relates to a claim or part of a claim which is secured[1]. A secured creditor is entitled to vote in respect of the unsecured part of his claim[2]. If he votes in respect of the secured part of his claim he impliedly, if not expressly, surrenders his rights as a secured creditor[3]. There mere act of voting should be sufficient to effect a surrender of the security provided it is not a mistake on the part of the creditor; certainly as soon as the creditor accepts the dividends under the arrangement the (previously secured) debt is discharged[4].

The creditors' meeting may not approve any proposal or modification which affects the rights of a secured creditor of the debtor to enforce his security, except with the secured creditor's concurrence[5]. There is, however, a distinction to be made between the debt owed to the creditor and the security the creditor holds to enforce the discharge of the debt. The language of IA 1986, s 4(3) (CVA), Sch A1, para 31(4) (CVA with moratorium), s 258(4) (IVA), protecting as it does 'the right of a secured creditor of the debtor to enforce his security' without reference to the debt in respect of which the creditor holds his security, lends itself to the argument that an arrangement may adversely affect the creditors' underlying debt while leaving untouched his right to enforce his security. Were this the case the secured creditor would find himself in a worse position in a voluntary arrangement than he would be in a liquidation or bankruptcy, where he would be entitled to enforce his security to the full extent of the debt. This despite the fact that the secured creditor cannot vote on the proposal or any modification to the extent that his debt is secured. This can hardly have been intended by Parliament[6]. However, in *Re Naeem*[7] the court, having stated that a landlord's right of re-entry provides him with security for payment of the rent and that the effect of the arrangement was to modify the landlord's claim for arrears of rent in the same way as other creditors' claims were modified, stated that 'it does not appear … to be unfairly prejudicial that after such modification the right to forfeit should only stand as security for the recovery of the modified debt rather than the original one'. It is now clear that a landlord's right of re-entry is not a security for the purposes of IA 1986[8], and it suggested that for established forms of security the reasoning that the security may be divorced from the debt secured and permitted to stand only for the modified debt will not be followed.

An execution creditor on whose behalf goods are seized under a writ of fieri facias[9] is a secured creditor for the purposes of voluntary arrangements despite the fact that the goods have not yet been sold[10].

Difficulties may arise where the value of the secured creditor's security fluctuates, especially where the secured creditor's vote as to the unsecured part of his debt may determine the outcome of the creditors' meeting whether or not to approve the arrangement. The relevant date for valuing the creditor's security will be the date of the creditors' meeting[11], or the beginning of the moratorium[12]. In cases of dispute the chairman will have to assess the value of the unsecured part of the secured creditor's claim by reference to the value of the security and allow the creditor to vote on this amount subject to any subsequent appeal.

After approval and implementation of a voluntary arrangement the value of the security will affect the secured creditor's right to dividends in respect of the unsecured balance of his claim. Many voluntary arrangements deal with the potential difficulties which follow a fluctuating value to the security by importing the provisions of IR 1986 as to revaluation, redemption and realisation of the security[13]. A secured creditor may claim in the arrangement in respect of any anticipated shortfall on a provisional basis (absent any express term to the contrary) without having to surrender the right to apply the proceeds of sale of its security towards the satisfaction of the whole of the unpaid balance of its debt[14]. Acceptance of a dividend will, of course, compromise any claim in respect of the unsecured portion of the debt. In the absence of a provision importing IR 1986 as to security into the arrangement, or of any express terms governing the position, it is suggested that neither the supervisor nor the secured creditor will be bound by any value the chairman put on the security for the purposes of voting, even where the creditor has agreed the valuation, provided always that there are reasonable grounds for belief that the value of the security has changed by a significant margin. The supervisor will be well advised to adopt a generous valuation[15] for the purpose of paying dividends, while retaining sufficient reserves to pay more in the event that the creditor mounts a successful application to the court complaining of the valuation adopted[16]. Once a supervisor has paid dividend money away to a secured creditor he will have a restitutionary remedy to recover any excess as money paid under a mistake[17], but the costs involved may well be substantial and may fall on the supervisor.

1 IR 1986, r 1.19(3)(b) (CVA without moratorium), r 1.52(4)(b) (CVA with moratorium), r 5.23(3)(b) (IVA).
2 *Calor Gas v Piercy* [1994] BCC 69.
3 *Khan v Permayer* [2001] BPIR 95.
4 See *Khan v Permayer* [2001] BPIR 95; the security here was a second charge on a lease which at the time of the proposal was worth less than the sum secured by the first charge.
5 IA 1986, s 4(3) (CVA), Sch A1, para 31(4) (CVA with moratorium), s 258(4) (IVA).
6 Although it may be noted that Parliament did not take the opportunity presented by the passage of the bill which became IA 2000 to amend IA 1986, ss 4(3) and 258(4).
7 [1990] 1 WLR 48.
8 *Christopher Moran Holdings Ltd v Bairstow* [2000] 2 AC 172 at 186, HL; this is a decision on IA 1986, s 248 (corporate insolvency) but will apply to IA 1986, s 383(2) (bankruptcy); see *Razzaq v Pala* [1997] 1 WLR 1336 (Lightman J on IA 1986, s 383(2)) and *Re Lomax Leisure Ltd* [1999] 2 BCLC 126 (Neuberger J on IA 1986, s 10(1)(b), company administration).
9 As to the nature of the security right derived from the writ of fieri facias, see *Ex parte Williams, Re Davies, ex p Williams* (1872) LR 7 Ch App 314.
10 *Peck v Craighead* [1995] 1 BCLC 33. Compare the position in liquidation or bankruptcy where an execution creditor who has not completed his execution or attachment at the date of the bankruptcy order is not entitled to retain the benefit of the execution or attachment as against the trustee: IA 1986, s 183(1) (liquidation), s 346(1) (bankruptcy).
11 IR 1986, r 1.17(2) (CVA without moratorium), r 1.49(2) (CVA with moratorium), r 5.21(2) (IVA) except where the debtor is in formal insolvency in which event the date for valuing the security will be the date of the relevant insolvency order, whether administration, liquidation or bankruptcy.
12 IR 1986, r 1.49(2).
13 IR 1986, rr 4.95–4.99 (liquidation), rr 6.115–6.119 (bankruptcy).
14 *Whitehead v Household Mortgage Corpn plc* [2002] EWCA Civ 1657, [2003] 1 All ER 319 at [26], where a mortgagee with a debt of £102,110 valued its security at £65,000 and accepted dividends on an unsecured balance of £37,110. The property was eventually sold for £137,000 when the mortgage debt had reached £118,000. As the mortgagee had

not abandoned its security it was entitled to insist that the security be redeemed for the full amount of the mortgage debt.

15 Ie a valuation at the top of the bracket of realistic valuations.

16 The creditor will be able to apply under IA 1986, s 7(3) (CVA), Sch A1, para 39(3) (CVA with moratorium), s 263(3) (IVA): see para 10.4 below.

17 *Whitehead v Household Mortgage Corpn plc* [2002] EWCA Civ 1657, [2003] 1 All ER 319; see at [24].

6.13 Approval of arrangements. The voluntary arrangement is approved if it secures the necessary majority in the creditors' meeting[1], and, in a CVA, a majority of the members voting in the company meeting[2]. In an IVA where there is only the creditors' meeting the voluntary arrangement takes effect, duly approved, as if made by the debtor at the creditors' meeting on the necessary majority being secured[3]. In a CVA, with both creditors' and company meetings, it will take effect if approved by both meetings[4], but there is the risk of divergent decisions. If the CVA is approved by the creditors' meeting but rejected by the company meeting it stands approved and comes into effect as if made by the company at the creditors' meeting[5]. However, if the meetings come to different decisions a member of the company may apply to the court[6]. On the member's application the court may order the decision of the company meeting to have effect instead of the decision of the creditors' meeting, or make such other order as it thinks fit[7]. The member's application must be made within 28 days of the date on which the creditors' meeting decision was taken, or, if later, the date on which the company meeting decision was taken[8]. The Financial Services Authority is entitled to be heard where the application relates to a regulated company[9].

The essential aim of the legislation in allowing a member of the company to apply to the court where the decisions of the creditors' and company meetings differ is to allow the member to object to a CVA being approved and implemented against the wishes of the company members expressed in the company meeting. Before the implementation of the amendments introduced by IA 2000 the company meeting could veto a CVA by voting against the proposal. It is easy to envisage circumstances in which the members of an insolvent company do not agree with the directors that the company should prolong its life with a CVA. On changing the law and giving the creditors' meeting primacy it is understandable that Parliament should give the members the opportunity to persuade the court that the voluntary arrangement should not take effect despite its approval by the creditors. The court will be slow to overturn the creditors' approval but circumstances in which it is appropriate to do so may occasionally arise. The legislation is, however, drafted more widely than this. IA 1986, s 4A(1) provides that the section applies 'to a decision … with respect to the approval of a proposed voluntary arrangement' which in ordinary language means a decision either way. IA 1986, s 4A(3) enables a member of the company to apply to the court 'if the decision taken by the creditors' meeting differs from that taken by the company meeting', and so is not restricted to cases where the creditors' meeting approves but the company meeting rejects the proposal. IA 1986, s 4A(6)(a) provides that the court may 'order the decision of the company meeting to have effect instead of the decision of the creditors' meeting' and so places no requirement on orders that they reject approval. The result is that the legislation allows a member to apply to the court where the company meeting has approved the voluntary arrangement to overturn the decision of the creditors' meeting to reject the proposal, a most unlikely scenario. Even were a situation to arise where it would be appropriate for the court to impose a voluntary arrangement on the creditors, only a member could apply for the order. Creditors may challenge the approval of arrangements but not their rejection[10]. It seems strange that if Parliament does wish to give the court the final word so as to do justice in extreme cases it does not permit a creditor to make the necessary application.

1 See para 6.10 above.
2 See para 6.11 above.
3 IA 1986, s 260(2)(a).
4 IA 1986, s 4A(2)(a) (CVA without moratorium), Sch A1 para 36(2)(a) (CVA with moratorium).
5 IA 1986, s 4A(2)(b) (CVA without moratorium), Sch A1 para 36(2)(b) (CVA with moratorium).
6 IA 1986, s 4A(3) (CVA without moratorium), Sch A1 para 36(3) (CVA with moratorium).
7 IA 1986, s 4A(6) (CVA without moratorium), Sch A1 para 36(5) (CVA with moratorium).
8 IA 1986, s 4A(4) (CVA without moratorium), Sch A1 para 36(4) (CVA with moratorium); as to this 28-day time limit generally see para 7.8 below.
9 IA 1986, s 4A(5) (CVA without moratorium), Sch A1 para 44(10) (CVA with moratorium); 'regulated company' means a company which is or has been an authorised person or an appointed representative under s 31 or s 39 Financial Services and Markets Act 2000 or is carrying on or has carried on a regulated activity within s 22 of that Act in contravention of the general prohibition contained in s 19. The FSA must be summoned to the creditors' meeting of any regulated company: see para 3.1 above.
10 Under IA 1986, s 6 (CVA without moratorium), Sch A1, para 38 (CVA with moratorium) see para 7.1 below.

6.14 Appointment of supervisor. On approving a proposal the creditors' meeting may pass a resolution providing that an authorised practitioner[1] other than the nominee be appointed supervisor of the voluntary arrangement, or that two or more authorised practitioners be appointed to act as supervisor[2].

It is usual for the nominee to be appointed supervisor, but it is not unknown for substantial creditors to make it a condition of supporting an arrangement that their preferred candidate becomes the supervisor. Where a resolution is moved to make an alternative appointment there must first be produced to the chairman at or before the creditors' meeting the written consent of the proposed supervisor to act and his written confirmation that he is qualified or authorised to act as a practitioner in relation to the debtor's voluntary arrangement[3]. Should two or more insolvency practitioners be appointed joint supervisors the creditors' meeting may resolve whether acts to be done in connection with the arrangement may be done by any one of them or must be done by both or all of them[4].

1 See para 1.12 above, an 'authorised practitioner' is an insolvency practitioner or a practitioner who is a member of a body authorised by the Secretary of State under IA 1986, s 389A to act in relation to voluntary arrangements.
2 See IR 1986, r 1.22(1) (all CVAs, by virtue of r 1.54(2) where a moratorium is in force), r 5.25(1) (IVA).
3 IR 1986, r 1.22(3) (all CVAs), r 5.25(2) (IVA).
4 IR 1986, r 1.22(1) (all CVAs), r 5.25(1) (IVA).

6.15 Chairman's report to the court. The chairman must prepare a report of the creditors' meeting for the court. No form is prescribed under IR 1986, but the report must contain the following information:

(a) whether the proposed voluntary arrangement was approved, if appropriate specifying any modifications made, or rejected. In CVA the report must state whether the approval was by the creditors of the company alone, or by both the creditors and the company;
(b) each resolution taken at the meeting, setting them out, and the decision in each case;

(c) a list of all the creditors present or represented with the value of the debts, and how they voted on each resolution;
(d) whether the EC Regulation applies to the voluntary arrangement and if so whether the proceedings are main proceedings or territorial proceedings[1]; and
(e) such further information as the chairman considers appropriate to make known to the court[2].

A copy of the chairman's report must be filed in court within four days of the meeting being held[3], and notice of the result of the meeting(s) must be given to all those who were sent notice of the meeting(s) immediately after the copy report is filed in court[4]. In IVA where the debtor is a bankrupt, notice of the result of the creditors' meeting must be sent to the official receiver and any trustee[5]. In CVA notice must be sent to the registrar of companies, but only if the decision was one to approve the voluntary arrangement[6].

In CVA, in keeping with the general approach of the legislation not to involve the court unless it is necessary to do so, the moratorium ends automatically at the end of the day on which the meetings finally decide whether or not to approve the proposed voluntary arrangement[7], unless it has come to an end earlier[8]. It is open for the meeting of the creditors, with or without the concurrence of the company meeting, to bring the moratorium to an end without closing further consideration of the proposal, although this would appear to be a rather unlikely scenario[9].

In IVA if the report is that the meeting has declined to approve the debtor's proposal the court may, and in practice will, discharge any interim order which is in force in relation to the debtor[10]. A final order on consideration of the chairman's report may be made without the attendance of the parties provided the chairman's report has been filed and complies with the rules[11]. The order records the effect of the chairman's report and discharges the interim order[12]. Where no interim order was obtained, the court does not consider the chairman's report unless an application is made in relation to it[13].

The Secretary of State is required to keep a register of IVAs[14]. Immediately after the chairman of an IVA creditors' meeting has filed in court his report that the meeting has approved the IVA, he must report the prescribed details[15] to the Secretary of State. This register is open to public inspection[16]. The supervisor of the IVA is also required to give notice of his appointment as supervisor to the Secretary of State[17]. IR 1986 now provide for old arrangements to be deleted from the register. IVAs in which a revocation order[18] was made before 22 March 1999 or where the final completion or termination of the arrangement occurred more than two years prior to 22 March 1999 have now been deleted from the register[19]. In future, all entries in the register in respect of an IVA are deleted when the Secretary of State receives notice of a making of a revocation order[20], and after two years of receipt of notice of the full implementation or termination of an IVA[21] all entries in the register relating to that arrangement will be deleted[22].

1 See paras 1.14 above and 14.2, 14.3 below. Strictly speaking, the EC Regulation always applies. The report to the court should presumably be concerned with the possibility that EC Regulation cross border issues might arise. The debtor might have a 'centre of main interests' in another EU state, in which event the voluntary arrangement will be territorial proceedings. Alternatively, the debtor has a 'centre of main interests' in the UK but has an 'establishment' in another EU state in respect of which there are territorial proceedings to which the voluntary arrangement will be main proceedings.
2 IR 1986, r 1.24(1)(2) (all CVAs, r 1.54(2) applies r 1.24 where a moratorium is in force), r 5.27(1)(2) (IVA).

3 IA 1986, s 4(6) (CVA without moratorium), Sch A1, para 30(3) (CVA with moratorium), s 259(1) (IVA) require the chairman to report; the time limit of four days is provided for by IR 1986, r 1.24(3) (all CVAs), r 5.27(3) (IVA) which further specify that the court must endorse the filed copy with the date of filing.
4 IR 1986, r 1.24(4) (all CVAs), r 5.27(4) (IVA). IR 1986, r 5.27(4) further provides that the chairman must send notice of the result of the creditors' meeting to any other creditor of whom the chairman is aware who was not sent notice of the creditors' meeting.
5 IR 1986, r 5.27(4) the notice to creditors, the official receiver and any trustee must be sent immediately after the report is filed in court.
6 IR 1986, r 1.24(5) (all CVAs).
7 IA 1986, Sch A1, para 8(2) or para 8(5), if the moratorium has been extended under para 32, see para 3.16 above. Unnecessarily, perhaps, IA 1986, Sch A1, para 8(7) provides that if it has not already terminated the moratorium comes to an end at the end of the day on which a decision to approve it takes effect.
8 This may be , for example, because the meetings were adjourned but the moratorium was not extended over the adjournment: see IA 1986, Sch A1, para 8(3); see generally para 3.5 above.
9 See para 3.3 above.
10 IA 1986, s 259(2).
11 Ie IR 1986, r 1.24 (all CVAs), r 5.27(1) (IVA): see text to n 1 above.
12 *Practice Direction: Insolvency Proceedings* para 16.1(4), see Appendix 6. A similar direction may be given in CVA.
13 IR 1986, r 5.27(5).
14 IR 1986, r 5.28(1).
15 Namely: (a) the name and address of the debtor; (b) the date on which the arrangement was approved by the creditors; (c) the name and address of the supervisor; and (d) the court in which the chairman's report has been filed: see IR 1986, r 5.29(1).
16 IR 1986, r 5.28(5). An application to inspect the Register of Voluntary Arrangements should be made to the General Services Team, 5th Floor, West Wing, Ladywood House, 45–46 Stephenson Street, Birmingham B2 4UP, Tel 0121 698 4000, Fax 0121 698 4406. A request for a search may be made by post or fax but not by telephone. It is not unknown for practitioners to fail to make the required report, so it is not possible to obtain a complete picture of the number of voluntary arrangements by consulting the Register, neither can a negative search be relied on in any particular case.
17 IR 1986, r 5.29(2).
18 Under IA 1986, s 262.
19 IR 1986, r 5.28(2).
20 IR 1986, r 5.28(3); notice of a revocation order is given under IR 1986, r 5.30: see para 7.9 below.
21 Under IR 1986, r 5.34(3).
22 IR 1986, r 5.28(4).

Chapter 7

Challenge to arrangements

7.1 Grounds of challenge. An application to challenge the decision of the creditors' meeting may be made on one or both of two grounds, namely:

(a) that the arrangement as approved[1] unfairly prejudices the interests of a creditor, or, in CVA, the interests of a member or contributory[2] of the company;

(b) that there has been some material irregularity at or in relation to the meeting[3].

It is not open to a creditor or anyone else to assert that the meeting's decision is invalid by reason of any irregularity at or in relation to the meeting other than by a challenge under IA 1986, s 6 (CVA) or s 262 (IVA)[4]. The aim of the Act is to provided a short time period, 28 days[5], within which an application may be made to challenge the meeting's decision after which the arrangement may proceed without fear of subsequent challenge even if it subsequently transpires that there was an irregularity at or in relation to the meeting or that one or more creditors' interests are prejudiced by the arrangement. Before the amendments introduced by IA 2000, a creditor who had no notice of the creditors' meeting was not bound by any voluntary arrangements which were approved by the creditors. From 1 January 2003, however, every creditor of the debtor will be bound by voluntary arrangements which have been approved by the creditors whether or not he received notice of the creditors' meeting or was otherwise aware of the proposal for a voluntary arrangement[6]. A creditor who was ignorant of the proposal and the summoning of the creditors' meeting does, however, have a right of challenge on either of the above grounds which must be brought within 28 days of him becoming aware of the arrangement[7].

It is important to note the precise extent of these two grounds. Ground (a), that the arrangement as approved unfairly prejudices the interests of a creditor, relates only to unfairness brought about by the terms of the arrangement itself[8]. It does not cover the situation where a creditor is concerned that the proposal is in some way improper and unfair on creditors because, for example, the debtor's statement of affairs is not accurate and includes debts which are a sham or does not disclose all the debtor's assets. Where a creditor believes that the creditors' approval has been obtained under false pretences he may challenge the voluntary arrangement under ground (b) above or by presenting a petition for the insolvency of the debtor. In *Re a Debtor (87 of 1993) (No 2)*[9] the court decided that the provision of false or misleading information was information provided 'in relation to' the meeting, as this phrase covered documentation supplied in connection with the meeting. It was therefore open to a creditor to challenge the creditors' decision on the basis that there had been a material irregularity at or in relation to the meeting[10], ie ground (b) above. This approach does have the considerable advantage of flexibility. The court can exercise its powers[11] to give directions for a further meeting to consider revised proposals or reconsider the original proposal, and if the creditors so wish insolvency may be avoided.

The alternative is to challenge the voluntary arrangement by petitioning for insolvency. In IVA the ability of the creditor to petition for bankruptcy is clear enough. IA 1986 expressly permits a creditor bound by an approved IVA to present a petition where he can show that information which was false or misleading in any material particular or which contained misleading omissions was (i) contained in the debtor's statement of affairs or any other document supplied by the debtor to any person in the course of the approval of the IVA, or (ii) was in some way made available by the debtor to his creditors at or in connection with the creditors' meeting[12]. In CVA the position is not so clear, for there is no equivalent provision for a winding-up petition to be presented for default in a CVA. There would appear, however, to be no good reason why a winding-up petition on the original debt should not be presented, any compromise of this debt being void for misrepresentation or breach of duty of good faith[13], but the safest course may be for the creditor to mount a challenge to the CVA under IA 1986, s 6(1)(b), that is ground (b) above. The court may well refuse to entertain a petition for winding up brought more than 28 days after the approval of the CVA for to do so would defeat the scheme of the legislation to have certainty, so far as possible, after this period has expired.

Where a creditor wishes to challenge a debt as a sham he must do so by way of appeal against the chairman's decision to allow the claim for the purposes of voting[14], and not by way of challenge under IA 1986[15].

Ground (b) covers any material irregularity at or in relation to the creditors' meeting including irregularities involving voting in respect of which there may also be an appeal under the Rules[16]. Under this ground an application may be made to challenge a refusal of the creditors' meeting to approve the arrangements, as well as to an approval of the arrangements. The court has, however, no power to declare the arrangements approved. If satisfied that there was a material irregularity at or in relation to a meeting which rejected the proposed arrangements the court may give a direction for the summoning of a further meeting to reconsider the proposal with or without amendment[17].

It should be emphasised that the statutory scheme for voluntary arrangements is that once an arrangement has been approved by the creditors' meeting the only routes to challenge or circumvent that approval are by direct challenge under IA 1986, s 6, Sch A1, para 38, or s 262[18] or by indirect challenge by means of a winding-up[19] or bankruptcy petition under IA 1986, s 264(1)(c), s 276(1)[20]. The Court of Appeal therefore refused to order that the approval of a voluntary arrangement was void when the debtor had failed to disclose that some only of the creditors had been given secret inducements to support the arrangement[21]. At first instance[22] the court had held, by reference to pre-1986 authorities, that there was a strict duty of good faith on the part of the debtor as between all competing unsecured creditors. Finding a breach of that duty the court held that the approval of the arrangements at the creditors' meeting was void. While overturning the declaration that the approval was void, the Court of Appeal effectively endorsed the existence of the strict duty of good faith on the part of the debtor[23], and made a bankruptcy order on the basis that information provided by the debtor was false and misleading in a material particular.

1 Ie in CVA the arrangement which has effect under IA 1986, s 4A (CVA without moratorium) or Sch A1, para 36 (CVA with moratorium) following approval by both meetings or the creditors' meeting alone, or by order of the court (see para 6.13 above), or, in IVA, has been approved by the creditors' meeting.
2 A 'contributory' is any person liable to contribute to the assets of a company in the event of it being wound up: IA 1986, s 79(1). Persons who may be liable to contribute following a declaration of the court in respect of fraudulent or wrongful trading, or past directors and shareholders who may have a liability to make a contribution to a company's assets, are not contributories: IA 1986, s 79(2), (3).
3 IA 1986, s 6(1) (CVA without moratorium), Sch A1, para 38(1) (CVA with moratorium), s 262(1) (IVA).
4 IA 1986, s 6(7) (CVA without moratorium), Sch A1, para 38(9) (CVA with moratorium), s 262(8) (IVA).
5 See para 7.8 below as to this time limit, which may be extended in IVA: see para 7.8 below.
6 IA 1986, s 5(2) (CVA without moratorium), Sch A1, para 37(2) (CVA with moratorium), s 260(2) (IVA).
7 IA 1986, s 6(3)(b) (CVA without moratorium), Sch A1, para 38(3)(b) (CVA with moratorium), s 262(3)(b) (IVA), as amended by IA 2000.
8 *Re a Debtor (No 259 of 1990)* [1992] 1 WLR 226, Hoffmann J; and see *Cadbury Schweppes v Somji* [2001] 1 WLR 615, para 37, CA.
9 [1996] 1 BCLC 63.
10 See [1996] 1 BCLC 63 at 94–95.
11 Under IA 1986, s 6(4) (CVA without moratorium), Sch A1, para 38(4) (CVA with moratorium), s 262(4) (IVA).
12 IA 1986, ss 264(1)(c), 276(1)(b).
13 As to which see *Cadbury Schweppes v Somji* [2001] 1 WLR 615.
14 Under IR 1986, rr 1.17, 1.17A (CVA without moratorium), rr 1.49,1.50 (CVA with moratorium) rr 5.21, 5.22 (IVA).
15 *Re a Debtor* [1992] 1 WLR 226 at 229; the challenge would be under s 6 (CVA without moratorium), Sch A1, para 38 (CVA with moratorium) or s 262 (IVA);
16 IR 1986, r 1.17A(3) (CVA without moratorium), r 1.50(3) (CVA with moratorium), r 5.22(3) (IVA); and see para 6.8 above.
17 IA 1986, s 6(4) (CVA without moratorium), Sch A1 para 38(4) (CVA with moratorium), s 262(4) (IVA), and see para 7.9 below.
18 With its strict time limits, see para 7.8 below.
19 But query as to winding up petition, see text above.
20 As to which see para 11.2 below.
21 *Cadbury Schweppes v Somji* [2001] 1 WLR 615.
22 [2001] 1 BCLC 498.
23 [2001] 1 WLR 615 at para 25: 'The deputy judge's impressive survey of the old law shows that in relation to compositions and arrangements with creditors the court did impose a strict requirement of good faith as between competing unsecured creditors, and prohibited any secret inducement to one creditor even if that inducement did not come from the debtor's own estate. There is no strong presumption that a similar principle must be found in the new regime set out in Part VIII of the 1986 Act, but (to put it at its lowest) it would be no great surprise to find it there in one form or another', per Robert Walker LJ.

7.2 Challenge coupled with appeal from chairman's decision on voting. A challenge to the meeting's decision with respect to a proposed arrangement may be brought together with an appeal against the chairman's decision as to a creditor's entitlement to vote[1].

1 See eg *Re A Debtor (No 222 of 1990)* [1992] BCLC 137, and many other cases where both applications have been brought together.

7.3 Ground (a) : unfair prejudice. To constitute a good ground of challenge under this head the unfair prejudice complained of must result from the terms of the arrangement, and not the fact of the IVA or some other extraneous matter, such as the status of the debts or the conduct of other creditors; further, a creditor applicant must show that the prejudice is to his interests as a creditor and not in some other capacity[1]. Accordingly, a scheme which proposed a 10% dividend to all creditors could not be unfairly prejudicial on the basis that the debts of certain of the supporting creditors were suspicious[2]. It is not unfair prejudice that by entry into voluntary arrangement the debtor escapes the investigation into past business dealings, assets and debts that would follow liquidation or bankruptcy. The challenge should demonstrate that the scheme has been framed in a manner which prejudices a creditor or class of creditor in a way which is unfair compared to what would have been the position if the scheme had been framed in a different way[3].

Neither IA 1986 nor IR 1986 attempt a definition of 'unfair prejudice'. It is not a term which has been used in previous bankruptcy legislation. 'Prejudice' denotes something detrimental to existing rights[4]. All creditors who do not receive 100p in the £ will to that extent be prejudiced by the arrangement. A creditor's rights can, however, go beyond the actual amount of his debt; the date of payment, the right to require further transactions at existing rates, restrictions on other dealings, the availability of other remedies, and the ability to exploit licences all being examples. Where the terms of the arrangement provide for the release from liability of a co-debtor or surety, a creditor who loses his additional rights of recourse against co-debtor or surety may be unfairly prejudiced[5]. A voluntary arrangement does not affect proprietary rights such as the right of a landlord to forfeit a debtor's lease[6], although the terms of an arrangement might be drawn so as to restrict such a right with the consent of the landlord. The concept of 'unfairness' suggests a differential treatment as between creditors. Such prejudice may more obviously appear where one creditor is expected to receive a lower dividend under the arrangement than other creditors who have no better security for their debts. It is also possible, however, that prejudice is suffered by a particular creditor even where the dividends payable under the arrangement are equal. Where one creditor had rights under the Third Parties (Rights Against Insurers) Act 1930 he was unfairly prejudiced by an arrangement which might have prevented him proceeding to judgment for the full amount of his claim against the debtor, thus prejudicing his statutory rights against the debtor's insurers[7]. When considering the question of prejudice the court may wish to compare the position of dissenting creditors under the arrangement with that in the event of liquidation or bankruptcy, but such a comparison is not determinative[8]. Where the proposal provided for the Inland Revenue and the Customs & Excise to be paid a dividend of about 19% in priority to the remaining creditors whose debts were, however, not compounded, the proposal was held to be unfair. The result of the proposed arrangement would have been that the remaining creditors (all friends of the debtor) would have succeeded in removing £77,000 of competing debt at a cost of £15,000 against the wishes of the Crown creditors whose debts were eliminated. It was not rendered fair by the fact that the Crown creditors were likely to receive less in the event of the debtor's bankruptcy or the fact that the debtor had no assets immediately available with which to pay the remaining creditors[9].

Other examples of prejudice being suffered by a creditor despite receiving an equal dividend under the arrangement would include a creditor who is bound to pay a proportion of the original monies due from the debtor to a sub-contractor or agent who is not bound by the arrangement[10], or a creditor who is prevented by the arrangement from completing an execution[11]. The fact that the majority creditors have collateral benefits through, for example, friendship or the continued provision of specialist services, might result in unfair prejudice to the minority creditors who receive no such benefits even though all creditors receive an equal dividend[12]. In appropriate circumstances there may be unfair prejudice where the terms of the arrangement fail to discriminate in favour of a particular creditor or class of creditors[13]. Accordingly, there was unfair prejudice to a creditor whose claim against the debtor could be pursued against the debtor's insurers under the Third Parties (Rights Against Insurers) Act 1930 even though under the terms of the arrangement all unsecured creditors were treated the same[14].

The term 'unfairly prejudicial' is used in CA 1985, ss 459–461, the provisions designed to give protection to minority shareholders, but it is unlikely that assistance may be had from decisions under these provisions[15]. However, in voluntary arrangements as with minority protection cases the test of unfairness is an objective one[16]. Where members of the same class are not treated equally it will not be difficult to establish prejudice[17]. Equal treatment, however, does not preclude unfair prejudice, as noted above, and in rare cases it may be shown that there was an intention to discriminate which may in fact have given rise to unfairness[18].

A creditor may feel that the dividend proposed under the arrangement is so low as to be unfair in favour of the debtor. Whether, on the wording of IA 1986, s 6, Sch A1, para 38, s 262 (all in similar terms) an arrangement may be open to challenge on the basis that it unfairly prejudices the interests of all the creditors must be doubtful. The court will in any event be slow, however, to go behind an arrangement which has been approved by 75% of the creditors[19]. The possibility that some of the creditors will be unfairly inclined toward the debtor is taken into account in the Insolvency Rules. No arrangement may be approved where those voting against it at the creditors' meeting include more than half in value of the creditors ignoring the votes of creditors who to the best of the chairman's belief are connected to or are associates of the debtor[20]. There is little prospect therefore that a successful challenge to an arrangement may be mounted solely on the ground that it is unfairly weighted toward the debtor. Indeed, an arrangement which provides for a nil dividend to unsecured creditors is capable of being a valid arrangement under the Act[21].

The court looks to see whether the applicant has suffered practical prejudice; it is not sufficient that prejudice can be demonstrated in theory on an academic approach to the terms of the arrangement. Thus where the terms of a voluntary arrangement appeared to discriminate against two banks which alone of the unsecured creditors were required to forgo their rights against the debtor's wife, because the wife had no assets of her own and no separate income the banks were held not to have suffered unfair prejudice in being prevented from suing her[22]. Neither was it unfairly prejudicial for the arrangement to allow for future creditors whose co-operation for the continuation of the business was essential to be paid in full whereas other creditors would merely receive a dividend[23]. The court expressed the view that the distinction proposed between the categories of future creditors was a 'realistic and commercially sensible' distinction, and on this basis rejected the argument that the different treatment which the terms of the arrangement afforded these creditors amounted to unfair prejudice.

In *Swindon Town Properties Ltd v Swindon Town Football Co Ltd*[24] the applicant complained that a CVA entered into while the company was in administration unfairly prejudiced his rights as a debenture holder because under the CVA if implemented funds would be channelled to the CVA creditors rather than be paid to the applicant under its debenture. The CVA (as was to be expected) contemplated the discharge of the administration order. This would leave the debenture holder free to enforce its security. It did not wish to do so (football club cases have more than purely commercial considerations in play), but as the court observed the applicant could not have its cake and eat it. There was no basis for holding that the creditor was unfairly prejudiced by the fact that the company intended to trade for the purposes of the CVA and pay the proceeds of its trading to the CVA creditors.

1 *Re a Debtor (No 259 of 1990)* [1992] 1 WLR 226; *Re a Debtor (No 87 of 1993) (No 2)* [1996] 1 BCLC 63 at 86; *Doorbar v Alltime Securities Ltd* [1996] 1 WLR 456; *Re a Debtor (No 574 of 1995)* [1998] 2 BCLC 124; and see *Cadbury Schweppes v Somji* [2001] 1 WLR 615, at para 37, per Robert Walker LJ: 'It is sufficient to say that there is a fairly strong line of first-instance authority, starting with the decision of Hoffman J in *In re A Debtor (No 259 of 1990),* which is uniformly in favour of limiting the effect of the provision to unfairness brought about by the terms of the IVA itself. As Hoffman J pointed out in that case, at p 229, section 276(1) provides an alternative remedy in many cases of unfairness brought about by other causes.'

2 *Re a Debtor (No 259 of 1990)* [1992] 1 WLR 226; there might, however, have been a material irregularity at or in relation to the meeting: see para 7.6 below.

3 *Re a Debtor (No 259 of 1990)* [1992] 1 WLR 226; *Re a Debtor (No 574 of 1995)* [1998] 2 BCLC 124, sub nom *National Westminster Bank v Scher* [1998] BPIR 225.

4 See eg *Re a Company (No 4475 of 1982)* [1983] Ch 178 at 188.

5 *Johnson v Davies* [1998] 2 BCLC 252 at 270.

6 *Re Naeem (a bankrupt) (No 18 of 1988)* [1990] 1 WLR 48.

7 Sea *Voyager Maritime Inc v Bielecki* [1999] 1 All ER 628.

8 See *Re a Debtor (No 222 of 1990)* [1992] BCLC 137 at 145; *Re a Debtor (No 87 of 1993)* [1996] 1 BCLC 63 at 86.

9 *Re a Debtor (No 101 of 1999)* [2001] 1 BCLC 54. A further, inappropriate, proposal was then made, see *Re a Debtor (No 101 of 1999) (No 2)* [2001] BPIR 996.

10 See eg the facts in *Simon Container Machinery Ltd v Emba Machinery AB* [1998] 2 Lloyd's Rep 429.

11 Although if it could be shown that the creditor would not have been able to complete his execution before the date on which, but for the voluntary arrangement, the debtor would have been made insolvent he will not have been prejudiced: see IA 1986, s 183 (liquidation), s 346 (bankruptcy).

12 See eg *Re a Debtor (No 101 of 1999) (No 2)* [2001] BPIR 996, where the court refused to direct a further meeting to consider revised proposals after a successful challenge. Although all the creditors were to receive an equal dividend under the new proposal the court considered that a 75% majority of creditors could only be achieved through the votes of friends or creditors motivated by a desire that the debtor, a racehorse trainer, could continue to train their horses. Such collateral benefits were not available to the minority creditors, the Inland Revenue and Customs & Excise.

13 See eg *Re Primlaks (UK) Ltd (No 2)* [1990] BCLC 234 at 236-237; *Sea Voyager Maritime Inc v Bielecki* [1999] 1 All ER 628 at 642.

14 See *Sea Voyager Maritime Inc v Bielecki* [1999] 1 All ER 628. In the event, at a further meeting of creditors, a modification was approved permitting the relevant creditor to sue the debtor provided he undertook not to enforce any judgment obtained against the debtor's personal assets.

15 Note the comments of Peter Gibson LJ in *Doorbar v Alltime Securities Ltd* [1996] 1 BCLC 487 at 498h, and Robert Walker LJ in *Cadbury Schweppes v Somji* [2001] 1 WLR 615, para 37.

16 *Re R A Noble & Sons (Clothing) Ltd* [1983] BCLC 273 at 290.

17 *Re Carrington Viyella plc* (1983) 1 BCC 98 at 951; *Re A Company (No 002612 of 1984)* [1985] BCLC 801, but it does not necessarily follow that different treatment amounts to unfair prejudice: see *Re Cancol Ltd* [1996] 1 All ER 37, [1996] 1 BCLC 100.

18 *Re Cumana Ltd* [1986] BCLC 430, CA; *Re A Company* [1986] BCLC 362; *Re a Company (No 00370 of 1987), ex p Glossop* [1988] 1 WLR 1068.

19 See in the context of the acquisition of the shares of dissenting minority shareholder under CA 1985, s 428, *Re Bugle Press Ltd* [1961] Ch 270.

20 IR 1986, r 1.19(4) (CVA), r 5.18(4) (IVA).
21 *IRC v Adam & Partners Ltd* [2001] 1 BCLC 222, CA.
22 *Re A Debtor (No 574 of 1995)* [1998] 2 BCLC 124 at 131, sub nom *National Westminster Bank v Scher* [1998] BPIR 224 at 230 (it would appear that the banks would have been better advised to cross-examine the debtor in this case and perhaps sought disclosure against the wife: CPR 34.2); see also *Re a Debtor (No 259 of 1990)* [1992] 1 WLR 226; it is not a material irregularity to fail to notify the debtor's ex-wife who as an associate could not effectively vote against the IVA.
23 *Re Cancol Ltd* [1996] 1 BCLC 100, sub nom *Cazaly Irving Holdings v* Cancol [1996] BPIR 252.
24 [2002] All ER (D) 85 (4 July).

7.4 Unfair prejudice: position of debtor's landlord. Unless expressly agreed otherwise, the debtor's future liability to pay rent will be subject to the terms of the arrangement. The landlord will be bound to an approved arrangement in respect of future rent because, as a creditor with a future debt, he will be entitled to vote at the creditors' meeting. The chairman should make a proper assessment of the value of the landlord's prospective claim, but even if, for whatever reason, the chairman is unable to or fails to value this claim the Rules now provide that the claim is to be valued at £1 if no higher value is put upon it[1]. In addition to his right in debt to the rent, the landlord will have additional rights against his tenant under the lease in the nature of security. In particular the right to distrain for unpaid rent, and the right to re-enter and forfeit the lease in the event of non-payment of rent and, usually, in the case of insolvency of the tenant[2]. In *March Estates plc v Gunmark Ltd*[3] the court confirmed that the landlord's right to re-enter and the right to forfeit are security rights for the purposes of IA 1986. To the extent that he is a secured creditor the approval of an arrangement by the tenant's creditors may not affect the landlord's rights[4]. Any attempt to do so without the landlord's consent will amount to unfair prejudice, assuming that they are valid and bind the landlord at all[5]. An arrangement which provided that the lease should be sold as soon as possible was not unfairly prejudicial to the landlord, however, as on a proper construction of the arrangement it was only intended to bind the landlord in his capacity as creditor and did not affect his right to forfeit the lease[6]. As regards rent, however, the landlord is in no different position than other unsecured creditors. An arrangement may postpone, modify or even extinguish the landlord's rights both to arrears and future rent, without this being of itself unfair prejudice[7]. Although the landlord's right to recover future rent as a debt may be modified by the arrangement it would seem that the better view is that where the landlord seeks to forfeit the lease the debtor would only be entitled to relief against forfeiture by paying the reserved rent in full[8]. In valuing the landlord's claim for future rent for voting purposes the chairman is entitled to take into account the degree of likelihood that the landlord will exercise his right of re-entry. It was not a material irregularity therefore where the chairman restricted the landlord's future claim to one year's rent[9]. In *Doorbar v Alltime Securities Ltd (No 2)*[10] the landlord had a right to require the surety to take a new lease in the event that the tenant became bankrupt and the trustee disclaimed the lease. The landlord claimed that it was unfairly prejudiced by the arrangement as it would prevent the right to require the surety to take a new lease from coming into effect. Both at first instance and in the Court of Appeal it was held that the interest of the landlord in enforcing his right against the surety fell outside the scope of IA 1986, s 262, as it was a right exercisable against a person other than the debtor and which arose through disclaimer by the debtor's trustee. It was therefore a substitute for rather than a constituent part of the debtor's indebtedness[11].

The assignee of the reversion will be bound to a voluntary arrangement to the same extent as a landlord[12].

Where the tenant's interest under the lease has been assigned the original tenant and any intermediate assignor will usually remain liable on their covenants to the landlord in respect of rent for periods covered by the voluntary arrangement. The statutory binding which operates on creditors' claims is not the equivalent to a release by accord or satisfaction or a release under seal. Accordingly, the making of a voluntary arrangement by the assignee tenant does not operate to release the original tenant or subsequent assignors from liability to the landlord under their covenants[13]. If a tenant by assignment enters into a voluntary arrangement the original and any subsequent assignor tenants face the difficulty that there is no provision in IA 1986 to enable a vesting order to be made. The original and any subsequent assignor tenants should be given notice of the creditors' meeting as they will be contingent if not actual creditors[14]. The possibility may be canvassed at the creditors' meeting that the voluntary arrangement contains a provision for the re-vesting of the lease in the original or one of the subsequent assignor tenants[15].

1 IR 1986, r 1.17(3) (CVA without moratorium), r 1.49(3) (CVA with moratorium), r 5.21(3) (IVA): see para 6.7 above. Before 1 January 2003 it was necessary for the chairman to put a value on the claim if the landlord was to be bound to the arrangement: see *Doorbar v Alltime Securities* [1996] 1 WLR 456, overruling *Burford Midland Properties Ltd v Marley Extensions* [1994] BCC 604.
2 Note, however, that a landlord's right of re-entry is not a security for the purposes of IA 1986: *Christopher Moran Holdings Ltd v Bristow* [2000] 2 AC 172, HL; *Razzaq v Pala* [1997] 1 WLR 1336; *Re Lomax Leisure Ltd* [1999] 2 BCLC 126. See also, in connection with Rent Act tenancies, *Cadogan Estates v McMahon Ltd* [2001] 1 AC 378.
3 [1996] 2 BCLC 1.
4 IA 1986, s 4(3) (CVA without moratorium), Sch A1 para 31(4) (CVA with moratorium), s 258 (4) (IVA); *Doorbar v Alltime Securities Ltd* [1996] 1 WLR 456.
5 While the landlord may assert that any such provision must be invalid by reason of IA 1986, s 4(3), Sch A1, para 31(4) or s 258(4), as applicable, he must be careful not to act so as to give implied consent.
6 *Re Naeem (No 18 of 1988)* [1990] 1 WLR 48.
7 *Cazaly Irving Holdings v Cancol* [1996] 1 All ER 37, [1996] BPIR 252; *March Estates v Gunmark* [1996] 2 BCLC 1.
8 In *Re Naeem (No 18 of 1988)* [1990] 1 WLR 48 the court expressed the view that relief from forfeiture would be given on payment of the modified not reserved rent. This was doubted in *March Estates v Gunmark* [1996] 2 BCLC 1, where the court considered that the basis on which the Court of Appeal had decided *Doorbar v Alltime Securities Ltd* [1996] 1 WLR 456 was that the reserved rent would have to be paid to secure relief
9 *Doorbar v Alltime Securities Ltd (No 2)* [1995] 2 BCLC 513 at 527, upheld on appeal, see n 10 below.
10 [1995] 2 BCLC 513, Knox J; [1996] 1 WLR 456, 1 BCLC 487, CA.
11 See [1996] 1 BCLC 487 at 499.
12 *Burford Midland Properties Ltd v Marley Extrusions Ltd* [1995] 1 BCLC 102.
13 *R A Securities Ltd v Merchantile Credit Co Ltd* [1995] 3 All ER 581; *Mytre Investments Ltd v Reynolds* [1995] 3 All ER 588.
14 *Mytre Investments Ltd v Reynolds* [1995] 3 All ER 588.
15 *Mytre Investments Ltd v Reynolds* [1995] 3 All ER 588.

7.5 Unfair prejudice: IVA: position of spouse. A spouse or former spouse may be in a different position from other creditors in that any obligation arising under an order made in family proceedings or under a maintenance assessment made under the Child Support Act 1991 (a 'matrimonial debt') does not give rise to a debt provable in a bankruptcy[1] neither will a matrimonial debt be released on the bankrupt's discharge[2]. Although a matrimonial debt is not provable in bankruptcy it is nevertheless a debt on which a bankruptcy petition may be founded; it will only be in rare cases, however, that a bankruptcy order is made on such a petition[3]. A spouse with a matrimonial debt is a creditor to whom notice must be given of the creditors' meeting[4], and is a creditor capable of being bound by an IVA[5]. As a spouse has a right to assert a matrimonial debt notwithstanding the release of debts which accompanies the bankrupt's discharge, he or she has a right which is not enjoyed by creditors generally. That right is overridden by the terms of any arrangement which compel acceptance of a dividend in satisfaction of a matrimonial debt, and the spouse is unfairly prejudiced as a consequence[6].

It is a standard term in many arrangements that a creditor whose claim falls within the definition in IR 1986 of those debts which are not provable[7] is not entitled to vote in connection with or prove in the arrangement, and will not be a creditor entitled to make an application for the purposes of IA 1986, s 262. The aim of this standard term is to keep the IVA separate from matrimonial claims. However, in *Re a Debtor, JP v Debtor*[8] the proposal included the matrimonial debt as a liability in the statement of affairs. Sir John Vinelott held that the standard condition was by implication excluded by this inclusion of the debt in the proposal.

1 IR 1986, r 12.3(2).
2 IA 1986, s 281(5)(b).
3 *Russell v Russell* [1998] BPIR 259.
4 *Re Bradley-Hole, ex p Knight* [1995] 2 FLR 838, [1995] BCC 418; the point was conceded but Rimer J considered the concession to be well founded.
5 *Re a Debtor, JP v Debtor* [1999] BPIR 206; *Re Bradley-Hole, ex p Knight* [1995] 2 FLR 838, [1995] BCC 418.
6 *Re a Debtor, JP v Debtor* [1999] BPIR 206.
7 Ie IR 1986, r 12.3(2) (matrimonial debts, criminal fines, drugs trafficking, confiscation order obligations).
8 [1999] BPIR 206 at 217.

7.6 Ground (b): material irregularity. The second ground for an application to challenge the approval of a voluntary arrangement by the creditors' meeting is that there has been some material irregularity either at or in relation to the meeting. The court takes a practical approach. To be 'material' the irregularity must be one which, objectively assessed, prevented the possibility of a different conclusion to any of the essential votes taken at the creditors' meeting[1]. Possible irregularities include the failure of the nominee to notify one or more creditors of the meeting, or the full details of the proposal, or a change of venue without due notice. The fact that a creditor who is not notified of the meeting would not himself have had sufficient voting strength to alter the outcome of the vote which was taken at the meeting should not of itself necessarily render immaterial the irregularity in failing to give him notice. It will depend on the circumstances whether the creditor in question might be able to show that he may have been able to persuade other voters to change their minds. But many creditors adopt positions in advance, and submit proxy votes, and it will take strong evidence to establish that a creditor would have had a reasonable prospect of persuading other creditors to change their minds. It is not unusual for further information to become available after the proposal has been sent to creditors, often only at the meeting itself on questioning the debtor. This can cause difficulties with proxy votes sent in without the benefit of the further information. A nominee who obtains proxy votes in favour of the proposal should assess the possible impact of further information on the creditors and not cast the proxies without further reference to the creditors involved unless confident that it is proper to do so. When the new information is significant the nominee is duty bound to adjourn the meeting and report the new information to all creditors even if this means having to seek an extension of time for the holding of the meeting and any interim order or moratorium[2].

A proxy which is faxed to the chairman is valid for the purposes of voting, and the refusal of the chairman to admit it for voting is a material irregularity[3]. A creditor is entitled to alter the terms of the authority given by proxy, and the refusal of the chairman to admit the altered proxy for voting is a material irregularity[4].

Where the chairman of the meeting is guilty of misconduct which prejudices creditors this may constitute a material irregularity as well as constituting unfair prejudice[5]. Incorrect decisions of the chairman, for example as to the voting entitlement of a creditor, will in principle be an irregularity, and so give rise to an appeal both under IR 1986 and IA 1986[6]. Where a creditor attended the meeting although he had not been given notice of it he was entitled to vote; failure to allow the creditor to vote would have amounted to a material irregularity[7].

False or misleading information provided by the debtor in his proposal or statement of affairs is information supplied 'in relation to' the creditors' meeting and may therefore constitute a material irregularity on which a challenge may be made to the meeting's decision[8]. Indeed, any material irregularity in the proposal or statement of affairs will be a material irregularity in relation to the creditors' meeting[9]. Failure properly to identify creditors, or the creditor who was to purchase an asset of the debtor in settlement of his claim, was a material irregularity sufficient to justify revoking the arrangement[10].

1 *Doorbar v Alltime Securities Ltd (Nos 1 and 2)* [1996] 1 BCLC 487 at 498, CA; *Re a Debtor (No 259 of 1990)* [1992] 1 WLR 226 at 229, where notice was not given to a creditor whose vote could not have altered the result. See also *Cazaly Irving Holdings v Cancol* [1996] BPIR 252, where the complaint was that one creditor's representative had persuaded the chairman of the meeting to increase the value of the creditor's debt for voting purposes to a remarkable extent. Knox J stated that had the increase in voting rights been capable of affecting the outcome of the vote he would have stood the matter over for evidence as to how the debt was valued.
2 *Cadbury Schweppes v Somji* [2001] 1 WLR 615, para 25.
3 *IRC v Conbeer and White* [1996] BPIR 398; the point taken was that a form of proxy had to be signed: see IR 1986, r 8.2. Laddie J held that the faxed signature should be treated as authentic unless there are surrounding circumstances which indicate otherwise, and see at 404–405, where the learned judge considered that other forms of electronically generated signatures would be sufficient for the purposes of the rules.
4 *Re Cardona* [1997] BPIR 604.
5 *Re a Debtor (No 222 of 1990)* [1992] BCLC 137, and note the judgment on costs at [1993] BCLC 233.
6 *Re Cranley Mansions Ltd* [1994] 1 WLR 1610, where the chairman's arbitrary reduction of a creditor's claim from, an admittedly excessive, £900,000 to a nominal £1 without the creditors' agreement was held to be a breach of IR 1986, r 1.17(3) (r 1.49(3) where a moratorium is in force; r 5.21(3) in IVA) and a material irregularity. Ferris J held that the creditor had no entitlement to vote at all and was therefore not bound by the arrangement. Equally, this meant that she could not challenge the meeting's decision, as she was not 'a person entitled in accordance with the rules to vote at the [creditors'] meeting' see IA 1986, s 6(2), Sch A1, para 38(2), s 262(2); but see *Doorbar v Alltime Securities Ltd (Nos 1 and 2)* [1996] 1 WLR 456, CA. Also *Re Wisepark Ltd* [1994] BCC 221 at 223; *Re a Debtor (No 400-IO-1996)* [1997] 1 WLR 1319; *Re a Debtor (No 574 of 1995)* [1998] 2 BCLC 124 at 127, and see para 7.4 above. See also *Re Sweatfield Ltd* [1998] BPIR 276, where the chairman's decision on the value of the claim for voting purposes was held not to be an irregularity at all.
7 See eg *Re Debtors (Nos 400 and 401 of 1996)* [1997] BPIR 431, a case decided under what was IR 1986, r 5.17 (now r 5.21) not IA 1986, s 262.
8 *Re a Debtor (87 of 1993) (No 2)* [1996] 1 BCLC 63 at 94.
9 *Re a Debtor (87 of 1993) (No 2)* [1996] 1 BCLC 63 at 88–95, where Rimer J. considered the earlier cases.
10 *IRC v Duce* [1999] BPIR 189.

7.7 Applicant for relief. The persons entitled to apply to challenge the decision of the creditors' meeting are:

1. the individual debtor or, in CVA, anyone entitled to vote at the company meeting[1];
2. any person entitled, in accordance with the rules[2], to vote at the creditors' meeting;
3. any person who would have been entitled to vote at the creditors' meeting if he had been given notice of it[3];
4. the nominee or any authorised practitioner who has replaced him[4];
5. where the debtor is a company in formal insolvency or an undischarged bankrupt the administrator or liquidator, or the trustee or the official receiver, as appropriate[5].

The positions of the debtor and the creditor seem clear enough. The former may wish to challenge the refusal of the proposed arrangement, or a modification voted through by the creditors[6]. A creditor may be concerned to challenge a decision which binds him to an arrangement which unfairly prejudices him; he may wish to overturn a refusal of an arrangement on the ground of material irregularity where he is concerned that a liquidation or bankruptcy may follow under which he will receive less than under the proposed arrangement. The interest of the nominee in applying is not so clear. In IVA he may be concerned that a modification was approved without the consent of the debtor. He may indeed be concerned that the failure of the proposal will deprive him of the administration of the arrangement, but if this interest is primarily financial it will be unattractive. A liquidator, administrator or trustee in bankruptcy may consider that the arrangements as approved might prejudice his administration of the estate or the interests of one or more creditors in the insolvency. Why in IVA the official receiver in his capacity other than trustee might wish to apply for relief is far from obvious, and he receives no assistance from the Act or the Rules should he wish to do so. Neither he (nor a liquidator, administrator or trustee in bankruptcy) has any right to be given notice of the meeting under the Rules, nor do they have a right to attend the meeting.

1 See paras 6.3, 6.11 above.
2 See para 6.6, 6.7 above.
3 IA 1986, s 6(2)(aa) (CVA without moratorium), Sch A1, para 38(2)(b) (CVA with moratorium), s 262(2)(b)(ii) (IVA), as introduced by IA 2000.
4 See para 4.9 above.
5 IA 1986, s 6(2) (CVA), s 262(2) (IVA).
6 See para 6.5 .

7.8 Time for making application. The application must be made not later than 28 days beginning with the day on which the report of the creditors' meeting was made to the court[1]. The wording is to be noted. The first day is part of the 28-day period which therefore ends on the twenty-eighth day counting the day of the report, and not on the following day which would be the case with most time limits[2]. This short time limit for bringing challenges to approved arrangements follows the recommendation of the Cork Committee[3] that there should be only a short period within which a challenge could be brought in order that finality should be reached speedily. However, there is no provision in IA 1986, Pt VIII (which deals with IVAs) dis-applying the general provision in IA 1986 covering the law relating to individuals giving the court power to extend the time, either before or after it has expired, on any terms it thinks fit to impose[4]. In consequence it is open to an applicant to bring an application to challenge the meeting's decision on an IVA after the expiry of the 28-day limit[5]. There is no such provision in corporate insolvency. In CVA, and in IVA, time may be extended under IR 1986 importing as they do the relevant provisions of the CPR[6]. But this extends only to time for compliance with anything required to be done under the Rules. As the court pointed out in *Re Bournemouth and Boscombe Athletic Football Club Co Ltd*[7], this cannot give the court power to override was is in effect a limitation period provided for in a statute. The result is that the strict 28-day time limit applies in CVA, but not necessarily in IVA.

There is, however, a great merit in having certainty for all concerned with a voluntary arrangement, and in many instances it will be important to the success of the arrangement that it is implemented without delay. It is anticipated that the court will be slow to extend the time limit; an extension will require special circumstances[8]. In *Tager v Westpac Banking Corpn*[9] an approved arrangement was challenged by dissenting creditors on the ground that one of the supporting creditors should not have voted. The application was not served on the debtor until after the 28-day time limit had expired, and was upheld by the court some six weeks after the date of the report to the court. The debtor then discovered that one of the dissenting creditors had been allowed to vote for more than his true debt, and issued an application three weeks later, ie some nine weeks after the expiry of the 28-day time limit. In exercising its discretion to extend time the court considered the relevant factors to be (a) the length of the delay, (b) the reasons for the delay, (c) the apparent merits of the underlying application, and (d) the prejudice to each side other than the inevitable prejudice inherent in re-opening the matter[10]. In *Re a Debtor; JP v Debtor*[11] the time for making an application was extended ten months where the court was satisfied that the applicant wife was not responsible for the delay and where the debtor husband had not suffered any significant prejudice. In *Warley Continental Services v Johal*[12] the court noted the width of the power conferred by IA 1986, s 376 which led to the conclusion that any circumstance was of potential relevance in any particular case. This would include the conduct of the parties. For instance, on the applicant's side, any warning given of the application[13], and on the supervisor/debtor's side the promptness and openness shown in addressing concerns raised by potential applicants; this particularly bearing in mind the status of the supervisor as an independent professional responsible to the court. In the event an application to revoke or suspend the voluntary arrangement was issued some six weeks and two days out of time, and although the court considered that the merits of the case counted strongly in favour of the applicant this was outweighed by the significant delay for which there was no real justification.

It is always open to seek a review of a decision of the court under IA 1986, s 375(1), but this is not a mechanism for a late appeal[14].

Following the amendments introduced by IA 2000, a creditor who should have been but was not given notice of the creditors' meeting may make an application to challenge the decision within 28 days of his becoming aware that the creditors' meeting has taken place[15]. It is no bar to his making an application (within 28 days of his becoming aware of the meeting) that the arrangement has ceased to have effect, unless it came to an end prematurely[16]. The exclusion of arrangements which come to a premature end appears to arise from the view that a premature end must mean a resolution of the debtor's position and hence that of the creditors by bankruptcy or solvency. But there is no magic in a premature end. Coming to an end prematurely may have very different effects in different arrangements. The trusts on which the funds are held by the supervisor under an arrangement may or may not fail on the premature end of that arrangement depending upon the terms of the trust and nature of the end. The applicant creditor who had no notice of the arrangement may still be prejudiced therefore despite the premature end to the arrangement, and it is suggested ought to have the right to apply to set aside the arrangement.

In amending IA 1986 by IA 2000 and binding creditors to the arrangement who have had no notice of the creditors' meeting, Parliament is seeking to strengthen the statutory scheme for voluntary arrangements and keep debtors out of insolvency. Plainly, the creditors who are bound without their knowledge must be given an opportunity to appeal when they learn that an arrangement has been approved and implemented. But what of the original creditors? In most cases their position will be adversely affected by the inclusion of one or more new creditors of whose debts, almost certainly, the original creditors were unaware when approving the arrangement. The new creditors will now be entitled to share in the available funds. If the new creditors' debts are substantial in value the position may be reached where original creditors will say that had they known the true position they would not have voted for the arrangement. Failure by the debtor to inform the creditors of the true extent of his indebtedness by any significant degree is on its face a material irregularity at or in relation to the meeting. Should the court extend the time limit to allow the original creditors to challenge the approval of the arrangement? In any particular case the court may well feel that it should incline to supporting the arrangement and reject late applications to challenge. But for this to become general practice may have a serious impact on institutional creditors who may respond by opposing other debtor's proposals. To avoid such difficulties creditors would be well advised to consider a provision in the arrangement that it be reconsidered by the whole body of creditors should it transpire that additional creditors with debts of a value exceeding, say, 10% of the debts listed on the debtor's statement of affairs were in fact entitled to, but were not given, notice of the creditors' meeting.

1 IA 1986, s 6(3) (CVA without moratorium), Sch A1, para 38(3) (CVA with moratorium), s 262(3) (IVA); as to the report of the meeting to the court see IA 1986, s 4(6) (CVA without moratorium), Sch A1, para 30(3) (CVA with moratorium), s 259(1) (IVA) and para 6.13 above.

2 See *Re Bournemouth and Boscombe Athletic Football Club Co Ltd* [1998] BPIR 183; where it was noted that the same formula is used in IA 1986, s 5(4)(a) (CVA) which provides that the court should not make an order consequent upon an approval of a CVA at any time before the end of the period of 28 days beginning with the fist day on which each of the chairman's reports are made to the court, although this is to tie this provision in with the time limit for launching a challenge to the CVA.

3 The Review Committee on Insolvency Law and Practice, Cmnd 8558, published June 1982.

4 IA 1986, s 376. Note that this power enables the court to extend the 28-day time limit imposed by IR 1986, r 5.22(6) against the chairman's decision on entitlement to vote at the creditors' meeting.

5 *Tager v Westpac Banking Corpn* [1997] 1 BCLC 313; *Plant v Plant* [1998] 1 BCLC 38; and *Warley Continental Services Ltd v Johal* [2002] All ER (D) 224.

6 See IR 1986, r 12.9(2), which imports CPR, r 3.1(2)(a) into IR 1986 'so as to enable the court to extend or shorten the time for compliance with anything required or authorised to be done by the Rules'.

7 [1998] BPIR 183; a decision in July 1997, ie when the Rules of the Supreme Court rather than CPR were in force, but RSC Ord 3, r 5 was in equivalent terms to CPR r 3.2(2)(a).

8 See the observations of Carnwath J in *Plant v Plant* [1998] 1 BCLC 38 at 54, where he refused to say that the decision in *Tager v Westpac Banking Corpn* [1997] BPIR 543 (see below) was 'plainly wrong' while noting the policy arguments for treating the time limit as absolute.

9 [1997] BPIR 543.
10 [1997] BPIR 543 at 555; the guidelines are those suggested in *C M Van Stillevoldt BV v E L Carriers Inc* [1983] 1 WLR 207, CA.
11 [1999] BPIR 206.
12 [2002] All ER (D) 224 (Oct), (2002) Times, 28 October.
13 Although it cannot count for much that a warning is given within 28 days but no application is made within that time; it is of the essence of the short time period that all parties may treat a decision on a proposed voluntary arrangement as final 28 days after report to the court.
14 *Re Debtors (Nos VA 7 and 8), ex p Stevens* [1996] BPIR 101.
15 IA 1986, s 6(3)(b) (CVA without moratorium), Sch A1, para 38(3)(b) (CVA with moratorium), s 262(3)(b) (IVA).
16 IA 1986, s 6(3) (CVA without moratorium), Sch A1 para 38(3) (CVA with moratorium), s 262(3) (IVA). A voluntary arrangement comes to an end prematurely if, when it ceases to have effect, it has not been fully implemented in respect of all persons bound by the arrangement, IA 1986, s 7B (all CVAs), s 262C (IVA), as added by IA 2000.

7.9 Powers of the court on an application. Where the court is satisfied that either of the two grounds on which a challenge may be brought[1] is established it may do one or both of the following:

(a) revoke or suspend any approval given by the meeting;
(b) give a direction to any person for the summoning of a further meeting of the debtor's creditors, and in CVA of the company, to consider any revised proposal the debtor may make or, in a case of material irregularity, to reconsider the original proposal[2].

Although satisfied that one or both grounds of the application are made out, the court may conclude that no good purpose is served in summoning another meeting, for example, because of the implacable attitude of sufficient creditors, and refuse to give a direction under (b) above[3]. In considering whether or not to summon a further meeting the court should carry out a balancing exercise between the seriousness and the heinousness of the irregularity and the likely attitude of the other creditors[4]. Where the debtor wishes to put forward a revised proposal similar principles apply as with the original proposal; the court should not direct a further meeting unless there will be a serious and viable proposal, that is one with a reasonable prospect of approval and implementation, to put before the creditors[5]. In an appropriate case the court may direct that the applicant is not bound by the arrangement[6]. In IVA where the court makes a direction under (b) above, it may also give a direction continuing or, as appropriate, renewing the effect of any interim order relating to the debtor[7]. In most cases it will be advisable, if not essential, to renew the interim order pending the holding of the further meeting.

In the event that the court is satisfied that there is no intention on the part of the directors (or officer-holder) in CVA or the individual debtor in IVA to submit a revised proposal, or resubmit the original proposal, it must revoke the direction summoning a further meeting and revoke or suspend any approval given at the previous meeting[8].

The court has power to give supplemental directions as it may think fit in any case where it revokes or suspends an approval[9] or gives a direction under (b) above. In particular, such directions may relate to (i) things done under the voluntary arrangement since it took effect[10], and (ii) things done since the voluntary arrangement took effect as could not have been done if a moratorium or an interim order had been in force in relation to the debtor when they were done[11]. This power enables the court by direction to validate acts carried out under the voluntary arrangement, particularly by the supervisor, which when the arrangement is revoked or suspended may leave the supervisor or other person exposed to civil suit who thought at the time that he acted that he had the necessary authority. Similarly, the court may invalidate acts which would not have been permitted under the interim order. In either case third parties may be involved. There is no express provision in the rules requiring third parties who may be affected by any directions made to be given notice of the hearing, but the court will presumably wish to hear any third parties involved, especially where the effect of the directions may be final. An applicant who intends to seek such directions would be well advised to notify any potentially interested third party.

Further meetings summoned by direction of the court. Both in CVA with a moratorium and in IVA the statute is drafted so as to give a right of challenge to a voluntary arrangement approved by the original meetings or creditors' meeting[12]. On a strict interpretation a further meeting of creditors (and a company meeting in CVA) summoned on the court's direction would not come within this wording. A decision of this further meeting might therefore not be susceptible to challenge under IA 1986, Sch A1, para 38(1) or s 262. It would be advisable for the court when directing a further meeting to give a general liberty to apply which would enable the debtor, nominee or any creditor entitled to vote at the meeting to challenge any decision of the further meeting on either of the grounds specified in IA 1986, Sch A1, para 38(1) or s 262 as appropriate.

1 See para 7.1 above.
2 IA 1986, s 6(4) (CVA without moratorium), Sch A1, para 38(4) (CVA with moratorium), s 262(4) (IVA).
3 *Re a Debtor (No 83 of 1988)* [1990] 1 All ER 949, [1990] 1 WLR 707.
4 *IRC v Duce* [1999] BPIR 189 at 201.
5 *Re a Debtor (No 101 of 1999) (No 2)* [2001] BPIR 996, where the debtor whose IVA had been set aside on the application of the crown debtors (see para 7.3 above) then proposed that the original fund, which after depletion had fallen to £3,100 should be shared equally among the creditors whose debts amounted to £541,000. The court refused to direct a further meeting assuming that a vote in favour could only be achieved by friends voting through motives of friendship or through a wish that the debtor, a racehorse trainer, would continue to train their horses; ie a collateral matter which would not apply to the minority (Crown) creditors.
6 *Re Cranley Mansions Ltd* [1994] 1 WLR 1610 (no entitlement to vote).
7 IA 1986, s 262(6): 'for such period as may be specified in the direction.' The court has therefore a complete discretion as to how long the interim order will be extended but will doubtless wish to set a tight timetable bearing in mind the short time (14 days) allowed for an interim order by IA 1986, s 255(6) when first granted.
8 IA 1986, s 6(5) (CVA without moratorium), Sch A1, para 38(5) (CVA with moratorium), s 262(5) (IVA).
9 Whether under IA 1986, s 6(4)(a) or s 6(5) (CVA without moratorium), Sch A1, para 38(4)(a) or (5) (CVA with moratorium), s 262(4)(a) or s 262(5) (IVA).
10 In IVA 'things done since the meeting under any voluntary arrangement approved by the meeting': IA 1986, s 262(7)(a).
11 IA 1986, s 6(6) (CVA without moratorium), Sch A1, para 38(8) (CVA with moratorium), s 262(7) (IVA).
12 IA 1986, Sch A1, para 38(1) (CVA with moratorium), IA 1986, s 262(1) (IVA); in a CVA without moratorium different wording is used; the challenge is to a voluntary arrangement which takes effect under IA 1986, s 4A.

7.10 Procedure on application. An application to challenge the approval of the arrangement or any decision of the creditors' meeting is made by ordinary application in Form 7.2[1]. Where the application is on the grounds that the arrangement unfairly prejudices the interests of the applicant creditor, the nominee and other creditors should not ordinarily[2] be made respondents to the application (although it is advisable to give the nominee notice) and they should not be ordered to pay the costs[3]. The application is heard by the registrar or district judge in chambers, although in difficult cases it may be adjourned to the judge in open court.

Evidence is given on affidavit, subject to the court's direction that deponents attend for cross examination[4]. It should be borne in mind that in the absence of cross examination of the deponent the court may feel bound to accept the affidavit evidence of the witness[5]. The practice and procedure of the High Court applies with regard to the form, contents and procedure governing the use of affidavits[6]. Accordingly, affidavits may contain hearsay evidence[7], and service of the affidavit will constitute compliance with the notice requirements of the Civil Evidence Act 1995, s 2(1)[8]. An applicant may seek orders for further information[9] and disclosure[10]. The fact that documents have been released to the supervisor did not mean that the documents were in the public domain and accordingly available to applicants seeking to challenge the arrangements[11].

In determining disputes concerning the decisions of the chairman of the creditors' meeting the court is not confined to the evidence that was before the chairman at the meeting, but is entitled to consider whatever evidence on the issue the parties to the appeal choose to place before the court[12].

The nominee acts as agent for the debtor and the costs of a successful application will be paid out of the debtor's estate unless there has been some personal conduct on the part of the nominee which would justify an order for costs against him[13]. Where the ground of application is that there was a material irregularity at the meeting for which the nominee as chairman was responsible and the application is brought together with an appeal against his decision on a creditor's entitlement to vote[14], the chairman is not protected from an order for costs by reason of the provision in the rules that an order for costs cannot be made against the chairman's decision on voting rights[15]. Where the chairman acts in good faith, albeit in error, no order for costs will be made against him[16].

Where a court makes an order revoking or suspending the voluntary arrangement the applicant is required to serve sealed copies of the order on (i) (in CVA) the directors, liquidator or administrator (according to who made the proposal), or (in IVA) the debtor, and, if the debtor is in an undischarged bankrupt, the trustee and official receiver, and (ii) the supervisor of the voluntary arrangement[17]. The applicant must also serve notice of the order, if the court directs that a further creditors' meeting be held, (iii) on the person required to summon that meeting[18], and (iv) within seven days, on the registrar of companies (CVA) or the Secretary of State (IVA) [19]. The directors or individual debtor[20] are responsible for notifying all persons who were sent notice of the creditors' meeting which approve the arrangement or who appear to be affected by the order[21]. The debtor must also within seven days of receiving the order (or within such longer period as the court may allow) give notice to the court whether it is intended to make a revised proposal to creditors or to invite re-consideration of the original proposal[22].

1 IR 1986, r 7.2(1). This is the usual procedure. It is, however, arguable that at this stage there are no pending proceedings before the court, and so the application should be made by originating application in Form 7.1: IR 1986, r 7.2(1).

2 It is a different matter if misconduct is alleged against the nominee or another creditor.

3 *Re Naeem (a bankrupt) (No 18 of 1988)* [1990] 1 WLR 48 at 51, where Hoffman J observed that it was convenient that the nominee be given notice of the application but that it was not necessary for that purpose that he be made a respondent.

4 See eg *Re a Debtor (No 87 of 1993) (No 2)* [1996] 1 BCLC 63 at 73.

5 See eg *Re a Debtor (No 574 of 1995)* [1998] 2 BCLC 124, sub nom *National Westminster Bank v Scher* [1998] BPIR 224.
6 IR 1986, r 7.57, which has not been amended to allow witness statements.
7 Note that the decision in *Re A Debtor (No 87 of 1993) (No 1)* [1996] 1 BCLC 55 (hearsay not permitted as the court's decision on an application under IA 1986, s 262 is a final one and not an interlocutory one) was reached before the passing of the Civil Evidence Act 1995.
8 CPR Part 33.2(1). The CPR, save where inconsistent with IA 1986, apply to insolvency proceedings by virtue of IR 1986, r 7.51.
9 IR 1986, r 7.60, 'in accordance with CPR Part 18'.
10 IR 1986, r 7.60, and see *Re Primlaks (UK) Ltd (No 2)* [1990] BCLC 234 at 240-241 where disclosure was ordered so as to enable the creditor to know the facts of the transactions which he asserted were unfairly prejudicial toward him, the onus being on him to demonstrate that he had suffered prejudice, and that this was unfair to him individually.
11 *Plant v Plant* [1998] BPIR 243.
12 *Re a Company (No 4539 of 1993)* [1995] BCC 116; *Re a Debtor (No 574 of 1995)* [1998] 2 BCLC 124, sub nom *National Westminster Bank v Scher* [1998] BPIR 224.
13 *Re Naeem (A Bankrupt) (No 18 of 1988)* [1990] 1 WLR 48.
14 Under IR 1986, rr 1.17, 1.17A (CVA without moratorium), rr 1.49, 1.50 (CVA with moratorium), rr 5.21, 5.22 (IVA): see para 6.8 above.
15 See IR 1986, r 1.17A(7) (CVA without moratorium), r 1.50 (7) (CVA with moratorium), r 5.22(7) (IVA) and *Re a Debtor (No 222 of 1990)* [1992] BCLC 137 and, on costs, *Re a Debtor (No 222 of 1990) (No 2)* [1993] BCLC 233, where the chairman, whose refusal to allow substantial creditors to vote was the cause of the appeals, was ordered to pay one-half the standard costs of the appellants, the balance falling on the debtor who had resisted the appeals.
16 *Re Cranley Mansions Ltd* [1995] 1 BCLC 290 at 314–315.
17 IR 1986, r 1.25(2) (all CVAs, r 1.25 applying where a moratorium is in force by virtue of r 1.54), r 5.30(2) (IVA).
18 IR 1986, r 1.25(3) (all CVAs), r 5.30(3) (IVA).
19 IR 1986, r 1.25(5) (all CVAs), r 5.30(5) (IVA).
20 Or, where appropriate, the liquidator or administrator in CVA or in the case of an undischarged bankrupt the trustee or official receiver where no trustee.
21 IR 1986, r 1.25(4)(a) (all CVAs), r 5.30(4)(a) (IVA).
22 IR 1986, r 1.25(4)(b) (all CVAs), r 5.30(4)(b) (IVA).

7.11 Review by the court of its orders. Every court having jurisdiction to wind up companies or in bankruptcy may review, rescind or vary any order made by it in the exercise of its jurisdiction[1]. This power, which is unique to courts with an insolvency jurisdiction, applies to orders made in applications and appeals relating to voluntary arrangement matters. In the 1986 legislation the power is in almost identical terms to the provisions of previous Bankruptcy Acts[2], applied also in liquidation, but it now forms part of an insolvency regime with a very different philosophy from that of earlier times and rules established in earlier case law will not be followed unless justified under the present regime[3]. The power to review an order should be exercised with caution and only in exceptional circumstances[4]. It is a jurisdiction which may be exercised where events since the making of the order have rendered its terms inappropriate or where there is further evidence to put before the court in the light of which the court would not wish the original order to stand; the further evidence may relate to matters in existence at the time of the original order[5]. There is no restriction on the admission of fresh evidence on a review, which will give the review procedure an advantage over an appeal[6], but the admission of new evidence remains a matter of discretion[7]. Ordinarily, the review should be conducted by the same judge who made the order under review, but another judge of co-ordinate jurisdiction has power to conduct the review[8]. Where a decision has been arrived at after full argument, another judge of co-ordinate jurisdiction should not substitute his own decision save in the most exceptional circumstances[9]. It appears that a High Court judge may review an order made by the registrar. In *S N Group plc*[10] the vacation judge refused to review a winding-up order made by the registrar on the ground, amongst others, that the rôle of the High Court judge was restricted to an appellate function. However, in *Re Dollar Land (Feltham) Ltd*[11] the registrar's winding-up order was rescinded by the High Court judge without expressly considering the question of jurisdiction, and in *Re Piccadilly Property Management Ltd*[12] the deputy judge having addressed the point concluded that he did have jurisdiction to review the decision of an inferior court. He emphasised that a party seeking a review should ordinarily do so from the same judge or a judge of co-ordinate jurisdiction. Only rarely would it be proper to seek a review in a superior court and 'double-barrelled appeals-cum-applications to review' were to be firmly discouraged. There is no time limit for an application for a review, but if the application is in substance to be regarded as an appeal and is issued at a date when, if it had been an appeal, it would have been out of time, the court will not exercise its jurisdiction, unless satisfied that there are special circumstances which would make it proper to hear it, treating it as an appeal out of time[13].

1 IR 1986, r 7.47 (companies), IA 1986, s 375 (bankruptcy).
2 Bankruptcy Act 1869, s 71; Bankruptcy Act 1883, s 104(1); Bankruptcy Act 1914, s 108(1).
3 *Fitch v Official Receiver* [1996] 1 WLR 242 at 246, 248–249.
4 *Fitch v Official Receiver* [1996] 1 WLR 242; *Re Thirty-Eight Building Ltd (in liquidation) (No 2)* [2000] 1 BCLC 201.
5 *Re Dollar Land (Feltham) Ltd* [1995] 2 BCLC 370; *Re Piccadilly Property Management Ltd* [1999] 2 BCLC 145.
6 Although with the introduction of CPR the rules relating to the admission of fresh evidence on appeal have been relaxed to the extent that previous restrictions now represent principles rather than rules: *Hertfordshire Investments v Bubb* [2000] 1 WLR 2318 at 2325; see also *Lombard Natwest Factors Ltd v Arbis* [2000] BPIR 79.
7 *Re a Debtor (No 32-SD-1991)* [1993] 1 WLR 314.
8 *Mond v Hammond Suddards* [2000] Ch 40, CA.
9 *Re RS & M Engineering Co Ltd* [1999] 2 BCLC 485, CA.
10 [1994] 1 BCLC 319.
11 [1995] 2 BCLC 370.
12 [1999] 2 BCLC 145.
13 *Re Cohen* [1950] 2 All ER 36 at 39, CA.

7.12 Appeals. In voluntary arrangements, whether company or individual, decisions on procedural and substantive questions may be made in the county court by district judges or circuit judges, or in the High Court by registrars or judges of the High Court. From a decision of a county court, whether made by a district judge or a circuit judge, and from a decision of a company or bankruptcy registrar an appeal lies to a single judge of the High Court[1]. Such an appeal is referred to in the *Practice Direction: Insolvency Proceedings* as a 'first appeal'. No permission is required to make such an appeal[2].

Decisions by judges of the High Court in the exercise of their insolvency jurisdiction fall into two categories: (1) decisions made on appeals from a county court or a registrar (decisions made on a first appeal); or (2) original decisions made at first instance. From a decision made by a judge of the High Court on a first appeal, a further appeal to the Court of Appeal may be made only with the permission of the Court of Appeal[3]. An appeal from a decision of a judge of the High Court may be made to the Court of Appeal with the permission of that judge or the Court of Appeal[4].

The procedure and practice of the Supreme Court relating to appeals to the Court of Appeal applies to appeals in insolvency proceedings[5]. This procedure and practice is now contained in CPR Pt 52 and its Practice Direction, which need to be read in conjunction with the *Practice Direction: Insolvency Proceedings* para 17[6].

1 IR 1986, r 7.47(2) (CVA), IA 1986, s 375(2), IR 1986, r 7.48(2) (IVA).
2 *Practice Direction : Insolvency Proceedings* para 17.6.
3 IR 1986, r 7.47(2) (CVA), IA 1986, s 375(2), IR 1986, r 7.48(2) (IVA), as amended by the Access to Justice Act 1999, s 55, *Practice Direction: Insolvency Proceedings* para 17.3(1).
4 CPR 52.3; *Practice Direction: Insolvency Proceedings* para 17.3(2).
5 IR 1986, r 7.49(1).
6 See Appendix 6.

Chapter 8
Criminal liability in connection with voluntary arrangements

8.1 Acting as nominee or supervisor without qualification. As has been seen, a debtor may not proceed with a proposal for a voluntary arrangement without a nominee, and, once approved, no voluntary arrangement may be implemented except under the control of a supervisor. Only a person who is qualified to act as an insolvency practitioner or is authorised to act as nominee in relation to a voluntary arrangement may act as nominee[1] or a supervisor[2]. Qualification may be obtained through membership of a recognised professional body[3], or by authorisation by a competent authority, at present only the Secretary of State[4]. A person who acts as an insolvency practitioner in relation to a company or an individual at a time when he is not qualified to do so is liable to imprisonment or a fine or to both[5]. EA 2002 extends authority to act as a nominee or supervisor to the official receiver but only in respect of IVAs made by an undischarged bankrupt[6]. The official receiver does not, however, commit an offence if he does act as an insolvency practitioner when not authorised to do so[7].

1 IA 1986, s 1(2) (CVA with or without moratorium), s 253(2) (IVA).
2 IA 1986, s 388(1)(b), s389(1) (CVA with or without moratorium); s 388(2)(c), s 389(1) (IVA); s 388(2A)(c), s 389(1) (PVA).
3 IA 1986, s 391; and see Insolvency Practitioners (Recognised Professional Bodies) Order 1986, SI 1986/1764; the professional bodies which have been recognised are: the Chartered Association of Certified Accountants; the Insolvency Practitioners Association; the Institute of Chartered Accountants in England and Wales; and the Law Society.
4 IA 1986, s 392. For the requirements for authorisation, see Insolvency Practitioners Regulations 1990, SI 1990/439, as amended.
5 IA 1986, s 389(1). On indictment the maximum term is two years' imprisonment and or unlimited fine; on summary conviction the maximum term is six months and or the statutory maximum fine in a magistrates' court. IA 1986, s 389(1) does not apply to a person who while not an insolvency practitioner has been authorised to act as a nominee or supervisor to a voluntary arrangement: IA 1986, s 389A.
6 IA 1986, s 389B(1). The Secretary of State may extend this authority to all IVAs by statutory instrument: s 389B(2), (3)
7 IA 1986, s 389(2).

8.2 Criminal liability in the course of a moratorium. IA 1986 creates a number of offences designed to ensure that the technical requirements of the moratorium provisions are complied with by the directors[1], other officers of the company, and the nominee. Plainly, there must be a sanction where a statutory requirement is not followed. Parliament instinctively thinks in terms of the criminal law, while being reluctant to provide the funds necessary to monitor and enforce it. It may be that personal liability on the part of company officers to creditors who are prejudiced by a failure of such officers to comply with the technical requirements of the law would in some instances prove a more effective and appropriate sanction, but that is not the traditional approach of Parliament. The various offences which may be committed in the course of a moratorium have been noted where appropriate in the text, but they are listed here for convenience with a note of the maximum punishment which, under IA 1986, Sch 10, may be imposed on offenders on conviction:

1. Directors failing without reasonable excuse to notify the nominee of the beginning of the moratorium[2]: on indictment two years or a fine or both, summarily six months or the statutory maximum fine[3], or both.
2. Nominee failing without reasonable excuse to advertise or notify the beginning of the moratorium[4]: summary only, one-fifth of the statutory maximum.
3. Nominee failing without reasonable excuse to advertise or notify end of moratorium[5]: summary only, one-fifth of the statutory maximum.
4. Failure by the company or its officers (without reasonable excuse) to state in an invoice, order for goods or business correspondence that a moratorium is in force[6]: summary only, one-fifth of the statutory maximum.
5. Company obtaining credit without disclosing the existence of a moratorium[7]: on indictment a fine, summarily the statutory maximum fine.
6. Officer of company knowingly and wilfully authorising or permitting the obtaining of credit for the company without disclosing the existence of a moratorium[8]: on indictment two years or a fine or both, summarily six months or the statutory maximum fine, or both.
7. Company disposing of property otherwise than in the ordinary way of business without belief it will benefit the company and without approval of the nominee or moratorium committee[9]: on indictment a fine, summarily the statutory maximum fine.
8. Officer of company without reasonable excuse authorising or permitting disposal of company property otherwise than in ordinary way of business without belief it will benefit the company and without approval of the nominee or moratorium committee[10]: on indictment two years or a fine or both, summarily six months or the statutory maximum fine, or both.
9. Company making payments in respect of liabilities in existence before the beginning of moratorium without belief it will benefit the company and without approval of the nominee or moratorium committee[11]: on indictment a fine, summarily the statutory maximum fine.
10. Officer of company without reasonable excuse authorising or permitting payment of pre-existing liability without belief it will benefit the company and without approval of the nominee or moratorium committee[12]: on indictment two years or a fine or both, summarily six months or the statutory maximum fine, or both.
11. Failure by the directors without reasonable excuse to send the registrar of companies the office copy of the court order permitting disposal of charged property[13]: summarily only, one-fifth of the statutory maximum fine.
12. Company without leave disposing of any property subject to a security otherwise than in accordance with the terms of that security or disposing of any goods held under a hire-purchase agreement otherwise than in

accordance with the terms of that agreement[14]: on indictment a fine, summarily the statutory maximum fine.

13. Officer of company without reasonable excuse authorising or permitting a disposal by the company of secured property or hire-purchase goods as in 12 above[15]: on indictment two years or a fine or both, summarily six months or the statutory maximum fine, or both.
14. Company entering into a market contract or any other transaction specified in IA 1986, Sch A1, para 23(2) [16]: on indictment a fine, summarily the statutory maximum fine.
15. Officer of company authorising or permitting the company to enter into a transaction as in 14 above without reasonable excuse[17]: on indictment two years or a fine or both, summarily six months or the statutory maximum fine, or both.
16. Nominee failing without reasonable excuse to give notice of withdrawal of consent to act[18]: summarily only, one-fifth of the statutory maximum fine.
17. Nominee failing without reasonable excuse to give notice of extension of moratorium[19]: summarily only, one-fifth of the statutory maximum fine.

In PVA no criminal liability falls on an insolvent partnership in circumstances where a company may be criminally liable[20]. However, an officer of an insolvent partnership may be liable in the same manner as an officer of a company[21]. For the purposes of criminal liability in connection with PVA generally, including under IA 1986, Sch 10 (as above), (a) references to directors or members of a company are to be construed as references to the members of an insolvent partnership, and (b) references to officers of a company as references to officers of an insolvent partnership[22].

1 'Director' includes any person occupying the position of director, by whatever name called, IA 1986, s 251.
2 IA 1986, Sch A1, para 9(2); see para 3.6 above
3 The statutory maximum fine is at present £5,000: Criminal Justice Act 1982, s 37.
4 IA 1986, Sch A1, para 10(3); see para 3.6 above
5 IA 1986, Sch A1, para 11(2); see para 3.6 above
6 IA 1986, Sch A1, para 16(2); see para 3.8 above
7 IA 1986, Sch A1, para 17(3)(a); see para 3.8 above.
8 IA 1986, Sch A1, para 17(3)(b); see para 3.8 above.
9 IA 1986, Sch A1, para 18(3)(a); see para 3.9 above.
10 IA 1986, Sch A1, para 18(3)(b); see para 3.9 above.
11 IA 1986, Sch A1, para 19(3)(a); see para 3.9 above.
12 IA 1986, Sch A1, para 19(3)(b); see para 3.9 above.
13 IA 1986, Sch A1, para 20(9); see para 3.9 above.
14 IA 1986, Sch A1, para 22(1); see para 3.9 above.
15 IA 1986, Sch A1, para 22(2); see para 3.9 above.
16 IA 1986, Sch A1, para 23(1)(a); see para 3.8 above.
17 IA 1986, Sch A1, para 23(1)(b); see para 3.8 above.
18 IA 1986, Sch A1, para 25(6); see para 3.11 above.
19 IA 1986, Sch A1, para 34(3); see para 3.16 above.
20 IA 1986, s 1A(5) as added by the Insolvent Partnership (Amendment) Order 2002, SI 2002/2708 ('IPO 2002').
21 IA 1986, s 1A(6), as added by IPO 2002.
22 IA 1986, s 1A(7), as added by IPO 2002.

8.3 Criminal activity in connection with a moratorium. IA 2000 creates a wide range of criminal offences to cover possible impropriety in the obtaining of a moratorium and the management of the company's affairs while under the protection of a moratorium.

Obtaining a moratorium. An offence[1] is committed by any person who is an officer[2] of the company who either (a) makes any false representation, or (b) fraudulently does, or omits to do, anything for the purpose of obtaining a moratorium, or an extension of a moratorium[3]. The offence may be committed even if in the event no moratorium or extension is obtained[4].

Offences by officers relating to a moratorium. The following activities by any person who is an officer[5] of the company constitute criminal offences, whether they are committed during the moratorium or during the period of 12 months immediately preceding the moratorium[6]:

(a) concealing any part of the company's property to the value of £500[7] or more, or concealing any debt due to or from the company;
(b) fraudulently removing any part of the company's property to the value of £500 or more;
(c) concealing, destroying, mutilating or falsifying any book or paper affecting or relating to the company's property or affairs;
(d) making any false entry in any book or paper affecting or relating to the company's property or affairs;
(e) fraudulently parting with, altering or making any omission in any document affecting or relating to the company's property or affairs;
(f) pawning, pledging or disposing of any property of the company which has been obtained on credit and has not been paid for, unless the pawning, pledging or disposal was in the ordinary way of the company's business[8].

An officer of the company also commits an offence if he is privy to the doing by others of any of the activities referred to in (c), (d) or (e) above whether in the 12 months immediately preceding the moratorium[9] or during the moratorium[10].

Offences by others relating to a moratorium. An offence is committed by any person who takes in pawn or pledge or otherwise receives property of the company knowing it to be pawned, pledged or disposed of in circumstances which would amount to offence if a moratorium were obtained for the company within 12 months of the date of pawn, pledge or disposal[11].

Defences. For a person charged in respect of activities comprised in (a) or (f) above it is a defence to prove that he had no intent to defraud, and in respect of activities comprised in (c) or (d) that he had no intent to conceal the state of affairs of the company or to defeat the law[12], the defence of 'innocent intention'[13]. It may be noted that the offences to which this defence is not provided, ie (b) and (e) above, involve an element of fraud. Accordingly, the prosecution would have to prove the necessary fraudulent intent on the part of any accused who is to be convicted of the crime.

A person guilty of any of the above offences is liable to imprisonment or a fine or both[14].

1 Punishable by imprisonment or a fine or both: IA 1986, Sch A1, para 42(4).
2 'Officer' includes a shadow director: IA 1986, Sch A1, para 42(5). A 'shadow director' meaning a person in accordance with whose directions or instructions the directors of a company are accustomed to act (but excluding professional advisers): IA 1986, s 251.
3 IA 1986, Sch A1, para 42(1).
4 IA 1986, Sch A1, para 42(2).
5 IA 1986, Sch A1, para 41(5).
6 IA 1986, Sch A1, para 41(1), (2), (3).
7 The monetary amount in these offences may be increased or reduced by order of the Secretary of State under IA 1986, s 417A, Sch A1, para 41(9); IA 1986, s 417A is inserted by IA 2000, Sch 1, para 10.

8 IA 1986, Sch A1, para 41(4).
9 IA 1986, Sch A1, para 41(2)(b).
10 IA 1986, Sch A1, para 41(3)(b).
11 IA 1986, Sch A1, para 41(7).
12 IA 1986, Sch A1, para 41(6).
13 See para 8.4 below.
14 IA 1986, Sch A1, para 41(8). The maximum sentence the court may impose on conviction on indictment is seven years' imprisonment or a fine or both; six months' imprisonment or the statutory maximum fine or both on summary conviction: see IA 1986, Sch 10, as amended by IA 2000, Sch 1, para 12.

8.4 Defence of innocent intention. With respect to certain of the offences which may be committed by officers of the company or others during the 12 months immediately preceding or during the moratorium there is available the statutory defence of innocent intention. This replicates the defence available in certain offences which may be committed in anticipation of a winding-up[1] or to offences which may be committed by the bankrupt before or after bankruptcy[2]. The wording of the defence: 'It is a defence for a person charged [with an offence] to prove that he had no intent to defraud'[3] or 'to prove that he had no intent to conceal the state of affairs of the company or to defeat the law'[4] suggests that the burden of proof in relation to any dishonesty involved in the mens rea of the offence is transferred to the accused. The offences excepted from this defence are all offences which incorporate a specific dishonest mens rea element requiring the prosecution to prove dishonesty before the offence is made out. It remains a vexed question whether the transfer of the burden of proof in relation to the dishonesty element of the offence is permissible after the enactment of the Human Rights Act 1998.

1 See IA 1986, s 206(4).
2 IA 1986, s 352 .
3 IA 1986, Sch A1, para 41(6)(a), ie no intent to conceal or dispose of property (a) and (f) in para 8.3 above.
4 IA 1986, Sch A1, para 41(6)(b), ie no intent with respect to concealing or making false entries in books or papers, (c) and (d) in para 8.3 above.

8.5 The impact of the Human Rights Act 1998 on the defence of innocent intention. In the absence of the HRA 1998 the combined effect of the offence and the defence in IA 1986, Sch A1, para 41(4) and (5) is that the burden of proof is reversed on an essential element of the offence requiring the accused to prove lack of fraud or dishonesty[1]. The prosecution must first prove, beyond reasonable doubt, the elements of the offence with which the accused is charged. If he wishes to rely on the defence of innocent intention the accused then has to discharge a persuasive not merely an evidential burden of proof by showing on a balance of probabilities[2] that he had no intent to defraud or to conceal the state of the company's affairs[3]. The alternative construction is that the words 'for a person to prove' may be read as meaning 'for a person to adduce sufficient evidence to show'. This makes a considerable difference, at least in theory. The accused is required only to put evidence before the court which, if believed, could be taken by a reasonable jury to be a defence to the charge[4]; the legal or persuasive burden of proof remains on the prosecution to show that the defence is not made out. 'The weight of judicial authority … [immediately before the coming into force of HRA 1998] favoured the long established and conventional approach identified by Lord Clyde in *Lambert*', namely that the accused faced a persuasive or legal burden of proof to make good his defence, albeit at the lesser standard applicable where a burden of proof rests with an accused[5].

Article 6(2) of the European Convention on Human Rights provides that everyone charged with a criminal offence shall be presumed innocent until proved guilty according to law. Although drafted in apparently absolute terms, it has been held that the right under Art 6(2) does not prohibit rules which transfer the burden to the accused to establish a defence, provided that the overall burden of proof remains on the prosecution[6]. Nevertheless, there must be a strong argument that following the introduction of Convention rights into English law under the provisions of the HRA 1998 the common law position should be reversed, with the burden on the accused becoming only an evidential burden with a persuasive burden to disprove the defence remaining with the prosecution.

Within the context of insolvency the Court of Appeal has held that this is indeed now the position. In *R v Carass*[7] the court was concerned with the similarly worded defence in the provisions relating to the concealment of company debts in anticipation of a winding up, deeming concealment an offence subject to the accused proving that he had no intent to defraud. Waller LJ, giving the judgment of the court, stated that although the prosecution had to prove concealment of a debt, it would be unrealistic to argue that an intent to defraud was not an important element of the offence. The court saw the decision of the House of Lords in *Lambert*[8] as being that although it might be possible to justify imposing a legal or persuasive burden on the accused in appropriate cases, the onus is on those seeking to persuade the court that this is necessary in any particular case and is a high one. In the case of an offence of concealing company debts in anticipation of a winding up the court did not see that it was necessary to impose a persuasive burden on the accused and therefore determined that the burden imposed by the defence of innocent intention was evidential only. In its judgment the court stated that the relevant statutory provision should be read as if drafted as follows:

> 'It is a defence for a person charged under [paragraph (a) ...] to adduce evidence sufficient to raise an issue that he had no intent to defraud, unless, if he does so, the prosecution proves the contrary beyond reasonable doubt.'

This re-wording would apply equally to offences in connection with a moratorium.

1 See *R v Anthony Lala Daniel* [2002] EWCA Crim 959, [2003] 1 Cr App Rep 99 at [15]; the Court of Appeal was there considering the defence of innocent intention in bankruptcy: IA 1986, s 352.
2 *R v Carr-Briant* [1943] KB 607.
3 See *R v Lambert* [2001] UKHL 37, [2002] 2 AC 545 at [132] (Lord Clyde); a decision on guilty knowledge in cases arising under the Misuse of Drugs Act 1971.
4 See eg *R v Lambert* [2001] UKHL 37, [2002] 2 AC 545 at [90] (Lord Hope).
5 Per Auld LJ in *R v Anthony Lala Daniel* [2002] EWCA Crim 959 at [20].
6 *Brown v Stott* [2001] 2 WLR 817 at 825, citing *Salabiaku v France* (1988) 13 EHRR 379 at 388 (para 28).
7 [2001] EWCA Crim 4788, [2002] Crim LR 316.
8 [2001] [2001] UKHL 37, [2002] 2 AC 545.

8. 6 The alternative view: the accused's burden to make good the defence. In *R v Anthony Daniel*[1] the Court of Appeal accepted that the nature of the offence and reverse burden of proof defence in IA 1986, s 206 was sufficiently similar in form and purpose to that in IA 1986, s 354 and s 352 respectively (the defendant there being charged with concealing a debt which he was required to deliver up to the official receiver) as to make the context and the reasoning indistinguishable. The court therefore held that it was bound by the reasoning in *Carass*. In the event, however, the offence and the trial in *Daniel* pre-dated the coming into force of HRA 1998 and the appeal turned on the pre-HRA 1998 law[2]. The court's consideration of the effect of HRA 1998 and its being bound by *Carass* was obiter. Nevertheless, the court[3] delivered itself of strong views in opposition to those expressed in *Carass*. Quoting the words of Lord Devlin in *Jayasena v R*[4] to the effect that the phrase 'evidential burden of proof' was meaningless except as a convenient way of describing a requirement that a party adduce some evidence in support of his case on any particular issue before that issue is left to the jury, the court suggested the words of the statutory defence '[an accused] is not guilty if he proves'[5] or 'it is a defence for the [accused] to prove'[6] must, 'as a matter of plain English', mean more than the evidential raising of an issue for the prosecution to refute beyond reasonable doubt[7]. While noting that the courts are required, by HRA 1998, s 3(1), to strive for compatibility through the medium of interpretation the court stated that:

> 'where there is plain incompatibility between the ordinary and natural meaning of statutory words *whatever the context* and Art 6(2), the court should take care not to strive for compatibility by so changing the meaning of those words as to give them a sense that they cannot, in the sense intended by section 3(1), *possibly* bear[8].'

The court suggested that the distinction between what are *procedural* guarantees in Art 6(2) and the *substantive* elements of the offence has not been clearly made, quoting with apparent approval the suggestion[9] that Art 6(2) has no bearing on substantive law requirements. Accordingly, reversing the burden of proof on elements of the offence and even offences of strict or absolute liability would not be contrary to the accused's Art 6(2) Convention right.

This is a good example of the divergence of views which will inevitably arise on the extent to which courts should rewrite statutory provisions which are, or may be considered to be, incompatible with Convention rights. The court in *Carass* faced the problem squarely and actually provided the text for the rewritten statute. The court in *Daniel* considered that incompatibility, where it exists, should be acknowledged; the court should not be driven by an imperative to find compatibility at all costs. In the present case it may be that on a proper interpretation of Art 6(2) (ie providing a procedural guarantee only) there is no incompatibility at all. Regrettably, it seems unlikely that the House of Lords will agree, and that when the matter reaches the Lords, their Lordships, having found incompatibility, will prefer the *Carass* approach. It is hoped that any feeling that juries may find reverse burdens of proof difficult to understand and implement will play no part in the eventual determination of this issue. The experience of many charged with explaining such matters to juries suggests that most jurors readily comprehend the imposition of different burdens and standards of proof to different issues which fall for their determination.

1 [2002] EWCA Crim 959, [2003] 1 Cr App Rep 99.
2 The 1998 Act is not retrospective so as to enable an appellant convicted before its implementation to rely on incompatibility under HRA 1998, s 6 or to require an appellate court to apply HRA 1998, s 3(1) and read the statute compatibly with the right in Art 6(2) presuming innocence until proved guilty according to law: see *R v Lambert* [2001] UKHL 37, [2002] 2 AC 545; *R v Kansal (No 2)* [2001] UKHL 62, [2002] 2 AC 69; and *R v Benjafield* [2002] 2 WLR 234.
3 Auld LJ gave the judgment of the court, the other members being Newman J and Roderick Evans J.
4 [1970] AC 618 at 624C–E, PC, 'seemingly not cited in *Lambert*'.
5 IA 1986, s 352.
6 IA 1986, s 206(4) and Sch A1, para 41(6).
7 *R v Anthony Daniel* [2002] EWCA Crim 959, [2003] 1 Cr App Rep 99 at [26].
8 [2002] EWCA Crim 959, [2003] 1 Cr App Rep 99 at [28]; the emphasis is in the judgment of the court.

9 Made by Roberts in 'The Presumption of Innocence brought home? *Kebilene*' [2002] 118 LQR 41 at 50.

8.7 Fraud in obtaining voluntary arrangements. The popularity of individual voluntary arrangements has come with its fair share of dishonest behaviour. From the start of voluntary arrangements it has been an offence for a debtor to make any false representation or commit any other fraud for the purposes of obtaining the approval of his creditors to a proposed voluntary arrangement[1]. IA 2000 has replaced this offence in more specific terms, and has in addition placed a duty on the nominee or supervisor of an arrangement to report any possible offence to the Department of Trade. An officer of a corporate debtor or an individual debtor commits an offence if, for the purpose of obtaining the approval of the creditors (or members) to a proposal for a voluntary arrangement, he either (a) makes any false representation, or (b) fraudulently does, or omits to do, anything[2]. This wide wording should catch any fraudulent behaviour engaged in with the aim of securing a voluntary arrangement. An offence may be committed even if the proposal is not approved[3]. The penalty is imprisonment or a fine, or both[4]. A notable omission from these provisions is criminal liability in respect of false representations or fraudulent acts in connection with obtaining the approval of creditors to a variation to a voluntary arrangement.

In PVA there is an offence in similar terms[5]. It may be committed by any person who is an officer of the partnership or an officer (including shadow director[6]) of a corporate member who either (a) makes a false representation or (b) fraudulently does, or omits to do anything for the purposes of obtaining the approval of the members or creditors of an insolvent partnership or of the members or creditors of any of the insolvent partnership's members or creditors to a proposal for voluntary arrangement whether or not the proposal is approved.

1 IR 1986, r 1.30 (CVA), r 5.30 (IVA), now repealed.
2 IA 1986, s 6A(1) (all CVAs), s 262A(1) (IVA).
3 IA 1986, s 6A(2) (all CVAs), s 262A(2) (IVA).
4 On indictment, seven years, unlimited fine; on summary conviction six months or the statutory maximum, or both, IA 1986, Sch 10.
5 IA 1986, s 6A(1), as modified by IPO 2002. There is an immaterial difference. In IA 1986, s 6A(1) the offence is to make 'any' false representation. As modified, the offence is to make 'a' false representation.
6 That is a person in accordance with whose directions on instructions the directors of a company are accustomed to act, but excluding professional advisers: IA 1986, s 251.

8.8 Duty of nominee or supervisor to report fraud. A duty is imposed on the nominee or supervisor to report possible fraud where a moratorium has been obtained by a company or where a voluntary arrangement has been approved. This duty arises only where a voluntary arrangement has been approved by the creditors and has taken effect[1]. The nominee or supervisor must report any past or present officer of a corporate debtor or individual debtor where it appears to him that such an officer or debtor 'has been guilty of any offence' in connection with a moratorium or voluntary arrangement 'for which he is criminally liable'[2]. The report is to be made to the Secretary of State and is to be made 'forthwith', that is immediately upon it appearing to the nominee or supervisor that there is guilt on the part of an officer or individual debtor[3].

The duty to report is subject therefore to two restrictions which might be thought unnecessary. First, although an offence may be committed in connection with the obtaining of a voluntary arrangement whether or not the relevant proposal was in fact approved, the duty to report criminal behaviour arises only where the proposal is approved and the voluntary arrangement takes effect. Secondly, the duty is to report 'guilt of an offence for which he *is* criminally liable'. The distinction may therefore be made between clear cases of guilt and cases where the nominee or supervisor merely considers that there might be guilt on the part of an officer or individual debtor. It would make a nonsense of the duty to report criminal activity if insolvency practitioners, perhaps reluctant to become involved in a criminal investigation, were to stick rigidly to reporting only the clearest possible cases. It would have been possible for the duty to have been drafted in rather wider terms, and this may yet become necessary if the Secretary of State is determined to take a rather firmer line on criminality in connection with voluntary arrangements than has been the case in the past.

1 IA 1986, s 7A(1) (CVA), s 262B(1) (IVA).
2 IA 1986, s 7A(2) (CVA), s 262B(2) (IVA).
3 IA 1986, s 7A(2) (CVA), s 262B(2) (IVA). In CVA the Secretary of State is the 'appropriate authority' in England and Wales; where the company is registered in Scotland the 'appropriate authority' is the Lord Advocate, s 7A(2).

8.9 Duty to provide assistance. The nominee or supervisor is also obliged to assist in any prosecution which may follow his report of criminal behaviour. Any information of relevance must be provided to the Secretary of State if required of the relevant practitioner, and he must also give such access to and facilities for inspecting and taking copies of any relevant documents which may be in his possession or under his control[1]. In IVA cases, should either the Director of Public Prosecutions or the Secretary of State institute criminal proceedings following a report by the nominee or the supervisor, the practitioner concerned must give all assistance in connection with the prosecution which he is reasonably able to give[2]. The relevant practitioner may also be directed to assist in the prosecution by the court on the application of the prosecuting authority concerned[3].

In CVA cases the possibility is envisaged that a rather wider investigation of the company's affairs may be required. After receiving a report from a nominee or supervisor concerning criminality in connection with a moratorium or voluntary arrangement, the Secretary of State may exercise any of the powers available to inspectors who are appointed[4] to investigate a company's affairs[5]. In carrying out any investigation of a company's affairs the Secretary of State may rely on any of the provisions of CA 1985 relating to the production of documents or giving of information to or otherwise assisting inspectors, and this will oblige the relevant practitioner to provide such assistance as may properly be required of him[6]. Should the Director of Public Prosecutions institute criminal proceedings following a report by a practitioner, that practitioner and every officer or agent[7] of the company past and present (other than the defendant in the proceedings) must give all assistance in connection with the prosecution which he is reasonably able to give[8]. Should the practitioner fail to give assistance he may be directed to do so by the court on the application of the prosecution authority[9]. Where any person answers a question put to him in the course of an investigation into the company's affairs by the Secretary of State that answer may be used in evidence against that person[10]. However, in criminal proceedings against that person in connection with any offence other than perjury no evidence of such an answer may be adduced and no question relating to it may be asked by the prosecution unless evidence relating to it is first adduced or a question relating to it is first asked by the person concerned[11].

1 IA 1986, s 7A(2)(b) (CVA), s 262B(2)(b) (IVA).
2 IA 1986, s 262B(3).
3 IA 1986, s 262B(4).
4 Under CA 1985, s 431 or s 432.
5 IA 1986, s 7A(3).
6 IA 1986, s 7A(4).
7 'Agent' includes any banker or solicitor of the company and any person employed by the company as auditor, whether or not that person is an officer of the company: IA 1986, s 7A(8).
8 IA 1986, s 7A(8).
9 IA 1986, s 7A(9).
10 IA 1986, s 7A(5).
11 IA 1986, s 7A(6).

Chapter 9

Effect of approval of voluntary arrangement

9.1 The binding of creditors: the statutory hypothesis. The voluntary arrangement as approved by the creditor's meeting (a) takes effect as if made by the debtor at the meeting[1], and (b) binds every person who in accordance with IR 1986[2] (i) was entitled to vote at the creditors' meeting, whether or not he was present or represented at it, or (ii) would have been entitled to vote if he had had notice of the meeting, as if he were a party to the arrangement[3]. Prior to the amendments introduced by IA 2000 the creditor had actually to have had notice of the meeting in order to be bound by the arrangement[4], although so long as the notice was sent according to the rules and the creditor was in fact aware of the notice before the meeting, even if he learnt of the meeting by other means, he was treated as having had notice of the meeting[5]. IR 1986[6] require notices to be sent to creditors at least 14 days before the meeting[7]. Although a creditor is now bound to a voluntary arrangement even if he did not receive notice of the creditors' meeting, it remains of considerable importance that the debtor and his nominee ensure that all persons who have a claim against the debtor do receive the requisite notice. A creditor who discovers late that he was entitled to but did not receive notice has 28 days to challenge the meetings' decision[8], and the fact that he was not given notice may assist him in any challenge he may bring. Solicitors do not have implied authority to accept service of notices[9].

The legal analysis of the approved arrangement is that there is a consensual agreement between the debtor and all the creditors who were entitled to vote at the meeting; these creditors must be treated as consenting parties to the arrangement under the statutory hypothesis imposed by IA 1986[10] however they voted, if at all, and whatever their attitude to the arrangement[11]. As it forms an agreement between the debtor and the creditor questions as to any further consequences of the voluntary arrangement beyond it binding the debtor's creditors are to be determined on a construction of its terms. Thus, for example, co-debtors or sureties may or may not be discharged from liability to the principal creditor depending upon the precise terms of the arrangement[12]. The terms of the arrangement will also determine whether or not the creditor's claim against the debtor is extinguished. An investor who is bound by an IVA made by a financial adviser will lose his right to make a claim against the Investors Compensation Scheme[13] where the arrangement extinguishes the claim, as in a composition[14]. In a scheme of arrangement the terms of the scheme may be drawn so as not to extinguish the claim against the financial adviser in which event the investor may pursue his ICS claim, subject to the relevant rules.

Unless the voluntary arrangement is unusually drafted the effect of approval on a secured creditor is that he will not be able to sue the debtor for payment under his covenant. The secured creditor will, of course, be able to enforce his security if he has not abandoned it[15]. While the notice of the meeting may set out the debt or debts owed to the creditor at the date of the proposal or statement of affairs, it is the creditor who has to receive notice not the holder of each particular debt. Accordingly, where a further debt becomes due between the date of the interim order and the approval of the arrangement, the further debt should be included in the creditor's claim and will become subject to the arrangement[16].

A creditor who is not given notice of the creditors' meeting (an 'omitted creditor') may discover that he is bound to an arrangement which has been in place for some time. The arrangement may even have been implemented completely. Where the arrangement is ongoing an omitted creditor should be entitled to such dividends or other payments as are due to other creditors in the same class, and, subject always to the terms of the voluntary arrangement, all outstanding dividends should be paid to the omitted creditor before further payments are made to existing creditors. If the supervisor refuses to accept an omitted creditor, or the amount of his debt, or his entitlement to be paid all outstanding dividends, the omitted creditor may apply to the court for appropriate directions[17]. Where the arrangement has 'ceased to have any effect' the debtor becomes liable, as at the date that the arrangement so ceased, to pay 'the amount payable under the arrangement' to the omitted creditor[18]. This will be a debt recoverable by the omitted creditor in place of his original debt. Although the words used, 'ceased to have any effect', are very wide, they necessarily mean fully implemented according to the terms of the arrangement in respect of all the creditors who had notice of the meeting. This is because where the arrangement has not been fully implemented in respect of all persons bound by the arrangement who had notice of the creditors' meeting it has 'ended prematurely'[19] and in such cases no liability to pay a dividend to an omitted creditor arises. In this event the statute is silent as to the omitted creditor's position, and his rights to recover monies which may be held by the supervisor, or petition for insolvency, will depend on the terms of the arrangement and the reasons for its failure. The omitted creditor who discovers that he is bound by an arrangement which has ended prematurely will not be able to challenge the validity of the arrangement[20] and he is unlikely to be able to challenge any act, omission or decision of the former supervisor[21]. He may be able to bring proceedings against the debtor (and possibly the directors of the corporate debtor) for breach of duty of good faith in connection with the proposal and his exclusion from the list of creditors to be given notice of the creditors' meeting[22], but in most cases the premature end of the voluntary arrangement will lead to formal insolvency. Whether the omitted creditor is prejudiced by his not having had notice will then depend on the terms of the arrangement; if he has missed the opportunity to be paid dividends from a trust which has survived the insolvency and in which most of the debtor's assets have been placed the omitted creditor will be prejudiced and may well find there is nothing that he can do to recover the position[23].

The Deeds of Arrangement Act 1914 does not apply to the approved IVA[24].

1 IA 1986, s 5(2)(a) (CVA without moratorium), Sch A1, s 37(2)(a) (CVA with moratorium), s 260(2)(a) (IVA).

2 See paras 6.6 and 6.7 above.
3 IA 1986, s 5(2)(b) (CVA without moratorium), Sch A1, para 37(2)(b) (CVA with moratorium), s 260(2)(b) (IVA).
4 IA 1986, s 260(2) (prior to amendment): *Re a Debtor (No 64 of 1992)* [1994] BCC 55; *Skipton Building Society v Collins* [1998] BPIR 267.
5 *Beverly Group plc v McClue* [1996] BPIR 25.
6 IR 1986, r 1.17(2) (CVA without moratorium), r.1.49(2) (CVA with moratorium), r 5.17(2) (IVA).
7 Accordingly, it was not enough before the amendment to IA 1986 to bind the creditor to the arrangement that the creditor had some but insufficient notice *Mytre Investments Ltd v Reynolds (No 2)* [1996] BPIR 464, where Blackburne J rejected the suggestion that 'substantial compliance' was sufficient or that the period of notice could be computed back from the date of an adjourned meeting. Where a creditor satisfied the court that he had not received the notice, although there was evidence of posting, he was not bound to the IVA: *Re a Debtor (No 64 of 1992)* [1994] 1 WLR 264.
8 IA 1986, s 6(3)(b) (CVA without moratorium), Sch A1, para 38(3)(b) (CVA with moratorium), s 262(3)(b) (IVA).
9 *Re Munro and Rowe; Singer v Trustee* [1981] 1 WLR 1358 at 1361.
10 IA 1986, s 5(2) (CVA without moratorium), Sch A1, para 37(2) (CVA with moratorium), s 260(2) (IVA).
11 See *Johnson v Davies* [1999] Ch 117 at 138, CA, approved in *Raja v Rubin* [2000] Ch 274, CA. As these cases pre-date the changes introduced by IA 2000 the principle is there framed in terms that there is a consensual agreement between the debtor and all the creditors who *had notice of and* were entitled to vote at the meeting.
12 *Johnson v Davies* [1999] Ch 117 where on a proper construction of the IVA's terms the co-debtor and sureties were not released.
13 Operated by the Securities and Investment Board under the Financial Services Act 1986, s 14.
14 See rule 3.2 of the Financial Services Compensation Scheme made by the Financial Services Authority under the Financial Services and Markets Act 2000, s 213.
15 See *Whitehead v Household Mortgage Corpn plc* [2002] EWCA Civ 1657, [2003] 1 All ER 319 and generally para 6.12 above.
16 *Re Kenneth George Hoare* [1997] BPIR 683 at 694, where the deputy judge suggested that IA 1986, s 260 did not prevent the splitting of a creditor's overall debt so that a creditor might be bound to an arrangement in respect of one debt, but not bound in respect of another. Such a result could only arise in unusual circumstances even before the amendments introduced by IA 2000 binding creditors to the arrangement regardless of whether they had notice.
17 IA 1986, s 7(3) (CVA without moratorium), Sch A1, para 39(3)(4) (CVA with moratorium), s 263(3) (IVA).
18 IA 1986, s 5(2A) (CVA without moratorium), Sch A1, para 37(3) (CVA with moratorium), s 260(2A)(b) (IVA).
19 See IA 1986, s 7B (all CVAs), s 262C (IVA).
20 He is expressly precluded from doing so by the terms of IA 1986, s 6(3)(b) (CVA without moratorium), Sch A1, para 38(3)(b) (CVA with moratorium), or s 262(3) (IVA).
21 See para 10.4 below.
22 *Cadbury Schweppes v Somji* [2001] 1 WLR 615, CA (also [2001] 1 BCLC 498, where the judgment at first instance is reported). Robert Walker LJ, para 24, noted that the deputy judge's 'impressive survey of the old law shows that in relation to compositions and arrangements with creditors the court did impose a strict requirement of good faith as between competing unsecured creditors … There is no strong presumption that a similar principle must be found in the new regime [for voluntary arrangements] but (to put it at its lowest) it would be no great surprise to find it there in one form or another'. Good faith was owed not only between competing creditors but between the debtor and the creditors, and if the court does import these principles into CVAs and IVAs an action may lie where a lack of good faith can be shown by a creditor in respect of his omission from the creditors listed on the statement of affairs or of whom notice was given to the nominee.
23 It is suggested that the legislature should give further thought to the position of the omitted creditor. It should be straightforward enough to provide that the omitted creditor should be put into the position he would have been in, so far as may be practicable, had he been given the notice of the creditors' meeting to which he was entitled whether or not the voluntary arrangement ends prematurely. At the least he should be able to apply to the court for directions to do justice to his position whatever the eventual outcome for the debtor.
24 IA 1986, s 260(3).

9.2 Effect of approval on third parties. In most cases the approval of a voluntary arrangement will have no effect on persons who are not parties to it. Approval may, however, have an effect on third parties where they have joint liability on a debt with the debtor. Depending upon the terms of the original liability and the terms of the arrangement the compromise or discharge agreed with the debtor under the voluntary arrangement may discharge a third party liable on the same debt. In *Johnson v Davies*[1] the Court of Appeal considered whether co-debtors and sureties should be excluded from the operation of the general law relating to joint liability in case of voluntary arrangements, in a manner similar to that in formal insolvency. The court concluded that the drafting of IA 1986 indicated that Parliament intended that the general law should have effect. 'It is up to the debtor to propose, and for the creditors to accept or reject, proposals which either do or do not have the effect of releasing co-debtors and sureties. A creditor who is prejudiced by the decision of the majority to approve proposals which have the effect of releasing a co-debtor against whom he could otherwise have recourse can apply to the court [under IA 1986, s 262[2]] for the approval of the meeting to be revoked'[3].

A creditor may reserve his rights against co-debtors and sureties at the time when approval is given to the voluntary arrangement. It is not necessary that there is a provision in the contract of surety permitting a reservation of rights, neither is it necessary for the reservation to be included as a term of the voluntary arrangement[4]. Plainly, it would be advisable for a creditor to seek the addition of an appropriate provision in the terms of the arrangement but the other creditors may not be agreeable. In determining whether there has been a reservation the court should look at all the circumstances including the dealings and correspondence between the parties[5].

1 [1999] Ch 117.
2 Or IA 1986, s 6 (CVA without moratorium), or Sch A1, para 38 (CVA with moratorium).
3 Per Chadwick LJ on *Johnson v Davies* [1999] Ch 117 at 138.
4 *Greene King plc v Stanley* [2001] EWCA Civ 1966, [2002] BPIR 491: see paras 72 (no need for provision in contract of surety) and 83 (no need for provision in terms of arrangement).
5 *Greene King plc v Stanley* [2001] EWCA Civ 1966, [2002] BPIR 491, para 83.

9.3 End of moratorium or interim order. The approval of a CVA brings any moratorium then in force to an end[1]. Any interim order in force covering the debtor immediately before the end of the period of 28 days beginning with the day on which the report of the creditor's meeting was made to the court ceases to have effect at the end of that period[2]. Where bankruptcy proceedings have been stayed by an interim order which ceases to have effect following the approval of the arrangement the bankruptcy petition is deemed to be dismissed unless the court otherwise orders[3].

1 IA 1986, Sch A1, para 8(6)(c).
2 IA 1986, s 260(4).
3 IA 1986, s 260(5). The rules make no provision as to any costs incurred by the petitioning creditor on the deemed dismissal of the petition. The petitioning creditor would be advised to request that the payment of these costs be a term of the debtor's proposal for a voluntary arrangement.

9.4 Effect of approval on winding up or administration proceedings. Where a winding up petition has been presented but has been caught by a moratorium[1] it must be dismissed by the court on the approval of a voluntary arrangement[2]. Where a winding up or administration order has been made, the court may, on the approval of a voluntary arrangement, stay all proceedings in the winding up of the company or discharge the administration order; alternatively, the court may give such directions as it thinks appropriate for facilitating the implementation of the arrangement[3]. An application for such a stay or discharge or for directions is made direct to the judge and will be heard in public unless otherwise directed[4]. The court may not, however, make an order staying winding-up proceedings or discharging an administration order at any time during (a) the period within which creditors or members who were given notice of the creditors' meeting may bring a challenge to the arrangement[5], ie 28 days commencing with the day on which each of the reports required to be made by the chairmen of the meetings of the company and creditors have been filed in court, or (b) if an application to challenge the approval of the voluntary arrangement is made, during any time when such an application or an appeal is pending or in the period within which an appeal in respect of that application may be brought[6].

1 See para 3.7 above.
2 IA 1986, Sch A1, para 37(4), unless it is an excepted petition, ie a petition presented under IA 1986, s 124A, the Financial Services Act 1986, s 72(1)(b) or the Banking Act 1987, s 92(1)(b): see para 3.11 above. Note: the petition must not be dismissed until the time for challenging the meetings' decisions (28 days) has passed or, if a challenge is made, until the challenge has been determined: IA 1986, Sch A1, para 37(5).
3 IA 1986, s 5(3); the CVA will, of course, have been proposed and approved in the absence of a moratorium.
4 *Practice Direction: Insolvency Proceedings* para 5.1(8).
5 Under IA 1986, s 6(3) (CVA without moratorium), Sch A1, para 38(3) (CVA with moratorium), and see para 7.8 above.
6 IA 1986, s 5(4). The time limit for bringing an appeal is 14 days unless a longer is period is permitted by the lower court, such period not normally exceeding 28 days: IR 1986, rr 13.1, 13.7; CPR 52.4, PD 52 para 2.7.

9.5 Effect on interim order and bankruptcy order. Any interim order in force in relation to the debtor which does not come to end before the end of the 28-day period following the chairman's report of the meeting's result to the court[1] ceases to have effect at the end of that period[2]. In cases where bankruptcy proceedings have been stayed by an interim order which ceases to have effect after the approval of a voluntary arrangement the bankruptcy petition is deemed to be dismissed unless the court otherwise orders[3].

Under the amendments introduced by the Enterprise Act 2002 where the approved voluntary arrangement relates to a debtor who is an undischarged bankrupt, the court must annul the bankruptcy order on an application by the bankrupt, or, where he does not make the application within the prescribed period[4], by the official receiver[5]. The making of an annulment order lifts from the debtor the status of a bankrupt for such matters as disqualification and his position on any future bankruptcy[6]. It does not, however, invalidate any sale or other disposition of property, payment made or any other act duly performed in the bankruptcy before annulment by or under the authority of the official receiver or the bankrupt's trustee or the court[7]. In the event that any part of the bankrupt's estate is vested in the trustee at the date of the annulment the court may vest it in the supervisor or any other person it may appoint[8]. The court must not annul a bankruptcy order under this power before the end of the period of 28 days beginning with the day on which the report of the creditor's meeting was made to the court[9] or at any time while an application is pending to challenge the meeting's decision[10] or, after such an application has been heard, the period for an appeal has not expired or an appeal is pending[11].

1 See para 6.15 above.
2 IA 1986, s 260(4).
3 IA 1986, s 260(5).
4 This period will be fixed in the amendments to IR 1986 consequent on the introduction of the Engerprise Act 2002.
5 IA 1986, s 261(1)(2) (as amended by EA 2002).
6 Which, for example, will affect the date on which he obtains his discharge.
7 IA 1986, s 282(4)(a).
8 IA 1986, s 282(4)(b), in default of any appointment the property concerned reverts to the bankrupt on such terms (if any) as the court may direct.
9 Under IA 1986, s 259: see para 6.13 above. The amendment introduced by IA 2000 refers to 'the period specified in s 262(3)(a) during which the decision of the creditors' meeting can be challenged' in place of 'the period of 28 days beginning with the day on which the report of the creditors' meeting was made to the court under s 259'. The words replaced are those used in IA 1986, s 262(3)(a).
10 Under IA 1986, s 262: see paras 7.1, 7.8 above.
11 IA 1986, s 261(3) as to time limits for appealing: see para 9.4 above.

9.6 Foreign creditors. Within England and Wales foreign creditors will be treated as any other creditor. They will be bound to the arrangement whether or not they voted and irrespective of how they voted. Within the foreign creditors' own jurisdiction local rules will apply and it may not be possible for the supervisor to prevent a foreign creditor enforcing his debt in full against local assets particularly if he voted against the proposal. Foreign creditors who are habitually residence, domiciled or have a registered office within another member state of the EU, except Denmark, will be subject to the rights and obligations imposed on creditors under the EC Regulation[1]. All EU claims may be lodged (the wording is aimed at claims against insolvent estates) including claims from the tax and social security authorities of member states[2]. EU creditors are entitled to be told of the start of insolvency proceedings, which include voluntary arrangements, and to be given information as to the lodging of claims, and any applicable time limit[3]. In lodging a claim the creditor must give full details of the claim, its nature, amount and date on which it arose, and provide copies of any supporting documents. Any preference, security in rem or reservation of title asserted by the creditor must be specified[4]. Information provided to a foreign creditor may be in English, but the form used must be headed '*Invitation to lodge a claim. Time limits to be observed*' in all the official languages of the EU[5]. A creditor may lodge a claim in the official language of his state, but may be required to provide a translation into English[6].

1 Ie Council Regulation (EC) 1346/2000 of 29 May 2000 on Insolvency Proceedings which came into force on 31 May 2002: see para 14.6 below. Denmark is the sole EU state to which the EC Regulation does not apply.
2 EC Regulation, Art 39.
3 EC Regulation, Art 40.
4 EC Regulation, Art 41.
5 EC Regulation, Art 42(1).
6 EC Regulation, Art 42(2).

Chapter 10
Implementation of arrangement

10.1 The supervisor. Where an arrangement is approved by the creditors' meeting, the person who is for the time being carrying out in relation to the arrangement the functions conferred by virtue of that approval on the nominee or his replacement is known as the supervisor of the arrangement[1]. The supervisor must be authorised to act as supervisor in relation to the arrangement[2]. The supervisor will usually have been the nominee, but it is open to the creditors' meeting to appoint one or more other persons to replace or in addition to the practitioner who has acted as nominee provided the practitioner or practitioners concerned are qualified insolvency practitioners or are authorised to act as supervisor in relation to the arrangement[3]. The rôle of supervisor may be undertaken by two or more practitioners. In such a case the creditors may resolve whether acts to be done in connection with the arrangement may be done by any one of them, or must be done by both or all the relevant practitioners[4].

The supervisor implements the arrangement, and the terms of the arrangement will dictate what activities the supervisor undertakes in connection with it. Whether assets subject to a voluntary arrangement are held by the supervisor and if so on what terms will ultimately depend on the terms of the arrangement. The court should not be slow to find that the supervisor holds assets under the arrangement on trust[5]. The supervisor holds any funds which have been passed to him by or on behalf of the debtor for distribution under the arrangement on trust for the creditors whether or not he is formally constituted a trustee under the terms of the arrangement[6]. In *Welburn v Dipp Lupton Broomhead*[7] the debtor's entire estate, apart from his dwelling house was included in his IVA. A major asset of the estate was an arbitration claim against a third party. The terms of the IVA required the supervisor to oversee the progress of the arbitration with the debtor providing assistance in the prosecution of the claim. The Court of Appeal held that the supervisor held the chose in action representing the claim on trust for the creditors[8].

There is no statutory protection for a supervisor who carries on the debtor's business or who trades within the context of the arrangement. He will be liable under the general law in respect of any business dealings, or the administration or disposal of assets. If there is to be further trading in the debtor's business the supervisor is well advised to ensure that he does not become liable for trade liabilities, tax, business rates and other such liabilities. A voluntary arrangement does not of itself terminate contracts of employment where the debtor is employer or employee. There may, however, be express provision covering contracts of employment when the voluntary arrangement takes effect in the terms of the arrangement or, exceptionally, in the contract of employment. Where a supervisor obtains an interest in land under the terms of the arrangement he may register it as a caution against first registration in respect of unregistered land[9], or a notice where the land is registered[10]. The supervisor may seek the assistance of the court and apply for directions in relation to any particular matter arising under the arrangement[11].

The fees, costs, charges and expenses that may be incurred for any purposes of the arrangement are: (1) any disbursements made by the nominee prior to the approval of the arrangement, and any remuneration for his services as such agreed between himself and the debtor or, where appropriate, the office-holder[12]; (2) any fees, costs, charges and expenses which are sanctioned by the terms of the arrangement or would be payable, or correspond to those which would be payable, in the debtor's liquidation or bankruptcy[13]. The priority in respect of the trustee's fees, charges and expenses extends to the date on which the supervisor takes possession of the assets, but not to fees, charges and expenses incurred after that date[14].

As soon as the arrangement is approved by the creditor's meeting, the directors of the corporate debtor or the individual debtor, or in cases where the debtor is in insolvency, the relevant office-holder as appropriate, must do all that is required for putting the supervisor into possession of the assets included in the arrangement[15]. The supervisor becomes responsible for the discharge of any balance due to the relevant office-holder by way of remuneration on account of fees, costs, charges or expenses properly incurred in the insolvency, and any advances made in respect of the insolvent estate together with interest at judgment rate[16]. The supervisor may either discharge such sums as may be owing or give a written undertaking to do so out of the first realisation of assets. Until such sums are discharged the office-holder has a charge over the assets included in the arrangement[17]. The supervisor must also discharge any guarantees properly given by the office-holder for the benefit of the estate out of the realisation of the assets included in the arrangement[18].

There is no provision in IA 1986 or IR 1986 for the resignation of the supervisor. Such provision may be made within the terms of the arrangement or arranged with the consent of the debtor and the creditors. A supervisor who wishes to resign and who is unable to do so by agreement may apply to the court for an order to appoint a replacement[19]. In IVA any supervisor who vacates office, and any new appointee as supervisor, must give notice to the Secretary of State of his vacation of office or appointment as the case may be[20].

1 IA 1986, s 7(3) (CVA without moratorium), Sch A1, para 39(3) (CVA with moratorium), s 263(1), (2) (IVA).

2 Whether as a qualified insolvency practitioner or a member of a body specifically recognised for the purpose of its members acting as nominees or supervisors by the Secretary of State: IA 1986, s 388(1)(b), s 389A, as amended and added by IA 2000, s 4: see para 1.12 above.

3 IA 1986, s 4(2) (CVA without moratorium), Sch A1 para 31(3) (CVA with moratorium), s 258(3) (IVA) and IR 1986, r 1.22 (all CVAs, applying where a moratorium has been in force by virtue of r 1.54), r 5.25 (IVA); note it is the rules that permit more than one supervisor, the statute envisages only one.

4 IR 1986, r 1.22(1) (all CVAs), r 5.25(1) (IVA).

5 *Welburn v Dibb Lupton Broomhead* [2002] EWCA Civ 1601, [2002] All ER (D) 363 (Oct).

6 *Re Leisure Study Group Ltd* [1994] 2 BCLC 65; *Re Bradley-Hole* [1995] 1 WLR 1097; see also *Re N T Gallagher & Sons Ltd* [2002] EWCA Civ 404, [2002] 1 WLR 2380 at [29].

7 (24 October 2002, unreported) CA.
8 It followed that the debtor could not claim damages for loss resulting from the failure of his solicitors to recover an interim award before the insolvency of the respondent company against whom the award had been made. It was the creditors not the debtor who had suffered any loss.
9 See Land Registration Act 2002, s 15 (which comes into force 13 October 2003).
10 See Land Registration Act 2002, s 32 (which comes into force 13 October 2003). previously a class C(iv) land charge under the Land Registration Act 1925, s 54.
11 IA 1986, s 7(4) (CVA without moratorium), Sch A1, para 39(5) (CVA with moratorium), s 263(4) (IVA). Note that a supervisor is, by IA 1986, s 7(4)(b) or Sch A1, para 39(5)(b) included among the person who may apply to the court for the company to be put into administration or liquidation. As to the supervisor's power to present a petition for a bankruptcy order, see para 11.2 below.
12 Ie the administrator, liquidator, the official receiver or the trustee.
13 IR 1986, r 1.28 (all CVAs; see r 1.54), r 5.33 (IVA). As to the fees etc payable in insolvency, see IR 1986 r 4.128 (winding up) and IR 1986, r 6.224 (bankruptcy).
14 *Rooney v Cardona and Judd* [1999] BPIR 954.
15 IR 1986, r 1.23(1) (CVA), r 5.26(1) (IVA).
16 IR 1986, r 1.23(2) (CVA), r 5.26(2) (IVA).
17 IR 1986, r 1.21(3), (4) (CVA), r 5.26(3)(4) (IVA). In IVA any sums due to the official receiver take priority over those due to a trustee: IR 1986, r 5.26(4).
18 IR 1986, r 1.23(5) (CVA), r 5.21(5) (IVA).
19 Under IA 1986, s 7(5) (CVA without moratorium), Sch A1, para 39(6) (CVA with moratorium), s 263(5) (IVA): see para 10.5 below.
20 IR 1986, r 5.29(2).

10.2 Powers and responsibilities of the supervisor. The supervisor will have such powers, and only such powers, as are vested in him by the arrangement. In the rare case where the voluntary arrangement comprises territorial proceedings[1] for the purposes of the EC Regulation the supervisor must be conscious that his powers are restricted to assets situated in the UK, whatever provision may be made about them in the terms of the arrangement[2]. No powers are implied by IA 1986 or IR 1986[3]. It is important therefore that the arrangement contains sufficient powers to enable the supervisor to implement the arrangement, for example, powers to collect in assets, bring proceedings etc. This is an obligation falling primarily on the nominee when preparing the proposal. Should the supervisor find that he does not have any necessary power he should in the first instance refer the matter to the creditors. Provided all the creditors, or all the creditors who are affected, agree, or the terms of any express provision in the arrangement as to variation are complied with, it will be possible to amend the arrangement as necessary[4]. The supervisor may apply to the court for directions to assist him on any matter[5], but the court may not make any order which amounts to a variation of the arrangement which has been approved by the creditors[6].

As with any consensual agreement, the court will only imply terms when it is necessary to do so for the efficacy of the voluntary arrangement[7]. A strict approach is generally adopted on the question of necessity for the implication of a term into a voluntary arrangement[8]. The court will, it is suggested, readily imply a term in the arrangement to the effect that the directors or individual debtor should do all such acts as are necessary to enable the supervisor to carry the arrangement into effect. Such a term will enable the court, for example, to direct the directors or individual debtor to execute a power of attorney to enable the supervisor to bring proceedings against the third party where this is necessary for the implementation of the arrangement. In *Alman v Approach Housing Ltd*[9] a creditor with a small admitted claim wished to establish by action in the High Court a much larger claim for unliquidated damages which had been given only a nominal value for voting purposes by the chairman of the creditors' meeting. The corporate debtor contended that it was implicit that the pursuit of legal proceedings was prohibited by the terms of the CVA. The remedy for any creditor who could not persuade the supervisor to agree his debt was to apply to the court as a person dissatisfied with a decision of the supervisor[10]. The court held that it was not necessary to imply such a term. There was no express provision in the voluntary arrangement for dealing with claims nor was a machinery provided for determining disputed claims. The creditor was therefore permitted, albeit with some hesitation on the part of the court, to proceed with his action against the debtor. Where the proposal put before creditors is that the equity in specified properties would be available to meet good any shortfall in the event that trading over the period of the arrangement proved insufficient to generate enough funds to pay the promised dividend, it is implicit that the equity in the properties is maintained and not eroded by further charges or by allowing the sums due under existing charges to increase[11].

In the ordinary course, however, proceedings to recover or protect assets will be brought or defended by the debtor. Even if all the proceeds of the litigation will go to the creditors in the arrangement, it is unlikely that the debtor will be held to be a nominal claimant for the purposes of security for costs[12]. In *Envis v Thakkar*[13] the Court of Appeal held that the debtor had a genuine personal interest in such litigation. In the absence of any element of duplicity, the definition of nominal claimant did not extend to the debtor even though his interest may not be directly in the proceeds of the litigation but indirectly in the payment of his creditors through the proper implementation of the arrangement. There is no reason in principle why an individual debtor should not be entitled to funding from the Legal Services Commission[14] to bring or defend proceedings which benefit the arrangement; whether he will receive it is quite another matter.

The supervisor has power to petition for the debtor's administration or liquidation[15], or bankruptcy[16].

1 See para 14.3 below.
2 EC Regulation, Art 3(2).
3 There is no power in the supervisor to disclaim leases or other onerous contracts, and no such power can, of course, be vested in the supervisor by a provision in the arrangement.
4 *Raja v Rubin and Goodman* [2000] Ch 274.
5 IA 1986, s 7(4) (CVA without moratorium), Sch A1, para 39(5) (CVA with moratorium), s 263(4) (IVA).
6 *Re Alpa Lighting Ltd* [1997] BPIR 341.
7 *Liverpool Corpn v Irwin* [1977] AC 239.
8 See eg *Johnson v Davies* [1999] Ch 117 at 128.
9 [2001] 1 BCLC 530.
10 See para 10.4 below.
11 *Harris v Gross* [2001] BPIR 586 at 598.
12 For the power to award security for costs see CPR 25.12, which applies to insolvency proceedings by virtue of IR 1986, r 7.51.
13 [1997] BPIR 189.
14 Civil legal aid.
15 IA 1986, s 7(4)(b) (CVA without moratorium), Sch A1, para 39(5)(b) (CVA with moratorium).
16 IA 1986, s 264(1)(c).

10.3 Liability of supervisor. In carrying out his duties as nominee, convener or chairman of the creditors' meeting and supervisor of the arrangement, the relevant insolvency practitioner (or other person authorised to act as supervisor in relation to the arrangement[1]) should ensure that he complies with good practice and in particular the guidance given by: (a) the Statement of Insolvency Practice 3, produced by the Society of Practitioners of Insolvency[2]; (b) the Guide to Professional Conduct and Ethics, issued by the Insolvency Practitioners Association; and (c) the 'Dear IP' notices issued by the Insolvency Service[3]. The supervisor's decisions may well impact on a number of people; the debtor, the creditors and a range of third parties who have or have had dealings with the debtor. It has been held that no private law right of action exists in the debtor, creditor or third party against the supervisor for breach of statutory duty. In *King v Anthony*[4] the Court of Appeal noted that IA 1986, Pt VIII comprised a self-contained scheme including express powers in the court to give appropriate directions if complaint is made to the court of the conduct of the supervisor. Since IA 1986 provides an effective means of enforcing the duty of a supervisor, this indicates that the statutory right was intended to be enforceable by application under IA 1986, s 263[5] and not by private right of action[6]. Funds held by the supervisor for distribution to the creditors under the arrangement will be held by him as trustee, whether or not the supervisor is formally constituted a trustee under the arrangement[7], and the liabilities of a trustee will therefore attach to the supervisor with regard to such funds.

1 See para 1.12 above.
2 Now called the Association of Business Rescue Professionals. See Appendix 8.
3 These are now collected together in the 'Dear IP' millennium edition. Chapter 24 covers voluntary arrangements: see Appendix 7.
4 [1998] 2 BCLC 517, [1999] BPIR 73.
5 This is an IVA case but is equally applicable in CVA.
6 See [1999] BPIR 73 at 78–79. To the extent that the supervisor is performing private functions this decision survives HRA 1998. However, in complying with the directions of the court the supervisor is a public authority for the purposes of HRA 1998, s 6 and a complaint arising out of his acts or omissions in this regard may be the subject matter of a private right of action at the suit of a victim: HRA 1998, s 7.
7 *Re Leisure Study Group Ltd* [1994] 2 BCLC 65.

10.4 Control by the court: who may apply. The court may exercise control over the arrangement by giving directions or by removing the supervisor or appointing a further supervisor to assist in the implementation of the arrangement[1]. IA 1986 gives the court a complete discretion to give directions in relation to any matter arising under the arrangement on the application of the supervisor[2]. An application to challenge any act, omission, or decision of the supervisor may be made by the debtor, any of his creditors, or any other person who is dissatisfied by the relevant act, omission or decision. On such an application the court may: (a) confirm, reverse or modify any act or decision of the supervisor; (b) give him directions; or (c) make such other order as it thinks fit[3]. The existence of this summary remedy on the part of any dissatisfied applicant will preclude private rights of action against the supervisor by any claimant who may bring such an application[4].

'Dissatisfied' is not a word used in previous insolvency legislation. It replaces 'aggrieved' in earlier legislation. In *Re Sidebotham, ex p Sidebotham*[5] James LJ said that:

> 'A person aggrieved must be a man who has suffered a legal grievance, a man against whom a decision has been pronounced which has wrongfully deprived him of something, or wrongfully refused him something or wrongfully affected his title to something.'

But the definition of James LJ is not to be regarded as exhaustive. The words 'person aggrieved' are of wide import and should not be subjected to a restrictive interpretation. They do not include, of course, a mere busybody who is interfering in things which do not concern him; but they do include a person who has a genuine grievance because an order has been made which prejudicially affects his interests'[6]. It is uncertain whether 'dissatisfied' is used as a more modern equivalent of 'aggrieved' or whether it was intended to alter the scope of possible applicant. The likelihood is that the change in wording brings no change in substance[7]. It would be unrealistic to suppose that the court will entertain an application by a person whose dissatisfaction arose merely through general concern at the manner in which the supervisor was implementing the proposal rather than through his being prejudicially affected by a particular act, omission or decision of the supervisor. There must be a limit to the class of persons who can make such an application. But any person who is directly affected by any act, omission or decision is likely to come within the class of potential applicant[8].

Within the context of formal insolvency, the equivalent provisions by which the court may exercise control over liquidators and trustees in bankruptcy have been interpreted restrictively. In compulsory liquidation IA 1986, s 168(5) entitles 'any person' aggrieved by an act or decision of the liquidator to apply to the court. This may be compared with the entitlement in IA 1986, s 167(3) of 'any creditor or contributory' to apply to the court with respect to the exercise or purported exercise by the liquidator of any of his powers. The courts recognise that the class of potential applicant under IA 1986, s 168(5) is wider than that under IA 1986, s 167(3), but nevertheless have stated that no 'outsider' to the liquidation has locus standi to make an application[9]. Accordingly, a person denied an opportunity to purchase an asset of a company in compulsory liquidation sold by the liquidator may not apply[10], neither may a surety bring an application in respect of acts or decisions affecting the assets of the company when his subrogation rights do not in any way depend on the company being in liquidation[11].

> 'It could not have been the intention of Parliament that any outsider to the liquidation, dissatisfied with some act or decision of the liquidator, could attack that act or decision by the special procedure of s 168(5). However, I would accept that someone, like the landlord in *Re Hans Place Ltd*[12], who is directly affected by the exercise of a power given specifically to liquidators, and who would not otherwise have any right to challenge the exercise of that power, can utilise s 168(5). It may be that other persons can properly bring themselves within the subsection.' [13]

It is suggested that these authorities do not bear directly on applications in respect of acts, omissions and decisions of supervisors while implementing the voluntary arrangement, at least when the context is very different. In a composition where assets are assigned to the supervisor to realise and distribute the proceeds the supervisor's task will be little different to that of a liquidator or trustee in bankruptcy. But in 'trading out' voluntary arrangements and other schemes of arrangement the supervisor may have a more commercial rôle and may have to deal with a wide variety of third parties over a range of matters. It would be inappropriate to deny a third party the opportunity to complain to the court about the supervisor simply on the basis that he is 'an outsider' to the voluntary arrangement, particularly as he is unable to challenge the supervisor by private right of action. Any person who (a) is directly affected by the acts, omissions or decisions of the supervisor in undertaking his rôle in the voluntary arrangement, and (b) has no other right of challenge, should be able to apply to the court for relief[14].

Although the court has a wide discretion on an application in respect of a supervisor's acts, omissions or decisions, it has no power to vary the terms of the arrangement[15]. Extending the duration of the arrangement amounts to a variation[16].

Subject to this important limitation the court's jurisdiction is extensive[17]. Nevertheless, the court should be careful not to allow the width of the jurisdiction to control the supervisor to be used as a means for allowing the expensive and time consuming ventilation of claims which are likely to be fruitless[18].

1 IA 1986, s 7(4), (5) (CVA without moratorium), Sch A1, para 39(5), (6) (CVA with moratorium), s 263(4), (5) (IVA).
2 IA 1986, s 7(3) (CVA without moratorium), Sch A1, para 39(3), (4) (CVA with moratorium), s 263(3) (IVA).
3 IA 1986, s 7(3) (CVA without moratorium), Sch A1, para 39(4) (CVA with moratorium), s 263(3) (IVA).
4 See *King v Anthony* [1998] 2 BCLC 517, and, generally, as to the liability of nominee or supervisor, para 4.17 above.
5 (1880) 14 Ch D 458 at 465.
6 *A-G of Gambia v N'Jie* [1961] AC 617 at 634, per Lord Denning.
7 '"Dissatisfied" is certainly no narrower than "aggrieved", and is arguably wider', per Stanley Burnton QC in *Re Dennis Michael Cook* [1999] BPIR 881 at 883.
8 A former solicitor of the bankrupt who had received a letter from the trustee authorising him to assist the SFO in inquiries into the affairs of the bankrupt and who faced prosecution by the SFO if he refused to answer questions and proceedings by the bankrupt for breach of professional privilege if he did was a person dissatisfied by the trustee's letter of authority for the purposes of IA 1986, s 303: *Re Dennis Michael Cook* [1999] BPIR 881.
9 'In the latter capacity alone, like any other outsider to the liquidation, they would not have the locus standi to apply under s 168(5)', per Nourse LJ in *Re Edennote Ltd* [1996] 2 BCLC 389 at 393, quoted by Peter Gibson LJ in *Mahommed v Morris* [2000] 2 BCLC 536, para 24.
10 *Re Edennote Ltd* [1996] 2 BCLC 389.
11 *Mahomed v Morris* [2000] 2 BCLC 536.
12 [1993] BCLC 768.
13 Per Peter Gibson LJ in *Mahomed v Morris* [2000] 2 BCLC 536, para 26.
14 See the passage quoted in the text from Peter Gibson LJ's judgment in *Mahomed v Morris* [2000] 2 BCLC 536.
15 *Re Alpa Lighting Ltd* [1997] BPIR 341, CA, impliedly overruling *Re FMS Financial Management Services Ltd* (1988) 5 BCC 191 where the court ordered that creditors who had been excluded from voting should be included in the voluntary arrangement and share in the sums paid as dividends.
16 *Re Alpa Lighting Ltd* [1997] BPIR 341, CA.
17 *King v Anthony* [1999] BPIR 73 at 78–79.
18 *Holdenhurst Securities plc v Cohen* [2001] 1 BCLC 460, quoting *Port v Auger* [1994] 1 WLR 862 at 874, but holding in the circumstances that there was a reasonable claim to be pursued.

10.5 Circumstances in which court will act on application. There is yet to be a case reported where the court has given detailed consideration to the principles on which it should interfere with the supervisor's implementation of a voluntary arrangement. In general terms it may be expected that similar principles will be applied as apply to the control of other office-holders by the court[1], having due regard to the fact that the supervisor will be implementing an arrangement which is designed to enable the debtor keep out of formal insolvency to the advantage of his creditors as opposed to administering an insolvent estate for the benefit of creditors in accordance with the general principles applicable to liquidation or bankruptcy. In formal insolvency cases the court has been slow to act, being concerned to allow office-holders to exercise their powers and their discretion without 'undue fetters'[2]. It may be noted that although bankruptcy and then company liquidation legislation has enabled 'any person … aggrieved by an act or decision of an [officer-holder]' to apply to the court for summary relief since 1869[3] there have been relatively few applications; certainly few reported decisions.

In *Re Peters, ex p Lloyd*[4] the trustee decided not to sell a contingent reversionary interest. The creditor applicant argued that a refusal to sell an asset of the estate was an absurd exercise of the discretion of the trustee but the Court of Appeal disagreed, stating that the court would not interfere unless the trustee is doing that which is so utterly unreasonable and absurd that no reasonable man would so act. It was the bankrupt who applied in *Re a Debtor (No 400 of 1940), ex p Debtor v Dodwell*[5]. On the debtor's bankruptcy the trustee found himself with a very substantial property portfolio in London, extremely difficult to realise and almost as difficult to manage because of the ongoing hostilities. The bankrupt made general complaints that the estate had been mismanaged by the trustee who had decided against making use of the bankrupt's offers of assistance, and he sought to restrain a sale of one property on the basis that it was a bad time of year to sell. Harman J noted that there must be circumstances in which the court would interfere but, without attempting to define what such circumstances were, stated that they could not '(in the absence of fraud) justify interference in the day to day administration of the estate, nor can they entitle the bankrupt to question the exercise by the trustee in good faith of his discretion, nor to hold him accountable for an error of judgment.' The court pointed out that the bankrupt had had ample time to put forward his own scheme for realising the portfolio and dismissed the application.

These cases were cited as applicable in liquidation by the court in *Leon v York-O-Matic Ltd*[6]. The company had operated a chain of launderettes. The liquidator contracted to sell all its properties in December 1965 for £47,000 having rejected an offer of £40,000 for only some of the properties from one of the former directors. The director commenced proceedings in March 1966 seeking to restrain completion of the sale, asserting that the properties were being sold at a gross undervalue. The court was not satisfied that the allegation of undervalue was made out, and expressed concern as to the delay in seeking relief. There was no question of fraud. In refusing the application the court stated that it was not satisfied either that the liquidator had not exercised his discretion bona fide or that he had acted in a way in which no reasonable liquidator could have acted. This decision was followed in *Pitman & Co v Top Business Systems (Nottingham) Ltd*[7], an application to strike out the statement of claim as disclosing no reasonable cause of action. The material allegation was that the liquidator had entered into a contract to sell intellectual property rights without a proper valuation of those rights and without the approval of the creditors. There was no allegation of fraud and no pleading that the liquidator had not exercised his discretion bona fide or that he was proposing to do something which was so utterly unreasonable and absurd that no reasonable man would do it. The court accepted that such a pleading was necessary, expressly making the point that it would not be enough to establish negligence[8], and struck out the pleading. The applicants in *Re Hans Place Ltd (in liquidation)*[9] were lessees of property which had been sub-let. The liquidator disclaimed the underlease thereby releasing the sureties[10] and the applicant sought an order setting the disclaimer aside. Counsel for the applicants argued that the previous authorities were all examples of a challenge being made to a commercial decision of the office-holder. While it was understandable that the court would not allow the routine challenge of such decisions, he argued that there should be no requirement of mala fides or perversity where the applicant could demonstrate that, as a landlord, he would be seriously affected by the decision to disclaim. The deputy judge disagreed and refused to interfere with the liquidator's decision.

A test which requires the court to find, before interfering, that the office-holder's actions were 'so utterly unreasonable and absurd that no reasonable man would have done it' is, conventionally expressed, the test for perversity. It suggests a test of such rigour that few challenges, absent fraud or bad faith, can hope to succeed. Success did, however, attend the application in *Re Edennote Ltd*[11]. The application concerned the assignment by the liquidator of the company's cause of action in existing proceedings concerning a football club over which various parties were wrangling. The applicant creditors of the company, effectively one of the competing parties, complained that the assignment was made to the other main competitor without an approach being made to them. They might well have made a more valuable offer for the assignment which would have been to the benefit of the creditors as a whole. The Court of Appeal affirmed the judge's view that the correct test was one of perversity[12] and held that it was perverse for the liquidator to assign the cause of action to one side of the dispute without inquiring whether a better offer might be obtained from the other side. If this is utterly unreasonable and absurd it is a less rigorous approach to perversity than might commonly be supposed would be applied by the court, and one to be welcomed. In this connection it is interesting to note two passages from the judgment. Counsel for the assignee had made the point that the possibility of a better offer for the cause of action had not been obvious to others. The learned judge referred to this and continued:

> 'While [counsel for the assignee] accepted that [the liquidator's] action must be judged objectively, he said, correctly, that the question was how a reasonable liquidator would have acted in the circumstances prevailing at the time, a question the court must answer eschewing the wisdom of hindsight.'[13]

The learned judge continued:

> 'I have felt the force of [counsel's] submissions on this question. But they overlook an important point. A reasonable liquidator must be taken to be one who is properly advised. If support be needed for that proposition it can be found in *Re Hans Place Ltd* [1993] BCLC 768 at 778 ... where [counsel] is recorded as having submitted that the court can only reverse a decision of a liquidator under s 168(5) where it is satisfied that it was taken in some way mala fide or 'was so perverse as to demonstrate that no liquidator properly advised could have taken it'. Although [the deputy judge's] acceptance of [counsel's] submissions (at 779) was a general one and not specifically directed to the need for proper advice, it nevertheless confirms the view that a reasonable liquidator must be taken to be one who has such advice where he needs it. Very often a liquidator will not need advice before he acts. Here he clearly did. If [the liquidator] had been properly advised, he would have been told that the applicants, once apprised of the possibility of an assignment to Mr Venables, would see that their application for security was likely to avail them nothing and, as the judge observed, that Mr Venables would acquire a very considerable nuisance value in the settlement of the action as a whole. Thus it would have become obvious to a liquidator in [this liquidator]'s position, properly advised, that an approach should be made to the applicants.'

It is difficult to disagree with the outcome of this case, but not so easy to analyse it in terms or perversity. As appears from the passage cited it was not a straightforward matter. Once appropriate advice was taken the matter would have become obvious, but how is the liquidator to know when he does and when he does not need advice? The liquidator was presumably rather pleased to receive £7,000 (and a promise of 10% of the proceeds) for assigning a cause of an action of no obvious interest to him or the company. Certainly, in the circumstances, it was unreasonable for the liquidator not to appreciate that he should seek an alternative offer from the applicants or at least obtain advice, even at some cost to the liquidation, as to the better realisation of the asset. But was it perverse?

In *Mitchell v Buckingham International plc*[14] the Court of Appeal was concerned with cross-border issues and the liquidator's decision as to restraining orders in America the effect of which was to prevent judgment creditors obtaining priority over other unsecured creditors. The court drew a distinction between liquidators exercising their administrative powers to realise assets 'where the court will be very slow to substitute its judgment for the liquidators' on what is essentially a businessman's decision'[15] and liquidators seeking, in effect, anti-execution relief from the court to prevent one creditor obtaining an advantage over others. 'That is eminently a matter for the Companies Court, or for liquidators acting under the control of the Companies Court. It is not a matter for the liquidators to decide at their own discretion in the way in which they might take decisions as to the disposal of their company's assets.' This has been referred to as 'the exception recognised in *Mitchell v Buckingham International plc* to the perversity test which the court in *Re Edennote Ltd* ... said was the appropriate test for justifying interference with the decisions of the liquidator'[16]. In *Mahomed v Morris*[17] the court on an application to strike out found that the issue was a decision by the liquidators on the realisation of assets of the company where a rival claim to the assets had been made. The compromise reached was a commercial decision to be decided by the liquidators at their own discretion. The court also rejected the submission that the liquidators should have consulted persons affected by their decision or obtain the approval of the Companies Court:

> 'I have never heard it suggested that a secured creditor who is contemplating realising the charged assets is under some duty to consult the debtor or the surety of the debtor, even if he is aware that the price he obtains on realisation may mean that the debt is not discharged and so there are no surplus proceeds which the surety may claim by subrogation' ... [Counsel for the applicants] could point to no authority in support of the alleged duty to consult. In my judgment to impose such an obligation on a secured creditor would impose a serious fetter on the freedom of the secured creditor to exercise his power of sale over the charged property at the time and in the manner he chooses ... The fact that the secured creditor happens to be in liquidation cannot alter the position. The same must apply to rival claims to such property. Nor could [counsel] point to any authority directly in point in support of the alleged duty to obtain the sanction of the court.'[18]

Another example of a successful application is that in *Hamilton v Official Receiver*[19]. In this case a contributory offered the liquidator £1,000 for the assignment of a speculative claim in negligence against solicitors which had been valued 'more in hope than through scientific analysis' at £500,000. His first offer was on the basis that the liquidator would receive 50% of the proceeds but with an indemnity against an adverse costs order of £3,000. This was rejected by the liquidator on the basis that he required a complete indemnity as to costs and 100% of the proceeds; 'a counter-offer which, on its face, could not have been accepted by any reasonable person'[20]. However, the learned judge suggested that it would have been legitimate for the contributory's offer to be turned down because of the limited nature of the indemnity. The contributory then offered to purchase the claim outright for £1,000. The liquidator refused this offer, concerned that to sell for £1,000 an asset which might eventually prove to be worth £500,000 would expose him to proceedings for creditors. It was, however, quite plain that the liquidator had no interest whatever in pursuing the negligence claim for reasons not only of substance but of limitation. The court took the view that –

> 'the refusal to accept a reasonable and indeed the only offer on the table for an asset which the [liquidator] has no interest now in realising is, within the meaning of the words as used in the *Re Hans Place* decision, perverse and in my view it is right that

I should make an order under the provisions of s 168(5) requiring him to assign the cause of action for £1,000.'[21]

It appears that the decision in *Re Peters, ex p Lloyd* was not cited to the court.

The approach, therefore, in applications against the commercial decisions of office-holders in liquidation or bankruptcy is one of non-interference except in cases of fraud, mala fides, or perversity, although it may be that the courts will construe perversity in a purposive manner giving due consideration to the commercial realities of the situation that the officer-holder finds himself in at the material time. In decisions relating to the formal conduct of the relevant insolvency procedure the court will interfere readily if necessary to ensure that the insolvency process duly complies with general principle. While a similar approach is to be anticipated in voluntary arrangement cases, it is to be hoped that the court will view the actions of the supervisor in commercial context and will not apply a perversity test with the utmost rigour.

Finally, it should be noted that there is no room for private rights of action against the supervisor, whether for breach of statutory duty or duty of care or otherwise, in carrying out his tasks under an approved voluntary arrangement. Any complaint about his acts, omissions or decisions must be brought under the 'self-contained statutory scheme' which precludes the existence of private rights of action against a supervisor[22].

1 See IA 1986, s 168(5) (control of liquidator in winding up by the court), s 303(1) (control of trustee in bankruptcy).
2 *Pitman v Top Business Systems* [1984] BCLC 593 at 597b.
3 Bankruptcy Act 1869, s 20 introduced the jurisdiction.
4 (1882) 47 LT 64 (the whole of the very short judgment is set out by Plowman J in his judgment in *Leon v York-O-Matic Ltd* [1966] 1 WLR 1450).
5 [1949] Ch 236.
6 [1966] 1 WLR 1450.
7 [1984] BCLC 593.
8 [1984] BCLC 593 at 597d.
9 [1993] BCLC 768.
10 But see now *Hindcastle v Barbara Attenborough Associates Ltd* [1997] AC 70.
11 [1996] 2 BCLC 389, CA, affirming on this point [1995] 2 BCLC 248.
12 The judge below applied a perversity test, and also referred to the administrative law principle of *Wednesbury* unreasonableness (see *Associated Provincial Picture Houses Ltd v Wednesbury Corpn* [1948] 1 KB 223). Nourse LJ with whom Millett LJ agreed suggested that this reference was unnecessary and possibly confusing: 'In general there seems to be something unrealistic in judging the propriety of the acts and decisions of a businessman [the learned judge had made the point that office-holders had to act as prudent businessmen in most of what they do] by asking whether he took into account something he ought not to have taken into account or failed to take into account something he ought to have taken into account.'
13 [1996] 2 BCLC 389 at 396b.
14 [1998] 2 BCLC 369.
15 Per Robert Walker LJ (giving the judgment of the court) at 391f.
16 Per Peter Gibson LJ in *Mahomed v Morris* [2000] 2 BCLC 536, para 31.
17 [2000] 2 BCLC 536.
18 [2000] 2 BCLC 536, paras 33, 35.
19 [1998] BPIR 602.
20 [1998] BPIR 602 at 604C, per Laddie J.
21 [1998] BPIR 602 at 605H, per Laddie J.
22 *King v Anthony* [1998] 2 BCLC 517.

10.6 Removal of supervisor. There is a general power in the court to make an order appointing as supervisor a person who is qualified to act as an insolvency practitioner or who is authorised to act as supervisor in relation to the arrangement whenever (a) it is expedient to make such an appointment and (b) it is inexpedient, difficult or impracticable for an appointment to be made without the assistance of the court[1]. The appointment may be either to replace an existing supervisor or to fill a vacancy[2], and may be used so as to increase the number of supervisors implementing the arrangement[3]. The condition that a court appointment should be made only where it is inexpedient, difficult or impracticable for the appointment to be made without the court's assistance recognises that many arrangements will make provision for the creditors to replace the supervisor within the terms of the arrangement.

Any interested person may apply for an order, the application being made in the first instance to the registrar or district judge[4]. The former partners of an insolvency practitioner were entitled to apply to remove the insolvency practitioner from offices he held jointly with other former partners and where he was a sole appointee. Although the appointments were personal, the reality was that the work was carried out by various members of the firm's staff, and it was impracticable for the practitioner to fulfil the obligations of the offices following his departure from the firm[5]. Unless the court so directs it will not be necessary to serve notice of the application on all creditors of the arrangement, but the possibility of substituting a new insolvency practitioner[6] for the existing supervisor should first be put to the creditors before any application is made[7]. Where a supervisor wishes to resign he may presumably make the application himself, and in other cases the debtor or a representative or dissatisfied creditor will make the application[8]. In situations where the supervisor wishes to retire from practice, or loses his qualification to act as an insolvency practitioner or authorisation to act as supervisor, it may be necessary for him, or the Secretary of State or relevant recognised professional body, to bring a block application to remove the insolvency practitioner from all his appointments and substitute him with one or more qualified insolvency practitioners. Such an application may be made to the High Court, to which all proceedings before county courts may be transferred pursuant to IR 1986 and the County Courts Act 1984[9]. Where the matter is contested, the High Court may order an insolvency practitioner who is substituted by a new supervisor to deliver up all documents and records relating to the arrangement[10]. It is helpful, when a block application for substitution of an insolvency practitioner is made for the court to be provided with a table detailing the appointments in question and the powers available to the court in each of the various insolvency cases[11].

1 IA 1986, s 7(5) (CVA without moratorium), Sch A1, para 39(6), s 263(5) (IVA).

2 IA 1986, s 7(5) (CVA without moratorium), Sch A1, para 39(6), s 263(5) (IVA). The power is expressly without prejudice to the Trustee Act 1925, s 41(2) (power of court to appoint trustees of deeds of arrangement).

3 IA 1986, s 7(6) (CVA without moratorium), Sch A1, para 39(7) (CVA with moratorium), s 263(6) (CVA). A sole appointee cannot be replaced by a joint appointment: *Re A & C Supplies Ltd* [1998] BPIR 303.

4 *Re John Abbot* [1998] BPIR 171 at 176.

5 *Re A & C Supplies Ltd* [1998] BPIR 303.

6 Or other person authorised to act as supervisor in relation to the arrangement: see para 1.12 above.

7 *Re Sankey Furniture Ltd* [1995] 2 BCLC 594. This decision can, however, give rise to a great deal of cost and might not necessarily be followed in every case depending upon the precise circumstances.

8 Strictly, by the time that an application is made to replace or add a further supervisor it is likely that there will be no 'pending proceedings before the court' for the purposes of IR 1986, r 7.1 and, accordingly, the application should be by originating application in Form 7.1: see Appendix 5. However, the court will usually entertain an application by 'ordinary application' under IR 1986, r 7.2; see Form 7.2 as there will by then have been relevant proceedings before the court.

9 IR 1986, r 7.11(4) and County Courts Act 1984, s 41(1); and see *Re Ballard and Taplin Ltd* [1996] BPIR 526; *Re John Abbot* [1998] BPIR 171; but cf *Re Bridgend Goldsmiths Ltd* [1995] BCC 226. Note in *Re A & C Supplies Ltd* [1998] BPIR 303 at 308, Blackburne J stated that the provisions of County Courts Act 1984, s 41 had not been drawn to his attention in *Re Bridgend Goldsmiths*.
10 *Re Stella Metals Ltd* [1997] BPIR 293, where the original insolvency practitioner was ordered to pay the costs.
11 *Re Supperstone v Auger* [1999] BPIR 152. For a suggested form of table, and notes, see [1999] BPIR 152 at 155–156.

10.7 Variation of arrangement. Many voluntary arrangements are approved on the basis that the debtor will make periodical contributions over a lengthy period, often five years. The chances that the debtor's situation will change during that period are significant and the ability to vary the arrangements as approved is often welcome. Many arrangements contain express provision for variation, usually on a 75% vote of the creditors in accordance with the provisions of IR 1986[1]. Such express provisions for variation are valid. In *Horrocks v Broome*[2] the court rejected the argument that the scheme of IA 1986 precluded variation in IVA, and the decision will apply equally in CVA. Various matters were raised in support of the argument, including the points that: (a) that the detailed safeguards in IA 1986 which applied to the implementation of the voluntary arrangement would be absent at the time of variation, and a dissentient creditor would not be able to challenge the arrangement at the time of its implementation because ex hypothesi he would not know at that stage whether the power to vary would be used so as to prejudice his interests; (b) if the arrangement was indeed subsequently varied in a manner prejudicial to the creditor he might have no remedy under IA 1986, s 263(3)[3] since the court would not normally entertain any challenge to the exercise of his discretion by the supervisor unless satisfied that it had been exercised improperly[4]; (c) there was nothing in IA 1986 or IR 1986 which suggested that Parliament had conceived of the possibility of variation, but rather the statute contemplated only a fresh proposal to the creditors which the debtor could not make within 12 months of the initial interim order[5]. Furthermore, the court had no power to sanction a variation[6]; (d) the criminal sanction[7] on the debtor in respect of false information supplied to the supervisor would not be available on a variation; and (e) the power to vary was ex facie bad since it would potentially permit provisions to be introduced into the arrangement which would not have been permissible in the original proposal, for example, varying the rights of a secured or preferential creditor.

While accepting that a variation might adversely affect the interests of a particular creditor, the court directed that the arrangement could be varied under the procedure contained in its terms, with the requisite 75% majority. The variation clause had to be construed as permitting only variations or modifications which could have been validly included in the original proposal. It was recognised that a challenge might be brought against an approved arrangement under IA 1986, s 262[8] on the grounds of potential substantial prejudice, and the court cautioned debtors and nominees to exercise care before including variation clauses to ensure that they were drafted to meet any objections that were likely to be taken.

The point made at (d) above needs to be kept in mind. A debtor or the directors of a corporate debtor may propose a variation to gain an ancillary advantage, for example to bring an arrangement to an earlier end than originally approved so as to avoid paying the fruits of a new business venture to the creditors. In proposing a variation the debtor will be subject to the general law as to misrepresentation and deceit, but it is uncertain to what extent he is obliged to disclose information without a specific request to do so[9]. It would be advisable for nominees to draft the arrangement so as to impose such a duty or for the supervisor or creditors to require disclosure before a proposal to vary the arrangement is put before the creditors.

In *Re Circuit Leisure Ltd, Larchstone Ltd v Eric Stonham*[10] the voluntary arrangement contained a provision that the supervisor might convene a meeting of creditors to consider whether amendments should be made to the arrangements if it appeared that there was no reasonable prospect of the voluntary arrangement being successfully completed. The court implied a term that the creditors' meeting so convened might vary the arrangements on a 75% majority vote in accordance with IR 1986, r 1.19.

1 Ie IR 1986, r 1.19(3)–(6) (CVA without moratorium), r 1.52(1)–(6) (CVA with moratorium), r 5.23(3)–(6) (IVA): see para 6.10 above.
2 [1999] BPIR 66.
3 Or IA 1986, s 7(3) (CVA without moratorium), Sch A1, para 39(3) (CVA with moratorium).
4 Cf *Re Edennote Ltd* [1996] 2 BCLC 389.
5 By virtue of IA 1986, s 255(1)(c); note that with the implementation of the amendments introduced by IA 2000 it will be possible for a debtor to propose a new IVA within 12 months of an existing IVA because he no longer needs to obtain an interim order before making his proposal to creditors: IA 1986, s 256A.
6 *Re Alpa Lighting* [1997] BPIR 341, and see para 10.4 above.
7 Previously IR 1986, r 5.30, now repealed and re-enacted in wider terms in IA 1986, s 262A, inserted by IA 2000. In CVA, IR 1986, r 1.30, now repealed and re-enacted in IA 1986, s 6A (all CVAs).
8 IA 1986, s 6 (CVA without moratorium), Sch A1, para 38 (CVA with moratorium).
9 There is a strong case to be made that the debtor or directors owe creditors a strict duty of good faith: see *Cadbury Schweppes v Somji* [2001] 1 WLR 615, para 25, reported with the decision at first instance at [2001] 1 BCLC 498. Parliament revised the criminal sanction against company officers or debtors who make false representations or are otherwise fraudulent in IA 2000; see IA 1986, s 6A (all CVAs), s 262A (IVA), para 8.7 above. However, these sanctions only apply where there is fraud 'for the purpose of obtaining the approval of creditors to a proposal for a voluntary arrangement'. The opportunity was therefore missed to introduce criminal sanctions in respect of fraud in connection with the implementation or variation of a voluntary arrangement.
10 (24 March 1999, unreported) (Miss E Gloster QC) Lawtel Doc No C9200093.

10.8 Variation where no express power. In the absence of express authorisation a term will not be implied into an arrangement permitting a variation by 75% of the creditors[1]. However, the Court of Appeal decided in *Raja v Rubin and Goodman*[2] that it is permissible for all the creditors, or all the creditors of a distinct class, to reach a consensual variation to the arrangement with the debtor which would be binding upon them all. Such a consensual arrangement would not have the effect of altering the original arrangement which would continue to have statutory force. If all the creditors and the debtor consent to the variation in the arrangement it proceeds as a binding agreement between them. If only a class of creditors agree to a variation as between themselves and the debtor, this variation not affecting the rights of creditors outside the class, the voluntary arrangement continues in its original form as between the debtor and any creditor not in the relevant class, but in its varied form as between the class creditors and the debtor. The court appreciated that this approach might give rise to uncertainty, in that no creditor at the start of the arrangement could be sure how the arrangement might develop through future amendment. But this consideration is outweighed by the advantages of allowing variation to which all affected creditors agree. The present law as to variation of voluntary arrangements may therefore be summarised as follows:

1. It is legitimate for a voluntary arrangement to contain an express provision for variation[3].
2. The fact that an arrangement as approved contains a variation provision might in appropriate (albeit, it is suggested, unusual) circumstances form the basis of a challenge under IA 1986[4].
3. Where a variation takes place pursuant to an express power the varied arrangement continues as if it were the arrangement approved in the creditors' meeting, subject always to rights accrued before the variation.
4. In the absence of an express power of variation the creditors as a whole, or any distinct class of creditors, may unanimously vary the terms of the arrangement provided that the rights of creditors not in the relevant class are not affected. For the creditors outside the class the arrangement continues as originally approved.
5. Where there is a consensual variation in the absence of an express power, any party who is affected by the variation may apply to the court to complain of the relevant act or decision of the supervisor which permitted the variation to proceed[5]. The court will then have power to disallow the variation.
6. Where there is any variation, whether under express power or otherwise, any person affected by its terms, even if not a party to the arrangement[6], may apply to the court to complain of the relevant act or decision of the supervisor which permitted the variation to proceed[7]. The court will then have power to disallow the variation.

1 *Raja v Rubin and Goodman* [1998] BPIR 647 (at first instance; there was no appeal on this point).
2 [2000] Ch 274.
3 If there is express provision for variation but no provision as to how the variation is to be agreed the court will imply the provisions of IR 1986, r 1.19 (CVA without moratorium), r 1.52 (CVA with moratorium), r 5.23 (IVA); *Re Circuit Leisure Ltd* (24 March 1999, unreported). See para 10.7 above.
4 IA 1986, s 6 (CVA without moratorium), Sch A1, para 38 (CVA with moratorium), s 262 (IVA). See paras 7.1, 7.3 above.
5 Under the provisions of IA 1986, s 7(3) (CVA without moratorium), Sch A1, para 39(3), (4) (CVA with moratorium), s 263(3) (IVA). See para 10.4 above.
6 See IA 1986, s 7(3) (CVA without moratorium), Sch A1, para 39(3),(4) (CVA with moratorium), s 263(3) (IVA), which permit *any* person dissatisfied by an act or decision of the supervisor to apply to the court.
7 See n 6 above.

10.9 The unco-operative debtor. In IVA where the supervisor or creditors find that the debtor is not giving the co-operation that is required to ensure the proper functioning of the arrangement the supervisor can bring that failure on the part of the debtor to the attention of the court by seeking directions[1]. Failure to comply with the court's directions will constitute contempt and can be punished by imprisonment or a fine. If the supervisor fails to act to seek appropriate directions one or more creditors may apply to the court as persons dissatisfied[2] with the supervisor's omission to seek directions from the court to remedy the debtor's default. Apart from seeking directions from the court the sanction available to the creditors against the unco-operative debtor is bankruptcy. A bankruptcy order made be made against the debtor, despite the existence of an IVA, on a petition by the supervisor or any creditor bound by the arrangements where the court is satisfied that the debtor has failed to do all such things for the purposes of the arrangement as have been reasonably required of him by the supervisor[3]. Apart from this draconian step the supervisor and creditors may ensure the compliance of the debtor with the arrangement by enforcing its terms as may be appropriate, seeking directions or other appropriate order from the court[4]. The terms of the voluntary arrangement will constitute a contract between the debtor and the creditors, and also the supervisor if the arrangements are so framed. The contract may be enforced by proceedings, subject to its terms, but the more convenient way to control the debtor will usually be by application to the insolvency court for directions.

In CVA it is less likely that the supervisor or creditors will face difficulties of co-operation on behalf of the company. The supervisor will normally be given all necessary powers under the voluntary arrangement to conduct the company's affairs as they may relate to the voluntary arrangement. Should difficulties arise the court should be in a position to give appropriate directions to overcome or circumvent the problem[5]. Ultimately, the court has power to make an order for administration or winding up, and IA 1986, s 7(4) expressly includes the supervisor among the persons who may apply for either such order.

1 Under IA 1986, s 263(4).
2 See para 10.4 above.
3 IA 1986, s 276(1)(c).
4 And see para 10.4 above; the supervisor may apply for appropriate directions under IA 1986, s 263(4) (IVA).
5 Under the powers given by IA 1986, s 7(3) (CVA without moratorium), Sch A1, para 39(3), (4) (CVA with moratorium).

10.10 Access to essential supplies. A supervisor of a voluntary arrangement is given power under IA 1986 to require the continuation of supplies by public utilities notwithstanding unpaid accounts due to the utility concerned by the debtor[1]. This power applies from the 'relevant day' which is the day on which the arrangement is approved by the creditors[2]. The utilities subject to these provisions are (a) those providing a supply of gas[3], (b) a public supply of electricity[4], (c) water supplied by a water undertaker[5], and (d) a supply of telecommunication services by a public telecommunications operator[6].

In IVA a request for a supply of any of these services may be made by or with the concurrence of the supervisor for the purposes of any business which is or has been carried on by the individual debtor, by a firm or partnership of which the individual is or was a member, or by an agent or manager for the individual or for such firm or partnership[7].

The public utility receiving a request for supplies from a supervisor of a CVA or an IVA is under its standard obligation[8] to provide or restore the supply in question, but may not make it a condition of providing the supply, or do anything which has the effect of making it a condition of the giving of the supply, that any outstanding charges in respect of a supply given to the individual before the relevant day are paid[9]. The utility is entitled to make it a condition of the supply that the supervisor personally guarantees the payment in respect of the supply[10].

1 See IA 1986, s 233(2)(b) (CVA), s 372(2)(b) (IVA).
2 IA 1986, s 233(1)(c), s 372(1)(b).
3 By a gas supplier within the meaning of the Gas Act 1986, Pt I: IA 1986, s 233(3) (CVA), s 372(4) (IVA).
4 Within the meaning of the Electricity Act 1989, Pt I.
5 IA 1986, s 233(3)(c) (CVA), s 372(4)(c) (IVA), as amended by the Water Act 1989, Sch 25, para 78.
6 IA 1986, s 233(3)(d) (CVA), s 372(4)(d) (IVA); 'telecommunication services' and 'public telecommunications operator' mean the same as in the Telecommunications Act 1984, except that the former does not include local delivery services within the meaning of the Broadcasting Act 1990, Pt II: IA 1986, ss 233(5), 374(5).

7 IA 1986, s 372(3).
8 The supervisor is in no better position than any other user.
9 IA 1986, s 233(2)(b) (CVA), s 372(2)(b) (IVA).
10 IA 1986, s 233(2)(a) (CVA), s 372(2)(a) (IVA).

10.11 Supervisor's accounts and reports. Where the arrangement authorises or requires the supervisor: (1) to carry on the debtor's business or to trade on his behalf or in his name; or (2) to realise the assets of the debtor[1]; or (3) otherwise to administer or dispose of any funds of the debtor or the estate, the supervisor must keep accounts and records of his acts and dealings in and in connection with the arrangement, including in particular records of all receipts and payment of money[2]. At least once every 12 months, beginning with the date of his appointment, the supervisor must prepare an abstract of these receipts and payments and send copies, accompanied by his comments on the progress and efficacy of the arrangement to the court, the debtor and all creditors bound by the arrangement, and, in CVA, to the Registrar of Companies, the members of the company, and (if the company is not in liquidation) the company's auditors[3]. The abstract must be sent out within two months of the end of the period to which it relates[4]. In the rare cases where the arrangement does not authorise the supervisor to trade, realise assets or administer or dispose of funds, the supervisor must send out a report on the progress and efficacy of the arrangement not less often than once in every 12 months[5]. On the application of the supervisor the court may vary the dates on which the obligation to send abstracts or reports arises[6].

At any time during the course of the arrangement or after its completion the Secretary of State may require the supervisor to produce for inspection (a) his records and accounts relating to the arrangement and (b) copies of his abstracts and reports[7]. Any accounts and records produced to the Secretary of State may be audited and the supervisor must give any further information and assistance as may be needed for the purposes of the audit[8].

The fees, costs, charges and expenses that may be incurred for any purposes of the arrangement are those which are sanctioned by its terms or which would or would correspond to those which would be payable in the debtor's insolvency[9]. Additionally, any disbursements made by the nominee prior to the arrangement's approval, and any remuneration for his services agreed between the nominee and the debtor, the liquidator or administrator, the official receiver or the trustee are also chargeable to the arrangement[10].

1 Or the assets belonging to the estate where the individual debtor is an undischarged bankrupt: IR 1986, r 5.31(1)(b).
2 IR 1986, r 1.26(1) (all CVAs, applying where a moratorium has been in force by virtue of IR 1986, r 1.54(2)), r 5.31(1) (IVA).
3 IR 1986, r 1.26(2) (all CVAs), r 5.31(2) (IVA). If during any period of 12 months no payments are made and there have been no receipts a statement must be sent to this effect: IR 1986, rr 1.26(2), 5.31(2).
4 IR 1986, r 1.26(3) (all CVAs), r 5.31(3) (IVA).
5 IR 1986, r 1.26(4) (all CVAs), r 5.31(4) (IVA), the report to be sent to the court, the debtor, and all creditors bound by the arrangement.
6 IR 1986, r 1.26(5) (all CVAs), r 5.31(5) (IVA). In CVA the court may dispense with sending abstracts or reports to members of the company either altogether or on the basis that the availability of a report is advertised to members.
7 IR 1986, r 1.27(1) (all CVAs, applying where a moratorium has been in force by virtue of r 1.54(2)), r 5.32(1) (IVA). Production may be required either at the supervisor's premises or elsewhere: rr 1.27(2), 5.32(2).
8 IR 1986, r 1.27(3) (all CVAs), r 5.32(3) (IVA).
9 IR 1986, r 1.28(1)(b) (all CVAs applying where a moratorium has been in force by virtue

of r 1.54(2)), r 5.33(b) (IVA); as to fees etc payable in insolvency see IR 1986, r 4.218 (winding up), IR 1986, r 6.224 (bankruptcy).

10 IR 1986, r 1.28(1) (all CVAs), r 5.33(1) (IVA).

10.12 Supervisor's duties on completion or termination of arrangement. Within 28 days of the final completion or termination[1] of the arrangement the supervisor must send to all creditors bound by the arrangement and the members of the corporate debtor or the individual debtor (a) a notice that the arrangement has been fully implemented or terminated as the case may be, and (b) a report summarising all receipts and payments made in the administration of the arrangement explaining any difference in the actual implementation of it as compared with the voluntary arrangement as approved, or, in the case of termination, explaining the reasons why the arrangement was not duly completed[2]. Should the debtor or any creditor be dissatisfied with the supervisor's summary the fact of or his explanation of any difference in the actual implementation of the arrangement from that envisaged, an application may be made to the court for an appropriate order or directions[3]. Also within this 28-day period the supervisor must send copies of the notice and report to the Registrar of Companies (CVA) or Secretary of State (IVA) and to the court, and until he does so he may not vacate his office[4].

The period of 28 days allowed for the notice and summary may be extended by the court on the supervisor's application[5].

1 Or 'come to an end prematurely' ie ceases to have effect before it has been fully implemented in respect of all persons bound to the arrangement: IA 1986, s 7B (all CVAs), s 262C (IVA).

2 IR 1986, r 1.29(1), (2) (all CVAs, applying where a moratorium has been in force by virtue of r 1.54(2)), r 5.34(1), (2) (IVA).

3 See IA 1986, s 7(3) (CVA without moratorium), Sch A1, para 39(3)(4) (CVA with moratorium), s 263(3) (IVA). See eg *Phillips v Stanley* (7 February 2003), Ch D (lawtel document AC 9200482) when the supervisor successfully appealed the declaration by the deputy district judge that the debtors had complied with all their obligations and that their failure to realise the equity in their domestic property or disclose the fact that they owned property in Spain were not material omissions.

4 IR 1986, r 1.29(3) (all CVAs), r 5.34(3) (IVA).

5 IR 1986, r 1.29(4) (all CVAs), r 5.34(4) (IVA).

Chapter 11

Failure of voluntary arrangements

11.1 When arrangement has failed. Whether, and if so when, a voluntary arrangement has failed will be a matter of construction of the terms of the arrangement. Neither culpability on the part of the debtor nor the views of the creditors are matters relevant to the proper construction of the terms[1]. Unless the terms have been drawn unusually, it will be open to any creditor to petition for insolvency or otherwise proceed to enforce his debt on the failure of the arrangement. 'Failure' of an arrangement will often be important in cases where the debtor, whether in trade or professional practice, has agreed to make periodic payments out of income to the supervisor for distribution among the creditors. In company voluntary arrangement such arrangements are not uncommon and are referred to as 'trading out' CVAs. Where a debtor in such an arrangement fails to make his promised payments there may be uncertainty and differing views among the arrangement creditors as to whether it will more advantageous to permit the arrangement to continue in the hope that payments will be made in the future or to bring the arrangement to an end and put the debtor into formal insolvency. The standard conditions of many arrangements provide that there is a failure of the arrangement on the happening of any one of a number of events; in particular where there is a breach of the debtor's obligations under the arrangement, or when it becomes possible for any person not bound by the arrangement to petition for the debtor's liquidation or bankruptcy, or something happens which renders it impossible for the supervisor to continue implementing the arrangement. Where an event of failure occurs such standard conditions usually require the supervisor to report the fact to the creditors and distribute any funds in his possession under the terms of the arrangement, and further provide that individual creditors cease to be bound by the arrangement. Two connected questions arise for consideration. First, whether the happening of an event of failure automatically brings the voluntary arrangement to an end irrespective of whether the supervisor is aware of the event and acts on it. Secondly, whether a requirement that the supervisor petitions for insolvency on learning that the debtor has failed to comply with the obligations of the arrangement is permissive or mandatory.

In considering the standard conditions of the arrangement applying to the company in CVA in *Welsby v Brelec Installations Ltd*[2] the court construed the condition specifying the events of failure as a threshold requirement to be satisfied before the supervisor took steps to bring the arrangement to an end, and not as a provision which automatically terminated the arrangement. Accordingly, it was only if the relevant event came to the notice of the supervisor and he then proceeded to take any unequivocal step to that end that the voluntary arrangement would terminate and the consequences of the arrangement failing would come into play. It was not to be supposed that the creditors in approving the voluntary arrangement had contemplated that any default, however trivial, might bring the arrangement to an end, and indeed do so without the supervisor or the creditors being aware of the fact. The decision in *Welsby v Brelec Installations Ltd* may be contrasted with that in *Re Maple Environmental Services Ltd*[3] where it had been suggested that where a company was involved in a 'trading out' arrangement any failure by the company to comply with its ongoing obligations would represent a failure of the voluntary arrangement. Much may depend in any particular case on the precise wording of the voluntary arrangement.

While the question of automatic termination can present difficulties it might be thought that the terms of the voluntary arrangement would be conclusive one way or the other on the second question, whether the supervisor is or is not obliged to present a petition for winding up or bankruptcy in the event of failure of the debtor to meet obligations under the arrangement. The terms of an arrangement may indeed be drawn to as to make the presentation of a petition obligatory for breach of certain terms, but discretionary in the case of breach of other terms. In *Re Maple Environmental Services Ltd* the point was stressed that in circumstances where the company was not meeting its ongoing trading obligations continued payments to the CVA creditors could only be made to the prejudice of the post arrangement creditors, who may well be unaware that the company was in CVA. In these circumstances it was suggested that it could not be open to the supervisor to maintain that it is a matter for him to determine whether or not there has been a failure of the arrangement. In *Welsby*, however, the court considered that the fact that an arrangement had continued to function at the expense of the company's post-arrangement creditors did not of itself constitute some special circumstance which necessitated the termination of the arrangement and the revocation of the trusts under which the supervisor held the funds paid over by the company in favour of the CVA creditors. It was pointed out[4] that if the liquidator subsequently considered that the company was wrong to continue making payments to the CVA he could invoke the antecedent provisions of IA 1986[5] to seek to recover money which should not have been paid away[6]. Accordingly, although in apparently obligatory terms the requirements of the arrangements' conditions that the supervisor take steps to terminate the arrangement were held to be permissive not mandatory.

It is suggested that such a view should be treated with caution. The supervisor is as bound by the terms of the voluntary arrangement as is the debtor and any creditor. If on a true construction of those terms a failure of obligation on the part of the debtor results in the failure of the voluntary arrangement and a requirement that a petition for formal insolvency be presented then that is what should happen. In *Re N T Gallagher & Son Ltd*[7] the CVA was subject to the following term:

> 'The joint supervisors shall petition for the winding-up of the company immediately it fails in any of its obligations under the arrangement, the supervisors to retain sufficient funds at all times to do so.'

In due course the company fell into arrears with its contributions such that under the terms of the arrangement it was deemed to have failed. Notwithstanding, the supervisor, with the consent of the creditors' committee, allowed the CVA to continue on condition that the company complied with a revised contribution arrangement. The view was taken that the supervisors had a discretion whether to petition for the winding up of the company despite its failure to comply with its obligation to make contributions. The Court of Appeal[8] described the correctness of this view as 'dubious' but noted that it was not an issue in the appeal.

It may well be that if a supervisor allows a voluntary arrangement to continue and accepts further contributions from the debtor after the debtor is in breach of obligation despite a requirement to petition for insolvency, creditors whose debts post-date the voluntary arrangement are likely to be prejudiced in an eventual insolvency where the trusts on which the voluntary arrangement contributions are held survive the insolvency. It should be open to such creditors to apply to the court as persons dissatisfied with the acts of the supervisor[9] in the expectation that the court would order that all 'post-failure' contributions should be held for the benefit of all the debtors' creditors and not just those creditors who are bound to the voluntary arrangement.

If the terms of a voluntary arrangement provide that it should last for a fixed period of time subject to extension with the consent of the creditors in a creditors' meeting it is not open to the creditors to extend the voluntary arrangement after the expiry of its fixed period. The creditors cannot extend a voluntary arrangement which has ceased to exist[10].

1 *Re Keenan* [1998] BPIR 205.
2 [2000] 2 BCLC 576.
3 [2000] BCC 93.
4 [2000] 2 BCLC 576 at 589c.
5 That is the provisions enabling a liquidator to seek an order restoring the position to what it would have been had the company not made a transaction at undervalue: IA 1986, s 238, or given a preference, IA 1986, s 239.
6 Or seek to render the directors personally accountable under IA 1986, s 214 for any wrongful trading which may have occurred. This plainly does not arise in personal insolvency. It is suggested that it is by no means clear that sums paid to the voluntary arrangement creditors would be recoverable by the trustee or liquidator as transactions at an undervalue or preferences, and while the decision is likely to be followed this aspect of the reasoning will in many cases be inapplicable.
7 [2002] EWCA Civ 404, [2002] 1 WLR 2380.
8 [2002] EWCA Civ 404, [2002] 1 WLR 2380 at [20].
9 See para 10.4 above.
10 *Re Strongmaster Ltd* [2002] EWHC 444 (Ch), [2002] All ER (D) 157 (Mar).

11.2 Bankruptcy order despite IVA. There are two circumstances in which the existence of an arrangement does not protect the debtor against the presentation of a bankruptcy petition or the making of a bankruptcy order[1]. First, a creditor whose debt arose after the arrangement will not be affected by it and may present a petition against the debtor in the normal way. Secondly, a petition may be presented by the supervisor or any creditor bound by the arrangement where the debtor is in default[2].

A petitioner who presents a petition in connection with an IVA must satisfy one of three grounds, namely that: (a) the debtor has failed to comply with his obligations under the arrangement; (b) information which was false or misleading in any material particular or which contained material omissions (i) was contained in any statement of affairs or other document supplied by the debtor to any person in connection with the arrangement or (ii) was otherwise made available by the debtor to his creditors at or in connection with a creditors' meeting; or (c) the debtor has failed to do all such things as may for the purposes of the voluntary arrangement have been reasonably required of him by the supervisor[3].

For the purposes of (a) above, it is not necessary to show any degree of culpability on the part of the debtor with regard to the failure; failure is to be considered objectively[4]. The court is not bound to make a bankruptcy order, however, and in cases where the failure is not serious and there is no culpability on the part of the debtor may refuse to do so[5]. Where there is a significant default by the debtor, and the underlying scheme of the voluntary arrangement is that if it is not properly carried out by the debtor bankruptcy will follow, then the court will only refuse a bankruptcy order in exceptional cases whatever the view of the creditors[6]. It may be noted that the requirement of IA 1986, s 276(1)(a) is that the court is satisfied that the debtor 'has failed' to comply with his obligation. There is no requirement that this failure persist at the date of the bankruptcy order[7], and accordingly a bankruptcy order may be made in respect of a past failure remedied before the date of the hearing of the petition[8].

For the purposes of (b) above, an omission is 'material' if it would be likely to have made a material difference to the way in which the creditors would have considered and assessed the terms of the proposed arrangement[9]. The court should apply this as an objective test[10]. Whether the debtor acted deliberately or was otherwise culpable is immaterial. It should also be borne in mind that where new information of a significant nature comes to light a nominee who holds proxies should adjourn the creditors' meeting so that the new information may be reported to all creditors[11]. Failure to do so on the part of the nominee would constitute a material omission, or result in information before creditors becoming misleading or even false. It is a material omission not to inform all creditors that some creditors had been offered an inducement by a third party to vote for the debtor's arrangement[12]. A similar approach will be applied to a consideration as to whether information was materially false or materially misleading.

There remains a discretion in the court as to whether it is appropriate to make a bankruptcy order. This discretion must be exercised in accordance with the principle that a creditor is entitled to payment of his debt; if it is not paid in full by the hearing of the petition, the petition should not be adjourned except on the basis that there was a reasonable prospect of payment within a reasonable time[13].

It is open to a supervisor to petition for bankruptcy even after the expiry of the period for which the IVA was to run, although if there is unjustified delay in the presentation of the petition that would be a factor which would be taken into account by the court when considering whether or not to make a bankruptcy order[14]. An appeal against an order of the registrar or district judge making or refusing a bankruptcy order is a true appeal and the judge will not interfere with the decision unless satisfied that there was a wrongful exercise of discretion[15].

1 Before the implementation of the amendments introduced by IA 2000 there was a third. A creditor whose debt ante-dated the arrangement was not bound by the arrangement if he was not given notice of the creditors' meeting. If he was unwilling or unable to join the arrangement he could present a petition against the debtor.
2 IA 1986, ss 264(1)(c), 276.
3 IA 1986, s 276(1).
4 *Re Keenan* [1998] BPIR 205.
5 See *Re Keenan* [1998] BPIR 205 and *Vadher v Weisgard* [1998] BPIR 295.
6 *Harris v Gross* [2001] BPIR 586; where at a meeting called by the supervisor to consider the position 69% in value of the creditors voted against bankruptcy.

7 This in contrast with the provisions of IA 1986, s 271(1)(a): 'the court shall not make a bankruptcy order on a creditors' petition unless it is satisfied that one or more of the petition debts ... has neither been paid or compounded for.'
8 *Carter-Knight v Peat* [2000] BPIR 968, the court rejecting the argument that the effect of IR 1986 rr 6.6 and 6.25 was that there must be an outstanding default under the IVA on the date of the hearing before a bankruptcy order could be made. The case was, however, remitted for rehearing because the judge below had not given sufficient reasons for making the order to demonstrate the basis on which he had proceeded.
9 *Apton New Homes v Tack* (19 June 1998) [2000] BPIR 164, referred to in *Cadbury Schweppes plc v Somji* [2001] 1 WLR 615, para 25.
10 *Cadbury Schweppes plc v Somji* [2001] 1 WLR 615, para 25.
11 *Cadbury Schweppes plc v Somji* [2001] 1 WLR 615, para 25.
12 *Cadbury Schweppes plc v Somji* [2001] 1 WLR 615.
13 *Judd v Williams* [1998] BPIR 88. Lloyd J made the point that the granting of repeated adjournments of the petition thereby allowing the debtor to make payment by instalments imposed an ad hoc voluntary arrangement on the creditor without his consent and without the protection afforded by a true IVA. If a bankruptcy order was made on another creditor's petition the sums paid under the initial petition might have to be returned.
14 *Harris v Gross* [2001] BPIR 586.
15 *Vadher v Weisgard* [1998] BPIR 295.

11.3 The effect of a winding up or bankruptcy order on a voluntary arrangement. A voluntary arrangement does not protect the debtor from liquidation or bankruptcy either at the petition of a creditor not bound to the arrangement[1], or at the petition of the supervisor or a creditor in respect of a breach by the debtor of obligations arising under the arrangement. If an order is made on the petition the vexed question arises as to the effect the order has on the existing voluntary arrangement. No assistance on this question may be found in IA 1986 or IR 1986. There is no provision at all concerning a corporate debtor in CVA entering into liquidation. In personal insolvency, although IA 1986 envisages that a bankruptcy order may be made against a debtor who is subject to an arrangement, it makes no provision with respect to the arrangement on the making of such an order[2]. It would not appear to be open to the supervisor to apply to the court for directions to determine the arrangement solely on the basis that a bankruptcy order has been made, as this is not a matter 'arising under the arrangement'[3]. It may be possible to seek directions, however, where the arrangement requires the debtor to make continuing payments to the creditors and he is prevented from doing so by his bankruptcy.

Where a voluntary arrangement comprises a composition, the amount for which the voluntary arrangement creditors will be able to prove will depend on the terms of the arrangement. It is standard practice for the terms to provide that the debtor is released from the creditors' debts only when he has completed his payments due under the arrangement. Creditors are well advised to ensure that a term of this nature is included in the arrangement, for otherwise they may find that they are only able to prove for such amounts as are due from the debtor under the voluntary arrangement at the commencement of the liquidation or bankruptcy, as opposed to their full pre-voluntary arrangement debt. In cases where the voluntary arrangement comprises a scheme of arrangement involving no more than a moratorium, the formal insolvency of the debtor is unlikely to be of any particular consequence. The moratorium will end and the creditors will participate in the payment of dividends in the liquidation or bankruptcy. There may be more important considerations at stake where the arrangement comprises a scheme of arrangement involving the debtor creating a trust over assets[4], or assigning assets to the supervisor, for realisation and distribution to the creditors. The likelihood is that the voluntary arrangement creditors will require a substantial proportion of the debtors' assets to be transferred to the voluntary arrangement. On the debtor entering liquidation or becoming bankrupt shortly afterwards the cupboard could be largely bare. If the trust over or assignment of assets to the supervisor is unimpeachable by the liquidator or trustee the voluntary arrangement creditors are likely to have a distinct advantage over the non-voluntary arrangement creditors in terms of dividend. This may be a real matter of concern on the part of a creditor whose debt arose after the arrangement, and who was unaware of the arrangement or its terms[5]. The prospects of a liquidator or trustee in bankruptcy being able to set aside the transfer of assets under the arrangement as a transaction at an undervalue, or a transaction in fraud of creditors[6], will be minimal. Neither will there normally be any realistic prospect of a successful challenge to the arrangement as a preference.

The critical question thus arises whether the trusts on which the voluntary arrangement assets are held survive the liquidation or bankruptcy. This issue has arisen not infrequently and, in differing circumstances, some 12 decisions[7] of the courts at first instance had been reported before the Court of Appeal considered the matter in *Re N T Gallagher & Son Ltd*[8]. These decisions showed a divergence of approach, and could be reconciled, if at all, only by drawing careful distinctions between the forms of liquidation in CVA cases and the identity of the petitioner in IVA as well as CVA cases.

The Court of Appeal in *N T Gallagher & Son Ltd* considered all these cases and concluded that such distinctions were misplaced. The court noted that the starting point for the determination of the question whether the voluntary arrangement trusts survived the liquidation or bankruptcy had to be the terms of the arrangement itself. The court went on to state that, as a matter of policy, in the absence of any provision in the voluntary arrangement as to what should happen to trust assets on liquidation or bankruptcy the court should prefer a default rule which furthers rather than hinders what might be taken to be the statutory purpose of IA 1986. Parliament plainly intended to encourage debtors and creditors to enter into voluntary arrangements so as to provide creditors with a means of recovering what they are owed without recourse to the more expensive means provided by formal insolvency, thereby giving some debtors the opportunity to trade[9]. The rescue aspects of these observations are only heightened by the implementation of IA 2000 and the enactment of EA 2002. As for the rights of the voluntary arrangement creditors to prove in the liquidation or bankruptcy if on the facts of a particular case the voluntary arrangement should fail, the Court of Appeal could see no substantial basis for the analysis of the court at first instance in *Re N T Gallagher & Son Ltd* that the voluntary arrangement creditors' rights were analogous to the rights of secured creditors who are only entitled to prove if they abandon their security. Accordingly, if the terms of the arrangement are appropriately drafted, the voluntary arrangement creditors both retain the benefit of the assets transferred to the arrangement and may also prove for any sums remaining due to them on the failure of the voluntary arrangement should, on the facts, the arrangement have failed. Careful drafting of voluntary arrangements will ensure that the voluntary arrangement creditors should have both the benefits of the assets transferred to the voluntary arrangement and the ability to prove for the full amount of their voluntary arrangement debts. The result is that a post-voluntary arrangement creditor may be hard hit on a liquidation or bankruptcy. The Court of Appeal met this head on:

> 'Whilst we acknowledge the possibility that there will be post-CVA creditors who are unaware of the CVA and its terms, in practice there is likely to be a considerable

> overlap between the CVA creditors and the post-CVA creditors. Further, save for the Crown and local authorities in respect of fiscal liabilities (and they are likely to be CVA creditors), no one is forced to become a creditor of a company without making such inquiries as are thought appropriate to ascertain the financial position of the company. We do not therefore accept that to treat a trust created by a CVA as continuing notwithstanding the liquidation of the company is productive of such unfairness that the court should conclude that liquidation brings the trust to an end. Such a conclusion would run counter to the general law which leaves trusts of assets not held for a company unaffected by its liquidation.' [10]

It is understandable that the court should have resolved the questions thrown up by the formal insolvency of voluntary arrangement debtors in this way. There is, however, always the possibility that potential trading partners will in future be careful to avoid giving credit to any company known to be in CVA, and this will impede, perhaps prevent, the opportunities for its rescue. But, as the court pointed out, in most cases there will be a considerable overlap between the pre and post-voluntary arrangement creditors.

The Court of Appeal in *Re N T Gallagher & Son Ltd* provided a helpful summary of its conclusions as follows[11]:

1. Where a CVA or IVA provides for moneys or other assets to be paid to or transferred or held for the benefit of CVA or IVA creditors, this will create a trust of those moneys or assets for those creditors.
2. The effect of the liquidation of the company or the bankruptcy of the debtor on a trust created by the CVA or IVA will depend on the provisions of the CVA or IVA relating thereto.
3. If the CVA or IVA provides what is to happen on liquidation or bankruptcy (or the failure of the CVA or IVA), effect must be given thereto.
4. If the CVA or IVA does not so provide, the trust will continue notwithstanding the liquidation, bankruptcy or failure and must take effect according to its terms.
5. The CVA or IVA creditors can prove in the liquidation or bankruptcy for so much of their debt as remains after payment of what has been or will be recovered under the trust.

1 As all pre-voluntary arrangement creditors are now bound whether or not they receive notice of the creditors' meeting such a petition will now come only from a post-voluntary arrangement creditor.

2 The draftsman of the Act evidently proceeded upon the basis that the IVA would come to an end on the making of a bankruptcy order on a petition by a supervisor or creditor subject to an IVA for default, for provision is made that in this event any expenses properly incurred in the administration of the IVA should be a first charge on the bankrupt's estate: IA 1986, s 276(2) and see *Davis v Martin-Sklan* [1995] 2 BCLC 483 at 486–487. It would presumably be open to the court on an application by the supervisor under IA 1986, s 263(4) to direct that the IVA should be wound up and the assets transferred to the trustee.

3 See IA 1986, s 263(4).

4 A supervisor who holds money or other assets for the purpose of implementing the IVA will do so as a trustee: *Re Leisure Study Group Ltd* [1994] 2 BCLC 65.

5 Before IA 2000 amendments a creditor whose debt was antecedent to the IVA but who was not given notice of the arrangement could find himself in a particularly unfortunate position. Making the debtor bankrupt would have no financial advantage. His best course was to apply to the supervisor to join the arrangement and if he was refused then apply to the court as a person dissatisfied with a decision of the supervisor for an appropriate direction or order to enable him to join the arrangement, subject always to the terms of the relevant arrangements.

6 See IA 1986, ss 339–342C.

7 *Re McKeen (a debtor)* [1995] BCC 412; *Re Bradley-Hole (a bankrupt)* [1995] 1 WLR 1097; *Davis v Martin-Sklan* [1995] 2 BCLC 483; *Re Halson Packaging Ltd* [1997] BPIR

194; *Re Arthur Rathbone Kitchens Ltd* [1997] 2 BCLC 280; *Re Excalibur Airways Ltd* [1998] 1 BCLC 436; *Kings v Cleghorn* [1998] BPIR 463; *Re Maple Environmental Services Ltd* [2000] BCC 93; *Welsby v Brelec Installations Ltd* [2000] 2 BCLC 576; *Re Kudos Glass Ltd* [2001] 1 BCLC 390; and *Re N T Gallagher & Son Ltd* at first instance reported at [2002] 1 BCLC 224.

8 [2002] EWCA Civ 404, [2002] 1 WLR 2380.

9 [2002] EWCA Civ 404, [2002] 1 WLR 2380 at [50]. This being a CVA case, the court here refers to the position of companies and their creditors, but similar considerations must also apply to individual debtors even though they will not always be traders.

10 [2002] EWCA Civ 404, [2002] 1 WLR 2380 at [49].

11 [2002] EWCA Civ 404, [2002] 1 WLR 2380 at [54].

Chapter 12

Death of the debtor

12.1 General. A debtor who is involved with voluntary arrangements will presumably be insolvent in the event of his death, that is his estate when realised will be insufficient to meet in full all debts and other liabilities to which it is subject[1]. Where an estate is found to be or is likely to be insolvent after an individual's death it has to be administered for the benefit of the deceased's creditors and not for those entitled under a will or on intestacy until all the debts are paid. Insolvent estates are regulated by the Administration of Insolvent Estates of Deceased Persons Order 1986, SI 1986/1999 ('DPO 1986')[2] and in the case of any conflict between the provisions of IA 1986 and those of DPO 1986 the latter prevail[3].

An insolvency administration order under DPO 1986 may be made on the petition of any of the deceased debtor's creditors or by the supervisor or any person who is bound by an IVA[4]. Once an order is made the estate is administered and distributions made in the same way as any bankrupt's estate. The administration will be subject to the control of the bankruptcy court which will have the same powers and the same procedures as in bankruptcy[5]. The trustee of the estate will stand in the same position toward the supervisor of an IVA as would a trustee of a living bankrupt.

An insolvent estate does not have to be administered under an insolvency administration order. An executor or administrator may if he wishes administer the estate outside formal bankruptcy for so long as no insolvency administration order is made[6]. If he does, he must comply with the bankruptcy rules as to the administration of the estate, the rights of secured and unsecured creditors, proof of debts, priority of debts and payments and all other rules applicable to the particular administration[7]. It is open to the personal representative to present a petition for an insolvency administration order if he does not wish to administer or continue with the administration of the estate, and provided the estate is indeed insolvent the court must make an insolvency administration order on the personal representative's petition[8].

1 IA 1986, s 421(4).
2 Made by the Lord Chancellor, with the concurrence of the Secretary of State, by virtue of the provisions of IA 1986, s 421. These provisions enable the statutory instrument to apply those provisions of IA 1986 which are considered relevant to the administration of the insolvent estates with any modifications which are considered appropriate.
3 DPO 1986, art 3(2).
4 IA 1986, s 264, modified by DPO 1986, art 3, Sch 1, Pt II, para 2.
5 DPO 1986, art 3, Sch 1, Pt II, para 30.

6 DPO 1986, art 4(1).
7 DPO 1986, art 4(1).
8 IA 1986, s 273, substituted by DPO 1986, art 3, Sch 1, Pt II, para 7.

12.2 Death of debtor before IVA is approved. DPO 1986 brings a proposed IVA to an end if the arrangements have not been approved by the creditors before the death of the debtor making the proposal for the IVA. Thus, where an interim order has been made but the debtor dies before he has submitted his proposal the nominee must give notice to the court of the death of the debtor[1], and on receiving this notice the court must discharge the interim order[2]. Where an interim order has been made and the court has been satisfied by the nominee's report that a creditors' meeting should be held to consider the debtor's proposal, but the debtor dies before the creditors' meeting can be held, the meeting is cancelled[3]. If at the date of his death the debtor was an undischarged bankrupt, the personal representative shall give notice of the death to the trustee of his estate and the official receiver[4].

1 IA 1986, s 256(1A), added by DPO 1986, art 3, Sch 1, Pt III, para 1.
2 IA 1986, s 256(1B), added by DPO 1986, art 3, Sch 1, Pt III, para 1.
3 IA 1986, s 257, added by DPO 1986, art 3, Sch 1, Pt III, para 2.
4 IA 1986, s 257, added by DPO 1986, art 3, Sch 1, Pt III, para 2.

12.3 Death after approval of voluntary arrangement. Where the creditors' meeting summoned to consider the IVA approves the proposals and the chairman of the meeting has report the result to the court, the voluntary arrangement takes effect and, subject to any provision in the arrangement to the effect that the death of the debtor brings the IVA to an end, is then implemented by the supervisor notwithstanding the subsequent death of the debtor[1]. It would appear, however, that if the debtor dies after the approval by the creditors' meeting, but before the report to the court, then the voluntary arrangement cannot be enforced as a valid and binding arrangement. This is because IA 1986, ss 260–262 are disapplied on the death of the debtor[2]. The court may not act on the basis of the approval[3], and the approval cannot be challenged by any of the interested parties[4]. It is somewhat strange that DPO 1986 should apparently permit an IVA to continue after approval by creditors but only if the chairman has reported the meetings' decision to the court. The report to the court would seem to be merely an administrative function so that, if appropriate, the court may discharge the interim order. It is not for the court to review or interfere with the creditors' decision. In the ordinary course the IVA takes effect as if made by the debtor at the meeting[5], not when the result of the meeting is reported to the court.

Provided, therefore, that the chairman has reported the approval of the IVA by the creditors' meeting to the court, there is no statutory reason why the IVA should not continue. Whether it does or not will depend on the terms of the arrangement, and in particular any term which makes specific provision in the event of the debtor's death[6]. Where the IVA involves a scheme under which the debtor assigns specific property to the supervisor as trustee to realise and distribute among the creditors the death of the debtor will have little impact. The position is clearly otherwise where the debtor has committed himself to make periodic payments throughout the life of the IVA. Many debtors will have life assurance policies with significant sums payable on death. Nominees preparing proposals, and creditors considering the implications of any proposal, would be well advised to ensure that the proposal has an after acquired assets clause which expressly includes (or excludes) the proceeds of any life or term assurance policies under which benefits accrue during the currency of the IVA. A further point for nominees and creditors to consider is whether insurance might be obtained to cover the continuing payments covenanted by a debtor under an IVA in the event of death or incapacity.

On the death of the debtor after the arrangement has been approved, the personal representative succeeds to the deceased debtor's rights to challenge any act or decision of the supervisor in the course of his implementation of the IVA[7]. The supervisor must give notice to the court that the debtor has died[8].

1 IA 1986, s 263, modified by DPO 1986, art 3, Sch 1, Pt III, para 5.
2 DPO 1986, art 3, Sch 1, Pt III, para 4.
3 Under IA 1986, s 261 (disapplied, as above).
4 Under IA 1986, s 262 (disapplied, as above).
5 See IA 1986, s 260(2).
6 See generally the cases on failure of a voluntary arrangement after bankruptcy or winding-up order, para 11.5 above, and in particular *Re N T Gallagher & Sons Ltd* [2002] EWCA Civ 404, [2002] 2 BCLC 133.
7 IA 1986, s 263, modified by DPO 1986, art 3, Sch 1, Pt III, para 5(a).
8 IA 1986, s 263, modified by DPO 1986, art 3, Sch 1, Pt III, para 5(b).

Chapter 13

Partnership voluntary arrangements

13.1 Statutory framework. Under the law prior to the coming into force of IA 1986 insolvent partnerships were dealt with under the law of bankruptcy[1]. IA 1986 brought partnerships as entities separate from the members who make up the partnership into the general legal framework for corporate insolvency[2].

The first order made was the Insolvent Partnerships Order 1986[3] ('IPO 1986'). It introduced the concept that an insolvent partnership could be wound up as an unregistered company under IA 1986, s 221, with the partners liable as contributories where the partnership assets were insufficient to meet its liabilities. IPO 1986, however, provided no mechanism for the partnership as opposed to its members to enter into voluntary arrangements. Although the practice developed of arranging IVAs for all members of the partnership[4] with identical provision for the partnership assets and debts and a common supervisor ('interlocking IVAs'), it was often difficult to arrange for large partnerships. This omission was remedied by the replacement of IPO 1986, with effect from 1 December 1994, with the Insolvent Partnerships Order 1994[5] ('IPO 1994').

1 See Bankruptcy Act 1914, s 116; Bankruptcy Rules 1952, rr 279–296; a firm comprising eight or more partners could be wound up as an unregistered company: CA 1985, ss 665(1), 665.

2 This is achieved through subordinate legislation. IA 1986, s 420 empowers the Lord Chancellor, with the concurrence of the Secretary of State, to make an order providing that specified provisions of IA 1986 should apply to insolvent partnerships with such modifications as may be considered appropriate.

3 SI 1986/2142.

4 A company voluntary arrangement could be proposed by any corporate members of the partnership.

5 SI 1994/2421.

13.2 Partnership voluntary arrangement. Introduced by IPO 1994, the partnership voluntary arrangement ('PVA') treated the partnership as if it were a limited company, and applies the provisions of IA 1986, Pt I relating to company voluntary arrangements to the insolvent partnership. There is, however, no bar to an individual partner proposing an individual voluntary arrangement either by himself or as one of a group of partners acting together proposing a series of interlocking IVAs which have similar provisions in the case of joint debts and the availability to the creditors of the joint estate together with individual provisions tailored to the needs of separate debts and the separate estates. The fact that any individual debtor is liable on his debts jointly with others is no bar to his obtaining an interim order and proceeding to an IVA[1]. The partner of an insolvent partnership and any insolvency practitioner advising him must take into account the fact that a PVA will protect the individual partner's estate from the claims of joint (ie partnership) creditors, but will not protect the individual's estate from the claims of any separate creditor. The entry into an IVA by one partner does not, of course, protect the other partners from enforcement procedures by a partnership creditor against their separate estates[2].

The PVA procedure under IPO 1994, based as it was on CVA, did not incorporate the interim order available in IVA to protect the partner against pressing creditors while the arrangements are put in place. The PVA regime has now been amended in line with the amendments introduced into CVA by IA 2000. This is achieved through the Insolvent Partnerships (Amendment) (No 2) Order 2002[3] ('IPO 2002). IPO 2002 operates by replacing IPO 1994, art 4 with the provisions of IA 1986, Pt I and Sch A1, suitably modified for insolvent partnerships. For convenience of reference, the provisions of IA 1986, Pt I as they apply to insolvent partnerships are set out in full in IPO 2002. This course has not been adopted, however, with Sch A1[4], although where individual paragraphs have been modified these paragraphs have been set out in full[5]. There is little by way of modification needed. For most of its provisions Sch A1 may be applied to partnership voluntary arrangements by appropriate construction. IA 1986, s 1A(7) (as modified by IPO 2002) provides that in applying Sch A1 and Sch 10 (which relates to offences which may be committed in relation to PVAs):

(a) references to the directors or members of a company shall be construed as references to the members of an insolvent partnership;
(b) references to officers of a company shall be construed as references to the officers of an insolvent partnership;
(c) references to a meeting of a company shall be construed as references to a meeting of the members of an insolvent partnership;
(d) references to a floating charge shall be construed as references to a floating charge created under the Agricultural Credits Act 1928, s 5.

Insolvent partnerships, in making voluntary arrangements or being wound up as unregistered companies, come within the scope of the EC Regulation[6].

IR 1986 apply to insolvent partnerships 'with such modifications as the context requires for the purpose of giving effect to the provisions of [IA 1986]' by virtue of IPO 1994, art 18. The above canons of construction are not applied expressly to the provisions of IR 1986, but it is anticipated that the court will use them as the context may require when construing IR 1986 in PVA.

1 *Re Cupit* [1996] BPIR 560n, CA.
2 *Schooler v Customs and Excise Comrs* [1995] 2 BCLC 610 at 616.
3 SI 2002/2708. The Insolvent Partnerships (Amendment) Order 2002, SI 2002/1308 introduced minor amendments to IPO 1994 to take account of the coming into force of the EC Regulation.
4 Ie the provisions enabling companies to propose and enter CVAs either without a moratorium (IA 1986, Pt I) or with a moratorium (IA 1986, Sch A1).
5 These are paras 3, 4, 12, 20, 37, 40, and 42, and even here the actual modifications to the company text, while important, are few in number.
6 See Chapter 14 below.

13.3 Limited liability partnership. A limited liability partnership ('LLP') may propose for voluntary arrangement, with the designated members making the proposal in place of the directors. The designated members will be acting on behalf of the LLP which, it is assumed, will have agreed to the proposal for a voluntary arrangement in accordance with its own decision-making procedures. Accordingly, no meetings of the LLP need be held, only a meeting of the LLP's creditors. In the event that the meeting of creditors approves the proposal with modifications these have to be agreed by the LLP as a whole. Any member of the LLP is entitled to challenge the decision of the creditors' meeting[1].

1 Limited Liability Partnership Regulations 2001, SI 2001/1090, reg 5, Sch 3, which modify the provisions of IA 1986 governing CVAs.

13.4 Jurisdiction. The PVA procedure under IPO 1994 applies to any partnership which the courts in England and Wales have jurisdiction to wind up[1]. Two conditions must be met before the courts of England and Wales have jurisdiction to wind up an insolvent partnership as an unregistered company:

1. the partnership must have or at any time have had:
   (a) a principal place of business in England or Wales (this need not be the firm's only principal place of business); or
   (b) a place of business in England or Wales at which business is or has been carried on[2] in the course of which the debt (or part of the debt) arose which forms the basis of the winding up petition[3].
2. The partnership must have been carrying on business at any time during the period of three years ending on the day on which the winding-up petition is presented[4].

In the case of a partnership which also has a principal place of business in Scotland or Northern Ireland, there is no jurisdiction in the English courts unless the partnership has had a principal place of business in England and Wales within the periods of one year and three years respectively ending with the day on which the winding-up petition is presented[5].

An application for a PVA may be made after a winding-up order against the partnership, and an individual partner who has been made bankrupt or a corporate partner which has had a winding-up order made against it may also make proposals for an IVA or CVA alongside the partnership's application for a PVA[6].

1 IPO 1994, art 1(2).
2 For the meaning of 'carrying on business within England and Wales', see *Re A Company (No 007816 of 1994)* [1995] 2 BCLC 539; *Scher v Policyholders Protection Board (No 2)* [1994] 2 AC 57; *Grant v Anderson & Co* [1892] 1 QB 108, CA; *Re Dagnall* [1896] 2 QB 407; *Theophile v Solicitor-General* [1950] AC 186; *Bird v IRC* [1962] 1 WLR 686; *Re a Debtor (No 784 of 1991)* [1992] Ch 554. Note that a business continues to be carried on even after direct operational activity has ceased until all debts are paid and all other liabilities have been met.
3 IA 1986, s 221(1), as modified by IPO 1994.
4 IA 1986, s 221(2), modified by IPO 1994.
5 IA 1986, s 221(3), modified by IPO 1994.
6 IPO 1994, art 5(1).

13.5 PVA procedure. As noted above, insolvent partnerships are treated as unregistered companies and may propose and implement voluntary arrangements either with or without a moratorium. For a moratorium in PVA, see Chapter 3 above. The various paragraphs of Chapter 3 apply to PVA with the references to directors, members, officers meetings and to a floating charge construed as provided for by IA 1986, s 1A(7)[1]. In the few instances where provisions applicable to CVA are not applicable to PVA, this is noted in the footnotes. Where a PVA proceeds without a moratorium, Chapter 4 will apply with the relevant construction given to company references. As with companies, a proposal may be made for a PVA where the partnership is being wound up, the administrator or liquidator making the proposal and either acting as nominee or arranging for another qualified practitioner to act as nominee. Additionally, a proposal may be made for PVA after an order is made on a petition under IPO 1994, art 11. This is where all the members of a partnership, all being individuals, jointly petition for bankruptcy. On an order being made, a single trustee is appointed and this trustee may propose a PVA in suitable cases. Such a proposal proceeds in precisely the same way as a proposal by an administrator or liquidator.

The consideration of a proposal for PVA proceeds as does a proposal for CVA by meetings of both creditors and the members of the partnership; see Chapter 6. Similar considerations apply as in CVA to any challenge that might be brought to an approved PVA (Chapter 7), to the effect of an approved PVA (Chapter 9), the implementation of an approved PVA (Chapter 10), and the failure of a PVA (Chapter 11)[2]. An insolvent partnership is exempt from criminal liability, but its officers will criminally liable in the same circumstances as would company officers (Chapter 8).

1 As modified by IPO 2002 and set out in para 13.2 above.
2 For these purposes it is noted that IPO 1994, art 4(2), (3) provides that the provisions of IA 1986 which relate to the supply of essential services (s 233), definitions (ss 247, 248, 249, 251 and 436), preferential debts (ss 386, 387), qualification of insolvency practitioners (ss 388–389), the making of rules and regulations (ss 411, 413, 414, 419), co-operation between insolvency courts (s 426) and the definition of associate (s 435) all apply to PVA procedures.

13.6 Members. For the purposes of IPO 1994 a 'member' of a partnership is defined as 'a member of a partnership and any person who is liable as a partner within the meaning of section 14 of the Partnership Act 1890'. The Partnership Act 1890, s 14 enacts the principle of partnership through 'holding out': 'Every one who by words spoken or written or by conduct represents himself, or who knowingly suffers himself to be represented, as a partner in a particular firm, is liable as a partner to any one who has on the faith of any such representation given credit to the firm, whether the representation has or has not been made or communicated to the person so giving credit by or with the knowledge of the apparent partner making the representation or suffering it to be made'[1]. An apparent partner may well be liable only to one or more of the partnership's creditors and then only in respect of part of the partnership liability. There is nothing in IPO 1994 to extend such liability as he may have as an apparent partner, but in all respects he is treated as a member of the partnership in the PVA regime without restriction.

It is 'the members' of the insolvent partnership who, formally at least, make the proposal for a voluntary arrangement[2]. This cannot mean the entire membership for otherwise there would be little purpose in summoning a members' meeting to consider the proposal[3]. Subject to the partnership deed specifying expressly how such a proposal should be made, an unlikely event, the ordinary management provisions of the deed or other agreement between the partners will apply. In default of express agreement the partnership will be governed by the provisions of the Partnership Act 1890. It is possible that terms of voluntary arrangement might be proposed that would constitute a change in the nature of the partnership business, in which event the consent of all existing partners would be required for its proposal[4]. In most instances, however, the proposed PVA will not involve a change to the nature of the partnership business and, accordingly, any decision to make the proposal may made by a majority of the partners[5].

At the meeting of the partnership's members, voting will be in accordance with the voting rights in the partnership[6], a simple majority being sufficient to approve the PVA for the purposes of the members' meeting[7]. Where there is a partnership deed with provision for voting rights those provisions will apply. Otherwise, partners will be entitled to vote in accordance with their rights to share in capital and profits, this right being equal as between the partners where there is no agreement expressed or implied to the contrary[8]. There may be partners, for example, 'salaried partners', who have no right to vote within the partnership. Prior to 1 January 2003 they were nevertheless entitled to vote for or against the proposal or any modification of it[9]. Such a vote was not be counted towards the majority needed to approve the PVA, but the importance of having the right to vote was that it carried with it the right to challenge the meeting's decision[10]. Since 1 January 2003 a member with no right to vote at the members' meeting in unable to challenge the approval of a PVA.

1 Partnership Act 1890, s 14(1); s 14(2) protects the estate of any deceased partner in whose name the partnership business continues.
2 IA 1986, s 1(1), as modified by IPO 2002.
3 As envisaged by IA 1986, ss 2(2), 3(1), as modified by IPO 2002.
4 Partnership Act 1890, s 24(8).
5 Partnership Act 1890, s 24(8).
6 IR 1986, r 1.18(1).
7 IR 1986, r 1.20(1), ignoring the vote of any member who has no right to vote in the partnership but is exercising his statutory right to vote under r 1.18(2).
8 Partnership Act 1890, s 24(1).
9 By virtue of IR 1986, r 1.18(2) (now repealed).
10 IA 1986, s 6(2)(a), as modified by IPO 94, art 4, Sch 1.

Chapter 14
EC Regulation on insolvency proceedings

14.1 General. Council Regulation (EC) 1346/2000 of 29 May 2000 on Insolvency Proceedings ('the EC Regulation') was adopted by the Council of the European Union on 29 May 2000 and came into effect throughout the EU (except in Denmark) on 31 May 2002. The EC Regulation makes no attempt to harmonise the insolvency laws of individual member states. Rather, it controls the exercise of the jurisdiction to commence insolvency proceedings in any member state and regulates the law applicable to insolvency proceedings by means of uniform rules for the choice of law. The aim is to improve the efficiency and effectiveness of cross-border insolvencies by removing or simplifying previously existing formalities as to recognition and enforcement. As a council regulation the EC Regulation is directly applicable to the law of member states, and will prevail in the event of any incompatibility with the national law. The EC Regulation applies only where the debtor has his 'centre of main interests' within the EU and is concerned only with jurisdiction within the EU[1]. It does not apply to insurance undertakings, credit institutions or investment undertakings which hold funds or securities for third parties[2].

The EC Regulation applies to 'collective insolvency proceedings which entail the partial or total divestment of a debtor and the appointment of a liquidator'[3]. These proceedings are specified to be those listed in Annex A to the EC Regulation and (for the UK) include 'Voluntary arrangements under insolvency legislation'[4]. It is immaterial, therefore, that some forms of voluntary arrangement do not in fact entail even the partial divestment of the debtor. Any debtor is included within the scope of the EC Regulation whether 'a natural person or a legal person, a trader or an individual'[5]. The term 'liquidator' is used throughout the EC Regulation to cover any office-holder: 'any person whose function is to administer or liquidate assets of which the debtor has been divested or to supervise the administration of his affairs. Those persons and bodies are listed in Annex C'[6]. There is also a wide definition for the term 'court' and the term 'judgment'. 'Court' means the judicial body or any other competent body of a member state empowered to open insolvency proceedings or to take decisions in the course of such proceedings[7]; 'judgment' in relation to the opening of insolvency proceedings or the appointment of a liquidator shall include the decision of any court empowered to open such proceedings or to appoint a liquidator[8].

1 EC Regulation, Art 3, recital 14.
2 EC Regulation, Art 1(2).
3 EC Regulation, Art 1(1).
4 EC Regulation, Art 2(a).
5 EC Regulation, recital 9; note that a recital to a Council Regulation may be used for the purposes of interpretation.
6 EC Regulation, Art 2(b); a 'supervisor of a voluntary arrangement' is listed in Annex C.
7 EC Regulation, Art 2(d).
8 EC Regulation, Art 2(e).

14.2 Main proceedings under the EC Regulation. The EC Regulation specifies three types of proceedings, main, territorial and secondary. A court (as widely defined[1]) in a member state may open two types of proceedings; main proceedings, which have primary competence, and territorial proceedings, which are proceedings restricted to those assets of the debtor which are situated in the territory of the state of the court which opens them. 'Main proceedings' may be opened only in the member state where the debtor has his 'centre of main interests'[2]. The EC Regulation attempts no definition of 'centre of main interests' although some assistance may be found in recital 13 which provides that 'the centre of main interests should correspond to the place where the debtor conducts the administration of his interests on a regular basis and is therefore ascertainable by third parties'. In most instances it will be clear where the debtor's centre of main interests is situated, and difficult cases are only likely to arise in the corporate field where companies have administration centres[3] in more than one member state. As the EC Regulation provides that in the case of a company the place of the registered office is to be presumed to be the centre of its main interests in the absence of proof to the contrary[4], this presumption will operate in all those cases where one of the company's administrative centres is in the state of its registered office. The proof required to displace the presumption is not indicated in the EC Regulation; there will a heavy onus on an applicant seeking to establish a centre of main interests in a member state other than the one in which the company has its registered office. This leaves uncertain the position of companies which have a registered office but no or little by way of administrative centre in one state and administrative centres in two or more other member states. Such companies will be few and far between.

As soon as main proceedings are opened they have effect throughout the EU. This fundamental principle of recognition operates automatically in all the other member states from the time that it becomes effective in the state in which the proceedings are opened[5], subject to the right of any member state to refuse to recognise another state's insolvency proceedings or a judgment handed down in such proceedings where the effects would be manifestly contrary to that state's public policy[6]. There are two important aspects to this automatic recognition of main proceedings. First, 'the judgment' (widely defined[7]) opening the main proceedings produces, *with no further formalities,* the same effects in any other member state as under the law of the state in which the main proceedings have been opened, provided no secondary proceedings are opened in that other member state and except as the EC Regulation provides[8]. Secondly, the liquidator appointed by the court in which the main proceedings are opened may exercise all the powers conferred on him by the law of the main proceedings state in any other member state provided that no secondary proceedings have been opened in that state nor any preservation measure implemented contrary to any power which the liquidator wishes to exercise pursuant to a request for the opening of secondary proceedings in that state[9]. This enables the liquidator to take steps both in the courts of other member states and out of court to protect and realise the assets of the debtor, although in doing so he must comply with the law of the local state 'in particular with regard to procedures for the realisation of assets'[10]. The liquidator may prove his appointment by a certified copy of the original decision appointing him or by any other certificate issued by the court which had jurisdiction[11].

1 See para 14.1 above.
2 EC Regulation, Art 3(1).
3 In the light of recital 13, it is an administration centre which is important rather than a place of operations, should the two be separated.
4 EC Regulation, Art 3(1).
5 EC Regulation, Art 16(1).
6 EC Regulation, Art 26; 'in particular its fundamental principles or the constitutional rights and liberties of the individual'.
7 See para 14.1 above.
8 EC Regulation, Art 17(1).
9 EC Regulation, Art 18(1).
10 EC Regulation, Art 18(2), (3).
11 EC Regulation, Art 19(1).

14.3 Territorial proceedings. Territorial proceedings may be opened against a debtor in a member state other than that in which the debtor's centre of main interests is situated provided the debtor has an establishment within that state[1]. The effects of such proceedings must be restricted to those assets of the debtor which are situated within the state in which the territorial proceedings are opened[2]. For the purpose of this jurisdiction 'establishment' means 'any place of operations where the debtor carries out a non-transitory economic activity with human means and goods'[3]. This definition may well prove somewhat elusive. However, the presence of assets within the jurisdiction is insufficient to amount to an establishment without accompanying economic activity, neither will a base for only occasional operations amount to an establishment for these purposes.

Territorial proceedings may be opened before main insolvency proceedings but only (a) if main proceedings cannot be opened in the state where the debtor has his centre of main interests because of a condition laid down by the law of that state or (b) where the opening of territorial proceedings is requested by a creditor who is domiciled or habitually resident or has its registered office in the territorial state or whose claim arises from the operation of the debtor's establishment[4]. It is the express intention of the EC Regulation to restrict territorial proceedings opened in the absence of main proceedings to what is absolutely necessary[5]. The main thrust of the EC Regulation is to ensure that cross border insolvencies are controlled by main proceedings undertaken in the member state in which the debtor has his centre of main interests, and that all other proceedings should be of subsidiary competence to the main proceedings. Where territorial proceedings are opened when main proceedings are in existence they must be secondary proceedings and must be winding-up proceedings and not part of a rescue or rehabilitation process[6]. In cases where main proceedings are opened after the opening of territorial proceedings the effect of EC Regulation, Art 36 would appear to be that the territorial proceedings are to be treated as secondary proceedings to the subsequent main proceedings so far as the progress of the territorial proceedings permits.

1 EC Regulation, Art 3(2).
2 EC Regulation, Art 3(2).
3 EC Regulation, Art 2(h).
4 EC Regulation, Art 3(4).

5 EC Regulation, recital 17.
6 EC Regulation, Art 3(3).

14.4 Secondary proceedings. Once main insolvency proceedings have been opened in a member state, secondary insolvency proceedings may be opened in any other state without the need for the debtor's insolvency to be examined or adjudicated upon by that other state[1]. The aim is to improve the efficiency and effectiveness of the proceedings in cross-border insolvencies. As primacy is afforded to the main proceedings the mere opening of those proceedings is sufficient to establish the debtor's insolvency for secondary proceedings. Such proceedings may be opened at the request of the liquidator in the main proceedings or by any person empowered to request the opening of insolvency proceedings in the secondary state[2]. Subject to the provisions of the EC Regulation ensuring primacy to the main proceedings, secondary proceedings are subject to the law of the secondary state[3]. To secure this primacy the EC Regulation imposes a duty on liquidators to co-operate with and communicate information with each other[4], and provides the main proceedings liquidator with powers to open other secondary proceedings[5], request the stay of the process of realisation of assets in secondary proceedings[6], propose a rescue plan or composition in secondary proceedings[7], and request that pre-existing territorial proceedings be converted into winding-up proceedings[8]. In order that supervisors of voluntary arrangements should comply with the duty to co-operate with a liquidator (as widely defined[9]) appointed in another member state, IR 1986 provide that the supervisor must give notice or provide copies of the relevant documents to a member state liquidator whenever he is obliged by the rules to give notice or provide copies of documents to the court or the official receiver, or in CVA cases to the registrar of companies[10].

1 EC Regulation, Art 27.
2 EC Regulation, Art 29.
3 EC Regulation, Art 28.
4 EC Regulation, Art 31.
5 EC Regulation, Art 29(a).
6 EC Regulation, Art 33.
7 EC Regulation, Art 34, where the secondary state law allows it. It follows that a liquidator in foreign main proceedings could propose a voluntary arrangement in England and Wales.
8 EC Regulation, Art 37.
9 See para 14.1 above.
10 IR 1986, r 1.34 (CVA), r 5.38 (IVA).

14.5 Applicable law. It is unnecessary for the purposes of this work to consider in any detail the provisions of the EC Regulation relating to applicable law, recognition of proceedings and enforceability of judgments. The general rule is that the national law of the state in which the proceedings are opened is the applicable law both on procedural matters and in substantive matters not expressly covered by the EC Regulation. There are, however, a number of substantive conflicts of laws provisions contained in Arts 5–15 of the EC Regulation. These cover third parties' rights in rem, set-off, reservation of title, contracts relating to real property, financial markets and payment systems, contracts of employment, rights subject to registration, community patents and trade marks, avoidance of detrimental acts, protection of third-party purchasers of immovable or registered property, and the effect of insolvency on pending law suits. Insolvency proceedings are now recognised without formality in all EU states and certain judgments may now be recognised without formality and may be enforced in accordance with the Brussels Convention.

14.6 Provision of information for creditors and lodging of claims. The provisions of the EC Regulation in relation to the provision of information to creditors and the proving of claims will apply where there are foreign creditors. They are straightforward but will have some impact on existing practice. Any creditor who has his habitual residence, domicile or registered office in a member state other than the state in which the proceedings are opened has the right to lodge claims in any insolvency proceedings in writing[1]. The granting of a right to lodge claims is more applicable to formal insolvency procedures than voluntary arrangements but notifying the nominee of a debt or other liability owed by the debtor amounts to a lodging of a claim. Of importance in this provision is the express inclusion of tax authorities and social security authorities of member states. To the extent that the rule in *Government of India v Taylor*[2] still applies, it no longer has any effect where the claimant is a member state of the EU.

As soon as insolvency proceedings are opened in a member state, the court concerned or the liquidator appointed by it is under a duty to inform all known creditors who have habitual residences, domiciles or registered offices in other member states of the proceedings[3]. Each creditor must receive an individual notice, informing him of any applicable time limits, any penalties in regard to such time limits, the body authorised to accept claims, whether creditors with preferential claims or holding securities need to lodge claims and 'the other measures laid down'[4]. This information is to be provided in the, or one of the, official languages in the state in which the proceedings were opened[5]. When lodging his claim a creditor must send copies of any supporting documents, and indicate the nature of his claim, the date on which it arose and its amount. He must also state whether he alleges preference, any security in rem or a reservation of title in respect of the claim and what assets are covered by any guarantee he is invoking[6]. A creditor lodging his claim may do so in his own state's official language, provided that the claim is headed '*Lodgement of claim*' in the, or one of the, official languages of the state of the proceedings. He may be required to provide a translation of his claim[7].

1 EC Regulation, Art 39.
2 [1955] AC 491, HL.
3 EC Regulation, Art 40(1).
4 EC Regulation, Art 40(2).
5 EC Regulation, Art 42(1): a form must be used bearing the heading 'Invitation to lodge a claim. Time limits to be observed' in all the official languages of the institutions of the EU.
6 EC Regulation, Art 41.
7 EC Regulation, Art 42(2).

14.7 Conversion of voluntary arrangement into liquidation or bankruptcy. As has been noted above, Art 37 of the EC Regulation entitles the liquidator in main proceedings to request that secondary proceedings in another member state be converted into winding-up proceedings[1] 'if this proves to be in the interests of the creditors in the main proceedings'. This clearly subordinates the interests of the creditors of a voluntary arrangement to the creditors in the main proceedings, although as there is no territorial restriction to the debts which are subject to voluntary arrangements there is likely to be considerable overlap between the arrangement creditors and the creditors in the main proceedings. It may be that cases will arise where the English court may be satisfied that it is in the interests of the main proceedings creditors to order a conversion on the basis of dividend likely to be received alone. More likely, however, the main proceedings liquidator will be relying on the need for the investigatory procedures of formal insolvency to be employed coupled with the court's powers to set aside or make orders in respect of antecedent transactions. The 'interests of creditors' in Art 37 plainly extend beyond the size of their dividends.

Procedurally, a main proceedings liquidator seeking the conversion of a voluntary arrangement to a winding up or bankruptcy is required to make an originating application supported by an affidavit which must be served on both the debtor and the supervisor[2]. The affidavit must be sworn by or on behalf of the main proceedings liquidator[3]. It must state: (1) that main proceedings have been opened in relation to the debtor in a member state other than the UK[4]; (2) the deponent's belief that the conversion to liquidation or bankruptcy would prove to be in the interests of the creditors in the main proceedings; and (3) all other matters which in the opinion of the main proceedings liquidator would assist the court in deciding whether or not to make a conversion order and if so what consequential provisions would be necessary or desirable[5]. A CVA may be converted either into a voluntary liquidation or a winding up by the court. The main proceedings liquidator should specify in his affidavit which form of winding up is in his opinion the more appropriate[6].

The court has a discretion whether or not to make the order[7], and if an order is made it may contain all such consequential provisions as the court considers necessary or desirable[8]. In the case of a conversion of a CVA to voluntary liquidation a direction may be included that the winding up proceed as if a resolution for winding up[9] was passed on the day on which the order is made[10]. If a conversion order is made in any particular case any expenses properly incurred as expenses of the administration of the voluntary arrangement become a first charge on the company's assets or individual debtor's estate[11].

1 Which term includes bankruptcy proceedings: Art 2(c).
2 IR 1986, r 1.31 (CVA), r 5.35 (IVA).
3 IR 1986, r 1.32 (2) (CVA), r 5.36(2) (IVA).
4 Note that Denmark remains outside the scope of the EC Regulation.
5 IR 1986, r 1.32(1) (CVA), r 5.36(1) (IVA).
6 IR 1986, r 1.32(1)(c).
7 IR 1986, r 1.33(1) (CVA), r 5.37(1) (IVA).
8 IR 1986, r 1.33(2) (CVA), r 5.37(2) (IVA).
9 Under IA 1986, s 84.
10 IR 1986, r 1.33(3).
11 IR 1986, r 1.33(4) (CVA), r 5.37(3) (IVA).

Appendix I

Insolvency Act 1986*

PART I
COMPANY VOLUNTARY ARRANGEMENTS

The proposal

1 Those who may propose an arrangement

(1) The directors of a company (other than one for which an administration order is in force, or which is being wound up) may make a proposal under this Part to the company and to its creditors for a composition in satisfaction of its debts or a scheme of arrangement of its affairs (from here on referred to, in either case, as a "voluntary arrangement").

(2) A proposal under this Part is one which provides for some person ("the nominee") to act in relation to the voluntary arrangement either as trustee or otherwise for the purpose of supervising its implementation; and the nominee must be a person who is qualified to act as an insolvency practitioner [or authorised to act as nominee, in relation to the voluntary arrangement].

(3) Such a proposal may also be made—
  (a) where an administration order is in force in relation to the company, by the administrator, and
  (b) where the company is being wound up, by the liquidator.

---

* **Commencement of amendments**
Unless otherwise stated, amendments made by the Insolvency Act 2000 came into effect on 1 January 2003, see SI 2002/2711, art 2; for transitional provisions, see arts 3 and 4 thereof. Similarly, unless otherwise stated, amendments made by SI 2002/1555 came into effect on 3 July 2002, see SI 2002/1555, art 1. The commencement dates of other amendments are noted below the relevant provision.

[(4) In this Part a reference to a company includes a reference to a company in relation to which a proposal for a voluntary arrangement may be made by virtue of Article 3 of the EC Regulation.]

NOTES

Amendment
Sub-s (2): words "or authorised to act as nominee, in relation to the voluntary arrangement" in square brackets substituted by the Insolvency Act 2000, s 2(a), Sch 2, Pt I, paras 1, 2.
Sub-s (4): inserted by SI 2002/1240, regs 3, 4.
Date in force: 31 May 2002: see SI 2002/1240, reg 1.

[1A Moratorium]

[(1) Where the directors of an eligible company intend to make a proposal for a voluntary arrangement, they may take steps to obtain a moratorium for the company.

(2) The provisions of Schedule A1 to this Act have effect with respect to—
- (a) companies eligible for a moratorium under this section,
- (b) the procedure for obtaining such a moratorium,
- (c) the effects of such a moratorium, and
- (d) the procedure applicable (in place of sections 2 to 6 and 7) in relation to the approval and implementation of a voluntary arrangement where such a moratorium is or has been in force.]

NOTES

Amendment
Inserted by the Insolvency Act 2000, s 1, Sch 1, paras 1, 2.

2 Procedure where nominee is not the liquidator or administrator

(1) This section applies where the nominee under section 1 is not the liquidator or administrator of the company [and the directors do not propose to take steps to obtain a moratorium under section 1A for the company].

(2) The nominee shall, within 28 days (or such longer period as the court may allow) after he is given notice of the proposal for a voluntary arrangement, submit a report to the court stating—
- (a) [whether, in his opinion, the proposed voluntary arrangement has a reasonable prospect of being approved and implemented,
- (aa)] whether, in his opinion, meetings of the company and of its creditors should be summoned to consider the proposal, and
- (b) if in his opinion such meetings should be summoned, the date on which, and time and place at which, he proposes the meetings should be held.

(3) For the purposes of enabling the nominee to prepare his report, the person intending to make the proposal shall submit to the nominee—
- (a) a document setting out the terms of the proposed voluntary arrangement, and
- (b) a statement of the company's affairs containing—
  - (i) such particulars of its creditors and of its debts and other liabilities and of its assets as may be prescribed, and
  - (ii) such other information as may be prescribed.

[(4) The court may—

(a) on an application made by the person intending to make the proposal, in a case where the nominee has failed to submit the report required by this section or has died, or

(b) on an application made by that person or the nominee, in a case where it is impracticable or inappropriate for the nominee to continue to act as such,

direct that the nominee be replaced as such by another person qualified to act as an insolvency practitioner, or authorised to act as nominee, in relation to the voluntary arrangement.]

NOTES

Amendment

Sub-s (1): words from "and the directors" to "for the company" in square brackets inserted by the Insolvency Act 2000, s 1, Sch 1, paras 1, 3.

Sub-s (2): in para (a) words from "whether, in his" to "approved and implemented," and subsequent reference to "(aa)" in square brackets inserted by the Insolvency Act 2000, s 2(a), Sch 2, Pt I, paras 1, 3(a).

Sub-s (4): substituted by the Insolvency Act 2000, s 2(a), Sch 2, Pt I, paras 1, 3(b).

3 Summoning of meetings

(1) Where the nominee under section 1 is not the liquidator or administrator, and it has been reported to the court that such meetings as are mentioned in section 2(2) should be summoned, the person making the report shall (unless the court otherwise directs) summon those meetings for the time, date and place proposed in the report.

(2) Where the nominee is the liquidator or administrator, he shall summon meetings of the company and of its creditors to consider the proposal for such a time, date and place as he thinks fit.

(3) The persons to be summoned to a creditors' meeting under this section are every creditor of the company of whose claim and address the person summoning the meeting is aware.

Consideration and implementation of proposal

4 Decisions of meetings

(1) The meetings summoned under section 3 shall decide whether to approve the proposed voluntary arrangement (with or without modifications).

(2) The modifications may include one conferring the functions proposed to be conferred on the nominee on another person qualified to act as an insolvency practitioner [or authorised to act as nominee, in relation to the voluntary arrangement].

But they shall not include any modification by virtue of which the proposal ceases to be a proposal such as is mentioned in section 1.

(3) A meeting so summoned shall not approve any proposal or modification which affects the right of a secured creditor of the company to enforce his security, except with the concurrence of the creditor concerned.

(4) Subject as follows, a meeting so summoned shall not approve any proposal or modification under which—

(a) any preferential debt of the company is to be paid otherwise than in priority to such of its debts as are not preferential debts, or

(b) a preferential creditor of the company is to be paid an amount in respect of a preferential debt that bears to that debt a smaller proportion than is borne to another preferential debt by the amount that is to be paid in respect of that other debt.

However, the meeting may approve such a proposal or modification with the concurrence of the preferential creditor concerned.

(5) Subject as above, each of the meetings shall be conducted in accordance with the rules.

(6) After the conclusion of either meeting in accordance with the rules, the chairman of the meeting shall report the result of the meeting to the court, and, immediately after reporting to the court, shall give notice of the result of the meeting to such persons as may be prescribed.

(7) References in this section to preferential debts and preferential creditors are to be read in accordance with section 386 in Part XII of this Act.

NOTES

Amendment

Sub-s (2): words "or authorised to act as nominee, in relation to the voluntary arrangement" in square brackets substituted by the Insolvency Act 2000, s 2(a), Sch 2, Pt I, paras 1, 4.

[4A Approval of arrangement]

[(1) This section applies to a decision, under section 4, with respect to the approval of a proposed voluntary arrangement.

(2) The decision has effect if, in accordance with the rules—

(a) it has been taken by both meetings summoned under section 3, or

(b) (subject to any order made under subsection (4)) it has been taken by the creditors' meeting summoned under that section.

(3) If the decision taken by the creditors' meeting differs from that taken by the company meeting, a member of the company may apply to the court.

(4) An application under subsection (3) shall not be made after the end of the period of 28 days beginning with—

(a) the day on which the decision was taken by the creditors' meeting, or

(b) where the decision of the company meeting was taken on a later day, that day.

(5) Where a member of a regulated company, within the meaning given by paragraph 44 of Schedule A1, applies to the court under subsection (3), the Financial Services Authority is entitled to be heard on the application.

(6) On an application under subsection (3), the court may—

(a) order the decision of the company meeting to have effect instead of the decision of the creditors' meeting, or

(b) make such other order as it thinks fit.]

NOTES

Amendment
Inserted by the Insolvency Act 2000, s 2(a), Sch 2, Pt I, paras 1, 5.

Sub-s(2)(b)
The text of the Act refers to 'sub-section (4)' as printed above. However this reference should have been amended to refer to 'sub-section (6)' when sub-sections (4) and (5) were added during the passage of the Insolvency Bill 2000.

5 Effect of approval

[(1) This section applies where a decision approving a voluntary arrangement has effect under section 4A.]

(2) The . . . voluntary arrangement—
- (a) takes effect as if made by the company at the creditors' meeting, and
- [(b) binds every person who in accordance with the rules—
  - (i) was entitled to vote at that meeting (whether or not he was present or represented at it), or
  - (ii) would have been so entitled if he had had notice of it,

  as if he were a party to the voluntary arrangement.

(2A) If—
- (a) when the arrangement ceases to have effect any amount payable under the arrangement to a person bound by virtue of subsection (2)(b)(ii) has not been paid, and
- (b) the arrangement did not come to an end prematurely,

the company shall at that time become liable to pay to that person the amount payable under the arrangement.]

(3) Subject as follows, if the company is being wound up or an administration order is in force, the court may do one or both of the following, namely—
- (a) by order stay or sist all proceedings in the winding up or discharge the administration order;
- (b) give such directions with respect to the conduct of the winding up or the administration as it thinks appropriate for facilitating the implementation of the . . . voluntary arrangement.

(4) The court shall not make an order under subsection (3)(a)—
- (a) at any time before the end of the period of 28 days beginning with the first day on which each of the reports required by section 4(6) has been made to the court, or
- (b) at any time when an application under the next section or an appeal in respect of such an application is pending, or at any time in the period within which such an appeal may be brought.

NOTES

Amendment
Sub-s (1): substituted by the Insolvency Act 2000, s 2(a), Sch 2, Pt I, paras 1, 6(a).
Sub-s (2): word omitted repealed by the Insolvency Act 2000, ss 2(a), 15(1), Sch 2, Pt I, paras 1, 6(b), Sch 5.
Sub-s (2): para (b) substituted, together with sub-s (2A), by the Insolvency Act 2000, s 2(a), Sch 2, Pt I, paras 1, 6(c).
Sub-s (2A): substituted, together with sub-s (2)(b), for sub-s (2)(b) as originally enacted, by the Insolvency Act 2000, s 2(a), Sch 2, Pt I, paras 1, 6(c).

Sub-s (3): in para (b) word omitted repealed by the Insolvency Act 2000, s 2(a), Sch 2, Pt I, paras 1, 6(b), s 15(1), Sch 5.

6 Challenge of decisions

(1) Subject to this section, an application to the court may be made, by any of the persons specified below, on one or both of the following grounds, namely—

(a) that a voluntary arrangement [which has effect under section 4A] unfairly prejudices the interests of a creditor, member or contributory of the company;

(b) that there has been some material irregularity at or in relation to either of the meetings.

(2) The persons who may apply under this section are—

(a) a person entitled, in accordance with the rules, to vote at either of the meetings;

[(aa) a person who would have been entitled, in accordance with the rules, to vote at the creditors' meeting if he had had notice of it;]

(b) the nominee or any person who has replaced him under section 2(4) or 4(2); and

(c) if the company is being wound up or an administration order is in force, the liquidator or administrator.

(3) An application under this section shall not be made[—

(a)] after the end of the period of 28 days beginning with the first day on which each of the reports required by section 4(6) has been made to the court, [or

(b) in the case of a person who was not given notice of the creditors' meeting, after the end of the period of 28 days beginning with the day on which he became aware that the meeting had taken place,

but (subject to that) an application made by a person within subsection (2)(aa) on the ground that the voluntary arrangement prejudices his interests may be made after the arrangement has ceased to have effect, unless it came to an end prematurely].

(4) Where on such an application the court is satisfied as to either of the grounds mentioned in subsection (1), it may do one or both of the following, namely—

(a) revoke or suspend [any decision approving the voluntary arrangement which has effect under section 4A] or, in a case falling within subsection (1)(b), any [decision taken by the meeting in question which has effect under that section];

(b) give a direction to any person for the summoning of further meetings to consider any revised proposal the person who made the original proposal may make or, in a case falling within subsection (1)(b), a further company or (as the case may be) creditors' meeting to reconsider the original proposal.

(5) Where at any time after giving a direction under subsection (4)(b) for the summoning of meetings to consider a revised proposal the court is satisfied that the person who made the original proposal does not intend to submit a revised proposal, the court shall revoke the direction and revoke or suspend any [decision approving the voluntary arrangement which has effect under section 4A].

(6) In a case where the court, on an application under this section with respect to any meeting—

(a) gives a direction under subsection (4)(b), or

(b) revokes or suspends an approval under subsection (4)(a) or (5),

the court may give such supplemental directions as it thinks fit and, in particular, directions with respect to things done [under the voluntary arrangement since it took effect].

(7) Except in pursuance of the preceding provisions of this section, [a decision taken] at a meeting summoned under section 3 is not invalidated by any irregularity at or in relation to the meeting.

NOTES

Amendment

Sub-s (1): in para (a) words "which has effect under section 4A" in square brackets substituted by the Insolvency Act 2000, s 2(a), Sch 2, Pt I, paras 1, 7(1), (2).
Sub-s (2): para (aa) inserted by the Insolvency Act 2000, s 2(a), Sch 2, Pt I, paras 1, 7(1), (3).
Sub-s (3): reference to "—(a)" in square brackets inserted by the Insolvency Act 2000, s 2(a), Sch 2, Pt I, paras 1, 7(1), (4)(a).
Sub-s (3): para (b) and word "or" immediately preceding it and words from "but (subject to that)" to "an end prematurely" in square brackets inserted by the Insolvency Act 2000, s 2(a), Sch 2, Pt I, paras 1, 7(1), (4)(b).
Sub-s (4): in para (a) words "any decision approving the voluntary arrangement which has effect under section 4A" in square brackets substituted by the Insolvency Act 2000, s 2(a), Sch 2, Pt I, paras 1, 7(1), (5)(a).
Sub-s (4): in para (a) words "decision taken by the meeting in question which has effect under that section" in square brackets substituted by the Insolvency Act 2000, s 2(a), Sch 2, Pt I, paras 1, 7(1), (5)(b).
Sub-s (5): words "decision approving the voluntary arrangement which has effect under section 4A" in square brackets substituted by the Insolvency Act 2000, s 2(a), Sch 2, Pt I, paras 1, 7(1), (6).
Sub-s (6): words "under the voluntary arrangement since it took effect" in square brackets substituted by the Insolvency Act 2000, s 2(a), Sch 2, Pt I, paras 1, 7(1), (7).
Sub-s (7): words "a decision taken" in square brackets substituted by the Insolvency Act 2000, s 2(a), Sch 2, Pt I, paras 1, 7(1), (8).

[6A False representations, etc]

[(1) If, for the purpose of obtaining the approval of the members or creditors of a company to a proposal for a voluntary arrangement, a person who is an officer of the company—

(a) makes any false representation, or
(b) fraudulently does, or omits to do, anything,

he commits an offence.

(2) Subsection (1) applies even if the proposal is not approved.

(3) For purposes of this section "officer" includes a shadow director.

(4) A person guilty of an offence under this section is liable to imprisonment or a fine, or both.]

NOTES

Amendment

Inserted by the Insolvency Act 2000, s 2(a), Sch 2, Pt I, paras 1, 8.

7 Implementation of proposal

(1) This section applies where a voluntary arrangement [has effect under section 4A].

(2) The person who is for the time being carrying out in relation to the voluntary arrangement the functions conferred—

[(a) on the nominee by virtue of the approval given at one or both of the meetings summoned under section 3,]

(b) by virtue of section 2(4) or 4(2) on a person other than the nominee,

shall be known as the supervisor of the voluntary arrangement.

(3) If any of the company's creditors or any other person is dissatisfied by any act, omission or decision of the supervisor, he may apply to the court; and on the application the court may—

(a) confirm, reverse or modify any act or decision of the supervisor,

(b) give him directions, or

(c) make such other order as it thinks fit.

(4) The supervisor—

(a) may apply to the court for directions in relation to any particular matter arising under the voluntary arrangement, and

(b) is included among the persons who may apply to the court for the winding up of the company or for an administration order to be made in relation to it.

(5) The court may, whenever—

(a) it is expedient to appoint a person to carry out the functions of the supervisor, and

(b) it is inexpedient, difficult or impracticable for an appointment to be made without the assistance of the court,

make an order appointing a person who is qualified to act as an insolvency practitioner [or authorised to act as supervisor, in relation to the voluntary arrangement], either in substitution for the existing supervisor or to fill a vacancy.

(6) The power conferred by subsection (5) is exercisable so as to increase the number of persons exercising the functions of supervisor or, where there is more than one person exercising those functions, so as to replace one or more of those persons.

NOTES

Amendment

Sub-s (1): words "has effect under section 4A" in square brackets substituted by the Insolvency Act 2000, s 2(a), Sch 2, Pt I, paras 1, 9(a).
Sub-s (2): para (a) substituted by the Insolvency Act 2000, s 2(a), Sch 2, Pt I, paras 1, 9(b).
Sub-s (5): words "or authorised to act as supervisor, in relation to the voluntary arrangement" in square brackets substituted by the Insolvency Act 2000, s 2(a), Sch 2, Pt I, paras 1, 9(c).

[7A Prosecution of delinquent officers of company]

[(1) This section applies where a moratorium under section 1A has been obtained for a company or the approval of a voluntary arrangement in relation to a company has taken effect under section 4A or paragraph 36 of Schedule A1.

(2) If it appears to the nominee or supervisor that any past or present officer of the company has been guilty of any offence in connection with the moratorium or, as the case may be, voluntary arrangement for which he is criminally liable, the nominee or supervisor shall forthwith—

(a) report the matter to the appropriate authority, and

(b) provide the appropriate authority with such information and give the authority such access to and facilities for inspecting and taking copies of documents (being information or documents in the possession or under the control of the nominee or supervisor and relating to the matter in question) as the authority requires.

In this subsection, "the appropriate authority" means—

(i) in the case of a company registered in England and Wales, the Secretary of State, and

(ii) in the case of a company registered in Scotland, the Lord Advocate.

(3) Where a report is made to the Secretary of State under subsection (2), he may, for the purpose of investigating the matter reported to him and such other matters relating to the affairs of the company as appear to him to require investigation, exercise any of the powers which are exercisable by inspectors appointed under section 431 or 432 of the Companies Act to investigate a company's affairs.

(4) For the purpose of such an investigation any obligation imposed on a person by any provision of the Companies Act to produce documents or give information to, or otherwise to assist, inspectors so appointed is to be regarded as an obligation similarly to assist the Secretary of State in his investigation.

(5) An answer given by a person to a question put to him in exercise of the powers conferred by subsection (3) may be used in evidence against him.

(6) However, in criminal proceedings in which that person is charged with an offence to which this subsection applies—

(a) no evidence relating to the answer may be adduced, and

(b) no question relating to it may be asked,

by or on behalf of the prosecution, unless evidence relating to it is adduced, or a question relating to it is asked, in the proceedings by or on behalf of that person.

(7) Subsection (6) applies to any offence other than—

(a) an offence under section 2 or 5 of the Perjury Act 1911 (false statements made on oath otherwise than in judicial proceedings or made otherwise than on oath), or

(b) an offence under section 44(1) or (2) of the Criminal Law (Consolidation) (Scotland) Act 1995 (false statements made on oath or otherwise than on oath).

(8) Where a prosecuting authority institutes criminal proceedings following any report under subsection (2), the nominee or supervisor, and every officer and agent of the company past and present (other than the defendant or defender), shall give the authority all assistance in connection with the prosecution which he is reasonably able to give.

For this purpose—

"agent" includes any banker or solicitor of the company and any person employed by the company as auditor, whether that person is or is not an officer of the company,

"prosecuting authority" means the Director of Public Prosecutions, the Lord Advocate or the Secretary of State.

(9) The court may, on the application of the prosecuting authority, direct any person referred to in subsection (8) to comply with that subsection if he has failed to do so.]

NOTES

Amendment
Inserted by the Insolvency Act 2000, s 2(a), Sch 2, Pt I, paras 1, 10.

[7B Arrangements coming to an end prematurely]

[For the purposes of this Part, a voluntary arrangement the approval of which has taken effect under section 4A or paragraph 36 of Schedule A1 comes to an end prematurely if, when it ceases to have effect, it has not been fully implemented in respect of all persons bound by the arrangement by virtue of section 5(2)(b)(i) or, as the case may be, paragraph 37(2)(b)(i) of Schedule A1.]

NOTES

Amendment
Inserted by the Insolvency Act 2000, s 2(a), Sch 2, Pt I, paras 1, 10.

[SCHEDULE A1
Moratorium Where Directors Propose Voluntary Arrangement]

NOTES

Amendment
Inserted by the Insolvency Act 2000, s 1, Sch 1, paras 1, 4.
Date in force (for certain purposes): 11 May 2001: see SI 2001/1751, art 2.
Date in force (for remaining purposes): 1 January 2003: see SI 2002/2711, art 2.

PART I
INTRODUCTORY

NOTES

Amendment
Inserted by the Insolvency Act 2000, s 1, Sch 1, paras 1, 4.
Date in force (for certain purposes): 11 May 2001: see SI 2001/1751, art 2.
Date in force (for remaining purposes): 1 January 2003: see SI 2002/2711, art 2.

Interpretation

1

In this Schedule—

"the beginning of the moratorium" has the meaning given by paragraph 8(1),
"the date of filing" means the date on which the documents for the time being referred to in paragraph 7(1) are filed or lodged with the court,
"hire-purchase agreement" includes a conditional sale agreement, a chattel leasing agreement and a retention of title agreement,
"market contract" and "market charge" have the meanings given by Part VII of the Companies Act 1989,
. . .
"moratorium" means a moratorium under section 1A,
"the nominee" includes any person for the time being carrying out the functions of a nominee under this Schedule,

. . .
"the settlement finality regulations" means the Financial Markets and Insolvency (Settlement Finality) Regulations 1999,
"system-charge" has the meaning given by the Financial Markets and Insolvency Regulations 1996.

Eligible companies

2

(1) A company is eligible for a moratorium if it meets the requirements of paragraph 3, unless—
- (a) it is excluded from being eligible by virtue of paragraph 4, or
- (b) it falls within sub-paragraph (2).

(2) A company falls within this sub-paragraph if—
- [(a) it effects or carries out contracts of insurance, but is not exempt from the general prohibition, within the meaning of section 19 of the Financial Services and Markets Act 2000, in relation to that activity,
- (b) it has permission under Part IV of that Act to accept deposits,
- (bb) it has a liability in respect of a deposit which it accepted in accordance with the Banking Act 1979 (c 37) or 1987 (c 22),]
- (c) it is a party to a market contract. . . or any of its property is subject to a market charge. . . or a system-charge, or
- (d) it is a participant (within the meaning of the settlement finality regulations) or any of its property is subject to a collateral security charge (within the meaning of those regulations).

[(3) Paragraphs (a), (b) and (bb) of sub-paragraph (2) must be read with—
- (a) section 22 of the Financial Services and Markets Act 2000;
- (b) any relevant order under that section; and
- (c) Schedule 2 to that Act.]

3

(1) A company meets the requirements of this paragraph if the qualifying conditions are met—
- (a) in the year ending with the date of filing, or
- (b) in the financial year of the company which ended last before that date.

(2) For the purposes of sub-paragraph (1)—
- (a) the qualifying conditions are met by a company in a period if, in that period, it satisfies two or more of the requirements for being a small company specified for the time being in section 247(3) of the Companies Act 1985, and
- (b) a company's financial year is to be determined in accordance with that Act.

(3) Subsections (4), (5) and (6) of section 247 of that Act apply for the purposes of this paragraph as they apply for the purposes of that section.

[(4) A company does not meet the requirements of this paragraph if it is a holding company of a group of companies which does not qualify as a small group or a medium-sized group in respect of the financial year of the company which ended last before the date of filing.

(5) For the purposes of sub-paragraph (4) "group" has the meaning given by section 262 of the Companies Act 1985 (c 6) (definitions for Part VII) and a group qualifies as small or medium-sized if it qualifies as such under section 249 of the Companies Act 1985 (qualification of group as small or medium-sized).]

4

(1) A company is excluded from being eligible for a moratorium if, on the date of filing—

- (a) an administration order is in force in relation to the company,
- (b) the company is being wound up,
- (c) there is an administrative receiver of the company,
- (d) a voluntary arrangement has effect in relation to the company,
- (e) there is a provisional liquidator of the company,
- (f) a moratorium has been in force for the company at any time during the period of 12 months ending with the date of filing and—
  - (i) no voluntary arrangement had effect at the time at which the moratorium came to an end, or
  - (ii) a voluntary arrangement which had effect at any time in that period has come to an end prematurely, or
- (g) a voluntary arrangement in relation to the company which had effect in pursuance of a proposal under section 1(3) has come to an end prematurely and, during the period of 12 months ending with the date of filing, an order under section 5(3)(a) has been made.

(2) Sub-paragraph (1)(b) does not apply to a company which, by reason of a winding-up order made after the date of filing, is treated as being wound up on that date.

[Capital market arrangement

4A

A company is also excluded from being eligible for a moratorium if, on the date of filing, it is a party to an agreement which is or forms part of a capital market arrangement under which—

- (i) a party has incurred, or when the agreement was entered into was expected to incur, a debt of at least £10 million under the arrangement, and
- (ii) the arrangement involves the issue of a capital market investment.

Public private partnership

4B

A company is also excluded from being eligible for a moratorium if, on the date of filing, it is a project company of a project which—

- (i) is a public-private partnership project, and
- (ii) includes step-in rights.

Liability under an arrangement

4C

(1) A company is also excluded from being eligible for a moratorium if, on the date of filing, it has incurred a liability under an agreement of £10 million or more.

(2) Where the liability in sub-paragraph (1) is a contingent liability under or by virtue of a guarantee or an indemnity or security provided on behalf of another person, the amount of that liability is the full amount of the liability in relation to which the guarantee, indemnity or security is provided.

(3) In this paragraph—
- (a) the reference to "liability" includes a present or future liability whether, in either case, it is certain or contingent,
- (b) the reference to "liability" includes a reference to a liability to be paid wholly or partly in foreign currency (in which case the sterling equivalent shall be calculated as at the time when the liability is incurred).

Interpretation of capital market arrangement

4D

(1) For the purposes of paragraph 4A an arrangement is a capital market arrangement if—
- (a) it involves a grant of security to a person holding it as trustee for a person who holds a capital market investment issued by a party to the arrangement, or
- (b) at least one party guarantees the performance of obligations of another party, or
- (c) at least one party provides security in respect of the performance of obligations of another party, or
- (d) the arrangement involves an investment of a kind described in articles 83 to 85 of the Financial Services and Markets Act 2000 (Regulated Activities) Order 2001 (SI 2001/544) (options, futures and contracts for differences).

(2) For the purposes of sub-paragraph (1)—
- (a) a reference to holding as trustee includes a reference to holding as nominee or agent,
- (b) a reference to holding for a person who holds a capital market investment includes a reference to holding for a number of persons at least one of whom holds a capital market investment, and
- (c) a person holds a capital market investment if he has a legal or beneficial interest in it.

(3) In paragraph 4A, 4C, 4J and this paragraph—

"agreement" includes an agreement or undertaking effected by—
- (a) contract,
- (b) deed, or
- (c) any other instrument intended to have effect in accordance with the law of England and Wales, Scotland or another jurisdiction, and

"party" to an arrangement includes a party to an agreement which—

(a) forms part of the arrangement,
(b) provides for the raising of finance as part of the arrangement, or
(c) is necessary for the purposes of implementing the arrangement.

Capital market investment

4E

(1) For the purposes of paragraphs 4A and 4D, an investment is a capital market investment if—

(a) it is within article 77 of the Financial Services and Markets Act 2000 (Regulated Activities) Order 2001 (SI 2001/544) (debt instruments) and
(b) it is rated, listed or traded or designed to be rated, listed or traded.

(2) In sub-paragraph (1)—

"listed" means admitted to the official list within the meaning given by section 103(1) of the Financial Services and Markets Act 2000 (c 8) (interpretation),
"rated" means rated for the purposes of investment by an internationally recognised rating agency,
"traded" means admitted to trading on a market established under the rules of a recognised investment exchange or on a foreign market.

(3) In sub-paragraph (2)—

"foreign market" has the same meaning as "relevant market" in article 67(2) of the Financial Services and Markets Act 2000 (Financial Promotion) Order 2001 (SI 2001/1335) (foreign markets),
"recognised investment exchange" has the meaning given by section 285 of the Financial Services and Markets Act 2000 (recognised investment exchange).

4F

(1) For the purposes of paragraphs 4A and 4D an investment is also a capital market investment if it consists of a bond or commercial paper issued to one or more of the following—

(a) an investment professional within the meaning of article 19(5) of the Financial Services and Markets Act 2000 (Financial Promotion) Order 2001,
(b) a person who is, when the agreement mentioned in paragraph 4A is entered into, a certified high net worth individual in relation to a communication within the meaning of article 48(2) of that order,
(c) a person to whom article 49(2) of that order applies (high net worth company, &c.),
(d) a person who is, when the agreement mentioned in paragraph 4A is entered into, a certified sophisticated investor in relation to a communication within the meaning of article 50(1) of that order, and
(e) a person in a State other than the United Kingdom who under the law of that State is not prohibited from investing in bonds or commercial paper.

(2) For the purposes of sub-paragraph (1)—

(a) in applying article 19(5) of the Financial Services and Markets Act 2000 (Financial Promotion) Order 2001 for the purposes of sub-paragraph (1)(a)—
 (i) in article 19(5)(b), ignore the words after "exempt person",

(ii) in article 19(5)(c)(i), for the words from "the controlled activity" to the end substitute "a controlled activity", and
(iii) in article 19(5)(e) ignore the words from "where the communication" to the end, and

(b) in applying article 49(2) of that order for the purposes of sub-paragraph (1)(c), ignore article 49(2)(e).

(3) In sub-paragraph (1)—

"bond" shall be construed in accordance with article 77 of the Financial Services and Markets Act 2000 (Regulated Activities) Order 2001 (SI 2001/544), and

"commercial paper" has the meaning given by article 9(3) of that order.

Debt

4G

The debt of at least £10 million referred to in paragraph 4A—

(a) may be incurred at any time during the life of the capital market arrangement, and

(b) may be expressed wholly or partly in a foreign currency (in which case the sterling equivalent shall be calculated as at the time when the arrangement is entered into).

Interpretation of project company

4H

(1) For the purposes of paragraph 4B a company is a "project company" of a project if—

(a) it holds property for the purpose of the project,
(b) it has sole or principal responsibility under an agreement for carrying out all or part of the project,
(c) it is one of a number of companies which together carry out the project,
(d) it has the purpose of supplying finance to enable the project to be carried out, or
(e) it is the holding company of a company within any of paragraphs (a) to (d).

(2) But a company is not a "project company" of a project if—

(a) it performs a function within sub-paragraph (1)(a) to (d) or is within sub-paragraph (1)(e), but
(b) it also performs a function which is not—
  (i) within sub-paragraph (1)(a) to (d),
  (ii) related to a function within sub-paragraph (1)(a) to (d), or
  (iii) related to the project.

(3) For the purposes of this paragraph a company carries out all or part of a project whether or not it acts wholly or partly through agents.

Public-private partnership project

4I

(1) In paragraph 4B "public-private partnership project" means a project—

(a) the resources for which are provided partly by one or more public bodies and partly by one or more private persons, or
(b) which is designed wholly or mainly for the purpose of assisting a public body to discharge a function.

(2) In sub-paragraph (1) "resources" includes—
(a) funds (including payment for the provision of services or facilities),
(b) assets,
(c) professional skill,
(d) the grant of a concession or franchise, and
(e) any other commercial resource.

(3) In sub-paragraph (1) "public body" means—
(a) a body which exercises public functions,
(b) a body specified for the purposes of this paragraph by the Secretary of State, and
(c) a body within a class specified for the purposes of this paragraph by the Secretary of State.

(4) A specification under sub-paragraph (3) may be—
(a) general, or
(b) for the purpose of the application of paragraph 4B to a specified case.

Step-in rights

4J

(1) For the purposes of paragraph 4B a project has "step-in rights" if a person who provides finance in connection with the project has a conditional entitlement under an agreement to—
(i) assume sole or principal responsibility under an agreement for carrying out all or part of the project, or
(ii) make arrangements for carrying out all or part of the project.

(2) In sub-paragraph (1) a reference to the provision of finance includes a reference to the provision of an indemnity.

"Person"

4K

For the purposes of paragraphs 4A to 4J, a reference to a person includes a reference to a partnership or another unincorporated group of persons.]

5

The Secretary of State may by regulations modify the qualifications for eligibility of a company for a moratorium.

NOTES

Amendment

Inserted by the Insolvency Act 2000, s 1, Sch 1, paras 1, 4.
Date in force (for the purposes of para 5): 11 May 2001: see SI 2001/1751, art 2.
Date in force (for remaining purposes): 1 January 2003: see SI 2002/2711, art 2.

Para 1: definitions ""money market contract" and "money market charge"" and "related contract" (omitted) repealed by virtue of SI 2002/1555, art 28(1), (2).
Para 2: sub-para (2)(a), (b), (bb) substituted, for sub-para (2)(a), (b) as previously enacted, by virtue of SI 2002/1555, art 29(1), (2).
Para 2: in sub-para (2)(c) words omitted repealed by virtue of SI 2002/1555, art 28(1), (3).
Para 2: sub-para (3) inserted by virtue of SI 2002/1555, art 29(1), (3).
Para 3: sub-paras (4), (5) inserted by SI 2002/1990, reg 3(1), (2).
Date in force: 1 January 2003 (being the date on which the Insolvency Act 2000, s 1 came into force for remaining purposes): see SI 2002/2711, art 2.
Paras 4A–4K: inserted by SI 2002/1990, reg 3(1), (3).
Date in force: 1 January 2003 (being the date on which the Insolvency Act 2000, s 1 came into force for remaining purposes): see SI 2002/2711, art 2.

PART II
OBTAINING A MORATORIUM

NOTES

Amendment
Inserted by the Insolvency Act 2000, s 1, Sch 1, paras 1, 4.

Nominee's statement

6

(1) Where the directors of a company wish to obtain a moratorium, they shall submit to the nominee—
- (a) a document setting out the terms of the proposed voluntary arrangement,
- (b) a statement of the company's affairs containing—
  - (i) such particulars of its creditors and of its debts and other liabilities and of its assets as may be prescribed, and
  - (ii) such other information as may be prescribed, and
- (c) any other information necessary to enable the nominee to comply with sub-paragraph (2) which he requests from them.

(2) The nominee shall submit to the directors a statement in the prescribed form indicating whether or not, in his opinion—
- (a) the proposed voluntary arrangement has a reasonable prospect of being approved and implemented,
- (b) the company is likely to have sufficient funds available to it during the proposed moratorium to enable it to carry on its business, and
- (c) meetings of the company and its creditors should be summoned to consider the proposed voluntary arrangement.

(3) In forming his opinion on the matters mentioned in sub-paragraph (2), the nominee is entitled to rely on the information submitted to him under sub-paragraph (1) unless he has reason to doubt its accuracy.

(4) The reference in sub-paragraph (2)(b) to the company's business is to that business as the company proposes to carry it on during the moratorium.

Documents to be submitted to court

7

(1) To obtain a moratorium the directors of a company must file (in Scotland, lodge) with the court—

- (a) a document setting out the terms of the proposed voluntary arrangement,
- (b) a statement of the company's affairs containing—
  - (i) such particulars of its creditors and of its debts and other liabilities and of its assets as may be prescribed, and
  - (ii) such other information as may be prescribed,
- (c) a statement that the company is eligible for a moratorium,
- (d) a statement from the nominee that he has given his consent to act, and
- (e) a statement from the nominee that, in his opinion—
  - (i) the proposed voluntary arrangement has a reasonable prospect of being approved and implemented,
  - (ii) the company is likely to have sufficient funds available to it during the proposed moratorium to enable it to carry on its business, and
  - (iii) meetings of the company and its creditors should be summoned to consider the proposed voluntary arrangement.

(2) Each of the statements mentioned in sub-paragraph (1)(b) to (e), except so far as it contains the particulars referred to in paragraph (b)(i), must be in the prescribed form.

(3) The reference in sub-paragraph (1)(e)(ii) to the company's business is to that business as the company proposes to carry it on during the moratorium.

(4) The Secretary of State may by regulations modify the requirements of this paragraph as to the documents required to be filed (in Scotland, lodged) with the court in order to obtain a moratorium.

Duration of moratorium

8

(1) A moratorium comes into force when the documents for the time being referred to in paragraph 7(1) are filed or lodged with the court and references in this Schedule to "the beginning of the moratorium" shall be construed accordingly.

(2) A moratorium ends at the end of the day on which the meetings summoned under paragraph 29(1) are first held (or, if the meetings are held on different days, the later of those days), unless it is extended under paragraph 32.

(3) If either of those meetings has not first met before the end of the period of 28 days beginning with the day on which the moratorium comes into force, the moratorium ends at the end of the day on which those meetings were to be held (or, if those meetings were summoned to be held on different days, the later of those days), unless it is extended under paragraph 32.

(4) If the nominee fails to summon either meeting within the period required by paragraph 29(1), the moratorium ends at the end of the last day of that period.

(5) If the moratorium is extended (or further extended) under paragraph 32, it ends at the end of the day to which it is extended (or further extended).

(6) Sub-paragraphs (2) to (5) do not apply if the moratorium comes to an end before the time concerned by virtue of—

- (a) paragraph 25(4) (effect of withdrawal by nominee of consent to act),
- (b) an order under paragraph 26(3), 27(3) or 40 (challenge of actions of nominee or directors), or
- (c) a decision of one or both of the meetings summoned under paragraph 29.

(7) If the moratorium has not previously come to an end in accordance with sub-paragraphs (2) to (6), it ends at the end of the day on which a decision under paragraph 31 to approve a voluntary arrangement takes effect under paragraph 36.

(8) The Secretary of State may by order increase or reduce the period for the time being specified in sub-paragraph (3).

Notification of beginning of moratorium

9

(1) When a moratorium comes into force, the directors shall notify the nominee of that fact forthwith.

(2) If the directors without reasonable excuse fail to comply with sub-paragraph (1), each of them is liable to imprisonment or a fine, or both.

10

(1) When a moratorium comes into force, the nominee shall, in accordance with the rules—

- (a) advertise that fact forthwith, and
- (b) notify the registrar of companies, the company and any petitioning creditor of the company of whose claim he is aware of that fact.

(2) In sub-paragraph (1)(b), "petitioning creditor" means a creditor by whom a winding-up petition has been presented before the beginning of the moratorium, as long as the petition has not been dismissed or withdrawn.

(3) If the nominee without reasonable excuse fails to comply with sub-paragraph (1)(a) or (b), he is liable to a fine.

Notification of end of moratorium

11

(1) When a moratorium comes to an end, the nominee shall, in accordance with the rules—

- (a) advertise that fact forthwith, and
- (b) notify the court, the registrar of companies, the company and any creditor of the company of whose claim he is aware of that fact.

(2) If the nominee without reasonable excuse fails to comply with sub-paragraph (1)(a) or (b), he is liable to a fine.

NOTES

Amendment
Inserted by the Insolvency Act 2000, s 1, Sch 1, paras 1, 4.

Part III
Effects of Moratorium

NOTES

Amendment
Inserted by the Insolvency Act 2000, s 1, Sch 1, paras 1, 4.

Effect on creditors, etc

12

(1) During the period for which a moratorium is in force for a company—
- (a) no petition may be presented for the winding up of the company,
- (b) no meeting of the company may be called or requisitioned except with the consent of the nominee or the leave of the court and subject (where the court gives leave) to such terms as the court may impose,
- (c) no resolution may be passed or order made for the winding up of the company,
- (d) no petition for an administration order in relation to the company may be presented,
- (e) no administrative receiver of the company may be appointed,
- (f) no landlord or other person to whom rent is payable may exercise any right of forfeiture by peaceable re-entry in relation to premises let to the company in respect of a failure by the company to comply with any term or condition of its tenancy of such premises, except with the leave of the court and subject to such terms as the court may impose,
- (g) no other steps may be taken to enforce any security over the company's property, or to repossess goods in the company's possession under any hire-purchase agreement, except with the leave of the court and subject to such terms as the court may impose, and
- (h) no other proceedings and no execution or other legal process may be commenced or continued, and no distress may be levied, against the company or its property except with the leave of the court and subject to such terms as the court may impose.

(2) Where a petition, other than an excepted petition, for the winding up of the company has been presented before the beginning of the moratorium, section 127 shall not apply in relation to any disposition of property, transfer of shares or alteration in status made during the moratorium or at a time mentioned in paragraph 37(5)(a).

(3) In the application of sub-paragraph (1)(h) to Scotland, the reference to execution being commenced or continued includes a reference to diligence being carried out or continued, and the reference to distress being levied is omitted.

(4) Paragraph (a) of sub-paragraph (1) does not apply to an excepted petition and, where such a petition has been presented before the beginning of the moratorium or is presented during the moratorium, paragraphs (b) and (c) of that sub-paragraph do not apply in relation to proceedings on the petition.

(5) For the purposes of this paragraph, "excepted petition" means a petition under—
- (a) section 124A of this Act,

(b) section 72 of the Financial Services Act 1986 on the ground mentioned in subsection (1)(b) of that section, or
(c) section 92 of the Banking Act 1987 on the ground mentioned in subsection (1)(b) of that section,
[(d) section 367 of the Financial Services and Markets Act 2000 on the ground mentioned in subsection (3)(b) of that section].

13

(1) This paragraph applies where there is an uncrystallised floating charge on the property of a company for which a moratorium is in force.

(2) If the conditions for the holder of the charge to give a notice having the effect mentioned in sub-paragraph (4) are met at any time, the notice may not be given at that time but may instead be given as soon as practicable after the moratorium has come to an end.

(3) If any other event occurs at any time which (apart from this sub-paragraph) would have the effect mentioned in sub-paragraph (4), then—
(a) the event shall not have the effect in question at that time, but
(b) if notice of the event is given to the company by the holder of the charge as soon as is practicable after the moratorium has come to an end, the event is to be treated as if it had occurred when the notice was given.

(4) The effect referred to in sub-paragraphs (2) and (3) is—
(a) causing the crystallisation of the floating charge, or
(b) causing the imposition, by virtue of provision in the instrument creating the charge, of any restriction on the disposal of any property of the company.

(5) Application may not be made for leave under paragraph 12(1)(g) or (h) with a view to obtaining—
(a) the crystallisation of the floating charge, or
(b) the imposition, by virtue of provision in the instrument creating the charge, of any restriction on the disposal of any property of the company.

14

Security granted by a company at a time when a moratorium is in force in relation to the company may only be enforced if, at that time, there were reasonable grounds for believing that it would benefit the company.

Effect on company

15

(1) Paragraphs 16 to 23 apply in relation to a company for which a moratorium is in force.

(2) The fact that a company enters into a transaction in contravention of any of paragraphs 16 to 22 does not—
(a) make the transaction void, or
(b) make it to any extent unenforceable against the company.

Company invoices, etc

16

(1) Every invoice, order for goods or business letter which—
- (a) is issued by or on behalf of the company, and
- (b) on or in which the company's name appears,

shall also contain the nominee's name and a statement that the moratorium is in force for the company.

(2) If default is made in complying with sub-paragraph (1), the company and (subject to sub-paragraph (3)) any officer of the company is liable to a fine.

(3) An officer of the company is only liable under sub-paragraph (2) if, without reasonable excuse, he authorises or permits the default.

Obtaining credit during moratorium

17

(1) The company may not obtain credit to the extent of £250 or more from a person who has not been informed that a moratorium is in force in relation to the company.

(2) The reference to the company obtaining credit includes the following cases—
- (a) where goods are bailed (in Scotland, hired) to the company under a hire-purchase agreement, or agreed to be sold to the company under a conditional sale agreement, and
- (b) where the company is paid in advance (whether in money or otherwise) for the supply of goods or services.

(3) Where the company obtains credit in contravention of sub-paragraph (1)—
- (a) the company is liable to a fine, and
- (b) if any officer of the company knowingly and wilfully authorised or permitted the contravention, he is liable to imprisonment or a fine, or both.

(4) The money sum specified in sub-paragraph (1) is subject to increase or reduction by order under section 417A in Part XV.

Disposals and payments

18

(1) Subject to sub-paragraph (2), the company may only dispose of any of its property if—
- (a) there are reasonable grounds for believing that the disposal will benefit the company, and
- (b) the disposal is approved by the committee established under paragraph 35(1) or, where there is no such committee, by the nominee.

(2) Sub-paragraph (1) does not apply to a disposal made in the ordinary way of the company's business.

(3) If the company makes a disposal in contravention of sub-paragraph (1) otherwise than in pursuance of an order of the court—

(a) the company is liable to a fine, and
(b) if any officer of the company authorised or permitted the contravention, without reasonable excuse, he is liable to imprisonment or a fine, or both.

19

(1) Subject to sub-paragraph (2), the company may only make any payment in respect of any debt or other liability of the company in existence before the beginning of the moratorium if—
(a) there are reasonable grounds for believing that the payment will benefit the company, and
(b) the payment is approved by the committee established under paragraph 35(1) or, where there is no such committee, by the nominee.

(2) Sub-paragraph (1) does not apply to a payment required by paragraph 20(6).

(3) If the company makes a payment in contravention of sub-paragraph (1) otherwise than in pursuance of an order of the court—
(a) the company is liable to a fine, and
(b) if any officer of the company authorised or permitted the contravention, without reasonable excuse, he is liable to imprisonment or a fine, or both.

Disposal of charged property, etc

20

(1) This paragraph applies where—
(a) any property of the company is subject to a security, or
(b) any goods are in the possession of the company under a hire-purchase agreement.

(2) If the holder of the security consents, or the court gives leave, the company may dispose of the property as if it were not subject to the security.

(3) If the owner of the goods consents, or the court gives leave, the company may dispose of the goods as if all rights of the owner under the hire-purchase agreement were vested in the company.

(4) Where property subject to a security which, as created, was a floating charge is disposed of under sub-paragraph (2), the holder of the security has the same priority in respect of any property of the company directly or indirectly representing the property disposed of as he would have had in respect of the property subject to the security.

(5) Sub-paragraph (6) applies to the disposal under sub-paragraph (2) or (as the case may be) sub-paragraph (3) of—
(a) any property subject to a security other than a security which, as created, was a floating charge, or
(b) any goods in the possession of the company under a hire-purchase agreement.

(6) It shall be a condition of any consent or leave under sub-paragraph (2) or (as the case may be) sub-paragraph (3) that—
(a) the net proceeds of the disposal, and
(b) where those proceeds are less than such amount as may be agreed, or determined by the court, to be the net amount which would be realised on

a sale of the property or goods in the open market by a willing vendor, such sums as may be required to make good the deficiency,

shall be applied towards discharging the sums secured by the security or payable under the hire-purchase agreement.

(7) Where a condition imposed in pursuance of sub-paragraph (6) relates to two or more securities, that condition requires—

(a) the net proceeds of the disposal, and

(b) where paragraph (b) of sub-paragraph (6) applies, the sums mentioned in that paragraph,

to be applied towards discharging the sums secured by those securities in the order of their priorities.

(8) Where the court gives leave for a disposal under sub-paragraph (2) or (3), the directors shall, within 14 days after leave is given, send an office copy of the order giving leave to the registrar of companies.

(9) If the directors without reasonable excuse fail to comply with sub-paragraph (8), they are liable to a fine.

21

(1) Where property is disposed of under paragraph 20 in its application to Scotland, the company shall grant to the disponee an appropriate document of transfer or conveyance of the property, and

(a) that document, or

(b) where any recording, intimation or registration of the document is a legal requirement for completion of title to the property, that recording, intimation or registration,

has the effect of disencumbering the property of, or (as the case may be) freeing the property from, the security.

(2) Where goods in the possession of the company under a hire-purchase agreement are disposed of under paragraph 20 in its application to Scotland, the disposal has the effect of extinguishing, as against the disponee, all rights of the owner of the goods under the agreement.

22

(1) If the company—

(a) without any consent or leave under paragraph 20, disposes of any of its property which is subject to a security otherwise than in accordance with the terms of the security,

(b) without any consent or leave under paragraph 20, disposes of any goods in the possession of the company under a hire-purchase agreement otherwise than in accordance with the terms of the agreement, or

(c) fails to comply with any requirement imposed by paragraph 20 or 21,

it is liable to a fine.

(2) If any officer of the company, without reasonable excuse, authorises or permits any such disposal or failure to comply, he is liable to imprisonment or a fine, or both.

Market contracts, etc

23

(1) If the company enters into any transaction to which this paragraph applies—
- (a) the company is liable to a fine, and
- (b) if any officer of the company, without reasonable excuse, authorised or permitted the company to enter into the transaction, he is liable to imprisonment or a fine, or both.

(2) A company enters into a transaction to which this paragraph applies if it—
- (a) enters into a market contract, . . .
- (b) gives a transfer order,
- (c) grants a market charge. . . or a system-charge, or
- (d) provides any collateral security.

(3) The fact that a company enters into a transaction in contravention of this paragraph does not—
- (a) make the transaction void, or
- (b) make it to any extent unenforceable by or against the company.

(4) Where during the moratorium a company enters into a transaction to which this paragraph applies, nothing done by or in pursuance of the transaction is to be treated as done in contravention of paragraphs 12(1)(g), 14 or 16 to 22.

(5) Paragraph 20 does not apply in relation to any property which is subject to a market charge, . . . a system-charge or a collateral security charge.

(6) In this paragraph, "transfer order", "collateral security" and "collateral security charge" have the same meanings as in the settlement finality regulations.

NOTES

Amendment
Inserted by the Insolvency Act 2000, s 1, Sch 1, paras 1, 4.
Para 12: sub-para (5)(d) inserted by virtue of SI 2002/1555, art 30.
Para 23: in sub-para (2)(a) words omitted repealed by virtue of SI 2002/1555, art 28(1), (4)(a).
Para 23: in sub-para (2)(c) words omitted repealed by virtue of SI 2002/1555, art 28(1), (4)(b).
Para 23: in sub-para (5) words omitted repealed by virtue of SI 2002/1555, art 28(1), (4)(c).

PART IV
NOMINEES

NOTES

Amendment
Inserted by the Insolvency Act 2000, s 1, Sch 1, paras 1, 4.

Monitoring of company's activities

24

(1) During a moratorium, the nominee shall monitor the company's affairs for the purpose of forming an opinion as to whether—

(a) the proposed voluntary arrangement or, if he has received notice of proposed modifications under paragraph 31(7), the proposed arrangement with those modifications has a reasonable prospect of being approved and implemented, and
(b) the company is likely to have sufficient funds available to it during the remainder of the moratorium to enable it to continue to carry on its business.

(2) The directors shall submit to the nominee any information necessary to enable him to comply with sub-paragraph (1) which he requests from them.

(3) In forming his opinion on the matters mentioned in sub-paragraph (1), the nominee is entitled to rely on the information submitted to him under sub-paragraph (2) unless he has reason to doubt its accuracy.

(4) The reference in sub-paragraph (1)(b) to the company's business is to that business as the company proposes to carry it on during the remainder of the moratorium.

Withdrawal of consent to act

25

(1) The nominee may only withdraw his consent to act in the circumstances mentioned in this paragraph.

(2) The nominee must withdraw his consent to act if, at any time during a moratorium—
(a) he forms the opinion that—
(i) the proposed voluntary arrangement or, if he has received notice of proposed modifications under paragraph 31(7), the proposed arrangement with those modifications no longer has a reasonable prospect of being approved or implemented, or
(ii) the company will not have sufficient funds available to it during the remainder of the moratorium to enable it to continue to carry on its business,
(b) he becomes aware that, on the date of filing, the company was not eligible for a moratorium, or
(c) the directors fail to comply with their duty under paragraph 24(2).

(3) The reference in sub-paragraph (2)(a)(ii) to the company's business is to that business as the company proposes to carry it on during the remainder of the moratorium.

(4) If the nominee withdraws his consent to act, the moratorium comes to an end.

(5) If the nominee withdraws his consent to act he must, in accordance with the rules, notify the court, the registrar of companies, the company and any creditor of the company of whose claim he is aware of his withdrawal and the reason for it.

(6) If the nominee without reasonable excuse fails to comply with sub-paragraph (5), he is liable to a fine.

Challenge of nominee's actions, etc

26

(1) If any creditor, director or member of the company, or any other person affected by a moratorium, is dissatisfied by any act, omission or decision of the nominee during the moratorium, he may apply to the court.

(2) An application under sub-paragraph (1) may be made during the moratorium or after it has ended.

(3) On an application under sub-paragraph (1) the court may—
- (a) confirm, reverse or modify any act or decision of the nominee,
- (b) give him directions, or
- (c) make such other order as it thinks fit.

(4) An order under sub-paragraph (3) may (among other things) bring the moratorium to an end and make such consequential provision as the court thinks fit.

27

(1) Where there are reasonable grounds for believing that—
- (a) as a result of any act, omission or decision of the nominee during the moratorium, the company has suffered loss, but
- (b) the company does not intend to pursue any claim it may have against the nominee,

any creditor of the company may apply to the court.

(2) An application under sub-paragraph (1) may be made during the moratorium or after it has ended.

(3) On an application under sub-paragraph (1) the court may—
- (a) order the company to pursue any claim against the nominee,
- (b) authorise any creditor to pursue such a claim in the name of the company, or
- (c) make such other order with respect to such a claim as it thinks fit,

unless the court is satisfied that the act, omission or decision of the nominee was in all the circumstances reasonable.

(4) An order under sub-paragraph (3) may (among other things)—
- (a) impose conditions on any authority given to pursue a claim,
- (b) direct the company to assist in the pursuit of a claim,
- (c) make directions with respect to the distribution of anything received as a result of the pursuit of a claim,
- (d) bring the moratorium to an end and make such consequential provision as the court thinks fit.

(5) On an application under sub-paragraph (1) the court shall have regard to the interests of the members and creditors of the company generally.

Replacement of nominee by court

28

(1) The court may—

(a) on an application made by the directors in a case where the nominee has failed to comply with any duty imposed on him under this Schedule or has died, or
(b) on an application made by the directors or the nominee in a case where it is impracticable or inappropriate for the nominee to continue to act as such,

direct that the nominee be replaced as such by another person qualified to act as an insolvency practitioner, or authorised to act as nominee, in relation to the voluntary arrangement.

(2) A person may only be appointed as a replacement nominee under this paragraph if he submits to the court a statement indicating his consent to act.

NOTES

Amendment
Inserted by the Insolvency Act 2000, s 1, Sch 1, paras 1, 4.

PART V
CONSIDERATION AND IMPLEMENTATION OF VOLUNTARY ARRANGEMENT

NOTES

Amendment
Inserted by the Insolvency Act 2000, s 1, Sch 1, paras 1, 4.

Summoning of meetings

29

(1) Where a moratorium is in force, the nominee shall summon meetings of the company and its creditors for such a time, date (within the period for the time being specified in paragraph 8(3)) and place as he thinks fit.

(2) The persons to be summoned to a creditors' meeting under this paragraph are every creditor of the company of whose claim the nominee is aware.

Conduct of meetings

30

(1) Subject to the provisions of paragraphs 31 to 35, the meetings summoned under paragraph 29 shall be conducted in accordance with the rules.

(2) A meeting so summoned may resolve that it be adjourned (or further adjourned).

(3) After the conclusion of either meeting in accordance with the rules, the chairman of the meeting shall report the result of the meeting to the court, and, immediately after reporting to the court, shall give notice of the result of the meeting to such persons as may be prescribed.

Approval of voluntary arrangement

31

(1) The meetings summoned under paragraph 29 shall decide whether to approve the proposed voluntary arrangement (with or without modifications).

(2) The modifications may include one conferring the functions proposed to be conferred on the nominee on another person qualified to act as an insolvency practitioner, or authorised to act as nominee, in relation to the voluntary arrangement.

(3) The modifications shall not include one by virtue of which the proposal ceases to be a proposal such as is mentioned in section 1.

(4) A meeting summoned under paragraph 29 shall not approve any proposal or modification which affects the right of a secured creditor of the company to enforce his security, except with the concurrence of the creditor concerned.

(5) Subject to sub-paragraph (6), a meeting so summoned shall not approve any proposal or modification under which—
- (a) any preferential debt of the company is to be paid otherwise than in priority to such of its debts as are not preferential debts, or
- (b) a preferential creditor of the company is to be paid an amount in respect of a preferential debt that bears to that debt a smaller proportion than is borne to another preferential debt by the amount that is to be paid in respect of that other debt.

(6) The meeting may approve such a proposal or modification with the concurrence of the preferential creditor concerned.

(7) The directors of the company may, before the beginning of the period of seven days which ends with the meetings (or either of them) summoned under paragraph 29 being held, give notice to the nominee of any modifications of the proposal for which the directors intend to seek the approval of those meetings.

(8) References in this paragraph to preferential debts and preferential creditors are to be read in accordance with section 386 in Part XII of this Act.

Extension of moratorium

32

(1) Subject to sub-paragraph (2), a meeting summoned under paragraph 29 which resolves that it be adjourned (or further adjourned) may resolve that the moratorium be extended (or further extended), with or without conditions.

(2) The moratorium may not be extended (or further extended) to a day later than the end of the period of two months which begins—
- (a) where both meetings summoned under paragraph 29 are first held on the same day, with that day,
- (b) in any other case, with the day on which the later of those meetings is first held.

(3) At any meeting where it is proposed to extend (or further extend) the moratorium, before a decision is taken with respect to that proposal, the nominee shall inform the meeting—

(a) of what he has done in order to comply with his duty under paragraph 24 and the cost of his actions for the company, and
(b) of what he intends to do to continue to comply with that duty if the moratorium is extended (or further extended) and the expected cost of his actions for the company.

(4) Where, in accordance with sub-paragraph (3)(b), the nominee informs a meeting of the expected cost of his intended actions, the meeting shall resolve whether or not to approve that expected cost.

(5) If a decision not to approve the expected cost of the nominee's intended actions has effect under paragraph 36, the moratorium comes to an end.

(6) A meeting may resolve that a moratorium which has been extended (or further extended) be brought to an end before the end of the period of the extension (or further extension).

(7) The Secretary of State may by order increase or reduce the period for the time being specified in sub-paragraph (2).

33

(1) The conditions which may be imposed when a moratorium is extended (or further extended) include a requirement that the nominee be replaced as such by another person qualified to act as an insolvency practitioner, or authorised to act as nominee, in relation to the voluntary arrangement.

(2) A person may only be appointed as a replacement nominee by virtue of sub-paragraph (1) if he submits to the court a statement indicating his consent to act.

(3) At any meeting where it is proposed to appoint a replacement nominee as a condition of extending (or further extending) the moratorium—
(a) the duty imposed by paragraph 32(3)(b) on the nominee shall instead be imposed on the person proposed as the replacement nominee, and
(b) paragraphs 32(4) and (5) and 36(1)(e) apply as if the references to the nominee were to that person.

34

(1) If a decision to extend, or further extend, the moratorium takes effect under paragraph 36, the nominee shall, in accordance with the rules, notify the registrar of companies and the court.

(2) If the moratorium is extended, or further extended, by virtue of an order under paragraph 36(5), the nominee shall, in accordance with the rules, send an office copy of the order to the registrar of companies.

(3) If the nominee without reasonable excuse fails to comply with this paragraph, he is liable to a fine.

Moratorium committee

35

(1) A meeting summoned under paragraph 29 which resolves that the moratorium be extended (or further extended) may, with the consent of the nominee, resolve

that a committee be established to exercise the functions conferred on it by the meeting.

(2) The meeting may not so resolve unless it has approved an estimate of the expenses to be incurred by the committee in the exercise of the proposed functions.

(3) Any expenses, not exceeding the amount of the estimate, incurred by the committee in the exercise of its functions shall be reimbursed by the nominee.

(4) The committee shall cease to exist when the moratorium comes to an end.

Effectiveness of decisions

36

(1) Sub-paragraph (2) applies to references to one of the following decisions having effect, that is, a decision, under paragraph 31, 32 or 35, with respect to—
- (a) the approval of a proposed voluntary arrangement,
- (b) the extension (or further extension) of a moratorium,
- (c) the bringing of a moratorium to an end,
- (d) the establishment of a committee, or
- (e) the approval of the expected cost of a nominee's intended actions.

(2) The decision has effect if, in accordance with the rules—
- (a) it has been taken by both meetings summoned under paragraph 29, or
- (b) (subject to any order made under sub-paragraph (5)) it has been taken by the creditors' meeting summoned under that paragraph.

(3) If a decision taken by the creditors' meeting under any of paragraphs 31, 32 or 35 with respect to any of the matters mentioned in sub-paragraph (1) differs from one so taken by the company meeting with respect to that matter, a member of the company may apply to the court.

(4) An application under sub-paragraph (3) shall not be made after the end of the period of 28 days beginning with—
- (a) the day on which the decision was taken by the creditors' meeting, or
- (b) where the decision of the company meeting was taken on a later day, that day.

(5) On an application under sub-paragraph (3), the court may—
- (a) order the decision of the company meeting to have effect instead of the decision of the creditors' meeting, or
- (b) make such other order as it thinks fit.

Effect of approval of voluntary arrangement

37

(1) This paragraph applies where a decision approving a voluntary arrangement has effect under paragraph 36.

(2) The approved voluntary arrangement—
- (a) takes effect as if made by the company at the creditors' meeting, and
- (b) binds every person who in accordance with the rules—
  - (i) was entitled to vote at that meeting (whether or not he was present or represented at it), or

(ii) would have been so entitled if he had had notice of it,
as if he were a party to the voluntary arrangement.

(3) If—
(a) when the arrangement ceases to have effect any amount payable under the arrangement to a person bound by virtue of sub-paragraph (2)(b)(ii) has not been paid, and
(b) the arrangement did not come to an end prematurely,

the company shall at that time become liable to pay to that person the amount payable under the arrangement.

(4) Where a petition for the winding up of the company, other than an excepted petition within the meaning of paragraph 12, was presented before the beginning of the moratorium, the court shall dismiss the petition.

(5) The court shall not dismiss a petition under sub-paragraph (4)—
(a) at any time before the end of the period of 28 days beginning with the first day on which each of the reports of the meetings required by paragraph 30(3) has been made to the court, or
(b) at any time when an application under paragraph 38 or an appeal in respect of such an application is pending, or at any time in the period within which such an appeal may be brought.

Challenge of decisions

38

(1) Subject to the following provisions of this paragraph, any of the persons mentioned in sub-paragraph (2) may apply to the court on one or both of the following grounds—
(a) that a voluntary arrangement approved at one or both of the meetings summoned under paragraph 29 and which has taken effect unfairly prejudices the interests of a creditor, member or contributory of the company,
(b) that there has been some material irregularity at or in relation to either of those meetings.

(2) The persons who may apply under this paragraph are—
(a) a person entitled, in accordance with the rules, to vote at either of the meetings,
(b) a person who would have been entitled, in accordance with the rules, to vote at the creditors' meeting if he had had notice of it, and
(c) the nominee.

(3) An application under this paragraph shall not be made—
(a) after the end of the period of 28 days beginning with the first day on which each of the reports required by paragraph 30(3) has been made to the court, or
(b) in the case of a person who was not given notice of the creditors' meeting, after the end of the period of 28 days beginning with the day on which he became aware that the meeting had taken place,

but (subject to that) an application made by a person within sub-paragraph (2)(b) on the ground that the arrangement prejudices his interests may be made after the arrangement has ceased to have effect, unless it came to an end prematurely.

(4) Where on an application under this paragraph the court is satisfied as to either of the grounds mentioned in sub-paragraph (1), it may do any of the following—

(a) revoke or suspend—

(i) any decision approving the voluntary arrangement which has effect under paragraph 36, or

(ii) in a case falling within sub-paragraph (1)(b), any decision taken by the meeting in question which has effect under that paragraph,

(b) give a direction to any person—

(i) for the summoning of further meetings to consider any revised proposal for a voluntary arrangement which the directors may make, or

(ii) in a case falling within sub-paragraph (1)(b), for the summoning of a further company or (as the case may be) creditors' meeting to reconsider the original proposal.

(5) Where at any time after giving a direction under sub-paragraph (4)(b)(i) the court is satisfied that the directors do not intend to submit a revised proposal, the court shall revoke the direction and revoke or suspend any decision approving the voluntary arrangement which has effect under paragraph 36.

(6) Where the court gives a direction under sub-paragraph (4)(b), it may also give a direction continuing or, as the case may require, renewing, for such period as may be specified in the direction, the effect of the moratorium.

(7) Sub-paragraph (8) applies in a case where the court, on an application under this paragraph—

(a) gives a direction under sub-paragraph (4)(b), or

(b) revokes or suspends a decision under sub-paragraph (4)(a) or (5).

(8) In such a case, the court may give such supplemental directions as it thinks fit and, in particular, directions with respect to—

(a) things done under the voluntary arrangement since it took effect, and

(b) such things done since that time as could not have been done if a moratorium had been in force in relation to the company when they were done.

(9) Except in pursuance of the preceding provisions of this paragraph, a decision taken at a meeting summoned under paragraph 29 is not invalidated by any irregularity at or in relation to the meeting.

Implementation of voluntary arrangement

39

(1) This paragraph applies where a voluntary arrangement approved by one or both of the meetings summoned under paragraph 29 has taken effect.

(2) The person who is for the time being carrying out in relation to the voluntary arrangement the functions conferred—

(a) by virtue of the approval of the arrangement, on the nominee, or

(b) by virtue of paragraph 31(2), on a person other than the nominee,

shall be known as the supervisor of the voluntary arrangement.

(3) If any of the company's creditors or any other person is dissatisfied by any act, omission or decision of the supervisor, he may apply to the court.

(4) On an application under sub-paragraph (3) the court may—
- (a) confirm, reverse or modify any act or decision of the supervisor,
- (b) give him directions, or
- (c) make such other order as it thinks fit.

(5) The supervisor—
- (a) may apply to the court for directions in relation to any particular matter arising under the voluntary arrangement, and
- (b) is included among the persons who may apply to the court for the winding up of the company or for an administration order to be made in relation to it.

(6) The court may, whenever—
- (a) it is expedient to appoint a person to carry out the functions of the supervisor, and
- (b) it is inexpedient, difficult or impracticable for an appointment to be made without the assistance of the court,

make an order appointing a person who is qualified to act as an insolvency practitioner, or authorised to act as supervisor, in relation to the voluntary arrangement, either in substitution for the existing supervisor or to fill a vacancy.

(7) The power conferred by sub-paragraph (6) is exercisable so as to increase the number of persons exercising the functions of supervisor or, where there is more than one person exercising those functions, so as to replace one or more of those persons.

NOTES

Amendment
Inserted by the Insolvency Act 2000, s 1, Sch 1, paras 1, 4.

Part VI
Miscellaneous

NOTES

Amendment
Inserted by the Insolvency Act 2000, s 1, Sch 1, paras 1, 4.
Date in force (for certain purposes): 11 May 2001: see SI 2001/1751, art 2.
Date in force (for remaining purposes): 1 January 2003: see SI 2002/2711, art 2.

Challenge of directors' actions

40

(1) This paragraph applies in relation to acts or omissions of the directors of a company during a moratorium.

(2) A creditor or member of the company may apply to the court for an order under this paragraph on the ground—

(a) that the company's affairs, business and property are being or have been managed by the directors in a manner which is unfairly prejudicial to the interests of its creditors or members generally, or of some part of its creditors or members (including at least the petitioner), or
(b) that any actual or proposed act or omission of the directors is or would be so prejudicial.

(3) An application for an order under this paragraph may be made during or after the moratorium.

(4) On an application for an order under this paragraph the court may—
(a) make such order as it thinks fit for giving relief in respect of the matters complained of,
(b) adjourn the hearing conditionally or unconditionally, or
(c) make an interim order or any other order that it thinks fit.

(5) An order under this paragraph may in particular—
(a) regulate the management by the directors of the company's affairs, business and property during the remainder of the moratorium,
(b) require the directors to refrain from doing or continuing an act complained of by the petitioner, or to do an act which the petitioner has complained they have omitted to do,
(c) require the summoning of a meeting of creditors or members for the purpose of considering such matters as the court may direct,
(d) bring the moratorium to an end and make such consequential provision as the court thinks fit.

(6) In making an order under this paragraph the court shall have regard to the need to safeguard the interests of persons who have dealt with the company in good faith and for value.

(7) In relation to any time when an administration order is in force in relation to the company, or the company is being wound up, in pursuance of a petition presented before the moratorium came into force, no application for an order under this paragraph may be made by a creditor or member of the company; but such an application may be made instead by the administrator or (as the case may be) liquidator.

Offences

41

(1) This paragraph applies where a moratorium has been obtained for a company.

(2) If, within the period of 12 months ending with the day on which the moratorium came into force, a person who was at the time an officer of the company—
(a) did any of the things mentioned in paragraphs (a) to (f) of sub-paragraph (4), or
(b) was privy to the doing by others of any of the things mentioned in paragraphs (c), (d) and (e) of that sub-paragraph,

he is to be treated as having committed an offence at that time.

(3) If, at any time during the moratorium, a person who is an officer of the company—

(a) does any of the things mentioned in paragraphs (a) to (f) of sub-paragraph (4), or
(b) is privy to the doing by others of any of the things mentioned in paragraphs (c), (d) and (e) of that sub-paragraph,

he commits an offence.

(4) Those things are—
(a) concealing any part of the company's property to the value of £500 or more, or concealing any debt due to or from the company, or
(b) fraudulently removing any part of the company's property to the value of £500 or more, or
(c) concealing, destroying, mutilating or falsifying any book or paper affecting or relating to the company's property or affairs, or
(d) making any false entry in any book or paper affecting or relating to the company's property or affairs, or
(e) fraudulently parting with, altering or making any omission in any document affecting or relating to the company's property or affairs, or
(f) pawning, pledging or disposing of any property of the company which has been obtained on credit and has not been paid for (unless the pawning, pledging or disposal was in the ordinary way of the company's business).

(5) For the purposes of this paragraph, "officer" includes a shadow director.

(6) It is a defence—
(a) for a person charged under sub-paragraph (2) or (3) in respect of the things mentioned in paragraph (a) or (f) of sub-paragraph (4) to prove that he had no intent to defraud, and
(b) for a person charged under sub-paragraph (2) or (3) in respect of the things mentioned in paragraph (c) or (d) of sub-paragraph (4) to prove that he had no intent to conceal the state of affairs of the company or to defeat the law.

(7) Where a person pawns, pledges or disposes of any property of a company in circumstances which amount to an offence under sub-paragraph (2) or (3), every person who takes in pawn or pledge, or otherwise receives, the property knowing it to be pawned, pledged or disposed of in circumstances which—
(a) would, if a moratorium were obtained for the company within the period of 12 months beginning with the day on which the pawning, pledging or disposal took place, amount to an offence under sub-paragraph (2), or
(b) amount to an offence under sub-paragraph (3),

commits an offence.

(8) A person guilty of an offence under this paragraph is liable to imprisonment or a fine, or both.

(9) The money sums specified in paragraphs (a) and (b) of sub-paragraph (4) are subject to increase or reduction by order under section 417A in Part XV.

42

(1) If, for the purpose of obtaining a moratorium, or an extension of a moratorium, for a company, a person who is an officer of the company—

(a) makes any false representation, or
(b) fraudulently does, or omits to do, anything,

he commits an offence.

(2) Sub-paragraph (1) applies even if no moratorium or extension is obtained.

(3) For the purposes of this paragraph, "officer" includes a shadow director.

(4) A person guilty of an offence under this paragraph is liable to imprisonment or a fine, or both.

Void provisions in floating charge documents

43

(1) A provision in an instrument creating a floating charge is void if it provides for—

(a) obtaining a moratorium, or
(b) anything done with a view to obtaining a moratorium (including any preliminary decision or investigation),

to be an event causing the floating charge to crystallise or causing restrictions which would not otherwise apply to be imposed on the disposal of property by the company or a ground for the appointment of a receiver.

(2) In sub-paragraph (1), "receiver" includes a manager and a person who is appointed both receiver and manager.

Functions of the Financial Services Authority

44

(1) This Schedule has effect in relation to a moratorium for a regulated company with the modifications in sub-paragraphs (2) to (16) below.

(2) Any notice or other document required by virtue of this Schedule to be sent to a creditor of a regulated company must also be sent to the Authority.

(3) The Authority is entitled to be heard on any application to the court for leave under paragraph 20(2) or 20(3) (disposal of charged property, etc).

(4) Where paragraph 26(1) (challenge of nominee's actions, etc) applies, the persons who may apply to the court include the Authority.

(5) If a person other than the Authority applies to the court under that paragraph, the Authority is entitled to be heard on the application.

(6) Where paragraph 27(1) (challenge of nominee's actions, etc) applies, the persons who may apply to the court include the Authority.

(7) If a person other than the Authority applies to the court under that paragraph, the Authority is entitled to be heard on the application.

(8) The persons to be summoned to a creditors' meeting under paragraph 29 include the Authority.

(9) A person appointed for the purpose by the Authority is entitled to attend and participate in (but not to vote at)—

(a) any creditors' meeting summoned under that paragraph,
(b) any meeting of a committee established under paragraph 35 (moratorium committee).

(10) The Authority is entitled to be heard on any application under paragraph 36(3) (effectiveness of decisions).

(11) Where paragraph 38(1) (challenge of decisions) applies, the persons who may apply to the court include the Authority.

(12) If a person other than the Authority applies to the court under that paragraph, the Authority is entitled to be heard on the application.

(13) Where paragraph 39(3) (implementation of voluntary arrangement) applies, the persons who may apply to the court include the Authority.

(14) If a person other than the Authority applies to the court under that paragraph, the Authority is entitled to be heard on the application.

(15) Where paragraph 40(2) (challenge of directors' actions) applies, the persons who may apply to the court include the Authority.

(16) If a person other than the Authority applies to the court under that paragraph, the Authority is entitled to be heard on the application.

(17) This paragraph does not prejudice any right the Authority has (apart from this paragraph) as a creditor of a regulated company.

(18) In this paragraph—

"the Authority" means the Financial Services Authority, and

"regulated company" means a company which—

(a) is, or has been, an authorised person within the meaning given by section 31 of the Financial Services and Markets Act 2000,
(b) is, or has been, an appointed representative within the meaning given by section 39 of that Act, or
(c) is carrying on, or has carried on, a regulated activity, within the meaning given by section 22 of that Act, in contravention of the general prohibition within the meaning given by section 19 of that Act.

Subordinate legislation

45

(1) Regulations or an order made by the Secretary of State under this Schedule may make different provision for different cases.

(2) Regulations so made may make such consequential, incidental, supplemental and transitional provision as may appear to the Secretary of State necessary or expedient.

(3) Any power of the Secretary of State to make regulations under this Schedule may be exercised by amending or repealing any enactment contained in this Act (including one contained in this Schedule) or contained in the Company Directors Disqualification Act 1986.

(4) Regulations (except regulations under paragraph 5) or an order made by the Secretary of State under this Schedule shall be made by statutory instrument

subject to annulment in pursuance of a resolution of either House of Parliament.

(5) Regulations under paragraph 5 of this Schedule are to be made by statutory instrument and shall only be made if a draft containing the regulations has been laid before and approved by resolution of each House of Parliament.

NOTES

Amendment
Inserted by the Insolvency Act 2000, s 1, Sch 1, paras 1, 4.
Date in force (for the purposes of para 45(1)–(3), (5)): 11 May 2001: see SI 2001/1751, art 2.
Date in force (for remaining purposes): 1 January 2003: see SI 2002/2711, art 2.

THE SECOND GROUP OF PARTS
INSOLVENCY OF INDIVIDUALS; BANKRUPTCY

PART VIII
INDIVIDUAL VOLUNTARY ARRANGEMENTS

Moratorium for insolvent debtor

252 Interim order of court

(1) In the circumstances specified below, the court may in the case of a debtor (being an individual) make an interim order under this section.

(2) An interim order has the effect that, during the period for which it is in force—
(a) no bankruptcy petition relating to the debtor may be presented or proceeded with,
[(aa) no landlord or other person to whom rent is payable may exercise any right of forfeiture by peaceable re-entry in relation to premises let to the debtor in respect of a failure by the debtor to comply with any term or condition of his tenancy of such premises, except with the leave of the court] and
(b) no other proceedings, and no execution or other legal process, may be commenced or continued [and no distress may be levied] against the debtor or his property except with the leave of the court.

NOTES

Amendment
Sub-s (2): para (aa) inserted by the Insolvency Act 2000, s 3, Sch 3, paras 1, 2(a).
Sub-s (2): in para (b) words "and no distress may be levied" in square brackets inserted by the Insolvency Act 2000, s 3, Sch 3, paras 1, 2(b).

Extent
This Part does not extend to Scotland: see s 440(2)(b).

253 Application for interim order

(1) Application to the court for an interim order may be made where the debtor intends to make a proposal [under this Part, that is, a proposal] to his creditors for

a composition in satisfaction of his debts or a scheme of arrangement of his affairs (from here on referred to, in either case, as a "voluntary arrangement").

(2) The proposal must provide for some person ("the nominee") to act in relation to the voluntary arrangement either as trustee or otherwise for the purpose of supervising its implementation [and the nominee must be a person who is qualified to act as an insolvency practitioner, or authorised to act as nominee, in relation to the voluntary arrangement].

(3) Subject as follows, the application may be made—
- (a) if the debtor is an undischarged bankrupt, by the debtor, the trustee of his estate, or the official receiver, and
- (b) in any other case, by the debtor.

(4) An application shall not be made under subsection (3)(*a*) unless the debtor has given notice of [the proposal] to the official receiver and, if there is one, the trustee of his estate.

(5) An application shall not be made while a bankruptcy petition presented by the debtor is pending, if the court has, under section 273 below, appointed an insolvency practitioner to inquire into the debtor's affairs and report.

NOTES

Amendment
Sub-s (1): words "under this Part, that is, a proposal" in square brackets inserted by the Insolvency Act 2000, s 3, Sch 3, paras 1, 3(a).
Sub-s (2): words from "and the nominee" to "the voluntary arrangement" in square brackets inserted by the Insolvency Act 2000, s 3, Sch 3, paras 1, 3(b).
Sub-s (4): words "the proposal" in square brackets substituted by the Insolvency Act 2000, s 3, Sch 3, paras 1, 3(c).

254 Effect of application

(1) At any time when an application under section 253 for an interim order is pending,
- [(a) no landlord or other person to whom rent is payable may exercise any right of forfeiture by peaceable re-entry in relation to premises let to the debtor in respect of a failure by the debtor to comply with any term or condition of his tenancy of such premises, except with the leave of the court, and
- (b)] the court may [forbid the levying of any distress on the debtor's property or its subsequent sale, or both, and] stay any action, execution or other legal process against the property or person of the debtor.

(2) Any court in which proceedings are pending against an individual may, on proof that an application under that section has been made in respect of that individual, either stay the proceedings or allow them to continue on such terms as it thinks fit.

NOTES

Amendment
Sub-s (1): para (a) and subsequent reference to "(b)" inserted by the Insolvency Act 2000, s 3, Sch 3, paras 1, 4(a).
Sub-s (1): in para (b) words "forbid the levying of any distress on the debtor's property or its subsequent sale, or both, and" in square brackets inserted by the Insolvency Act 2000, s 3, Sch 3, paras 1, 4(b).

255 Cases in which interim order can be made

(1) The court shall not make an interim order on an application under section 253 unless it is satisfied—

- (a) that the debtor intends to make [a proposal under this Part];
- (b) that on the day of the making of the application the debtor was an undischarged bankrupt or was able to petition for his own bankruptcy;
- (c) that no previous application has been made by the debtor for an interim order in the period of 12 months ending with that day; and
- (d) that the nominee under the debtor's proposal . . . is willing to act in relation to the proposal.

(2) The court may make an order if it thinks that it would be appropriate to do so for the purpose of facilitating the consideration and implementation of the debtor's proposal.

(3) Where the debtor is an undischarged bankrupt, the interim order may contain provision as to the conduct of the bankruptcy, and the administration of the bankrupt's estate, during the period for which the order is in force.

(4) Subject as follows, the provision contained in an interim order by virtue of subsection (3) may include provision staying proceedings in the bankruptcy or modifying any provision in this Group of Parts, and any provision of the rules in their application to the debtor's bankruptcy.

(5) An interim order shall not, in relation to a bankrupt, make provision relaxing or removing any of the requirements of provisions in this Group of Parts, or of the rules, unless the court is satisfied that that provision is unlikely to result in any significant diminution in, or in the value of, the debtor's estate for the purposes of the bankruptcy.

(6) Subject to the following provisions of this Part, and interim order made on an application under section 253 ceases to have effect at the end of the period of 14 days beginning with the day after the making of the order.

NOTES

Amendment

Sub-s (1): in para (a) words "a proposal under this Part" in square brackets substituted by the Insolvency Act 2000, s 3, Sch 3, paras 1, 5(a).

Sub-s (1): in para (d) words omitted repealed by the Insolvency Act 2000, ss 3, 15(1), Sch 3, paras 1, 5(b), Sch 5.

256 Nominee's report on debtor's proposal

(1) Where an interim order has been made on an application under section 253, the nominee shall, before the order ceases to have effect, submit a report to the court stating—

- (a) [whether, in his opinion, the voluntary arrangement which the debtor is proposing has a reasonable prospect of being approved and implemented,
- (aa)] whether, in his opinion, a meeting of the debtor's creditors should be summoned to consider the debtor's proposal, and
- (b) if in his opinion such a meeting should be summoned, the date on which, and time and place at which, he proposes the meeting should be held.

(2) For the purpose of enabling the nominee to prepare his report the debtor shall submit to the nominee—

(a) a document setting out the terms of the voluntary arrangement which the debtor is proposing, and
(b) a statement of his affairs containing—
  (i) such particulars of his creditors and of his debts and other liabilities and of his assets as may be prescribed, and
  (ii) such other information as may be prescribed.

[(3) The court may—
(a) on an application made by the debtor in a case where the nominee has failed to submit the report required by this section or has died, or
(b) on an application made by the debtor or the nominee in a case where it is impracticable or inappropriate for the nominee to continue to act as such,

direct that the nominee shall be replaced as such by another person qualified to act as an insolvency practitioner, or authorised to act as nominee, in relation to the voluntary arrangement.

(3A) The court may, on an application made by the debtor in a case where the nominee has failed to submit the report required by this section, direct that the interim order shall continue, or (if it has ceased to have effect) be renewed, for such further period as the court may specify in the direction.]

(4) The court may, on the application of the nominee, extend the period for which the interim order has effect so as to enable the nominee to have more time to prepare his report.

(5) If the court is satisfied on receiving the nominee's report that a meeting of the debtor's creditors should be summoned to consider the debtor's proposal, the court shall direct that the period for which the interim order has effect shall be extended, for such further period as it may specify in the direction, for the purpose of enabling the debtor's proposal to be considered by his creditors in accordance with the following provisions of this Part.

(6) The court may discharge the interim order if it is satisfied, on the application of the nominee—
(a) that the debtor has failed to comply with his obligations under subsection (2), or
(b) that for any other reason it would be inappropriate for a meeting of the debtor's creditors to be summoned to consider the debtor's proposal.

NOTES

Amendment
Sub-s (1): in para (a) words from "whether, in his" to "approved and implemented," and subsequent reference to "(aa)" in square brackets inserted by the Insolvency Act 2000, s 3, Sch 3, paras 1, 6(a).
Sub-ss (3), (3A): substituted, for sub-s (3) as originally enacted, by the Insolvency Act 2000, s 3, Sch 3, paras 1, 6(b).

[Procedure where no interim order made]

NOTES

Amendment
Inserted by the Insolvency Act 2000, s 3, Sch 3, paras 1, 7.

[256A Debtor's proposal and nominee's report]

[(1) This section applies where a debtor (being an individual)—

(a) intends to make a proposal under this Part (but an interim order has not been made in relation to the proposal and no application for such an order is pending), and

(b) if he is an undischarged bankrupt, has given notice of the proposal to the official receiver and, if there is one, the trustee of his estate,

unless a bankruptcy petition presented by the debtor is pending and the court has, under section 273, appointed an insolvency practitioner to inquire into the debtor's affairs and report.

(2) For the purpose of enabling the nominee to prepare a report to the court, the debtor shall submit to the nominee—

(a) a document setting out the terms of the voluntary arrangement which the debtor is proposing, and

(b) a statement of his affairs containing—

(i) such particulars of his creditors and of his debts and other liabilities and of his assets as may be prescribed, and

(ii) such other information as may be prescribed.

(3) If the nominee is of the opinion that the debtor is an undischarged bankrupt, or is able to petition for his own bankruptcy, the nominee shall, within 14 days (or such longer period as the court may allow) after receiving the document and statement mentioned in subsection (2), submit a report to the court stating—

(a) whether, in his opinion, the voluntary arrangement which the debtor is proposing has a reasonable prospect of being approved and implemented,

(b) whether, in his opinion, a meeting of the debtor's creditors should be summoned to consider the debtor's proposal, and

(c) if in his opinion such a meeting should be summoned, the date on which, and time and place at which, he proposes the meeting should be held.

(4) The court may—

(a) on an application made by the debtor in a case where the nominee has failed to submit the report required by this section or has died, or

(b) on an application made by the debtor or the nominee in a case where it is impracticable or inappropriate for the nominee to continue to act as such,

direct that the nominee shall be replaced as such by another person qualified to act as an insolvency practitioner, or authorised to act as nominee, in relation to the voluntary arrangement.

(5) The court may, on an application made by the nominee, extend the period within which the nominee is to submit his report.]

NOTES

Amendment

Inserted by the Insolvency Act 2000, s 3, Sch 3, paras 1, 7.

[Creditors' meeting]

NOTES

Amendment
Inserted by the Insolvency Act 2000, s 3, Sch 3, paras 1, 7.

257 Summoning of creditors' meeting

(1) Where it has been reported to the court under section 256 [or 256A] that a meeting of the debtor's creditors should be summoned, the nominee (or his replacement under section [256(3) or 256A(4)]) shall, unless the court otherwise directs, summon that meeting for the time, date and place proposed in his report.

(2) The persons to be summoned to the meeting are every creditor of the debtor of whose claim and address the person summoning the meeting is aware.

(3) For this purpose the creditors of a debtor who is an undischarged bankrupt include—

- (a) every person who is a creditor of the bankrupt in respect of a bankruptcy debt, and
- (b) every person who would be such a creditor if the bankruptcy had commenced on the day on which notice of the meeting is given.

NOTES

Amendment
Sub-s (1): words "or 256A" in square brackets inserted by the Insolvency Act 2000, s 3, Sch 3, paras 1, 8(a).
Sub-s (1): words "256(3) or 256A(4)" in square brackets substituted by the Insolvency Act 2000, s 3, Sch 3, paras 1, 8(b).

Consideration and implementation of debtor's proposal

258 Decisions of creditors' meeting

(1) A creditors' meeting summoned under section 257 shall decide whether to approve the proposed voluntary arrangement.

(2) The meeting may approve the proposed voluntary arrangement with modifications, but shall not do so unless the debtor consents to each modification.

(3) The modifications subject to which the proposed voluntary arrangement may be approved may include one conferring the functions proposed to be conferred on the nominee on another person qualified to act as an insolvency practitioner [or authorised to act as nominee, in relation to the voluntary arrangement].

But they shall not include any modification by virtue of which the proposal ceases to be a proposal [under this Part].

(4) The meeting shall not approve any proposal or modification which affects the right of a secured creditor of the debtor to enforce his security, except with the concurrence of the creditor concerned.

(5) Subject as follows, the meeting shall not approve any proposal or modification under which—

- (a) any preferential debt of the debtor is to be paid otherwise than in priority to such of his debts as are not preferential debts, or

(b) a preferential creditor of the debtor is to be paid an amount in respect of a preferential debt that bears to that debt a smaller proportion than is borne to another preferential debt by the amount that is to be paid in respect of that other debt.

However, the meeting may approve such a proposal or modification with the concurrence of the preferential creditor concerned.

(6) Subject as above, the meeting shall be conducted in accordance with the rules.

(7) In this section "preferential debt" has the meaning given by section 386 in Part XII; and "preferential creditor" is to be construed accordingly.

NOTES

Amendment

Sub-s (3): words "or authorised to act as nominee, in relation to the voluntary arrangement" in square brackets substituted by the Insolvency Act 2000, s 3, Sch 3, paras 1, 9.
Sub-s (3): words "under this Part" in square brackets substituted by the Insolvency Act 2000, s 3, Sch 3, paras 1, 9.

259 Report of decisions to court

(1) After the conclusion in accordance with the rules of the meeting summoned under section 257, the chairman of the meeting shall report the result of it to the court and, immediately after so reporting, shall give notice of the result of the meeting to such persons as may be prescribed.

(2) If the report is that the meeting has declined (with or without modifications) to approve the debtor's proposal, the court may discharge any interim order which is in force in relation to the debtor.

260 Effect of approval

(1) This section has effect where the meeting summoned under section 257 approves the proposed voluntary arrangement (with or without modifications).

(2) The approved arrangement—
(a) takes effect as if made by the debtor at the meeting, and
[(b) binds every person who in accordance with the rules—
(i) was entitled to vote at the meeting (whether or not he was present or represented at it), or
(ii) would have been so entitled if he had had notice of it,
as if he were a party to the arrangement.

(2A) If—
(a) when the arrangement ceases to have effect any amount payable under the arrangement to a person bound by virtue of subsection (2)(b)(ii) has not been paid, and
(b) the arrangement did not come to an end prematurely,

the debtor shall at that time become liable to pay to that person the amount payable under the arrangement.]

(3) The Deeds of Arrangement Act 1914 does not apply to the approved voluntary arrangement.

(4) Any interim order in force in relation to the debtor immediately before the end of the period of 28 days beginning with the day on which the report with

respect to the creditors' meeting was made to the court under section 259 ceases to have effect at the end of that period.

This subsection applies except to such extent as the court may direct for the purposes of any application under section 262 below.

(5) Where proceedings on a bankruptcy petition have been stayed by an interim order which ceases to have effect under subsection (4), the petition is deemed, unless the court otherwise orders, to have been dismissed.

NOTES

Amendment

Sub-s (2): para (b) substituted, together with sub-s (2A), by the Insolvency Act 2000, s 3, Sch 3, paras 1, 10.

Sub-s (2A): substituted, together with sub-s (2)(b), for sub-s (2)(b) as originally enacted, by the Insolvency Act 2000, s 3, Sch 3, paras 1, 10.

261 Effect where debtor an undischarged bankrupt

(1) Subject as follows, where the creditors' meeting summoned under section 257 approves the proposed voluntary arrangement (with or without modifications) and the debtor is an undischarged bankrupt, the court may do one or both of the following, namely—

- (a) annul the bankruptcy order by which he was adjudged bankrupt;
- (b) give such directions with respect to the conduct of the bankruptcy and the administration of the bankrupt's estate as it thinks appropriate for facilitating the implementation of the approved voluntary arrangement.

(2) The court shall not annul a bankruptcy order under subsection (1)—

- (a) at any time before the end of the period of 28 days beginning with the day on which the report of the creditors' meeting was made to the court under section 259, or
- (b) at any time when an application under section 262 below, or an appeal in respect of such an application, is pending or at any time in the period within which such an appeal may be brought.

262 Challenge of meeting's decision

(1) Subject to this section, an application to the court may be made, by any of the persons specified below, on one or both of the following grounds, namely—

- (a) that a voluntary arrangement approved by a creditors' meeting summoned under section 257 unfairly prejudices the interests of a creditor of the debtor;
- (b) that there has been some material irregularity at or in relation to such a meeting.

(2) The persons who may apply under this section are—

- (a) the debtor;
- [(b) a person who—
  - (i) was entitled, in accordance with the rules, to vote at the creditors' meeting, or
  - (ii) would have been so entitled if he had had notice of it;]
- (c) the nominee (or his replacement under section [256(3), 256A(4)] or 258(3)); and
- (d) if the debtor is an undischarged bankrupt, the trustee of his estate or the official receiver.

(3) An application under this section shall not be made—

[(a)] after the end of the period of 28 days beginning with the day on which the report of the creditors' meeting was made to the court under section 259, [or

(b) in the case of a person who was not given notice of the creditors' meeting, after the end of the period of 28 days beginning with the day on which he became aware that the meeting had taken place,

but (subject to that) an application made by a person within subsection (2)(b)(ii) on the ground that the arrangement prejudices his interests may be made after the arrangement has ceased to have effect, unless it has come to an end prematurely].

(4) Where on an application under this section the court is satisfied as to either of the grounds mentioned in subsection (1), it may do one or both of the following, namely—

(a) revoke or suspend any approval given by the meeting;

(b) give a direction to any person for the summoning of a further meeting of the debtor's creditors to consider any revised proposal he may make or, in a case falling within subsection (1)(b), to reconsider his original proposal.

(5) Where at any time after giving a direction under subsection (4)(b) for the summoning of a meeting to consider a revised proposal the court is satisfied that the debtor does not intend to submit such a proposal, the court shall revoke the direction and revoke or suspend any approval given at the previous meeting.

(6) Where the court gives a direction under subsection (4)(b), it may also give a direction continuing or, as the case may require, renewing, for such period as may be specified in the direction, the effect in relation to the debtor of any interim order.

(7) In any case where the court, on an application made under this section with respect to a creditors' meeting, gives a direction under subsection (4)(b) or revokes or suspends an approval under subsection (4)(a) or (5), the court may give such supplemental directions as it thinks fit and, in particular, directions with respect to—

(a) things done since the meeting under any voluntary arrangement approved by the meeting, and

(b) such things done since the meeting as could not have been done if an interim order had been in force in relation to the debtor when they were done.

(8) Except in pursuance of the preceding provisions of this section, an approval given at a creditors' meeting summoned under section 257 is not invalidated by any irregularity at or in relation to the meeting.

NOTES

Amendment

Sub-s (2): para (b) substituted by the Insolvency Act 2000, s 3, Sch 3, paras 1, 11(1)(a).
Sub-s (2): in para (c) reference to "256(3), 256A(4)" in square brackets substituted by the Insolvency Act 2000, s 3, Sch 3, paras 1, 11(1)(b).
Sub-s (3): reference to "(a)" in square brackets inserted by the Insolvency Act 2000, s 3, Sch 3, paras 1, 11(2)(a).

Sub-s (3): para (b) and word "or" immediately preceding it and words from "but (subject to that)" to "an end prematurely" in square brackets inserted by the Insolvency Act 2000, s 3, Sch 3, paras 1, 11(2)(b).

[262A False representations etc]

[(1) If for the purpose of obtaining the approval of his creditors to a proposal for a voluntary arrangement, the debtor—
- (a) makes any false representation, or
- (b) fraudulently does, or omits to do, anything,

he commits an offence.

(2) Subsection (1) applies even if the proposal is not approved.

(3) A person guilty of an offence under this section is liable to imprisonment or a fine, or both.]

NOTES

Amendment
Inserted by the Insolvency Act 2000, s 3, Sch 3, paras 1, 12.

[262B Prosecution of delinquent debtors]

[(1) This section applies where a voluntary arrangement approved by a creditors' meeting summoned under section 257 has taken effect.

(2) If it appears to the nominee or supervisor that the debtor has been guilty of any offence in connection with the arrangement for which he is criminally liable, he shall forthwith—
- (a) report the matter to the Secretary of State, and
- (b) provide the Secretary of State with such information and give the Secretary of State such access to and facilities for inspecting and taking copies of documents (being information or documents in his possession or under his control and relating to the matter in question) as the Secretary of State requires.

(3) Where a prosecuting authority institutes criminal proceedings following any report under subsection (2), the nominee or, as the case may be, supervisor shall give the authority all assistance in connection with the prosecution which he is reasonably able to give.

For this purpose, "prosecuting authority" means the Director of Public Prosecutions or the Secretary of State.

(4) The court may, on the application of the prosecuting authority, direct a nominee or supervisor to comply with subsection (3) if he has failed to do so.]

NOTES

Amendment
Inserted by the Insolvency Act 2000, s 3, Sch 3, paras 1, 12.

[262C Arrangements coming to an end prematurely]

[For the purposes of this Part, a voluntary arrangement approved by a creditors' meeting summoned under section 257 comes to an end prematurely if, when it ceases to have effect, it has not been fully implemented in respect of all persons bound by the arrangement by virtue of section 260(2)(b)(i).]

NOTES

Amendment
Inserted by the Insolvency Act 2000, s 3, Sch 3, paras 1, 12.

263 Implementation and supervision of approved voluntary arrangement

(1) This section applies where a voluntary arrangement approved by a creditors' meeting summoned under section 257 has taken effect.

(2) The person who is for the time being carrying out, in relation to the voluntary arrangement, the functions conferred by virtue of the approval on the nominee (or his replacement under section [256(3), 256A(4)] or 258(3)) shall be known as the supervisor of the voluntary arrangement.

(3) If the debtor, any of his creditors or any other person is dissatisfied by any act, omission or decision of the supervisor, he may apply to the court; and on such an application the court may—

- (a) confirm, reverse or modify any act or decision of the supervisor,
- (b) give him directions, or
- (c) make such other order as it thinks fit.

(4) The supervisor may apply to the court for directions in relation to any particular matter arising under the voluntary arrangement.

(5) The court may, whenever—

- (a) it is expedient to appoint a person to carry out the functions of the supervisor, and
- (b) it is inexpedient, difficult or impracticable for an appointment to be made without the assistance of the court,

make an order appointing a person who is qualified to act as an insolvency practitioner [or authorised to act as supervisor, in relation to the voluntary arrangement], either in substitution for the existing supervisor or to fill a vacancy.

This is without prejudice to section 41(2) of the Trustee Act 1925 (power of court to appoint trustees of deeds of arrangement).

(6) The power conferred by subsection (5) is exercisable so as to increase the number of persons exercising the functions of the supervisor or, where there is more than one person exercising those functions, so as to replace one or more of those persons.

NOTES

Amendment
Sub-s (2): reference to "256(3), 256A(4)" in square brackets substituted by the Insolvency Act 2000, s 3, Sch 3, paras 1, 13(a).
Sub-s (5): words "or authorised to act as supervisor, in relation to the voluntary arrangement" in square brackets substituted by the Insolvency Act 2000, s 3, Sch 3, paras 1, 13(b).

* * * *

249 "Connected" with a company

For the purposes of any provision in [the parts of the Insolvency Act dealing with company insolvency], a person is connected with a company if—

(a) he is a director or shadow director[1] of the company or an associate of such a director or shadow director, or
(b) he is an associated of the company;

and 'associate' has the meaning given by section 435 of this Act.

NOTES
1 A 'shadow director' means a person in accordance with whose directions or instructions the directors of the company are accustomed to act (but so that a person is not deemed a shadow director by reason only that the directors act on advice given by him in a professional capacity); IA 1986, s 251.

Modification
Modified by the Building Societies Act 1986, s 90, Sch 15, and the Friendly Societies Act 1992, s 23, Sch 10.

* * * *

PART XVIII
INTERPRETATION

435 Meaning of "associate"

(1) For the purposes of this Act any question whether a person is an associate of another person is to be determined in accordance with the following provisions of this section (any provision that a person is an associate of another person being taken to mean that they are associates of each other).

(2) A person is an associate of an individual if that person is the individual's husband or wife, or is a relative, or the husband or wife of a relative, of the individual or of the individual's husband or wife.

(3) A person is an associate of any person with whom he is in partnership,[1] and of the husband or wife or a relative of any individual with whom he is in partnership; and a Scottish firm is an associate of any person who is a member of the firm.

(4) A person is an associate of any person whom he employs or by whom he is employed.[2]

(5) A person in his capacity as trustee of a trust other than-
(a) a trust arising under any of the second Group of Parts of the Bankruptcy (Scotland) Act 1985, or
(b) a pension scheme or an employees' share scheme (within the meaning of the Companies Act),

is an associate of another person if the beneficiaries of the trust include, or the terms of the trust confer a power that may be exercised for the benefit of, that other person or an associate of that other person.[3]

(6) A company is an associate of another company-
(a) if the same person has control of both, or a person has control of one and persons who are his associates, or he and persons who are his associates, have control of the other, or
(b) if a group of two or more persons has control of each company, and the groups either consists of the same persons or could be regarded as

consisting of the same persons by treating (in one or more cases) a member of either group as replaced by a person of whom he is an associate.

(7) A company is an associate of another person if that person has control of it or if that person and persons who are his associates together have control of it.

(8) For the purposes of this section a person is a relative of an individual if he is that individual's brother, sister, uncle, aunt, nephew, niece, lineal ancestor or lineal descendant, treating–

(a) any relationship of the half blood as a relationship of the whole blood and the stepchild or adopted child of any person as his child, and

(b) an illegitimate child as the legitimate child of his mother and reputed father;[4]

and references in this section to a husband or wife include a former[5] husband or wife and a reputed[6] husband or wife.

(9) for the purposes of this section any director or other officer[7] of a company is to be treated as employed by that company.

(10) For the purposes of this section a person is to be taken as having control of a company if–

(a) the directors of the company or of another company which has control of it (or any of them) are accustomed to act in accordance with his directions or instructions, or

(b) he is entitled to exercise, or control the exercise of, one third or more of the voting power at any general meeting of the company or of another company which has control of it;

and where two or more persons together satisfy either of the above conditions, they are to be taken as having control of the company.

(11) In this section 'company' includes any body corporate (whether incorporated in Great Britain or elsewhere); and references to directors and other officers of a company and to voting power at any general meeting of a company have effect with any necessary modifications.

NOTES

1 Note the present tense 'is in partnership'. It follows that a former partner, even where the partnership is dissolved only a day or two before the relevant vote or transaction is not an associate, unless, presumably, the court is able to conclude that the dissolution of the partnership was a sham. Thus where a former partner, who had been in partnership with the debtor until only a few days before the date of the interim order, voted in favour of and was responsible for carrying in the proposed voluntary arrangements he was not treated as an associate for the purposes of the vote, *Barclays Bank plc v Getter* (4 March 1993, unreported), per Mr Registrar Scott.

2 Again the present tense is to be noted. Former employees are not associates, unless presumably the termination of employment can be shown to be a sham, that is an act intended by the persons involved to give to third parties or to the court the appearance of creating between the parties legal rights and obligations different from the actual legal rights and obligations which the parties intend to create, *Snook v London & West Riding Investments Ltd* [1967] 1 All ER 518, CA at 528.

3 A pension scheme trustee is not an associate, *Re Thirty-Eight Building Ltd* [1999] 1 BCLC 416.

4 In the case of reputed fathers it is suggested that the intention of parliament is to go further than a reputed blood relationship and cover any man who is apparently the father in the light of his relationship with the subject and the subject's mother.

5 Former husband and wife will include not only spouses from whom there has been a divorce but also deceased husband and wife. Thus the relatives of a deceased or divorced spouse come within the definition of associate; IA 1986, s 435(2).

6 The use of 'reputed' which is not a term of art in family law is reminiscent of the concept of reputed ownership under the Bankruptcy Acts. In the case of reputed husband and wife Parliament is presumably intending to cover 'common law' spouses or co-habitees. It may be argued that co-habitation is not enough; the strict words of the Act require that there be a reputation of marriage itself, ie that the couple have indeed undergone a ceremony of marriage. It is suggested that this would be too literal an approach to interpretation. The plain aim of the section is to cover persons with whom the subject may have close ties such that transactions between them or votes in respect of the subject may not be at arm's length. The ceremony of marriage is irrelevant here. What matters is the bond between the subject and the associate. However, in the course of the passage of the Insolvency Bill an unsuccessful attempt was made to introduce the Scots Law concept of 'conjunct or confident person' into the definition of Associate. The expressed aim was to include persons living together and mistresses. It is by no means clear that the failure of this amendment leads to the conclusion that Parliament intended that co-habitees should be excluded from the definition of associate, but the point is arguable. Mistresses, and other lovers, are outside the scope of the definition.This may be thought to be a significant lacuna, but drafting a provision to cover such persons would not be straightforward. For the debate on the Insolvency Bill, see *Hansard* (HL) Vol 459 col 1272, 7 February 1985.

7 For the purposes of the Companies Act 1985 'officer' includes a director, manager or secretary, CA 1985, s 744. The openness of this definition enables any person with an appropriate degree of control or influence to be held to be an officer. See generally *Re Liberator Permanent Benefit Building Society* (1894) 71 LT 406, 407 DC.

435 Limited Liability Partnerships

(3A) A member of a limited liability partnership is an associate of that limited liability partnership and of every other member of that limited liability partnership and of the husband or wife or relative of every other member of that limited liability partnership.[1]

NOTES

1 As inserted by the Limited Liability Partnerships Regulations 2001 SI 2001/1090, reg 5, Sch 3.

Appendix 2

Insolvency Rules 1986,* SI 1986/1925

PART 1
COMPANY VOLUNTARY ARRANGEMENTS

Chapter 1
Preliminary

1.1 Scope of this Part; interpretation

(1) The Rules in this Part apply where, pursuant to Part I of the Act, it is intended to make, and there is made, a proposal to a company and its creditors for a voluntary arrangement, that is to say, a composition in satisfaction of its debts or a scheme of arrangement of its affairs.

(2) In this Part—

[(a) Chapter 2 applies where the proposal for the voluntary arrangement is made by the directors of the company and
  (i) the company is neither in liquidation nor is an administration order (under Part II of the Act) in force in relation to it; and
  (ii) no steps have been taken to obtain a moratorium under Schedule A1 to the Act in connection with the proposal;]

(b) Chapter 3 applies where the company is in liquidation or an administration order is in force, and the proposal is made by the liquidator or (as the case may be) the administrator, he in either case being the nominee for the purposes of the proposal;

[(c) Chapter 4 applies in the same case as Chapter 3, but where the nominee is not the liquidator or administrator;

(d) Chapter 5 applies in all the three cases mentioned in sub-paragraphs (a) to (c) above;

(e) Chapters 7 and 8 apply to all voluntary arrangements with or without a moratorium; and

---

* **Commencement of amendments**
Unless otherwise stated, amendments made by SI 2002/1307 came into effect on 31 May 2002, see SI 2002/1307, r 1. Those amendments made by SI 2002/2712 came into effect on 1 January 2003, see SI 2002/2712, r 1. The commencement dates of other amendments are noted below the relevant provisions.

(f) Chapter 9 applies where the proposal is made by the directors of an eligible company with a view to obtaining a moratorium].

(3) In Chapters 3, 4 and 5, the liquidator or the administrator is referred to as "the responsible insolvency practitioner".

[(4) In this Part, a reference to an "eligible company" is to a company that is eligible for a moratorium in accordance with paragraph 2 of Schedule A1 to the Act.]

NOTES

Amendment

Para (2): sub-para (a) substituted by SI 2002/2712, r 3(1), Schedule, Pt 1, para 1(a).
Para (2): sub-paras (c)–(f) substituted, for sub-paras (c), (d) as originally enacted, by SI 2002/2712, r 3(1), Schedule, Pt 1, para 1(b).
Para (4): inserted by SI 2002/2712, r 3(1), Schedule, Pt 1, para 1(c).

Chapter 2
Proposal by Directors

1.2 Preparation of proposal

The directors shall prepare for the intended nominee a proposal on which (with or without amendments to be made under Rule 1.3 below) to make his report to the court under section 2.

1.3 Contents of proposal

(1) The directors' proposal shall provide a short explanation why, in their opinion, a voluntary arrangement under Part I of the Act is desirable, and give reasons why the company's creditors may be expected to concur with such an arrangement.

(2) The following matters shall be stated, or otherwise dealt with, in the directors' proposal—

- (a) the following matters, so far as within the directors' immediate knowledge—
  - (i) the company's assets, with an estimate of their respective values,
  - (ii) the extent (if any) to which the assets are charged in favour of creditors,
  - (iii) the extent (if any) to which particular assets are to be excluded from the voluntary arrangement;
- (b) particulars of any property, other than assets of the company itself, which is proposed to be included in the arrangement, the source of such property and the terms on which it is to be made available for inclusion;
- (c) the nature and amount of the company's liabilities (so far as within the directors' immediate knowledge), the manner in which they are proposed to be met, modified, postponed or otherwise dealt with by means of the arrangement, and (in particular)—
  - (i) how it is proposed to deal with preferential creditors (defined in section 4(7)) and creditors who are, or claim to be, secured,
  - (ii) how persons connected with the company (being creditors) are proposed to be treated under the arrangement, and
  - (iii) whether there are, to the directors' knowledge, any circumstances giving rise to the possibility, in the event that the company should go into liquidation, of claims under—

section 238 (transactions at an undervalue),
section 239 (preferences),
section 244 (extortionate credit transactions), or
section 245 (floating charges invalid);
and, where any such circumstances are present, whether, and if so how, it is proposed under the voluntary arrangement to make provision for wholly or partly indemnifying the company in respect of such claims;

(d) whether any, and if so what, guarantees have been given of the company's debts by other persons, specifying which (if any) of the guarantors are persons connected with the company;
(e) the proposed duration of the voluntary arrangement;
(f) the proposed dates of distributions to creditors, with estimates of their amounts;
[(fa) how it is proposed to deal with the claim of any person who is bound by the arrangement by virtue of section 5(2)(b)(ii);]
(g) the amount proposed to be paid to the nominee (as such) by way of remuneration and expenses;
(h) the manner in which it is proposed that the supervisor of the arrangement should be remunerated, and his expenses defrayed;
(j) whether, for the purposes of the arrangement, any guarantees are to be offered by directors, or other persons, and whether (if so) any security is to be given or sought;
(k) the manner in which funds held for the purposes of the arrangement are to be banked, invested or otherwise dealt with pending distribution to creditors;
(l) the manner in which funds held for the purpose of payment to creditors, and not so paid on the termination of the arrangement, are to be dealt with;
(m) the manner in which the business of the company is proposed to be conducted during the course of the arrangement;
(n) details of any further credit facilities which it is intended to arrange for the company, and how the debts so arising are to be paid;
(o) the functions which are to be undertaken by the supervisor of the arrangement; . . .
[(p) the name, address and qualification of the person proposed as supervisor of the voluntary arrangement, and confirmation that he is either qualified to act as an insolvency practitioner in relation to the company or is an authorised person in relation to the company][; and
(q) whether the EC Regulation will apply and, if so, whether the proceedings will be main proceedings, secondary proceedings or territorial proceedings].

(3) With the agreement in writing of the nominee, the directors' proposal may be amended at any time up to delivery of the former's report to the court under section 2(2).

NOTES

Amendment
Para (2): sub-para (fa) inserted by SI 2002/2712, r 3(1), Schedule, Pt 1, para 2(a).
Para (2): in sub-para (o) word omitted revoked by SI 2002/1307, rr 3(1), 4(2)(a).
Para (2): sub-para (p) substituted by SI 2002/2712, r 3(1), Schedule, Pt 1, para 2(b).

Para (2): sub-para (q) and word "; and" immediately preceding it inserted by SI 2002/1307, rr 3(1), 4(2)(b).

1.4 Notice to intended nominee

(1) The directors shall give to the intended nominee written notice of their proposal.

(2) The notice, accompanied by a copy of the proposal, shall be delivered either to the nominee himself, or to a person authorised to take delivery of documents on his behalf.

(3) If the intended nominee agrees to act, he shall cause a copy of the notice to be endorsed to the effect that it has been received by him on a specified date; and the period of 28 days referred to in section 2(2) then runs from that date.

(4) The copy of the notice so endorsed shall be returned by the nominee forthwith to the directors at an address specified by them in the notice for that purpose.

1.5 Statement of affairs

(1) The directors shall, within 7 days after their proposal is delivered to the nominee, or within such longer time as he may allow, deliver to him a statement of the company's affairs.

(2) The statement shall comprise the following particulars (supplementing or amplifying, so far as is necessary for clarifying the state of the company's affairs, those already given in the directors' proposal)—

- (a) a list of the company's assets, divided into such categories as are appropriate for easy identification, with estimated values assigned to each category;
- (b) in the case of any property on which a claim against the company is wholly or partly secured, particulars of the claim and its amount, and of how and when the security was created;
- (c) the names and addresses of the company's preferential creditors (defined in section 4(7)), with the amounts of their respective claims;
- (d) the names and addresses of the company's unsecured creditors, with the amounts of their respective claims;
- (e) particulars of any debts owed by or to the company to or by persons connected with it;
- (f) the names and addresses of the company's members, with details of their respective shareholdings;
- (g) such other particulars (if any) as the nominee may in writing require to be furnished for the purposes of making his report to the court on the directors' proposal.

(3) The statement of affairs shall be made up to a date not earlier than 2 weeks before the date of the notice to the nominee under Rule 1.4.

However, the nominee may allow an extension of that period to the nearest practicable date (not earlier than 2 months before the date of the notice under Rule 1.4); and if he does so, he shall give his reasons in his report to the court on the directors' proposal.

(4) The statement shall be certified as correct, to the best of their knowledge and belief, by two or more directors of the company, or by the company secretary and at least one director (other than the secretary himself).

1.6 Additional disclosure for assistance of nominee

(1) If it appears to the nominee that he cannot properly prepare his report on the basis of information in the directors' proposal and statement of affairs, he may call on the directors to provide him with—

(a) further and better particulars as to the circumstances in which, and the reasons why, the company is insolvent or (as the case may be) threatened with insolvency;

(b) particulars of any previous proposals which have been made in respect of the company under Part I of the Act;

(c) any further information with respect to the company's affairs which the nominee thinks necessary for the purposes of his report.

(2) The nominee may call on the directors to inform him, with respect to any person who is, or at any time in the 2 years preceding the notice under Rule 1.4 has been, a director or officer of the company, whether and in what circumstances (in those 2 years or previously) that person—

(a) has been concerned in the affairs of any other company (whether or not incorporated in England and Wales) which has become insolvent, or

(b) has himself been adjudged bankrupt or entered into an arrangement with his creditors.

(3) For the purpose of enabling the nominee to consider their proposal and prepare his report on it, the directors must give him access to the company's accounts and records.

1.7 Nominee's report on the proposal

(1) With his report to the court under section 2 the nominee shall deliver—

(a) a copy of the directors' proposal (with amendments, if any, authorised under Rule 1.3(3)); and

(b) a copy or summary of the company's statement of affairs.

(2) If the nominee makes known his opinion [that the directors' proposal has a reasonable prospect of being approved and implemented and] that meetings of the company and its creditors should be summoned under section 3, his report shall have annexed to it his comments on the proposal.

If his opinion is otherwise, he shall give his reasons for that opinion.

(3) The court shall cause the nominee's report to be endorsed with the date on which it is filed in court. Any director, member or creditor of the company is entitled, at all reasonable times on any business day, to inspect the file.

(4) The nominee shall send a copy of his report, and of his comments (if any), to the company.

NOTES

Amendment

Para (2): words "that the directors' proposal has a reasonable prospect of being approved and implemented and" in square brackets inserted by SI 2002/2712, r 3(1), Schedule, Pt 1, para 3.

[1.8 Replacement of nominee]

[(1) Where a person other than the nominee intends to apply to the court under section 2(4) for the nominee to be replaced, (except in any case where the nominee has died) he shall give to the nominee at least 7 days' notice of his application.

(2) Where the nominee intends to apply to the court under section 2(4) of the Act to be replaced, he shall give at least 7 days' notice of his application to the person intending to make the proposal.

(3) No appointment of a replacement nominee shall be made by the court unless there is filed in court a statement by the replacement nominee—
- (a) indicating his consent to act, and
- (b) that he is qualified to act as an insolvency practitioner in relation to the company or is an authorised person in relation to the company.]

NOTES

Amendment
Substituted by SI 2002/2712, r 3(1), Schedule, Pt 1, para 4.

1.9 Summoning of meetings under s 3

(1) If in his report the nominee states that in his opinion meetings of the company and its creditors should be summoned to consider the directors' proposal, the date on which the meetings are to be held shall be not less than 14, nor more than 28, days from that on which the nominee's report is filed in court under Rule 1.7.

(2) Notices calling the meetings shall be sent by the nominee, at least 14 days before the day fixed for them to be held—
- (a) in the case of the creditors' meeting, to all the creditors specified in the statement of affairs, and any other creditors of the company of whom he is otherwise aware; and
- (b) in the case of the meeting of members of the company, to all persons who are, to the best of the nominee's belief, members of it.

(3) Each notice sent under this Rule shall specify the court to which the nominee's report under section 2 has been delivered and shall state the effect of Rule 1.19(1), (3) and (4) (requisite majorities (creditors)); and with each notice there shall be sent—
- (a) a copy of the directors' proposal;
- (b) a copy of the statement of affairs or, if the nominee thinks fit, a summary of it (the summary to include a list of creditors and the amount of their debts); and
- (c) the nominee's comments on the proposal.

Chapter 3
Proposal by Administrator or Liquidator (Himself the Nominee)

1.10 Preparation of proposal

(1) The responsible insolvency practitioner's proposal shall specify—
- (a) all such matters as under Rule 1.3 in Chapter 2 the directors of the company would be required to include in a proposal by them[, with the addition, where the company is subject to an administration order, of the names and addresses of the company's preferential creditors (defined in section 4(7)), with the amounts of their respective claims], and
- (b) such other matters (if any) as the insolvency practitioner considers appropriate for ensuring that members and creditors of the company are enabled to reach an informed decision on the proposal.

(2) Where the company is being wound up by the court, the insolvency practitioner shall give notice of the proposal to the official receiver.

NOTES

Amendment

Para (1): words in square brackets inserted by SI 1987/1919, r 3(1), Schedule, Part 1, para 3.

1.11 Summoning of meetings under s 3

(1) The responsible insolvency practitioner shall fix a venue for the creditors' meeting and the company meeting, and give at least 14 days' notice of the meetings—

(a) in the case of the creditors' meeting, to all the creditors specified in the company's statement of affairs, and to any other creditors of whom the insolvency practitioner is aware; and

(b) in the case of the company meeting, to all persons who are, to the best of his belief, members of the company.

(2) Each notice sent out under this Rule shall state the effect of Rule 1.19(1), (3) and (4) (requisite majorities (creditors)); and with it there shall be sent—

(a) a copy of the responsible insolvency practitioner's proposal, and

(b) a copy of the statement of affairs or, if he thinks fit, a summary of it (the summary to include a list of creditors and the amounts of their debts).

Chapter 4
Proposal by Administrator or Liquidator (Another Insolvency Practitioner the Nominee)

1.12 Preparation of proposal and notice to nominee

(1) The responsible insolvency practitioner shall give notice to the intended nominee, and prepare his proposal for a voluntary arrangement, in the same manner as is required of the directors, in the case of a proposal by them, under Chapter 2.

(2) Rule 1.2 applies to the responsible insolvency practitioner as it applies to the directors; and Rule 1.4 applies as regards the action to be taken by the nominee.

(3) The content of the proposal shall be as required by Rule 1.3 [(and, where relevant, Rule 1.10)], reading references to the directors as referring to the responsible insolvency practitioner.

(4) Rule 1.6 applies in respect of the information to be furnished to the nominee, reading references to the directors as referring to the responsible insolvency practitioner.

(5) With the proposal the responsible insolvency practitioner shall provide a copy of the company's statement of affairs.

(6) Where the company is being wound up by the court, the responsible insolvency practitioner shall send a copy of the proposal to the official receiver, accompanied by the name and address of the insolvency practitioner [or authorised person] who has agreed to act as nominee.

(7) Rules 1.7 to 1.9 apply as regards a proposal under this Chapter as they apply to a proposal under Chapter 2.

NOTES

Amendment
Para (3): words in square brackets inserted by SI 1987/1919, r 3(1), Schedule, Part 1, para 4.
Para (6): words "or authorised person" in square brackets inserted by SI 2002/2712, r 3(1), Schedule, Pt 1, para 5.

Chapter 5
Proceedings on a Proposal made by the Directors, or by the Administrator, or by the Liquidator

Section A: Meetings of Company´s Creditors and Members

1.13 Summoning of meetings

(1) Subject as follows, in fixing the venue for the creditors' meeting and the company meeting, the person summoning the meeting ("the convener") shall have regard primarily to the convenience of the creditors.

(2) Meetings shall in each case be summoned for commencement between 10.00 and 16.00 hours on a business day.

[(3) The meetings may be held on the same day or on different days. If held on the same day, the meetings shall be held in the same place, but in either case the creditors' meeting shall be fixed for a time in advance of the company meeting.

(4) Where the meetings are not held on the same day, they shall be held within 7 days of each other.]

(4) With every notice summoning either meeting there shall be sent out forms of proxy.

NOTES

Amendment
Para (3), First Para (4): substituted, for para (3) as originally enacted, by SI 2002/2712, r 3(1), Schedule, Pt 1, para 6.

Miscellaneous
The substituted first para (4) is numbered as it appears in the Queen's Printer's copy. This is understood to be a drafting error.

1.14 The chairman at meetings

(1) Subject as follows, at both the creditors' meeting and the company meeting, and at any combined meeting, the convener shall be chairman.

(2) If for any reason he is unable to attend, he may nominate another person to act as chairman in his place; but a person so nominated must be . . .—
- [(a) a person qualified to act as an insolvency practitioner in relation to the company;
- (b) an authorised person in relation to the company; or
- (c) an employee of the convenor or his firm who is experienced in insolvency matters].

NOTES

Amendment
Para (2): word omitted revoked by SI 2002/2712, r 3(1), Schedule, Pt 1, para 7(a).
Para (2): sub-paras (a)–(c) substituted, for sub-paras (a), (b) as originally enacted, by SI 2002/2712, r 3(1), Schedule, Pt 1, para 7(b).

1.15 The chairman as proxy-holder

The chairman shall not by virtue of any proxy held by him vote to increase or reduce the amount of the remuneration or expenses of the nominee or the supervisor of the proposed arrangement, unless the proxy specifically directs him to vote in that way.

1.16 Attendance by company officers

(1) At least 14 days' notice to attend the meetings shall be given by the convener—

(a) to all directors of the company, and
(b) to any persons in whose case the convener thinks that their presence is required as being officers of the company, or as having been directors or officers of it at any time in the 2 years immediately preceding the date of the notice.

(2) The chairman may, if he thinks fit, exclude any present or former director or officer from attendance at a meeting, either completely or for any part of it; and this applies whether or not a notice under this Rule has been sent to the person excluded.

Section B: Voting Rights and Majorities

[1.17 Entitlement to vote (creditors)]

[(1) Subject as follows, every creditor who has notice of the creditors' meeting is entitled to vote at the meeting or any adjournment of it.

(2) Votes are calculated according to the amount of the creditor's debt as at the date of the meeting or, where the company is being wound up or is subject to an administration order, the date of its going into liquidation or (as the case may be) of the administration order.

(3) A creditor may vote in respect of a debt for an unliquidated amount or any debt whose value is not ascertained and for the purposes of voting (but not otherwise) his debt shall be valued at £1 unless the chairman agrees to put a higher value on it.]

NOTES

Amendment
Substituted, together with r 1.17A, for r 1.17 as originally enacted, by SI 2002/2712, r 3(1), Schedule, Pt 1, para 8.

[1.17A Procedure for admission of creditors' claims for voting purposes]

[(1) Subject as follows, at any creditors' meeting the chairman shall ascertain the entitlement of persons wishing to vote and shall admit or reject their claims accordingly.

(2) The chairman may admit or reject a claim in whole or in part.

(3) The chairman's decision on any matter under this Rule or under paragraph (3) of Rule 1.17 is subject to appeal to the court by any creditor or member of the company.

(4) If the chairman is in doubt whether a claim should be admitted or rejected, he shall mark it as objected to and allow votes to be cast in respect of it, subject to such votes being subsequently declared invalid if the objection to the claim is sustained.

(5) If on an appeal the chairman's decision is reversed or varied, or votes are declared invalid, the court may order another meeting to be summoned, or make such order as it thinks just.

The court's power to make an order under this paragraph is exercisable only if it considers that the circumstances giving rise to the appeal give rise to unfair prejudice or material irregularity.

(6) An application to the court by way of appeal against the chairman's decision shall not be made after the end of the period of 28 days beginning with the first day on which the report required by section 4(6) has been made to the court.

(7) The chairman is not personally liable for any costs incurred by any person in respect of an appeal under this Rule.]

NOTES

Amendment
Substituted, together with r 1.17, for r 1.17 as originally enacted, by SI 2002/2712, r 3(1), Schedule, Pt 1, para 8.

1.18 Voting rights (members)

(1) Subject as follows, members of the company at their meeting vote according to the rights attaching to their shares respectively in accordance with the articles.

(2) . . .

(3) References in this Rule to a person's shares include any other interest which he may have as a member of the company.

NOTES

Amendment
Para (2): revoked by SI 2002/2712, r 3(1), Schedule, Pt 1, para 9.

1.19 Requisite majorities (creditors)

(1) Subject as follows, at the creditors' meeting for any resolution to pass approving any proposal or modification there must be a majority in excess of three-quarters in value of the creditors present in person or by proxy and voting on the resolution.

(2) The same applies in respect of any other resolution proposed at the meeting, but substituting one-half for three-quarters.

(3) In the following cases there is to be left out of account a creditor's vote in respect of any claim or part of a claim—

- (a) where written notice of the claim was not given, either at the meeting or before it, to the chairman or convener of the meeting;

(b) where the claim or part is secured;
(c) where the claim is in respect of a debt wholly or partly on, or secured by, a current bill of exchange or promissory note, unless the creditor is willing—
  (i) to treat the liability to him on the bill or note of every person who is liable on it antecedently to the company, and against whom a bankruptcy order has not been made (or in the case of a company, which has not gone into liquidation), as a security in his hands, and
  (ii) to estimate the value of the security and (for the purpose of entitlement to vote, but not of any distribution under the arrangement) to deduct it from his claim.

(4) Any resolution is invalid if those voting against it include more than half in value of the creditors, counting in these latter only those—
(a) to whom notice of the meeting was sent;
(b) whose votes are not to be left out of account under paragraph (3); and
(c) who are not, to the best of the chairman's belief, persons connected with the company.

(5) It is for the chairman of the meeting to decide whether under this Rule—
(a) a vote is to be left out of account in accordance with paragraph (3), or
(b) a person is a connected person for the purposes of paragraph (4)(c);

and in relation to the second of these two cases the chairman is entitled to rely on the information provided by the company's statement of affairs or otherwise in accordance with this Part of the Rules.

(6) If the chairman uses a proxy contrary to Rule 1.15, his vote with that proxy does not count towards any majority under this Rule.

[(7) The chairman's decision on any matter under this Rule is subject to appeal to the court by any creditor or member and paragraphs (5) to (7) of Rule 1.17A apply as regards such an appeal.]

NOTES

Amendment
Para (7): substituted by SI 2002/2712, r 3(1), Schedule, Pt 1, para 10.

1.20 Requisite majorities (members)

(1) Subject as follows, and to any express provision made in the articles, at a company meeting any resolution is to be regarded as passed if voted for by more than one-half [in value] of the members present in person or by proxy and voting on the resolution.

[The value of members is determined by reference to the number of votes conferred on each member by the company's articles.]

(2) . . .

(3) If the chairman uses a proxy contrary to Rule 1.15, his vote with that proxy does not count towards any majority under this Rule.

NOTES

Amendment
Para (1): words in square brackets inserted by SI 1987/1919, r 3(1), Schedule, Part 1, para 5.
Para (2): revoked by SI 2002/2712, r 3(1), Schedule, Pt 1, para 11.

[1.21 Proceedings to obtain agreement on the proposal]

[(1) If the chairman thinks fit, the creditors' meeting and the company meeting may be held together.

(2) The chairman may, and shall if it is so resolved at the meeting in question, adjourn that meeting for not more than 14 days.

(3) If there are subsequently further adjournments, the final adjournment shall not be to a day later than 14 days after the date on which the meeting in question was originally held.

(4) In the case of a proposal by the directors, if the meetings are adjourned under paragraph (2), notice of the fact shall be given by the nominee forthwith to the court.

(5) If following the final adjournment of the creditors' meeting the proposal (with or without modifications) has not been approved by the creditors, it is deemed rejected.]

NOTES

Amendment
Substituted by SI 2002/2712, r 3(1), Schedule, Pt 1, para 12.

Section C: Implementation of the Arrangement

1.22 Resolutions to follow approval

[(1) If the voluntary arrangement is approved (with or without modifications) by the creditors' meeting, a resolution may be taken by the creditors, where two or more supervisors are appointed, on the question whether acts to be done in connection with the arrangement may be done by any one or more of them, or must be done by all of them.]

(2) . . .

(3) If at either meeting a resolution is moved for the appointment of some person other than the nominee to be supervisor of the arrangement, there must be produced to the chairman, at or before the meeting—

- (a) that person's written consent to act (unless he is present and then and there signifies his consent), and
- (b) his written confirmation that he is qualified to act as an insolvency practitioner in relation to the company [or is an authorised person in relation to the company].

NOTES

Amendment
Para (1): substituted by SI 2002/2712, r 3(1), Schedule, Pt 1, para 13(a).
Para (2): revoked by SI 2002/2712, r 3(1), Schedule, Pt 1, para 13(b).
Para (3): in sub-para (b) words "or is an authorised person in relation to the company" in square brackets inserted by SI 2002/2712, r 3(1), Schedule, Pt 1, para 13(c).

[1.22A Notice of order made under section 4A(6)]

[(1) This Rule applies where the court makes an order under section 4A(6).

(2) The member of the company who applied for the order shall serve sealed copies of it on—

(a) the supervisor of the voluntary arrangement; and
(b) the directors of the company.

(3) Service on the directors may be effected by service of a single copy on the company at its registered office.

(4) The directors or (as the case may be) the supervisor shall forthwith after receiving a copy of the court's order, give notice of it to all persons who were sent notice of the creditors' or company meetings or who, not having been sent such notice, are affected by the order.

(5) The person on whose application the order of the court was made shall, within 7 days of the order, deliver an office copy to the registrar of companies.]

NOTES

Amendment
Inserted by SI 2002/2712, r 3(1), Schedule, Pt 1, para 14.

1.23 Hand-over of property etc to supervisor

(1) [Where the decision approving the voluntary arrangement has effect under section 4A—]
(a) the directors, or
(b) where the company is in liquidation or is subject to an administration order, and a person other than the responsible insolvency practitioner is appointed as supervisor of the voluntary arrangement, the insolvency practitioner,

shall forthwith do all that is required for putting the supervisor into possession of the assets included in the arrangement.

(2) Where the company is in liquidation or is subject to an administration order, the supervisor shall on taking possession of the assets discharge any balance due to the insolvency practitioner by way of remuneration or on account of—
(a) fees, costs, charges and expenses properly incurred and payable under the Act or the Rules, and
(b) any advances made in respect of the company, together with interest on such advances at the rate specified in section 17 of the Judgments Act 1838 at the date on which the company went into liquidation or (as the case may be) became subject to the administration order.

(3) Alternatively, the supervisor must, before taking possession, give the responsible insolvency practitioner a written undertaking to discharge any such balance out of the first realisation of assets.

(4) The insolvency practitioner has a charge on the assets included in the voluntary arrangement in respect of any sums due as above until they have been discharged, subject only to the deduction from realisations by the supervisor of the proper costs and expenses of such realisations.

(5) The supervisor shall from time to time out of the realisation of assets discharge all guarantees properly given by the responsible insolvency practitioner for the benefit of the company, and shall pay all the insolvency practitioner's expenses.

(6) References in this Rule to the responsible insolvency practitioner include, where a company is being wound up by the court, the official receiver, whether or not in his capacity as liquidator; and any sums due to the official receiver take priority over those due to a liquidator.

NOTES

Amendment

Para (1): words "Where the decision approving the voluntary arrangement has effect under section 4A—" in square brackets substituted by SI 2002/2712, r 3(1), Schedule, Pt 1, para 15.

1.24 Report of meetings

(1) A report of the meetings shall be prepared by the person who was chairman of them.

(2) The report shall—

[(a) state whether the proposal for a voluntary arrangement was approved by the creditors of the company alone or by both the creditors and members of the company and in either case whether such approval was with any modifications;]

(b) set out the resolutions which were taken at each meeting, and the decision on each one;

(c) list the creditors and members of the company (with their respective values) who were present or represented at the meetings, and how they voted on each resolution; . . .

[(ca) state whether, in the opinion of the supervisor, (i) the EC Regulation applies to the voluntary arrangement and (ii) if so, whether the proceedings are main proceedings, secondary proceedings or territorial proceedings; and]

(d) include such further information (if any) as the chairman thinks it appropriate to make known to the court.

(3) A copy of the chairman's report shall, within 4 days of the meetings being held, be filed in court; and the court shall cause that copy to be endorsed with the date of filing.

(4) In respect of each of the meetings, the persons to whom notice of its result is to be sent by the chairman under section 4(6) are all of those who were sent notice of the meeting under this Part of the Rules.

The notice shall be sent immediately after a copy of the chairman's report is filed in court under paragraph (3).

(5) [If the decision approving the voluntary arrangement has effect under section 4A] (whether or not in the form proposed), the supervisor shall forthwith send a copy of the chairman's report to the registrar of companies.

NOTES

Amendment

Para (2): sub-para (a) substituted by SI 2002/2712, r 3(1), Schedule, Pt 1, para 16(a).
Para (2): in sub-para (c) word omitted revoked by SI 2002/1307, rr 3(1), 4(3)(a).
Para (2): sub-para (ca) inserted by SI 2002/1307, rr 3(1), 4(3)(b).
Para (5): words "If the decision approving the voluntary arrangement has effect under section 4A" in square brackets substituted by SI 2002/2712, r 3(1), Schedule, Pt 1, para 16(b).

1.25 Revocation or suspension of the arrangement

(1) This Rule applies where the court makes an order of revocation or suspension under section 6.

(2) The person who applied for the order shall serve sealed copies of it—

(a) on the supervisor of the voluntary arrangement, and
(b) on the directors of the company or the administrator or liquidator (according to who made the proposal for the arrangement).

Service on the directors may be effected by service of a single copy of the order on the company at its registered office.

(3) If the order includes a direction by the court under section 6(4)(b) for any further meetings to be summoned, notice shall also be given (by the person who applied for the order) to whoever is, in accordance with the direction, required to summon the meetings.

(4) The directors or (as the case may be) the administrator or liquidator shall—
(a) forthwith after receiving a copy of the court's order, give notice of it to all persons who were sent notice of the creditors' and company meetings or who, not having been sent that notice, appear to be affected by the order;
(b) within 7 days of their receiving a copy of the order (or within such longer period as the court may allow), give notice to the court whether it is intended to make a revised proposal to the company and its creditors, or to invite re-consideration of the original proposal.

(5) The person on whose application the order of revocation or suspension was made shall, within 7 days after the making of the order, deliver a copy of the order to the registrar of companies.

1.26 Supervisor's accounts and reports

(1) Where the voluntary arrangement authorises or requires the supervisor—
(a) to carry on the business of the company or trade on its behalf or in its name, or
(b) to realise assets of the company, or
(c) otherwise to administer or dispose of any of its funds,

he shall keep accounts and records of his acts and dealings in and in connection with the arrangement, including in particular records of all receipts and payments of money.

(2) The supervisor shall, not less often than once in every 12 months beginning with the date of his appointment, prepare an abstract of such receipts and payments, and send copies of it, accompanied by his comments on the progress and efficacy of the arrangement, to—
(a) the court,
(b) the registrar of companies,
(c) the company,
(d) all those of the company's creditors who are bound by the arrangement,
(e) subject to paragraph (5) below, the members of the company who are so bound, and
(f) if the company is not in liquidation, the company's auditors for the time being.

If in any period of 12 months he has made no payments and had no receipts, he shall at the end of that period send a statement to that effect to all those specified in sub-paragraphs (a) to (f) above.

(3) An abstract provided under paragraph (2) shall relate to a period beginning with the date of the supervisor's appointment or (as the case may be) the day following the end of the last period for which an abstract was prepared under this Rule; and copies of the abstract shall be sent out, as required by paragraph

(2), within the 2 months following the end of the period to which the abstract relates.

(4) If the supervisor is not authorised as mentioned in paragraph (1), he shall, not less often than once in every 12 months beginning with the date of his appointment, send to all those specified in paragraph (2)(a) to (f) a report on the progress and efficacy of the voluntary arrangement.

(5) The court may, on application by the supervisor—
- (a) dispense with the sending under this Rule of abstracts or reports to members of the company, either altogether or on the basis that the availability of the abstract or report to members is to be advertised by the supervisor in a specified manner;
- (b) vary the dates on which the obligation to send abstracts or reports arises.

1.27 Production of accounts and records to Secretary of State

(1) The Secretary of State may at any time during the course of the voluntary arrangement or after its completion [or termination] require the supervisor to produce for inspection—
- (a) his records and accounts in respect of the arrangement, and
- (b) copies of abstracts and reports prepared in compliance with Rule 1.26.

(2) The Secretary of State may require production either at the premises of the supervisor or elsewhere; and it is the duty of the supervisor to comply with any requirement imposed on him under this Rule.

(3) The Secretary of State may cause any accounts and records produced to him under this Rule to be audited; and the supervisor shall give to the Secretary of State such further information and assistance as he needs for the purposes of his audit.

NOTES

Amendment
Para (1): words "or termination" in square brackets inserted by SI 2002/2712, r 3(1), Schedule, Pt 1, para 17.

1.28 Fees, costs, charges and expenses

(1) The fees, costs, charges and expenses that may be incurred for any of the purposes of the voluntary arrangement are—
- (a) any disbursements made by the nominee prior to the [decision approving the arrangement taking effect under section 4A], and any remuneration for his services as such agreed between himself and the company (or, as the case may be, the administrator or liquidator);
- (b) any fees, costs, charges or expenses which—
  - (i) are sanctioned by the terms of the arrangement, or
  - (ii) would be payable, or correspond to those which would be payable, in an administration or winding up.

NOTES

Amendment
Para (1): in sub-para (a) words "decision approving the arrangement taking effect under section 4A" in square brackets substituted by SI 2002/2712, r 3(1), Schedule, Pt 1, para 18.

[1.29 Completion or termination of the arrangement]

[(1) Not more than 28 days after the final completion or termination of the voluntary arrangement, the supervisor shall send to creditors and members of the company who are bound by it a notice that the voluntary arrangement has been fully implemented or (as the case may be) has terminated.

(2) With the notice there shall be sent to each creditor and member a copy of a report by the supervisor summarising all receipts and payments made by him in pursuance of the arrangement, and explaining in relation to implementation of the arrangement any departure from the proposals as they originally took effect, or (in the case of termination of the arrangement) explaining the reasons why the arrangement has terminated.

(3) The supervisor shall, within the 28 days mentioned above, send to the registrar of companies and to the court a copy of the notice to creditors and members under paragraph (1), together with a copy of the report under paragraph (2), and the supervisor shall not vacate office until after such copies have been sent.]

NOTES

Amendment
Substituted by SI 2002/2712, r 3(1), Schedule, Pt 1, para 19.

Chapter 6

. . .

NOTES

Amendment
Revoked by SI 2002/2712, r 3(1), Schedule, Pt 1, para 20.

1.30 . . .

. . .

NOTES

Amendment
Revoked by SI 2002/2712, r 3(1), Schedule, Pt 1, para 20.

Chapter 7

EC Regulation—Conversion of Voluntary Arrangement into Winding up

NOTES

Amendment
Chapters 7 and 8 inserted by SI 2002/1307, rr 3(1), 4(4).

1.31 Application for conversion into winding up

(1) Where a member State liquidator proposes to apply to the court for the conversion under Article 37 of the EC Regulation (conversion of earlier proceedings) of a voluntary arrangement into a winding up, an affidavit complying with Rule 1.32 must be prepared and sworn, and filed in court in support of the application.

(2) An application under this Rule shall be by originating application.

(3) The application and the affidavit required under this Rule shall be served upon—

(a) the company; and
(b) the supervisor.

1.32 Contents of affidavit

(1) The affidavit shall state—

(a) that main proceedings have been opened in relation to the company in a member State other than the United Kingdom;
(b) the deponent's belief that the conversion of the voluntary arrangement into a winding up would prove to be in the interests of the creditors in the main proceedings;
(c) the deponent's opinion as to whether the company ought to enter voluntary winding up or be wound up by the court; and
(d) all other matters that, in the opinion of the member State liquidator, would assist the court—
    (i) in deciding whether to make such an order, and
    (ii) if the court were to do so, in considering the need for any consequential provision that would be necessary or desirable.

(2) An affidavit under this Rule shall be sworn by, or on behalf of, the member State liquidator.

1.33 Power of court

(1) On hearing the application for conversion into winding up the court may make such order as it thinks fit.

(2) If the court makes an order for conversion into winding up the order may contain all such consequential provisions as the court deems necessary or desirable.

(3) Without prejudice to the generality of paragraph (1), an order under that paragraph may provide that the company be wound up as if a resolution for voluntary winding up under section 84 were passed on the day on which the order is made.

(4) Where the court makes an order for conversion into winding up under paragraph (1), any expenses properly incurred as expenses of the administration of the voluntary arrangement in question shall be a first charge on the company's assets.

Chapter 8
EC Regulation—Member State Liquidator

1.34 Interpretation of creditor and notice to member State liquidator

(1) This Rule applies where a member State liquidator has been appointed in relation to the company.

(2) Where the supervisor is obliged to give notice to, or provide a copy of a document (including an order of court) to, the court, the registrar of companies or the official receiver, the supervisor shall give notice or provide copies, as appropriate, to the member State liquidator.

(3) Paragraph (2) is without prejudice to the generality of the obligations imposed by Article 31 of the EC Regulation (duty to cooperate and communicate information).

Chapter 9
Obtaining a Moratorium
Proceedings during a Moratorium
Nominees
Consideration of Proposals where Moratorium Obtained

NOTES

Amendment
Chapter 9 inserted by SI 2002/2712, r 3(1), Schedule, Pt 1, para 21.

Section A: Obtaining a Moratorium

1.35 Preparation of proposal by directors and submission to nominee

(1) The document containing the proposal referred to in paragraph 6(1)(a) of Schedule A1 to the Act shall—

- (a) be prepared by the directors;
- (b) comply with the requirements of paragraphs (1) and (2) of Rule 1.3 (save that the reference to preferential creditors shall be to preferential creditors within the meaning of paragraph 31(8) of Schedule A1 to the Act); and
- (c) state the address to which notice of the consent of the nominee to act and the documents referred to in Rule 1.38 shall be sent.

(2) With the agreement in writing of the nominee, the directors may amend the proposal at any time before submission to them by the nominee of the statement required by paragraph 6(2) of Schedule A1 to the Act.

1.36 Delivery of documents to the intended nominee etc

(1) The documents required to be delivered to the nominee pursuant to paragraph 6(1) of Schedule A1 to the Act shall be delivered to the nominee himself or to a person authorised to take delivery of documents on his behalf.

(2) On receipt of the documents, the nominee shall forthwith issue an acknowledgement of receipt of the documents to the directors which shall indicate the date on which the documents were received.

1.37 Statement of affairs

(1) The statement of the company's affairs required to be delivered to the nominee pursuant to paragraph 6(1)(b) of Schedule A1 to the Act shall be delivered to the nominee no later than 7 days after the delivery to him of the document setting out the terms of the proposed voluntary arrangement or such longer time as he may allow.

(2) The statement of affairs shall comprise the same particulars as required by Rule 1.5(2) (supplementing or amplifying, so far as is necessary for clarifying the state of the company's affairs, those already given in the directors' proposal).

(3) The statement of affairs shall be made up to a date not earlier than 2 weeks before the date of the delivery of the document containing the proposal for the voluntary arrangement to the nominee under Rule 1.36(1).

However, the nominee may allow an extension of that period to the nearest practicable date (not earlier than 2 months before the date of delivery of the documents referred to in Rule 1.36(1)) and if he does so, he shall give a statement of his reasons in writing to the directors.

(4) The statement of affairs shall be certified as correct, to the best of their knowledge and belief, by two or more directors of the company, or by the company secretary and at least one director (other than the secretary himself).

1.38 The nominee's statement

(1) The nominee shall submit to the directors the statement required by paragraph 6(2) of Schedule A1 to the Act within 28 days of the submission to him of the document setting out the terms of the proposed voluntary arrangement.

(2) The statement shall have annexed to it—

(a) the nominee's comments on the proposal, unless the statement contains an opinion in the negative on any of the matters referred to in paragraph 6(2)(a) and (b) of Schedule A1 to the Act, in which case he shall instead give his reasons for that opinion, and

(b) where he is willing to act in relation to the proposed arrangement, a statement of his consent to act.

1.39 Documents submitted to the court to obtain moratorium

(1) Where pursuant to paragraph 7 of Schedule A1 to the Act the directors file the document and statements referred to in that paragraph in court, those documents shall be delivered together with 4 copies of a schedule listing them within 3 working days of the date of the submission to them of the nominee's statement under paragraph 6(2) of Schedule A1 to the Act.

(2) When the directors file the document and statements referred to in paragraph (1), they shall also file—

(a) a copy of any statement of reasons made by the nominee pursuant to Rule 1.37(3); and

(b) a copy of the nominee's comments on the proposal submitted to them pursuant to Rule 1.38(2).

(3) The copies of the schedule shall be endorsed by the court with the date on which the documents were filed in court and 3 copies of the schedule sealed by the court shall be returned by the court to the person who filed the documents in court.

(4) The statement of affairs required to be filed under paragraph 7(1)(b) of Schedule A1 to the Act shall comprise the same particulars as required by Rule 1.5(2).

1.40 Notice and advertisement of beginning of a moratorium

(1) After receiving the copies of the schedule endorsed by the court under Rule 1.39(3), the directors shall forthwith serve 2 of them on the nominee and one on the company.

(2) Forthwith after receiving the copies of the schedule pursuant to paragraph (1) the nominee shall advertise the coming into force of the moratorium once in the Gazette, and once in such newspaper as he thinks most appropriate for ensuring that its coming into force comes to the notice of the company's creditors.

(3) The nominee shall forthwith notify the registrar of companies, the company and any petitioning creditor of the company of whose claim he is aware of the coming into force of the moratorium and such notification shall specify the date on which the moratorium came into force.

(4) The nominee shall give notice of the coming into force of the moratorium specifying the date on which it came into force to—

- (a) any sheriff or other officer who, to his knowledge, is charged with an execution or other legal process against the company or its property; and
- (b) any person who, to his knowledge, has distrained against the company or its property.

1.41 Notice of extension of moratorium

(1) The nominee shall forthwith notify the registrar of companies and the court of a decision taking effect pursuant to paragraph 36 of Schedule A1 to the Act to extend or further extend the moratorium and such notice shall specify the new expiry date of the moratorium.

(2) Where an order is made by the court extending or further extending or renewing or continuing a moratorium, the nominee shall forthwith after receiving a copy of the same give notice to the registrar of companies and with the notice shall send an office copy of the order.

1.42 Notice and advertisement of end of moratorium

(1) After the moratorium comes to an end, the nominee shall forthwith advertise its coming to an end once in the Gazette, and once in such newspaper as he thinks most appropriate for ensuring that its coming to an end comes to the notice of the company's creditors, and such notice shall specify the date on which the moratorium came to an end.

(2) The nominee shall forthwith give notice of the ending of the moratorium to the registrar of companies, the court, the company and any creditor of the company of whose claim he is aware and such notice shall specify the date on which the moratorium came to an end.

Section B: Proceedings during a Moratorium

1.43 Disposal of charged property etc during a moratorium

(1) This Rule applies in any case where the company makes an application to the court under paragraph 20 of Schedule A1 to the Act for leave to dispose of property of the company which is subject to a security, or goods in possession of the company under an agreement to which that paragraph relates.

(2) The court shall fix a venue for the hearing of the application and the company shall forthwith give notice of the venue to the person who is the holder of the security or, as the case may be, the owner under the agreement.

(3) If an order is made, the company shall forthwith give notice of it to that person or owner.

(4) The court shall send 2 sealed copies of the order to the company, who shall send one of them to that person or owner.

Section C: Nominees

1.44 Withdrawal of nominee's consent to act

Where the nominee withdraws his consent to act he shall, pursuant to paragraph 25(5) of Schedule A1 to the Act, forthwith give notice of his withdrawal and the reason for withdrawing his consent to act to—

(a) the registrar of companies;
(b) the court;
(c) the company; and
(d) any creditor of the company of whose claim he is aware.

1.45 Replacement of nominee by the court

(1) Where the directors intend to make an application to the court under paragraph 28 of Schedule A1 to the Act for the nominee to be replaced, they shall give to the nominee at least 7 days' notice of their application.

(2) Where the nominee intends to make an application to the court under that paragraph to be replaced, he shall give to the directors at least 7 days' notice of his application.

(3) No appointment of a replacement nominee shall be made by the court unless there is filed in court a statement by the replacement nominee indicating his consent to act.

1.46 Notification of appointment of a replacement nominee

Where a person is appointed as a replacement nominee, he shall forthwith give notice of his appointment to—

(a) the registrar of companies;
(b) the court (in any case where he was not appointed by the court); and
(c) the person whom he has replaced as nominee.

1.47 Applications to court under paragraphs 26 or 27 of Schedule A1 to the Act

Where any person intends to make an application to the court pursuant to paragraph 26 or 27 of Schedule A1 to the Act, he shall give to the nominee at least 7 days' notice of his application.

Section D: Consideration of proposals where Moratorium obtained

1.48 Summoning of meetings; procedure at meetings etc

(1) Where the nominee summons meetings of creditors and the company pursuant to paragraph 29(1) of Schedule A1 to the Act, each of those meetings shall be summoned for a date that is not more than 28 days from the date on which the moratorium came into force.

(2) Notices calling the creditors' meetings shall be sent by the nominee to all creditors specified in the statement of affairs and any other creditors of the company of whose address he is aware at least 14 days before the day fixed for the meeting.

(3) Notices calling the company meeting shall be sent by the nominee to all persons who are, to the best of the nominee's belief, members of the company at least 14 days before the day fixed for the meeting.

(4) Each notice sent under this Rule shall specify the court in which the documents relating to the obtaining of the moratorium were filed and state the effect of paragraphs (1), (3) and (4) of Rule 1.52 (requisite majorities (creditors)) and with each notice there shall be sent—

- (a) a copy of the directors' proposal;
- (b) a copy of the statement of the company's affairs or, if the nominee thinks fit, a summary of it (the summary to include a list of creditors and the amount of their debts); and
- (c) the nominee's comments on the proposal.

(5) The provisions of Rules 1.13 to 1.16 shall apply.

1.49 Entitlement to vote (creditors)

(1) Subject as follows, every creditor who has notice of the creditors' meeting is entitled to vote at the meeting or any adjournment of it.

(2) Votes are calculated according to the amount of the creditor's debt as at the beginning of the moratorium, after deducting any amounts paid in respect of that debt after that date.

(3) A creditor may vote in respect of a debt for an unliquidated amount or any debt whose value is not ascertained and for the purposes of voting (but not otherwise) his debt shall be valued at £1 unless the chairman agrees to put a higher value on it.

1.50 Procedure for admission of creditors' claims for voting purposes

(1) Subject as follows, at any creditors' meeting the chairman shall ascertain the entitlement of persons wishing to vote and shall admit or reject their claims accordingly.

(2) The chairman may admit or reject a claim in whole or in part.

(3) The chairman's decision on any matter under this Rule or under paragraph (3) of Rule 1.49 is subject to appeal to the court by any creditor or member of the company.

(4) If the chairman is in doubt whether a claim should be admitted or rejected, he shall mark it as objected to and allow votes to be cast in respect of it, subject to such votes being subsequently declared invalid if the objection to the claim is sustained.

(5) If on an appeal the chairman's decision is reversed or varied, or votes are declared invalid, the court may order another meeting to be summoned, or make such order as it thinks just.

The court's power to make an order under this paragraph is exercisable only if it considers that the circumstances giving rise to the appeal are such as give rise to unfair prejudice or material irregularity.

(6) An application to the court by way of appeal against the chairman's decision shall not be made after the end of the period of 28 days beginning with the first day on which the report required by paragraph 30(3) of Schedule A1 to the Act has been made to the court.

(7) The chairman is not personally liable for any costs incurred by any person in respect of an appeal under this Rule.

1.51 Voting rights (members)

Rule 1.18 shall apply.

1.52 Requisite majorities (creditors)

(1) Subject as follows, at the creditors' meeting for any resolution to pass approving any proposal or modification there must be a majority in excess of three-quarters in value of the creditors present in person or by proxy and voting on the resolution.

(2) The same applies in respect of any other resolution proposed at the meeting, but substituting one-half for three-quarters.

(3) At a meeting of the creditors for any resolution to pass extending (or further extending) a moratorium, or to bring a moratorium to an end before the end of the period of any extension, there must be a majority in excess of three quarters in value of the creditors present in person or by proxy and voting on the resolution. For this purpose paragraph (4)(b) below shall not apply and a secured creditor is entitled to vote in respect of the amount of his claim without deducting the value of his security.

(4) In the following cases there is to be left out of account a creditor's vote in respect of any claim or part of a claim—

- (a) where written notice of the claim was not given, either at the meeting or before it, to the chairman or convenor of the meeting;
- (b) where the claim or part is secured;
- (c) where the claim is in respect of a debt wholly or partly on, or secured by, a current bill of exchange or promissory note, unless the creditor is willing—
  - (i) to treat the liability to him on the bill or note of every person who is liable on it antecedently to the company, and against whom a bankruptcy order has not been made (or, in the case of a company, which has not gone into liquidation), as a security in his hands, and
  - (ii) to estimate the value of the security and (for the purpose of entitlement to vote, but not of any distribution under the arrangement) to deduct it from his claim.

(5) Any resolution is invalid if those voting against it include more than half in value of the creditors, counting in these latter only those—

- (a) who have notice of the meeting;
- (b) whose votes are not to be left out of account under paragraph (4); and
- (c) who are not, to the best of the chairman's belief, persons connected with the company.

(6) It is for the chairman of the meeting to decide whether under this Rule—

- (a) a vote is to be left out of account in accordance with paragraph (5), or
- (b) a person is a connected person for the purposes of paragraph (5)(c);

and in relation to the second of these two cases the chairman is entitled to rely on the information provided by the statement of the company's affairs or otherwise in accordance with this Part of the Rules.

(7) If the chairman uses a proxy contrary to Rule 1.15 as it applies by virtue of Rule 1.48(4), his vote with that proxy does not count towards any majority under this Rule.

(8) The chairman's decision on any matter under this Rule is subject to appeal to the court by any creditor or member and paragraphs (5) to (7) of Rule 1.50 apply as regards such an appeal.

1.53 Requisite majorities (members) and proceedings to obtain agreement on the proposal

(1) Rule 1.20 shall apply.

(2) If the chairman thinks fit, the creditors' meeting and the company meeting may be held together.

(3) The chairman may, and shall if it is so resolved at the meeting in question, adjourn that meeting, but any adjournment shall not be to a day which is more than 14 days after the date on which the moratorium (including any extension) ends.

(4) If the meetings are adjourned under paragraph (3), notice of the fact shall be given by the nominee forthwith to the court.

(5) If following the final adjournment of the creditors' meeting the proposal (with or without modifications) has not been approved by the creditors, it is deemed rejected.

1.54 Implementation of the arrangement

(1) Where a decision approving the arrangement has effect under paragraph 36 of Schedule A1 to the Act, the directors shall forthwith do all that is required for putting the supervisor into possession of the assets included in the arrangement.

(2) Subject to paragraph (3), Rules 1.22, 1.22A and 1.24 to 1.29 apply.

(3) The provisions referred to in paragraph (2) are modified as follows—
- (a) in paragraph (1) of Rule 1.22A the reference to section 4A(6) is to be read as a reference to paragraph 36(5) of Schedule A1 to the Act;
- (b) in paragraph (4) of Rule 1.24 the reference to section 4(6) is to be read as a reference to paragraph 30(3) of Schedule A1 to the Act;
- (c) in paragraph (5) of Rule 1.24 the reference to section 4A is to be read as a reference to paragraph 36 of Schedule A1 to the Act;
- (d) in paragraph (1) of Rule 1.25 the reference to section 6 is to be read as a reference to paragraph 38 of Schedule A1 to the Act and the references in paragraphs (2) and (4) to the administrator or liquidator shall be ignored;
- (e) in paragraph (3) of Rule 1.25 the reference to section 6(4)(b) is to be read as a reference to paragraph 38 (4)(b) of Schedule A1 to the Act; and
- (f) in sub-paragraph (a) of paragraph (1) of Rule 1.28 the reference to section 4A is to be read as a reference to paragraph 36 of Schedule A1 to the Act.

*****

THE SECOND GROUP OF PARTS
INDIVIDUAL INSOLVENCY; BANKRUPTCY

PART 5
INDIVIDUAL VOLUNTARY ARRANGEMENTS

NOTES

Amendment
Part 5 (rr 5.1–5.38) substituted for rr 5.1–5.5, 5.5A (as inserted by SI 1987/1919, r 3(1), Schedule, Pt I, para 85), 5.6–5.30, 5.31–5.34 (as inserted by SI 2002/1307, rr 3(1), 7(3)), by SI 2002/2712, r 5(1), Schedule, Pt 3, para 24.

Chapter 1
Preliminary

5.1 Introductory

(1) The Rules in this Part apply in relation to a voluntary arrangement under Part VIII of the Act.

(2) In this Part—
- (a) Chapter 2 applies in all cases;
- (b) Chapter 3 applies in cases where an application for an interim is order is made;
- (c) Chapter 4 applies in cases where no application for an interim order is or is to be made; and
- (d) except where otherwise stated, Chapters 5, 6 and 7 apply in all cases.

Chapter 2
Preparation of the Debtor's Proposal

5.2 Preparation of proposal

The debtor shall prepare for the intended nominee a proposal on which (with or without amendments to be made under Rule 5.3(3) below) to make his report to the court under section 256 or section 256A.

5.3 Contents of proposal

(1) The debtor's proposal shall provide a short explanation why, in his opinion, a voluntary arrangement under Part VIII is desirable, and give reasons why his creditors may be expected to concur with such an arrangement.

(2) The following matters shall be stated, or otherwise dealt with, in the proposal—
- (a) the following matters, so far as within the debtor's immediate knowledge—
  - (i) his assets, with an estimate of their respective values,
  - (ii) the extent (if any) to which the assets are charged in favour of creditors,
  - (iii) the extent (if any) to which particular assets are to be excluded from the voluntary arrangement;

(b) particulars of any property, other than assets of the debtor himself, which is proposed to be included in the arrangement, the source of such property and the terms on which it is to be made available for inclusion;

(c) the nature and amount of the debtor's liabilities (so far as within his immediate knowledge), the manner in which they are proposed to be met, modified, postponed or otherwise dealt with by means of the arrangement and (in particular)—

 (i) how it is proposed to deal with preferential creditors (defined in section 258(7)) and creditors who are, or claim to be, secured,

 (ii) how associates of the debtor (being creditors of his) are proposed to be treated under the arrangement, and

 (iii) in any case where the debtor is an undischarged bankrupt, whether, to the debtor's knowledge, claims have been made under section 339 (transactions at an undervalue), section 340 (preferences) or section 343 (extortionate credit transactions), or where the debtor is not an undischarged bankrupt, whether there are circumstances which would give rise to the possibility of such claims in the event that he should be adjudged bankrupt,

and, where any such circumstances are present, whether, and if so how, it is proposed under the voluntary arrangement to make provision for wholly or partly indemnifying the insolvent estate in respect of such claims;

(d) whether any, and if so what, guarantees have been given of the debtor's debts by other persons, specifying which (if any) of the guarantors are associates of his;

(e) the proposed duration of the voluntary arrangement;

(f) the proposed dates of distributions to creditors, with estimates of their amounts;

(g) how it is proposed to deal with the claims of any person who is bound by the arrangement by virtue of section 260(2)(b)(ii);

(h) the amount proposed to be paid to the nominee (as such) by way of remuneration and expenses;

(j) the manner in which it is proposed that the supervisor of the arrangement should be remunerated, and his expenses defrayed;

(k) whether, for the purposes of the arrangement, any guarantees are to be offered by any persons other than the debtor, and whether (if so) any security is to be given or sought;

(l) the manner in which funds held for the purposes of the arrangement are to be banked, invested or otherwise dealt with pending distribution to creditors;

(m) the manner in which funds held for the purpose of payment to creditors, and not so paid on the termination of the arrangement, are to be dealt with;

(n) if the debtor has any business, the manner in which it is proposed to be conducted during the course of the arrangement;

(o) details of any further credit facilities which it is intended to arrange for the debtor, and how the debts so arising are to be paid;

(p) the functions which are to be undertaken by the supervisor of the arrangement;

(q) the name, address and qualification of the person proposed as supervisor of the voluntary arrangement, and confirmation that he is, so far as the debtor is aware, qualified to act as an insolvency practitioner in relation to him or is an authorised person in relation to him; and

(r) whether the EC Regulation will apply and, if so, whether the proceedings will be main proceedings or territorial proceedings.

(3) With the agreement in writing of the nominee, the debtor's proposal may be amended at any time up to the delivery of the former's report to the court under section 256 or section 256A.

5.4 Notice to the intended nominee

(1) The debtor shall give to the intended nominee written notice of his proposal.

(2) The notice, accompanied by a copy of the proposal, shall be delivered either to the nominee himself, or to a person authorised to take delivery of documents on his behalf.

(3) If the intended nominee agrees to act, he shall cause a copy of the notice to be endorsed to the effect that it has been received by him on a specified date.

(4) The copy of the notice so endorsed shall be returned by the nominee forthwith to the debtor at an address specified by him in the notice for that purpose.

(5) Where the debtor is an undischarged bankrupt and he gives notice of his proposal to the official receiver and (if any) the trustee, the notice must contain the name and address of the insolvency practitioner or (as the case may be) authorised person who has agreed to act as nominee.

5.5 Statement of Affairs

(1) Subject to paragraph (2), the debtor shall, within 7 days after his proposal is delivered to the nominee, or such longer time as the latter may allow, deliver to the nominee a statement of his (the debtor's) affairs.

(2) Paragraph (1) shall not apply where the debtor is an undischarged bankrupt and he has already delivered a statement of affairs under section 272 (debtor's petition) or 288 (creditor's petition) but the nominee may require the debtor to submit a further statement supplementing or amplifying the statement of affairs already submitted.

(3) The statement of affairs shall comprise the following particulars (supplementing or amplifying, so far as is necessary for clarifying the state of the debtor's affairs, those already given in his proposal)—

(a) a list of his assets, divided into such categories as are appropriate for easy identification, with estimated values assigned to each category;
(b) in the case of any property on which a claim against the debtor is wholly or partly secured, particulars of the claim and its amount, and of how and when the security was created;
(c) the names and addresses of the debtor's preferential creditors (defined in section 258(7)), with the amounts of their respective claims;
(d) the names and addresses of the debtor's unsecured creditors, with the amounts of their respective claims;
(e) particulars of any debts owed by or to the debtor to or by persons who are associates of his;
(f) such other particulars (if any) as the nominee may in writing require to be furnished for the purposes of making his report to the court on the debtor's proposal.

(4) The statement of affairs shall be made up to a date not earlier than 2 weeks before the date of the notice to the nominee under Rule 5.4.

However, the nominee may allow an extension of that period to the nearest practicable date (not earlier than 2 months before the date of the notice under Rule 5.4); and if he does so, he shall give his reasons in his report to the court on the debtor's proposal.

(5) The statement shall be certified by the debtor as correct, to the best of his knowledge and belief.

5.5A . . .

. . .

5.6 Additional disclosure for assistance of nominee

(1) If it appears to the nominee that he cannot properly prepare his report on the basis of information in the debtor's proposal and statement of affairs, he may call on the debtor to provide him with—

- (a) further and better particulars as to the circumstances in which, and the reasons why, he is insolvent or (as the case may be) threatened with insolvency;
- (b) particulars of any previous proposals which have been made by him under Part VIII of the Act;
- (c) any further information with respect to his affairs which the nominee thinks necessary for the purposes of his report.

(2) The nominee may call on the debtor to inform him whether and in what circumstances he has at any time—

- (a) been concerned in the affairs of any company (whether or not incorporated in England and Wales) which has become insolvent, or
- (b) been adjudged bankrupt, or entered into an arrangement with his creditors.

(3) For the purpose of enabling the nominee to consider the debtor's proposal and prepare his report on it, the latter must give him access to his accounts and records.

Chapter 3

Cases in which an Application for an Interim Order is made

5.7 Application for interim order

(1) An application to the court for an interim order under Part VIII of the Act shall be accompanied by an affidavit of the following matters—

- (a) the reasons for making the application;
- (b) particulars of any execution or other legal process or levying of any distress which, to the debtor's knowledge, has been commenced against him;
- (c) that he is an undischarged bankrupt or (as the case may be) that he is able to petition for his own bankruptcy;
- (d) that no previous application for an interim order has been made by or in respect of the debtor in the period of 12 months ending with the date of the affidavit; and
- (e) that the nominee under the proposal (naming him) is willing to act in relation to the proposal and is a person who is either qualified to act as an insolvency practitioner in relation to the debtor or is authorised to act as nominee in relation to him.

(2) A copy of the notice to the intended nominee under Rule 5.4, endorsed to the effect that he agrees so to act, and a copy of the debtor's proposal given to the nominee under that Rule, shall be exhibited to the affidavit.

(3) On receiving the application and affidavit, the court shall fix a venue for the hearing of the application.

(4) The applicant shall give at least 2 days' notice of the hearing—
- (a) where the debtor is an undischarged bankrupt, to the bankrupt, the official receiver and the trustee (whichever of those three is not himself the applicant),
- (b) where the debtor is not an undischarged bankrupt, to any creditor who (to the debtor's knowledge) has presented a bankruptcy petition against him, and
- (c) in either case, to the nominee who has agreed to act in relation to the debtor's proposal.

5.8 Court in which application to be made

(1) Except in the case of an undischarged bankrupt, an application to the court under Part VIII of the Act shall be made to a court in which the debtor would be entitled to present his own petition in bankruptcy under Rule 6.40.

(2) The application shall contain sufficient information to establish that it is brought in the appropriate court.

(3) In the case of an undischarged bankrupt, such an application shall be made to the court having the conduct of his bankruptcy and shall be filed with the bankruptcy proceedings.

5.9 Hearing of the application

(1) Any of the persons who have been given notice under Rule 5.7(4) may appear or be represented at the hearing of the application.

(2) The court, in deciding whether to make an interim order on the application, shall take into account any representations made by or on behalf of any of those persons (in particular, whether an order should be made containing such provision as is referred to in section 255(3) and (4)).

(3) If the court makes an interim order, it shall fix a venue for consideration of the nominee's report. Subject to the following paragraph, the date for that consideration shall be not later than that on which the interim order ceases to have effect under section 255(6).

(4) If under section 256(4) an extension of time is granted for filing the nominee's report, the court shall, unless there appear to be good reasons against it, correspondingly extend the period for which the interim order has effect.

5.10 Action to follow making of order

(1) Where an interim order is made, at least 2 sealed copies of the order shall be sent by the court to the person who applied for it; and that person shall serve one of the copies on the nominee under the debtor's proposal.

(2) The applicant shall also forthwith give notice of the making of the order to any person who was given notice of the hearing pursuant to Rule 5.7(4) and was not present or represented at it.

5.11 Nominee's report on the proposal

(1) Where the nominee makes his report to the court under section 256, he shall deliver 2 copies of it to the court not less than 2 days before the interim order ceases to have effect.

(2) With his report the nominee shall deliver—
- (a) a copy of the debtor's proposal (with amendments, if any, authorised under Rule 5.3(3)); and
- (b) a copy or summary of any statement of affairs provided by the debtor.

(3) If the nominee makes known his opinion that the debtor's proposal has a reasonable prospect of being approved and implemented, and that a meeting of the debtor's creditors should be summoned under section 257, his report shall have annexed to it his comments on the debtor's proposal.

If his opinion is otherwise, he shall give his reasons for that opinion.

(4) The court shall upon receipt of the report cause one copy of the report to be endorsed with the date of its filing in court and returned to the nominee.

(5) Any creditor of the debtor is entitled, at all reasonable times on any business day, to inspect the file.

(6) Where the debtor is an undischarged bankrupt, the nominee shall send to the official receiver and (if any) the trustee—
- (a) a copy of the debtor's proposal,
- (b) a copy of his (the nominee's) report and his comments accompanying it (if any), and
- (c) a copy or summary of the debtor's statement of affairs.

(7) Where the debtor is not an undischarged bankrupt, the nominee shall send a copy of each of the documents referred to in paragraph (6) to any person who has presented a bankruptcy petition against the debtor.

5.12 Replacement of nominee

(1) Where the debtor intends to apply to the court under section 256(3) for the nominee to be replaced, he shall give to the nominee at least 7 days' notice of his application.

(2) No appointment of a replacement nominee shall be made by the court unless there is filed in court a statement by the replacement nominee indicating his consent to act.

5.13 Consideration of nominee's report

(1) At the hearing by the court to consider the nominee's report, any of the persons who have been given notice under Rule 5.7(4) may appear or be represented.

(2) Rule 5.10 applies to any order made by the court at the hearing.

Chapter 4
Cases where no Interim Order is to be Obtained

5.14 Nominee's report to the court

(1) The nominee shall deliver 2 copies of his report to the court (as defined in Rule 5.15) under section 256A within 14 days (or such longer period as the court may allow) after receiving from the debtor the document and statement mentioned in section 256A(2) but the court shall not consider the report unless an application is made under the Act or these Rules in relation to the debtor's proposal.

(2) With his report the nominee shall deliver—
- (a) a copy of the debtor's proposal (with amendments, if any, authorised under Rule 5.3(3));
- (b) a copy or summary of any statement of affairs provided by the debtor; and
- (c) a copy of the notice referred to in Rule 5.4(3),

together with 2 copies of Form 5.5 listing the documents referred to in (a) to (c) above and containing a statement that no application for an interim order under section 252 is to be made.

(3) If the nominee makes known his opinion that the debtor's proposal has a reasonable prospect of being approved and implemented, and that a meeting of the debtor's creditors should be summoned under section 257, his report shall have annexed to it his comments on the debtor's proposal.

If his opinion is otherwise, he shall give his reasons for that opinion.

(4) The court shall upon receipt of the report and Form 5.5 cause one copy of the form to be endorsed with the date of its filing in court and returned to the nominee.

(5) Any creditor of the debtor is entitled, at all reasonable times on any business day, to inspect the file.

(6) Where the debtor is an undischarged bankrupt, the nominee shall send to the official receiver and (if any) the trustee—
- (a) a copy of the debtor's proposal,
- (b) a copy of his (the nominee's) report and his comments accompanying it (if any), and
- (c) a copy or summary of the debtor's statement of affairs.

(7) Where the debtor is not an undischarged bankrupt, the nominee shall send a copy of each of the documents referred to in paragraph (6) to any person who has presented a bankruptcy petition against the debtor.

(8) The filing in court of the report under section 256A shall constitute an insolvency proceeding for the purpose of Rule 7.27 and Rule 7.30.

5.15 Filing of reports made under section 256A—appropriate court

(1) Except where the debtor is an undischarged bankrupt, the court in which the nominee's report under section 256A is to be filed is the court in which the debtor would be entitled to present his own petition in bankruptcy under Rule 6.40.

(2) The report shall contain sufficient information to establish that it is filed in the appropriate court.

(3) Where the debtor is an undischarged bankrupt, such report shall be filed in the court having the conduct of his bankruptcy and shall be filed with the bankruptcy proceedings.

5.16 Applications to the court

(1) Any application to court in relation to any matter relating to a voluntary arrangement or a proposal for a voluntary arrangement shall be made in the court in which the nominee's report was filed.

(2) Where the debtor intends to apply to the court under section 256A(4)(a) or (b) for the nominee to be replaced, he shall give to the nominee at least 7 days' notice of the application.

(3) Where the nominee intends to apply to the court under section 256A(4)(b) for his replacement as nominee, he shall give to the debtor at least 7 days' notice of the application.

(4) No appointment of a replacement nominee shall be made by the court unless there is filed in court a statement by the replacement nominee indicating his consent to act.

Chapter 5
Creditors' Meetings

5.17 Summoning of creditors' meeting

(1) If in his report the nominee states that in his opinion a meeting of creditors should be summoned to consider the debtor's proposal, the date on which the meeting is to be held shall be—
- (a) in a case where an interim order has not been obtained, not less than 14 days and not more than 28 days from that on which the nominee's report is filed in court under Rule 5.14; and
- (b) in a case where an interim order is in force, not less than 14 days from the date on which the nominee's report is filed in court nor more than 28 days from that on which the report is considered by the court.

(2) Notices calling the meeting shall be sent by the nominee, at least 14 days before the day fixed for it to be held, to all the creditors specified in the debtor's statement of affairs, and any other creditors of whom the nominee is otherwise aware.

(3) Each notice sent under this Rule shall specify the court to which the nominee's report on the debtor's proposal has been delivered and shall state the effect of Rule 5.23(1), (3) and (4) (requisite majorities); and with it there shall be sent—
- (a) a copy of the proposal,
- (b) a copy of the statement of affairs or, if the nominee thinks fit, a summary of it (the summary to include a list of the creditors and the amounts of their debts), and
- (c) the nominee's comments on the proposal.

5.18 Creditors' meeting: supplementary

(1) Subject as follows, in fixing the venue for the creditors' meeting, the nominee shall have regard to the convenience of creditors.

(2) The meeting shall be summoned for commencement between 10.00 and 16.00 hours on a business day.

(3) With every notice summoning the meeting there shall be sent out forms of proxy.

5.19 The chairman at the meeting

(1) Subject as follows, the nominee shall be chairman of the creditors' meeting.

(2) If for any reason the nominee is unable to attend, he may nominate another person to act as chairman in his place; but a person so nominated must be—

- (a) a person qualified to act as an insolvency practitioner in relation to the debtor;
- (b) an authorised person in relation to the debtor; or
- (c) an employee of the nominee or his firm who is experienced in insolvency matters.

5.20 The chairman as proxy-holder

The chairman shall not by virtue of any proxy held by him vote to increase or reduce the amount of the remuneration or expenses of the nominee or the supervisor of the proposed arrangement, unless the proxy specifically directs him to vote in that way.

5.21 Entitlement to vote

(1) Subject as follows, every creditor who has notice of the creditors' meeting is entitled to vote at the meeting or any adjournment of it.

(2) A creditor's entitlement to vote is calculated as follows—

- (a) where the debtor is not an undischarged bankrupt and an interim order is in force, by reference to the amount of the debt owed to him as at the date of the interim order;
- (b) where the debtor is not an undischarged bankrupt and an interim order is not in force, by reference to the amount of the debt owed to him at the date of the meeting; and
- (c) where the debtor is an undischarged bankrupt, by reference to the amount of the debt owed to him as at the date of the bankruptcy order.

(3) A creditor may vote in respect of a debt for an unliquidated amount or any debt whose value is not ascertained, and for the purposes of voting (but not otherwise) his debt shall be valued at £1 unless the chairman agrees to put a higher value on it.

5.22 Procedure for admission of creditors' claims for voting purposes

(1) Subject as follows, at the creditors' meeting the chairman shall ascertain the entitlement of persons wishing to vote and shall admit or reject their claims accordingly.

(2) The chairman may admit or reject a claim in whole or in part.

(3) The chairman's decision on any matter under this Rule or under paragraph (3) of Rule 5.21 is subject to appeal to the court by any creditor or by the debtor.

(4) If the chairman is in doubt whether a claim should be admitted or rejected, he shall mark it as objected to and allow votes to be cast in respect of it, subject

to such votes being subsequently declared invalid if the objection to the claim is sustained.

(5) If on an appeal the chairman's decision is reversed or varied, or votes are declared invalid, the court may order another meeting to be summoned, or make such order as it thinks just.

The court's power to make an order under this paragraph is exercisable only if it considers that the circumstances giving rise to the appeal are such as give rise to unfair prejudice or material irregularity.

(6) An application to the court by way of appeal against the chairman's decision shall not be made after the end of the period of 28 days beginning with the first day on which the report required by section 259 is made to the court.

(7) The chairman is not personally liable for any costs incurred by any person in respect of an appeal under this Rule.

5.23 Requisite majorities

(1) Subject as follows, at the creditors' meeting for any resolution to pass approving any proposal or modification there must be a majority in excess of three-quarters in value of the creditors present in person or by proxy and voting on the resolution.

(2) The same applies in respect of any other resolution proposed at the meeting, but substituting one-half for three-quarters.

(3) In the following cases there is to be left out of account a creditor's vote in respect of any claim or part of a claim—
- (a) where written notice of the claim was not given, either at the meeting or before it, to the chairman or the nominee;
- (b) where the claim or part is secured;
- (c) where the claim is in respect of a debt wholly or partly on, or secured by, a current bill of exchange or promissory note, unless the creditor is willing—
  - (i) to treat the liability to him on the bill or note of every person who is liable on it antecedently to the debtor, and against whom a bankruptcy order has not been made (or, in the case of a company, which has not gone into liquidation), as a security in his hands, and
  - (ii) to estimate the value of the security and (for the purpose of entitlement to vote, but not of any distribution under the arrangement) to deduct it from his claim.

(4) Any resolution is invalid if those voting against it include more than half in value of the creditors, counting in these latter only those—
- (a) who have notice of the meeting;
- (b) whose votes are not to be left out of account under paragraph (3); and
- (c) who are not, to the best of the chairman's belief, associates of the debtor.

(5) It is for the chairman of the meeting to decide whether under this Rule—
- (a) a vote is to be left out of account in accordance with the paragraph (3), or
- (b) a person is an associate of the debtor for the purposes of paragraph (4)(c);

and in relation to the second of these cases the chairman is entitled to rely on the information provided by the debtor's statement of affairs or otherwise in accordance with this Part of the Rules.

(6) If the chairman uses a proxy contrary to Rule 5.20, his vote with that proxy does not count towards any majority under this Rule.

(7) The chairman's decision on any matter under this Rule is subject to appeal to the court by any creditor or by the debtor and paragraphs (5) to (7) of Rule 5.22 apply as regards such an appeal.

5.24 Proceedings to obtain agreement on the proposal

(1) On the day on which the creditors' meeting is held, it may from time to time be adjourned.

(2) If on that day the requisite majority for the approval of the voluntary arrangement (with or without modifications) has not been obtained, the chairman may, and shall if it is so resolved, adjourn the meeting for not more than 14 days.

(3) If there are subsequently further adjournments, the final adjournment shall not be to a day later than 14 days after that on which the meeting was originally held.

(4) If the meeting is adjourned under paragraph (2), notice of the fact shall be given by the chairman forthwith to the court.

(5) If following any final adjournment of the meeting the proposal (with or without modifications) is not agreed to, it is deemed rejected.

Chapter 6
Implementation of the Arrangement

5.25 Resolutions to follow approval

(1) If the voluntary arrangement is approved (with or without modifications), a resolution may be taken by the creditors, where two or more individuals are appointed to act as supervisor, on the question whether acts to be done in connection with the arrangement may be done by any one of them, or must be done by both or all.

(2) If at the creditors' meeting a resolution is moved for the appointment of some person other than the nominee to be supervisor of the arrangement, there must be produced to the chairman, at or before the meeting—

- (a) that person's written consent to act (unless he is present and then and there signifies his consent), and
- (b) his written confirmation that he is qualified to act as an insolvency practitioner in relation to the debtor or is an authorised person in relation to the debtor.

5.26 Hand-over of property, etc to supervisor

(1) Forthwith after the approval of the voluntary arrangement, the debtor or, where the debtor is an undischarged bankrupt, the official receiver or the debtor's trustee, shall do all that is required for putting the supervisor into possession of the assets included in the arrangement.

(2) On taking possession of the assets in any case where the debtor is an undischarged bankrupt, the supervisor shall discharge any balance due to the official receiver and (if other) the trustee by way of remuneration or on account of—

(a) fees, costs, charges and expenses properly incurred and payable under the Act or the Rules, and
(b) any advances made in respect of the insolvent estate, together with interest on such advances at the rate specified in section 17 of the Judgments Act 1838 at the date of the bankruptcy order.

(3) Alternatively where the debtor is an undischarged bankrupt, the supervisor must, before taking possession, give the official receiver or the trustee a written undertaking to discharge any such balance out of the first realisation of assets.

(4) Where the debtor is an undischarged bankrupt, the official receiver and (if other) the trustee has a charge on the assets included in the voluntary arrangement in respect of any sums due as above until they have been discharged, subject only to the deduction from realisations by the supervisor of the proper costs and expenses of realisation.

Any sums due to the official receiver take priority over those due to a trustee.

(5) The supervisor shall from time to time out of the realisation of assets discharge all guarantees properly given by the official receiver or the trustee for the benefit of the estate, and shall pay all their expenses.

5.27 Report of creditors' meeting

(1) A report of the creditors' meeting shall be prepared by the chairman of the meeting.

(2) The report shall—
(a) state whether the proposal for a voluntary arrangement was approved or rejected and, if approved, with what (if any) modifications;
(b) set out the resolutions which were taken at the meeting, and the decision on each one;
(c) list the creditors (with their respective values) who were present or represented at the meeting, and how they voted on each resolution;
(d) whether in the opinion of the supervisor,
(i) the EC Regulation applies to the voluntary arrangement, and
(ii) if so, whether the proceedings are main proceedings or territorial proceedings; and
(e) include such further information (if any) as the chairman thinks it appropriate to make known to the court.

(3) A copy of the chairman's report shall, within 4 days of the meeting being held, be filed in court; and the court shall cause that copy to be endorsed with the date of filing.

(4) The persons to whom notice of the result is to be given, under section 259(1), are all those who were sent notice of the meeting under this Part of the Rules and any other creditor of whom the chairman is aware, and where the debtor is an undischarged bankrupt, the official receiver and (if any) the trustee.

The notice shall be sent immediately after a copy of the chairman's report is filed in court under paragraph (3).

(5) In a case where no interim order has been obtained the court shall not consider the chairman's report unless an application is made to the court under the Act or the Rules in relation to it.

5.28 Register of voluntary arrangements

(1) The Secretary of State shall maintain a register of individual voluntary arrangements, and shall enter in it all such matters as are reported to him in pursuance of Rules 5.29 and 5.34 and orders of suspension made under section 262 reported to him in pursuance of Rule 5.30.

(2) Where the Secretary of State has received notice of the making of a revocation order or that an arrangement has been fully implemented in pursuance of Rules 5.30 or 5.34 or has otherwise received written notice of the termination of an arrangement from the supervisor and—

(a) the revocation order under section 262 was made prior to 22nd March 1999, or

(b) the final completion or termination of the arrangement occurred more than 2 years prior to 22nd March 1999,

the Secretary of State shall delete from the register all matters entered in it relating to such arrangement.

(3) Where the Secretary of State receives notice under Rule 5.30(5) of the making of a revocation order in respect of an individual voluntary arrangement of which entry is made in the register, the Secretary of State shall delete from the register all matters entered in it relating to that arrangement.

(4) Where the Secretary of State receives notice under Rule 5.34(3) of the full implementation or termination of an individual voluntary arrangement of which entry is made in the register, the Secretary of State shall, on the expiry of 2 years after the final completion or termination of such individual voluntary arrangement, delete from the register all matters entered in it relating to that arrangement.

(5) The register shall be open to public inspection.

5.29 Reports to Secretary of State

(1) Immediately after the chairman of the creditors' meeting has filed in court a report that the meeting has approved the voluntary arrangement, he shall report to the Secretary of State the following details of the arrangement—

(a) the name and address of the debtor;

(b) the date on which the arrangement was approved by the creditors;

(c) the name and address of the supervisor; and

(d) the court in which the chairman's report has been filed.

(2) A person who is appointed to act as supervisor of an individual voluntary arrangement (whether in the first instance or by way of replacement of another person previously appointed) shall forthwith give written notice to the Secretary of State of his appointment.

If he vacates office as supervisor, he shall forthwith give written notice of that fact also to the Secretary of State.

5.30 Revocation or suspension of the arrangement

(1) This Rule applies where the court makes an order of revocation or suspension under section 262.

(2) The person who applied for the order shall serve sealed copies of it—

(a) in a case where the debtor is an undischarged bankrupt, on the debtor, the official receiver and the trustee;

(b) in any other case, on the debtor; and
(c) in either case, on the supervisor of the voluntary arrangement.

(3) If the order includes a direction by the court under section 262(4)(b) for any further creditors' meeting to be summoned, notice shall also be given (by the person who applied for the order) to whoever is, in accordance with the direction, required to summon the meeting.

(4) The debtor or (where the debtor is an undischarged bankrupt) the trustee or (if there is no trustee) the official receiver shall—
(a) forthwith after receiving a copy of the court's order, give notice of it to all persons who were sent notice of the creditors' meeting which approved the voluntary arrangement or who, not having been sent that notice, are affected by the order;
(b) within 7 days of their receiving a copy of the order (or within such longer period as the court may allow), give notice to the court whether it is intended to make a revised proposal to creditors, or to invite reconsideration of the original proposal.

(5) The person on whose application the order of revocation or suspension was made shall, within 7 days after the making of the order, give written notice of it to the Secretary of State and shall, in the case of an order of suspension, within 7 days of the expiry of any suspension order, given written notice of such expiry to the Secretary of State.

5.31 Supervisor's accounts and reports

(1) Where the voluntary arrangement authorises or requires the supervisor—
(a) to carry on the debtor's business or to trade on his behalf or in his name, or
(b) to realise assets of the debtor or (in a case where the debtor is an undischarged bankrupt) belonging to the estate, or
(c) otherwise to administer or dispose of any funds of the debtor or the estate,

he shall keep accounts and records of his acts and dealings in and in connection with the arrangement, including in particular records of all receipts and payments of money.

(2) The supervisor shall, not less often than once in every 12 months beginning with the date of his appointment, prepare an abstract of such receipts and payments, and send copies of it, accompanied by his comments on the progress and efficacy of the arrangement, to—
(a) the court,
(b) the debtor, and
(c) all those of the debtor's creditors who are bound by the arrangement.

If in any period of 12 months he has made no payments and had no receipts, he shall at the end of that period send a statement to that effect to all who are specified in sub-paragraphs (a) to (c) above.

(3) An abstract provided under paragraph (2) shall relate to a period beginning with the date of the supervisor's appointment or (as the case may be) the day following the end of the last period for which an abstract was prepared under this Rule; and copies of the abstract shall be sent out, as required by paragraph (2), within the 2 months following the end of the period to which the abstract relates.

(4) If the supervisor is not authorised as mentioned in paragraph (1), he shall, not less often than once in every 12 months beginning with the date of his appointment, send to all those specified in paragraph 2(a) to (c) a report on the progress and efficacy of the voluntary arrangement.

(5) The court may, on application by the supervisor, vary the dates on which the obligation to send abstracts or reports arises.

5.32 Production of accounts and records to Secretary of State

(1) The Secretary of State may at any time during the course of the voluntary arrangement or after its completion require the supervisor to produce for inspection—
- (a) his records and accounts in respect of the arrangement, and
- (b) copies of abstracts and reports prepared in compliance with Rule 5.31.

(2) The Secretary of State may require production either at the premises of the supervisor or elsewhere; and it is the duty of the supervisor to comply with any requirement imposed on him under this Rule.

(3) The Secretary of State may cause any accounts and records produced to him under this Rule to be audited; and the supervisor shall give to the Secretary of State such further information and assistance as he needs for the purposes of his audit.

5.33 Fees, costs, charges and expenses

The fees, costs, charges and expenses that may be incurred for any purposes of the voluntary arrangement are—
- (a) any disbursements made by the nominee prior to the approval of the arrangement, and any remuneration for his services as such agreed between himself and the debtor, the official receiver or the trustee;
- (b) any fees, costs, charges or expenses which—
  - (i) are sanctioned by the terms of the arrangement, or
  - (ii) would be payable, or correspond to those which would be payable, in the debtor's bankruptcy.

5.34 Completion or termination of the arrangement

(1) Not more than 28 days after the final completion or termination of the voluntary arrangement, the supervisor shall send to all creditors of the debtor who are bound by the arrangement, and to the debtor, a notice that the arrangement has been fully implemented or (as the case may be) terminated.

(2) With the notice there shall be sent to each of those persons a copy of a report by the supervisor summarising all receipts and payments made by him in pursuance of the arrangement, and explaining any difference in the actual implementation of it as compared with the proposal as approved by the creditors' meeting or (in the case of termination of the arrangement) explaining the reasons why the arrangement has not been implemented in accordance with the proposal as approved by the creditors' meeting.

(3) The supervisor shall, within the 28 days mentioned above, send to the Secretary of State and to the court a copy of the notice under paragraph (1), together with a copy of the report under paragraph (2), and he shall not vacate office until after such copies have been sent.

(4) The court may, on application by the supervisor, extend the period of 28 days under paragraphs (1) and (3).

Chapter 7
EC Regulation: Conversion of Voluntary Arrangement into Bankruptcy

5.35 Application for conversion of voluntary arrangement into bankruptcy

(1) Where a member State liquidator proposes to apply to the court for conversion under Article 37 of the EC Regulation (conversion of earlier proceedings) of a voluntary arrangement into a bankruptcy, an affidavit complying with Rule 5.36 must be prepared and sworn, and filed in court in support of the application.

(2) An application of the kind referred to in paragraph (1) shall be by originating application.

(3) The application and the affidavit required under this Rule shall be served upon—
- (a) the debtor; and
- (b) the supervisor.

5.36 Contents of affidavit

(1) The affidavit shall state—
- (a) that main proceedings have been opened in relation to the debtor in a member State other than the United Kingdom;
- (b) the deponent's belief that the conversion of the voluntary arrangement into a bankruptcy would prove to be in the interests of the creditors in the main proceedings; and
- (c) all other matters that, in the opinion of the member State liquidator, would assist the court—
  - (i) in deciding whether to make an order under Rule 5.37, and
  - (ii) if the court were to do so, in considering the need for any consequential provision that would be necessary or desirable.

(2) An affidavit under this Rule shall be sworn by, or on behalf of, the member State liquidator.

5.37 Power of court

(1) On hearing an application for conversion of a voluntary arrangement into a bankruptcy, the court may make such order as it thinks fit.

(2) If the court makes an order for conversion of a voluntary arrangement into a bankruptcy under paragraph (1), the order may contain all such consequential provisions as the court deems necessary or desirable.

(3) Where the court makes an order for conversion of a voluntary arrangement into a bankruptcy under paragraph (1), any expenses properly incurred as expenses of the administration of the voluntary arrangement in question shall be a first charge on the bankrupt's estate.

5.38 Notices to be given to member State liquidator

(1) This Rule applies where a member State liquidator has been appointed in relation to the debtor.

(2) Where the supervisor is obliged to give notice to, or provide a copy of a document (including an order of the court) to, the court or the official receiver, the supervisor shall give notice or provide copies, as appropriate, to the member State liquidator.

Appendix 3

Insolvent Partnerships (Amendment) (No 2) Order 2002, SI 2002/2708

1 Citation and commencement

This Order may be cited as the Insolvent Partnerships (Amendment) (No 2) Order 2002 and shall come into force on 1st January 2003.

2 Interpretation

(1) In this Order,

"the Act" means the Insolvency Act 1986,

"rule" means a rule of the Insolvency Rules 1986,

"the 1994 Order" means the Insolvent Partnerships Order 1994.

(2) In this Order a reference to a "modified section" means a section of the Act as modified by, and set out in, the 1994 Order.

3 Amendment to section 388 of the Insolvency Act 1986

For section 388(2A)(c) of the Act substitute—

"(c) where a voluntary arrangement in relation to the insolvent partnership is proposed or approved under Part I of the Act, as nominee or supervisor.".

4 Amendment to Article 4 of the Insolvent Partnerships Order 1994

For article 4(1) of the 1994 Order (voluntary arrangement of insolvent partnership) substitute—

"(1) The provisions of Part I of, and Schedule A1 to, the Act shall apply in relation to an insolvent partnership, certain of those provisions being modified in such manner that, after modification, they are as set out in Schedule 1 to this Order.".

5 Amendment to Article 19 of the Insolvent Partnerships Order 1994

In article 19(4) of the 1994 Order (supplemental and transitional provisions), after "enactment" insert—

"except where paragraph 12 of Schedule A1 to the Act, as applied by this Order, has the effect of preventing a petition being so presented".

6 Substitution of Schedule 1 to the Insolvent Partnerships Order 1994

For Schedule 1 to the 1994 Order (modified provisions of Part I of the Act) substitute the Schedule set out in Schedule 1 to this Order.

7 Amendments to Schedule 2 to the Insolvent Partnerships Order 1994

(1) Schedule 2 to the 1994 Order (modified provisions of Part II of the Act) is amended as follows.

(2) In paragraph 2 (section 8: power of court to make order), after modified section 8(6) insert—

"(7) In this Part a reference to an insolvent partnership includes a reference to an insolvent partnership in relation to which an administration order may be made by virtue of Article 3 of the EC Regulation.".

(3) In paragraph 4 (section 10: effect of application), after modified section 10(1)(a) insert—

"(aa) no landlord or other person to whom rent is payable may exercise any right of forfeiture by peaceable re-entry in relation to premises forming part of the partnership property or let to one or more officers of the partnership in their capacity as such in respect of a failure by the partnership or one or more officers of the partnership to comply with any term or condition of the tenancy of such premises, except with the leave of the court and subject to such terms as the court may impose;".

(4) In paragraph 5 (section 11: effect of order), after modified section 11(3)(d) insert—

"(da) no landlord or other person to whom rent is payable may exercise any right of forfeiture by peaceable re-entry in relation to premises forming part of the partnership property or let to one or more officers of the partnership in their capacity as such in respect of a failure by the partnership or one or more officers of the partnership to comply with any term or condition of the tenancy of such premises, except with the consent of the administrator or the leave of the court and subject (where the court gives leave) to such terms as the court may impose;".

NOTES

Initial Commencement
Specified date
Specified date: 1 January 2003: see art 1.

8 Amendment to Schedule 3 to the Insolvent Partnerships Order 1994

In paragraph 3 of Part I of Schedule 3 to the 1994 Order (section 221: winding up of unregistered companies), after modified section 221(7)(c) insert—

"(d) at the time at which a moratorium for the insolvent partnership under section 1A comes to an end, no voluntary arrangement approved under Part I of this Act has effect in relation to the insolvent partnership.

(7A) A winding-up petition on the ground set out in section 221(7)(d) may only be presented by one or more creditors.".

9 Amendment to Schedule 4 to the Insolvent Partnerships Order 1994

(1) Schedule 4 to the 1994 Order (modified provisions of the Act applying for purposes of Article 8) is amended as follows.

(2) In paragraph 3 of Part I (section 221: winding up of unregistered companies), for modified section 221(8) substitute—

"(8) The circumstances in which an insolvent partnership may be wound up as an unregistered company are as follows—

(a) the partnership is unable to pay its debts,

(b) at the time at which a moratorium for the insolvent partnership under section 1A comes to an end, no voluntary arrangement approved under Part I of this Act has effect in relation to the insolvent partnership.".

(3) In paragraph 6(a) of Part II (circumstances in which members of insolvent partnerships may be wound up or made bankrupt by the court), for modified section 122 substitute—

"122

A corporate member or former corporate member of an insolvent partnership may be wound up by the court if—

(a) it is unable to pay its debts,

(b) there is a creditor, by assignment or otherwise, to whom the insolvent partnership is indebted and the corporate member or former corporate member is liable in relation to that debt and at the time at which a moratorium for the insolvent partnership under section 1A comes to an end, no voluntary arrangement approved under Part I of this Act has effect in relation to the insolvent partnership.".

(4) In paragraph 6(b) of Part II (circumstances in which members of insolvent partnerships may be wound up or made bankrupt by the court),

(a) in modified section 267(2) after "Subject to", insert "subsection (2A) below and",

(b) after modified section 267(2) insert—

"(2A) A creditor's petition may be presented to the court in respect of a joint debt or debts if at the time at which a moratorium for the insolvent partnership under section 1A comes to an end, no voluntary arrangement approved under Part I of this Act has effect in relation to the insolvent partnership.".

10 Forms

For Forms 5, 6 and 7 contained in Schedule 9 to the 1994 Order substitute Forms 5, 6 and 7 contained in Schedule 2 to this Order.

11 Transitional provisions

(1) The amendments to the 1994 Order set out in articles 3, 4, 5, 6, 8, 9 and 10 of, and Schedules 1 and 2 to, this Order do not apply where, in relation to a voluntary arrangement under Part I of the Act, as the case may be, a proposal is made by—

(a) the members of a partnership and before this Order comes into force the intended nominee has endorsed a copy of the written notice of the proposal under rule 1.4(3),

(b) the liquidator or the administrator (acting as nominee) and before this Order comes into force the liquidator or administrator (as the case may be) has sent out a notice summoning the meetings under section 3 of the Act as required by rule 1.11, or

(c) the liquidator or the administrator of a partnership (not acting as the nominee) and before this Order comes into force the intended nominee has endorsed a copy of the written notice of the proposal under rule 1.12(2).

(2) The amendments to the 1994 Order set out in article 7 of this Order do not apply where a petition for an administration order in relation to an insolvent partnership has been presented before this Order comes into force.

(3) Where, by virtue of the 1994 Order, provisions of the Act apply in a case falling within paragraph (1) or (2), those provisions shall continue to have effect as if this Order had not been made.

Irvine of Lairg, C

22nd October 2002

I concur, on behalf of the Secretary of State

Melanie Johnson,

Parliamentary Under-Secretary of State for Competition, Consumers and Markets,

Department of Trade and Industry

29th October 2002

SCHEDULE 1

Article 6

"SCHEDULE 1
Modified Provisions of Part I of, and Schedule A1 to, the Act (Company Voluntary Arrangements) as Applied by Article 4

Article 4

PART I
MODIFIED PROVISIONS OF SECTIONS 1 TO 7B OF THE ACT

For sections 1 to 7B of the Act there shall be substituted:—

"PART I
PARTNERSHIP VOLUNTARY ARRANGEMENTS

The proposal

1

THOSE WHO MAY PROPOSE AN ARRANGEMENT

(1) The members of an insolvent partnership (other than one for which an administration order is in force, or which is being wound up as an unregistered company, or in respect of which an order has been made by virtue of article 11 of the Insolvent Partnerships Order 1994) may make a proposal under this Part to the partnership's creditors for a composition in satisfaction of the debts of the partnership or a scheme of arrangement of its affairs (from here on referred to, in either case, as a "voluntary arrangement").

(2) A proposal under this Part is one which provides for some person ("the nominee") to act in relation to the voluntary arrangement either as trustee or otherwise for the purpose of supervising its implementation; and the nominee must be a person who is qualified to act as an insolvency practitioner or authorised to act as nominee, in relation to the voluntary arrangement.

(3) Such a proposal may also be made—
- (a) where an administration order is in force in relation to the partnership, by the administrator,
- (b) where the partnership is being wound up as an unregistered company, by the liquidator, and
- (c) where an order has been made by virtue of article 11 of the Insolvent Partnerships Order 1994, by the trustee of the partnership.

(4) In this Part a reference to an insolvent partnership includes a reference to an insolvent partnership in relation to which a proposal for a voluntary arrangement may be made by virtue of Article 3 of the EC Regulation.

1A

MORATORIUM

(1) Where the members of an eligible insolvent partnership intend to make a proposal for a voluntary arrangement, they may take steps to obtain a moratorium for the insolvent partnership.

(2) Subject to subsections (3), (4), (5), (6) and (7), the provisions of Schedule A1 to this Act have effect with respect to—

- (a) insolvent partnerships eligible for a moratorium under this section,
- (b) the procedure for obtaining such a moratorium,
- (c) the effects of such a moratorium, and
- (d) the procedure applicable (in place of sections 2 to 6 and 7) in relation to the approval and implementation of a voluntary arrangement where such a moratorium is or has been in force.

(3) Certain of the provisions applied in relation to insolvent partnerships by virtue of subsection (2) are modified in their application in relation to insolvent partnerships in such manner that, after modification, they are as set out in Part II of Schedule 1 to the Insolvent Partnerships Order 1994.

(4) Paragraphs 4A, 4B, 4C, 4D, 4E, 4F, 4G, 4H, 4I, 4J, 4K, 5, 7(4), 8(8), 32(7), 34(2), 41(5) and 45 of Schedule A1 to this Act shall not apply.

(5) An insolvent partnership is not liable to a fine under paragraphs 16(2), 17(3), 18(3), 19(3), 22 or 23(1) of Schedule A1 to the Act.

(6) Notwithstanding subsection (5) an officer of an insolvent partnership may be liable to imprisonment or a fine under the paragraphs referred to in that subsection in the same manner as an officer of a company.

(7) In the application of Schedule A1, and the application of the entries in Schedule 10 relating to offences under Schedule A1, to insolvent partnerships—

- (a) references to the directors or members of a company shall be construed as references to the members of an insolvent partnership,
- (b) references to officers of a company shall be construed as references to the officers of an insolvent partnership,
- (c) references to a meeting of a company shall be construed as references to a meeting of the members of an insolvent partnership, and
- (d) references to a floating charge shall be construed as references to a floating charge created under section 5 of the Agricultural Credits Act 1928.

2

PROCEDURE WHERE NOMINEE IS NOT THE LIQUIDATOR, ADMINISTRATOR OR TRUSTEE

(1) This section applies where the nominee under section 1 is not the liquidator, administrator or trustee of the insolvent partnership and the members of the partnership do not propose to take steps to obtain a moratorium under section 1A for the insolvent partnership.

(2) The nominee shall, within 28 days (or such longer period as the court may allow) after he is given notice of the proposal for a voluntary arrangement, submit a report to the court stating—

(a) whether, in his opinion, the proposed voluntary arrangement has a reasonable prospect of being approved and implemented,
(b) whether, in his opinion, meetings of the members of the partnership and of the partnership's creditors should be summoned to consider the proposal, and
(c) if in his opinion such meetings should be summoned, the date on which, and time and place at which, he proposes the meetings should be held.

(3) The nominee shall also state in his report whether there are in existence any insolvency proceedings in respect of the insolvent partnership or any of its members.

(4) For the purposes of enabling the nominee to prepare his report, the person intending to make the proposal shall submit to the nominee—
(a) a document setting out the terms of the proposed voluntary arrangement, and
(b) a statement of the partnership's affairs containing—
(i) such particulars of the partnership's creditors and of the partnership's debts and other liabilities and of the partnership property as may be prescribed, and
(ii) such other information as may be prescribed.

(5) The court may—
(a) on an application made by the person intending to make the proposal, in a case where the nominee has failed to submit the report required by this section or has died, or
(b) on an application made by that person or the nominee, in a case where it is impracticable or inappropriate for the nominee to continue to act as such,

direct that the nominee be replaced as such by another person qualified to act as an insolvency practitioner, or authorised to act as nominee, in relation to the voluntary arrangement.

3

SUMMONING OF MEETINGS

(1) Where the nominee under section 1 is not the liquidator, administrator or trustee of the insolvent partnership, and it has been reported to the court that such meetings as are mentioned in section 2(2) should be summoned, the person making the report shall (unless the court otherwise directs) summon those meetings for the time, date and place proposed in the report.

(2) Where the nominee is the liquidator, administrator or trustee of the insolvent partnership, he shall summon meetings of the members of the partnership and of the partnership's creditors to consider the proposal for such a time, date and place as he thinks fit.

(3) The persons to be summoned to a creditors' meeting under this section are every creditor of the partnership of whose claim and address the person summoning the meeting is aware.

Consideration and implementation of proposal

4

DECISIONS OF MEETINGS

(1) The meetings under section 3 shall decide whether to approve the proposed voluntary arrangement (with or without modifications).

(2) The modifications may include one conferring the functions proposed to be conferred on the nominee on another person qualified to act as an insolvency practitioner, or authorised to act as nominee, in relation to the voluntary arrangement.

But they shall not include any modification by virtue of which the proposal ceases to be a proposal such as is mentioned in section 1.

(3) A meeting so summoned shall not approve any proposal or modification which affects the right of a secured creditor of the partnership to enforce his security, except with the concurrence of the creditor concerned.

(4) Subject as follows, a meeting so summoned shall not approve any proposal or modification under which—

- (a) any preferential debt of the partnership is to be paid otherwise than in priority to such of its debts as are not preferential debts, or
- (b) a preferential creditor of the partnership is to be paid an amount in respect of a preferential debt that bears to that debt a smaller proportion than is borne to another preferential debt by the amount that is to be paid in respect of that other debt.

However, the meeting may approve such a proposal or modification with the concurrence of the preferential creditor concerned.

(5) Subject as above, each of the meetings shall be conducted in accordance with the rules.

(6) After the conclusion of either meeting in accordance with the rules, the chairman of the meeting shall report the result of the meeting to the court, and, immediately after reporting to the court, shall give notice of the result of the meeting to all those who were sent notice of the meeting in accordance with the rules.

(7) References in this section to preferential debts and preferential creditors are to be read in accordance with section 386 in Part XII of this Act.

4A

APPROVAL OF ARRANGEMENT

(1) This section applies to a decision, under section 4, with respect to the approval of a proposed voluntary arrangement.

(2) The decision has effect if, in accordance with the rules—

- (a) it has been taken by both meetings summoned under section 3, or
- (b) (subject to any order made under subsection (6)) it has been taken by the creditors' meeting summoned under that section.

(3) If the decision taken by the creditors' meeting differs from that taken by the meeting of the members of the partnership, a member of the partnership may apply to court.

(4) An application under subsection (3) shall not be made after the end of the period of 28 days beginning with—
- (a) the day on which the decision was taken by the creditors' meeting, or
- (b) where the decision of the meeting of the members of the partnership was taken on a later day, that day.

(5) Where a member of an insolvent partnership which is regulated applies to the court under subsection (3), the Financial Services Authority is entitled to be heard on the application.

(6) On an application under subsection (3), the court may—
- (a) order the decision of the meeting of the members of the partnership to have effect instead of the decision of the creditors' meeting, or
- (b) make such other order as it thinks fit.

(7) In this section "regulated" in relation to an insolvent partnership means a person who—
- (a) is, or has been, an authorised person within the meaning given by section 31 of the Financial Services and Markets Act 2000,
- (b) is, or has been, an appointed representative within the meaning given by section 39 of that Act, or
- (c) is carrying on, or has carried on, a regulated activity, within the meaning given by section 22 of that Act, in contravention of the general prohibition within the meaning given by section 19 of that Act.

5

EFFECT OF APPROVAL

(1) This section applies where a decision approving a voluntary arrangement has effect under section 4A.

(2) The voluntary arrangement—
- (a) takes effect as if made by the members of the partnership at the creditors' meeting, and
- (b) binds every person who in accordance with the rules—
  - (i) was entitled to vote at that meeting (whether or not he was present or represented at it), or
  - (ii) would have been so entitled if he had had notice of it,

  as if he were a party to the voluntary arrangement.

(2A) If—
- (a) when the arrangement ceases to have effect any amount payable under the arrangement to a person bound by virtue of subsection 2(b)(ii) has not been paid, and
- (b) the arrangement did not come to an end prematurely,

the insolvent partnership shall at that time become liable to pay to that person the amount payable under the arrangement.

(3) Subject as follows, if the partnership is being wound up as an unregistered company, or an administration order or an order by virtue of article 11 of the Insolvent Partnerships Order 1994 is in force, the court may do one or both of the following, namely—
- (a) by order—

(i) stay all proceedings in the winding up or in the proceedings under the order made by virtue of the said article 11 (as the case may be), including any related insolvency proceedings of a member of the partnership in his capacity as such, or

(ii) discharge the administration order;

(b) give such directions as it thinks appropriate for facilitating the implementation of the voluntary arrangement with respect to—

(i) the conduct of the winding up, the proceedings by virtue of the said article 11 or the administration (as the case may be), and

(ii) the conduct of any related insolvency proceedings as referred to in paragraph (a)(i) above.

(4) The court shall not make an order under subsection (3)(a)—

(a) at any time before the end of the period of 28 days beginning with the first day on which each of the reports required by section 4(6) has been made to the court, or

(b) at any time when an application under the next section or an appeal in respect of such an application is pending, or at any time in the period within which such an appeal may be brought.

6

CHALLENGE OF DECISIONS

(1) Subject to this section, an application to the court may be made, by any of the persons specified below, on one or both of the following grounds, namely—

(a) that a voluntary arrangement which has effect under section 4A unfairly prejudices the interests of a creditor, member or contributory of the partnership;

(b) that there has been some material irregularity at or in relation to either of the meetings.

(2) The persons who may apply under this section are—

(a) a person entitled, in accordance with the rules, to vote at either of the meetings;

(b) a person who would have been entitled, in accordance with the rules, to vote at the creditors' meeting if he had had notice of it;

(c) the nominee or any person who has replaced him under section 2(5) or 4(2); and

(d) if the partnership is being wound up as an unregistered company or an administration order or order by virtue of article 11 of the Insolvent Partnerships Order 1994 is in force, the liquidator, administrator or trustee of the partnership.

(3) An application under this section shall not be made—

(a) after the end of the period of 28 days beginning with the first day on which each of the reports required by section 4(6) has been made to the court, or

(b) in the case of a person who was not given notice of the creditors' meeting, after the end of the period of 28 days beginning with the day on which he became aware that the meeting had taken place,

but (subject to that) an application made by a person within subsection (2)(b) on the ground that the voluntary arrangement prejudices his interests may be made after the voluntary arrangement has ceased to have effect, unless it came to an end prematurely.

(4) Where on such an application the court is satisfied as to either of the grounds mentioned in subsection (1), it may do one or both of the following, namely—

(a) revoke or suspend any decision approving the voluntary arrangement which has effect under section 4A or, in a case falling within subsection (1)(b), any decision taken by the meeting in question which has effect under that section;

(b) give a direction to any person for the summoning of further meetings to consider any revised proposal the person who made the original proposal may make or, in a case falling within subsection (1)(b), a further meeting of the members of the partnership or (as the case may be) of the partnership's creditors to reconsider the original proposal.

(5) Where at any time after giving a direction under subsection (4)(b) for the summoning of meetings to consider a revised proposal the court is satisfied that the person who made the original proposal does not intend to submit a revised proposal, the court shall revoke the direction and revoke or suspend any decision approving the voluntary arrangement which has effect under section 4A.

(6) In a case where the court, on an application under this section with respect to any meeting—

(a) gives a direction under subsection (4)(b), or

(b) revokes or suspends an approval under subsection (4)(a) or (5),

the court may give such supplemental directions as it thinks fit, and, in particular, directions with respect to things done under the voluntary arrangement since it took effect.

(7) Except in pursuance of the preceding provisions of this section, a decision taken at a meeting summoned under section 3 is not invalidated by any irregularity at or in relation to the meeting.

6A

FALSE REPRESENTATIONS, ETC

(1) If, for the purpose of obtaining the approval of the members or creditors of an insolvent partnership or of the members or creditors of any of its members to a proposal for a voluntary arrangement in relation to the partnership or any of its members, a person who is an officer of the partnership or an officer (which for this purpose includes a shadow director) of a corporate member in relation to which a voluntary arrangement is proposed—

(a) makes a false representation, or

(b) fraudulently does, or omits to do, anything,

he commits an offence.

(2) Subsection (1) applies even if the proposal is not approved.

(3) A person guilty of an offence under this section is liable to imprisonment or a fine, or both.

7

IMPLEMENTATION OF PROPOSAL

(1) This section applies where a voluntary arrangement has effect under section 4A.

(2) The person who is for the time being carrying out in relation to the voluntary arrangement the functions conferred—

- (a) on the nominee by virtue of the approval given at one or both of the meetings summoned under section 3, or
- (b) by virtue of section 2(5) or 4(2) on a person other than the nominee,

shall be known as the supervisor of the voluntary arrangement.

(3) If any of the partnership's creditors or any other person is dissatisfied by any act, omission or decision of the supervisor, he may apply to the court; and on the application the court may—

- (a) confirm, reverse or modify any act or decision of the supervisor,
- (b) give him directions, or
- (c) make such other order as it thinks fit.

(4) The supervisor—

- (a) may apply to the court for directions in relation to any particular matter arising under the voluntary arrangement, and
- (b) is included among the persons who may apply to the court for the winding up of the partnership as an unregistered company or for an administration order to be made in relation to it.

(5) The court may, whenever—

- (a) it is expedient to appoint a person to carry out the functions of the supervisor, and
- (b) it is inexpedient, difficult or impracticable for an appointment to be made without the assistance of the court,

make an order appointing a person who is qualified to act as an insolvency practitioner or authorised to act as supervisor, in relation to the voluntary arrangement, either in substitution for the existing supervisor or to fill a vacancy.

(6) The power conferred by subsection (5) is exercisable so as to increase the number of persons exercising the functions of supervisor or, where there is more than one person exercising those functions, so as to replace one or more of those persons.

7A

PROSECUTION OF DELINQUENT OFFICERS OF PARTNERSHIP

(1) This section applies where a moratorium under section 1A has been obtained for an insolvent partnership or the approval of a voluntary arrangement in relation to an insolvent partnership has taken effect under section 4A or paragraph 36 of Schedule A1.

(2) If it appears to the nominee or supervisor that any past or present officer of the insolvent partnership has been guilty of any offence in connection with the moratorium or, as the case may be, voluntary arrangement for which such officer is criminally liable, the nominee or supervisor shall forthwith—

- (a) report the matter to the Secretary of State, and
- (b) provide the Secretary of State with such information and give him such access to and facilities for inspecting and taking copies of documents (being information or documents in the possession or under the control of the nominee or supervisor and relating to the matter in question) as the Secretary of State requires.

(3) Where a prosecuting authority institutes criminal proceedings following any report under subsection (2), the nominee or supervisor, and every officer and agent of the insolvent partnership past or present (other than the defendant), shall give the authority all assistance in connection with the prosecution which he is reasonably able to give.

For this purpose—

"agent" includes any banker or solicitor of the insolvent partnership and any person employed by the insolvent partnership as auditor, whether that person is or is not an officer of the insolvent partnership,

"prosecuting authority" means the Director of Public Prosecutions or the Secretary of State.

(4) The court may, on the application of the prosecuting authority, direct any person referred to in subsection (3) to comply with that subsection if he has failed to do so.

7B

ARRANGEMENTS COMING TO AN END PREMATURELY

For the purposes of this Part, a voluntary arrangement the approval of which has taken effect under section 4A or paragraph 36 of Schedule A1 comes to an end prematurely if, when it ceases to have effect, it has not been fully implemented in respect of all persons bound by the arrangement by virtue of section 5(2)(b)(i) or, as the case may be, paragraph 37(2)(b)(i) of Schedule A1."

PART II
MODIFIED PROVISIONS OF SCHEDULE A1 TO THE ACT

The following provisions of Schedule A1 to the Act are modified so as to read as follows:

"3

(1) An insolvent partnership meets the requirements of this paragraph if the qualifying conditions are met—
- (a) in the year ending with the date of filing, or
- (b) in the tax year of the insolvent partnership which ended last before that date.

(2) For the purposes of sub-paragraph (1) the qualifying conditions are met by an insolvent partnership in a period if, in that period, it satisfies two or more of the requirements set out in sub-paragraph (3).

(3) The qualifying conditions referred to in this paragraph are—
- (a) turnover of not more than £2.8 million,
- (b) assets of not more than £1.4 million, and
- (c) no more than 50 employees.

(4) For the purposes of sub-paragraph (3)—
- (a) the total of turnover is the amount which is or would be, as the case may be, entered as turnover in the partnership's tax return,
- (b) the total of assets is the amount which—
  - (i) in the case of the period referred to in paragraph 3(1)(a), is entered in the partnership's statement of affairs which must be filed with the court under paragraph 7(1)(b), or

(ii) in the case of the period referred to in paragraph 3(1)(b), would be entered in the partnership's statement of affairs had it prepared such a statement on the last day of the period to which the amount for turnover is calculated for the purposes of paragraph 3(4)(a),

(c) the number of employees is the average number of persons employed by the insolvent partnership—

(i) in the case of the period referred to in paragraph 3(1)(a), in the period ending with the date of filing,

(ii) in the case of the period referred to in paragraph 3(1)(b), in the period to which the amount for turnover is calculated for the purposes of paragraph 3(4)(a).

(5) Where the period covered by the qualifying conditions in respect of the insolvent partnership is not a year the total of turnover referred to in paragraph 3(3)(a) shall be proportionately adjusted.

(6) The average number of persons employed by the insolvent partnership shall be calculated as follows—

(a) by ascertaining the number of persons employed by it under contracts of service for each month of the year (whether throughout the month or not),

(b) by adding those figures together, and

(c) by dividing the resulting figure by the number of months during which persons were so employed by it during the year.

(7) In this paragraph—

"tax return" means a return under section 12AA of the Taxes Management Act 1970,

"tax year" means the 12 months beginning with 6th April in any year.

4

(1) An insolvent partnership is excluded from being eligible for a moratorium if, on the date of filing—

(a) an administration order is in force in relation to the insolvent partnership,

(b) the insolvent partnership is being wound up as an unregistered company,

(c) there is an agricultural receiver of the insolvent partnership,

(d) a voluntary arrangement has effect in relation to the insolvent partnership,

(e) there is a provisional liquidator of the insolvent partnership,

(f) a moratorium has been in force for the insolvent partnership at any time during the period of 12 months ending with the date of filing and—

(i) no voluntary arrangement had effect at the time at which the moratorium came to an end, or

(ii) a voluntary arrangement which had effect at any time in that period has come to an end prematurely,

(g) a voluntary arrangement in relation to the insolvent partnership which had effect in pursuance of a proposal under section 1(3) has come to an end prematurely and, during the period of 12 months ending with the date of filing, an order under section 5(3)(a) has been made, or

(h) an order has been made by virtue of article 11 of the Insolvent Partnerships Order 1994.

(2) Sub-paragraph (1)(b) does not apply to an insolvent partnership which, by reason of a winding-up order made after the date of filing, is treated as being wound up on that date.

Effect on creditors, etc

12

(1) During the period for which a moratorium is in force for an insolvent partnership—

(a) no petition may be presented for the winding-up of the insolvent partnership as an unregistered company,

(b) no meeting of the members of the partnership may be called or requisitioned except with the consent of the nominee or the leave of the court and subject (where the court gives leave) to such terms as the court may impose,

(c) no order may be made for the winding-up of the insolvent partnership as an unregistered company,

(d) no petition for an administration order in relation to the insolvent partnership may be presented,

(e) no agricultural receiver of the partnership may be appointed except with the leave of the court and subject to such terms as the court may impose,

(f) no landlord or other person to whom rent is payable may exercise any rights of forfeiture by peaceable re-entry in relation to premises forming part of the partnership property or let to one or more officers of the partnership in their capacity as such in respect of a failure by the partnership or one or more officers of the partnership to comply with any term or condition of the tenancy of such premises, except with the leave of the court and subject to such terms as the court may impose,

(g) no other steps may be taken to enforce any security over the partnership property, or to repossess goods in the possession, under any hire-purchase agreement, of one or more officers of the partnership in their capacity as such, except with the leave of the court and subject to such terms as the court may impose,

(h) no other proceedings and no execution or other legal process may be commenced or continued, and no distress may be levied, against the insolvent partnership or the partnership property except with the leave of the court and subject to such terms as the court may impose,

(i) no petition may be presented, and no order may be made, by virtue of article 11 of the Insolvent Partnerships Order 1994, and

(j) no application or order may be made under section 35 of the Partnership Act 1890 in respect of the insolvent partnership.

(2) Where a petition, other than an excepted petition, for the winding-up of the insolvent partnership has been presented before the beginning of the moratorium, section 127 shall not apply in relation to any disposition of partnership property, any transfer of an interest in the insolvent partnership or alteration in status of a member of the partnership made during the moratorium or at a time mentioned in paragraph 37(5)(a).

(3) Paragraph (a) of sub-paragraph (1) does not apply to an excepted petition and, where such a petition has been presented before the beginning of the moratorium or is presented during the moratorium, paragraphs (b) and (c) of that sub-paragraph do not apply in relation to proceedings on the petition.

(4) For the purposes of this paragraph, "excepted petition" means a petition under—

(a) article 7(1) of the Insolvent Partnerships Order 1994 presented by the Secretary of State on the grounds mentioned in subsections (b), (c) and (d) of section 124A of this Act,
(b) section 72 of the Financial Services Act 1986 on the ground mentioned in subsection (1)(b) of that section,
(c) section 92 of the Banking Act 1987 on the ground mentioned in subsection (1)(b) of that section, or
(d) section 367 of the Financial Services and Markets Act 2000 on the ground mentioned in subsection (3)(b) of that section.

Disposal of charged property, etc

20

(1) This paragraph applies where—
(a) any partnership property of the insolvent partnership is subject to a security, or
(b) any goods are in possession of one or more officers of the partnership in their capacity as such under a hire-purchase agreement.

(2) If the holder of the security consents, or the court gives leave, the insolvent partnership may dispose of the property as if it were not subject to the security.

(3) If the owner of the goods consents, or the court gives leave, the insolvent partnership may dispose of the goods as if all rights of the owner under the hire-purchase agreement were vested in the members of the partnership.

(4) Where property subject to a security which, as created, was a floating charge is disposed of under sub-paragraph (2), the holder of the security has the same priority in respect of any partnership property directly or indirectly representing the property disposed of as he would have had in respect of the property subject to the security.

(5) Sub-paragraph (6) applies to the disposal under sub-paragraph (2) or (as the case may be) sub-paragraph (3) of—
(a) any property subject to a security other than a security which, as created, was a floating charge, or
(b) any goods in the possession of one or more officers of the partnership in their capacity as such under a hire-purchase agreement.

(6) It shall be a condition of any consent or leave under sub-paragraph (2) or (as the case may be) sub-paragraph (3) that—
(a) the net proceeds of the disposal, and
(b) where those proceeds are less than such amount as may be agreed, or determined by the court, to be the net amount which would be realised on a sale of the property or goods in the open market by a willing vendor, such sums as may be required to make good the deficiency,

shall be applied towards discharging the sums secured by the security or payable under the hire-purchase agreement.

(7) Where a condition imposed in pursuance of sub-paragraph (6) relates to two or more securities, that condition requires—
(a) the net proceeds of the disposal, and
(b) where paragraph (b) of sub-paragraph (6) applies, the sums mentioned in that paragraph,

to be applied towards discharging the sums secured by those securities in the order of their priorities.

(8) In this paragraph "floating charge" means a floating charge created under section 5 of the Agricultural Credits Act 1928.

Effect of approval of voluntary arrangement

37

(1) This paragraph applies where a decision approving a voluntary arrangement has effect under paragraph 36.

(2) The approved voluntary arrangement—
- (a) takes effect as if made by the members of the partnership at the creditors' meeting, and
- (b) binds every person who in accordance with the rules—
  - (i) was entitled to vote at that meeting (whether or not he was present or represented at it), or
  - (ii) would have been so entitled if he had had notice of it,

  as if he were a party to the voluntary arrangement.

(3) If—
- (a) when the arrangement ceases to have effect any amount payable under the arrangement to a person bound by virtue of sub-paragraph (2)(b)(ii) has not been paid, and
- (b) the arrangement did not come to an end prematurely,

the insolvent partnership shall at that time become liable to pay to that person the amount payable under the arrangement.

(4) Where a petition for the winding-up of the insolvent partnership as an unregistered company or a petition by virtue of article 11 of the Insolvent Partnerships Order 1994, other than an excepted petition within the meaning of paragraph 12, was presented before the beginning of the moratorium, the court shall dismiss the petition.

(5) The court shall not dismiss a petition under sub-paragraph (4)—
- (a) at any time before the end of the period of 28 days beginning with the first day on which each of the reports of the meetings required by paragraph 30(3) has been made to the court, or
- (b) at any time when an application under paragraph 38 or an appeal in respect of such an application is pending, or at any time in the period within which such an appeal may be brought.

Challenge of actions of officers of insolvent partnership

40

(1) This paragraph applies in relation to acts or omissions of the officers of a partnership during a moratorium.

(2) A creditor or member of the insolvent partnership may apply to the court for an order under this paragraph on the ground—

(a) that the partnership's affairs and business and partnership property are being or have been managed by the officers of the partnership in a manner which is unfairly prejudicial to the interests of its creditors or members generally, or of some part of its creditors or members (including at least the petitioner), or
(b) that any actual or proposed act or omission of the officers of the partnership is or would be so prejudicial.

(3) An application for an order under this paragraph may be made during or after the moratorium.

(4) On an application for an order under this paragraph the court may—
(a) make such order as it thinks fit for giving relief in respect of the matters complained of,
(b) adjourn the hearing conditionally or unconditionally, or
(c) make an interim order or any other order that it thinks fit.

(5) An order under this paragraph may in particular—
(a) regulate the management by the officers of the partnership of the partnership's affairs and business and partnership property during the remainder of the moratorium,
(b) require the officers of the partnership to refrain from doing or continuing an act complained of by the petitioner, or to do an act which the petitioner has complained they have omitted to do,
(c) require the summoning of a meeting of creditors or members of the partnership for the purpose of considering such matters as the court may direct,
(d) bring the moratorium to an end and make such consequential provision as the court thinks fit.

(6) In making an order under this paragraph the court shall have regard to the need to safeguard the interests of persons who have dealt with the insolvent partnership in good faith and for value.

(7) In relation to any time when an administration order is in force in relation to the insolvent partnership, or the insolvent partnership is being wound up as an unregistered company or an order by virtue of article 11 of the Insolvent Partnerships Order 1994 has been made, in pursuance of a petition presented before the moratorium came into force, no application for an order under this paragraph may be made by a creditor or member of the insolvent partnership; but such an application may be made instead by the administrator or (as the case may be) trustee or liquidator.

42

(1) If, for the purpose of obtaining a moratorium, or an extension of a moratorium, for an insolvent partnership or any of its members (a moratorium meaning in the case of an individual the effect of an application for, or the making of, an interim order under Part VIII of the Act), a person who is an officer of an insolvent partnership or an officer (which for this purpose includes a shadow director) of a corporate member in relation to which a voluntary arrangement is proposed—
(a) makes any false representation, or
(b) fraudulently does, or omits to do, anything,

he commits an offence.

(2) Sub-paragraph (1) applies even if no moratorium or extension is obtained.

(3) A person guilty of an offence under this paragraph is liable to imprisonment or a fine, or both."

SCHEDULE 2

Article 10

"Form 5

Creditor's Petition to Wind Up Partnership (Presented in Conjunction with Petitions against Members)

Schedule 4, para 8
s 124(1)(a)

(a) Insert name of partnership	**In the matter of (a)** ______________________________ ______________________________
	(hereinafter referred to as "the partnership") and in the matter of the Insolvent Partnerships Order 1994
(b) Insert title of court and number of proceedings (to be allocated by court)	To (b) ______________________________ ______________ No: __________ of __________
(c) Insert full name(s) and address(es) of petitioner(s)	The petition of (c) ______________________________ ______________________________ ______________________________
(d) Insert the nature of the partnership's business	1 The nature of the partnership's business is/was (d) ______________________________ ______________________________
(e) Delete as appropriate	2 (e) [The centre of main interests] [An establishment] of the partnership is at (f) ______________________________ within the jurisdiction of the court
	OR
(f) Insert address of business applicable to show jurisdiction of the court	(e) [The principal place of business of the partnership] [A place of business at which business was carried on by the partnership in the course of which the debt (or part of the debt) arose which forms the basis of this petition] is at (f) ______________________________ ______________________________ within the jurisdiction of the court.

If the partnership has a principal place of business in both England and Wales and in Scotland the relevant period is 1 year. In any other case it is 3 years.	3 The partnership has carried on its business in England and Wales at some time during the period of (e) [3 years] [1 year] ending with the day on which this petition is presented. 4 The partnership is/is not (e) [an insurance undertaking;] [a credit institution;] [an investment undertaking providing services involving the holding of funds or securities for third parties;] or [a collective investment undertaking] referred to in Article 1.2 of the EC Regulation.
(g) Insert name of person swearing affidavit (h) Insert whether main, secondary or territorial proceedings	5 For the reasons stated in the affidavit of (g) ______________________________ filed in support hereof it is considered that the EC Regulation (e) will/will not apply (e) [and that these proceedings will be (h) ________________________________ proceedings as defined in Article 3 of the EC Regulation].
	6 The partnership is justly and truly indebted to me/us in the aggregate sum of £ ________________. The above-mentioned debt is for a liquidated sum payable immediately.
(j) Insert date of service (k) State manner of service of demand	(e) [On (j) _________________ a demand was served upon the partnership by (k)________________________________ ________________________________ in respect of the above-mentioned debt. To the best of my knowledge and belief the demand has not been complied with.]
(l) Insert full name of member or members	(e) [On (j) _________________ (e) [a demand was] [demands were] served upon (l) ________________________________ [a] member[s] of the partnership by (k)________________________________ ________________________________ in respect of the above-mentioned debt. To the best of my knowledge and belief the demand[s] has not/have not been complied with.]
(m) Delete (1) or (2) as appropriate	7 The partnership (m)— [(1) is unable to pay its debts,] or [(2) at the time at which a moratorium for the insolvent partnership under section 1A of the Insolvency Act 1986 came to an end, no voluntary arrangement approved under Part I had effect in relation to the insolvent partnership,] and in the circumstances the partnership should be wound up. The petitioner[s] therefore pray[s] as follows:

(1) that (a) ____
may be wound up by the court under the provisions of the Insolvency Act 1986 as modified by the Insolvent Partnerships Order 1994.

OR

(2) that such other order may be made as the court thinks fit.

Under the EC Regulation:

(i) The centre of main interest should correspond to the place where the debtor conducts the administration of his interests on a regular basis.

(ii) Establishment is defined as "any place of operations where the debtor carries out a non-transitory economic activity with human means and goods".

NOTE 1:
Petitions are also being presented against the following members of the partnership:

NAME	ADDRESS	TYPE OF PETITION (WINDING-UP OR BANKRUPTCY)	DATE DEMAND SERVED (if applicable)

NOTE 2:
It is intended to serve this petition on the partnership.

(n) Delete as applicable

(o) Insert name and address of court

ENDORSEMENT

This petition having been presented to the court on ______________________ will be heard at (n) [Royal Courts of Justice, Strand, London WC2A 2LL] [(o) ______________________ County Court

____

______________________]

on:

Date ______________________

Time ______________________
(or as soon thereafter as the petition can be heard)

The solicitor to the petitioner is:

Name ______________________

Address ______________________

____

____

Tel No ______________________

Reference ______________________

[whose agents are:

Name ______________________

Address ______________________

____

____

Tel No ______________________

Reference ______________________]

Form 6
Creditor's Petition to Wind Up Corporate Member (Presented in Conjunction with Petition against Partnership)

Schedule 4, para 8
s 124(1)(b)

(a) Insert name of corporate member subject to winding-up petition

In the matter of (a) ______________________________________

____

(hereinafter referred to as "the company") and in the matter of the Insolvent Partnerships Order 1994

(b) Insert title of court and number of proceedings (to be allocated by court)

To (b) ______________________________________

____________________ No: ______________ of ____________

(c) Insert full name(s) and address(es) of petitioner(s)

The petition of (c) ______________________________________

____

____

(d) Insert date of incorporation

1 The company was incorporated on (d) ______________________________________ under the Companies Act 19 .

(e) Insert address of registered office

2 The registered office of the company is at (e)

____

____

____

3 The nominal capital of the company is £ ____________________ divided into ____________ shares of £ ____________ each. The amount of the capital paid up or credited as paid up is £ ______________

4 The principal objects for which the company was established are as follows:—

____

____

____

____

and other objects stated in the memorandum of association of the company.

(f) Delete as appropriate

5 The company is/is not (f)[an insurance undertaking;] [a credit institution;] [an investment undertaking providing services involving the holding of funds or securities for third parties;] or [a collective investment undertaking] referred to in Article 1.2 of the EC Regulation.

(g) Insert name of person swearing affidavit (h) Insert whether main, secondary or territorial proceedings	6 For the reasons stated in the affidavit of (g) ________________ filed in support hereof it is considered that the EC Regulation (f) will/will not apply (f) [and that these proceedings will be (h) ________________ proceedings as defined in Article 3 of the EC Regulation].
(j) Insert full name of partnership against which winding-up petition has been presented to this court	7 The subject of this petition is a member of (j) ________________________________ which has carried on business in England and Wales at some time during the period of (f) [3 years] [1 year] ending with (k) ________________, the day on which a winding-up petition was presented to this court against the partnership.
If the partnership has a principal place of business in both England and Wales and in Scotland the relevant period is 1 year. In any other case it is 3 years. (k) Insert appropriate date (l) State manner of service of demand	8 The partnership is justly and truly indebted to me/us in the aggregate sum of £ ________________. The above-mentioned debt is for a liquidated sum payable immediately. (f) [On (k) ________________ a demand was served upon the company and the partnership by (l) ________________ ________________________________ in respect of the above-mentioned debt. To the best of my knowledge and belief the demand has not been complied with.]
(m) Delete (1) or (2) as appropriate	The partnership (m) [(1) is unable to pay its debts,] [(2) at the time at which a moratorium for the insolvent partnership under section 1A of the Insolvency Act 1986 came to an end, no voluntary arrangement approved under Part I had effect in relation to the insolvent partnership,] and in the circumstances the corporate member should be wound up. The petitioner[s] therefore pray[s] as follows:

(1) that (a) ________________________________
may be wound up by the court under the provisions of the Insolvency Act 1986 as modified by the Insolvent Partnerships Order 1994.

OR

(2) that such other order may be made as the court thinks fit.

NOTE 1:
Petitions are also being presented against the following members of the partnership:

NAME	ADDRESS	TYPE OF PETITION (WINDING-UP OR BANKRUPTCY)	DATE DEMAND SERVED (if applicable)

NOTE 2:
It is intended to serve this petition on (a)

____

____

(n) Delete as applicable

(o) Insert name and address of court

ENDORSEMENT

This petition having been presented to the court
on ______________________________________ will be heard at (n)
[Royal Courts of Justice, Strand, London WC2A 2LL]
[(o) __________________________________ County Court

____

____]

on:

Date ____

Time ____
(or as soon thereafter as the petition can be heard)

The solicitor to the petitioner is:

Name ____

Address ____

____

____

Tel No ____

Reference ____

[whose agents are:

Name ____

Address ____

____

____

Tel No ____

Reference ____]

FORM 7

Creditor's Bankruptcy Petition against Individual Member (Presented in Conjunction with Petition against Partnership)

Schedule 4, para 8
s 124(1)(c)

(a) Insert name of individual member subject of petition	**In the matter of (a)** ______________________________ ______________________________ **and in the matter of the Insolvent Partnerships Order 1994**
(b) Insert title of court and number of proceedings (to be allocated by court)	To (b) ______________________________ ______________ No: ____________ of __________
(c) Insert full name(s) and address(es) of petitioner(s)	I/We (c) ______________________________ ______________________________ ______________________________ ______________________________
(d) Insert full name, place of residence and occupation of individual member	petition the court that a bankruptcy order may be made against (d) ______________________________ ______________________________ ______________________________ ______________________________
(e) Insert in full any other name(s) by which the member is or has been known	[also known as (e) ______________________________ ______________________________]
(f) Insert trading name (adding "with another or others", if this is so), business address and nature of business	[and carrying on business as (f) ______________________________ ______________________________ ______________________________ ______________________________]
(g) Insert any former address(es) at which the member has resided after the time at which the petition debt of the partnership (k) was incurred	[and lately residing at (g) ______________________________ ______________________________ ______________________________ ______________________________]

(h) Give the same details as specified in note (f) above for any other businesses which have been carried on at or after the time at which the petition debt of the partnership (k) was incurred or at which the member may have incurred debts or liabilities still unpaid or unsatisfied	[and lately carrying on business as (h) ____________________ ____ ____]
(j) Delete as appropriate	(j) [His centre of main interests is] [He has an establishment] at ____ **OR** He carries on business as (j) [an insurance undertaking;] [a credit institution;] [an investment undertaking providing services involving the holding of funds or securities for third parties;] or [a collective investment undertaking] referred to in Article 1.2 of the EC Regulation. **OR** His centre of main interests is not within a member State.
(k) Insert full name of partnership against which a winding-up petition has been presented to this court. If the partnership has a principal place of business in both England and Wales and in Scotland the relevant period is 1 year. In any other case it is 3 years.	On the grounds that:— he is a member of (k) ______________________________ which has carried on business in England and Wales at some time during the period of (j) [3 years] [1 year] ending with (l) ________________, the day on which a winding-up petition was presented to this court against the partnership. The partnership is justly and truly indebted to me/us in the aggregate sum of £____________________
(l) Insert appropriate date	The above-mentioned debt is for a liquidated sum payable immediately.

(m) State date and manner of service of demand

(j) [on (1) ________________ a demand was served upon the member and the partnership by (m)

____

____

____

in respect of the above-mentioned debt.]

(j) [To the best of my knowledge and belief the demand has neither been complied with nor set aside in accordance with the Rules and no application made to set it aside is outstanding.]

(n) Delete (1) or (2) as appropriate

The partnership (n)
[(1) is unable to pay its debts,] or
[(2) at the time at which a moratorium for the insolvent partnership under section 1A of the Insolvency Act 1986 came to an end, no voluntary arrangement under Part I had effect in relation to the insolvent partnership,]
and in the circumstances a bankruptcy order should be made against (a)

____

Under the EC Regulation:

(i) The centre of a debtor's main interests should correspond to the place where the debtor conducts the administration of his interests on a regular basis.

(ii) Establishment is defined as "any place of operations where the debtor carries out a non-transitory economic activity with human means and goods".

NOTE 1:
Petitions are also being presented against the following members of the partnership:

NAME	ADDRESS	TYPE OF PETITION (WINDING-UP OR BANKRUPTCY)	DATE DEMAND SERVED (if applicable)

NOTE 2:
It is intended to serve this petition on (a) ________________________________

____

ENDORSEMENT

This petition having been presented to the court on ____________________ it is ordered that the petition shall be heard as follows:

Date ____________________

Time ____________________

Place ____________________

(o) Insert name of member

and you, the above named (o) ____________________ are to take notice that if you intend to oppose the petition you must not later than 7 days before the date fixed for the hearing:

(i) file in court a notice in Form 6.19 of the Insolvency Rules 1986 specifying the grounds on which you object to the making of a bankruptcy order; and

(ii) send a copy of the notice to the petitioner or his solicitor.

(p) Only to be completed where the petitioning creditor is represented by a solicitor

The solicitor to the petitioner is (p):

Name ____________________

Address ____________________

____

____

Tel No ____________________

Reference ____________________

[whose agents are:

Name ____________________

Address ____________________

____

____

____

Tel No ____________________

Reference ____________________]

Appendix 4

4.1 Proposals for voluntary arrangements: introduction

There is no prescribed form for a proposal. The statutory requirement is contained in IR 1986, r 1.3 (CVAs and PVAs) or r 5.3 (IVAs) and is to provide a 'short' explanation as to why a voluntary arrangement is desirable, to give reasons why the creditors may be expected to concur with the arrangement proposed and to provide the information specified, under 17 separate heads.

Many proposals use a formal court heading, particularly in IVA where an interim order is obtained. A formal heading is not necessary, but may be useful in giving the document a more formal look thereby ensuring that it is given due consideration by the recipient creditors. The need to explain the desirability of the proposal can be used, where desirable, to put a more human face on the document and to give a summary of what will for many creditors be a lengthy and potentially indigestible legal document.

Occasionally proposals have to deal with commercially sensitive matters. This should be recognised by whoever drafts the proposal document, and it may be advisable in particular cases to refer to documents in the proposal which will be shown to individual creditors only in defined circumstances.

Of particular importance is that the proposal spells out precisely the terms of the composition or scheme of arrangement as the case may be. While in many cases it may readily be inferred that, for example, the dividend to be paid to creditors is in full and final settlement of all debts due as at the date of the arrangement taking effect this is not an aspect of the proposal that should be left to implication. There should be a section in the proposal which clearly sets out the terms as they affect the creditors' debts, so that a creditor reading the proposal should be in no doubt how the proposal, if it is approved, will affect his rights to enforce his debt against the debtor.

The 17 heads of information which have to be 'stated or otherwise dealt with in the proposal' (IR 1986, rr 1.3(2), 5.3(2)) can plainly be dealt with in any way the person drafting the document prefers. Many proposal documents have been drawn so as to group these heads of matter in what is considered to be a more convenient way than the order in which these heads appear in the Rules. It is imperative, however, that all these matters are dealt with, and proceeding (albeit laboriously) through the list in the order they appear in the Rule does have the advantage that it is readily apparent when all the particular matters have been dealt with. The most likely matter to be overlooked is the one which may be totally irrelevant to the proposal in point, but it must still be covered. Time is often very pressing. The debtor does not need his proposal returned because an assiduous clerk in the court office has spotted the (immaterial) omission, or to encounter problems because a difficult minor creditor takes issue with propriety of the document.

It is also important to remember that whatever the precise duties as to good faith there may be on those proposing a voluntary arrangement creditors are unlikely to vote in favour of a proposal where they have the feeling that they have not been given a complete and fair picture of the debtor's affairs. Consideration should therefore be given to providing general information (disclosure) about the debtor. This is conveniently done in an appendix with relevant documents referred to available for inspection.

The proposal may contain all the terms and conditions to which the approved arrangement will be subject. Many practitioners however rely on standard conditions covering what might be considered to be the technical aspects of the arrangement. These conditions are provided to the creditors in a separate document. This has the great advantage of keeping the proposal document down to more manageable proportions. There will be firms of Insolvency Practitioners and Solicitors who will prefer to keep to their own standard conditions. For everyone else there are the Standard Conditions produced by the Association of Business Recovery Professionals ('R3'). At present these conditions only cover IVAs. R3 anticipate producing Standard Conditions for CVAs in the course of Summer 2003. They will be available on the R3 website at www.r3.org.uk. It seems sensible to make use of these conditions, modifying or adding individual terms as may be considered appropriate in particular cases.

Four examples of proposals are offered below:

Appendix 4.2CVA –Peterson Plastics Limited	Various schemes of arrangement by traders
Appendix 4.3PVA – Classic Conservatories	
Appendix 4.4IVA – Vincent Tapping	
Appendix 4.5IVA – Barry Baldrick	A composition by a non-trader

Appendix 4.6 comprises various miscellaneous terms which might be useful for a debtor preparing a proposal or a creditor seeking to introduce modifications to an existing proposal.

Appendix 4.7 contains a brief commentary on the R3 Standard Conditions.

Appendix 4.8 sets out the standard modifications regularly proposed by VAS.

Appendix 4.9 contains proposed standard conditions for 'omitted' creditors.

Appendix 4.10 comprises the R3 Standard Conditions.

4.2 Proposal by directors for a Company Voluntary Arrangement

PETERSON PLASTICS LIMITED

PROPOSAL BY THE DIRECTORS FOR A VOLUNTARY ARRANGEMENT

BASIS OF PROPOSAL

The Company's core business, that of plastic extrusion moulding of household goods, has for over 10 years been and remains a strong viable business. Unfortunately the Company's attempt to expand its area of operations into the manufacture of plastic childrens' toys has resulted in heavy trading losses. A detailed assessment of the Company's prospects in the toy market has concluded that there is no realistic prospect that future trading will prosper. The Company sees no alternative but to abandon this venture and concentrate on its core business. This course will involve closure and redundancy costs. The Company has found new shareholders willing to invest in its business but only if the Company's creditors are prepared to compromise existing claims in accordance with these proposals. The Company's bankers, who have a debenture over all the Company's undertaking property and assets, are willing to support these proposals provided new capital is made available to support the Company's continuing operations. The Company's bankers have refused to extend the facilities currently available to the Company. At the present time the Company is unable to pay all its debts as they fall due. Accordingly, if these proposals do not prove acceptable to creditors the directors will have to cease trading and put the Company into insolvent liquidation.

The proposals involve:

- A moratorium for a period not exceeding 12 months on repayment of all debts due as at the date of this proposal.
- An issue of new share capital, fully paid, in the sum of £400,000.
- A strengthened management team.
- The closure and sale of the Company's factory at Saxon Trading Estate, Milton Keynes.
- The moratorium creditors to receive the net proceeds of sale of the factory and £200,000 from the new share capital in settlement of the moratorium debts.

The proposal should be attractive to creditors for two reasons.

First, the proposals offer the prospect of a dividend of about 55p in the £. Were the Company now to be placed in liquidation the creditors could expect a dividend of no more than 30p in the £.

Second, the Company has demonstrated over the years that it has a sound core business. Most of the creditors are long-term trading partners of the Company in connection with this business. If the Company survives there will be opportunities for further business with the Company. Creditors whose liabilities arise after the date of this proposal will be paid in the ordinary course of business after the termination of the moratorium which the directors have obtained under the provisions of the Insolvency Act 1986, Schedule A1.

The nominee for this proposal is John Smith of Harcourt House, King Street, Hertford HE 5 7IP. As nominee he will convene meetings of the creditors and of the company pursuant to the Insolvency Rules 1986 to consider this proposal.

STATEMENT OF PROPOSAL BY THE DIRECTORS

Definitions

The following definitions apply throughout this proposal unless the context otherwise requires:

'the Company'	Peterson Plastics Limited, registered in England no. ... whose registered office is at *(address).*
'the Moratorium Debts'	All actual and any contingent liabilities of the Company outstanding on the date of this proposal other than (1) liabilities to the Company's Bankers (Lloyds TSB Bank plc) or (2) preferential debts (as defined by the Insolvency Act 1986, s 386) or (3) liabilities to the extent they are secured (as defined by the Insolvency Act 1986, s 248).
'the Moratorium Creditors'	The creditors holding Moratorium Debts.
'the New Shareholders'	The persons named in Appendix 1.
'the Nominee'	John Smith of Harcourt House, King Street, Hertford HE5 7IP.
'the New Shares'	The 400,000 ordinary shares of £1 each in the Company now proposed to be issued to and subscribed for by the New Shareholders.
'the Supervisor'	The Nominee or such other person as the statutory meetings may elect.
'the Toy Factory Premises'	The Company's factory at Saxon Trading Estate, Milton Keynes MK3 4TP and all fixtures and fixed plant and machinery situated there at the date of this proposal.

The Terms of the Proposed Voluntary Arrangement

1. The Company will within 14 days of the approval of the arrangement issue and allot the New Shares to the New Shareholders in the proportions set out in Appendix 1 on terms that the shares are fully paid at par within 14 days of allotment. The allotment to be made as if the Companies Act 1985, s 89(1) did not apply to the allotment.
2. The Company will forthwith on receipt of the total consideration for the New Shares pay the sum of £200,000 to the Supervisor. The Company will retain the balance of £200,000 as working capital.
3. The Supervisor will as soon as practicable appoint one or more agents as he may be advised to market and sell the Toy Factory Premises.

4. The Company will cease the manufcature of toys and will undertake all steps reasonably required of it by the Supervisor to facilitate the sale of the Toy Factory Premises.
5. The Company's bankers have a debenture over all its undertaking property and assets. They have agreed to permit the sale of the Toy Factory Premises if the arrangement is approved by the Moratorium creditors, on condition that £200,000 additional working capital is injected into the Company. A copy of a letter dated *(date)* from the company's bankers agreeing to the above is annexed hereto as appendix 3.
6. The Company acting by the Supervisor will sell the Toy Factory Premises for the best price reasonably obtainable. The Supervisor may for this purpose incur the reasonable fees of a surveyor and a conveyancing solicitor in addition to selling agents' fees.
7. The Moratorium Creditors are to grant the Company a moratorium for an initial period not exceeding 12 months during which time the Company, acting by the Supervisor, will market and sell the Toy Factory Premises. During the period of the moratorium, each Moratorium Creditor undertakes in respect of any Moratorium Debt not to present any petition for the winding up of the Company, commence or continue any proceedings, execution or other legal process nor levy distress against the Company, or take any step to enforce any security over the Company's property or repossess any goods in the Company's possession under any hire-purchase agreement.
8. If the Supervisor is unable, despite all reasonable endeavours, to sell the Toy Factory Premises within 12 months of the approval of the arrangement he may ask the Moratorium Creditors to extend the Moratorium.
9. Subject to any extension agreed by the Moratorium Creditors, the moratorium will end on *(date)* or, if earlier, 42 days after completion of the sale of the Toy Factory Premises.
10. The sum of £200,000 to be paid to the Supervisor from the consideration received for the New Shares together with the net proceeds of sale of the Toy Factory Premises will be distributed by way of pro rata dividend to the Moratorium Creditors who agree to accept such dividends in full and final settlement of their respective Moratorium Debts. The management of the Company is to be reorganised by the resignation of *(names)* from the board of directors and the appointment of *(name)* as marketing director and *(name)* as non-executive director.
11. The full terms of the voluntary arrangement will comprise this proposal together with the standard conditions of company voluntary arrangement annexed in appendix 4 hereto, subject to such modifications, if any, as the creditors may approve in the creditors' meeting and to which the company shall agree.

STATUTORY AND OTHER MATERIAL INFORMATION

(pursuant to the Insolvency Rules 1986, rule 1.3)

Statement of Responsibility

The present directors of the Company, whose names are listed below, are responsible for the information contained in this document. To the best of the knowledge and belief of the directors the information contained in this proposal is full, true and accurate.

Directors : *(list directors and give their position; eg Chairman, Managing Director, Finance Director, Non-executive director, Secretary)*

1. Assets of the Company

The assets of the Company as at *(date)* were as follows:

Assets	*Estimated value (going concern)*	*Estimated value (forced sale)*
The Toy Factory premises	...	...
Other Freehold property	...	...
(Freehold) premises in Spain	...	...
Leasehold premises	...	...
Plant and machinery	...	...
Stock in own warehouse	...	...
Stock in distributors' warehouse	...	...
Stock in Spain	...	...
Debtors	...	...
Shares	...	...
Misc other	...	...

The assets included in the proposed voluntary arrangement are the Toy Factory Premises and £200,000 from the proposed issue of New Shares. All other assets are to be excluded from the arrangement. All the assets listed above are subject to existing charges to the Company's bankers, but, as stated above, the Company's bankers have agreed to permit the sale of the Toy Factory Premises and the distribution of the proceeds of sale to the Moratorium Creditors.

2. Property not belonging to the Company to be included in the arrangement

No property not belonging to the Company is proposed to be included in the arrangement.

3. Liabilities of the Company

The liabilities of the Company as at *(date)* were as follows:

Nature of liability	Amount	Preferential or Secured	Name of guarantor (if any)
VAT	£...	Up to £... preferential[1]	–
PAYE	£...	all preferential[1]	–

1 Note that on the coming into force of s 251 of the Enterprise Act 2002 Crown debts will no longer be preferential.

Wages	£...	all preferential	–
Bank	£...	secured on assets	Mr Philip Peterson
Trade creditors	£...	–	–
Claim by former Sales representative	£...	*(this claim is contested)*	

Under the proposal, £... of the above liabilities will be Moratorium Debts. Preferential creditors will continue to be paid in the ordinary course of business. The secured creditors will retain their security, save for the Company's bankers who have agreed to waive their security over the Toy Factory Premises.

To the knowledge of the directors, in the event that the Company goes into liquidation there are no circumstances which would justify a claim under any of the following sections of the Insolvency Act 1986:
Section 238 (transactions at an undervalue)
Section 239 (preferences)
Section 244 (extortionate credit transactions)
Section 245 (floating charges invalid)

4. Guarantees of the Company's debts

Apart from the liabilities to the Company's bankers which are guaranteed by Mr.Philip Peterson subject to a limit of £350,000 including interest, no liabilities of the Company are guaranteed.

5. Duration of voluntary arrangement

The arrangement will continue until the final distribution is made following the completion of the sale of the Toy Factory Premises. If this does not occur within 12 months of the date of this proposal the arrangement will terminate unless continued by the Moratorium Creditors.

6. Proposed distributions to Moratorium Creditors

An interim dividend is proposed from the proceeds of the allotment of the New Shares on *(date)* estimated to be ...p in the £. A final distribution will be made within 28 days of the completion of the sale of the Toy Factory Premises, the amount of which is estimated to be ...p in the £.[2]

7. Creditors bound without notice

Should the existence of any creditor bound to the arrangement by reason of the fact that he would have been entitled in accordance with the rules to vote at the

2 For commercial reasons this dividend will have to be calculated by reference to the asking price of the Toy Factory Premises, whatever views may be held privately as to the need to accept a lower price, provided always that the asking price is not wholly unrealistic.

creditors' meeting had he had notice of it ('an omitted creditor') come to the attention of the Supervisor before the arrangement has been fully implemented it is proposed that the omitted creditor should be admitted to the arrangement, as soon as may be practicable, on the same terms and with the same benefits as he would have been subject to and enjoyed had he had notice of the meeting. If by the time of his admission to the arrangement the Supervisor has paid the interim dividend an equivalent dividend shall be paid to the omitted creditor before payment is made of the final dividend.

In the event that the total value of any debts or liabilities owed by the Company to one or more omitted creditors amount to more than [10%] of the value of the debts and liabilities disclosed by the Company by the date of the creditors' meeting, the existing creditors will be given the opportunity to terminate the arrangement prematurely.

8. The Nominee's remuneration and expenses

The Nominee is nominee for the arrangement. The Company has agreed to pay a fee of £2,500 plus VAT for acting as nominee. All expenses incurred by the Nominee in connection with the voluntary arrangement will be paid out of the assets of the Company. The Company has deposited with the Nominee the sum of £ ... generally on account of his fee and expenses.

9. The Supervisor's remuneration and expenses

The Nominee is nominated to act as Supervisor. The Supervisor is to be paid a fee calculated monthly at the hourly charging out rate from time to time used by his firm, together with out of pocket expenses. The fee will be payable from the assets of the arrangement. All expenses incurred by the Supervisor in connection with the arrangement will be paid out of the assets of the Company.

10. Guarantees for the purpose of the arrangement

No guarantees are offered by the Company's directors for the purposes of the arrangement.

11. Banking of arrangement funds

Pending distribution to creditors the Supervisor will deposit arrangement funds in a specified interest bearing account with a reputable bank. The Supervisor will be responsible for selecting the account which pays the best rate of interest reasonably obtainable for the purpose.

12. Funds held on termination of arrangement

All funds received under the terms of the arrangement will be distributed to the Moratorium Creditors. Any funds remaining unclaimed after the expiry of the period of 12 months following the termination of the arrangement will be distributed to the remaining creditors.

13. Management of the business

The names of the present directors and secretary of the Company and the positions which they hold are set out above. If the directors' proposals are approved, the directors propose to appoint *(name)* as marketing director and *(name)* as non-executive director of the Company. Both have confirmed that they will accept appointment to the board. *(Names)* have tendered their resignation as directors. During the course of the arrangement it is proposed that the business of the Company be conducted under the control of its new board. The Supervisor will perform the functions set out in paragraph 15 below. The board of directors will delegate the entire responsibility for the marketing and sale of the Toy Factory Premises to the Supervisor, and will render all necessary assistance required by him to ensure the effective marketing and most advantageous sale of the Toy Factory Premises.

14. Further credit facilities

There are no present plans to arrange further credit facilities for the Company. The Company's bankers have agreed to continue the Company's current facilities at least for the period of the arrangement.

15. The functions to be undertaken by the supervisor

The functions of the Supervisor will be to:

1. Take possession of the Toy Factory Premises, instruct agents as appropriate and supervise the sale of the Toy Factory Premises, including the fixtures plant and machinery and the collection of the proceeds of sale.
2. Take possession of the sum of £200,000 from the proceeds of the New Shares.
3. Ascertain the creditors owed the Moratorium Debts and the amount of such Debts owed to each creditor.
4. Hold the sums which are to be distributed in a specified interest bearing account pending distribution.
5. Calculate and distribute the interim and final dividends to the Moratorium Creditors.
6. Undertake all such further acts and matters as may be necessary to give effect to the terms of the arrangement.

The Supervisor will not be concerned in the management of the business of the Company.

16. Name, address and qualification of supervisor

The proposed supervisor is the Nominee, John Smith of Harcourt House, King Street, Hertford HE5 7IP. John Smith is a fellow of the Institute of Chartered Accountants in England and Wales and the Insolvency Partner of Smith & Stringer, accountants of the above address. He has confirmed to the directors that he is qualified under the Insolvency Act 1986 to act as nominee and supervisor in relation to the Company.

17. EC Regulation

The EC Regulation applies in that the Company have a distribution centre which may constitute an establishment (for the purposes of the EC Regulation) in Seville, Spain. The company has its main centre of interests in England. These proceedings will be main proceedings.

Further information

Details of certain material contracts, litigation, director's interests in the Company and other matters which creditors and shareholders may consider material are set out in Appendix 2. The Company currently has ... employees. If the proposal is implemented the workforce will be reduced to ... employees. The directors estimate that the losses of the Company in the year to *(date)* will be not less than £... After that the Company should return to profitability. Audited accounts for the year to *(date)* will be filed at Companies House not later than *(date)*. No dividends will be paid in respect of the financial year just past and this financial year.

(signed)

Philip Peterson : Chairman

Paul Watson : Finance Director and Secretary

[*date*]

APPENDIX 1 : THE NEW SHAREHOLDERS

1.	Name	Number of shares
2.	Name	Number of shares
3.	Name	Number of shares

APPENDIX 2 : GENERAL INFORMATION REGARDING THE COMPANY

Share capital: ...

The business: ...

Directors' interests: ...

Directors' service agreements: ...

Litigation: The Company is the defendant in an action brought by *(name)* relating to his claim for commissions due as a sales representative. He is seeking damages in the sum of £... The claim has been denied. Counsel has advised that in his opinion the claim is ill-founded and will fail. The company is not involved in any other litigation or arbitration and no claim has been notified to the Company or its solicitors.

Material contracts : ...	
Consents :	[The Company's auditors *(name)* have given and have not withdrawn their written consent to the issue of this document with their name included in the form and context in which it appears.]
Documents for inspection :	Copies of the following documents will be available for inspection at the offices of the Company's solicitor *(name and address)* during normal business hours on 24 hours' notice until the proposal is approved or lapses: (1) the memorandum and articles of the company, (2) the audited accounts of the Company for the last 3 financial years, (3) the consents and material contracts referred to above.

APPENDIX 3 : LETTER FROM COMPANY'S BANKERS

Letter dated *(date)* from the Company's bankers agreeing to the sale of the Toy Factory Premises free of all charges, and the distribution of the proceeds of sale to the Moratorium Creditors.

APPENDIX 4 : STANDARD CONDITIONS FOR COMPANY VOLUNTARY ARRANGEMENT

4.3 Proposal for Partnership Voluntary Arrangement

IN THE HIGH COURT OF JUSTICE
COMPANIES COURT

IN THE MATTER OF AB, CD, and EF
trading as CLASSIC CONSERVATORIES

AND IN THE MATTER OF THE INSOLVENCY ACT 1986
AND IN THE MATTER OF THE INSOLVENT PARTNERSHIPS ORDER 1994

PROPOSAL FOR A PARTNERSHIP VOLUNTARY ARRANGEMENT

1. Background to proposal

The partnership Classic Conservatories was formed in 1988 by AB and CD. Both these partners had some five years' experience of selling conservatories made by one of the leading manufacturers in the field, Betta Bryta Build plc. When this company decided to make its salesforce redundant AB and CD entered into an agency agreement to sell Betta Bryta conservatories in the south-west of England. In 1992 EF joined the partnership. EF is a skilled joiner and glazier and was able to customise conservatories where individual customers or planning authorities required adaptations to standard Betta Bryta models. The business traded successfully until last year. Classic Conservatories had secured two substantial contracts for Georgian Estates (Wessex) plc to build conservatories for some 30 new high value properties. The terms of the agreement with Georgian Estate (Wessex) plc gave credit terms to this company which the partners now appreciate were too favourable. In August last year Georgian Estates (Wessex) plc went into creditors' voluntary liquidation leaving the partnership with substantial cash flow problems. The partnership was unable to pay sums due to Betta Bryta Build plc, as a result of which all credit facilities were withdrawn and Betta Bryta Build plc declined to deliver further supplies. Classic Conservatories obtained alternative supplies from New England Conservatories Ltd, but although this supplier produces excellent product delivery is often late. This has resulted in reduced payments and claims from customers. Despite every effort by the partners to remain solvent it has not been possible to avoid the financial difficulties in which the partnership finds itself at present. The partners still have a substantial order book and are confident that provided the immediate difficulties can be surmounted the business will return to long term profitability.

2. Desirability of a partnership voluntary arrangement

It is expected that this proposal will yield appreciably more for creditors than a winding up of the partnership and/or the bankruptcy of the partners. The partners believe this for the following reasons:

(a) The partnership's business has a strong profile in the high value end of the market. The goodwill is the principal asset of the partnership. On a winding up it is likely that the remaining assets of the partnership will realise little on a forced sale. The goodwill of the partnership depends on the continued involvement of the partners.

(b) The partners have little by way of personal assets remaining uncharged to the partnership's bankers.

(c) Under the terms of the proposal it is anticipated that preferential creditors will receive 100p in the £ and that unsecured creditors will receive a dividend of approximately 30p in the £. In the event of a winding up of the partnership and/or the bankruptcy of the partners the unsecured creditors will at best receive a dividend of about 10p in the £.

(d) It is likely that the fees and expenses of a supervisor would be less than those which would be charged if the equivalent assets were administered in a winding up of the partnership or the bankruptcy of the partners.

3. The Proposal

The partners propose that the partnership will pay sums amounting to a total of some £xx to the Supervisor for distribution among the creditors. This total sum will be made up of two components. First, the partnership has an admitted claim in the winding-up of Georgian Estates (Wessex) plc which the liquidator has estimated is worth £20,000 on a dividend of 15p in the £. Secondly, the partnership proposes to make monthly payments to the Supervisor out of the profits of continued trading as set out below:

Year 1 £x per month	=	£12x
Year 2 £xy per month	=	£12xy
Year 3 £xy per month	=	£12xy
Year 4 £xx per month	=	£12xx
Year 5 £xxx per month	=	£12xxx
Total		£xxxx

These payments will be financed in part by a staff redundancy in the office, and in part by lower drawings by all the partners. The administrative work will now be undertaken by Mrs AB and Mrs CD who both have office experience. The payments will commence one month after the chairman's report to the court following any approval of the proposal by the creditors.

The supervisor will distribute the sums received by him by way of five annual payments of dividend to the creditors. The creditors will accept these dividends in full and final satisfaction of their claims against the partnership or the partners individually. The creditors will release the partnership and the partners from any claims for interest which they may have against them such that no interest will be claimed from the date of the meeting of creditors at which any resolution approving this proposal (with or without modifications) is passed.

No proceedings, execution, distress or other process shall be commenced or continued by any creditor against the partners or the partnership in relation to any debt or liability existing at the date of approval of the PVA.

4. The Nominee

The nominee is Mr IP, a chartered accountant and licensed insolvency practitioner and a partner in the firm of IP & Co. Mr IP has confirmed to the partners, and it is their belief, that he is qualified to act in relation to this proposal. The Nominee's fees are £1,500 plus VAT. These have been paid by the partnership.

5. The Supervisor

It is proposed that the Nominee will act as supervisor of the proposed PVA.

6. Information required by the Insolvency Rules not provided above

6.1 Details of the partnership's assets together with an estimate of their respective values appear from the statement of affairs annexed hereto (Appendix 1). The statement of affairs reflects the financial position of the partnership as at *(date – within two months).* The partnership's freehold premises at The Mayor's Trading Estate, Casterbridge are charged to the partnership's bankers. The valuation annexed hereto (Appendix 3) from Freethwaite & Co indicates that there is no equity in the premises. None of the remaining assets of the partnership is subject to any charge.

6.2 The only property which it is proposed should be included in the PVA is the partnership's claim the subject of its proof of debt in the liquidation of Georgian Estates (Wessex) plc. All partnership assets are excluded as they are required for the continuation of the partnership business.

6.3 The nature and amount of the partnership's liabilities (so far as they are within the knowledge of the partners) appear from the statement of affairs annexed hereto. Also annexed hereto (Appendix 2) is a list of the names and addresses of the creditors of the partnership together with details of the sums estimated to be due to each of them. No creditor is a person connected with the partnership by reason of being an associate of the partners or any of them.

6.4 It is proposed that preferential creditors be paid in full.

6.5 To the best of the partners' knowledge and belief there are no circumstances which would, in the event of the winding up of the partnership, give rise to any claims under the Insolvency Act 1986, section 238 (transactions at an undervalue), section 239 (preferences), section 244 (extortionate credit transactions), or section 245 (invalid floating charges)

6.6 No guarantees have been given in respect of the partnership's debts by any other persons. No guarantees are to be given or offered by the partners or any other person in connection with this PVA.

6.7 The duration of the PVA shall be 63 months from the date of the chairman's report to the court following approval at the meeting of creditors herein, three months being allowed for the supervisor properly and fully to implement the terms of the PVA after the last of the monthly payments has been made by the partnership.

6.8 It is proposed that (subject to agreement of creditors' claims) dividends be paid annually on the anniversary of the date of the chairman's report to the court following approval of the PVA or as soon thereafter as may be practicable.

6.9 Should the existence of any creditor bound to the arrangement by reason of the fact that he would have been entitled in accordance with the rules to vote at the creditors' meeting had he had notice of it ('an omitted creditor') come to the attention of the supervisor before the arrangement has been fully implemented it is proposed that the omitted creditor should be admitted to the arrangement, as soon as may be practicable, on the same terms and with the same benefits as he would have been subject to and enjoyed had he had notice of the meeting. If by the time of his admission to the arrangement any dividends have been received by other creditors equivalent dividends shall be paid to the omitted creditor on his admission before any further dividends are received by the existing creditors bound to the arrangement.

In the event that the value of any debts or liabilities owed by the partnership to one or more omitted creditors amounts to more than [10%] of the value of the debts and liabilities disclosed by the partners at the creditors' meeting the existing creditors will be given the opportunity to terminate the arrangement prematurely.

6.10 The supervisor's fees shall be calculated on a time cost basis in accordance with the charges usually made by his firm. These fees shall rank as a first charge on any funds paid into the PVA such that they shall be paid before any dividends are distributed to creditors. Any expenses incurred by the supervisor will be paid by the partnership.

6.11 Pending distribution to creditors, the supervisor shall pay any sums received into an interest bearing deposit account held in a UK clearing bank of his choice. Any funds remaining unclaimed on termination of this proposal will be distributed to the remaining creditors who have proved.

6.12 During the course of the arrangement the partnership business will be conducted by the partners as it has been to date with the partners alone being responsible for its trading and its affairs. The supervisor will monitor the financial performance of the partnership for which purpose the partners will make available to him such books and records as he requires them to produce for such purpose. The partners will not extend credit facilities to any customer beyond 30 days without first consulting the supervisor.

6.13 It is not intended that any further credit facilities will be arranged for the partnership in connection with this PVA. The partnership intends to rely on normal credit arrangements for the purpose of its continuing to trade in order to meet its obligations under the terms of its PVA.

6.14 The supervisor's functions shall be:

6.14.1 to investigate and agree creditors' claims for the purposes of dividend to the extent that the admission of any claim for the purpose of voting may require review in this connection; to investigate and agree the claim of any omitted creditor.

6.14.2 to maintain the partnership's claim and proof of debt in the liquidation of Georgian Estates (Wessex) plc, and to collect and invest such dividends as are paid in the liquidation;

6.14.3 to collect and invest the instalments to be made by the partnership as provided above;

6.14.4 to make distributions to creditors in accordance with the priorities provided for under the terms of the PVA and in accordance with law;

6.14.5 to monitor the financial performance of the partnership and to give advice as may be required as provided above;

6.14.6 to present a petition for the winding up of the partnership in the event of the partnership's failure to comply with its obligations under the terms hereof or to cooperate with him in his administration of the PVA;

6.14.7 to do all such things as may be necessary to give effect to the terms of the PVA.

6.15 The supervisor shall retain at all times sufficient funds to enable him to petition for the compulsory winding up of the partnership in the event of any default by the partnership in the performance of any of its obligations under the terms of the PVA, subject to the approval of the creditors.

6.16 The EC Regulation applies to this arrangement. The partnership's centre of main interest is in England. The partnership carries on no trading outside the UK. These proceedings are main proceedings as defined in Article 3 of the EC Regulation.

7. Committee of creditors

7.1 The creditors may resolve at any meeting of creditors to appoint a committee of creditors to assist and advise the supervisor.

7.2 The committee of creditors shall consist of no less than three and no more than five creditors whose claims have been allowed in whole or in part for the purpose of voting and dividend, or a representative of any such creditor.

7.3 The committee of creditors shall be entitled to fix the supervisor's remuneration.

7.4 The provisions of rules 4.152 to 4.170 (except rules 4.154 and 4.164) of the Insolvency Rules 1986 shall apply to the membership and functions of the committee of creditors, substituting as necessary therein 'supervisor' for 'liquidator', 'partnership voluntary arrangement' for 'liquidation' and 'committee of creditors' for 'liquidation committee' and with such modifications as may be necessary to give proper effect to the rules for the purpose of a PVA.

8. Completion of the PVA

The PVA shall be completed when the partnership has performed its obligations in full and the supervisor has done all that is necessary to perform his functions thereunder.

9. Terms of the arrangement

The arrangement shall comprise this proposal and the standard conditions of arrangement set forth in Appendix 4 hereto. In the event of inconsistency the provisions of this proposal shall prevail.

10. Warranty

Messrs AB, CD and EF warrant to the supervisor and to the creditors that a resolution has been passed by the partnership that the partnership should propose a PVA to its creditors in the foregoing terms and that nothing in the partnership deed of the partnership or in any other agreement made between the partners and one another or any other person prevents the partnership from proposing a PVA in the foregoing or any other terms.

Dated

Signed [AB] [CD][EF]

APPENDIX 1 :	Statement of affairs of the Partnership and each partner.
APPENDIX 2 :	List of all creditors of the partnership together with their addresses and details of the sum or sums owed to each of them.
APPENDIX 3 :	Freethwaite & Co valuation.
APPENDIX 4 :	Standard Conditions of Arrangement.

4.4 Proposal by Debtor (trader) for Individual Voluntary Arrangement

IN THE HIGH COURT OF JUSTICE

IN BANKRUPTCY

IN THE MATTER OF VINCENT TAPPING

AND IN THE MATTER OF THE INSOLVENCY ACT 1986

PROPOSAL FOR AN INDIVIDUAL VOLUNTARY ARRANGEMENT

I, VINCENT TAPPING of 23 Acacia Avenue, London SW11 make this proposal for the purposes of Part VIII of the Insolvency Act 1986 and the Insolvency Rules 1986.

As appears from the statement of affairs annexed to this proposal as Appendix 1 it is clear that I am insolvent. I am unable to pay my debts as they fall due and my liabilities, including prospective and contingent liabilities, exceed my present and prospective assets. I am in a position to petition for my own bankruptcy, but I seek a voluntary arrangement with my creditors. I believe that my creditors may be expected to approve my proposed arrangement because it will secure them a higher dividend than that they would receive if I became bankrupt.

Relevant history

I am married with two children aged 5 and 3. In 1980 I left school and undertook a 3 year apprentice as a car mechanic and body work repairer with Sanders Supercars plc. Having completed my apprenticeship I worked for the company for three years. I then formed a partnership with a cousin to trade as motor repairers in the Wimbledon area. The business was successful and we took on two employees. I came to specialise in older and rarer cars. In 1990 my cousin emigrated to Australia and I continued the business on my own. In 1992 I began dealing in older cars and opened a small showroom staffed by two employees. In 1994 I was offered work by D Direct Insurance Company plc repairing cars which had been involved in accidents. This resulted in a substantial increase in the volume of work and I expanded the business, taking on five further employees and moving my premises to the South Battersea Park Trading Estate. However, during the past few years D Direct Insurance Company plc has put increasing pressure on me to reduce my repair charges for this accident work. It has become increasingly uneconomic. At the beginning of this year D Direct Insurance Company plc refused to renew my annual contract with them except at prices for work which will not cover the costs. I refused to renew and had to make five employees redundant. At the same time a substantial creditor for my old cars, King's Cross Films plc, went into administrative receivership and insolvent liquidation without paying several instalments amounting to £180,000 due under an agreement for the sale of ten American cars of the 1930s era worth £350,000. I believe I have a valid retention of title clause in this contract but this is being disputed by the Administrative Receivers who have in fact (wrongly) disposed of the cars. I do not have enough private work coming in to meet my overheads and redundancy costs. Hence my present predicament. I believe that I can rebuild my private customer work and return to profitability provided I am able to continue trading. This will enable me to pay a better dividend to my unsecured ordinary creditors than would be payable in the event of my bankruptcy.

On *(date)* I was served with a bankruptcy petition by HM Customs and Excise in respect of unpaid VAT. Since then I have made some five payments totalling £2,000 to the petitioning creditor who has agreed to adjourn the petition hearing due to be heard on *(date)* in order that my proposal for an individual voluntary arrangement can be considered by my creditors. I have been advised that these payments could, in the event of my bankruptcy, be construed as voidable transactions. However, this is not certain and, indeed, the offer I am willing to make to my creditors is greater than they would receive, even if the voidable transaction were reversed.

My accountant has had discussions with both HM Customs and Excise and the Inland Revenue and has sent them draft accounts for all outstanding accounting periods. My financial affairs will be brought completely up to date over the next three months and I will continue to meet my future tax liabilities as and when they fall due throughout the period of the arrangement.

The terms of the proposed voluntary arrangement[1]

1. Vincent Tapping ('the Debtor') will continue to trade and make voluntary contributions of £400 per month over the next four years (total contributions of £19,200). The first contribution will be made 28 days after approval of this voluntary arrangement.
2. The Debtor's father in law, Dr Robert Black, will contribute the sum of £20,000 to the arrangement to be paid in full within 42 days of the approval of this voluntary arrangement. This sum represents the highest figure which has been put on the Debtor's share of the equity of the matrimonial home by Sich, Mole and Freedman, estate agents and valuers of Putney whose valuation report is annexed to this proposal as Appendix 4.
3 The Debtor will, if requested to do so, assign his cause of action against the Administrative Receivers of King's Cross Films plc for wrongful interference with the ten American cars referred to above. Further or alternatively the Debtor will contribute to the arrangement such sum as he may receive by way of dividend in the liquidation of King's Cross Films plc.
4. The Debtor will contribute to the arrangement anything which he may receive during the period of arrangement by way of legacy, gift, windfall or any other such benefit, limited to such sum as will produce for the creditors a dividend of 100p in the £.
5. The supervisor of the voluntary arrangement will hold all sums paid for the purposes of the arrangement as trustee. He will make annual distributions pro rata to all creditors whose claims have been admitted of all such sums as he holds on behalf of the arrangement at the time the distribution is made, save that he shall retain sufficient sums to enable him

1 Although this proposal uses the first person singular for the history and the provision of information, the Terms of the arrangement are more formally drawn. It may be preferred to use the third person throughout.

to petition for the Debtor's bankruptcy and to ensure that he is able properly to perform his obligations as supervisor.

6. Every creditor of the Debtor as at the date on which the voluntary arrangement is approved, whatever the nature of the debt or liability owed to him, shall accept the distributions made by the Supervisor in full and final settlement of the entirety of his claim or claims against the Debtor provided that the arrangement does not terminate prematurely.
7. During the currency of the arrangement each creditor bound thereto agrees not to present any petition for the bankruptcy of the Debtor, nor commence or continue any proceedings, execution or other legal process against the Debtor.

Information required by the Insolvency Rules

1. Assets

A summary of my assets appears from my statement of affairs which is annexed to this proposal at appendix 1. I presently live with my wife and children at 23 Acacia Avenue London SW11. The property is in the joint beneficial ownership of myself and my wife. It is mortgaged to the Runcorn Building Society and the sum of £145,000 is presently outstanding on this mortgage. I have had a valuation carried out by local valuers Sich, Mole and Freedman. They have valued the property at £175,000 to £185,000 on a sale by private treaty. In order to save the family home for his daughter and grand-children my father-in-law is prepared to pay the full amount of my equity to the supervisor for the benefit of the arrangement.

I ask that my household furniture, which is jointly owned with my wife and which is necessary for my domestic needs, be excluded from the proposal. I understand that if I were subject to a bankruptcy order that such items would be protected by the Insolvency Act 1986, s 283(2).

My business premises are leasehold and are charged to the bank. There is no equity in these premises. I also ask that the Ford motor car, Bedford pick-up truck and stock referred to in my statement of affairs and which I use for my business be excluded. Finally, I have a life policy which I wish to continue. It has a current surrender value of £2,500. The contributions I am offering my creditors have been calculated to cover the surrender value of the policy, so this is also to be excluded.

2. Property to be included in arrangement from third parties

My father-in-law is a retired consultant surgeon and medical practitioner. He has offered £20,000 from his savings to compensate creditors for the exclusion of the matrimonial home from the arrangement. The money is offered without conditions other than that the proposal is approved by creditors, and will be paid within 42 days of the approval of this arrangement.

3. Liabilities

My liabilities appear from the statement of affairs, Appendix 1. The preferential creditors, Inland Revenue and HM Customs and Excise[2] will be paid in full but

2 Note that on the coming into force of s 251 of the Enterprise Act 2002 the Crown will cease to be a preferential creditor.

they have agreed to defer payment of their claim in accordance with the letter from the Voluntary Arrangements Service *(dated)* a copy of which is annexed to this proposal.

I have one creditor who is an associate. My brother Stephen lent me the sum of £1,000 to pay wages on *(date)*. He has agreed to accept the same dividend as is received by other creditors but postponed to the end of the arrangement.

To the best of my knowledge and belief there are no circumstances which would, in the event of my bankruptcy, give rise to any claims under the Insolvency Act 1986 section 339 (transactions at an undervalue), s 340 (preferences), or section 343 (extortionate credit transactions), save that I have paid the sum of £2,000 to HM Customs and Excise in respect of their claim to secure an adjournment of their bankruptcy petition to enable me to propose this voluntary arrangement.

4. Guarantees

No guarantees have been provided by third parties in respect of my debts.

5. Duration

It is proposed that the voluntary arrangement should last for a period of four years

6. Proposed dates of distribution

It is proposed that the supervisor should make an annual distribution to creditors of all such sums as he then holds, save for such sum as he reasonably requires to present a petition for my bankruptcy should this become necessary and a reasonable sum to cover fees and expenses. The first distribution will include the sum of £20,000 to be paid by my father-in-law. The estimated amount of this distribution will therefore be *x*p in the £. The remaining distributions are estimated at *y*p in the £ subject to increase in the event that any sums are paid to the supervisor under provisions 3 and 4 of my proposal above.

7. Persons bound to the arrangement without notice

Should the existence of any creditor bound to the arrangement by reason of the fact that he would have been entitled in accordance with the rules to vote at the creditors' meeting had he had notice of it ('an omitted creditor') come to the attention of the supervisor before the arrangement has been fully implemented it is proposed that an omitted creditor should be admitted to the arrangement, as soon as may be practicable, on the same terms and with the same benefits as he would have been subject to and enjoyed had he had notice of the meeting. If by the time of his admission to the arrangement any dividends have been received by other creditors equivalent dividends shall be paid to the omitted creditor on his admission before any further dividends are received by the existing creditors bound to the arrangement.

In the event that the value of any debts or liabilities owed by me to one or more omitted creditors amounts to more than [10%] of the value of the debts and liabilities disclosed by me at the date of the creditors' meeting the existing creditors will be given the opportunity to terminate the arrangement prematurely.

8. Nominee's remuneration and expenses

The nominee will be paid a fee of £1,500. The sum of £750 has been paid. The balance of £750 together with any expenses reasonably incurred in assisting with the preparation of the proposal, acting as chairman of the creditors' meeting, and reporting to the court will be paid by me within 28 days of that report.

9. Supervisor's remuneration

The supervisor will be paid fees calculated on a time cost basis in accordance with his firm's usual charges. These fees together with any reasonable expenses incurred in the administration of the arrangement will be met by me.

10. Guarantees for the arrangement

Dr Robert Black, my father-in-law, has agreed to guarantee the periodic payments due under the arrangement. A letter sufficient to comprise the necessary memorandum in writing has been signed by him and is in the possession of the Nominee. No security for this guarantee has been offered and none will be sought.

11. Arrangement funds

Pending distribution to creditors the supervisor will pay all sums received into an interest bearing designated client account with the Royal Bank of Scotland.

12. Funds not distributed

Any funds remaining unclaimed after the expiry of the period of 12 months following the termination of the arrangement will be distributed to the remaining creditors who have proved their claims.

13. Conduct of business

I will be solely responsible for the conduct of the business during the period of the arrangement. I will concentrate on his private client repair work and car sales. I have no present plans to resume insurance company contract repair work and undertake not to do so in the future without first obtaining the supervisor's approval to the terms on which such work is undertaken.

14. Credit facilities

I have a bank overdraft facility of £20,000. I do not intend to enter into any further credit arrangements and will not do so without first consulting the supervisor.

15. Functions to be undertaken by the Supervisor

(1) To collect and invest the instalments made by me under the arrangement;
(2) To collect the sum of £20,000 to be contributed by Robert Black;
(3) To arrange for the completion of a formal guarantee by Robert Black of the instalments which I have agreed to pay;
(4) To pursue in my name the action for wrongful interference against the Administrative Receivers of King's Cross Films plc referred to above. The

supervisor will in this regard instruct junior counsel experienced in such matters of at least 10 years' call and act in accordance with counsel's advice. If so advised the supervisor will prove in the liquidation of King's Cross Films plc;

(5) To collect and invest any sums received in the litigation or liquidation referred to above;

(6) To require declarations every 12 months as to any legacies, gifts, windfalls or other such benefits which I may have received during the period of the arrangement and to collect any resulting monies for the arrangement;

(7) To calculate and distribute dividends to creditors;.

(8) To do all such further acts and undertake all such further enquiries as may in his opinion be required for the proper implementation of the arrangement;

(9) The supervisor shall retain at all times sufficient funds to enable him to petition for my bankruptcy in the event of any default by me in the performance of any of my obligations under the terms of the IVA, subject to the approval of the creditors.

The supervisor shall hold all funds received in connection with this arrangement as trustee.

16. The Supervisor

It is proposed that the Nominee, David Appleton of Paul Williams & Co, St Mary's Axe, London EC3 7TY, should be the supervisor of the arrangement if approved. David Appleton is a licensed insolvency practitioner authorised to act in relation to me as debtor.

17. EC Regulation

The EC Regulation appliesd to this arrangement. These are main proceedings as defined by Article 3 of the EC Regulation. I do not carry on any trading outside the United Kingdom. My centre of main interest is in England.

Debtor's undertaking

I undertake to procure the payment by Dr Robert Black of the sum of £20,000 within 42 days of the approval of this arrangement.

Additional information for creditors

There is set out in Appendix 2 an estimate of the likely outcome of the voluntary arrangement compared with the position as it is likely to be in the event of bankruptcy.

Appendix 3 contains an estimate of my projected income and expenditure in the next full year should the arrangement be approved.

Standard Conditions

It is proposed that the terms of the arrangement should comprise this proposal and the standard conditions for individual voluntary arrangements produced by the Association of Business Recovery Professionals, subject to the variations to these standard conditions set forth in appendix 6 hereto and any modification lawfully made by the creditors and agreed by myself at the creditors' meeting.

APPENDIX 1

[Estimated] Statement of Affairs as at (date not more than 14 days before the date endorsed by the nominee on the notice accompanying the proposal, see IR 1986, r 5.4)

Assets (specifically charged)

Matrimonial home

Less value of charge (mortgage)

Business premises (leasehold)

Less value of bank's charge

Assets (not specifically charged)

Life policy – surrender value

Stock

Motor car

Pick-up truck

Claim against Administrative Receivers

Preferential creditors

Inland Revenue

HM Customs and Excise

Outstanding wages

Surplus as regards preferential creditors

Unsecured creditors (see list attached)

HM Customs and Excise

Deficiency as regards creditors

APPENDIX 2

COMPARISON BETWEEN BANKRUPTCY AND IVA

	Bankruptcy	IVA
Share of matrimonial home equity		
Payment by Robert Black		
Claim against King's Cross admin receivers		
Life policy surrender value		
Stock		
Motor car		
Pick-up Truck		
Voluntary contributions		

	Bankruptcy	IVA
Voidable transaction		
Fees		
Petitioning creditors' costs		
Supervisor's fees		
Total costs		
Balance available to creditors		
Less: preferential creditors		
Unsecured creditors		
Claim of HM Customs		

APPENDIX 3

ESTIMATED PROJECTED INCOME AND EXPENDITURE

Income
Net Profit
Personal Expenses
- — Mortgage
- — Light and heat
- — Telephone
- — Council tax and water rates
- — Food and clothes
- — Motor running costs
- — Accountancy and book-keeping
- — Secretarial fees
- — Insurance

Monthly contribution
Balance for all remaining expenses

APPENDIX 4

Valuation report on 23 Acacia Avenue, London SW 11 by Sich, Mole and Freedman

APPENDIX 5

Letter from Dr Robert Black FRCP

(confirming offer to pay £20,000 into arrangement within 42 days of approval and guarantee of debtor's voluntary payments)

APPENDIX 6

Variations proposed to the standard conditions for individual voluntary arrangements produced by the Association of Business Recovery Professionals.

4.5 Proposal by Debtor (non-trader) for Individual Voluntary Arrangement

IN THE HIGH COURT OF JUSTICE

IN BANKRUPTCY

IN THE MATTER OF BARRY BALDRICK

AND IN THE MATTER OF THE INSOLVENCY ACT 1986

PROPOSAL FOR AN INDIVIDUAL VOLUNTARY ARRANGEMENT

1. Introduction

I, Barry Baldrick of The Gatehouse, Little Paignton, Devon wish to make a proposal to my creditors for a voluntary arrangement. For 35 years I have worked as a personal assistant to the well-known impresario, Sir Edmund Blackadder. I have also worked as a barman when I had some free time, and I also undertook individual business deals when the opportunity arose. My wages were modest but for many years Sir Edmund paid me a substantial Christmas bonus on which I counted for my business transactions. Shortly before last Christmas Sir Edmund was arrested on charges of downloading inappropriate material from the internet. I lost my employment and I did not receive my anticipated bonus. Unfortunately I had bought long on a number of commodity options in anticipation that I would be able to make any necessary payments from my bonus. In the event I was unable to meet my obligations. I have been unable to find alternative employment and am now dependent on state benefits.

2. Terms of Proposed Arrangement

(1) I will assign to my supervisor, for realisation and division of the proceeds to my creditors, all my assets other than personal effects, namely 37 cases of wine, a fine Margaux Premier Cru, 14 eighteenth-century silver topped black canes, a penny-farthing bicycle, and 23 assorted artefacts previously belonging to Sir Montague Blackadder (1623-1687) which were given to me by my previous employer in lieu of wages;

(2) Lady Sarah Millward, cousin to my former employer, will contribute the sum of £5,000 to the assets of the arrangement;

(3) All my creditors are to accept a pro rata dividend paid from the above realisations and money contribution in full and final satisfaction of all claims against me existing as at the date of the approval of the arrangement.

3. The interest of my creditors

Under the terms of the arrangement the likely dividend is in the region of 24p in the £. Were I to be adjudged bankrupt my creditors would receive less than 10p in the £ by way of dividend. I believe therefore that they are likely to accept my proposal.

4. Assets and liabilities

4.1 I have no assets apart from personal effects of little value and the assets comprised in my proposed terms of arrangement, as above. I estimate the wine to have a value of £14,000, the silver canes to be worth £820, the penny-farthing bicycle £600 and the assorted artefacts formerly the property of Sir Montagu Blackadder, £8,200.

4.2 Lady Sarah Millward will contribute £5,000 to the arrangement in recognition of the services I have provided to her cousin my former employer.

4.3 I have no assets which are the subject of any charge.

4.4 My liabilities amount to £118,350 as listed in my statement of affairs.

4.5 I have no liabilities to preferential creditors.

4.6 None of my creditors is an associate.

4.7 I can envisage no circumstances which could rise to the possibility of claims under the Insolvency Act, ss 339, 340 or 343. My nominee has carefully explained the effects of these statutory provisions to me.

5. Further information

5.1 No guarantees have been given by any other person in respect of my debts.

5.2 The expected duration of the arrangement is six months being the time it will take my supervisor to agree all creditors' claims, realise the property I have assigned to him and pay a full and final dividend to all creditors.

5.3 One dividend will be paid, on about *(date)*, subject to the creditors agreeing an extension of time if the assets have not been realised advantageously by that date.

5.4 If there are any of my creditors who were entitled to but were not given notice of the arrangement, then, upon them making themselves known to the supervisor I propose that they be admitted to the arrangement and receive their appropriate dividend.

5.5 The nominee's fee, which I have already paid, is £750 plus VAT.

5.6 The supervisor will be paid on a time-cost basis. He has estimated his fees to be no more than £1,000 plus VAT and disbursements.

5.7 No guarantees are to be given by any third party for the purposes of the implementation of this arrangement.

5.8 Pending distribution to my creditors, any money held by the supervisor will be paid into an interest-bearing nominated deposit account with the Bank of Ireland.

5.9 Any unclaimed dividends will be distributed pro rata among the creditors who are entitled to receive a dividend.

5.10 I do not propose to conduct a business during the currency of my voluntary arrangement.

5.11 I do not propose to arrange any credit facilities during the currency of my voluntary arrangement.

5.12 The supervisor's functions will be:

(1) to agree and if necessary investigate creditors' claims;

(2) to realise the assets I assign to him for the purpose of the arrangement;

(3) to collect the sum of £5,000 from Lady Sarah Millward;

(4) to distribute the funds among the creditors whose claims have been admitted for dividend;

(5) to do all such other things as may be required to implement the terms of my arrangement.

5.13 The proposed supervisor's name is Paul Peters, of Peters & Co. 139 St John's Street, Exeter. He is a chartered accountant and has confirmed to me that he is duly qualified to act as nominee and supervisor in relation my voluntary arrangement.

5.14 The EC Regulation applies to this voluntary arrangement. My main centre of interest is in England. I have not traded outside the United Kingdom. These proceedings are main proceedings as defined in Article 3 of the EC Regulation.

6. Miscellaneous

6.1 I undertake to procure the payment by Lady Sarah Millward of the sum of £5,000 within 2 months of the approval of this proposal.

6.2 I propose that the terms of the arrangement should comprise this proposal and the standard conditions for individual voluntary arrangements prepared by the Association of Business Recovery Professionals. In the event of conflict the terms of this proposal shall prevail.

Dated:

Signed:

STATEMENT OF AFFAIRS

4.6 Additional terms for use in a proposal

The following miscellaneous terms are offered more for consideration than immediate use reflecting the sort of terms that might be required or found to be useful in a proposal. Both the appropriateness of any term and the law underlying it will have to be checked before it is used in practice. The first section comprises terms drafted for use with a CVA or PVA ('Company' being replaced by 'Partnership') and the second section has terms aimed at an IVA. The CVA terms may readily be transposed to an IVA by changing 'Company' to 'Debtor' and making any other necessary amendments.

(1) Terms for CVA or PVA proposals

Disputed claims

The Company disputes each of the claims listed in Appendix Z for the reasons there stated on the basis of legal advice. This advice is and remains confidential to the Company. Following the approval of the arrangement the supervisor will endeavour to agree these claims. Whether he contests any claim which cannot be agreed will be a matter for the discretion of the supervisor. He may, if he so decides, take legal or other advice for the purpose of assessing or contesting any claim [as an expense of the arrangement], but he is under no obligation to incur any cost in such assessment or contestation.

Litigation

The Supervisor may if he considers fit commence, continue or defend any legal proceedings in the Company's name to recover any property or money due to the Company which if recovered would form part of the assets of the arrangement, or to protect any property or money forming part of the assets of the arrangement. [The cost of any such proceedings will be an expense of the arrangement.] The Company, by its directors and employees, will give all such assistance as may reasonably be required by the Supervisor for this purpose.

Preference

On *(date)* the Company paid the sum of £x and relinquished its claim for payment of invoice 456913 in settlement of a claim made by Vicious Sid plc. The division of the Company responsible for the dealings with Vicious Sid plc did not consider that its claim was well founded, and this was duly reported to the board of directors. Nevertheless, the Company agreed to make the payment in order to stave off the threats of litigation and bad publicity made by Vicious Sid plc. In making the payment and settling the claim the Company had no intention to putting Vicious Sid plc in a better position than it would have enjoyed in the event of the Company's insolvent liquidation. Nevertheless, the Company has been advised that this settlement may constitute a preference.

Property valuation by independent valuer

On *(date)* the Company obtained a valuation of the property High Trees House, Clapham Common, London SW11 from Messrs Sich, Mole and Freedman property agents and valuers of High Street, Putney ('the Valuers'). The valuation was obtained for the purpose of seeking further financial facilities and the valuation report was given by the Valuers strictly on the basis that no other use could be made of it. The directors have asked the Valuers to permit the use of this report for the purpose of this proposal. The Valuers have indicated that they will give their permission provided that no liability on their part may attach to such use. A copy of this report will be provided on request to any creditor listed on the Company's statement of affairs but only on receipt of confirmation that the creditor accepts that it is received and considered by him without responsibility on the part of the Valuers.

Third Party (Rights against Insurers) Act 1930

The Company has public liability, product liability, and occupiers' liability policies of insurance. In the event that any creditor considers that he has a claim against the Company which may be covered by any of these insurances he should notify the supervisor of such claim. Provided that the creditor first gives the supervisor his written undertaking not to enforce any judgment or award he may obtain against the Company, he may commence or continue any legal proceedings against the Company for the purposes of establishing his rights for the purposes of the Third Party (Rights against Insurers) Act 1930. The provisions of this term shall not constitute an admission of liability on the part of the Company, nor preclude the Company (at the instance of its insurers or of its own volition) from defending any such proceedings brought by the creditor, nor prevent the creditor proving in the arrangement to the extent to which he may be entitled in the event that he is unable to recover his claim in full against insurers.

(2) Terms for IVA proposals

After-acquired assets

The Debtor will notify the Supervisor of any property with a value likely to exceed [£500] or any sum of money in excess of [£250] which is acquired by or which devolves on him during the currency of the arrangement, within 21 days of the receipt by him of the relevant item of property or money. In the case of money the Debtor will pay the same over to the Supervisor at the time he gives notice. In the case of property, if it appears to the Supervisor that the property concerned would not be excluded under s 283(2) of the Insolvency Act 1986 from the Debtor's estate were he to be bankrupt he will so inform the Debtor who will then transfer the property to the Supervisor forthwith for the benefit of the arrangement.

Debtor's action for personal injuries

The Debtor has a cause of action against [former employers] for damages for personal injury. A claim has been commenced. The heads of damage sought in the claim include damages for loss of earnings. The Nominee has seen an opinion from counsel stating that this head of damage (and this head alone) would vest in a trustee were the Debtor to be adjudged bankrupt. If this proposal is approved the Debtor will procure an undertaking from the solicitors having conduct of this claim to pay such sum as is received in respect of the claim for loss of earnings (whether pursuant to an order of the court or a settlement) to the supervisor for the benefit of the arrangement. [The Debtor will in addition pay a further sum to the supervisor amounting to 25% of any sums received in respect of his remaining heads of damage pursued in this claim limited to £10,000]. Any such payment will be made within 14 days of receipt by the Debtor.

Discretionary trust beneficiary

The Debtor is one of the beneficiaries under a discretionary trust dated 14th March 1958 created by his grandfather who died on 30th May 1958. The terms of this trust provide that the Debtor has no absolute entitlement in any circumstance to any of the capital or income of the trust. In their letter dated *(date)* the trustees have indicated that there is no realistic prospect that they will they exercise their discretion in favour of the Debtor should he become bankrupt. However, they will be prepared to pay the supervisor by way of an advance to the Debtor the sum of [£10,000] should this arrangement be approved. Such a payment will form part of the arrangement funds to be distributed among the creditors.

Life and pension policies

The Debtor has a life policy with Topaz Assurance Company, numbered TCP-345-ilk-978466588. The present surrender value of the policy is £ ... as appears from a letter dated *(date)* from Topaz Assurance Company a copy of which forms part of Appendix Z. Within 14 days of the commencement of the arrangement the debtor will execute an assignment of the benefits payable under this policy to the Supervisor. The policy will be maintained in force until the 4th anniversary of the arrangement. During the 5th year of the arrangement the Supervisor will, on a date of his choosing, surrender the policy. [The Debtor undertakes to execute all such deeds or documents as may be necessary to effect the surrender.] [Within 14 days of the commencement of the arrangement the Debtor will execute an irrevocable power of attorney in terms which will authorise the Supervisor to surrender the policy.]

The Debtor has a life policy with Utopia Assurance Company, numbered U2-876, which is charged in favour of the mortgagees of the Debtor's matrimonial home, the New Age Building Society. In the event that the proceeds of sale of the matrimonial home, together with the proceeds of the endowment policies assigned to the New Age Building Society (referred to in paragraph [x] above) are sufficient to discharge the sum due to the Building Society, policy U2-876 will be surrendered and the proceeds paid forthwith on receipt to the Supervisor for the purposes of the arrangement. The Debtor has provided the Nominee with a written undertaking to execute all such deeds and documents as may be necessary to effect the surrender. The present surrender value is £ ... as appears from the letter dated *(date)* from Utopia Assurance Company a copy of which comprises Appendix Z. The Debtor's wife has agreed to waive any claim that she may have against the policy or its proceeds of sale, as appears from her letter dated *(date)* a copy of which is contained in Appendix Z.

For the benefit of an arrangement the Debtor has agreed, within 21 days of the approval of this proposal, to effect a term assurance policy with Headstone Insurance Company plc in the sum of £... The premium will be £.. and will be paid [from the assets of the arrangement][from the Debtor's own resources]. The insured sum has been assessed by reference to the total value of the assets of the arrangement. The policy will be held on trust for the supervisor on behalf of the arrangement. In the event of the Debtor's death before the conclusion of the arrangement, the sum assured will be paid to the supervisor in order to enable him to pay a total dividend of ...p in the £. Any surplus then remaining from the sum paid under the Headstone

Insurance Company plc policy or the assets of the arrangement will be paid to the Debtor's personal representatives for the benefit of his estate.

The Debtor has the various retirement annuity and personal pension policies listed in Appendix Z. On *(date)* the Debtor will be entitled to tax free sums and annuities under the terms of these policies estimates of which are provided in Appendix Z. The Debtor has provided the Nominee with a written undertaking that he will do all such things as may be necessary to ensure that the lump sums payable under the policies are paid to the Supervisor as funds for the voluntary arrangement. The Debtor will also contribute £... per month from the annuities he receives under the policies.

Low value home

The Debtor's [sole or principal] residence, 14 Acacia Avenue, Pinner, Middlesex HA5 5NL ('the property'), is a property which, at the date of this proposal, is either in negative equity or is a low value home for the purposes of s 313A Insolvency Act 1986. For this reason it has been excluded from the arrangement. [A copy of a valuation by Sich, Mole & Freedman, valuers, and a statement from the New Albion Building Society showing the present position are annexed hereto in Appendix Z.] If during the period of the arrangement the Debtor sells the property he shall pay any net proceeds of sale to the Supervisor for the benefit of the arrangement, limited to such sum as will together with all other assets of the arrangement produce for the creditors a dividend of ... p in the £.

The Debtor shall be under no obligation to sell the property [unless the value of the property increases beyond the sum outstanding to the said mortgagees to the extent that the Defendant has an equity of not less than [£20,000] in the property. In this event the Supervisor may require the Debtor to sell the property, having frist obtained a valuation of the property from Sich, Mole & Freedman or, in the event of their unavailability some other reputable firm of valuers, which demonstrates the specified equity. The Debtor will, at the request of the Supervisor, obtain a statement of sums owing to the said mortgagee at any time during the period of the arrangement.][The Debtor undertakes not to grant any further charge or other security over the property.]

Power of attorney

If so required by the Supervisor, the Debtor will execute a power of attorney [in any appropriate form][in the form annexed in appendix Z][irrevocable during the currency of the arrangement] authorising the Supervisor to perform any act on behalf of the Debtor which is necessary for the proper implementation of the arrangement.

Sale of matrimonial home – concurrence of co-owner and adult in occupation

The Debtor occupies the matrimonial home, the Red House, Appleton, Gloucestershire with his wife, who owns half the beneficial interest in the property, and adult daughter, who has no such beneficial interest. Both the Debtor's wife and daughter will co-operate fully in the sale of the property. Further, although she has been advised that she has an equity of exoneration, the Debtor's wife has agreed that one half of the net proceeds of sale may be paid to the supervisor for the purposes of the arrangement. The Debtor's wife and daughter have obtained independent legal advice from Messrs Gilliatt, solicitors, as to their respective rights in connection with the matrimonial home. A copy of a letter dated *(date)* from Messrs Gilliatt, confirming the above, is annexed hereto as Appendix Z.

Shareholder in family company

The Debtor holds 350 shares representing 20% of the total equity in Horsted Humpers Ltd, a private company founded by his great grandfather in 1882. The Debtor has been advised that it is not possible to value these shares. The Articles of Association of this company place severe restrictions on the disposal of these shares. They have been offered to all the family members who are entitled to buy the shares but none are willing to pay more than a nominal price for them. The Debtor has given the Nominee a power of attorney, irrevocable during the period of any approved voluntary arrangement, by which the Supervisor may offer these shares for sale in accordance with the company's Articles of Association on behalf of the Debtor. If the company's trading improves during the currency of the voluntary arrangement it may be possible to obtain a worthwhile sum for them which will then be paid into the arrangement. However the company's prospects do not look particularly good at present.

Third party obligations

The Debtor hereby guarantees the performance of all obligations falling on third parties in this proposal, other than obligations falling on the Nominee or Supervisor.

4.7 Commentary on the R3 Standard Conditions for IVAs

The Association of Business Recovery Professionals (R3) have produced a set of standard conditions for Individual Voluntary Arrangements ('the R3 Conditions') which is in widespread use. No set of conditions will please everyone, but the R3 Conditions are well drafted, with an eye to equivalent provisions in the Insolvency Rules, and are extensive, covering most situations that might arise in the course of the implementation of an arrangement. The R3 Conditions are readily available, either in hard copy from the Association or on the web (www.r3.org.uk) and the time will soon come, if it has not come already, when reference may be made to the R3 Conditions in the same way as with standard conditions of sale, setting out only those amendments, if any, which are to be made for the particular arrangement under consideration. It is understood that R3 expect to publish a set of standard conditions for company voluntary arrangements in summer 2003. The IVA R3 Conditions can indeed be readily adapted for use in CVA or PVA.

The R3 Conditions are set out at appendix 4.10 below. The following observations are offered on these conditions.

Paragraph 11: Termination of Arrangement. This condition provides that the trusts created under the arrangement should survive the termination of the arrangement. This will almost always be in the interests of the arrangement creditors, but thought should be given as to whether under the particular proposed arrangement it would be preferable for the trusts not to survive termination, see the text at paragraph 11.3 above. In this respect it may be important for a creditor to ensure that his claim is not compromised until all payments under the voluntary arrangement have been made in full. In the case of arrangements which depend on continued trading, consideration needs to be given as to whether the effect of the approved arrangement may be to deter essential trading partners of the debtor from continued involvement with him, particularly on credit terms.

It may be noted that VAS (as to which see the text at paragraph 4.12 above) have in a number of cases stated that if they are to vote for the arrangement they require

(a) the deletion of the words 'none of which circumstances shall affect the trusts created under paragraph 29' in paragraph 11, and
(b) the replacement of paragraph 29(3) with the following:

> '**29(3) Effect upon Trusts of termination of Arrangement]** Upon termination of the arrangement [within the meaning of paragraph 11] the trusts referred to in sub-paragraphs (1) and (2) shall cease save that assets already realised shall [after provision for supervisor's fees and disbursements] be distributed to arrangement creditors.'

The effect of this replacement paragraph will be to put post-arrangement creditors in a less disadvantageous position on a subsequent insolvency.

Paragraph 17: Supervisor's fees. A sensitive subject. A creditor should perhaps investigate the possibility that the debtor will accept responsibility for fees, costs and expenses which under the R3 Conditions fall on the assets of the arrangement. If this is not a practicable proposition thought should be given to insisting on a cap on fees, adding to clause 17(1): 'such fees not in any event to exceed [x%] of the assets of the arrangement'.

Paragraph 26: Debtor's acknowledgement. The previous Rule 5.30 has now been omitted from the Insolvency Rules following the introduction of s 262A Insolvency Act 1986. Paragraph 26(3) therefore requires amending as follows:

> **26(3) [Section 262A]** The Debtor acknowledges that he commits an offence if he makes any false representation or fraudulently does, or omits to do, anything for the purpose of obtaining the approval of his Creditors to the Arrangement.

Paragraph 27: Arrangement assets. This paragraph defines arrangement assets very widely, putting the onus (quite properly perhaps) on the debtor to ensure that assets to be excluded from the arrangement are clearly spelt out in the proposal. It is important that the debtor appreciates the width of this provision.

Paragraph 28: After-acquired assets. This paragraph may not be sufficiently tightly drawn for some creditors. VAS (see paragraph 4.12) have their own clause which they sometimes seek to insert into the conditions as follows:

> '28 After-acquired assets
>
> **28(1) [After-acquired Property subject to Arrangement]** Should the Debtor inherit any Property or receive or become entitled to any Property which had not been foreseen by the proposal then such Property shall become an asset of the Arrangement upon the Debtor's become entitled to it ('After-Acquired Assets').
>
> **28(2) [After-Acquired Assets to be supplementary]** After-Acquired Assets shall be sold or realised to the extent necessary to effect full repayment of the Creditors together with interest, if any, to which Creditors are entitled pursuant to the Arrangement and as such will be supplementary to any other contribution or Property which the Debtor is to include in the Arrangement.
>
> **28(3) [Continuance of Debtor's obligations]** Until the issue of a Completion Certificate all the Debtor's obligations under the Arrangement, including any obligations to make contributions or realise Property, continue notwithstanding the realisation of any After-Acquired Assets.'

PART VI: CLAIMS: Paragraphs 31 to 44 provide a full code for the submission of claims for the purpose of participation in the arrangement. Creditors will however have already submitted claims to the chairman of the creditors' meeting for voting purposes. Many may consider it unnecessary to submit a further claim where their claim has already been accepted by the chairman of the meeting, who of course will in most cases be the same person as the Supervisor. It might be preferable to amend paragraph 31 by adding, after the existing paragraph 31 renumbered as 31(1), paragraph 31(2) as follows:

> **'31(2) [Claim accepted for voting]** Where the creditor has submitted a claim to the chairman of the creditors' meeting and that claim has been admitted by the chairman for the purposes of voting ('the existing claim'), the Notice to Submit Claims shall state the amount of the existing claim and whether the Supervisor is content to accept it for the purposes of dividend or other participation in the arrangement. If the Supervisor is so content and the creditor does not wish to alter the existing claim, the creditor may return the Notice to Submit Claims duly endorsed to that effect and no further submission will be required for the claim to be admitted for dividend.'

PART VIIA : OMITTED CREDITORS: The R3 Conditions do not cover the position of the creditor who was not given notice of the meeting but is nevertheless bound to the arrangement by reason of the provisions of IA 1986, s 5(2)(b) (CVA without moratorium), Sch A1, para 37(2)(b) (CVA with moratorium), or s 260(2)(b) (IVA). Standard conditions to cover the position of the 'omitted creditor' are offered in appendix 4.9 below.

PART X: PROVISIONS FOLLOWING BREACH. The R3 Conditions advisedly leave open the question of termination of the arrangement following breach by the debtor. This will often be in the interests of the creditors who may find themselves worse off in formal insolvency should the arrangement be terminated. Nevertheless in some circumstances the creditors may prefer to insist on automatic termination on breach by the debtor.

Paragraph 70: Variation of the Arrangement. As explained in paragraphs 10.7 and 10.8 of the text above it is advisable to have a provision permitting variation of the terms of the arrangement. It should nevertheless be borne in mind that unless the variation provision requires unanimity among the creditors there is the possibility that including a variation provision in the arrangement terms may leave the approval of the arrangement open to challenge. Paragraph 70 permits variation and, by paragraph 61(2), a 75% resolution will suffice to vary the arrangement, provided not more than half in value of the creditors who are not associates do not vote against the resolution, paragraph 61(3). In the vast majority of cases this will be the appropriate course to adopt. Consideration should however be given in each individual case to the possibility that paragraph 61(2) should be varied to require a unanimous vote before a variation is permitted.

Creditors are well advised to take care when a Debtor proposes a variation. There have been cases where a Debtor whose arrangement is due to last, say, 5 years appreciates that he is likely to acquire a considerable sum of money in the 4th or 5th year of the arrangement, by reason of a business opportunity or a new job or other reason. It is then tempting for him to propose a variation to bring the Arrangement to an end early 'for the purposes of finality' or whatever. The creditors may be offered an increased dividend for the 4th year of the arrangement to support a variation to reduce the length of the arrangement. A friend or relative (apparently) may offer a capital sum for this purpose. Although it is suggested that the common law would impose a duty of good faith in these circumstances the legal position is not clear. This potentially important area is not covered by the legislation. It is suggested that the following clause might be added to paragraph 70.

> '**70(6) [Debtor's duty on variation]** In the event that the Debtor or any Creditor proposes a variation to the Arrangement the Debtor must disclose to the creditors in writing, not less than [14] days before the meeting called to consider the proposed variation is held, every material fact and circumstance known to the Debtor. A fact or circumstance is material if it might influence the judgment of a reasonable creditor who is not an associate of the Debtor in deciding whether to support or oppose the proposed variation.'

4.8 Standard modifications proposed by Voluntary Arrangements Service (VAS) on behalf of Inland Revenue (IR) and Customs & Excise (C & E)

The Voluntary Arrangements Service (VAS) and its influence on proposals and voluntary arrangements has been commented upon in the text at paragraph 4.12. In almost every case it will be important for the nominee and or the Debtor (or company directors or partners) to make contact with the VAS at an early stage of the procedure to discuss the proposal with them and ascertain what terms or modifications they will wish to have in the arrangement if they are to support it. The influence of VAS will diminish somewhat when the crown ceases to be a preferential creditor on the coming into force of s 251 of the Enterprise Act 2002. Nevertheless, it is likely that VAS will remain an influential creditor at the creditors' meeting for the reasons discussed in paragraph 4.12. In addition to the modifications set out in Appendix 4.7 the following are modifications which VAS usually wish to see accepted if they are not to vote against the proposal.

VAS. Specific IVA modifications:

1. Where a modification to the proposal is approved by creditors and accepted by the debtor, the entire proposal shall be construed in the light of the modification and read to give effect to that modification such that any contrary or potentially contrary provisions in the proposal shall either be ignored, or interpreted, in order that the intention of the modification is given priority and effect.
2. The IR provisional claim in the IVA will include both SA payments on account due for the year in which the arrangement was approved, PAYE/NIC due to the date of approval, plus any earlier unpaid liabilities.
   - 2.1 The IR final claim in the IVA will additionally include the SA balancing adjustment due following submission of the SA return for the period to the 5 April following the date of approval.
   - 2.2 The IR final claim in the IVA will not include SA/NIC on any source of income that commences after the date of approval. Payment of liability arising on this post approval source will be the debtor's responsibility.
3. The C & E claim in the IVA is made on present information and will include assessed tax or duty due to the date of the meeting. If returns are made or under declarations of tax or duty come to light following the approval the claim will be adjusted accordingly.
4. All SA/VAT returns (and any tax levy or duty returns due to C & E) or P35s/CIS36s and payments due for periods post approval shall be rendered when they fall due.
5. All outstanding P35s/SC35s/CIS36s accounts, tax/VAT returns (and any tax levy or duty return due to C & E) to the date of the creditors' meeting and any other information or explanations required by an Inspector of Taxes or Customs Officer must be provided within three months of the approval date.

6. The debtor's monthly provision for income tax/NIC as it appears in the income and expenditure statement shall, from the date of approval of the IVA to the following 5 April, be paid to the Supervisor for the benefit of the arrangement creditors.
7. Where prior to payment of a dividend, VAS has not notified a final claim under the arrangement the Supervisor is to calculate the dividend by reference to the VAS provisional claim and hold this amount in reserve until such time as the final claim has been received.
8. No distribution will be made until:
   8.1 the SA return for the year in which the arrangement was approved; and
   8.2 a VAT return (or other tax levy or duty return(s) due to C & E) up to the date of the meeting, have been filed; or
   8.3 an Inland Revenue Determination or a Customs assessment has been made and final claims have been received by the supervisor.
9. CGT or VAT due on sale of assets included in the arrangement will be regarded as an expense of realising the asset and payable immediately out of the net sale proceeds.
10. During the currency of the arrangement, any tax/excise/VAT repayments that relate to a period prior to the date of approval of the arrangement shall be offset rateably against the appropriate department's preferential and non-preferential claims in the arrangement. Any remaining surplus shall be similarly applied to the claims of other government departments before being offered to the Supervisor for the benefit of arrangement creditors. Any repayments relating to a period after the approval of the arrangement shall be offset against any post approval tax debts. Any remaining surplus will then be treated as a windfall and offered to the Supervisor for the benefit of creditors in the arrangement.
11. IR and C & E distress/petition costs are to be paid as an expense of the arrangement, in priority to the nominee's fees and supervisor's fees, remuneration and disbursements.
12. The release of the Debtor from liability to creditors by the terms of the IVA shall not operate as a release of any co Debtor for the same debt.

4.9 Standard conditions for omitted creditors

A creditor who would have been entitled to vote at the creditors' meeting if he had had notice of it but who was not given notice (the 'omitted creditor') has 28 days from his becoming aware that the meeting has taken place to challenge the decision of the meeting on the ground of unfair prejudice or material irregularity at or in relation to the meeting (see paras 7.1, 7.8 above). As to 'unfair prejudice' it is hard to resist the conclusion that if the voluntary arrangement does not permit the omitted creditor to participate in and benefit under its terms to the same extent as he would have enjoyed had he been given notice the omitted creditor will be unfairly prejudiced. As to 'material irregularity' the mere fact that the omitted creditor has not been given notice will not amount to a material irregularity in the light of the amendments to the IA 1986 introduced by IA 2000. However the omission to give notice should be held to be a material irregularity if the omitted creditor can show that his omission was deliberate, although the court will only revoke or suspend the voluntary arrangement if the omitted creditor can show that his vote by itself would have made a difference to the eventual outcome or that had he been present at the creditors' meeting he is likely to have persuaded sufficient other creditors to change their votes to ensure a different outcome.

The Rules now require the proposal to state how it is proposed to deal with the claim of an omitted creditor[1]. It is suggested that there will have to be very special circumstances indeed to justify the omitted creditor's claim being dealt with in any way other than the way in which it would have been dealt with had he had notice of the creditors' meeting. The proposal should so provide, and it should also provide that in the event that the omitted creditor is admitted late to the arrangement he will be entitled to receive such dividends or other benefits to which he would have been entitled as have been received by the other creditors before any further dividends are paid or other benefits received by the other creditors.

It is also necessary to consider the position of the other creditors. They will have voted for the arrangement without knowledge of the omitted creditor's claim. Where, as in most voluntary arrangements, a dividend is to be paid, the existence of one or more additional claims will result in a dilution of that dividend. The existing creditors should be entitled to review the arrangement in the light of the additional claims, and if appropriate bring the voluntary arrangement to an early termination. They may wish to require the debtor to pay a further sum into the arrangement to save it from termination. On a practical level it is suggested that the omitted creditor's claim should amount to a significant proportion of the total claims before the voluntary arrangement may be terminated; creditors will be able to decide for themselves what that proportion should be.

The following drafts are offered for both proposal and terms of the arrangement to be amended as necessary to take account of individual circumstances and the views of the creditors in particular cases.

1 IR 1986, r 1.3(2)(fa) (all CVAs), r 5.3(2)(fa) (IVA).

Paragraph to be added to proposal[2]

Should the existence of any creditor bound to the arrangement by reason of the fact that he would have been entitled in accordance with the rules to vote at the creditors' meeting had he had notice of it ('an omitted creditor') come to the attention of the supervisor before the arrangement has been fully implemented it is proposed that the omitted creditor should be admitted to the arrangement, as soon as may be practicable, on the same terms and with the same benefits as he would have been subject to and enjoyed had he had notice of the meeting. If by the time of his admission to the arrangement any dividends [and or other benefits][3] have been received by other creditors [in his class][4] equivalent dividends shall be paid [and or other benefits provided][3] to the omitted creditor on his admission before any further dividends [and or other benefits][3] are received by the existing creditors bound to the arrangement.

In the event that the value of any debts or liabilities owed by the debtor to one or more omitted creditors amounts to more than [10%] of the value of the debts and liabilities disclosed by the debtor by the date of the creditors' meeting, the existing creditors will be given the opportunity to terminate the arrangement prematurely.

Additional terms of arrangement (which may be used in conjunction with the R3 terms)

PART VIIA : OMITTED CREDITORS

52A Creditors not receiving notice of Creditors' Meeting

52A(1)[Debtor's duty] The Debtor has warranted[5] that he has disclosed full and complete particulars of all his debts and liabilities and has therefore warranted that he has identified all creditors who are or who might be entitled to vote at the meeting of creditors summoned to consider the Proposal. Failure to notify the existence of any such creditor, whether involving culpability on the part of the Debtor or not, shall, without prejudice to any other remedy which may be available in respect of such failure, amount to a breach of the terms of the Arrangement [for the purposes of paragraph 66][but only if the debt or liability owed to such creditor either by itself or in conjunction with the debt or liability owed to any other creditor of whose existence no notice was given to the creditors' meeting amounts to more than [10%] of the total of the Creditors' claims admitted for the purposes of the Arrangement].

2 A much simpler approach is offered in the proposal by Barry Baldrick, Appendix 4.5, para 5.4.
3 Include only if necessary, that is where benefits other than dividends are to be provided to or distributed to the creditors.
4 Include only if necessary, that is where distinctions are made in the proposal between different classes of creditors.
5 Paragraph 22.

52A(2) [Notification of terms] If at any time during the currency of the Arrangement the Supervisor learns of the existence of a creditor who would have been entitled to vote at the creditors' meeting had he received notice of it, but who was not given notice of the creditors' meeting, for whatever reason, (an 'omitted creditor') he shall forthwith sent to the omitted creditor a copy of the Proposal, these Conditions and the report to the court submitted by the chairman of the creditors' meeting. The Supervisor shall further send the omitted creditor a Notice to Submit Claims informing him that his claim will be considered provided that it is submitted within [28] days and drawing his attention to Part VI of these Conditions.

52A(3) [Examination of claim] The Supervisor, within 14 days of receiving a claim from an omitted creditor, shall examine the same and determine whether the claim should be admitted for the purposes of the arrangement and if so in what amount.

52A(4) [Assistance of debtor] The Debtor shall render the Supervisor all necessary assistance for the purpose of his examination of any claim submitted by an omitted creditor.

52A(5) [Notification of creditors] After reaching a determination of a claim submitted by an omitted creditor the Supervisor shall (a) notify the omitted creditor who submitted the claim of his determination and (b) notify all Creditors that the claim has been submitted and the outcome of his determination. If the Supervisor is of the opinion that the omitted creditor is entitled to or should participate in any dividend payable under the Arrangement, or should in any other way participate in the Arrangement, he should inform the Creditors (i) of the likely effect on their dividends or other benefits under the Arrangement of the participation of the omitted creditor, and (ii) the payments, if any, he proposes to make to the omitted creditor to ensure that he is not unfairly prejudiced by his late admission to the Arrangement. The Supervisor may, if he considers it advisable to do so, summon a meeting of Creditors to consider the participation in the Arrangement of the omitted creditor and or whether to resolve that the Supervisor do issue a Certificate of Termination for the purposes of paragraph 67(3).

52A(6) [Calling of meeting] On receipt of such notice from the Supervisor any one or more Creditors [the value of whose debts amount to not less than [10]% of the total debts of the existing Creditors] may, within seven days of such receipt, requisition a meeting of the Creditors to consider the participation in the Arrangement of the omitted creditor and or whether to resolve that the Supervisor do issue a Certificate of Termination for the purposes of paragraph 67(3).

52A(7) [Decision of meeting] In the event that the meeting of Creditors summoned by the Supervisor or requisitioned by Creditors:

(a) resolves that the omitted creditor should participate in the Arrangement, the meeting shall also consider what payments, if any, should be made by the Supervisor to the omitted creditor under the Arrangement to ensure that the omitted creditor is not unfairly prejudiced by his late admission to the Arrangement;

(b) resolves that the Supervisor do issue a Certificate of Termination, the meeting shall also consider what, if any, payments should be made to the omitted creditor in order to ensure that he is not unfairly prejudiced by the implementation of the Arrangement to the date of its termination.

52A(8) [Supervisor's actions] If no meeting of creditors is summoned or requisitioned within the time allowed, or if a meeting of creditors fails to reach any decision in relation to the admission of the omitted creditor or the termination of the Arrangement, the Supervisor will proceed to admit the omitted creditor to the Arrangement and make such payments as may be necessary to ensure that the omitted creditor is not unfairly prejudiced by his late admission to the Arrangement.

52A(9) [Termination by creditors] In the event that the value of the omitted creditor's claim admitted by the Supervisor either by itself or in conjunction with the value of other claims from omitted creditors admitted by the Supervisor amounts to more than [10%] of the value of the debts and liabilities disclosed by the debtor by the date of the creditors' meeting at which the Arrangement was approved, the Supervisor shall issue a Notice of Breach under paragraph 67(1). As this breach will not be capable of remedy the Supervisor shall then proceed to convene, as soon as practicable, a meeting of creditors under paragraph 67(3).

4.10 Standard conditions for Individual Voluntary Arrangements

Produced by the Association of Business Recovery Professionals (R3)

TABLE OF CONTENTS

PART I: INTERPRETATION

1 Miscellaneous definitions

1 In the Arrangement, except where the context otherwise demands:

(a) "**the Act**" means the Insolvency Act 1986 as amended;

(b) "**the Arrangement**" means the Proposal and the Conditions read together;

(c) "**Associate**" shall have the meaning given to it in section 435 of the Act;

(d) "**the Conditions**" are these Conditions;

(e) "**the Court**" means any court having jurisdiction in respect of the Arrangement;

(f) "**Creditor**" is a person bound by the Arrangement to whom a Debt is owed;

(g) "**Debt**" has the meaning given to it in section 382 of the Act with the modifications necessary to refer to a voluntary arrangement;

(h) "**the Debtor**" means the person who makes the Proposal;

(i) **"Dividend"** means a distribution to Creditors;

(j) "**Excluded Assets**" are those assets identified in the Proposal as being excluded from the Arrangement;

(k) "**Paragraphs**" are Paragraphs of these Conditions; and Sub-paragraph shall be construed accordingly;

(l) **"Preferential Creditor"** is a Creditor with a Debt falling within section 386 of the Act and "**Preferential Debt**" shall be construed accordingly;

(m) "**Property**" has the meaning given to it in section 436 of the Act;

(n) "**the Proposal**" is the document annexed hereto together with modifications and documents incorporated thereto, being a proposal under Part VIII of the Act;

(o) "**the Rules**" means the Insolvency Rules 1986 as amended;

(p) "**Security**" has the meaning given to it in section 383 of the Act; and "Secured Creditor" shall be construed accordingly;

(q) "**the Supervisor**" is the person or persons for the time being appointed to supervise the implementation of the Arrangement.

2 The Conditions

2 The Conditions are an integral part of the Arrangement. In the event of any ambiguity or conflict between the Conditions and the Proposal and any modifications to it, the Proposal as modified shall prevail.

PART II: COMMENCEMENT, EFFECT, AND
DURATION OF ARRANGEMENT

3 Commencement of Arrangement

3 The Arrangement shall come into effect upon the approval thereof by the Creditors pursuant to the provisions of the Act and Rules.

4 Nature and effect of the Arrangement

4(1) [Nature of Arrangement] The Arrangement is a proposal under Part VIII of the Act for a scheme of arrangement of the Debtor's affairs or a composition in full and final satisfaction of the Debtor's Debts.

4(2) [Claims against third parties] Unless the Proposal indicates to the contrary, nothing in the Arrangement shall be construed as effecting a composition or satisfaction of any Debt owed by a person other than the Debtor, whether that Debt is owed jointly by the Debtor or otherwise.

4(3) [Restriction on Creditor's rights] After the commencement of the Arrangement, no Creditor shall, in respect of any Debt which is subject to the Arrangement:

(a) have any remedy against the property or person of the Debtor;

(b) commence or continue any action or other legal proceeding against the Debtor.

4(4) [Saving for certain rights] Nothing in this Paragraph or elsewhere in the Conditions shall be construed as affecting the following rights:

(a) the right of any Secured Creditor to enforce his Security, except with the Secured Creditor's consent;

(b) the right of the Supervisor or any Creditor to present a bankruptcy petition under section 264(1)(c) of the Act for default in connection with the Arrangement;

(c) the right of any Creditor to bring or continue legal proceedings against the Debtor and to obtain a judgment against the Debtor in the full amount of its Debt for the sole purpose of making a claim against an insurer of the Debtor by virtue of the Third Party (Rights Against Insurers) Act 1930.

5 Existing proceedings against Debtor

5(1) [Discontinuance of existing proceedings] Legal proceedings against the Debtor in existence at the commencement of the Arrangement in respect of Debts which are subject to the Arrangement shall, unless they are of a type contemplated by Paragraph 4(4), be discontinued by the Creditor as soon after the commencement of the Arrangement as is practicable.

5(2) [Costs of existing proceedings] Legal costs of a Creditor in proceedings other than bankruptcy referred to in Sub-paragraph (1) shall be a Debt falling within the Arrangement.

5(3) [Costs of bankruptcy proceedings] Petition costs of a Creditor who presented a bankruptcy petition against the Debtor prior to the commencement of the Arrangement shall be treated as an expense of the Arrangement to rank after the costs of the Nominee but before those of the Supervisor.

5(4) [Prior distress] Where any person has distrained on the goods or effects of the Debtor in the period of three months prior to the making of the interim order, those goods or effects, or the proceeds of their sale, shall be charged with the Preferential Debts of the Debtor to the extent that the assets of the Arrangement are insufficient for meeting those debts.

6 Existing execution against Debtor's assets

6(1) [Partly-completed execution] A Creditor who, before the commencement of the Arrangement, has issued execution against the goods or land of the Debtor in respect of a Debt which is subject to the Arrangement, or has attached a Debt due to the Debtor from another person in respect of such a Debt shall, unless the execution or attachment was completed before the commencement of the Arrangement, discontinue the execution or attachment as soon after the commencement of the Arrangement as is practicable.

6(2) [Completion of execution or attachment] For the purposes of Sub-paragraph (1):

(a) an execution against goods is completed by seizure and sale or by the making of a charging order absolute under section 1 of the Charging Orders Act 1979;

(b) an execution against land is completed by seizure, by the appointment of a receiver or by the making of a charging order absolute under section 1 of the Charging Orders Act 1979;

(c) an attachment of a Debt is completed by the receipt of the Debt.

7 Mutual credit and set-off

7(1) [Application] This Paragraph applies where before the commencement of the Arrangement there have been mutual credits, mutual Debts or other mutual dealings between the Debtor and any Creditor.

7(2) [Account to be taken] An account shall be taken of what is due from each party to the other in respect of the mutual dealings and the sums due from one party shall be set-off against the sums due from the other.

7(3) [No account where Creditor has notice] Sums due from the Debtor to another party shall not be included in the account taken under Sub-paragraph (2) if that other party had notice at the time they became due that a bankruptcy petition relating to the Debtor was pending or that an interim order was made in relation to the Debtor.

7(4) [Restriction on post-commencement set-off] Other than as provided for in this Paragraph, set-off shall not be available in respect of any Debt or item of Property.

7(5) [Balance provable or to be paid] Only the balance (if any) of the account taken under Sub-paragraph (2) is provable in the Arrangement or, as the case may be, to be paid to the Debtor or, if the Proposal so provides, to the Supervisor.

8 Duration of Arrangement

8(1) [General rule] Unless extended under the provisions of these Conditions, the Arrangement shall continue until the end of the period stated in the Proposal.

8(2) [Extension of duration by Supervisor] The Supervisor may, if he thinks fit for the purposes of finalising the administration of the Arrangement, extend the duration of the Arrangement by sending a notice to this effect ("an Extension Notice") to the Debtor and all Creditors. This may be done on up to two occasions: for a period of up to 6 months in the first instance and for a period of up to three months in the second instance.

8(3) [Extension Notice] An Extension Notice shall be sent not less than seven days prior to the date upon which the Arrangement is otherwise due to complete and must state the reason or reasons for the extension.

8(4) [Effect of extension] In the event of an Extension Notice being sent, the Arrangement shall continue for the period specified therein, or for the maximum allowable period for that extension (being six months for a first extension and three months for a second extension) commencing on the date immediately after that on which the Arrangement would otherwise have completed, whichever is sooner.

8(5) [Supervening notice calling a meeting of Creditors] In the event that a meeting of Creditors has been called by the Supervisor for a time after the

Arrangement would otherwise have expired, the duration of the Arrangement shall be extended to the date of that meeting and to any adjournment thereof.

8(6) [Further extension] Any extension for a period longer than that provided for under Paragraph 8(2) shall require approval as a variation in accordance with Paragraph 70.

9 Completion of Arrangement

9(1) [The Completion Certificate] Upon the expiration of the Arrangement, the Supervisor shall, if the Debtor has complied with his obligations under the Arrangement, issue a certificate ("the Completion Certificate") stating that the Proposal has been fully implemented.

9(2) [Effect of Completion Certificate] Save to the extent provided in Paragraph 4(4), upon the issue by the Supervisor of a Completion Certificate, the Debtor shall be released from all Debts which are subject to the Arrangement.

9(3) [Notification of issue of Completion Certificate] Copies of the Completion Certificate issued under this Paragraph shall be sent by the Supervisor to the Debtor, the Creditors, the Secretary of State for Trade and Industry and the Court together with the Supervisor's report under Rule 5.29 (completion or termination of Arrangement).

10 Substantial Compliance

10(1) [Issue of certificate where substantial compliance] The Supervisor may, if he thinks fit, issue a Completion Certificate notwithstanding the fact that the Debtor has not complied with all of his obligations under the Arrangement provided that the Debtor has:

(a) made all payments required of him under the terms of the Arrangement;

(b) provided a full explanation of any breach of the terms of the Arrangement required by the Supervisor;

(c) paid to the Supervisor such sum (if any) as the Supervisor shall reasonably have required to compensate the Creditors for any reduction in Dividend caused by the Debtor's breach of the terms of the Arrangement.

10(2) [Notification to creditors] Where the Supervisor proposes to issue a Completion Certificate under Sub-paragraph 1 he shall notify the Creditors accordingly and invite them to submit any comments within 21 days from the date of notification.

10(3) [Treatment as full implementation] If the Supervisor issues a Completion Certificate under Sub-paragraph (1), the Arrangement shall be treated as fully implemented.

11 Termination of Arrangement

11(1) [Termination in certain circumstances] The Arrangement shall terminate upon:

(a) the Supervisor issuing a Certificate of Termination under Paragraph 67;

(b) the making of a bankruptcy order against the Debtor;

(c) the Debtor's death,

none of which circumstances shall affect the trusts created under Paragraph 29.

11(2) [Notice of termination] The Supervisor shall, on discovering the occurrence of a terminating event, but in any event not more than 28 days after such discovery, give notice of such termination and the reason therefor to the Debtor (or, if the Debtor has died, his representative) and Creditors.

PART III: SUPERVISOR'S FUNCTIONS, POWERS ETC

12 Supervisor's functions

12(1) [Primary function] The Supervisor's primary function is to supervise the Debtor's performance of his obligations under the Arrangement and to administer the Arrangement.

12(2) [Other functions] The Supervisor shall also undertake such functions as are given to him in the Proposal, Act and Rules.

13 Supervisor's powers

13 Subject to those powers more particularly given to him in the Arrangement, Act and Rules, the Supervisor shall have the following powers:

13(1) [*Getting in assets*] power to take possession of, collect, get in and hold any or all of the assets which, under the terms of the Arrangement, he is to hold as trustee;

13(2) [*Realisation of assets*] power to sell or otherwise dispose of any asset referred to in Sub-paragraph (1) in such manner as may seem to him expedient;

13(3) [*Putting funds on deposit*] power to place money coming into his hands during the course of the Arrangement on deposit with any established United Kingdom clearing bank or building society;

13(4) [*Appointing agents*] power to engage legal representatives, managers, agents and other persons to assist the Supervisor in the performance of his functions under the Arrangement;

13(5) [*Delegation*] power to delegate to his firm and any appropriate partner, employee or agent thereof any or all of his duties and functions under the Arrangement save those which by law he is required to perform personally;

13(6) [*Insurance*] power to effect and maintain insurances in respect of any asset subject to the Arrangement;

13(7) [*Power to claim*] power to prove, rank, claim and draw a Dividend in respect of such Debts owed to the Debtor as fall within the Arrangement;

13(8) [*Power to direct Debtor*] power, in the event that the Supervisor is unable or it is impracticable for him to do any act or thing which he is empowered to do himself, to direct the Debtor to do that act or thing on his behalf;

13(9) [*Ancillary power*] power to do any other act or thing which is necessary or expedient for the purposes of exercising the above powers or for carrying out his functions under the Arrangement.

14 Supervisor's powers upon completion/termination

14(1) [Exercise of powers after completion/termination] Completion and/ or termination of the Arrangement shall not affect the Supervisor's power to carry out such of his functions and to exercise such of his powers as are necessary for him to fully carry out his duties, obligations and responsibilities under the Arrangement, Act and Rules and to resolve such matters as may have arisen during the course of the Arrangement.

14(2) [Retention of funds by Supervisor] Upon completion and/or termination of the arrangement, the Supervisor shall be entitled to retain for such period as he reasonably deems necessary from any funds under his control such moneys as he reasonably thinks fit on account of his fees, costs, charges, liabilities and expenses, and shall advise Creditors and the Debtor in writing of the quantum of the funds so retained and the reasons why.

15 Exercise of Supervisor's functions and powers

15(1) [Application of bankruptcy provisions] In the event that the Arrangement does not provide guidance to the Supervisor as to what action he should take in any given situation, the Supervisor shall apply the provisions of the Act and Rules in so far as they relate to bankruptcy with necessary modifications.

15(2) [Consultation of Creditors] If the Supervisor is uncertain as to what action he should take in any situation, or wishes to ascertain the wishes of Creditors on a matter concerning the Arrangement, he may seek the advice and/or direction of the Creditors' Committee and/or the majority or most material of the Creditors and he may act upon such advice and/or direction.

15(3) [Directions from the Court] This Paragraph is without prejudice to the Supervisor's right to refer matters concerning the Arrangement to the Court for guidance and/or directions if, in his discretion, he shall think fit.

16 Restriction upon Supervisor's duty and liability

16(1) [Supervisor's duty] The Supervisor shall be under no obligation to perform any act or carry out any function save for those expressly provided for in the Arrangement, the Act or Rules.

16(2) [Supervisor's liability] Neither the Supervisor, his firm or any of his agents or employees shall incur any personal liability in negligence or otherwise for any act or omission carried out by him or any of them in connection with the Arrangement, unless such act or omission constitutes one of dishonesty or a breach of the Supervisor's obligations under the Act, Rules or the Arrangement.

17 Supervisor's fees, costs and expenses

17(1) [Amount of fees] The Supervisor shall be entitled to charge fees for his services in accordance with the time actually and reasonably expended by him and his staff in carrying out the Supervisor's functions under the Arrangement by reference to the ordinary hourly rates of the Supervisor and his staff as shall apply from time to time.

17(2) [Payment of fees, costs and expenses] The fees, costs, charges and expenses of the Supervisor shall be paid out of the assets of the Arrangement from time to time as the Supervisor thinks fit. The Supervisor shall provide such information to any Creditors' committee appointed in relation to the Arrangement as is reasonably necessary to explain how the fees, costs, charges and expenses were determined or incurred, as the case may be.

17(3) [Supervisor's right of recourse to Court] If the Supervisor is dissatisfied with a determination of the Creditors Committee or a meeting of Creditors on a matter involving his fees, costs, charges and/or expenses, he shall have the right to refer the matter to the Court, whose decision on the matter shall bind all parties.

18 Supervisor's resignation

18(1) [Methods of resignation] A Supervisor may resign from office with the approval of a meeting of Creditors or with the leave of the Court.

18(2) [Grounds of Supervisor's resignation] The Supervisor may only resign from office on one or more of the following grounds:

(a) ill health;

(b) cessation of practice as an insolvency practitioner;

(c) change of circumstances rendering it impracticable for him to continue in office;

(d) impracticability to have the present number of persons acting as Supervisor to the Arrangement.

18(3) [Report of Supervisor's administration] The notice to Creditors convening a meeting for the purpose of receiving his resignation shall specify the grounds upon which the Supervisor wishes to resign and shall be accompanied by a report of the Supervisor's administration of the Arrangement which includes an up to date summary of his receipts and payments.

19 Removal of Supervisor from Office

19(1) [Methods of removal] On cause being shown, the Supervisor may be removed from office by the Court or by a resolution of a meeting of Creditors.

19(2) [Notice of requisitioned meeting] Any notice served by a Creditor upon the Supervisor under Paragraph 56(2) (notice requisitioning meeting) for the purpose of convening a meeting of Creditors to remove the Supervisor from office must set out the grounds upon which his removal is sought.

19(3) [Report of Supervisor's administration] The notice sent out by the Supervisor to Creditors convening such a requisitioned meeting shall specify the grounds upon which his removal is sought and shall be accompanied by a report of the Supervisor's administration of the Arrangement including an up to date summary of his receipts and payments.

20 Vacation of Office by Supervisor

20(1) [Resignation/removal of Supervisor where more than one acting] If the Creditors resolve to accept the resignation of a Supervisor, or to remove a Supervisor from office, and there will be another person in the office of Supervisor for the time being, the Supervisor who is resigning or being removed shall vacate office immediately.

20(2) [Resignation/removal of Supervisor where no other acting] If the Creditors resolve to accept a Supervisor's resignation or to remove a Supervisor from office, and there is no other person in the office of Supervisor for the time being, that resignation and/or removal shall not take effect and the Supervisor shall not vacate office unless and until a meeting of Creditors or the Court appoints a replacement Supervisor.

20(3) [Loss of qualification] The Supervisor shall vacate office immediately if he ceases to be a person who is for the time being qualified to act as an insolvency practitioner.

20(4) [Notice of vacation of Office] A Supervisor who, for any reason, vacates office shall forthwith give notice of that fact to the Court, the Debtor the Creditors and the Secretary of State for Trade and Industry.

20(5) [Duties of Supervisor upon vacation of Office] A Supervisor who, for any reason, vacates office shall, as soon as practicable, deliver up to his successor Supervisor or Supervisors all books, records and papers relating to the Arrangement and his administration thereof together with all assets of which he is a trustee under the terms of the Arrangement.

20(6) [Continuing duty of former Supervisor] Former Supervisors shall be obliged to give such assistance to the Supervisor of the Arrangement from time to time as he may reasonably require for ascertaining what transpired during the tenure of office by the former Supervisor.

21 Vacancy in the Office of Supervisor

21(1) [Meeting of Creditors to fill vacancy] If, for any reason, there is a vacancy in the office of Supervisor, that vacancy may be filled by a meeting of Creditors or by the Court.

21(2) [Convening a meeting where no Supervisor acting] If no Supervisor is in office, such a meeting of Creditors may be convened by the Debtor, any Creditor, any person who was in partnership with the Supervisor immediately before the vacancy occurred, or by the former Supervisor's authorising body.

21(3) [Chairman where no Supervisor acting] In the event that a meeting of Creditors is called when no Supervisor is in office, the person who convened the meeting shall act as chairman of that meeting.

PART IV: DEBTOR'S WARRANTY, DUTIES & OBLIGATIONS

22 Debtor's warranty

22(1) [Disclosure in Proposal] The Debtor warrants that he has disclosed in the Proposal full and complete particulars of all matters required of him under the Act and Rules including (without prejudice to the generality of the foregoing) particulars of all of his assets, Debts and liabilities, whether actual, contingent or prospective.

22(2) [Accuracy of Proposal] The Debtor warrants that the contents of the Proposal are true and accurate in all material respects as at the date of the commencement of the Arrangement, subject only to those qualifications that may be disclosed by the Debtor at the meeting of Creditors held to approve the arrangement, which qualifications shall be recorded by the Supervisor in his report to the Court under Rule 5.22 (report of Creditors' meeting).

22(3) [Disclosure of third party information] The Debtor authorises any creditor to disclose to the Supervisor such information relating to the Debtor, his dealings or property as may reasonably be required to assist in the implementation of the Arrangement.

23 Debtor's duties in relation to Supervisor

23(1) [Duty to co-operate with Supervisor] The Debtor undertakes and agrees that during the subsistence of the Arrangement he will:

(a) give to the Supervisor such information as to his assets, liabilities and other affairs;

(b) attend on the Supervisor, his agents, representatives or nominees at such times; and

(c) do all such other things;

as the Supervisor shall reasonably require for the purpose of carrying out his functions and duties under the Arrangement.

23(2) [Duty to submit accounts] The Debtor undertakes and agrees to furnish the Supervisor with accounts relating to his affairs of such nature, as at such date and for such period as the Supervisor may reasonably require.

23(3) [Notice of after-acquired assets and increased income] Where at any time during the subsistence of the Arrangement After-Acquired Property of a description falling within Paragraph 28 is acquired by or devolves upon the Debtor, or there is an increase in the Debtor's income if the Debtor is under an obligation to make contributions out of income, the Debtor shall forthwith give the Supervisor notice of the property or, as the case may be, of the increase.

24 Duty to hand over property to Supervisor

24 Forthwith after the Commencement of the Arrangement, and subject to the provisions of the Proposal, the Debtor shall do all that is required for putting the Supervisor into possession of the assets included in the Arrangement.

25 Further Documents

25 Without prejudice to the generality of the Debtor's other duties under the Arrangement, the Debtor shall, at the request of the Supervisor, execute such Mortgages, Charges, Deeds, Transfers, Trusts, Powers of Attorney or other documents as may reasonably be required by the Supervisor for the protection and/or realisation of assets, to secure the Debtor's compliance with his obligations under the Arrangement, or otherwise to facilitate the implementation of the Arrangement.

26 Debtor's acknowledgement

26(1) [Agreement to be bound] The Debtor undertakes to carry out the obligations imposed upon him under the Arrangement in full and at the times provided for.

26(2) [Consequences of breach] The Debtor acknowledges that the likely consequence of his failure to comply with his obligations hereunder in full and at the times provided for is that the Arrangement will fail and he will be adjudged bankrupt on a petition presented by the Supervisor.

26(3) [Rule 5.30] The Debtor acknowledges that he commits an offence if he makes any false representation or commits any other fraud for the purpose of obtaining the approval of his Creditors to the Arrangement.

PART V: ARRANGEMENT ASSETS

27 Arrangement assets

27 Property other than Excluded Assets belonging to or vested in the Debtor at the date of commencement of the Arrangement which would form part of the Debtor's estate in a bankruptcy shall be subject to the Arrangement and be an asset thereof.

28 After-acquired assets

28(1) [After-acquired property subject to Arrangement] Subject to the following Sub-paragraphs, the Supervisor may claim as an asset of the Arrangement any Property acquired by the Debtor between the commencement date of the Arrangement and the date of its completion and/or termination which would have been capable of being an asset of the Arrangement if it belonged to or was vested in the Debtor at the date of commencement of the Arrangement ("After-Acquired Assets"). Any such asset shall be subject to the Arrangement and be an asset thereof.

28(2) [Limit on assets which may be claimed] Sub-paragraph (1) shall not apply to:

(a) such equipment, stock or other effects as are necessary to the debtor for use personally by him in his employment, business or vocation;

(b) such clothing, bedding, furniture, household equipment and provisions as are necessary for supplying the domestic needs of the debtor and his family.

28(3) [Proviso for excess assets] After-Acquired Assets shall only be sold or realised to the extent necessary to repay the Creditors in full together with interest, if any, to which Creditors are entitled pursuant to the Arrangement.

29 Trust of Arrangement assets

29(1) [Assets in the possession of the Debtor] Property constituting an asset of the Arrangement in the possession, custody or control of the Debtor shall be held by the Debtor upon trust for the purposes of the Arrangement until realisation thereof (if so provided) in accordance with the Arrangement.

29(2) [Assets in the possession of the Supervisor] Property constituting an asset of the Arrangement in the possession, custody or control of the Supervisor shall be held by the Supervisor upon trust for the purposes of the Arrangement.

29(3) [Trusts to survive termination of Arrangement] The trusts referred to in Sub-paragraphs (1) and (2) shall not come to an end upon termination of the Arrangement. Instead those assets shall be got in and realised by the Supervisor, and any proceeds applied and distributed in accordance with the terms of the Arrangement.

30 Restriction on dispositions

30 The Debtor shall not sell, charge or otherwise dispose of any interest he may have in any asset subject to the Arrangement without the Supervisor's written consent.

PART VI: CLAIMS

31 Notice to submit claims

31 As soon as practicable after the commencement of the Arrangement, and provided no application under Section 262 of the Act (challenge of meeting's decision) or an appeal under Rule 5.17(5) (appeal from chairman's decision) is pending, the Supervisor shall send a notice ("a Notice to Submit Claims") to every Creditor and other person to whom the Debtor may be indebted of whom he has notice requiring them to provide such details of their claims as the Supervisor thinks fit.

32 Submission of claims

32 Any Creditor, or other person who wishes and agrees to participate in and be bound by the Arrangement, shall submit his claim in writing to the Supervisor in the form, if any, required by the Supervisor, or one which is substantially similar.

33 Variation of claims

33 A Creditor's claim may at any time be withdrawn or varied.

34 Production of documents

34 The Supervisor may call for any document or other evidence to be produced to him, where he thinks it necessary, for the purpose of substantiating the whole or any part of the claim.

35 Affidavit substantiating claim

35 The Supervisor may, if he thinks it necessary, require a claim to be verified by affidavit.

36 Supervisor to allow inspection of claims

36 The Supervisor shall, so long as claims lodged with him are in his hands, allow them to be inspected, at all reasonable times on any business day, by:

(a) any Creditor who has submitted his claim (unless that claim has been wholly rejected for the purposes of Dividend or otherwise); and

(b) the Debtor.

37 Admission and rejection of claims for Dividend

37(1) [Admission] A claim may be admitted for Dividend either for the whole of the amount claimed by the Creditor, or for part of that amount.

37(2) [Rejection] If the Supervisor rejects a claim in whole or in part, he shall prepare a written statement of his reasons for so doing and send it to the Creditor.

38 Appeal against decision on claim

38(1) [Application by Creditor] If a Creditor is dissatisfied with the Supervisor's decision with respect to his claim or its ranking he may apply to the Court, within 21 days (or such longer period as the Court shall, in the special circumstances, allow) of receiving the statement sent under Paragraph 37(2) for the decision to be reversed or varied.

38(2) [Application by Debtor or other Creditor] The Debtor or any other Creditor may, if dissatisfied with the Supervisor's decision admitting or rejecting the whole or any part of a claim, make such an application within 21 days (or such longer period as the Court shall, in the special circumstances, allow) of becoming aware of the Supervisor's decision.

38(3) [Costs of appeal] The Supervisor is not personally liable for the costs incurred by any person in respect of an appeal under this Paragraph unless the Court so orders.

39 Debts of uncertain value

39(1) [Estimation of Debt or liability] The Supervisor shall estimate the value of any Debt which, by reason of its being subject to a contingency or for any other reason, does not bear a certain value.

39(2) [Notification to Creditor] The Supervisor shall notify the Creditor in writing of any such estimate. If the Creditor is dissatisfied with the Supervisor's decision he may exercise his rights under paragraph 38.

39(3) [Claim of Debts of uncertain value] Where the value of any Debt is estimated by the Supervisor under Sub-paragraph (1), the amount provable in the Arrangement shall be the amount of the estimate.

40 Secured Creditors

40(1) [Proving for balance of Debt] A Secured Creditor may claim for the balance of his Debt (if any), after deducting the value of his Security.

40(2) [Voluntary surrender of Security] If a Secured Creditor voluntarily surrenders his Security for the general benefit of the Creditors, he may claim for his whole Debt, as if it were unsecured.

40(3) [Altering value of Security] A Secured Creditor may, with the agreement of the Supervisor or the leave of the Court, at any time alter the value which he has, in his claim, put upon his Security.

40(4) [Test of Security's value] If the Supervisor is dissatisfied with the value which a Secured Creditor puts on his Security (whether in his claim or by way of re-valuation), he may require the Security to be professionally valued by a person agreed as between the Creditor and the Supervisor, or in default of such agreement by the Court.

40(5) [Professional valuation treated as amended valuation] Where a professional valuation has been carried out under the previous Sub-paragraph, that valuation shall be treated as an amended valuation of the Creditor.

40(6) [Realisation of Security] If a Creditor who has valued his Security subsequently realises it:

(a) the Creditor shall forthwith notify the Supervisor and shall give the Supervisor such information relating thereto as he may reasonably require;

(b) the net amount realised shall be substituted for the value previously put by the Creditor on the Security, and

(c) that amount shall be treated in all respects as an amended valuation by him.

41 Foreign currency Debts

41(1) [Conversion into sterling] For the purpose of claiming for a Debt incurred or payable in a currency other than sterling, the amount of the Debt shall be converted into sterling at the official exchange rate prevailing on the date of the commencement of the Arrangement.

41(2) [The official exchange rate] The official exchange rate is the middle market rate at the Bank of England, as published for the date in question. In the absence of any such published rate, it is such rate as the Supervisor and Creditor agree or, in default of such agreement, the Court determines.

42 Debts payable at future time

42 Subject to Paragraph 51 (adjustment of Dividend where payment made before time) a Creditor may claim for a Debt of which payment was not yet due at the date of commencement of the Arrangement.

43 Interest on Debts

43 Where a Debt bears interest, that interest may be claimed as part of the Debt except in so far as it is payable in respect of any period after the commencement of the Arrangement.

44 Cost of submitting claims

44(1) [Creditor bears cost of submitting claim] Every Creditor bears the cost of submitting his own claim, including such cost as may be incurred in obtaining valuations, providing documents, affidavits or other evidence to the Supervisor.

44(2) [Supervisor's costs] Costs incurred by the Supervisor in estimating the value of a Debt of uncertain value shall be an expense of the Arrangement

PART VII: PAYMENT OF DIVIDENDS

45 Distribution by Dividend

45(1) [Duty to declare and distribute Dividends] At the time or times specified in the Proposal or, if none, whenever the Supervisor has sufficient funds in hand for the purpose, the Supervisor shall, subject to the retention of such sums as he considers necessary for payment of the expenses of the Arrangement, declare and distribute Dividends among the Creditors in respect of those of their claims which have been admitted.

45(2) [Calculation and distribution of Dividend] In the calculation and distribution of a Dividend the Supervisor shall make provision:

(a) for any Debts which are the subject of claims which have not yet been determined; and

(b) for disputed claims.

46 Notice of intended Dividend

46(1) [Notice to Creditors who have not claimed] No more than three months before declaring a Dividend to non-preferential Creditors, the Supervisor shall give notice of his intention to do so to all such Creditors whose addresses are known to him and who have not submitted their claims.

46(2) [Last date for submitting claims] Any notice sent out to Creditors under Sub-paragraph (1) shall specify a date ("the Last Date for Submitting Claims") up to which claims may be lodged. The Last date for Submitting Claims shall be the same for all Creditors, and not less than 21 days from the date of the notice.

47 Notice of declaration

47(1) [Notice to Creditors who have claimed] The Supervisor shall give notice of the Dividend to all Creditors who have submitted their claims.

47(2) [Particulars in notice] The notice shall include the following particulars:

(a) amounts realised from the sale of assets subject to the Arrangement and/or amounts paid by the Debtor to the Supervisor under the Arrangement;

(b) payments made by the Supervisor during the course of the Arrangement;

(c) provision (if any) made for unsettled claims, and funds (if any) retained for particular purposes;

(d) the total amount to be distributed, and the rate of Dividend;

(e) whether, and if so when, any further Dividend is expected to be declared.

47(3) [Simultaneous distribution] The Dividend may be distributed simultaneously with the notice declaring it.

47(4) [Method of payment] Payment of Dividend may be made by post, or arrangements may be made with any Creditor for it to be paid in another way, or held for his collection.

47(5) [Endorsement in negotiable instrument] Where a Dividend is paid on a bill of exchange or other negotiable instrument, the amount of the Dividend shall be endorsed on the instrument, or on a certified copy of it, if required to be produced by the holder for that purpose.

48 Claim altered after payment of Dividend

48(1) [Amount claimed increased] If, after payment of Dividend, the amount claimed by a Creditor is increased, the Creditor is not entitled to disturb the distribution of the Dividend; but he is entitled to be paid, out of any money for the time being available for the payment of any further Dividend, any Dividend or Dividends which he has failed to receive before that money is applied to the payment of any such further Dividend.

48(2) [Claim withdrawn, disallowed, reduced] If, after a Creditor's claim has been admitted, the claim is withdrawn or disallowed, or the amount of it is reduced, the Creditor shall repay to the Supervisor any amount overpaid by way of Dividend.

49 Secured Creditors

49(1) [Application of Paragraph] The following applies where a Creditor re-values his Security at a time when a Dividend has been declared.

49(2) [Reduction in unsecured claim] If the re-valuation results in a reduction of his unsecured claim ranking for Dividend, the Creditor shall, as soon as practicable, repay to the Supervisor any amount received by him as Dividend in excess of that to which he would be entitled having regard to the re-valuation of the Security.

49(3) [Increase of unsecured claim] If the re-valuation results in an increase of his unsecured claim, the Creditor is entitled to receive from the Supervisor, out of any money for the time being available for the payment of a further Dividend, before any such Dividend is paid, any Dividend or Dividends which he has failed to receive, having regard to the re-valuation of the Security. However, the Creditor is not entitled to disturb any Dividend declared (whether or not distributed) before the date of the revaluation.

50 Assignment of Debts or rights to Dividend

50(1) [Notice of assignment] If a person entitled to a Dividend gives notice to the Supervisor that he wishes the Dividend to be paid to another person, or that he has assigned his entitlement or Debt to another person, the Supervisor shall pay the Dividend to that other person accordingly.

50(2) [Contents of notice] A notice given under this Paragraph must specify the name and address of the person to whom payment is to be made.

51 Debts payable at future time

51(1) [Entitlement to Dividend] Where a Creditor has claimed for a Debt of which payment is not due at the date of the declaration of Dividend, he is entitled to Dividend equally with other Creditors, but subject as follows.

51(2) [Calculation of amount of reduction] For the purpose of Dividend (and for no other purpose), the amount of the Creditor's admitted claim (or, if a distribution has previously been made to him, the amount remaining outstanding in respect of his admitted claim) shall be reduced by a percentage calculated as follows:

$$\frac{I \times M}{12}$$

where I is 5 per cent and M is the number of months (expressed, if need be, as or as including, fractions of months) between the declaration of Dividend and the date when payment of the Creditor's Debt would otherwise be due.

52 Debts of unpaid Creditors

51(1) [Creditors not entitled to Dividend] Creditors who do not claim in the Arrangement shall not be entitled to receive any Dividend.

52(2) [Unclaimed Dividends paid to Debtor] Dividends due to Creditors who have claimed in the Arrangement but who have not claimed or been paid their Dividends shall, at the end of the Arrangement, be paid to the Debtor.

52(3) [Debtor liable for unclaimed Dividends] Once a Dividend has been paid to the Debtor under the previous Sub-paragraph, the Creditor must claim it from the Debtor and no other person.

PART VIII: PRIORITY OF PAYMENTS AND DISTRIBUTIONS

53 Costs and Expenses of the Arrangement

53(1) [Expenses to be paid first] Subject to Paragraph 5(3) the fees, costs, charges, expenses and liabilities properly charged or incurred by or on behalf of the Nominee or the Supervisor are expenses of the Arrangement and shall be paid in priority to all other charges, expenses, liabilities and Debts.

53(2) [Charge in relation to expenses] The Supervisor shall have a charge on the assets subject to the Arrangement in respect of the expenses of the Arrangement.

54 Priority of Debts and application of surplus

54(1) [Priority of preferential Debts] In the distribution of sums due to be paid to Creditors under the terms of the Arrangement, Preferential Debts shall be paid in priority to other Debts.

54(2) [Ranking of preferential Debts] Preferential Debts rank equally between themselves after the expenses of the Arrangement.

54(3) [Ranking of ordinary Debts] Debts other than Preferential Debts rank equally between themselves and, after the Preferential Debts, shall be paid in full unless the sums due to be paid to Creditors are insufficient for meeting them, in which case they abate in equal proportions between themselves.

54(4) [Surplus after payment] Any surplus remaining after the payment of the Preferential and other Debts shall first be applied in paying interest on those Debts in respect of the periods during which they have been outstanding since the commencement of the Arrangement (for this purpose interest on Preferential Debts ranks equally with interest on Debts other than Preferential Debts) and thereafter returned to the Debtor.

54(5) [Interest rate on surplus] The rate of interest payable under Sub-paragraph (4) in respect of any Debt is whichever is the greater of the following:

(a) the rate specified in section 17 of the Judgments Act 1838 at the commencement of the Arrangement; and

(b) the rate applicable to that Debt apart from the Arrangement.

PART IX: THE CREDITORS COMMITTEE AND MEETINGS OF CREDITORS

55 The Creditors' Committee

55(1) [Establishment] Any meeting of Creditors may establish a committee ("the Creditors' Committee"), consisting of not less than 3 and not more than 5 members to represent the interests of the Creditors and to provide such assistance and guidance to the Supervisor as he may reasonably require.

55(2) [Eligibility] All the members of the Creditors' Committee must be Creditors of the Debtor; and any Creditor (other than one who is fully secured) may be a member, so long as:

(a) he has lodged a claim, and

(b) his claim has neither been wholly disallowed for voting purposes, nor wholly rejected for the purposes of distribution or Dividend.

55(3) [Application of Rules] The Rules relating to the Creditors' Committee in a bankruptcy contained in Rules 6.151 to 6.163 shall apply to the Arrangement with the modifications necessary to apply those rules to a voluntary arrangement.

55(4) [Expenses of members] The reasonable travelling expenses directly incurred by any member of the Creditors' Committee or their representatives in respect of their attendance at the meetings of the Creditors' Committee, or otherwise on the Creditors' Committee's business, shall rank as an expense of the Arrangement.

56 Power to call/requisition meetings of Creditors

56(1) [Supervisor's power to call meetings] The Supervisor may, if he thinks it desirable, summon and conduct meetings of Creditors for any purpose connected with the Arrangement.

56(2) [Power to requisition a meeting] If requested in writing by the Debtor, or by Creditors with not less than one-quarter in value of the total amount of Debts subject to the Arrangement, the Supervisor shall, unless relieved by the Court from so doing, convene a meeting of Creditors within 21 days from the receipt of such request.

56(3) [Content of notice requisitioning meeting] A notice served upon the Supervisor under Sub-paragraph (2) shall state the purpose for which the meeting is to be held.

57 Calling Creditors' meetings

57(1) [Notice of meeting] Notice of a Creditor's meeting shall be given by the person convening the meeting to the Debtor and every Creditor whose address is known to him or identified in the Proposal at least 14 days before the date fixed for the meeting, or such shorter period as the Court may allow.

57(2) [Contents of notice] The notice to Creditors shall specify the purpose for which the meeting is convened and a time and date (not earlier than 4.00 p.m. on the business day before the meeting) by which Creditors must lodge proxies and those who have not already lodged claims must do so, in order to be entitled to vote at the meeting.

57(3) [Forms of proxy] With every notice convening a Creditors' meeting there shall be sent out forms of proxy.

57(4) [Venue of meeting] In fixing the venue for a meeting of Creditors, the person convening it shall have regard to the convenience of the parties who may wish to attend.

57(5) [Time of meeting] Meetings of Creditors shall be convened for commencement between the hours of 10.00 and 16.00 on a business day, unless the Court otherwise directs.

57(6) [Chairman of meeting] Unless Paragraph 21(3) (chairman where no Supervisor acting) applies, the Supervisor, or a person experienced in insolvency matters and nominated by him, shall be chairman of the meeting.

58 Cost of summoning meetings

58(1) [Security for payment of expenses] Subject to Sub-paragraph (3) below, the cost of summoning and holding a meeting of Creditors at the instance of the Debtor or Creditors under Paragraph 56(2) shall be paid by that person or persons, who shall deposit security for their payment with the Supervisor.

58(2) [Appropriate security] The sum to be deposited shall be such as the Supervisor determines to be appropriate; and the Supervisor shall be under no obligation to act without the deposit having been paid.

58(3) [Vote for cost to be an expense of arrangement] Where a meeting is so summoned, it may vote that the expenses of convening and holding it shall rank as an expense of the Arrangement.

58(4) [Repayment of deposit] To the extent that any deposit made under this Paragraph is not required for the payment of expenses of convening and holding the meeting, it shall be repaid to the person who made it.

59 Entitlement to vote

59(1) [Conditions for voting] Subject as follows, at a meeting of Creditors a person is entitled to vote as a Creditor only if:

(a) he has duly lodged his claim by the time and date stated in the notice of the meeting, and

(b) the claim has been admitted under the next Paragraph for the purpose of entitlement to vote, and there has been lodged, by that time and date, any proxy requisite for that entitlement.

59(2) [Unliquidated and unascertained claims] A Creditor shall not vote in respect of a Debt for an unliquidated amount, or any Debt whose value is not ascertained, except where the Chairman agrees to put upon the Debt an estimated minimum value for the purpose of entitlement to vote.

59(3) [Secured Creditors] A Secured Creditor is entitled to vote only in respect of the balance (if any) of his Debt after deducting the value of his Security as estimated by him.

60 Admission and rejection of claim

60(1) [Chairman's discretion] The chairman has power to admit or reject a Creditor's claim for the purpose of his entitlement to vote, and the power is exercisable with respect to the whole or any part of the claim.

60(2) [Appeal from chairman's decision] The chairman's decision on entitlement to vote is subject to appeal to the Court by any Creditor, or by the Debtor, within 21 days of the meeting of Creditors at which the decision was made, or such longer period as the Court shall, in the special circumstances, allow.

60(3) [Voting subject to objection] If the chairman is in doubt whether a claim should be admitted or rejected, he shall mark it objected to and allow the Creditor to vote, subject to his vote being subsequently declared invalid if the objection to the claim is sustained.

60(4) [Where chairman's decision reversed] If, on an appeal, the chairman's decision is reversed or varied, or a Creditor's vote is declared invalid, the Court may order another meeting to be summoned, or make such other order as it thinks fit, provided that the Court considers the matter is such as to give rise to unfair prejudice or a material irregularity.

60(5) [Costs of appeal] The chairman is not personally liable for the costs incurred by any person in respect of an appeal under this Paragraph unless the Court so orders.

61 Majorities required to pass resolutions

61(1) [Resolutions by majority in value] Subject as follows, at a meeting of Creditors a resolution is passed when a majority in value of Creditors present and voting, in person or by proxy, have voted in favour of the resolution.

61(2) [Resolutions varying terms of Arrangement] In the case of a resolution varying the terms of the Arrangement, a majority in excess of three-quarters in value of those present and voting, in person or by proxy, is required to pass the resolution.

61(3) [Votes rendering resolution invalid] Any resolution is invalid if those voting against it include more than half in value of the Creditors who are not, to the best of the chairman's belief, Associates of the Debtor.

61(4) [Resolution for the appointment of Supervisor] In the case of a resolution for the appointment of a Supervisor:

(a) if on any vote there are 2 nominees for appointment, the person who obtains the most support is appointed, provided that such support represents a majority in value of all those present (in person or by proxy) at the meeting and entitled to vote; and

(b) if there are 3 or more nominees, and one of them has a clear majority over both or all of the others together, that one is appointed; and

(c) in any other case, the chairman shall continue to take votes (disregarding at each vote any nominee who has withdrawn and, if no nominee has withdrawn, the nominee who obtained the least support last time), until a clear majority is obtained for any one nominee.

61(5) [Resolution for joint appointment] The chairman may at any time put to the meeting a resolution for the joint appointment of any 2 or more nominees if he thinks it appropriate.

62 Chairman of meeting as proxy-holder

62 Where the chairman at a meeting holds a proxy for a Creditor which requires him to vote for a particular resolution, and no other person proposes that resolution, he shall himself propose it.

63 Suspension/adjournment of meeting

63(1) [Suspension] Once only in the course of any meeting, the chairman may, in his discretion and without an adjournment, declare the meeting suspended for any period up to one hour.

63(2) [Adjournment] The chairman at any meeting may, in his discretion, and shall, if the meeting so resolves, adjourn it to such time and place as seems to him to be appropriate in the circumstances; provided that if the chairman is the Supervisor and a resolution has been proposed for his removal, the chairman shall not adjourn the meeting without the consent of at least one half in value of the Creditors present (in person or by proxy) and entitled to vote.

63(3) [Period of adjournment] An adjournment under this Paragraph shall not be for a period of more than 21 days, or such longer period as the Court may allow.

63(4) [Use of claims and proxies at adjourned meeting] Where a meeting is adjourned under this Paragraph, claims and proxies may be used if lodged at any time up to 4.00 p.m. on the business day immediately before the adjourned meeting.

64 Record of proceedings

64(1) [Minutes of proceedings] The chairman of any Creditors' meeting shall cause minutes of the proceedings at the meeting, signed by him, to be retained as part of the records of the Arrangement.

64(2) [List of Creditors attending] The chairman shall also cause to be made and kept a list of all the Creditors who attended the meeting either in person or by proxy and the amount of their claims for voting purposes.

64(3) [Record of resolutions] The minutes of the meeting shall include a record of the resolutions which were taken at the meeting and the decision on each one.

64(4) [List of creditors to be circulated] The list of Creditors referred to in Sub-paragraph (2) shall be sent with the chairman's report to Creditors, the Debtor and the Court.

65 Postal resolutions

65(1) [Application of procedure] The following procedure may be utilised by the Supervisor, if he thinks fit, for the purposes of ascertaining the wishes of Creditors on any matter concerning the Arrangement other than the removal of the Supervisor.

65(2) [Notice of proposed resolution] The Supervisor may send to the Debtor and every Creditor whose address is known to him or identified in the Proposal a notice containing a copy of any proposed resolution on which a decision is sought, which shall be set out in a such a way that agreement with or dissent from each separate resolution may be indicated by the recipient on the copy so sent.

65(3) [Contents of notice] The notice must specify a date ("the Last Date for Voting"), not less that 21 days after the date of sending thereof, by which Creditors must lodge their votes with the Supervisor and those who have not already lodged claims must do so, in order to be entitled to vote.

65(4) [Creditors requiring meeting] Creditors with one-quarter in value of the total amount of Debts subject to the Arrangement may, within 14 days from the date upon which the Supervisor sent out the resolution, request the Supervisor in writing to summon a meeting of Creditors to consider the matters raised by the resolution and, if they so request, the Supervisor shall call a meeting of Creditors for that purpose.

65(5) [Deemed passing of resolution] In the absence such a request, the resolution is deemed to have been carried at a duly convened meeting of Creditors, if, of the written votes received by the Supervisor by the end of the Last Date for Voting, a sufficient majority of Creditors as defined in Paragraph 61 entitled to vote on the resolution have indicated their consent to the resolution in writing.

65(6) [Application of voting rights and majorities] The provisions of Paragraphs 59 (entitlement to vote), 60 (admission and rejection of claim) and 61 (majorities required to pass resolutions) shall apply to postal votes as they do to votes at meetings of Creditors.

65(7) [Copy of resolutions] A copy of every resolution taken under this Paragraph, together with copies of the votes of Creditors received by the Supervisor endorsed by the Supervisor with the date upon which the vote was received by him, shall be kept with the records of the Arrangement.

PART X: PROVISIONS FOLLOWING BREACH OF THE ARRANGEMENT

66 Breach by the Debtor of the terms of the Arrangement

66 The Debtor shall be regarded as in breach of the Arrangement if:

(a) he fails to comply with any of his obligations under the Arrangement;

(b) information which was false or misleading in any material particular or contains any material omissions:

- (i) was contained in any statement of affairs or other document supplied by the Debtor under Part VIII under the Act to any person, or
- (ii) was otherwise made available by the Debtor to his Creditors at or in connection with any meeting of Creditors held, or any postal resolution taken, in connection with the Arrangement, or

(c) the Debtor fails to do all such things as may for the purposes of the Arrangement have been reasonably required of him by the Supervisor.

67 Procedure following breach

67(1) [Notice of Breach] If, at any time, it appears to the Supervisor that the Debtor is in breach of the Arrangement, then, unless such breach is remedied forthwith, he shall as soon as practicable issue to the Debtor a notice ("Notice of Breach") identifying the breach and requiring the Debtor within one month of sending the notice:

(a) to remedy the breach if it is capable of being remedied, and, if he thinks fit

(b) to give a full explanation of the breach.

67(2) [Remedy of breach] If, within the one month period referred to in Sub-paragraph (1), or such longer period not exceeding a further one month as the Supervisor shall reasonably allow, the Debtor:

(a) remedies his breach of the Arrangement;

(b) if so required in the Notice of Breach, provides a full explanation of the breach, and

(c) pays to the Supervisor such sum (if any) as the Supervisor may reasonably require to compensate the Creditors for any reduction in Dividend caused by the Debtor's breach,

no further action shall be taken against the Debtor save that the Supervisor shall report the breach to the Creditors when he next sends his comments to Creditors on the progress and efficacy of the Arrangement under Rule 5.26 (Supervisor's accounts and reports), or on the next convenient occasion, if earlier.

67(3) [Certificate of Termination/bankruptcy petition] If the Debtor has not done those things specified in Sub-paragraph (2) by the time specified or allowed, the Supervisor shall as soon as practicable convene a meeting of Creditors to resolve whether or not to do the following things:

(i) issue a certificate ("Certificate of Termination") terminating the Arrangement by reason of the Debtor's breach;

(ii) present a petition for the Debtor's bankruptcy;

(iii) vary the terms of the arrangement under Paragraph 70;

(iv) take no action.

67(4) [Supervisor's duty] If the Creditors resolve to issue a Certificate of Termination and/or to present a bankruptcy petition against the Debtor, the Supervisor shall do so as soon as practicable.

67(5) [Copies of Certificate of Termination] A copy of any Certificate of Termination issued by the Supervisor shall be sent to the Debtor and Creditors together with the notice under Paragraph 11.

68 Retention of funds by Supervisor

68 The Supervisor shall, at all times during the course of the Arrangement, retain sufficient of the funds coming into his hands as represents his best estimate of the costs of petitioning for the Debtor's bankruptcy should the Creditors so direct under the previous Paragraph hereof. Such costs shall be provided for in priority to any other costs of the Arrangement.

PART XI: MISCELLANEOUS PROVISIONS

69 Third Party obligations

68(1) [Application of Paragraph] This Paragraph applies where the Proposal includes any obligation on the part of a person other than the Supervisor or Debtor to pay moneys, transfer assets or do any other thing.

69(2) [Evidence of agreement] The third party shall sign the Proposal or such other document evidencing his agreement to be bound by the obligation as the Supervisor shall reasonably require.

69(3) [Enforcement of obligation] The obligations of the third party shall be enforceable by the Supervisor, or by the Debtor at the direction of the Supervisor.

69(4) [Failure a default of arrangement] The failure by the third party to carry out the obligation when due shall constitute a breach of the arrangement.

70 Variation of the Arrangement

70(1) [Variation with Creditor's approval] The provisions of this Arrangement may be amended with the approval of a meeting of Creditors.

70(2) [Consent of Debtor/third party to variation required] No variation of the terms of the Arrangement shall be of any effect unless made with the consent of the Debtor and any third party affected thereby.

70(3) [Saving for certain rights] No variation which restricts the following rights shall be of effect:

(a) the right of any Secured Creditor to enforce his Security, except with the Secured Creditor's consent;

(b) the right of any Creditor to present a bankruptcy petition under section 264(1)(c) of the Act for default in connection with Arrangement;

(c) the right of a Preferential Creditor to be paid in priority to other Creditors, except with that Creditor's consent;

(d) the right of a Preferential Creditor to be paid pro rata with other Preferential Creditors, except with that Creditor's consent.

70(4) [Unfair prejudice and material irregularity] No variation shall be of effect if it unfairly prejudices the rights of any Creditor or if there has been any material irregularity in the operation of the provisions of this Paragraph.

70(5) [Restriction on variation] No variation shall be of effect if it causes the Arrangement to cease to be a voluntary arrangement within Part VIII of the Act.

71 Tax liabilities arising on realisations

70(1) [Tax to be paid out of proceeds] Taxation liabilities of the Debtor arising on the sale or other realisation of any asset subject to the Arrangement shall, in so far as those proceeds are sufficient, be discharged out of the sale proceeds of the asset in question.

72 Invalidity and/or illegality

72 If any provision or part of the Arrangement is found to be contrary to the Act or Rules, illegal, invalid or contrary to public policy, that will not affect the validity of the remainder of the Arrangement and the provision or part of the Arrangement in question shall be construed accordingly.

CONDITIONS OF USE

1. Copyright of the attached Standard Conditions is the property of the Association of Business Recovery Professionals (hereinafter referred to as 'R3').

2. No liability attaches to R3 in respect of the use of the Standard Conditions or any consequence thereof or in respect of any proposed or approved arrangement of which the Standard Conditions form a part.

3. R3 licenses all its members to use the Standard Conditions without payment of a fee subject as follows:

   – the Standard Conditions must be used in their entirety, or alternatively

   – the proposal of which they form part must draw attention to any omissions or variations and give reasons for them.

4. Members of R3 may authorise the use of the Standard Conditions by debtors, but subject to the conditions set out in paragraph 3.

5. Other persons wishing to use the Standard Conditions may obtain a licence to do so from R3, for which a fee may be charged. Use of the Standard Conditions by other persons is subject to the conditions set out in paragraph 3.

6. If the Standard Conditions are used in any published work the conditions of use must be made clear.

7. If R3 amends the Standard Conditions users must specify the version they are using.

8. Use of the Standard Conditions does not relieve the nominee of the requirement to issue a full copy of the proposal, including the Standard Conditions, to every creditor.

9. Where the Standard Conditions are used they must be fully explained to the debtor.

10. Any variations to the Standard Conditions should not seek to affect statutory rights or obligations.

Association of Business Recovery Professionals

March 2002

4.11 Originating and Ordinary Applications (Form 7.1) (Form 7.2)

There are two forms of application[1] which may be used in proceedings relating to voluntary arrangements:

(1) an originating application which is an application to the court which is not an application in pending proceedings before the court[2]; and

(2) an ordinary application which is any other application to the court.

An originating application should be used where proceedings are being commenced in which some new substantive relief is sought or new substantive issue raised for determination. An ordinary application is akin to an application made under CPR Pt 23 or, in the old terminology, an interlocutory summons or motion[3].

As to the heading of an application the formal requirement of the Rules is that every proceeding under IA 1986, Pt I 'shall, with any necessary additions, be intituled 'IN THE MATTER OF (*naming the company to which the proceedings relate*) AND IN THE MATTER OF THE INSOLVENCY ACT 1986'[4]. The Rules make no requirement as to the heading of applications under Pt VIII. It is common practice to title IVA proceedings 'IN BANKRUPTCY'[5] and to add IN THE MATTER OF (*name of debtor*).

An application must be in writing and must state[6]:

(a) the names of the parties;

(b) the nature of the relief or order applied for or the directions sought from the court;

(c) the names and addresses of the persons (if any) on whom it is intended to serve the application or state that no person is intended to be served;

(d) where IA 1986 or IR 1986 required that notice of the application is to be given to specified persons, the names and addresses of all those persons, so far as known to the applicant; and

(e) the applicant's address for service.

The application must be signed by the applicant if he is acting in person, or by or on behalf of his solicitor if one is acting for the applicant[7]. An originating application must set out the grounds on which the applicant claims to be entitled to the relief or other order sought[8].

1 Forms may be obtained on the internet published by the Insolvency Service, see www.insolvency.gov.uk/information/forms.htm.
2 IR 1986, r 7.1, 7.2; Forms 7.1 and 7.2.
3 See *Port v Auger* [1994] 1 WLR 862.
4 IR 1986, r 7.26(1).
5 Which is the title required for proceedings under IA 1986, Pts IX–XI, IR 1986, r 7.26(2).
6 IR 1986, r 7.3(1).
7 IR 1986, r 7.3(3).
8 IR 1986, r 7.3(2).

Evidence is usually given by affidavit. In the absence of specific provision or direction the applicant is to file in court and serve his affidavit evidence on the respondent not less than 14 days before the date set for the hearing; the respondent should file and serve his affidavit evidence in opposition not less than seven days before the hearing date[9]. Evidence may be by witness statement verified by a statement of truth as an alternative to an affidavit[10].

ORIGINATING APPLICATION

IN THE HIGH COURT OF JUSTICE

[CHANCERY DIVISION

COMPANIES COURT]

[IN BANKRUPTCY]

[IN THE DINGLEY DELL COUNTY COURT]

IN THE MATTER OF [PETERSON PLASTICS LIMITED] [BARRY BALDRICK]

AND IN THE MATTER OF THE INSOLVENCY ACT 1986

Between:

[*name of applicant*]

Applicant

– and –

[*name of respondent*]

Respondent

Let [*respondent*] of [*address*] attend before the Judge / Registrar / District Judge on:

Date:

Time:

Place:

9 IR 1986, r 7.8(1).
10 IR 1986, r 7.57(5).

On the hearing of an application by [*applicant*], the applicant for:

[*set out the order(s)or directions sought*]

The grounds on which the applicant claims to be entitled to the order / directions sought are: [*set out grounds*]

Or

[The grounds on which the applicant claims to be entitled to the order / directions sought are set out in the affidavit [witness statement] of the applicant dated *(date).*

The names and addresses of the persons upon whom it is intended to serve this application are [*name and address of respondent and any other person who is to be served eg office-holder*]

Or

It is not intended to serve any person with this application.

The Applicant's address for service is [*set out applicant's address or that of his solicitors where he is represented*]

Dated ... ...

... ...

(signature)

[Solicitor for the] Applicant

If you do not attend, the Court may make such order as it thinks fit.

ORDINARY APPLICATION

IN THE HIGH COURT OF JUSTICE
[CHANCERY DIVISION
COMPANIES COURT]
[IN BANKRUPTCY]

[IN THE DINGLEY DELL COUNTY COURT]

IN THE MATTER OF [PETERSON PLASTICS LIMITED] [BARRY BALDRICK]

AND IN THE MATTER OF THE INSOLVENCY ACT 1986

Between:

[*name of applicant*]

Applicant

– and –

[*name of respondent*]

Respondent

Take notice that I, [*applicant*] intend to apply to the Judge / Registrar / District Judge on:

Date:

Time:

Place:

For: [*state nature and grounds of application*]

Dated:

Signed:

[Solicitor for the] Applicant

My address for service is [*address*]

To: [*name and address of respondent and any other person(s) on whom it is intended to serve the application*]

Or

It is not intended to serve any person with this application.

If you do not attend, the Court may make such order as it thinks fit.

4.12 Originating application seeking interim order by a debtor who is not an undischarged bankrupt

IN THE DINGLEY DELL COUNTY COURT No. 200 of 2003

IN BANKRUPTCY[1]

In the matter of the Insolvency Act 1986, Part VIII[2]

Re Alfred Debtor

Alfred Debtor

Applicant

– and –

(1) Brian Nominee[3]

[(2) Charles Creditor][4]

Respondents

Let Brian Nominee of Pickwick Court, St Mary Street, Dingley Dell, DD3 4TY, and Charles Creditor of 23 Broadmead, Tangley, Essex CM4 7KH attend before the District Judge on:

Date:

Time:

Place:

On the hearing of an application by Alfred Debtor, the applicant for

1. an interim order pursuant to section 252 of the Insolvency Act 1986 in respect of the applicant; and
2. a direction pursuant to section 256 of the Insolvency Act 1986 that the period for which the interim order has effect shall be extended until *(date)*

1 This is not necessary, and strictly wrong, because the Rules, IR 1986, r 7.26(2) require the use of 'In Bankruptcy' only for applications in bankruptcy. Nevertheless, the title is often used in IVA applications.

2 This is not a requirement of the Rules, see IR 1986, r 7.26, but is often used.

3 The nominee must be given notice, IR 1986, r 5.4(c).

4 Notice must be given to any creditor who (to the debtor's knowledge) has presented a petition against him IR 1986, r 5.4(d).

for the purpose of enabling the applicant's proposal to be considered by his creditors[5].

The grounds on which the applicant claims to be entitled to the order are set out in the witness statement[6] of the applicant dated *(date)*.

The names and addresses of the persons upon whom it is intended to serve this application are

(1) Brian Nominee of Pickwick Court, St Mary Street, Dingley Dell, DD3 4TY, and

(2) Charles Creditor of 23 Broadmead, Tangley, Essex CM4 7KH

The applicant's address for service is [*address*]

Dated:

Signed :

(Solicitor for the) Applicant

If you do not attend the Court may make such order as it thinks fit.

5 Where by the time the application is made the nominee has already prepared his report and recommends that the debtor's proposal be put to his creditors, it is appropriate to seek the direction extending the period for which the interim order has effect until after the date on which the creditors' meeting is to be held. If the interim order is sought before the nominee's report is prepared, this direction cannot be sought and a further hearing will be necessary at which the court will consider the report and direct that the period be extended if appropriate.

6 Evidence may be by affidavit, IR 1986, r 7.7, or by witness statement, IR 1986, r 7.57(5), subject to any specific direction of the court.

4.13 Witness statement in support of application for interim order

IN THE DINGLEY DELL COUNTY COURT — No. 200 of 2003

IN BANKRUPTCY

In the matter of the Insolvency Act 1986, Part VIII

Re Alfred Debtor

Alfred Debtor

Applicant

– and –

(1) Brian Nominee

(2) Charles Creditor

Respondents

I, Alfred Debtor, of 92 Carey Street, Dingley Dell, DD3 4TY state as follows[1]:

1. I am the applicant in this matter. I make this witness statement in support of my application for an interim order pursuant to section 252 of the Insolvency Act 1986.
2. Attached to this statement marked 'AD-1' is a copy of my proposal for an individual voluntary arrangement and a copy of the notice to the intended nominee, Brian Nominee, duly endorsed with his agreement to act in relation to my proposed voluntary arrangement. Mr Nominee is a person qualified to act as an insolvency practitioner in relation to my affairs.
3. My reasons for seeking an individual voluntary arrangement are set out in my proposal.
4. A bankruptcy petition was presented against me on *(date)* by Charles Creditor of 23 Broadmead, Tangley, Essex CM4 7KH in respect of an undisputed debt of £20,000 due as rent for business premises at Unit 13, Weller Park, Tangley. No execution or other legal process has, to my knowledge, been commenced against me.
5. I am able to petition for my own bankruptcy.

1 For the required contents of the witness statement (or affidavit) see IR 1986, r 5.5(1).

6. No previous application for an interim order has been made by or in respect of me in the period of 12 months ending with the date of this application.

I believe that the facts stated in this witness statement are true.

.... (signed)

Alfred Debtor

4.14 Interim order including extension[1]

IN THE DINGLEY DELL COUNTY COURT No. 200 of 2003

IN BANKRUPTCY

District Judge Plowden

Re Alfred Debtor

Alfred Debtor

Applicant

– and –

(1) Brian Nominee

(2) Charles Creditor

Respondents

Upon the application of Alfred Debtor, of 92 Carey Street, Dingley Dell, DD3 4TY

An upon hearing [counsel/the solicitor for] the debtor and the nominee [and (counsel/the solicitor for) the second respondent]

And upon reading the evidence

It is ordered that during the period of [14[2]] days beginning with the day after the date of this order and during any extended period for which this interim order has effect:

1. no bankruptcy petition relating to the debtor may be presented or proceeded with;
2. proceedings upon the petition presented against the debtor on *(date)* by the second respondent are stayed;
3. no other proceedings, and no execution or other legal process may be commenced or continued against the debtor or his property except with the leave of the court.

And the court having this day considered the report of the nominee submitted pursuant to section 256 of the Insolvency Act 1986 and filed on *(date)*

It is ordered that the period for which the interim order hereby made has effect be extended to *(date)* to enable a meeting of the debtor's creditors to be summoned to consider the debtor's proposal, such meeting as proposed by the nominee to be held on:

1 Adapted from IR 1986, Sch 4, Forms 5.2 and 5.3.

2 14 days unless an extension is granted on the application of the nominee.

Date:

Time:

Place:

And it is order that this application is adjourned to:

Date:

Time:

Place:

For consideration of the report of the chairman of the creditors' meeting.

Dated *(date)*

4.15 Ordinary application by debtor challenging the right of creditor to vote[1]

IN THE DINGLEY DELL COUNTY COURT No. 200 of 2003

In the Matter of the Insolvency Act 1986

Re Alfred Debtor

Alfred Debtor

Applicant

-- and –

Derek Claimant

Respondent

Take notice that Alfred Debtor intends to apply to the District Judge on:

Date:

Time:

Place:

for the following:

1. a declaration that the respondent's vote in respect of an asserted debt of £100,000 at the meeting of creditors held on *(date)* to consider the applicant's proposal for an individual voluntary arrangement was invalid;
2. alternatively, a declaration that the debt owed by the applicant to the respondent be valued at £35,000 or such other sum as the court may determine;
3. an order that the resolution passed at the meeting of creditors held on *(date)* to reject the applicant's proposal be revoked;
4. a direction that a further meeting of the applicant's creditors be held to reconsider the applicant's proposal;
5. such further or other orders as the court may think just.

1 As to the right of the debtor or any creditor to apply to the court by way of appeal against the chairman's decision on voting see para 6.8 above.

Dated:

Signed:

(Solicitor for the) Applicant

My address for service is [*address*]

To: [*name and address of respondent*]

If you do not attend, the Court may make such order as it thinks fit.

4.16 Originating application by creditor challenging acts and omissions of directors during a moratorium

IN THE HIGH COURT OF JUSTICE

CHANCERY DIVISION

COMPANIES COURT

In the Matter of Peterson Plastics Limited

And in the Matter of the Insolvency Act 1986

Between:

New Age Plastics plc

Applicant

– and –

(1) Peterson Plastics Limited

(2) Philip Peterson

(3) Paul Watson

(4) Stephen Philpot

(5) John Smith

Respondents

Let (1) Peterson Plastics Limited of [*registered office*], (2) Philip Peterson of [*address*], (3) Paul Watson of [*address*], (4) Stephen Philpot of [*address*], (5) John Smith of [*address*], nominee, attend before the Registrar on:

Date:

Time:

Place:

On the hearing of an application by [*applicant*], the applicant for:

1. A direction that the First Respondent, ('the Company') do not enter into an agreement with Superbos Plasticos SA to manufacture and supply plastic toys;

2. A direction that the Company do forthwith re-deliver to the Applicant all remaining cartons of plastic granules grade R4 supplied to the Company by the Applicant under the terms of contract number NAP-457834-No.3;

3. A direction that the Company do not enter into an agreement with Superbos Plasticos (Marbella) SA for the sale of any of the 3 Stanislav-V moulding machine registred numbers StV-MMC-014, StV-MMC-015 or StV-MMC-016, and do not part with possession of the said machines to Superbos Plasticos (Marbella) SA or to any other person, company or firm.

4. An order that the costs of this application be paid by the First to Fourth Respondents.

5. Such further or other relief as the Court may think fit.

The grounds on which the Applicant claims to be entitled to the relief sought are:

(1) On [*date*] the Second and Third Respondents as directors of the Company made a proposal for a voluntary arrangement for the Company. An essential term of this proposal is the cessation by the Company of the manufacture of plastic toys for children, an area of operations in which the Company has made heavy trading losses.

(2) The Company proposes to enter into an agreement with Superbos Plasticos SA to manufacture and supply plastic toys. This agreement in the course of negotaion by the the Fourth Respondent. If it is entered into this will be because of the close relationship between the Second, Third and Fourth Respondents and the directors of Superbos Plasticos SA. It is not a profitable contract for the Company but will result in further trading losses.

(3) The Company is in possession of a number of cartons of plastic granules grade R4 being the remainder of the 500 cartons supplied to the Company by the Applicant under the terms of contract number NAP-457834-No 3 on [*date*]. Under the terms of the contract the cartons remain the property of the Applicant until all outstanding invoices have been paid in full. The invoice for the said cartons, in addition to another invoice number NAP-457832 for goods supplied to the Company by the Applicant, remains unpaid. The Applicant has sought an undertaking from the Company that the cartons will be returned or held to the Applicant's order, but the Company has refused to give the undertaking sought.

(4) The Company is the owner of three Stanislav-V moulding machines registered numbers StV-MMC-014, StV-MMC-015 and StV-MMC-016. These machines have been charged to the Applicant as security for the Company's outstanding indebtedness, and such charge has been duly registered as a Bill of Sale.

(5) The Company is proposing to sell these machines to Superbos Plasticos SA without first paying the sums due under the Applicant's said security.

The names and addresses of the persons upon whom it is intended to servie this application are [*names and addresses as above, Superbos Plasticos SA and Superbos Plasticos (Marbella) SA*].

The Applicant's address for service is [*address*]

Dated ……………………..

(signed)………………..

[Solicitor for the] Applicant

If you do not attend, the Court may make such order as it thinks fit.

4.17 Originating application by creditor challenging the decision of the meeting to approve the partnership's proposal

IN THE BARCHESTER COUNTY COURT

In the Matter of Warden Pies (a firm)

And in the Matter of the Insolvency Act 1986

And in the Matter of the Insolvent Partnerships Order 1994

Between:

Christopher Creditor

Applicant

– and –

(1) Peter Warden

(2) Paul Warden

(3) Clifford Chairman

Respondents

Let (1) Peter Warden of [*address*]; (2) Paul Warden of [*address*] and (3) Clifford Chairman of [*address*] attend before the District Judge on:

Date:

Time:

Place:

On the hearing of an application by Christopher Creditor, the applicant, for:

1. An order that the approval of the voluntary arrangement given by the meetings of creditors and the partnership held on [*date*] be revoked or suspended on such terms as shall to this court seem just.
2. Further or alternatively, a direction that the Third Respondent or such other person as the court considers fit do within 14 days convene a further meeting of creditors to consider the partnership's proposal for a voluntary arrangement filed herein.
3. A direction that at any further meeting convened to consider the partnership's proposal the chairman of the creditors' meeting to admit for voting the Applicant's claim in the sum of £ ...
4. A direction that the expense of convening such further meeting and of this application shall be an expense of the voluntary arrangement or shall be paid by the First and Second Respondents as the court shall consider fit.

The grounds on which the Applicant clams to be entitled to the order and directions sought are set out in the affidavit of the Applicant dated [*date*].

The names and addresses of the persons upon whom it is intended to serve this application[1] are [*names and addresses of Respondents*].

The Applicant's address for service is [*address*].

Dated ....

(signed)................

[Solicitor for the] Applicant

If you do not attend, the Court may make such order as it thinks fit

1 The court may require all the creditors bound to the arrangement to be served depending upon the precise grounds of the application.

4.18 Originating application by creditor challenging chairman's decision on voting and the decision of the meeting to approve the debtor's proposal

IN THE DINGLEY DELL COUNTY COURT

In the Matter of the Insolvency Act 1986

Re Alfred Debtor

Between:

Harold Hawkeye

Applicant

– and –

(1) Alfred Debtor

(2)Brian Nominee

(3) Clive Confederate

Respondents

Let (1) Alfred Debtor of 92 Carey Street, Dingley Dell DD3 4RZ; (2) Brian Nominee of Pickwick Court, St Mary Street, Dingley Dell DD3 4TY and (3) Clive Confederate of The Hollows, Cow Lane, Tangley, Essex CM4 3RT attend before the Registrar on:

Date:

Time:

Place:

On the hearing of an application by Harold Hawkeye, the applicant for:

1. A declaration that the Third Respondent, Clive Confederate, is an associate of First Respondent ('the Debtor') being the Debtor's sister's husband;
2. A declaration that the debt asserted to be due from the Debtor to the Third Respondent of £180,000 arising out of an alleged liability to pay damages for breach of contract is a sham and should not have been admitted for voting by the Second Respondent as chairman of the meeting of creditors;
3. A declaration that the resolution approving the Debtor's proposal is invalid on the ground that the Third Respondent's debt should not have been admitted for voting by the Second Respondent as chairman of the meeting;

4. Alternatively a declaration that the resolution approving the Debtor's proposal is invalid on the ground that as the Third Respondent is an associate of the Debtor more than one half in value of the creditors as defined in rule 5.23(4) of the Insolvency Rules 1986 voted against the proposal;
5. Such further or other orders as the court may think just.

The grounds on which the applicant claims to be entitled to the relief sought are set out in the affidavit of the applicant dated *(date)* which is served herewith.

To (1) Alfred Debtor of 92 Carey Street, Dingley Dell DD3 4RZ; (2) Brian Nominee of Pickwick Court, St Mary Street, Dingley Dell DD3 4TY, and (3) Clive Confederate of The Hollows, Cow Lane, Tangley, Essex CM4 3RT

The applicant's address for service is [*address*].

Dated:

Signed:

(Solicitor for the) Applicant

If you do not attend, the Court may make such order as it thinks fit.

4.19 Originating application by creditor bound to arrangement without notice of the creditors' meeting challenging the approval of the proposal

IN THE HIGH COURT OF JUSTICE

CHANCERY DIVISION

COMPANIES COURT

In the Matter of Peterson Plastics Limited

And in the Matter of the Insolvency Act 1986

Between:

Industrial Supplied Limited

Applicant

– and –

(1) Peterson Plastics Limited

(2) Philip Peterson

(3) Paul Watson

(4) John Smith

Respondents

Let (1) Peterson Plastics Limited of [*registered office*], (2) Philip Peterson of [*address*], (3) Paul Watson of [*address*], and (4) John Smith of [*address*] attend before the Registrar on:

Date:

Time:

Place:

On the hearing of an application by Industrial Supplies Limited, the applicant, for:

1. An order that the approval of the proposal dated *(date)* made by the Second and Third Respondents for a voluntary arrangement by the First Respondent ('the Company') given by the meetings of creditors and of the Company held on *(date)* be revoked or suspended on such terms as this Court shall consider just;
2. A direction that the Fourth Respondent as supervisor or such other person as the Court shall consider fit do within 14 days convene a further meeting

of creditors to consider the said proposal of the Second and Third Respondents;

3. a declaration that the Applicant be permitted to vote at any further meeting in the full amount of his claim in the sum of £ …
4. an order that the expense of convening such further meeting and that the costs of this applciation shall be paid by the First, Second and Third Respondents.

The grounds on which the applicant claims to be entitled to the relief sought are:

(1) The Applicant is creditor of the Company and has been since [*date*] when it supplied goods and services to the Company at an agreed price of £ … in pursuance of an agreement dated [*date*]. Thereafter, at three monthly intervals the Applicant has rendered invoices to the Company, each invoice setting out the Applicant's address at [*address*].

(2) At all material times before [*date of proposal*] the Applicant has conducted business at [*address*]. At no time did the Applicant receive notice of the proposal dated [*date*] for a company voluntary arrangement by the Company, nor of the creditors' meeting summoned to consider the said proposal, nor any other indication that the company might enter into a voluntary arrangement.

(3) The Applicant learnt of the Company's voluntary arrangement in the following circumstances [*state circumstances*].

(4) It appears therefore that the failure of the Second and Third Respondents to include the Applicant's debt among the liabilities of the Company stated in the proposal or otherwise inform the Fourth Respondent and the creditors of the existence of the Applicant's debt amounts to a material irregularity in relation to the creditors' meeting.

(5) The Applicant wrote to the Fourth Respondent, as supervisor of the Company's voluntary arrangement, on [*date*] and asked to be admitted to the voluntary arrangement.

(6) The Fourth Respondent however refused to admit the Applicant to the voluntary arrangement except on terms that the Applicant reduced its claim by 33% and did not participate in any dividends already paid to the creditors under the arrangement.

(7) The voluntary arrangement approved at the creditors' and company meetings, taking effect as it has without the full inclusion of the Applicant, unfairly prejudices the interests of the Applicant as a creditor of the Company.

The names and addresses of the persons upon whom it is intended to serve this application are (1) Peterson Plastics Limited of [*registered office*]

(2) Philip Peterson of [*address*]

(3) Paul Watson of [*address*]

(4) John Smith of [*address*]

The Applicant's address for service is [*address*]

Dated ……………….

………………….. (signed)

[Solicitor for the] Applicant

If you do not attend, the Court may make such order as it thinks fit.

4.20 Originating application by creditor dissatisfied with act or omission of supervisor in relation to a matter arising under the voluntary arrangement

IN THE CASTERBRIDGE COUNTY COURT

In the Matter of Flanders Fetes (a firm)

And in the Matter of the Insolvency Act 1986

And in the Matter of the Insolvent Partnerships Order 1994

Between:

Empire Marquees Limited

Applicant

– and –

(1) John Prefect

(2) Peter Flanders

(3) Paul Flanders

(4) Clifford Inns plc

Respondents

Let (1) John Prefect of [*address*], (2) Peter Flanders of [*address*], (3) Paul Flanders of [*address*] and (4) Clifford Inns plc of [*registered office address*] attend before the District Judge on:

Date:

Time:

Place:

On the hearing of an application by Empire Marquees Limited, the applicant, for the following relief, namely:

1. A declaration that the Fourth Respondent was not a creditor of the business conducted by the Second and Third Respondents trading as Flanders Fetes ('the Partnership') on [*date*] the date on which the voluntary arrangement proposed in respect of the Partnership was approved;
2. A declaration that the Fourth Respondent was wrongly admitted to the voluntary arrangement as a creditor who was entitled to but did not receive notice of the creditors' meeting by the First Respondent as supervisor thereof;

3. An order that the Fourth Respondent do repay to the First Respondent the sums received by way of dividend under the voluntary arrangement together with interest thereon such sums to be held for the benefit of the voluntary arrangement.
4. Such further or other relief as the court considers fit.
5. An order that the costs occasioned by the admission of the Fourth Respondent to the voluntary arrangement and of this application should be paid by the Second, Third and Fourth Respondents.

The grounds on which the Applicant clams to be entitled to the order and directions sought are set out in the affidavit of the Applicant dated [*date*] and the witness statement of Stephen George Steadman dated [*date*].

The names and addresses of the persons upon whom it is intended to serve this application are [*names and addresses of Respondents*].

The Applicant's address for service is [*address*].

Dated ....

(signed)................

[Solicitor for the] Applicant

If you do not attend, the Court may make such order as it thinks fit.

Appendix 5

Forms

5.1 Moratorium documents
Documents to be submitted to court to obtain moratorium (Form 1.9)
- (i) Terms of proposed voluntary arrangement (see Appendix 4)
- (ii) Statement of affairs (Form 1.6)
  Form of Statement of affairs (Form 4.17)
- (iii) Statement of eligibility (Form 1.7)
- (iv) Statement of consent to act by nominee (Form 1.8)
- (v) Nominee's statement of opinion (Form 1.5)
- (vi) Nominee's comments under Rule 1.38(2) (no form provided in the Rules)
- (vii) Statement of reasons for the extension of the period to which the Statement of affairs is made up (no form provided in the Rules)

5.2 Interim Order of Court under Insolvency Act 1986, s 252 (Form 5.2)
5.3 Order extending effect of Interim Order (Form 5.3)
5.4 Chairman's Report to the Court (PVA)
5.5 Chairman's Report to the Court (IVA)
5.6 Proof of Debt (Form 6.37)
5.7 Affidavit of Debt (Form 6.39)
5.8 Form of Proxy (Form 8.1)
5.9 Bankruptcy petition for default in connection with voluntary arrangement (Form 6.10)
5.10 Affidavit in support of the petition
5.11 Notice to creditors under r 6.10(6)

5.1 Documents to be submitted to court to obtain moratorium (Form 1.9)

Form 1.9

Rule 1.39

Documents to be submitted to court to obtain moratorium

Company number

Name of company

(a) Insert full name of company

(a) Limited.

We, the directors of the above-named company, hereby file the following—

(b) Insert date

(i) the document setting out the terms of the proposed voluntary arrangement dated (b) ;

(ii) the statement of the company's affairs as at (b) ;

(iii) the statement that the company is eligible for a moratorium;

(iv) the statement that the nominee has given his consent to act;

(v) the statement of opinion from the nominee;

(vi) the nominee's comments under Rule 1.38(2); and

(vii) a statement of the reasons for the extension of the period under Rule 1.37(3) (delete if not applicable).

Signed____________________________Director

(c) Delete as applicable

Signed____________________________Director/Secretary (c)

Date __________

(d) To be completed by the court

(e) Insert date

(f) Insert name of court

Endorsement (d)

This form and the attached documents have been filed on (e) at (f)

5.1(ii) Statement of affairs (Form 1.6)

Form 1.6

Rules 1.37 and 1.39

Statement of Affairs

(a) Insert full name of company

(b) Insert date

Statement as to the affairs of (a)____________________________ Limited as at (b) _______________________ . The pages attached hereto are to the best of our knowledge and belief a full, true and complete statement as to the affairs of the above-named company (c).

(c) The attached pages should set out the details referred to in Rule 1.37(2) and 1.39(4).

Signed________________________________(Director)

(d) Delete as applicable

Signed________________________________(Director/Secretary) (d)

Date________________________________

5.1(ii)(*cont'd*) Form of Statement of affairs (Form 4.17)[1]

Rule 4.33 **Form 4.17**

Statement of Affairs

(TITLE)

NOTE:
These details will be the same as those shown at the top of the winding-up petition

In the ______________________ No. __________ of ______

STATEMENT OF AFFAIRS OF

____

*Delete as appropriate

on the ______________ the date of the winding-up order (or date directed by the Official Receiver)*

The 'Guidance notes' booklet tells you how to complete this form easily and correctly

Show the company's current financial position by completing all the pages of this form which will then be your statement of the company's affairs.

Affidavit

This affidavit must be sworn or affirmed before a Solicitor or Commissioner of Oaths or an officer of the court duly authorised to administer oaths when you have completed the rest of this form.

(a) Insert full name and occupation

I (a) ____

____

(b) Insert full address

of (b) ____

____

Make oath and say that the several pages exhibited hereto and marked ________

are to the best of my knowledge and belief a full, true and complete statement as to the affairs of the above named company as at ______________ the date of the winding-up order (or the date directed by the Official Receiver)

and that the said company carried on business as ______________

Sworn at ______________________

Date ______________________

Signature(s)______________

Before me ______________

____

A Solicitor or Commissioner of Oaths or Duly authorised officer

Before swearing the affidavit the Solicitor or Commissioner is particularly requested to make sure that the full name, address and description of the Deponent are stated, and to initial any crossings-out or other alterations in the printed form. A deficiency in the affidavit in any of the above respects will mean that it is refused by the court, and will need to be re-sworn.

1 This is the prescribed form for use in compulsory liquidation, see IR 1986, r 4.33. It is suitable for use in CVA or PVA. Note however that no form is prescribed for the Statement of Affairs to be submitted for a moratorium.

A—Summary of Assets

Assets	Book Value £	Estimated to Realise £
Assets specifically pledged:—		
Assets not specifically pledged:—		
Estimated total assets available for preferential creditors £		

Signature ______________________ Date ____________

A1—Summary of liabilities

			Estimated to realise £
Estimated total assets available for preferential creditors (carried from page A)		£	
Liabilities			
Preferential creditors:—	£		
Estimated deficiency/surplus as regards preferential creditors		£	
Debts secured by a floating charge:—	£		
Estimated deficiency/surplus of assets available for non-preferential creditors		£	
Non-preferential claims:—	£		
Estimated deficiency/surplus as regards creditors		£	
Issued and called up capital:—	£		
Estimated total deficiency/surplus as regards members		£	

Signature ______________________ Date ______________

B
Company Creditors

NOTE You must identify creditors under hire-purchase, chattel leasing or conditional sale agreements *and* customers claiming amounts paid in advance of the supply of goods or services *and* creditors claiming retention of title over property in the company's possession.

Name of creditor or claimant	Address (with postcode)	Amount of debt £	Details of any security held by creditor	Date security given	Value of security £

Signature ______________________ Date __________

C
Shareholders

NOTE: If more convenient, a list of the company's shareholders may be attached to this page.

1 No	2 Name of Shareholder	3 Address (with postcode)	4 Type of shares held	5 Nominal amount of share £	6 Number of shares held	7 Amount per share called up £	8 Total amount called up £
						TOTAL	

Signature ______________________ Date ___________

5.1(iii) Statement of eligibility (Form 1.7)

Form 1.7

Rule 1.39

Statement of eligibility for a moratorium pursuant to paragraph 7(1)(c) of Schedule A1 to the Insolvency Act 1986

Name of company

(a) Insert full name of company

(a)

Limited

The following statement of eligibility for a moratorium under section 1A of the Insolvency Act 1986 is made by the directors of the above-named company-

1. The company meets the requirements of of paragraph 3 of Schedule A1 to the Insolvency Act 1986, and is not a company which falls within paragraph 2 (2) of that Schedule.

(b) Insert date

2. The company, as at (b) , the date of filing in court of this statement, is not excluded from being eligible for a moratorium by virtue of paragraph 4 of Schedule A1 to the Insolvency Act 1986.

Signed ______________________ Director

(c) Delete as applicable

Signed ______________________ Director/Secretary (c)

Date ______________________

5.1(iv) Statement of consent to act by nominee (Form 1.8)

Rules 1.8, 1.38, 1.39 and 1.45

Paragraphs 7(1)(d) and 28 (2) of Schedule A1 to the Insolvency Act 1986

Form 1.8

Statement of consent to act by nominee

(a) Insert full name of company

Name of company

(a)

Limited

(b) Insert full name, address and qualification of person making the statement

I (b)

have consented to act as nominee in relation to proposals for a voluntary arrangement between the above-named company and its creditors pursuant to Part I of the Insolvency Act 1986.

Signed Date

5.1(v) Nominee's statement of opinion (Form 1.5)

Form 1.5

Rules 1.38 and 1.39

Nominee's statement of opinion pursuant to paragraph 6(2) of Schedule A1 to the Insolvency Act 1986

Name of company

(a) Insert full name of company

(a) ______________________________ Limited

(b) Insert full name and address

I (b)

make this statement pursuant to paragraph 6(2) of the Schedule A1 to the Insolvency Act 1986.

In my opinion:

(c) Insert date

(d) Delete as applicable

(a) the proposed voluntary arrangement in relation to the above-named company, the terms of which are set out in the document dated (c) prepared by the directors [has] [does not have] (d) a reasonable prospect of being approved and implemented;

(b) the company [is] [is not] (d) likely to have sufficient funds available to it during the proposed moratorium to enable it to carry on its business; and

(c) meetings of the company and its creditors [should] [should not] (d) be summoned to consider the proposed voluntary arrangement.

Signed Date

5.2 Interim Order of Court under Insolvency Act 1986, s 252 (Form 5.2)

Form 5.2

Rule 5.10 **Interim Order of Court under section 252 of the Insolvency Act 1986**

(Title)

(a) Insert full name and address of applicant

Upon the application of (a) ____________________

And upon hearing ____________________

And upon reading the evidence ____________________

(b) Delete as applicable

(b) [And upon the application of ____________________, the nominee, for an extension of the period for which the interim order shall have effect pursuant to section 256(4) of the Insolvency Act 1986.]

(c) 14 days unless an extension is granted on the application of the nominee

It is ordered that during the period of (c) _______ days beginning with the day after the date of this order and during any extended period for which this interim order has effect:

(d) Insert name of debtor

(i) no bankruptcy petition relating to the above-named (d)____________________ ____________________ (the debtor) may be presented or proceeded with, and

(ii) no other proceedings, and no execution or other legal process, may be commenced or continued against the debtor or his property except with the leave of the court.

(e) Date to be 2 business days before the day on which the report is to be considered

And it is ordered that the report of the nominee be submitted and delivered by him to the court not later than (e) ____________________

(f) Insert details of any orders made under section 255(3) and (4) of the Insolvency Act 1986

[And it is ordered that (f) ____________________]

And it is ordered that ____________________

(g) Delete if debtor is not a bankrupt or if he is a bankrupt but the applicant is the official receiver

(g) [And it is ordered that the applicant forthwith serve a copy of this order on the official receiver.]

Date ____________________

Time ____________________ hours

Place ____________________

be appointed for consideration of the nominee's report.

Dated ____________________

5.3 Order extending effect of Interim Order (Form 5.3)

Form 5.3

Section 256 **Order extending effect of Interim Order**

(Title)

(a) Insert full name and address of applicant

Upon the application of (a) ______________________

And upon hearing ______________________

And upon reading the evidence ______________________

(b) Insert date of filing

And the court having this day considered the report of the nominee submitted pursuant to section 256 of the Insolvency Act 1986 and filed on (b) ______________

(c) Insert date

It is ordered that the period for which the interim order made on (c) __________ has effect be extended to (c) ______________ to enable a meeting of the debtor's creditors to be summoned to consider the debtor's proposals, such meeting as proposed by the nominee to be held on:—

(d) Date to be not less than 14 days from date of filing of report under Rule 5.13 nor more than 28 days from date of consideration of report under Rule 5.12

(e) Time to be between 10.00 and 16.00 hours on a business day (Rule 5.14(2))

Date (d) ______________________

Time (e) ______________________ hours

Place ______________________

And it is ordered that this application be adjourned to:—

Date ______________________

Time ______________________ hours

Place ______________________

for consideration of the report of the chairman of the creditors' meeting.

Dated ______________________

5.4 Report of chairman on meeting of creditors to approve partnership voluntary arrangement

IN THE HIGH COURT OF JUSTICE

COMPANIES COURT

IN THE MATTEROF AB, CD, and EF

Trading as CLASSIC CONSERVATORIES

AND IN THE MATTER OF THE INSOLVENCY ACT 1986

AND IN THE MATTER OF THE INSOLVENT PARTNERSHIPS ORDER 1994

CHAIRMAN'S REPORT TO THE COURT

REPORT by IP on the meeting of creditors held at [*address*] at ... am / pm on [*date*].

IP of IP & Co, chartered accountant and licensed insolvency practitioner advised the meeting of creditors that it had been summoned to consider and vote on the proposal of the partners pursuant to section 3 of the Insolvency Act 1986.

IP explained the statutory provisions relating to partnership voluntary arrangements and the effect of the changes brought about by the Insolvency Act 2000. He explained that he was the chairman of the meeting and was responsible for agreeing creditors' claims for the purposes of voting, and further explained the majorities required for the approval of the arrangement. Having dealt with all issues outstanding on creditors' claims for voting IP then took the meeting in detail through the terms of the proposal and the nominee's report.

The partners AB, CD, and EF were introduced to the meeting and answered questions raised by creditors. IP reported to the creditors that a meeting of the partnership had been duly convened and held [earlier that day][on *date*] and that the proposal had been approved and the nominee's report adopted.

AFTER DELIBERATION IT WAS RESOLVED THAT the proposal be approved subject to the following modifictions:

1. that in years 1 and 3 of the arrangement the partnership should make monthly payments of £xy and £xx per month respectively, and not £x and £xy per month as proposed;
2. that should the partnership or any partner be the recipient of any funds or assets (not being assets required for the business of the partnership) of a value in excess of £500 not anticipated at the time of the approval of the arrangement, such funds or assets would be paid to or delivered to the supervisor for realisation for the purpose of increasing the dividend paid to creditors, limited to such sum as would produce for the creditors a dividend to 100p in the £;

3. that all outstanding VAT returns should be completed and forwarded to HM Customs and Excise within 2 months of the creditors' meeting;
4. that all future VAT returns should be completed, returned and paid by their due dates; and
5. that the supervisor should throughout the period of the arrangement retain sufficient funds to petition for the winding up of the partnership in the event that the partnership was in default of the terms of the arrangement.

The creditors appointed IP as supervisor of the voluntary arrangement and resolved that his fees should be calculated on a time cost basis in accordance with the charges usually made by his firm, a copy of which charges being circulated at the meeting.

A list of the creditors present or represented at the meeting, together with the amounts of their claims and the manner in which they voted on each resolution, is attached hereto.

It is the opinion of IP that the EC Regulation applies to this voluntary arrangement and that the proceedings are main proceedings.

IP further confirms that the voluntary arrangement was duly approved in accordance with the Insolvency Rules 1986 by the required majorities.

[Signed]........................

IP: Chairman of the meeting

5.5 Report of chairman on meeting of creditors to approve individual voluntary arrangement

IN THE PAIGNTON COUNTY COURT

IN BANKRUPTCY

IN THE MATTER OF BARRY BALDRICK

AND IN THE MATTER OF THE INSOLVENCY ACT 1986

CHAIRMAN'S REPORT TO THE COURT

Dear Sir,

I would inform you at that the meeting of the creditors of Barry Baldrick of The Gatehouse, Little Paignton, Devon held at [*address*] on [*date*] at [*time*] a resolution was passed approving the debtor's proposal subject to the modifications set out below. A resolution was further passed to appoint Paul Peters of Peters & Co as supervisor of the arrangement.

Modifications to the proposal

(1) The debtor will contribute to the arrangement anything which he may receive by way of legacy, gift, windfall, or any other such benefit, limited to such sum as will produce for the creditors a dividend of 100p in the £.

(2) The debtor should make a full return of all profits made on trading during the past three years to the Inland Revenue within three months. After the profits, if any, so disclosed are agreed with the Inland Revenue such profits will be admitted as debts in the arrangement;

(3) The debtor should assign to the supervisor the silver tea set of 15 pieces belonging to him but currently in the possession of his nephew Colin Baldrick to be realised and for the benefit of creditors;

(4) The supervisor should retain sufficient funds to petition for the bankruptcy of the debtor in the event that he is in default of the terms of the arrangement, and should present such a petition in the event of any breach of the arrangement by the debtor.

Creditors present or represented at the meeting

Modification (1)

Creditors voting for in person £	creditors in person against £
F1	X1 ......
F2	X2 ......
F3	X3 ......

Creditors voting for by proxy £	creditors by proxy against £
F4	X4 ...
F5	X5 ...

Modification (2)

(etc)

Modification (3)

(etc)

Modification (4)

(etc)

Creditors voting for approval	Creditors voting for rejection
In person	In person
By proxy	By proxy

The following creditors (F2, F5) were associates of the debtor.

In accordance with Rule 5.23 a majority in excess of 75% in value of those creditors present in person or by proxy voted in favour of the resolution and the creditors voting against acceptance did not amount to 50 % of those voting who were not associates of the debtor. The proposal was therefore duly approved by the creditors.

In my opinion the EC Regulation applies to this individual voluntary arrangement. These proceedings are main proceedings.

Signed.......................

Paul Peters – chairman of the meeting

5.6 Proof of Debt (Form 6.37)

Rule 6.96 Form 6.37

Proof of Debt - General Form
(TITLE)

Date of Bankruptcy Order

1	Name of Creditor	
2	Address of Creditor	
3	Total amount of claim, including any Value Added Tax and outstanding uncapitalised interest as at the date of the bankruptcy order	
4	Details of any documents by reference to which the debt can be substantiated. [Note: the liquidator may call for any document or evidence to substantiate the claim at his discretion]	
5	If the total amount shown above includes Value Added Tax, please show:- (a) amount of Value Added Tax (b) amount of claim NET of Value Added Tax	 £ £
6	If total amount above includes outstanding uncapitalised interest, please state amount	£
7	If you have filled in both box 3 and box 5, please state whether you are claiming the amount shown in box 3 or the amount shown in box 5(b)	
8	Give details of whether the whole or any part of the debt falls within any (and if so which) of the categories of preferential debts under section 386 of, and schedule 6 to, the Insolvency Act 1986 (as read with schedule 3 to the Social Security Pensions Act 1975)	Catergory Amount(s) claimed as preferential £
9	Particulars of how and when debt incurred	

10	Particulars of any security held, the value of the security, and the date it was given	
11	Particulars of any reservation of title claimed, including details of goods supplied, their value and when supplied	
12	Signature of creditor or person authorised to act on his behalf ________________ Name in BLOCK LETTERS ________________ Position with or relation to creditor ________________	

Admitted to vote for

£

Date

Official Receiver/Trustee

Admitted preferentially for

£

Date

Trustee

Admitted non-preferentially for

£

Date

Trustee

5.7 Affidavit of Debt (Form 6.39)

Rule 6.96, 6.99 **Affidavit of Debt** **Form 6.39**

(TITLE)

(a) Insert full name, address and description of person making oath

I (a)

make oath and say:

(b) Delete as applicable

(1) That (b) [I am a creditor of the above-named bankrupt] [I am (c)

(c) State capacity eg director, secretary, solicitor etc

of (d)

(d) Insert full name and address of creditor

a creditor of the above-named bankrupt.

(e) State means of knowledge of matters sworn to in affidavit

I have been concerned in this matter (e)

and am authorised by the creditor to make this affidavit on its/his behalf]

(f) Insert name of bankrupt

(2) That the said (f)

(g) Insert date

on (g) the date of the bankruptcy order, was and still is justly and truly indebted (b) [to me] [to the said creditor] in the sum of £ as shown in the proof of debt exhibited hereto marked "A".

Sworn at

5.8 Form of Proxy (Form 8.1)

Rule 8.1 **Form 8.1**

Proxy (company or individual voluntary arrangements)

Insolvency Act 1986

Notes to help completion of the form	
Please give full name and address for communication	Name of creditor/member .. ..
	Address .. ..
Please insert name of person (who must be 18 or over) or the "chairman of the meeting" (see note below). If you wish to provide for alternative proxy-holders in the circumstances that your first choice is unable to attend please state the name(s) of the alternatives as well	Name of proxy-holder .. ..
	1 .. ..
	2 .. ..
	3 .. ..
Please delete words in brackets if the proxy-holder is only to vote as directed ie he has no discretion	I appoint the above person to be my/the creditor's/member's proxy-holder at the meeting of creditors/members to be held on .. .. , or at any adjournment of that meeting. The proxy-holder is to propose or vote as instructed below (and in respect of any resolution for which no specific instruction is given, may vote or abstain at his/her discretion).
	Voting instructions for resolutions
*Please delete as appropriate	1 For the acceptance/rejection* of the proposed voluntary arrangement (with the following modifications:—)
Any other resolution which the proxy-holder is to propose or vote in favour of or against should be set out in numbered paragraphs in the space provided below Paragraph 1. If more room is required please use the other side of this form.	.. ..
	.. ..
This form must be signed	**Signature .. .. Date .. ..**
	Name in CAPITAL LETTERS .. ..
Only to be completed if the creditor/member has not signed in person	**Position with creditor/member or relationship to creditor/member or other authority for signature .. ..**
	Remember: there may be resolutions on the other side of this form.

5.9 Bankruptcy petition for default in connection with voluntary arrangement (Form 6.10)

Rule 6.6

Form 6.10

Bankruptcy Petition for Default in Connection with Voluntary Arrangement

(Title)

(a) Insert full name(s) and address(es) of petitioner(s)

(b) Insert full name, place of residence and occupation (if any) of debtor

(c) Insert in full any other name(s) by which the debtor is or has been known

(d) Insert trading name (adding "with another or others", if this is so), business address and nature of business

(e) Insert any other address or addresses at which the debtor has resided at or after the time the petition debt was incurred

(f) Give the same details as specified in note (d) above for any other businesses which have been carried on at or after the time the petition debt was incurred

(g) Delete as applicable

(h) Or as the case may be following the terms of Rule 6.9

I/We (a)____

____

____

petition the court that a bankruptcy order may be made against (b)____________

____

[also known as (c)________________________________]

[and carrying on business as (d)____________________________

____]

[and lately residing at (e)________________________________

________________________________]

[and lately carrying on business as (f)____________________________

____]

and say as follows:-

1. (g) [The debtor's centre of main interests has been][The debtor has had an establishment] at ________________________________

OR

The debtor carries on business as an insurance undertaking; a credit institution; an investment undertaking providing services involving the holding of funds or securities for third parties; or a collective investment undertaking as referred to in Article 1.2 of the EC Regulation

OR

The debtor's centre of main interests is not within a member State

2. The debtor has for the greater part of six months immediately preceding the presentation of this petition (g) [resided at] [carried on business at]

____

within the district of this court (h)

Under the EC Regulation:
(i) The centre of main interests should correspond to the place where the debtor conducts the administration of his interests on a regular basis.
(ii) Establishment is defined as "any place of operations where the debtor carries out a non-transitory economic activity with human means and goods".

(j) Insert date the debtor entered into voluntary arrangement

(k) Insert name of supervisor

3. On (j) ______________ a voluntary arrangement proposed by the debtor was approved by his creditors and I am (g) [a person who is for the time being bound by the said voluntary arrangement and (k) ______________ is the supervisor] [(k) ______________ the supervisor of the said voluntary arrangement]

(l) Give details of the default in connection with the composition or scheme, being the grounds under section 276(1) IA86 upon which the bankruptcy order is sought

(l)

Endorsement

This petition having been presented to the court on ______________ it is ordered that the petition shall be heard as follows:-

Date ______________

Time ______________ hours

Place ______________

(m) Insert name of debtor

and you, the above-named (m) ______________, are to take notice that if you intend to oppose the petition you must not later than 7 days before the date fixed for the hearing:

(i) file in court a notice (in Form 6.19) specifying the grounds on which you object to the making of a bankruptcy order; and

(ii) send a copy of the notice to the petitioner or his solicitor.

The solicitor to the petitioning creditor is:- (n)

(n) Only to be completed where the petitioning creditor is represented by a solicitor

Name ______________

Address ______________

____

Telephone Number ______________

Reference ______________

5.10 Affidavit in support of petition in default of individual voluntary arrangement

IN THE PAIGNTON COUNTY COURT

IN BANKRUPTCY

Re Barry Baldrick

AFFIDAVIT

I, Paul Peters of Peters & Co. 139 St John's Street, Exeter EX7 4PJ a chartered accountant and licensed insolvency practitioner, MAKE OATH and say as follows:

1. I make this affidavit in support of the bankruptcy petition herein a copy whereof is exhibited hereto marked 'PP1'. I myself prepared the petition on the basis of my own knowledge as nominee and supervisor of the debtor's individual voluntary arrangement. I confirm that the statements contained in the petition are true.
2. An interim order was made by the High Court of Justice on [*date*]. The matter was transferred to this court on [*date*]. The debtor's proposal, a copy of which is exhibited hereto marked 'PP2' was considered and duly approved at a meeting of the debtor's creditors on [*date*]. I filed a copy of my report as chairman of the creditors' meeting on [*date*] , and I became the supervisor of the arrangement.
3. The proposal provided, inter alia, that the debtor should assign to me as supervisor 23 assorted artefacts previously belonging to Sir Montague Blackadder. The debtor informed myself and the creditors that these artefacts, which had been valued at £8,200, had been given to him by his previous employer, Sir Edmund Blackadder, in lieu of wages.
4. On [*date*] I called on the debtor to assign and deliver this property to me under the terms of the arrangement. He failed so to. On [*date*] I received a letter from solicitors acting for Sir Edmund Blackadder, a copy of which is at pages 1–3 of exhibit 'PP3' hereto stating these items had at all times been and remained the property of their client and had been wrongly interfered with by the debtor. Further, the said solicitors produced receipts and other evidence which satisfied me that all wages due to the debtor had been paid in full by Sir Edmund Blackadder. Copies of these receipts are at pages 4-28 of exhibit PP3.
5. Further, on [*date*] I received a letter from Lady Sarah Millward, a copy of which is at pages 29–34 of exhibit PP3 stating that by his actions the debtor was in breach of the agreement with her under which she had agreed to pay £5,000 to the arrangement. In the light of this breach she was exercising her right not to pay the said sum.
6. The terms of the proposal, as modified at the creditors' meeting, provided that I as supervisor should retain sufficient funds to petition for the bankruptcy of the debtor in the event that he is in default of the terms of the arrangement, and that I should present such a petition in the event of any breach of the arrangement by the debtor.
7. By reason of the matters above it is apparent that the debtor is in default for the purposes of section 276(1)(a) and (c) of the Insolvency Act 1986 and I ask this court to make a bankruptcy order against the debtor.

8. On [*date*] I sent a copy of the notice under rule 6.10(6) to all the creditors of the debtor. I have received no replies.
9. I now produce marked 'PP4' a copy account showing all my receipts and payments to date. As indicated I am holding a balance of £... The costs of this petition are £... and I have outstanding fees and expenses as supervisor in the region of £... There will therefore be a balance of £ ... on the making of a bankruptcy order.

Sworn at

On [*date*]

Before me.........................

A person authorised to take oaths

5.11 Notice to Creditors under Rule 6.10(6)

IN THE PAIGNTON COUNTY COURT

IN BANKRUPTCY

Re Barry Baldrick

NOTICE TO CREDITORS

I, Paul Peters of 139 St.John's Street, Exeter, EX7 4PJ

DO HEREBY GIVE YOU NOTICE as follows:

1. I am the supervisor of the individual voluntary arrangement of the above-named debtor, Barry Baldrick, which voluntary arrangement was approved by creditors at a meeting held on [*date*].
2. You are a creditor bound by the said voluntary arrangement.
3. On [*date*], I presented to the Paignton County Court a bankruptcy petition against the debtor, based on his default in connection with the said voluntary arrangement. The petition is to be heard by the Paignton County Court on [*date*] at [*time*] am/pm.
4. The petition contains an application that, in the event of a bankruptcy order being made, I be appointed trustee in bankruptcy of the debtor, pursuant to the provisions of section 297(5) of the Insolvency Act 1986.
5. The provisions of rule 6.42(7) of the Insolvency Rules 1986 require that I give you written notification of my intention to seek appointment as the debtor's trustee in bankruptcy.
6. Not less than two days before the day appointed for hearing the petition I will file in court a report, with particulars of the date on which I gave creditors written notification of my intention to seek appointment as trustee and details of any response from creditors to this notice, including any objections to my appointment.
7. If you wish to respond to this notice, and raise any objections to my appointment as trustee in bankruptcy of the debtor then you should do so in writing addressed to me by not later than [*date*].

Dated this ... day of ......

Signed ....

Supervisor

Appendix 6

6.1 Practice Direction: Insolvency Proceedings

Contents of Practice Direction

PART ONE

1. GENERAL

1.1 In this Practice Direction:

(1) 'The Act' means the Insolvency Act 1986 and includes the Act as applied to limited liability partnerships by the Limited Liability Partnerships Regulations 2001;

(2) 'The Insolvency Rules' means the rules for the time being in force and made under s.411 and s.412 of the Act in relation to insolvency proceedings;

(3) 'CPR' means the Civil Procedure Rules and 'CPR' followed by a Part or rule by number means the Part or rule with that number in those Rules;

(4) 'RSC' followed by an Order by number means the Order with that number set out in Schedule 1 to the CPR;

(5) 'Insolvency proceedings' means any proceedings under the Act, the Insolvency Rules, the Administration of Insolvent Estates of Deceased Persons Order 1986 (S.I. 1986 No.1999), the Insolvent Partnerships Order 1986 (S.I. 1986 No. 2124), the Insolvent Partnerships Order 1994 (S.I. 1994 No. 2421) or the Limited Liability Partnerships Regulations 2001.

(6) References to a 'company' shall include a limited liability partnership and references to a 'contributory' shall include a member of a limited liability partnership.

1.2 This Practice Direction shall come into effect on 26th April 1999 and shall replace all previous Practice Notes and Practice Directions relating to insolvency proceedings.

1.3 Except where the Insolvency Rules otherwise provide, service of documents in insolvency proceedings in the High Court will be the responsibility of the parties and will not be undertaken by the court.

1.4 Where CPR Part 2.4 provides for the court to perform any act, that act may be performed by a Registrar in Bankruptcy for the purpose of insolvency proceedings in the High Court.

1.5 A writ of execution to enforce any order made in insolvency proceedings in the High Court may be issued on the authority of a Registrar.

1.6 (1) This paragraph applies where an insolvency practitioner ('the outgoing office holder') holds office as a liquidator, administrator, trustee or supervisor in more than one case and dies, retires from practice as an insolvency practitioner or is otherwise unable or unwilling to continue in office.

(2) A single application may be made to a Judge of the Chancery Division of the High Court by way of ordinary application in Form 7.2 for the appointment of a substitute office holder or office holders in all cases in which the outgoing office holder holds office,and for the transfer of each such case to the High Court for the purpose only of making such an order.

(3) The application may be made by any of the following:

(i) the outgoing office holder (if he is able and willing to do so);

(ii) any person who holds office jointly with the outgoing office holder;

(iii) any person who is proposed to be appointed as a substitute for the outgoing office holder; or

(iv) any creditor in the cases where the substitution is proposed to be made.

(4) The outgoing office holder (if he is not the applicant) and every person who holds office jointly with the office holder must be made a respondent to the application, but it is not necessary to join any other person as a respondent or to serve the application upon any other person unless the Judge or Registrar in the High Court so directs.

(5) The application should contain schedules setting out the nature of the office held, the identity of the Court currently having jurisdiction over each case and its name and number.

(6) The application must be supported by evidence setting out the circumstances which have given rise to the need to make a substitution and exhibiting the written consent to act of each person who is proposed to be appointed in place of the outgoing office holder.

(7) The Judge will in the first instance consider the application on paper and make such order as he thinks fit. In particular he may do any of the following:

(i) make an order directing the transfer to the High Court of those cases not already within its jurisdiction for the purpose only of the substantive application;

(ii) if he considers that the papers are in order and that the matter is straightforward, make an order on the substantive application;

(iii) give any directions which he considers to be necessary including (if appropriate) directions for the joinder of any additional respondents or requiring the service of the application on any person or requiring additional evidence to be provided;

(iv) if he does not himself make an order on the substantive application when the matter is first before him, give directions for the further consideration of the substantive application by himself or another Judge of the Chancery Division or adjourn the substantive application to the Registrar for him to make such order upon it as is appropriate.

(8) An order of the kind referred to in sub-paragraph (6)(i)[1] shall follow the draft order in Form PDIP 3 set out in the Schedule hereto and an order granting the substantive application shall follow the draft order in Form PDIP 4 set out in the schedule hereto (subject in each case to such modifications as may be necessary or appropriate).

(9) It is the duty of the applicant to ensure that a sealed copy of every order transferring any case to the High Court and of every order which is made on a substantive application is lodged with the court having jurisdiction over each case affected by such order for filing on the court file relating to that case.

1 Sub-paragraph 7(i) is meant; these forms are not reproduced here. They are available on the Court Service website www.courtservice.gov.uk.

(10) It will not be necessary for the file relating to any case which is transferred to the High Court in accordance with this paragraph to be sent to the High Court unless a Judge or Registrar so directs.

PART TWO: COMPANIES

[paragraphs 2–8 deal with winding up only]

PART THREE: PERSONAL INSOLVENCY

9. Distribution of Business

9.1 The following applications shall be made direct to the Judge and unless otherwise ordered shall be heard in public:

(1) Applications for the committal of any person to prison for contempt;

(2) Application for injunctions or for the modification or discharge of injunctions;

(3) Applications for interlocutory relief or directions after the matter has been referred to the Judge.

9.2 All other applications shall be made to the Registrar or the District Judge in the first instance. He shall give any necessary directions and may, if the application is within his jurisdiction to determine, in his discretion either hear and determine it himself or refer it to the Judge.

9.3 The following matters shall be heard in public:

(1) The public examination of debtors;

(2) Opposed applications for discharge or for the suspension or lifting of the suspension of discharge;

(3) Opposed applications for permission to be a director;

(4) In any case where the petition was presented or the receiving order or order for adjudication was made before the appointed day, those matters and applications specified in Rule 8 of the Bankruptcy Rules 1952;

(5) All matters and applications heard by the Judge, except matters and applications referred by the Registrar or the District Judge to be heard by the Judge in private or directed by the Judge to be so heard.

9.4 All petitions presented will be listed under the name of the debtor.

9.5 In accordance with Directions given by the Lord Chancellor the Registrar has authorised certain applications in the High Court to be dealt with by the Court Manager of the Bankruptcy Court pursuant to Insolvency Rule 13.2(2). The applications are:

(1) By petitioning creditors: to extend time for hearing petitions (s.376 of the Act).

(2) by the Official Receiver:

(a) To transfer proceedings from the High Court to a County Court (Insolvency Rule 7.13);

(b) To amend the full title of the proceedings (Insolvency Rules 6.35 and 6.47).

[NB In District Registries all such applications must be made to the District Judge] .

[paragraphs 10–15 deal with bankruptcy only]

16. Orders without attendance

16.1 In suitable cases the Court will normally be prepared to make orders under Part VIII of the Act (Individual Voluntary Arrangements), without the attendance of either party, provided there is no bankruptcy order in existence and (so far as is known) no pending petition. The orders are:

(1) A fourteen day interim order with the application adjourned 14 days for consideration of the nominee's report, where the papers are in order, and the nominee's signed consent to act includes a waiver of notice of the application or a consent by the nominee to the making of an interim order without attendance.

(2) A standard order on consideration of the nominee's report, extending the interim order to a date 7 weeks after the date of the proposed meeting, directing the meeting to be summoned and adjourning to a date about 3 weeks after the meeting. Such an Order may be made without attendance if the nominee's report has been delivered to the Court and complies with section 256(1) of the Act and Insolvency Rule 5.10(2) and (3)[2] and proposes a date for the meeting not less than 14 days from that on which the nominee's report is filed in Court under Insolvency Rule 5.10[3] nor more than 28 days from that on which that report is considered by the Court under Insolvency Rule 5.12[4].

(3) A 'concertina' Order, combining orders as under (1) and (2) above. Such an order may be made without attendance if the initial application for an interim order is accompanied by a report of the nominee and the conditions set out in (1) and (2) above are satisfied.

(4) A final order on consideration of the Chairman's report. Such an order may be made without attendance if the Chairman's report has been filed and complies with Insolvency Rule 5.22(1)[5]. The order will record the effect of the Chairman's report and may discharge the interim order.

16.2 Provided that the conditions as under 16.1(2) and (4) above are satisfied and that the appropriate report has been lodged with the Court in due time the parties need not attend or be represented on the adjourned hearing for consideration of the Nominee's report or of the Chairman's report (as the case may be) unless they are notified by the Court that attendance is required. Sealed copies of the order made (in all four cases as above) will be posted by the Court to the applicant or his Solicitor and to the Nominee.

2 Now IR 1986, r 5.11(2) and (3).
3 Now IR 1986, r 5.11.
4 Now IR 1986, r 5.13.
5 Now IR 1986, r 5.27(1); however the Practice Direction clearly meant to refer to r 5.22(2) now r 5.27(2) which sets out what the report should contain.

16.3 In suitable cases the Court may also make consent orders without attendance by the parties. The written consent of the parties will be required. Examples of such orders are as follows:

(1) On applications to set aside a statutory demand, orders:

(a) dismissing the application, with or without an order for costs as may be agreed (permission will be given to present a petition on or after the seventh day after the date of the order, unless a different date is agreed);

(b) setting aside the demand, with or without an order for costs as may be agreed; or

(c) giving permission to withdraw the application with or without an order for costs as may be agreed.

(2) On petitions: where there is a list of supporting or opposing creditors in Form 6.21, or a statement signed by or on behalf of the petitioning creditor that no notices have been received from supporting or opposing creditors, orders:

(a) dismissing the petition, with or without an order for costs as may be agreed, or

(b) if the petition has not been served, giving permission to withdraw the petition (with no order for costs).

(3) On other applications, orders:

(a) for sale of property, possession of property, disposal of proceeds of sale;

(b) giving interim directions;

(c) dismissing the application, with or without an order for costs as may be agreed;

(d) giving permission to withdraw the application, with or without an order for costs as may be agreed.

If, (as may often be the case with orders under subparagraphs (3)(a) or (b) above) an adjournment is required, whether generally with liberty to restore or to a fixed date, the order by consent may include an order for the adjournment. If adjournment to a date is requested, a time estimate should be given and the Court will fix the first available date and time on or after the date requested.

16.4 The above lists should not be regarded as exhaustive, nor should it be assumed that an order will be made without attendance as requested.

16.5 The procedure outlined above is designed to save time and costs but is not intended to discourage attendance.

16.6 Applications for consent orders without attendance should be lodged at least two clear working days (and preferably longer) before any fixed hearing date.

16.7 Whenever a document is lodged or a letter sent, the correct case number, code (if any) and year (for example 123/SD/99 or 234/99) should be quoted. A note should also be given of the date and time of the next hearing (if any).

16.8 Attention is drawn to paragraph 4.4(4) of the Practice Direction relating to CPR Part 44.

PART FOUR

17. Appeals in insolvency proceedings

17.1 This Part shall come into effect on 2nd May 2000 and shall replace and revoke Paragraph 17 of, and be read in conjunction with the Practice Direction : Insolvency Proceedings which came into effect on 26th April 1999 as amended.

17.2 (1) An appeal from a decision of a County Court (whether made by a District Judge or a Circuit Judge) or of a Registrar of the High Court in insolvency proceedings ('a first appeal') lies to a Judge of the High Court pursuant to s 375(2) of the Act and Insolvency Rules 7.47(2) and 7.48(2) (as amended by s 55 of the Access to Justice Act 1999).

(2) The procedure and practice for a first appeal are governed by Insolvency Rule 7.49 which imports the procedure and practice of the Court of Appeal. The procedure and practice of the Court of Appeal is governed by CPR Part 52 and its Practice Direction, which are subject to the provisions of the Act, the Insolvency Rules and this Practice Direction: see CPR Part 52 rule 1(4).

(3) A first appeal (as defined above) does not include an appeal from a decision of a Judge of the High Court.

17.3 (1) Section 55 of the Access to Justice Act 1999 has amended s 375(2) of the Act and Insolvency Rules 7.47(2) and 7.48(2) so that an appeal from a decision of a Judge of the High Court made on a first appeal lies, with the permission of the Court of Appeal, to the Court of Appeal.

(2) An appeal from a Judge of the High Court in insolvency proceedings which is not a decision on a first appeal lies, with the permission of the Judge or of the Court of Appeal, to the Court of Appeal (see CPR Part 52 rule 3);

(3) The procedure and practice for appeals from a decision of a Judge of the High Court in insolvency proceedings (whether made on a first appeal or not) are also governed by Insolvency Rule 7.49 which imports the procedure and practice of the Court of Appeal as stated at Paragraph 17.2(2) above.

17.4 CPR Part 52 and its Practice Direction and Forms apply to appeals from a decision of a Judge of the High Court in insolvency proceedings.

17.5 An appeal from a decision of a Judge of the High Court in insolvency proceedings requires permission as set out in Paragraph 17.3(1) and (2) above.

17.6 A first appeal does not require the permission of any court.

17.7 Except as provided in this Part, CPR Part 52 and its Practice Direction and Forms do not apply to first appeals, but Paragraphs 17.8 to 17.23 inclusive of this Part apply only to first appeals.

17.8 Interpretation:

(a) the expressions 'appeal court', 'lower court', 'appellant', 'respondent' and 'appeal notice' have the meanings given in CPR Part 52.1(3);

(b) 'Registrar of Appeals' means in relation to an appeal filed at the Royal Courts of Justice in London a Bankruptcy Registrar, and in relation to an appeal filed in a District Registry in accordance with Paragraph 17.10(2) and (3) below a District Judge of the relevant District Registry.

(c) 'appeal date' means the date fixed by the appeal court for the hearing of the appeal or the date fixed by the appeal court upon which the period within which the appeal will be heard commences.

17.9 An appellant's notice and a respondent's notice shall be in Forms PDIP 1 and PDIP 2 set out in the Schedule hereto.

17.10 (1) An appeal from a decision of a Registrar in Bankruptcy shall, or from any decision made in any County Court may, be filed at the Royal Courts of Justice in London.

(2) An appeal from a decision made in the County Court exercising jurisdiction over an area within the Birmingham, Bristol, Cardiff, Leeds, Liverpool, Manchester, Newcastle Upon Tyne or Preston Chancery District Registries may be filed in the Chancery District Registry of the High Court appropriate to the area in which the decision was made.

17.11 (1) Where a party seeks an extension of time in which to file an appeal notice it must be requested in the appeal notice and the appeal notice should state the reason for the delay and the steps taken prior to the application being made; the court will fix a date for the hearing of the application and notify the parties of the date and place of hearing;

(2) The appellant must file the appellant's notice at the appeal court within —

(a) such period as may be directed by the lower court; or

(b) where the court makes no such direction, 14 days after the date of the decision of the lower court which the appellant wishes to appeal.

(3) Unless the appeal court orders otherwise, an appeal notice must be served by the appellant on each respondent —

(a) as soon as practicable; and

(b) in any event not later than 7 days, after it is filed.

17.12 (1) A respondent may file and serve a respondent's notice.

(2) A respondent who wishes to ask the appeal court to uphold the order of the lower court for reasons different from or additional to those given by the lower court must file a respondent's notice.

(3) A respondent's notice must be filed within —

(a) such period as may be directed by the lower court; or

(b) where the court makes no such direction, 14 days after the date on which the respondent is served with the appellant's notice.

(4) Unless the appeal court orders otherwise a respondent's notice must be served by the respondent on the appellant and any other respondent —

(a) as soon as practicable; and

(b) in any event not later than 7 days, after it is filed.

17.13 (1) An application to vary the time limit for filing an appeal notice must be made to the appeal court.

(2) The parties may not agree to extend any date or time limit set by —

(a) this Practice Direction; or

(b) an order of the appeal court or the lower court.

17.14 Unless the appeal court or the lower court orders otherwise an appeal shall not operate as a stay of any order or decision of the lower court.

17.15 An appeal notice may not be amended without the permission of the appeal court.

17.16 A Judge of the appeal court may strike out the whole or part of an appeal notice where there is compelling reason for doing so.

17.17 (1) In relation to an appeal the appeal court has all the powers of the lower court.

(2) The appeal court has power to —

(a) affirm, set aside or vary any order or judgment made or given by the lower court;

(b) refer any claim or issue for determination by the lower court;

(c) order a new trial or hearing;

(d) make a costs order.

(3) The appeal court may exercise its powers in relation to the whole or part of an order of the lower court.

17.18 (1) Every appeal shall be limited to a review of the decision of the lower court.

(2) Unless it orders otherwise, the appeal court will not receive —

(a) oral evidence; or

(b) evidence which was not before the lower court.

(3) The appeal court will allow an appeal where the decision of the lower court was:

(a) wrong; or

(b) unjust because of a serious procedural or other irregularity in the proceedings in the lower court.

(4) The appeal court may draw any inference of fact which it considers justified on the evidence.

(5) At the hearing of the appeal a party may not rely on a matter not contained in his appeal notice unless the appeal court gives permission.

17.19 The following applications shall be made to a Judge of the appeal court:

(1) for injunctions pending a substantive hearing of the appeal;

(2) for expedition or vacation of the hearing date of an appeal;

(3) for an order striking out the whole or part of an appeal notice pursuant to Paragraph 17.16 above;

(4) for a final order on paper pursuant to Paragraph 17.22(8) below.

17.20 (1) All other interim applications shall be made to the Registrar of Appeals in the first instance who may in his discretion either hear and determine it himself or refer it to the Judge.

(2) An appeal from a decision of a Registrar of Appeals lies to a Judge of the appeal court and does not require the permission of either the Registrar of Appeals or the Judge.

17.21 The procedure for interim applications is by way of ordinary application (see Insolvency Rule 12.7 and Sch 4, Form 7.2).

17.22 The following practice applies to all first appeals to a Judge of the High Court whether filed at the Royal Courts of Justice in London, or filed at one of the other venues referred to in Paragraph 17.10 above:

(1) on filing an appellant's notice in accordance with Paragraph 17.11(2) above, the appellant must file:

(a) two copies of the appeal notice for the use of the court, one of which must be stamped with the appropriate fee, and a number of additional copies equal to the number of persons who are to be served with it pursuant to Paragraph 17.22(4) below;

(b) a copy of the order under appeal; and

(c) an estimate of time for the hearing.

(2) the above documents may be lodged personally or by post and shall be lodged at the address of the appropriate venue listed below:

(a) if the appeal is to be heard at the Royal Courts of Justice in London the documents must be lodged at Room 110, Thomas More Building, The Royal Courts of Justice, Strand, London WC2A 2LL;

(b) if the appeal is to be heard in Birmingham, the documents must be lodged at the District Registry of the Chancery Division of the High Court, 33 Bull Street, Birmingham B4 6DS;

(c) if the appeal is to be heard in Bristol the documents must be lodged at the District Registry of the Chancery Division of the High Court, Third Floor, Greyfriars, Lewins Mead, Bristol, BS1 2NR;

(d) if the appeal is to be heard in Cardiff the documents must be lodged at the District Registry in the Chancery Division of the High Court, First Floor, 2 Park Street, Cardiff , CF10 1ET;

(e) if the appeal is to be heard in Leeds the documents must be lodged at the District Registry of the Chancery Division of the High Court, The Court House, 1 Oxford Row, Leeds LS1 3BG;

(f) if the appeal is to be heard in Liverpool the documents must be lodged at the District Registry of the Chancery Division of the High Court, Liverpool Combined Court Centre, Derby Square, Liverpool L2 1XA;

(g) if the appeal is to be heard in Manchester the documents must be lodged at the District Registry of the Chancery Division of the High Court, Courts of Justice, Crown Square, Manchester, M60 9DJ;

(h) if the appeal is to be heard at Newcastle Upon Tyne the documents must be lodged at the District Registry of the Chancery Division of the High Court, The Law Courts, Quayside, Newcastle Upon Tyne NE1 3LA;

(i) if the appeal is to be heard in Preston the documents must be lodged at the District Registry of the Chancery Division of the High Court, The Combined Court Centre, Ringway, Preston PR1 2LL.

(3) if the documents are correct and in order the court at which the documents are filed will fix the appeal date and will also fix the place of hearing. That court will send letters to all the parties to the appeal informing them of the appeal date and of the place of hearing and indicating the time estimate given by the appellant. The parties will be invited to notify the court of any alternative or revised time estimates. In the absence of any such notification the estimate of the appellant will be taken as agreed. The court will also send to the appellant a document setting out the court's requirement concerning the form and content of the bundle of documents for the use of the Judge. Not later than 7 days before the appeal date the bundle of documents must be filed by the appellant at the address of the relevant venue as set out in sub-paragraph 17.22(2) above and a copy of it must be served by the appellant on each respondent. The bundle should include an approved transcript of the judgment of the lower court or, where there is no officially recorded judgment, the document(s) referred to in paragraph 5.12 of the Practice Direction pdp-52 to CPR Part 52.

(4) the appeal notice must be served on all parties to the proceedings in the lower court who are directly affected by the appeal. This may include the Official Receiver, liquidator or trustee in bankruptcy.

(5) the appeal notice must be served by the appellant or by the legal representative of the appellant and may be effected by:

(a) any of the methods referred to in CPR Part 6 rule 2; or

(b) with permission of the court, an alternative method pursuant to CPR Part 6 rule 8.

(6) service of an appeal notice shall be proved by a Certificate of Service in accordance with CPR Part 6 rule 10 (CPR Form N215) which must be filed at the relevant venue referred to at Paragraph 17.22(2) above immediately after service.

(7) skeleton arguments, accompanied by a written chronology of events relevant to the appeal, should be filed at the address of the appropriate venue as set out in sub-paragraph 17.22(2) above, at least two clear days before the date fixed for the hearing. Failure to lodge may result in an adverse costs order being made by the Judge on the hearing of the appeal.

(8) where an appeal has been settled or where an appellant does not wish to continue with the appeal, the appeal may be disposed of on paper without a hearing. It may be dismissed by consent but the appeal court will not make an order allowing an appeal unless it is satisfied that the decision of the lower court was wrong. Any consent order signed by each party or letters of consent from each party must be lodged not later than 24 hours before the date fixed for the hearing of the appeal at the address of the appropriate venue as set out in sub-paragraph 17.22(2) above and will be dealt with by the Judge of the appeal court. Attention is drawn to paragraph 4.4(4) of

the Practice Direction pdp-44 to CPR Part 44 regarding costs where an order is made by consent without attendance.

17.23 Only the following paragraphs of the Practice Direction pdp-52 to CPR Part 52, with any necessary modifications, shall apply to first appeals: 5.12 and 5.14 to 5.20 inclusive.

17.24 (1) Where, under the procedure relating to appeals in insolvency proceedings prior to the coming into effect of this Part of this Practice Direction, an appeal has been set down in the High Court or permission to appeal to the Court of Appeal has been granted before 2nd May 2000, the procedure and practice set out in this Part of this Practice Direction shall apply to such an appeal after that date.

(2) Where, under the procedure relating to appeals in insolvency proceedings prior to the coming into effect of this Part of this Practice Direction, any person has failed before 2nd May 2000 either:

(a) in the case of a first appeal, to set down in the High Court an appeal which relates to an order made (County Court) or sealed (High Court) after 27th March 2000 and before 2nd May 2000, or

(b) in the case of an appeal from a decision of a Judge of the High Court, to obtain any requisite permission to appeal to the Court of Appeal which relates to an order sealed in the same period,

the time for filing an appeal notice is extended to 16th May 2000 and application for any such permission should be made in the appeal notice.

17.25 This paragraph applies where a judge of the High Court has made a Bankruptcy order or a winding-up order or dismissed an appeal against such an order and an application is made for a stay of proceedings pending appeal.

(1) the judge will not normally grant a stay of all proceedings but will confine himself to a stay of advertisement of the proceedings.

(2) where the judge has granted permission to appeal any stay of advertisement will normally be until the hearing of the appeal but on terms that the stay will determine without further order if an appellant's notice is not filed within the period prescribed by the rules.

(3) where the judge has refused permission to appeal any stay of advertisement will normally be for a period not exceeding 28 days. Application for any further stay of advertisement should be made to the Court of Appeal.

Appendix 7

7.1 Dear IP Millennium Edition

CHAPTER 24 : VOLUNTARY ARRANGEMENTS

1. The Role of the Nominee and Application of Professional Judgement

The Service monitoring teams have encountered a number of instances where the nominee appears to have acted merely as a post-box for the proposal, and not queried the information presented. It is considered that such actions result in a high percentage of arrangements failing either at the first meeting of creditors or following approval.

The nominee must ensure that the proposal meets the criteria set out in the legislation, but that is not sufficient reason to conclude that the proposal is fit to be put to creditors: the practitioner must also use professional judgement in deciding whether or not the proposal is feasible.

Under Section 256 of the Insolvency Act 1986 it is the duty of the nominee to report to court on whether in his opinion a meeting of creditors should be summoned to consider the debtor's proposal. The clear implication is that as nominee you will consider the proposal, and make such enquiries as you consider necessary to satisfy yourself that the proposal ought to be put to creditors. For instance, the nominee's right of access, under Rule 5.9 (3), to the debtor's accounts and records, is there to be exercised, and was provided for that purpose.

Case law has reinforced this view, i.e. that the nominee must go further than merely ensuring that the proposal contains the matters required by the legislation. In *Re a debtor (No 222 of 1990)* it was held that a nominee in making his report to court, and acting as chairman of the meeting of creditors has a duty (arising from section 256) to exercise a professional independent judgement. That this judgement is required of an authorised insolvency practitioner, emphasises that the court requires a report from a qualified person, skilled and experienced, who is exercising his professional judgement as to whether the matter is, in his opinion, fit to go forward for consideration by the creditors.

In relation to each and every arrangement the Service would ask practitioners to consider the following:

Is it feasible?

Is it fair to the creditors?

Is it an acceptable alternative to formal insolvency?

Is it fit to be considered by the creditors? and

Is it fair to the debtor?

(First published in Dear IP no. 33. March 1995)

2. Failed Individual Voluntary Arrangements (IVA's)

Monitoring by the Service has highlighted the difficulty faced by some supervisors when an arrangement has failed. In several instances the proposal has failed but no further action has been taken to resolve the matter.

The set functions undertaken by the supervisor under the proposal should include any actions he is to take should the arrangement be deemed to have failed.

The Service is aware that the scope for action when an arrangement fails can be limited by lack of funds. However, in Re a debtor (No 222 of 1990) No 2, it was held that a supervisor must take some positive action if it appears that an arrangement is failing, either in accordance with the provisions of the proposal, or, where there are no such provisions, by seeking directions from the court, or petitioning for a bankruptcy order.

Monitoring has also revealed that not all practitioners are aware of their duty to notify the Secretary of State when an arrangement has failed. When notifying the Secretary of State it would be appreciated if you could indicate what further actions you intend to take as supervisor, e.g. in respect of petitioning for bankruptcy.

(First published in Dear IP no. 33, March 1995)

3. IVAs - Notices to the Official Receiver and the Secretary of State

Practitioners are reminded that at various points during the course of an individual voluntary arrangement (IVA) notices must be given to the OR and/or to the Secretary of State. The Insolvency Rules 1986, provide:

Rule 5.5(4) [*now Rule 5.7(4)*]

Where the debtor is an undischarged bankrupt, at least two days notice of the hearing of an application for an interim order must be given to the bankrupt, the OR, and any trustee.

Rule 5.7(2) [*now Rule 5.10(2)*]

Where an interim order is made the applicant must give notice of the fact to the bankrupt, the OR, and any trustee not present or represented at the hearing

Rule 5.10(5) [*now Rule 5.11(6)*]

Where the debtor is an undischarged bankrupt the nominee shall send the OR, a copy of the nominee's report and a copy, or summary, of the debtor's statement of affairs.

Rule 5.12 [*now Rule 5.13*]

Any of the persons given notice under Rule 5.5(4) [*now Rule 5.7(4)*] may appear to be represented at the hearing to consider the nominee's report, so notice of the hearing must be given to the bankrupt, the OR and any trustee.

Rule 5.22(4) [*now Rule 5.27(4)*]

Following the creditors' meeting the chairman is required [*by Rule 5.27(2)*] to prepare a report which shall:

1. state whether the proposal was approved or rejected, and if approved, with what (if any) amendments;
2. set out the resolutions taken and the decision on each one;
3. list the creditors (with their respective values) present or represented, and how they voted on each resolution; and
4. include such further information (if any) as the chairman thinks it appropriate to make known to the court.

Where the debtor is an undischarged bankrupt, a copy of the report is to be sent to the OR; and to any trustee.

Rule 5.24 [*now Rule 5.29*]

Immediately after the chairman of the creditors' meeting has filed his report in court that the proposal has been approved he shall report to the Secretary of State the following details:

1. the name and address of the debtor;
2. the date on which the arrangement was approved by the creditors;
3. the name and address of the supervisor; and
4. the court in which the chairman's report has been filed.

In addition, the supervisor must give written notice of his appointment to the Secretary of State.

Rule 5.25(2) and (5) [*now Rule 5.30*]

Where the court makes an order revoking or suspending an IVA a copy must be served on the debtor, the OR and any trustee by the applicant for that order.

The applicant is also required to give notice of the revocation or suspension to the Secretary of State, at the address given below. (see article 4 below)

Rule 5.29 [*now Rule 5.34*]

On completion of the arrangement the supervisor must within 28 days send to the Secretary of State at the address given below, a copy of the notice to creditors that the arrangement has been completed, and a copy of his report summarising all receipts and payments further to Rule 5.29(1)(2).

Address for matters to be reported to or filed with the Secretary of State

Insolvency Practitioners Section
5th Floor
Ladywood House
45/46 Stephenson Street
Birmingham
B2 4UY

In relation to registration of the IVA under Rule 5.24 [*now Rule 5.29*] there is a fee payable under the Insolvency Fees Order 1986 (as amended); cheques should be made payable to 'The Insolvency Service'.

(First published in Dear IP no. 30, March 1994)

4. Modification of Court Jurisdiction

It has been drawn to our attention that it is becoming increasingly common for terms to be inserted in proposals for individual voluntary arrangements which seek to exclude or vary the jurisdiction of the Court. Practitioners are reminded that any conditions seeking to exclude or vary jurisdiction will be void as being contrary to public policy, and accordingly should not be included in proposals.

(First published in Dear IP no. 34, October 1995)

5. Notification to Secretary of State Regarding IVAs

Article 3 above sets out the information to be sent to the Secretary of State. Where a debtor simply fails to adhere to an arrangement, and no action is taken by the supervisor, then the arrangement will still subsist, despite the debtor being in breach of its terms. In those circumstances, there is no obligation on the supervisor to notify the Secretary of State. There is no provision for the notification of, and entry onto, the register of details relating to the termination of an arrangement where the supervisor has petitioned for a bankruptcy order pursuant to Section 264(1)(c).

Rule 5.29 [*now Rule 5.34*] Insolvency Rules 1986

The Secretary of State must be notified not more than 28 days after final completion of the arrangement. The notification must be accompanied by a report summarising all receipts and payments made by him in pursuance of the arrangement, and explaining any difference in the actual implementation of it compared to the proposal as approved by the creditors meeting.

(First published in Dear IP no. 34, October 1995)

6. Position of Preferential Creditors

Practitioners are reminded that section 4(4) and 258(5) of the Insolvency Act 1986, provide that a meeting of creditors may not approve a proposal or modification which affects the rights of a preferential creditor without the approval of that preferential creditor.

HM Customs and Excise has informed the Service that in an increasing number of cases the proposal approved by creditors purports to affect Customs rights as preferential creditor, without approval, Customs will consider making an application to court, and reporting the matter to the practitioners authorising body, where the provisions of these sections have not been observed.

(First published in Dear IP no. 24, November 1992)

7. Receipts of Funds by Trustees Prior to an IVA

Where an individual voluntary arrangement (IVA) is proposed following the appointment of a trustee in bankruptcy, the trustee, acting as such, is still required to pay the proceeds of asset realisation into the ISA under Regulation 20 of the Insolvency Regulations 1984. These proceeds will attract the Secretary of State fee, which will not be rebated when the bankruptcy is subsequently replaced by an IVA.

Practitioners will wish to bear this in mind when formulating proposals for an IVA.

(First published in Dear IP no. 35, April 1996)

8. Individual Voluntary Arrangements following a Bankruptcy Order – Discharge of Official Receiver's Costs – Rule 5.21 [*now Rule 5.26*] of The Insolvency Rules 1986

In bankruptcy cases where an individual voluntary arrangement (IVA) is subsequently approved, Rule 5.21 [*now Rule 5.26*] of The Insolvency Rules 1986 provides that the supervisor must either discharge any balance due to the OR in respect of fees, costs, charges and expenses properly incurred, or give the OR a written undertaking to discharge any such debit balances out of the first realisation of assets.

Generally, no provision is made in the bankrupt's proposal to creditors for the discharge of the OR's costs as there is no mandatory requirement to do so under Rule 5.3, nor is it covered by current best practice guidance. Nonetheless, IPs are requested to consider including such provisions in any proposal prepared on behalf of a bankrupt, given the statutory requirement to discharge the OR's costs.

IPs should also be aware that Insolvency Practitioner Compliance Unit have responsibility for recovery of the OR's costs from the supervisor in cases where the bankruptcy order is annulled following the approval of the IVA.

Contact: Jane Knight, Insolvency Practitioners Control Unit, 5th Floor, Ladywood House, 45/46 Stephenson Street, Birmingham B2 4UZ. Tel: 0121 698 4098

(First published in Dear IP no. 46, July 1999)

9. Individual Insolvency Register – request for searches

The Individual Insolvency Register comprises two separate registers, one being the Bankruptcy register and the other the Individual Voluntary Arrangement register.

Requests for searches of the Individual Insolvency Register are dealt with by the General Services Team at 5th Floor, West Wing, Ladywood House, 45–46 Stephenson Street, Birmingham, B2 4UZ.

SUBMISSION OF REQUESTS

Requests can be made by either fax or post at the above address. Telephone requests cannot be accepted. The fax number for requests is 0121 698 4406 and search results will be returned by post.

Alternatively, search requests may be made in person at any OR's office.

RETURN OF SEARCH INFORMATION

Where there is an exact match of name and address and/or date of birth you have provided, you will receive a copy of the search report. Please note the more information you are able to provide the quicker the request can be processed.

Where there are no possible matches you may receive the reports provided the administrator dealing with your search is satisfied that the information is a close enough match.

Search requests are processed within three days of receipt.

Please note that under the provisions of the Data Protection Act 1998 it may not be possible to disclose additional personal details.

STANDARD REQUEST FORMS

Search requests can be made utilising a standard search request form which is available from the General Services Team. Should you require a copy of the form please contact us at:

General Services Team
5th floor
West Wing
45–46 Stephenson Street
Birmingham, B2 4UZ
Telephone:- 0121 698 4080 / 4081 / 4082

(First published in Dear IP no. 47, October 1999)

10. Individual Voluntary Arrangements – Reports of the Creditors Meeting to the Court and the Secretary of State in compliance with Rules 5.22 and 5.24 [*now Rules 5.27 and 5.29*] of the Insolvency Rules 1986

Practitioners are reminded that Rule 5.22 (3) [*now Rule 5.27(3)*] provides that following approval of an IVA a copy of the chairman's report shall, within 4 days of the meeting being held, be filed in court. Rule 5.24 [*now Rule 5.29*] provides that immediately after a copy of the report has been filed in court, the chairman shall report to the Secretary of State details of the arrangement, and the supervisor shall forthwith give written notice of his/her appointment to the Secretary of State. In practice these two requirements are generally undertaken jointly.

Details supplied to the Insolvency Practitioners Compliance Unit (IPCU) should include: the name and address of the debtor, the date that the arrangement was approved, the name and address of the supervisor and the court where the chairman's report has been filed. The information supplied is recorded on the IVA register, and is available for public inspection by search of the Individual Insolvency Register. It is therefore important that the information provided to IPCU is accurate and up to date.

The vast majority of reports and notices of appointment are received within a matter of days of the meeting, but there can be significant delays. IPCU considers that any reports/notices of appointment under Rule 5.24 [*now Rule 5.29*] will comply with requirements to lodge 'immediately' and 'forthwith' if they are received within 10 days of the meeting of creditors approving the IVA. Any reports received more than 10 days after the meeting will be treated as late, and a letter will be sent to the practitioner requesting an explanation for the delay. Details of insolvency practitioners who have a significant number of defaults, or where there are significant delays in complying with rule 5.24 [*now Rule 5.29*], will be provided to their authorising body, and the practitioner will be notified accordingly.

(First published in Dear IP no. 34, October 1995)

11. Individual Voluntary Arrangements – reports of the creditors' meeting to the Secretary of State in accordance with rule 5.24 [*now Rule 5.29*] of the Insolvency Rules 1986.

This article clarifies the information given in article 10.

Rule 5.24 [*now Rule 5.29*] provides that immediately after a copy of the chairman's report is filed in court the chairman shall report to the Secretary of State details of the arrangements, and the supervisor shall forthwith give written notice of his appointment to the Secretary of State. The article in Dear IP Millennium Issue described a 14 day deadline within which Insolvency Practitioners Compliance Unit (IPCU), in acting on behalf of the Secretary of State, expects to receive the chairman's report and notice of the supervisor's appointment. This deadline of 14 days from the meeting of creditors is, however, one that has been set by IPCU solely for its compliance purposes. The time scale gives insolvency practitioners (IPs) a known deadline which, if missed, will trigger appropriate compliance action. It is likely that the time scale will be reduced over time, although of course IPs will be notified in advance of any such reduction.

There is no statutory definition of the terms, 'immediately' and 'forthwith', which appear in rule 5.24 [*now Rule 5.29*] and elsewhere in the insolvency legislation. The 14 day time scale set by IPCU for rule 5.4 compliance purposes has no application whatsoever in any other context to any other part of the legislation where the words 'immediately' and 'forthwith' may appear.

Enquiries arising form the above should be addressed to:

Gareth Limb, IPCU, 5th Floor, Ladywood House, 45/6 Stephenson Street, Birmingham B2 4UZ.

Tel: 0121 698 4105. E-mail: gareth.limb@insolvency.gsi.gov.uk

12. Individual Voluntary Arrangements – notification of the completion or termination of the arrangement to the Secretary of State as required by rule 5.29 [*now Rule 5.34*] of the Insolvency Rules 1986 (as amended).

Insolvency Practitioners Compliance Unit (IPCU) act on behalf of the Secretary of State in maintaining the Register of Individual Voluntary Arrangements. IPs are reminded that when notifying IPCU of a completed or terminated voluntary arrangement, as required by rule 5.29(3) [*now Rule 5.34(3)*], a copy of both the supervisor's notice to creditors and the report to creditors should be provided.

Enquiries about this should be addressed to:

Gareth Limb, IPCU, 5th Floor, Ladywood House, 45/6 Stephenson Street, Birmingham B2 4UZ.

Tel: 0121 698 4105. E-mail: gareth.limb@insolvency.gsi.gov.uk.

13. CVA Voting Procedure – Rule 1.19, Requisite Majorities (Creditors)

An issue has arisen regarding the application of rule 1.19(4) of the Insolvency Rules 1986 rendering a resolution invalid at a meeting of creditors in a CVA. Rule 1.19(4) states that 'any resolution is invalid if those voting against it include more than half in value of the creditors, counting in these latter only those –

(a) to whom notice of the meeting was sent;

(b) whose votes are not to be left out of account under [rule1.19(3)]; and

(c) who are not, to the best of the chairman's belief, persons connected with the company.

The point at issue is the meaning of 'creditors' in the context of the phrase 'more than half in value of the creditors'. Our view is that the reference to rule 1.19(3) implies that the creditors for the purpose of the calculation are:

(a) unsecured;

(b) have been given notice of the meeting;

(c) have given written notice of their claim to the chairman, and

(d) he/she does not believe them to be connected with the company.

Enquiries arising from the above should be addressed to Gareth Limb, Insolvency Practitioners Compliance Unit, The Insolvency Service, 5th Floor, 45 Stephenson Street, Birmingham, B2 4UZ. Tel: 0121 698 4105.

e-mail: gareth.limb@insolvency.gsi.gov.uk.

14. Individual Voluntary Arrangements – Registration of an arrangement with the Secretary of State as required by rule 5.24, 5.25 and 5.29 [*now Rule 5.29, 5.30 and 5.34*] of the Insolvency Rules 1986.

Insolvency Practitioners Compliance Unit (IPCU) act on behalf of the Secretary of State in maintaining the Register of Individual Voluntary arrangements. IPCU has recently found several instances where IPs have failed to notify the Registrar of new arrangements or completion of the arrangement. Therefore, IPs are reminded of the requirement to report new arrangements to the Registrar immediately after the chairman of the creditors' meeting has filed in court a report that the meeting has approved the arrangement and within 28 days following the completion of the arrangement.

IPCU, as a result of these omissions by IPs, is concerned as to the accuracy and integrity of the data held on the register and is presently considering completing a review of the data held. The unit completed a similar exercise in 1998 and IPs were then provided with details of 'open' arrangements and were asked to confirm if these accurately reflected their own office records. Therefore, IPsmay wish to review their office records and advise IPCU of any omissions to the register in advance of this intended review.

Enquiries about this should be addressed to:

Pat Christopher, IPCU, 5th Floor West Wing, Ladywood House, 45/46 Stephenson Street, Birmingham B2 4UZ. Tel no: 0121 698 4104.

E mail pat.christopher@insolvency.gsi.gov.uk

Appendix 8

8.1 Statement of Insolvency Practice 3[1]

This statement of good practice has been issued by the Association of Business Recovery Professionals in conjunction with the recognised professional bodies for licencing insolvency practitioners. This statement is from time to time revised and is due to be revised to take into account the changes in the rules consequent on the introduction of the Insolvency Act 2000 amendments. The statement set out below is that issued in November 1997 with the inclusion (at paragraphs 3.7, 6.5 and 7.13) of the additional provisions of which notice was given in June 2002. [Annotations in square brackets note the changes made to the law on 1st January 2003]

VOLUNTARY ARRANGEMENTS

ENGLAND AND WALES

1. Introduction

1.1 This statement of insolvency practice is one of a series issued by the Council of the Society with a view to harmonising the approach of members to questions of insolvency practice. It should be read in conjunction with the Explanatory Foreword to the Statements of Insolvency Practice and Insolvency Technical Reminders issued in June 1996.

1.2 The statement has been prepared for the sole use of members in dealing with both company am individual voluntary arrangements in England and Wales. Members are reminded that SPI Statements of Insolvency Practice are for the purpose of guidance only and may not be relied upon as definitive statements. No liability attaches to the Council or anyone involved in the preparation or publication of Statements of Insolvency Practice.

1.3 The Insolvency Act 1986 (IA 1986) and associated Rules set out a procedure which enables the directors of a company to make a proposal for a voluntary arrangement (CVA) with its creditors. A similar procedure is set out which enables a debtor to make a proposal for a voluntary arrangement (IVA)

1 Reproduced with the kind permission of the Association of Business Recovery Professionals.

with his creditors. In the latter case, The Insolvency Rules 1986 (the Rules) specify two type of debtor:

'Case 1': an undischarged bankrupt;

'Case 2': not an undischarged bankrupt.[2]

The CVA procedure is also available to insolvent partnerships.

In the case of both CVAs and IVAs the arrangement must take the form of a composition in satisfaction of the company's or individual's debts or a scheme of arrangement of their affairs.

1.4 The objective of this statement is to set out best practice in relation to the work carried out by members in connection with voluntary arrangements (VAs). Due to the similarities in the law and practice of CVAs and IVAs, this statement is intended to apply to both types of VA, except where otherwise specifically indicated.

The statement has been prepared primarily to address the circumstances where a proposal for a VA is made by the directors of a company or by an individual debtor, but it should also be applied as appropriate where the proposal is made by an administrator or liquidator.

1.5 Members should refer to the relevant legislation, which for a CVA is contained in [Part I and schedule A1 of the IA 1986 and rules 1.1-1.53 (inclusive) of the Rules, as amended by the Insolvency (Amendment) No.2 Rules 2002]. IVAs are dealt with at [Part VIII IA 1986 and rules 5.1-5.38 (inclusive) of the Rules, as amended by the Insolvency (Amendment) No.2 Rules 2002].

In relation to CVAs for insolvent partnerships members should refer specifically to Part II of The Insolvent Partnerships Order 1994 which applies Part I of the Act (Company Voluntary Arrangements) with appropriate modifications [as amended by the Insolvent Partnerships (Amendment) (No 2) Order 2002].

2. Basis of the Arrangement

2.1 The terms of the VA will be contained in the proposal, as modified, which is eventually approved by the creditors. A comprehensive and accurately drafted proposal is therefore fundamental to the arrangement. In view of the importance of the proposal the member should, where the circumstances are complex, consider whether it should be prepared or approved by a lawyer. The contents of the proposal are given further consideration in section 5 and the Appendix.

2.2 In dealing with a VA the member should bear in mind his overriding duty to ensure a fair balance between the interests of the company/debtor, the creditors and any other parties involved. In considering whether to accept appointment as either nominee or supervisor the member should have regard to the ethical guidelines of his authorising body.

2 Note that the Case 1/Case 2 terminology does not survive the changes to the Rules as from 1 January 2003.

3. Initial Contact with the Directors/Debtor

3.1 The directors/debtor should be advised at the initial interview of the member's requirement to maintain independence. The nominee should consider the need for separate representation of any third parties who intend to inject funds or who are otherwise affected by the VA.

3.2 **[IVA]** Where there is a possibility that a VA may adversely affect a spouse, for example in relation to the matrimonial home, the spouse should be advised to take independent advice.

3.3 The member should explain his role as nominee in relation to the directors'/debtor's proposal and of his duty to perform an independent, objective review and assessment of the proposal for the purposes of reporting his opinion to the court and generally balancing the interests of the company/debtor and the creditors. This duty of independence and objectivity arises irrespective of the extent of the member's involvement in drafting the directors'/debtor's proposals. The member should make it clear to the directors/debtor that his duties as nominee cannot be fettered by any instructions of the directors/debtor or any third party.

3.4 It is advisable that the member send a letter of engagement to the directors/debtor setting out in writing their respective duties and responsibilities in relation to the proposal in order to minimise the scope for misunderstandings.

3.5 **[CVA]** In instances where the assets are not already protected by the presentation of an administration petition or by an administration or winding-up order, the member should give consideration to the need for early action to protect the assets. The procedure for a CVA, unlike that for an IVA, does not provide for the court to grant an Interim Order (IO) so as to stay actions and proceedings against the company. Where a stay of proceedings, execution and other legal processes is sought in the interim period, pending consideration of the proposal by the meetings of creditors and members, this would normally entail an application for an administration order but may exceptionally entail a petition for the winding up of the company and the appointment of a provisional liquidator. If, however, a winding-up petition has been presented against the company an application may be made for the court to stay actions and proceedings against the company under section 126 IA 1986.

3.6 **[IVA]** Where the assets are not already protected by a bankruptcy order the member should give consideration to the need for early action to protect the assets. This could involve the preparation of an estimated statement of affairs and an embryonic proposal so as to expedite the application for an IO and any other appropriate orders.

3.7 **[IVA]** The member should take all necessary steps to familiarise himself with the debtor's financial circumstances. He should satisfy himself that the debtor has received appropriate advice on his position and that all the options available to him and the consequences of his decision to propose an IVA have been fully explained to him. Unless there are exceptional circumstances, the member, or a suitably experienced member of his staff, should meet the debtor personally and should keep a written record of the meeting. The [attached] leaflet, 'Is a Voluntary Arrangement Right for Me?' explains the IVA procedure and sets out the alternatives available to insolvent debtors. Before deciding on a course of action the debtor should be provided with a copy of the leaflet and confirm in writing that he has read and understood it.

4. Statement of Affairs and Obtaining Additional Information

4.1 The statement of affairs should detail the nature and amount of all the company's / debtor's assets and liabilities, including the liabilities set out in paragraph 4.3(a)(i)–(vii) below. A misstatement of the amount of the assets and liabilities can constitute a 'material irregularity' (within the meaning of sections 6 and 262 IA 1986) being a ground on which an approved VA may be challenged by an aggrieved creditor. In addition, a director/debtor commits an offence if he makes any false representations or commits any other fraud for the purpose of obtaining the approval of the creditors to the proposed arrangement. The directors/debtor should be informed of these dangers.

4.2 **[IVA]** It should be noted that a Case I debtor [an undischarged bankrupt] who has delivered a statement of affairs under section 272 or section 288 need not deliver a further statement unless so required by the nominee.

4.3 The member's approach should cover the points listed below:

(a) Creditors

The member should require the directors/debtor to provide details of all known or possible liabilities including:

(i) claims which are fully or partly secured: the status of the accounts and the existence of any arrears should be established;

(ii) preferential claims;

(iii) guarantee liabilities;

(iv) claims for breach of contract, including claims in respect of faulty and incomplete work and hire purchase and leasing agreements;

(v) creditors who are:

[CVA] persons connected with the company ('connected persons', as defined in section 249 IA 1986);

[IVA] 'associates' (as defined in section 435 IA 1986);

(vi) guarantors of the company's/debtor's debts, including connected persons/associates;

(vii) debts for an unliquidated amount or any debt whose value is unascertained, including particularly:

contingent liabilities;

the potential for liabilities arising under property leases (of both present and past tenancies).

He should also:

(viii) identify any creditors who have commenced execution or any other legal process;

(ix) consider the possibility of early informal discussions with the key creditors, including government departments, to establish their views;

(x) obtain independent confirmation from any bank or other financial institution of their intention to continue to provide financial support to the company/debtor where this is necessary for the purpose of the arrangement;

(xi) establish whether connected persons/associates may consider withdrawing or deferring their claims.

(b) Assets

The member should take steps to satisfy himself that the value of the assets is appropriately reflected in the statement of affairs. Where the value of an asset is material to the outcome of the arrangement consideration should be given to obtaining corroborative evidence as to its value. The member should also ensure that a comprehensive schedule of non-trading assets in which the company/debtor has an interest has been prepared together with explanatory notes. If there is a business, the member should consider, in conjunction with the directors/debtor, the manner in which that business is to be dealt with.

If the business is to be continued by the company/debtor, a 'business plan' should be produced to justify this decision stating the assumptions on which it is based, and in appropriate detail having regard to the circumstances and size of the undertaking. The member should satisfy himself that the plan has a reasonable chance of success.

(c) Antecedent Transactions

The member should enquire as to:

(i) possible transactions at an undervalue (sections 238, 339 and 423 IA 1986);

(ii) payments which may be preferences (sections 239, 340 IA 1986);

(iii) **[CVA]** floating charges which would be invalid in the event of administration or liquidation (section 245 IA 1986);

(iv) **[CVA]** charges which would be void against a liquidator, administrator or creditor in the event of liquidation or administration (section 395 CA 1985);

(v) liabilities which may be extortionate credit transactions, both those outstanding and paid (sections 244, 343 IA 1986).

(d) General

The member should also consider:

(i) whether the person(s) making the proposal is/are credible and making a full disclosure. The member should explain the consequences of making false representations;

(ii) whether (any of) the directors/debtor has been involved in any previous business failure, either individual or corporate, and if so the details of that failure and the person's responsibility for it;

(iii) the timetable for the VA.

The extent of the member's enquiries into these issues is likely to vary according to the particular circumstances of the case but should be such as will enable the member to properly discharge his duty to report to the court as nominee (see section 6 below).

5. Consideration of the Proposal

5.1 Throughout his consideration of the above factors the member should be forming his opinion of the appropriate method of dealing with the company's/debtor's affairs. Although this will be partly a subjective review of the factors already referred to, the member should take into account:

(a) the directors'/debtor's attitude;

(b) the likelihood of the company/debtor adhering to the terms of the proposal;

(c) the extent of the control over the assets exercised by the company/ debtor as opposed to the supervisor of the proposal, bearing in mind that in a VA the assets do not automatically vest in the supervisor by operation of law;

(d) the removal/absence of the restrictions otherwise imposed by formal winding up/bankruptcy.

5.2 In view of the importance of the contents of the proposal the member should, prior to submitting his report and supporting comments to the court, satisfy himself that the proposal, as modified, is structured and drafted in such a way that the terms of the VA can be clearly understood and that the arrangement is likely to proceed to a successful conclusion.

5.3 The member should ensure that the proposal addresses all those matters prescribed by the Rules. The member should also consider the inclusion of appropriate other provisions in order to facilitate the practical implementation of the arrangement (see Appendix) but should bear in mind that the terms of a proposal cannot extend or fetter the jurisdiction of the court. The proposal should also set out what action is to be taken in the event of deviation from, or failure of, the arrangement.

6. The Nominee's Report and Comments

6.1 In the case of *Re A Debtor (No 140 10 of* 1995), *Greystoke v Hamilton-Smith and Others* ([1996] 2 BCLC 429; [1997] BPIR 24) the court set out three tests which the nominee should apply before concluding that a meeting should or should not be summoned and held that he should satisfy himself on all three counts. They are:

(a) that the company's/debtor's true position as to assets and liabilities is not materially different from that which it is represented to the creditors to be;

(b) that the directors'/debtor's proposal has a real prospect of being implemented in the way it is to be represented it will be;

(c) that there is no already-manifest yet unavoidable prospective unfairness.

6.2 If the nominee cannot satisfy himself that the above three conditions are met but still recommends that a meeting should be held, he should explain in his comments the basis on which he is making that recommendation and qualify his comments so that the fact that the conditions are not met is conspicuously brought to the attention of the court.

6.3 If the nominee reports that a meeting of creditors (and [CVA] the company) should be held he is required to set out his comments on the proposal and to annex them to his report to the court. The matters upon which the nominee will wish to comment will vary from case to case but they should normally include:

(a) the extent to which the nominee has investigated the company's/debtor's circumstances;

(b) the basis upon which assets have been valued;

(c) the extent to which the nominee considers that reliance can be placed upon the directors'/debtor's estimate of the liabilities to be included in the VA;

(d) information on the attitude adopted by the directors/debtor with particular reference to instances of failure to co-operate with the nominee;

(e) the result of any discussions between the nominee and secured creditors or other interested parties upon whose co-operation the performance of the VA will depend;

(f) information on the attitude of any major unsecured creditor which may affect the approval of the arrangement by creditors;

(g) details of any previous history of failures in which (any of) the directors/debtor has been involved, in so far as they are known to the nominee;

(h) an estimate of the result for the creditors if the VA is approved, explaining why it is more beneficial for creditors than any alternative insolvency proceeding;

(i) the likely effect of the proposal's rejection by the creditors;

(j) details of any claims which have come to his attention which might be capable of being pursued by a liquidator/administrator/trustee in bankruptcy if one were appointed;

(k) where the conditions set out in paragraph 6.1 above have not been met, the basis on which the nominee is recommending that a meeting be held.

6.4 If the nominee reports that meetings should not be held he must give his reasons for that opinion.

6.5 Either in the proposal or in the nominee's comments the following information should be provided:

(i) The source of any referrals to him or his firm in relation to the proposed VA.

(ii) Any payments made, or proposed to be made, to the source of such referrals.

(iii) Any payments made, or proposed to be made, to the nominee or his firm by the company/debtor whether in connection with the proposed VA or otherwise.

7. The Meeting of Creditors (and [CVA] of Members)

7.1 Notice of the meeting must be given to all creditors whether or not they are intended to be bound by the arrangement. There must be strict compliance with the Rules as to notice of the meeting(s) to ensure that all parties intended to be bound by the arrangement are so bound. The minimum notice period of fourteen days excludes the day of sending the notice and the day of the meeting.

7.2 An approved VA may not be binding on a creditor who claims not to have received notice of the creditors' meeting. When sending out notice of VA meetings the member should consider either obtaining certificates of postage (forms available from the Post Office) or himself providing a certificate under Rule 12.4(3) so that he can prove when and to whom notice was sent.

7.3 Before the creditors' meeting the nominee should take the following steps:

(a) record all proxies received in advance of the meeting, and details of claims;

(b) complete the meeting record as far as possible detailing the names and voting value of creditors;

(c) discuss with the directors/debtor any modifications suggested by creditors prior to the meeting;

(d) review the proposal in the light of creditors' responses and possible changes in circumstances;

(e) prepare a brief report for presentation at the meeting, summarising the proposal, outlining the likely effects of acceptance and rejection and giving details of any changes in circumstances which have arisen since the proposal was sent to creditors;

(f) consider voting rights and requisite majority.

7.4 The chairman must decide the amount for which creditors are to be allowed to vote. Particular care needs to be exercised in relation to debts for an unliquidated amount or whose value is not ascertained (e.g. contingent claims under property leases). Creditors have no voting entitlement in respect of such claims, and are thus not bound by the VA in respect of such claims, unless the chairman has admitted them to vote having placed upon them, in good faith, an estimated minimum value for voting purposes. Proxies and statements of claim to be used at the meeting may be lodged at any time, even during the course of the meeting (although the courts have taken the view that they have discretion to make orders varying the statutory provisions if the circumstances of the case require).

7.5 After the chairman has presented his report to the creditors' meeting he should allow creditors an opportunity to make comments, ask questions or propose modifications to the proposal.

7.6 **[IVA]** The nominee should request the debtor to attend the creditors' meeting in order to answer questions and to give consideration to proposed modifications. If the debtor is not available to consider modifications which are proposed, the meeting will have to be adjourned as his consent to them is required by law.

7.7 **[CVA]** Although it is not a statutory requirement for directors to consent to modifications, it is recommended that the nominee should find out and report to the meeting their views on any proposed modifications which they may be required to implement if approved.

7.8 If modifications are proposed by a creditor the chairman should give careful consideration to the manner in which he will use specific instructions given to him by creditors to vote for either the acceptance or the rejection of the original proposal. If the words in the proxy form allowing the exercise of discretion in the absence of specific instructions have not been deleted so as to entitle the proxy holder to vote only as directed, the proxy holder is entitled to vote or abstain on any modification at his discretion.

7.9 However, the chairman should consider most carefully the impact of the exercise of his discretion upon the expressed intentions of any creditor who has completed a proxy requiring a vote on any particular resolution. He should bear in mind that, if a creditor is aggrieved that a vote on proposed modifications has been taken and a decision reached which might have been different if creditors represented by proxy had been present at the meeting or had been given the opportunity of amending their proxy, the aggrieved creditor may challenge the decision by an application to the court (sections 6 and 262 IA 1986). Accordingly, the chairman should consider an adjournment or suspension of the meeting to give him an opportunity to explain the circumstances to the creditor or creditors from whom he holds a proxy and to obtain their further instructions.

7.10 If a majority for approval of the VA is not obtained at the creditors' meeting, the chairman may adjourn the meeting, and must adjourn it if it is so resolved. The maximum period for adjournment is 14 days from the original meeting date, but within this period there can be more than one adjournment. The chairman must give notice to the court that the meeting is adjourned. He should also consider the need to inform creditors of the adjournment and, where substantial modifications are proposed, of those modifications.

7.11 **[CVA]** If the chairman thinks fit for obtaining the simultaneous agreement of the meetings to the proposal, the meetings may be held together. There shall be no adjournment of either meeting unless the other is also adjourned to the same business day.

7.12 **[IVA]** In the event of an adjournment the chairman should consider the need to apply for an extension of the IO.

7.13 At the meeting of creditors held under section 3 [or schedule A1 paragraph 29] or section 257 the chairman should provide information on any changes in the circumstances of the debtor/company from that presented in the proposal which need to be brought to the attention of creditors.

8. Implementation Following the Meeting of Creditors

8.1 The supervisor's main duty is to ensure that the VA proceeds in accordance with the terms of the agreed proposal. In order to do this he should maintain regular contact with the directors/debtor, obtaining reports as may be appropriate to the case. If the supervisor or directors/debtor consider that the terms of the arrangement may not be achieved then the supervisor should take steps to discuss the situation with the directors/debtor. If actual events suggest a deviation from the terms of the arrangement, the supervisor should take appropriate action. Such action should correspond to further detailed provisions of the proposal. If he is authorised to exercise discretion in any area, and that discretion is exercised, the supervisor should explain the circumstances to creditors (and [CVA] members) at the next available opportunity.

9. Conclusion/Termination of the Arrangement

9.1 Where the arrangement has been fully implemented the supervisor should conclude his administration as expeditiously as possible.

9.2 In circumstances where the implementation of the arrangement becomes frustrated or the anticipated distribution to creditors is to be materially different from that indicated in the proposal, it will be necessary to consider how matters should proceed. The term 'failure of the scheme' or 'failure of the arrangement' is not an expression found in the Act or Rules and it is essential, as stated in paragraph 5.3 above, that the proposal should have set out in specific terms the circumstances in which it shall be deemed to have failed and state what action the supervisor is required to take in the event of failure. Where failure has occurred the supervisor should notify the creditors accordingly and advise them what action he has taken or proposes to take.

9.3 **[IVA]** Where the debtor commits an act of 'default' (within the meaning of section 276(1) IA), the supervisor is empowered by the Act to initiate bankruptcy proceedings against the debtor. Whilst 'failure' and 'default' will often be synonymous, this will not always be the case.

9.4 In the event of failure particular care must be taken to ascertain who is entitled to the remaining assets, and in the event of the presentation of a winding-up or bankruptcy petition, whether disposal of the assets would be void under section 127 or 284 of the Insolvency Act 1986.

9.5 Where a supervening winding-up/bankruptcy order is made against the company/debtor, the supervisor should advise the official receiver of the circumstances. If the effect of the order is that the VA is terminated, the supervisor should arrange for the prompt handover of assets, funds, books and records to the official receiver or liquidator/trustee in bankruptcy as appropriate.

9.6 So far as the supervisor's final account is concerned, the Rules envisage a situation whereby a VA is concluded essentially in accordance with what was proposed. If the VA 'fails', the notice to be sent to creditors (and [CVA] members) under the Rules that the VA has been 'fully implemented' should be modified to reflect the circumstances giving rise to termination of the VA.

Issued November 1997

Version 2 (England and Wales)

With June 2002 amendments and updating of statutory references

Appendix

Voluntary Arrangements: Contents of the Proposal

The proposal should include sections covering the following:

(a) the background to the arrangement, including details of the circumstances in which the company/debtor has become insolvent and including any relevant personal circumstances of the directors/debtor;

(b) the statement of affairs, which should include full details of business assets and business liabilities (and [IVA] also personal assets and liabilities). Creditors should be provided with a clear comparison of the estimated outcomes of the VA and of winding up/bankruptcy including comparative costs;

(c) the actual financial proposal to be put to the creditors. This section should include:

(i) details of assets to be realised for the benefit of creditors and details of those which are to be excluded from the proposal, together with the reasons for the exclusion and whether alternatives are to be suggested;

(ii) proposals regarding after-acquired assets and windfall gains;

(iii) proposals regarding future profit/ income over a specific period;

(iv) details of any contributions from the debtor (e.g. from future earnings) including the amounts (or the basis on which they are to be computed) and frequency;

(v) whether third party funds are to be injected;

(vi) [IVA] the debtor's specific proposals with regard to any interest he may have in his dwelling house;

(vii) details of creditors to be included in the arrangement. It is important that every creditor or potential creditor including preferential creditors, who will invariably form part of the arrangement, should be considered, to minimise the possibility of some creditors not being bound by the terms of the VA. Secured creditors should also be included if they are to form part of the proposal. If they are not, they should be provided with a copy of the proposal, since if this adversely affects such a creditor's security, their consent must be obtained. The date to which claims are to be calculated should be stated together with details of arrangements with regard to, if appropriate, secured creditors and hire purchase or leasing agreements;

(d) the intentions with regard to any business operated by the company/debtor stating in particular whether the business is to be continued, and if so, the extent to which, if any, the supervisor shall exercise any degree of control over the business. If the supervisor is not to exercise any degree of control, this should be specifically stated in the proposal. The purpose or aim of continued trading should be stated: have new opportunities been created that will generate profits to pay creditors; is the trade being wound down to generate funds from asset realisations or is the business being marketed (and if so, how) as a going concern? Consideration should be given to including a summary cash flow projection;

(e) the powers, duties and responsibilities of the supervisor. This will need to deal with the question of admission or rejection of claims, the manner in which funds are to be distributed to creditors and the basis on which the supervisor is to report to creditors;

(f) miscellaneous matters which under the Act or Rules need to be included.

Other matters which the member should consider in order to facilitate the practical implementation of the proposal:

(g) whether a committee of creditors is to be appointed and if so what will be its powers, duties and responsibilities;

(h) what will happen to surplus funds arising, for example, from more beneficial trading than was originally envisaged, when the VA is concluded;

(i) confirmation that when the terms of the VA have been successfully completed the creditors will no longer be entitled to pursue the company/

debtor for the balance of their claim: that the VA is in full and final settlement of their liabilities;

(j) what will happen to unclaimed dividends or unpresented cheques when the VA is concluded;

(k) how to deal with creditors who have not made claims;

(1) the power of the supervisor to summon ad hoc meetings of the VA creditors for the purpose of obtaining their views and in particular for obtaining their approval to proposed modifications to the VA;

(m) the requisite majorities required to pass resolutions at ad hoc meetings of creditors (and **[CVA]** members) summoned during the course of the VA;

(n) **[IVA]** the position with regard to maintenance orders or attachment of earnings orders in favour of the debtor's spouse, and with regard to fines;

(o) in view of the fact that the assets do not automatically vest in the supervisor it may be advisable for the proposal to provide for such vesting or for the supervisor to be granted a charge over assets, or to be given some other suitable form of security or for a declaration of trust or power of attorney to be executed;

(p) the attitude to be adopted with regard to contingent creditors;

(q) the situation with regard to overseas creditors;

(r) the circumstances in which the supervisor is to present a petition for a winding-up/bankruptcy order;

(s) the situation with regard to tax liabilities arising on disposal of the company's/debtor's assets, or the future income of or gifts to the company/debtor from a third party, that are applied towards the payment of creditors' claims;

(t) the approach to be adopted in respect of creditors who inadvertently do not receive notice and [are therefore not bound] [are bound without being able to vote on and without knowledge of the approval of the arrangement.]

(u) the inclusion of power for the supervisor or any creditor's committee to be able to determine that a VA has no future and petition for winding up/bankruptcy and authority to retain and use funds from the VA for such costs.

When considering these issues the member should have regard to any relevant decisions of the court which have clarified points of law where the statutory provisions are either silent or ambiguous.

Appendix 9*

9.1 Comparable statute provisions CVA / IVA

The provisions of the Insolvency Act governing CVA without moratorium, CVA with a moratorium and IVA are not invariably identical, but the differences where they occur are minor. This table sets out the comparable provisions.

Provision	*CVA (no moratorium)*	*CVA (+ moratorium)*	*IVA*
Proposal CVA/ apply interim order IVA	s 1	s 1	s 253
Moratorium /interim order	–	s 1A	s 252-255
Eligibility for moratorium	–	§§ 2-5	–
Obtaining a moratorium	–	§§ 6-11	–
Effects of moratorium	–	§§ 12-23	–
Nominee's rôle in moratorium	–	§§ 24-27	–
Procedure where nominee is not L or A	s 2	–	
Opinion of nominee re proposal	s 2(2)	§ 6(2)	s 256(1)/256A(3)
Submission to nominee for report	s 2(3)	§ 6(1)	s 256(2)/256A(2)
Replacement of nominee	s 2(4)	§ 28	s 256(3)(3A)/A(4)
Procedure where no interim order	–	–	s 256A
Summoning of meeting(s)	s 3	§ 29	s 257
Consideration and implementation			
Decisions of meetings consent	s 4(1)	§ 31(1)	s 258(1)(2)
Modification of nominee	s 4(2)	§ 31(2)	s 258(3)
Must remain a voluntary arrangement	s 4(2)	§ 31(3)	s 258(3)
No affect on secured creditor	s 4(3)	§ 31(4)	s 258(4)
No affect on preferential creditor	s 4(4)	§ 31(5)(6)	s 258(5)
Conduct in accordance with rules	s 4(5)	§ 30(1)	s 258(6)
Chairman report to court	s 4(6)	§ 30(3)	s 259(1)(2)
Directors may give notice of mods	–	§ 30(7)	–
Preferential debts = s 386	s 4(7)	§ 31(8)	s 258(7)

* The author acknowledges the kind assistance of the editors of *Atkins' Court Forms* in the provision of material on which tables in this appendix are based. See *Atkin's Court Forms* (2nd edn), vol 7(1) Bankruptcy and Insolvency (Pt 1) at pp 187-209 (IVA); vol 9(2) Companies Winding-up (Pt 1) at pp 178-186 (CVA); and vol 30(1) Partnerships and Firms – Insolvency at pp 91-101 (PVA).

Provision	*CVA (no moratorium)*	*CVA (+ moratorium)*	*IVA*
Approval of arrangement	s 4A	§ 36	–
Takes effect both / creditors meeting	s 4A(2)	§ 36(2)	–
Application to court if difference cr/cpy	s 4A(3)	§ 36(3)	–
Application only within 28 days	s 4A(4)	§ 36(4)	–
Rights of FSA	s 4A(5)	§ 44(10)	–
Power of court on application	s 4A(6)	§ 36(5)	–
Effect of approval	s 5	§ 37	s 260(1)
Takes effect as if by debtor at cred. meeting	s 5(2)(a)	§ 37(2)(a)	s 260(2)(a)
Binds those entitled or wd have been	s 5(2)(b)	§ 37(2)(b)	s 260(2)(b)
Cpy to pay dividend to wd have beens	s 5(2A)	§ 37(3)	s 260(2A)
Court may stay / directions if in L or Ad	s 5(3)	§ 37(4)	s 261(2)(4)
No (3) order until after 28 days or appeal	s 5(4)	§ 37(5)	s 261(3)
Challenge of decisions : two grounds	s 6(1)	§ 38(1)	s 262(1)
Applicant for challenge	s 6(2)	§ 38(2)	s 262(2)
No application after 28 days	s 6(3)	§ 38(3)	s 262(3)
Power of court on application	s 6(4)	§ 38(4)	s 262(4)
Revocation of new proposal order	s 6(5)	§ 38(5)	s 262(5)
Renewal of moratorium / int.order	–	§ 38(6)	s 262(6)
S upplemental directions on application	s 6(6)	§ 38(7)(8)	s 262(7)
Only route to challenge meetings	s 6(7)	§ 38(9)	s 262(8)
False representations	s 6A	s 6A/§41[1]	s 262A
Implementation of proposal	s 7	§ 39	s 263
Implementer – supervisor	s 7(2)	§ 39(2)	s 263(2)
Challenge to supervisor	s 7(3)	§ 39(3)(4)	s 263(3)
S upervisor may apply for directions	s 7(4)	§ 39(5)	s 263(4)
Power in court to replace supervisor	s 7(5)	§ 39(6)	s 263(5)
Power to increase no. of supervisors	s 7(6)	§ 39(7)	s 263(6)
Prosecution of delinquent officers	s 7A	s 7A	s 262B
Arrangements ending prematurely	s 7B	s 7B	s 262C
Fast-track individual voluntary arrangement[2]	–	–	s 263A/G

1 S 6A creates an offence of fraud for the purpose of obtaining approval to a CVA whether or not a moratorium is obtained; §41creates offences in connection with a moratorium

2 These sections are introduced by the Enterprise Act 2002 when it comes into force.

9.2 Comparative rule table

Following the amendment to the Rules consequent upon the changes introduced by the Insolvency Act 2000, (1) the CVA (without moratorium) rules have kept their existing numbering, with the rules governing CVAs with a moratorium being added on at the end of the Part 1; (2) the IVA rules have been renumbered with the new rules governing IVA without interim order being inserted at rr 5.14-5.16. This table gives a quick reference guide to the Rules as they now stand showing where the rules are (in some cases substantially but not exactly) similar between CVA and IVA and indicating the destination of the old IVA rules.

	CVA		IVA	
	without moratorium	*with moratorium*	*old*	*new*
Introductory	1.1	–	5.1	5.1
Preparation of proposal	1.2	1.35	5.2	5.2
Contents of proposal	1.3	[1.3][1]	5.3	5.3
Notice to intended nominee	1.4	1.36	5.4	5.4
Application for interim order	–	–	5.5	5.7
court in which application to be made	–	–	5.5A	5.8
Hearing of the application	–	–	5.6	5.9
Action to follow making of order	–	–	5.7	5.10
Statement of Affairs	1.5	1.37	5.8	5.5
Additional disclosure	1.6	[§6(1)(c)][2]	5.9	5.6
Nominee's report on proposal	1.7	–	5.10	5.11
Replacement of nominee	1.8*	–	5.11	5.12
Consideration of nominee's report	–	–	5.12	5.13
Nominee's report to court (no int.order)	–	–	–	5.14
Filing of report under s256A (no int.order)	–	–	–	5.15
Applications to the court (no int.order)	–	–	–	5.16
Preparation of proposal by L or A	1.10	–	–	–
Summoning of meeting by L or A	1.11	–	–	–
Preparation of proposal in L or A	1.12	–	–	–
The nominee's statement	–	1.38	–	–
Documents submitted for moratorium	–	1.39	–	–
Notice and advert of beginning of mora	–	1.40	–	–
Notice of extension of moratorium	–	1.41	–	–
Notice and advert of end of moratorium	–	1.42	–	–
Disposal of charged property during mora	–	1.43	–	–
Withdrawal of nominee's consent to act	–	1.44	–	–
Replacement of nominee by court	–	1.45	–	–

	CVA		IVA	
	without moratorium	*with moratorium*	*old*	*new*
Notification of appointment of replacement	–	1.46	–	–
Applications to court under §26 or §27	–	1.47	–	–
Summoning of creditors' meeting	1.9	1.48	5.13	5.17
Creditors' meeting : supplementary	1.13*	[1.13][3]	5.14	5.18
The chairman at the meeting	1.14	[1.14][3]	5.15	5.19
The chairman as proxy-holder	1.15	[1.15][3]	5.16	5.20
Attendance by company officers	1.16	[1.16][3]		– –
Voting rights [Entitlement to vote]	1.17*	1.49	5.17	5.21
[Procedure for admission of claim]	1.17A*	1.50	5.17	5.22
Voting rights (members)	1.18	[1.18][4]	–	–
Requisite majorities	1.19	1.52	5.18	5.23
Requisite majorities (members)	1.20	[1.20][5]	–	–
Proceedings to obtain agreement	1.21*	1.53	5.19	5.24
Resolutions to follow approval	1.22	[1.22][6]	5.20	5.25
Notice of order under s 4A(6)	1.22A	[1.22A][6]	–	–
Hand-over of property to supervisor	1.23	5.21	5.26	
Report of (creditors') meeting	1.24	[1.24][6]	5.22	5.27
Register of voluntary arrangements	–	–	5.23	5.28
Reports to Secretary of State	–	–	5.24	5.29
Revocation or suspension of arrangement	1.25	[1.25][6]	5.25	5.30
Supervisor's accounts and reports	1.26	[1.26][6]	5.26	5.31
Production of accounts and records	1.27	[1.27][6]	5.27	5.32
Fees, costs, charges, and expenses	1.28	[1.28][6]	5.28	5.33
Completion of the arrangement	1.29*	[1.29][6]	5.29	5.34
False representations	~~1.30~~	–	~~5.30~~	–
Application for conversion to w/u-b'cy	1.31	1.31	–	5.35
Contents of affidavit	1.32	1.32	–	5.36
Power of the Court	1.33	1.33	–	5.37
Notices to member state liquidator	1.34	1.34	–	5.38

* denotes a significant change to the pre-2003 rule

1 imported into r 1.35(1)
2 there is no 'additional disclosure' rule in CVA with moratorium but the nominee may require further information under IA SchA1 §6(1)(c)
3 incorporated by r 1.48(5)
4 incorporated by r 1.51
5 incorporated by r 1.53(1)
6 incorporated by r 1.54(2) with the modifications in r 1.54(3)

9.3 Procedural table: Company Voluntary Arrangements (without moratorium)

SUMMARY OF TABLE

Directors' proposal and statement of affairs (Steps 1- 5)

Nominee's report to the court (Steps 6 – 9)

Meetings of creditors and company (Steps 10 –13)

Where voluntary arrangement is approved (Steps 14 – 16)

Appeal to the court (Steps 17 – 29)

Application to challenge supervisor or by supervisor for directions (Steps 30 – 39)

Conversion of voluntary arrangement into winding up (Steps 40 – 43)

Action following completion or termination of the arrangement (Steps 44 – 45)

	Steps to be Taken	Insolvency Act 1986	Insolvency Rules 1986	Cross reference to text
1.	Directors instruct insolvency practitioner (or other person authorised to act as nominee in relation to the voluntary arrangement) to act as nominee, to give advice and assistance on preparation of proposal.		IR 1986, r 1.2	Para 4.1
2.	Proposal is prepared by or on behalf of the directors to enable nominee to prepare his report to the court. The proposal must include: (1) the terms of the proposed arrangement; (2) an explanation of why, in the opinion of the directors, a voluntary arrangement is desirable and why the creditors may be expected to concur with the arrangement; and	 IA 1986, s 2 (3)(a)	 IR 1986, r 1.3 (1)	Para 4.2 Para 4.4

	Steps to be Taken	Insolvency Act 1986	Insolvency Rules 1986	Cross reference to text
	(3) a statement dealing with the various matters set out in IR 1986, r 1.3(2)		IR 1986, r 1.3 (2)(a)–(q)	
	In the event that the nominee cannot properly prepare his report on the basis of the information in the directors' proposal, he may call on the directors:			
	(1) to provide him (inter alia)with any further information with respect to the Company's affairs which the nominee thinks necessary for his report; and		IR 1986, r 1.6 (1)(a)–(c)	
	(2) to inform him of any person who is or, during the two years preceding the giving of notice to the nominee of the proposal, has been a director or officer of the Company, whether and in what circumstances that person has been concerned in the affairs of any other Company which has become insolvent or has himself been adjudged bankrupt or entered into an arrangement with his creditors.		IR 1986, r 1.6 (2)(a), (b)	
	Where the proposal is made by an administrator or liquidator who himself is to be the nominee it must in addition specify such other matters as he considers appropriate to enable members and creditors to reach an informed decision on the proposal.		IR 1986 1.10 (1)	
3.	Directors give nominee written notice of their proposal.		IR 1986, r 1.4 (1)	Para 4.3
	The notice accompanied by a copy of the proposal must be delivered either to the nominee himself or to a person authorised to accept documents on his behalf.		IR 1986, r 1.4 (2)	

	Steps to be Taken	Insolvency Act 1986	Insolvency Rules 1986	Cross reference to text
	Where the company is being wound up by the Court the insolvency practitioner must give notice of the proposal to the Official Receiver.		IR 1986, r 1.10 (2)	
4.	Nominee, if he agrees to act, endorses receipt of notice with date of receipt and returns same to directors. The nominee has 28 days from this date to submit his report to the court		IR 1986, r 1.4 (3), (4)	Para 4.3
5.	Directors deliver statement of the company's affairs to nominee.	IA 1986, s 2 (3)(b)	IR 1986, r 1.5 (1)	Para 4.5
	Time: Within 7 days after delivery of proposal or such longer time as the nominee may allow.		IR 1986, r 1.5 (1)	
	The statement must comprise the following particulars:		IR 1986, r 1.5 (2)	
	(1) a list of the company's assets, divided into appropriate categories with estimated values assigned to each category;		IR 1986, r 1.5 (2)(a)	
	(2) particulars of any secured claim on the company's property, including the amount of the claim and how and when the security was created;		IR 1986, r 1.5 (2)(b)	
	(3) the names, addresses and amounts of the claims of preferential creditors;		IR 1986, r 1.5 (2)(c)	
	(4) the names, addresses and amounts of unsecured creditors;		IR 1986, r 1.5 (2)(d)	
	(5) particulars of debts owed by or to the company to or by persons connected with it;		IR 1986, r 1.5 (2)(e)	

	Steps to be Taken	Insolvency Act 1986	Insolvency Rules 1986	Cross reference to text
	(6) the names and addresses of the members of the company with details of their respective shareholdings; and		IR 1986, r 1.5 (2)(f)	
	(7) such other particulars as the nominee may in writing require to enable him to make his report to the Court on the directors' proposal.		IR 1986, r 1.5 (2)(g)	
	The statement of affairs must be made up to a date not earlier than 2 weeks before the date of the notice to the nominee (*see Step 3 above*) and must be certified as correct by 2 or more directors or by the secretary and at least one other director.		IR 1986, r 1.5 (3), (4)	
6.	Nominee reports to Court as to:			Paras 4.7, 4.8
	(1) whether, in his opinion, the proposed voluntary arrangement has a reasonable prospect of being approved and implemented	IA 1986, s 2 (2) (a)		
	(2) whether, in his opinion, meetings should be summoned of the company and its creditors to consider the proposal, and	IA 1986, s 2 (2) (aa)		
	(3) if so, the date, time and place at which he proposes the meetings should be held.	IA 1986, s 2 (2) (b)		
	Time: Within 28 days, or such longer period as the Court may allow, after being given notice of the proposal.	IA 1986, s 2 (2)		
	A copy of the directors' proposal and a copy or summary of the company's statement of affairs must be delivered with the report.		IR 1986, r 1.7 (1)	

	Steps to be Taken	Insolvency Act 1986	Insolvency Rules 1986	Cross reference to text
	If the nominee is of opinion that meetings should be summoned, he must also annex his comments to the proposal and if his opinion is otherwise, he must give his reasons. Where the nominee has failed to submit a report, the Court may on the application of the person intending to make the proposal direct that the nominee be replaced as such by another insolvency practitioner qualified to act in relation to the company.	 IA 1986, s 2 (4)	IR 1986, r 1.7 (2)	
7.	Court endorses the date of filing of the report and files it.		IR 1986, r 1.7 (3)	Para 4.7
8.	Nominee sends copy of report and his comments to the company.		IR 1986, r 1.7 (4)	Para 4.7
9.	The court may direct that the nominee be replaced by another person qualified to act as an insolvency practitioner or authorised to act as nominee in relation to the voluntary arrangement: (1) on application of directors making the proposal where nominee has failed to submit his report or has died (2) on application of directors making the proposal or nominee where it is impracticable or inappropriate for nominee to act as such	 IA 1986, s 2 (4) (a) IA 1986, s 2 (4) (b)		Para 4.9
10.	Where nominee reports that meetings should be summoned, then, unless the court otherwise orders, the	IA 1986, s 3 (1)		Para 6.3

	Steps to be Taken	Insolvency Act 1986	Insolvency Rules 1986	Cross reference to text
	person making the report summons meetings for the time, date and place proposed in the report.			
	The date of the meetings must be not less than 14 nor more than 28 days from the date on which the nominee's report was filed (*see Step 7 above*).		IR 1986, r 1.9 (1)	
	At least 14 days notice of the meetings must be given and it must state the effect of, r 1.19 (1), (3) and (4) as to majorities required to approve the arrangement or pass other resolutions and be accompanied by: (1) a copy of the directors' proposal; (2) a copy of the statement of affairs or, if the nominee thinks fit, a summary of it; and (3) the nominee's comments on the proposal; and (4) forms of proxy.		IR 1986, r 1.9 (2) IR 1986, r 1.9 (3) IR 1986, r 1.13 (4)	
	The meetings of the Company and of the creditors may be held on the same day or on different days. If held on the same day the meetings must be held in the same place. In either event the creditors' meeting must be held in advance of the company meeting.		IR 1986, r 1.13 (3)	Para 6.4
	Any officer of the company or any person who has been a director or officer in the previous 2 years may be required to attend the meeting.		IR 1986, r 1.16(1)(b)	
	If the meetings are not held on the same day they must be held within 7 days of each other.		IR 1986, r 1.13(4)	
11.	Creditors and members attend respective meetings and decide whether or not to approve the proposal (with or without modifications).	IA 1986, s 4 (1)		Paras 6.7 – 6.11

	Steps to be Taken	Insolvency Act 1986	Insolvency Rules 1986	Cross reference to text
	Conduct of the meetings.			
	(1) The nominee will be the chairman of the meetings. If he is unable to attend, he may nominate another insolvency practitioner or an employee who is experienced in insolvency matters to act as chairman		IR 1986, r 1.14	
	(2)The chairman's decision on entitlement to vote is subject to appeal to the court by any creditor or the debtor. An appeal shall not be made after the end of 28 days beginning with the day on which the chairman's report is filed in court. *The appeals procedure is set out in step 17 and following below.*		IR 1986, r 1.17A(3) IR 1986, r 1.17A(6)	
	(3) At the creditors' meeting, a majority in excess of three-quarters (in value) of the creditors present in person or by proxy and voting is necessary to pass a resolution approving or modifying the proposal but for any other resolution proposed at the meeting a majority of one-half (in value) is sufficient. Even with a 75% or 50% majority (as appropriate) a resolution is invalid if those voting against it include more than 50% in value of the creditors counting only those to whom notice of the meeting was sent, are not to be left out of account because their claim is secured, and are not persons connected with the company.		IR 1986, r 1.19(1) IR 1986, r 1.19(2) IR 1986, r 1.19(3)(4)	
	(4) At the company meeting, subject to any express provision made in the company's articles, a majority of more than one-half (in value) of the members present in		IR 1986, r 1.20	

	Steps to be Taken	Insolvency Act 1986	Insolvency Rules 1986	Cross reference to text
	person or by proxy and voting is necessary to pass any resolution. Value of members is determined by reference to the number of votes conferred on each member by the company's articles.			
	(5) If at the meeting, a majority for approval has not been obtained, the chairman may, and must if so resolved, adjourn the meeting for not more than 14 days. The meeting may be adjourned from time to time within the period of 14 days but the final adjournment must be to a day not later than 14 days after the first meeting. If the proposal is not approved at the final meeting, it is deemed rejected. Notice of any adjournments shall be given by the chairman forthwith to the court		IR 1986, r 1.21(2) IR 1986, r 1.21(3) IR 1986, r 1.21(5) IR 1986, r 1.21(4)	
	(6) Where a proposal is approved which provides for 2 or more insolvency practitioners to act as supervisors, the creditors may resolve as to whether they are to act jointly or separately and allocate their duties		IR 1986, r 1.22(1)	
	(7) If, at the meeting, it is proposed that a person other than the nominee be appointed the supervisor, there must be produced to the chairman written confirmation that the person is an insolvency practitioner and has consented to act. The consent may be given orally at the meeting.		IR 1986, r 1.22(3)	
12.	Approval of arrangement The arrangement is approved if the decision to approve it has been taken, in accordance with the rules, by both	IA 1986, s 4A(2)		Para 6.13

	Steps to be Taken	Insolvency Act 1986	Insolvency Rules 1986	Cross reference to text
	creditors' and company meetings, or by the creditors' meeting alone.			
	If the decision taken by the creditors' meeting differs from that taken by the company meeting, a member of the company may apply to the court.	IA 1986, s 4A(3)		
	Such an application may not be made after the end of the period of 28 days beginning with (1) the day on which the decision was taken by the creditors' meeting or (2) the day, if later, on which the decision was taken by the company meeting.	IA 1986, s 4A(6)		
	Where an order is made the member of the company who applied for it must (1) serve sealed copies of it on (a) the supervisor and (b) the directors, and (2) within 7 days of the order deliver an office copy to the registrar of companies.		IR 1986, r 1.22A(2) IR 1986, r 1.22A(3) IR 1986, r 1.22A(5)	
	The directors or the supervisor must forthwith after receiving a copy of the court's order give notice of it to all persons who were sent notice of the creditors' or company meetings or any person who is affected by the order even if he did not receive notice of the meetings.		IR 1986, r 1.22A(4)	
13.	Chairman of meetings reports results of meetings to the court and, immediately thereafter, gives notice of result of meetings to persons who were sent notice of meetings.	IA 1986, s 4 (6)	IR 1986, r 1.24 (4)	Para 6.15
	Time: Within 4 days of the meetings being held.		IR 1986, r 1.24 (3)	

	Steps to be Taken	Insolvency Act 1986	Insolvency Rules 1986	Cross reference to text
	The report must:			
	(1) state whether the proposal was approved by the creditors of the company alone, or by both the creditors and members of the company and, in either case, whether such approval was with any modifications;		IR 1986, r 1.24 (2)(a)	
	(2) set out the resolutions taken at each meeting and the decision on each;		IR 1986, r 1.24 (2)(b)	
	(3) list the creditors and members (with their respective values) present or represented at the meetings and how they voted on each resolution; and		IR 1986, r 1.24 (2)(c)	
	(4) state whether,in the opinion of the supervisor, the EC regulation applies to the voluntary arrangement and if so whether the proceedings are main proceedings or territorial proceedings.		IR 1986, r 1.24 (2)(ca)	
	(5) include such further information (if any) which the chairman thinks it appropriate to make known to the Court.		IR 1986, r 1.24 (2)(d)	
	Where the voluntary arrangement is approved at the meetings:			
14.	Supervisor sends copy of chairman's report to Registrar of Companies.		IR 1986, r 1.24 (5)	Para 6.15
15.	Directors or, if the company is in liquidation or is subject to an Administration Order and a person other than the liquidator or the administrator (as the case may be) is appointed to act as supervisor of the voluntary		IR 1986, r 1.23 (1)(a), (b)	Para 10.1

	Steps to be Taken	Insolvency Act 1986	Insolvency Rules 1986	Cross reference to text
	arrangement, the liquidator or the administrator does all that is required for putting the supervisor into possession of the assets included in the arrangement. *Time*: Forthwith.			
16.	Supervisor proceeds to put the voluntary arrangement into effect. If the company is being wound up or an Administration Order is in force, the court may, at any time after the period of 28 days beginning with the first day on which the chairman's report (*see Step 13 above*) has been made, stay all proceedings in the winding up or discharge the Administration Order, or give such directions with respect to the conduct of the winding up or the administration as it thinks appropriate for facilitating the implementation of the approved voluntary arrangement. It may not, however, make such an order if an application challenging the decision taken at the meetings, is pending or is the subject of an appeal.	IA 1986, s 5 (3), (4)(a) IA 1986, s 5 (4)(b)		Paras 10.1 – 10.3
	Application to the court to challenge a decision of the chairman or a decision taken at meetings of creditors and the company to consider a proposal for a voluntary arrangement.	IA 1986, s 6	IR 1986, r 1.17A(3) IR 1986, r 1.19(7)	
17.	Applicant issues originating application to reverse a decision of the chairman or the decision taken at meetings.		IR 1986 rr 7.2 (1), 7.4 (1)	

	Steps to be Taken	Insolvency Act 1986	Insolvency Rules 1986	Cross reference to text
	Time: Within 28 days after the filing of the chairman's report as to the result of the meetings, or, where application is made by a creditor who was not given notice of the creditors' meeting, within 28 days of the date on which he first became aware that the meeting had taken place.	IA 1986, s 6(3)(a) IA 1986, s 6(3)(b)	IR 1986, r 1.17A(6)	Para 6.8
	The Applicant may be: (1) any creditor or member of the company may make application in respect of decisions of the chairman as to: (a) entitlement to vote (b) whether a vote should be left out of account (c) whether a person is connected with the company.		IR 1986, r 1.17A(3) IR 1986, r 1.19(7)	
	(2) in the case of a challenge to the decisions of the meetings (a) a person entitled to vote at either of the meetings; (b) a person who would have been entitled to vote at the creditors' meeting if he had had notice of it. (c) the nominee or any person who has replaced him as such; or (d) if the Company is being wound up or is the subject of an Administration Order, the liquidator or the administrator.	IA 1986, s 6(2) (a)–(c)		Para 7.9

	Steps to be Taken	Insolvency Act 1986	Insolvency Rules 1986	Cross reference to text
	The grounds of the application to challenge the decision of the meeting will be that the voluntary arrangement unfairly prejudices the interests of a creditor, member or contributory of the company and/or that there has been some material irregularity at or in relation to either meeting. If the Applicant is the liquidator or the administrator the application will be without notice. If the Applicant is the nominee the application will be without notice unless the company is in liquidation or is the subject of an administration order when the liquidator or the administrator will be the Respondent. If the Applicant is a person entitled to vote the nominee will be the Respondent.	IA 1986, s 6 (1)(a), (b)		
18.	Unless the Court otherwise directs, Applicant serves sealed copy of the application upon Respondent (if any) endorsed with the venue for the hearing.		IR 1986, r 7.4(3)	Para 7.10
19.	Applicant files witness statement or affidavit in support and serves copy on any Respondent. *Time*: Not less than 14 days before the hearing.		IR 1986 rr 7.7(1), 7.8 (1)(a)	
20.	Respondent files witness statement or affidavit in reply and serves copy on Applicant. *Time*: Not less than 7 days before the hearing.		IR 1986, r 7.8(1)(b)	
21.	Parties attend hearing of application in Chambers before Registrar.			

	Steps to be Taken	Insolvency Act 1986	Insolvency Rules 1986	Cross reference to text
	The Registrar may give such directions as he thinks fit and adjourn the matter to be heard by the Judge in Court.		IR 1986, r 7.10(2) IR 1986, r 7.10(1)	
22.	Applicant lodges in Registrar's office: 1. copy application; and 2. original exhibits for use of Judge.			
23.	Parties attend adjourned hearing of application in Court. If the Court is satisfied on an application to challenge a decision of the chairman that the circumstances giving rise to the appeal give rise to unfair prejudice or material irregularity it may reverse or vary the decision, or, if the votes are declared invalid, order another meeting to be summoned or make such order as it thinks just. If the Court is satisfied as to either of the grounds of the application to challenge the decision of the meetings (*see Step 17 above*) it may: (1) revoke or suspend the approvals given by the meetings or any approval given at a meeting at which there was some material irregularity; and/or (2) direct the summoning of further meetings to consider any revised proposal or a further meeting in place of that at which there was an irregularity to reconsider the original proposal.	IA 1986, s 6 (4)(a) IA 1986, s 6 (4)(b)	IR 1986, r 1.17(5) IR 1986, r 1.19(7)	Para 6.8 Para 7.9

	Steps to be Taken	Insolvency Act 1986	Insolvency Rules 1986	Cross reference to text
	If at any time after directing further meetings to consider a revised proposal the Court is satisfied that no revised proposal is to be submitted, it must revoke the direction and revoke or suspend any approval given at the previous meetings.	IA 1986, s 6 (5)		
24.	Parties (if so required) attend the Court Associate to lodge Counsels' briefs properly endorsed.			
25.	Court draws up Order and sends copies to Applicant.			
26.	Applicant serves sealed copies of the Order on: (1) the supervisor of the voluntary arrangement; and (2) on the directors of the company or the administrator or the liquidator (depending upon who made the proposal for a voluntary arrangement). If the Order contains a direction for further meetings notice must also be given by the Applicant to whoever is required by the Order to summon the meetings.		IR 1986, r 1.25(2) IR 1986, r 1.25 (2)(a) IR 1986, r 1.25 (2)(b) IR 1986, r 1.25(3)	
27.	Directors or liquidator or administrator (as the case may be) give notice of the Order to all persons who were given notice of the meetings and to any other persons who appear to be affected by the Order. *Time:* Forthwith after receiving the copy of the Order.		IR 1986, r 1.25 (4)(a) IR 1986, r 1.25 (4)(a)	
28.	Directors or liquidator or administrator (as the case may be) give notice to Court whether it is intended to make a revised proposal or to invite re-consideration of the original proposal.		IR 1986, r 1.25 (4)(b)	

	Steps to be Taken	Insolvency Act 1986	Insolvency Rules 1986	Cross reference to text
	Time: Within 7 days after receiving the copy of the Order (or such longer period as the Court may allow).		IR 1986, r 1.25 (4)(b)	
29.	Applicant delivers copy Order to Registrar of Companies. *Time*: Within 7 days after the making of the Order.		IR 1986, r 1.25 (5) IR 1986, r 1.25 (5)	
30.	*Application to reverse or modify an act, omission or decision of a supervisor of a voluntary arrangement.*	IA 1986, s 7 (3)	IR 1986, rr 7.2 (1), 7.4 (1)	Paras 10.4, 10.5
	Applicant issues originating application to reverse or modify supervisor's decision. The Applicant may be a creditor or any other person dissatisfied by any act, omission or decision of the supervisor. The supervisor will be the Respondent to the application.	IA 1986, s 7 (3)		
31.	Unless the Court otherwise directs, Applicant serves sealed copy of application upon supervisor endorsed with the venue for the hearing.		IR 1986, r 7.4 (3)	
32.	Applicant files witness statement or affidavit supporting application and serves copy on supervisor.		IR 1986, rr7.7 (1), 7.8 (1)(a)	
33.	Follow Steps 20-24 above. The Court may: (1) confirm, reverse or modify any act or decision of the supervisor; (2) give directions to the supervisor; or (3) make such other order as it thinks fit.	IA 1986, s 7 (3)(a)–(c)		

	Steps to be Taken	Insolvency Act 1986	Insolvency Rules 1986	Cross reference to text
34.	Court draws up Order and sends a duplicate thereof to the Applicant.			
	The Supervisor may apply to the Court for directions in relation to any matter arising under the voluntary arrangement.	IA 1986, s 7 (4)(a)		
35.	Applicant issues ordinary (or originating) application.		IR 1986 rr 7.2 (1), 7.4 (1)	Para 10.2
36.	Unless the Court otherwise directs Applicant serves sealed copy of application on any person affected by the subject matter of application who should be Respondent endorsed with the venue for the hearing.		IR 1986, r 7.4 (3)	
37.	Applicant files witness statement or affidavit supporting application, and serves copy on Respondent.		IR 1986, r 7.8 (1)(a)	
38.	Follow Steps 20–24 above.			
39.	Court draws up order and sends copy to the Applicant.			
	Conversion of voluntary arrangement into winding up			
40.	On opening of main proceedings in member State other than UK the main proceedings liquidator must inform UK creditors whose claims have not been compromised that they may lodge claims in main proceedings, advising creditors of any time limits or other measures relevant to the lodging of claims.	EC Regulation Article 40(1) Article 40(2)		Para 14.7
41.	Member State liquidator seeking conversion of voluntary arrangement into winding up issues originating	EC Regulation Article 37	IR 1986, r 1.31(1)	

	Steps to be Taken	Insolvency Act 1986	Insolvency Rules 1986	Cross reference to text
	application and files affidavit in support. The affidavit must be sworn by or on behalf of the liquidator and state: (1) that main proceedings have been opened in relation to the company in another member State; (2) the liquidator's belief that the conversion of the voluntary arrangement into a winding up will prove to be in the interests of the creditors in the main proceedings; (3) the liquidator's opinion as to whether the company should enter compulsory or voluntary winding up; (4) all other matters which in the liquidator's opinion would assist the court in deciding whether or not to make a conversion order and, if an order were made, in considering the need for consequential provisions.		IR 1986, r 7.2 IR 1986, r 1.32(2) IR 1986, r 1.32(1)	
42.	The application and the affidavit must be served on the company and the supervisor		IR 1986, r 1.31(3)	
43.	On hearing liquidator's application the court may make such order as it thinks fit. The order may contain all necessary or desirable consequential provisions. The order may state that a company entering voluntary liquidation is to be wound up as if a resolution for winding up had been passed on the day the order is made.		IR 1986, r 1.33(3)	

	Steps to be Taken	Insolvency Act 1986	Insolvency Rules 1986	Cross reference to text
	Action following completion or termination of the arrangement			
44.	Within 28 days of the final completion or termination of the voluntary arrangement the supervisor must send a notice to all creditors and members bound by the arrangement that it has been fully implemented or, if it be the case, has terminated.		IR 1986, r 1.29(1)	Para 10.12
	The supervisor must prepare a report summarising all receipts and payments made by him under the arrangement explaining any departure from the proposal as approved and, if the arrangement has terminated before full implementation why this has happened. A copy of this report must be sent to each creditor and member bound by the arrangement.		IR 1986, r 1.29(2)	
45.	Within 28 days of the final completion or termination of the voluntary arrangement the supervisor must send copies of both the notice and report to the registrar of companies. Until this has been done the supervisor may not vacate his office as supervisor.		IR 1986, r 1.29(3)	

9.4 Procedural table: Company Voluntary Arrangements (with moratorium)

SUMMARY OF TABLE

Directors' proposal and statement of affairs (Steps 1- 6)

Obtaining a moratorium (Steps 7 – 15)

Challenge to nominee's actions (Steps 16 – 20)

Meetings of creditors and company (Steps 21 –25)

Where the voluntary arrangement is approved at the meetings (Steps 26 – 27)

Appeal to the court (Steps 28 – 40)

Application to challenge supervisor or by supervisor for directions (Steps 41 – 50)

	Steps to be Taken	Insolvency Act 1986	Insolvency Rules 1986[1]	Cross reference to text
1.	Directors instruct insolvency practitioner (or other person authorised to act as nominee in relation to the voluntary arrangement) to act as nominee, to give advice and assistance on preparation of proposal and a moratorium		IR 1986, r 1.2	Para 3.3
2.	Directors investigate if company eligible for moratorium. Qualifying conditions: company must satisfy 2 or more requirements for being a small company: (1) turnover not more than £2.8 million; (2) balance sheet total not more than £1.4 million; (3) employees not more than 50. Excluded companies: financial services, banking, companies with capital market arrangement, project companies in a public private partnership with step-in rights, companies in liquidation, administration, or administrative receivership, companies where a moratorium has been in force or an arrangement has had a premature end within previous 12 months.	CA 1985, s 247(3) IA 1986, Sch A1, paras 2 – 4K		Para 3.1 Para 3.2

	Steps to be Taken	Insolvency Act 1986	Insolvency Rules 1986[1]	Cross reference to text
3.	Directors deliver proposal to nominee.	IA 1986, Sch A1, para 6(1)		Para 3.3.
	Delivery of documents must be to the nominee or a person authorised to take delivery of documents on his behalf. On receipt of documents the nominee must forthwith issue a dated acknowledgement of receipt.		IR 1986, r 1.36	
	The proposal must include:			Para 3.4
	(1) the terms of the proposed arrangement;	IA 1986, Sch A1, para 6(1)(a)		
	(2) an explanation of why, in the opinion of the directors, a voluntary arrangement is desirable and why the creditors may be expected to concur with the arrangement; and		IR 1986, r 1.35(1)(b)	
	(3) a statement dealing with the various matters set out in IR 1986, r 1.3(2)		IR 1986, r 1.35 (1)(b)	
	(4) The address to which notice of the consent of the nominee to act and the nominee's statement should be sent.		IR 1986, r 1.35 (1)(c)	
4.	Directors deliver statement of the company's affairs to nominee.	IA 1986, Sch A1, para 6(1)(b)		Para 3.4
	Time: Within 7 days after delivery of proposal or such longer time as the nominee may allow.		IR 1986, r 1.37(1)	
	The statement must comprise the following particulars:		IR 1986, r 1.37(2) applying r 1.5(2)	
	(1) a list of the company's assets, divided into appropriate categories with estimated values assigned to each category;		IR 1986, r 1.5(2)(a)	
	(2) particulars of any secured claim on the company's property, including the amount of the claim and how and when the security was created;		IR 1986, r 1.5(2)(b)	

	Steps to be Taken	Insolvency Act 1986	Insolvency Rules 1986[1]	Cross reference to text
	(3) the names, addresses and amounts of the claims of preferential creditors;		IR 1986, r 1.5(2)(c)	
	(4) the names, addresses and amounts of unsecured creditors;		IR 1986, r 1.5(2)(d)	
	(5) particulars of debts owed by or to the company to or by persons connected with it;		IR 1986, r 1.5(2)(e)	
	(6) the names and addresses of the members of the company with details of their respective shareholdings; and		IR 1986, r 1.5(2)(f)	
	(7) such other particulars as the nominee may in writing require to enable him to make his report to the Court on the directors' proposal.		IR 1986, r 1.5(2)(g)	
	The statement of affairs must be made up to a date not earlier than 2 weeks before the date of delivery of the proposal, but the nominee may allow an extension of that period to not earlier than 2 months,		IR 1986, r 1.37(3)	
	The statement of affairs must be certified as correct by 2 or more directors or by the secretary and at least one other director.		IR 1986, r 1.37(4)	
5.	Directors provide any other information requested by the nominee to enable him prepare his nominee's statement.	IA 1986, Sch A1, para 6(1)(c)		Para 3.4
6.	Nominee prepares and submits to the directors a nominee's statement in prescribed form indicating:			Para 3.4
	(1) whether, in his opinion, the proposed voluntary arrangement has a reasonable prospect of being approved and implemented;	IA 1986, Sch A1, para 6(2)(a)		
	(2) whether the company is likely to have sufficient funds available to it to carry on the business it proposes to carry on during the proposed moratorium;	IA 1986, Sch A1, para 6(2)(b), (4)		

	Steps to be Taken	Insolvency Act 1986	Insolvency Rules 1986[1]	Cross reference to text
	(3) whether, in his opinion, meetings should be summoned of the company and its creditors to consider the proposal, and	IA 1986, Sch A1, para 6(2)(c)		
	Time: Within 28 days after submission of the proposal by the directors.		IR 1986, r 1.38(1)	
	A copy of the nominee's comments on the proposal must be annexed to the nominee's statement, unless he gives a negative opinion on any of the above 3 matters, in which event he must instead give reasons for his opinion.		IR 1986, r 1.38(2)(a)	
	The nominee should also annex a statement of his consent to act where he is willing to do so.		IR 1986, r 1.38(2)(b)	
	Obtaining a moratorium			
7.	The directors file the 5 'moratorium documents' in court, together with 4 copies of a schedule listing the documents, namely:	IA 1986, Sch A1, para 7(1)	IR 1986, r 1.39(1)	Para 3.3
	(1) the proposal (2) the company's statement of affairs (3) a statement that the company is eligible for a moratorium (4) a statement that the nominee has given his consent to act (5) the nominee's statement (*see step 6 above*)		Prescribed forms 1.5, 1.6, 1.7, 1.8, and 1.9	
	The directors must also file a copy of any statement of reasons for extending the period to which the statement of affairs is prepared made by the nominee, and a copy of the nominee's comments on the proposal.		IR 1986, r 1.39(2)	
	Time: within 3 working days of the date of receipt by them of the nominee's statement		IR 1986, r 1.39(1)	

	Steps to be Taken	Insolvency Act 1986	Insolvency Rules 1986[1]	Cross reference to text
8.	The copies of the schedule listing the moratorium documents are endorsed by the court and 3 sealed copies returned to the person who filed the documents in court.		IR 1986, r 1.39(3)	
9.	The moratorium comes into force on the filing of the moratorium documents in court.	IA 1986, Sch A1, para 8(1)		Para 3.5
	The directors must give the nominee immediate notice that the moratorium has come into effect. After receiving the copies of the schedule endorsed by the court (*see step 8 above*) the directors serve 2 of them on the nominee and one on the company.	IA 1986, Sch A1, para 9(1)	IR 1986, r 1.40(1)	
	The nominee forthwith after receiving his copies of the schedule advertises the coming into force of the moratorium in the Gazette, and in such newspaper as he thinks most appropriate for ensuring that the coming into force of the moratorium comes to the notice of the company's creditors.	IA 1986, Sch A1, para 10(1)	IR 1986, r 1.40(2)	Para 3.6
	The nominee also (forthwith) notifies the registrar of companies and any creditor petitioning for the company's winding up of whose claim he is aware of the coming into force of the moratorium specifying the date on which it came into force	IA 1986, Sch A1, para 10(1)(b)(2)	IR 1986, r 1.40(3)	
	The nominee must also give notice of the coming into force of the moratorium to any sheriff or other officer charged with an execution or other legal process against the company, and to any person who, to his knowledge, has distrained against the company or its property.		IR 1986, r 1.40(4)	
10.	The moratorium may be extended, or further extended, by the meetings of the creditors and the company, but not	IA 1986, Sch A1, para 32(1)		Para 3.5 Para 3.16

	Steps to be Taken	Insolvency Act 1986	Insolvency Rules 1986[1]	Cross reference to text
	beyond a period of 2 months beginning on the day on which the meetings of creditors and the company were first held, or if held on different days the day on which the later of those meetings was first held. The nominee must forthwith notify the registrar of companies and the court of any decision to extend the moratorium. Such notice must specify the new expiry date.		IR 1986, r 1.41(1)	
11.	The moratorium may be extended or further extended or renewed or continued by the court. The nominee must forthwith notify the registrar of companies and with the notice send an office copy of the order.	IA 1986, Sch A1, para 38(6)	IR 1986, r 1.41(2)	Para 3.16
12.	Where the company has property which is charged, or is in possession of goods under a hire-purchase agreement, the company may dispose of the property as if it were not subject to the security with the consent of the holder of the security. The company issues an originating application supported by an affidavit or witness statement. When the court fixes a venue for the hearing notice must be given forthwith to the holder of the security or the owner under the agreement. If an order is made the court sends 2 sealed copies of the order to the company, who must send one of them to the holder of the security or owner under the agreement.	IA 1986, Sch A1, para 20(1)	IR 1986, r 1.43(1) IR 1986, r 7.2 IR 1986, r 1.43(2) IR 1986, r 1.43(4) IR 1986, r 1.43(3)	Para 3.9
13.	Where the nominee withdraws his consent to act he must give notice of his withdrawal and the reasons for it to: (1) the registrar of companies;	IA 1986, Sch A1, para 25	IR 1986, r 1.44 Form 1.16, 1.17	Para 3.11

	Steps to be Taken	Insolvency Act 1986	Insolvency Rules 1986[1]	Cross reference to text
	(2) the court; (3) the company; (4) any creditor of the company of whose claim he is aware. On the withdrawal of the nominee the voluntary arrangement comes to an end.			
14.	Where the directors intend to make an application to the court to replace the nominee they must issue an originating application supported by affidavit or witness statement and give the nominee not less than 7 days' notice of the application. The originating application should specify the ground on which the replacement is sought; ie the failure by the nominee to comply with any duty imposed on him, or his death, or it being impracticable or inappropriate for him to continue as nominee. The court will not appoint a replacement nominee unless there is a statement by the proposed replacement indicating his consent to act filed in court. Where a person is appointed as a replacement nominee he must give immediate notice to (a) the registrar of companies (b) the court (if not appointed by the court) (c) the person he has replaced as nominee.	IA 1986, Sch A1, para 28(1)(a)(b)	IR 1986, r 1.45(1) IR 1986, r 1.45(3) IR 1986, r 1.46	Para 3.14
15.	Where the nominee intends to make an application to the court for his replacement on the ground that it is impracticable or inappropriate for him to continue acting he must issue an originating application supported by affidavit or	IA 1986, Sch A1, para 28(1)(b)	IR 1986, r 1.45(2)	Para 3.14

	Steps to be Taken	Insolvency Act 1986	Insolvency Rules 1986[1]	Cross reference to text
	witness statement and give the directors not less than 7 days' notice of his application. The court will not appoint a replacement nominee unless there is a statement by the proposed replacement indicating his consent to act filed in court.		IR 1986, r 1.45(3)	
16.	*Challenge to nominee's actions* Applicant issues originating application to reverse or modify nominee's act omission or decision or to give him directions. The applicant may be a creditor director or member of the company or any other person affected by the moratorium. The nominee will be the respondent to the application.	IA 1986, Sch A1, para 26(1)	IR 1986, rr 7.2(1), 7.4(1)	Para 3.12
17.	Unless the court otherwise directs, applicant serves sealed copy of application upon nominee endorsed with the venue for the hearing at least 7 days before the hearing date.		IR 1986, r 1.47	
18.	Applicant files affidavit or witness statement supporting application and serves copy on nominee. If only 7 days' notice is given evidence should ordinarily be served with application.		IR 1986, rr 7.7(1), 7.8(1)(a)	
19.	Respondent files affidavit or witness statement in reply and serves copy on applicant.		IR 1986, r 7.8(1)(b)	
20.	Parties attend registrar or district judge for hearing of application. The registrar or district judge may give directions and adjourn the matter to be heard by the Judge.		IR 1986, r 7.10	
21.	*Meetings of creditors and the company* The nominee summons meetings of the company and its creditors for such time and on such date as he thinks fit, but the date must not be more than 28 days from the date on	IA 1986, Sch A1, para 29(1)	IR 1986, r 1.48(1) IR 1986, r 1.13(1)	Para 3.16

	Steps to be Taken	Insolvency Act 1986	Insolvency Rules 1986[1]	Cross reference to text
	which the moratorium came into force, and the nominee must have regard primarily to the convenience of the creditors.			
22.	At least 14 days before the day fixed for the meetings: The nominee sends notices calling the creditors' meeting to all the creditors specified in the statement of affairs and any other creditors of whose address he is aware; The nominee sends notices calling the company meeting to all persons who are, to the best of his belief, members of the company. Each notice must specify the court in which the moratorium documents were filed and state the effect of the rules relating to the majorities necessary to approve the arrangement. Each notice must be accompanied by: (1) a copy of the proposal; (2) a copy of the statement of affairs, or if the nominee thinks fit, a summary of it; (3) the nominee's comments on the proposal.		IR 1986, r 1.48(2) IR 1986, r 1.48(3) IR 1986, r 1.48(4)	Para 6.3
23.	Creditors and members attend respective meetings and decide whether or not to approve the proposal (with or without modifications). Conduct of the meetings. (1) The nominee will be the chairman of the meetings. If he is unable to attend, he may nominate another insolvency practitioner or an employee who is experienced in insolvency matters to act as chairman (2)The chairman's decision on entitlement to vote is subject to appeal to the court by any creditor or the debtor. An	IA 1986, Sch A1, para 31(1)	IR 1986, r 1.14 applied by r 1.48(5) IR 1986, r 1.50(3) IR 1986, r 1.50(6)	Paras 6.7 – 6.11

	Steps to be Taken	Insolvency Act 1986	Insolvency Rules 1986[1]	Cross reference to text
	appeal shall not be made after the end of 28 days beginning with the day on which the chairman's report is filed in court. *The appeals procedure is set out in step 28 and following below.*			
	(3) At the creditors' meeting, a majority in excess of three-quarters (in value) of the creditors present in person or by proxy and voting is necessary to pass a resolution approving or modifying the proposal but for any other resolution proposed at the meeting a majority of one-half (in value) is sufficient. Even with a 75% or 50% majority (as required) a resolution is invalid if those voting against it include more than 50% in value of the creditors counting only those to whom notice of the meeting was sent, are not to be left out of account because claims are secured, and are not persons connected with the company.		IR 1986, r 1.52(1) IR 1986, r 1.52(2) IR 1986, r 1.52(3)(4)	
	(4) At the company meeting, subject to any express provision made in the company's articles, a majority of more than one-half (in value) of the members present in person or by proxy and voting is necessary to pass any resolution. Value of members is determined by reference to the number of votes conferred on each member by the company's articles.		IR 1986, r 1.20 applied by r 1.52	
	(5) If at the meeting, a majority for approval has not been obtained, the chairman may, and must if so resolved, adjourn the meeting for not more than 14 days. The meeting may be adjourned from time to time within the period of 14 days but the final adjournment must be to a day not later than 14 days after the first meeting. If the proposal is not approved at the final meeting, it is deemed rejected. Notice of any adjournments shall be given by the chairman forthwith to the court		IR 1986, r 1.53(3) IR 1986, r 1.53(3) IR 1986, r 1.53(5) IR 1986, r 1.53(4)	

	Steps to be Taken	Insolvency Act 1986	Insolvency Rules 1986[1]	Cross reference to text
	(6) Where a proposal is approved which provides for 2 or more insolvency practitioners to act as supervisors, the creditors may resolve as to whether they are to act jointly or separately and allocate their duties (7) If, at the meeting, it is proposed that a person other than the nominee be appointed the supervisor, there must be produced to the chairman written confirmation that the person is an insolvency practitioner and has consented to act. The consent may be given orally at the meeting.		IR 1986, r 1.22(1) applied by r 1.54 IR 1986, r 1.22(3) applied by r 1.54	
24.	Approval of arrangement The arrangement is approved if the decision to approve it has been taken, in accordance with the rules, by both creditors' and company meetings, or by the creditors' meeting alone. If the decision taken by the creditors' meeting differs from that taken by the company meeting, a member of the company may apply to the court. Such an application may not be made after the end of the period of 28 days beginning with (1) the day on which the decision was taken by the creditors' meeting or (2) the day, if later, on which the decision was taken by the company meeting. Where an order is made the member of the company who applied for it must (1) serve sealed copies of it on (a) the supervisor and (b) the directors, and (2) within 7 days of the order deliver an office copy to the registrar of companies. The directors or the supervisor must forthwith after receiving a copy of the court's order give notice of it to all persons who were sent notice of the creditors' or company meetings or	IA 1986, Sch A1, para 36(2) IA 1986, Sch A1, para 36(3) IA 1986, Sch 39 para 36(4)	IR 1986, r 1.22A(2) IR 1986, r 1.22A(3) IR 1986, r 1.22A(5) applied by r 1.54 IR 1986, r 1.22A(4) applied by r 1.54	Para 6.13

	Steps to be Taken	Insolvency Act 1986	Insolvency Rules 1986[1]	Cross reference to text
	any person who is affected by the order even if he did not receive notice of the meetings.			
25.	Chairman of meetings reports results of meetings to the court and, immediately thereafter, gives notice of result of meetings to persons who were sent notice of meetings. *Time*: Within 4 days of the meetings being held.	IA 1986, Sch A1, para 30(3)	IR 1986, r 1.24(4) applied by r 1.54 IR 1986, r 1.24(3) applied by r 1.54	Para 6.15
	The report must: (1) state whether the proposal was approved by the creditors of the company alone, or by both the creditors and members of the company and, in either case, whether such approval was with any modifications;		IR 1986, r 1.24 (2)(a) applied by r 1.54	
	(2) set out the resolutions taken at each meeting and the decision on each;		IR 1986, r 1.24 (2)(b) applied by r 1.54	
	(3) list the creditors and members (with their respective values) present or represented at the meetings and how they voted on each resolution; and		IR 1986, r 1.24 (2)(c) applied by r 1.54	
	(4) state whether, in the opinion of the supervisor, the EC regulation applies to the voluntary arrangement and if so whether the proceedings are main proceedings or territorial proceedings.		IR 1986, r 1.24 (2)(ca) applied by r 1.54	
	(5) include such further information (if any) which the chairman thinks it appropriate to make known to the Court.		IR 1986, r 1.24 (2)(d) applied by r 1.54	

	Steps to be Taken	Insolvency Act 1986	Insolvency Rules 1986[1]	Cross reference to text
	Where the voluntary arrangement is approved at the meetings:			
26.	Supervisor sends copy of chairman's report to Registrar of Companies.		IR 1986, r 1.24(5) applied by r 1.54	Para 6.15
27.	Supervisor proceeds to put the voluntary arrangement into effect.			Paras 10.1 –10.3
	If a petition has been presented against the company (other than an excepted petition – see Sch A1, para 12(5)) the court dismisses the petition.	IA 1986, Sch A1, para 37(4)		
	It may not, however, make such an order if an application challenging the decision taken at the meetings, is pending or is the subject of an appeal.	IA 1986, Sch A1, para 37(5)		
	Application to the court to challenge a decision of the chairman or a decision taken at meetings of creditors and the company to consider a proposal for a voluntary arrangement.	IA 1986, Sch A1, para 38	IR 1986, r 1.50(3) IR 1986, r 1.52(8)	
28.	Applicant issues originating application to reverse a decision of the chairman or the decision taken at meetings.		IR 1986, rr 7.2(1), 7.4 (1)	
	Time: Within 28 days after the filing of the chairman's report as to the result of the meetings, or, where application is made by creditor who was not given notice of the creditors' meeting, within 28 days of the date on which he first became aware that the meeting had taken place.	IA 1986, Sch A1, para 38(3)(a) IA 1986, Sch A1, para 38(3)(b)	IR 1986, r 1.50(6)	Para 7.8
	The Applicant may be: (1) any creditor or member of the company may make application in respect of decisions of the chairman as to: (a) entitlement to vote		IR 1986, r 1.50(3) IR 1986, r 1.52(8)	Para 6.8

	Steps to be Taken	Insolvency Act 1986	Insolvency Rules 1986[1]	Cross reference to text
	(b) whether a vote should be left out of account (c) whether a person is connected with the company.			Paras 7.7
	(2) in the case of a challenge of the decisions of the meetings (a) a person entitled to vote at either of the meetings; (b) a person who would have been entitled to vote at the creditors' meeting if he had had notice of it. (c) the nominee or any person who has replaced him as such.	IA 1986, Sch A1, para 38(2) (a)–(c)		
	The grounds of the application to challenge the decision of the meeting will be that the voluntary arrangement unfairly prejudices the interests of a creditor, member or contributory of the company and/or that there has been some material irregularity at or in relation to either meeting.	IA 1986, Sch A1, para 38(1)(a), (b)		
29.	Unless the Court otherwise directs, Applicant serves sealed copy of the application upon Respondent (if any) endorsed with the venue for the hearing.		IR 1986, r 7.4(3)	Para 7.10
30.	Applicant files witness statement or affidavit in support and serves copy on any Respondent. *Time*: Not less than 14 days before the hearing.		IR 1986, rr 7.7(1), 7.8 (1)(a)	
31.	Respondent files witness statement or affidavit in reply and serves copy on Applicant. *Time*: Not less than 7 days before the hearing.		IR 1986, r 7.8(1)(b)	
32.	Parties attend hearing of application in Chambers before Registrar.			

	Steps to be Taken	Insolvency Act 1986	Insolvency Rules 1986[1]	Cross reference to text
	The Registrar may give such directions as he thinks fit and adjourn the matter to be heard by the Judge in Court.		IR 1986, r 7.10(2) IR 1986, r 7.10(1)	
33.	Applicant lodges in Registrar's office: 1. copy application; and 2. original exhibits for use of Judge.			
34.	Parties attend adjourned hearing of application in Court.			
	If the Court is satisfied on an application to challenge a decision of the chairman that the circumstances giving rise to the appeal give rise to unfair prejudice or material irregularity it may reverse or vary the decision, or, if the votes are declared invalid, order another meeting to be summoned or make such order as it thinks just. If the Court is satisfied as to either of the grounds of the application (*see Step 28 above*) it may:		IR 1986, r 1.50(5) IR 1986, r 1.52(7)	Para 6.8
	(1) revoke or suspend the approvals given by the meetings or any approval given at a meeting at which there was some material irregularity; and/or	IA 1986, Sch A1, para 38(4)(a)		Para 7.9
	(2) direct the summoning of further meetings to consider any revised proposal or a further meeting in place of that at which there was an irregularity to reconsider the original proposal.	IA 1986, Sch A1, para 38(4)(b)		
	If at any time after directing further meetings to consider a revised proposal the Court is satisfied that no revised proposal is to be submitted, it must revoke the direction and revoke or suspend any approval given at the previous meetings.	IA 1986, Sch A1, para 38(5)		

	Steps to be Taken	Insolvency Act 1986	Insolvency Rules 1986[1]	Cross reference to text
35.	Parties (if so required) attend the Court Associate to lodge Counsels' briefs properly endorsed.			
36.	Court draws up Order and sends copies to Applicant.			
37.	Applicant serves sealed copies of the Order on: (1) the supervisor of the voluntary arrangement; and (2) the directors of the company If the Order contains a direction for further meetings notice must also be given by the Applicant to whoever is required by the Order to summon the meetings.		IR 1986, r 1.25 (2)(a) applied by r 1.54 IR 1986, r 1.25 (2)(b) applied by r 1.54 IR 1986, r 1.25(3) applied by r 1.54	
38.	Directors give notice of the Order to all persons who were given notice of the meetings and to any other persons who appear to be affected by the Order. *Time:* Forthwith after receiving the copy of the Order.		IR 1986, r 1.25 (4)(a) applied by r 1.54 IR 1986, r 1.25 (4)(a)	
39.	Directors give notice to Court whether it is intended to make a revised proposal or to invite re-consideration of the original proposal. *Time*: Within 7 days after receiving the copy of the Order (or such longer period as the Court may allow).		IR 1986, r 1.25 (4)(b) applied by r 1.54 IR 1986, r 1.25 (4)(b) applied by r 1.54	
40.	Applicant delivers copy Order to Registrar of Companies. *Time*: Within 7 days after the making of the Order.		IR 1986, r 1.25(5) applied by r 1.54 IR 1986, r 1.25(5) applied by r 1.54	

	Steps to be Taken	Insolvency Act 1986	Insolvency Rules 1986[1]	Cross reference to text
	Application to reverse or modify an act, omission or decision of a supervisor of a voluntary arrangement.	IA 1986, Sch A1, para 39(3)		
41.	Applicant issues ordinary application to reverse or modify supervisor's decision. The Applicant may be a creditor or any other person dissatisfied by any act, omission or decision of the supervisor. The supervisor will be the Respondent to the application.	IA 1986, Sch A1, para 39(3)	IR 1986, rr 7.2(1), 7.4(1)	Para 10.4, 10.5
42.	Unless the Court otherwise directs, Applicant serves sealed copy of application upon supervisor endorsed with the venue for the hearing.		IR 1986, r 7.4(3)	
43.	Applicant files witness statement or affidavit supporting application and serves copy on supervisor.		IR 1986, rr 7.7(1), 7.8 (1)(a)	
44.	Follow Steps 31-35 above. The Court may: (1) confirm, reverse or modify any act or decision of the supervisor; (2) give directions to the supervisor; or (3) make such other order as it thinks fit.	IA 1986, Sch A1, para 39(4)(a)–(c)		
45.	Court draws up Order and sends a duplicate thereof to the Applicant.			
	The Supervisor may apply to the Court for directions in relation to any matter arising under the voluntary arrangement.	IA 1986, Sch A1, para 39(5)		
46.	Applicant issues ordinary (or originating) application.		IR 1986, rr 7.2(1), 7.4 (1)	Para 10.2
47.	Unless the Court otherwise directs Applicant serves sealed copy of application on Respondent endorsed with the venue for the hearing.		IR 1986, r 7.4(3)	
48.	Applicant files witness statement or affidavit supporting application, and serves copy on Respondent.		IR 1986, r 7.8(1)(a)	

	Steps to be Taken	Insolvency Act 1986	Insolvency Rules 1986[1]	Cross reference to text
49.	Follow Steps 31-35 above.			
50.	Court draws up order and sends copy to the Applicant.			
	Conversion of voluntary arrangement into winding up			
51.	See table 9.3 company voluntary arrangement without moratorium steps 40 – 45.			Para 14.7

9.5 Procedural table: Individual Voluntary Arrangements

SUMMARY OF TABLE

Debtor's proposal and statement of affairs (Steps 1–6).

Cases where application made for Interim order (Steps 7–19).

Cases where no interim order is to be obtained (Steps 20-21).

Creditors' meeting (Steps 22–25).

Appeal to the court (Steps 26–33).

Proceedings subsequent to approval of arrangement (Steps 34–36).

For:

Application to challenge supervisor or by supervisor for directions : see table 9.3 CVA without moratorium steps 30 to 39 (for IVA rules see table 9.2)

Conversion of voluntary arrangement into bankruptcy : see table 9.3 CVA without moratorium steps 40 to 43 (for IVA rules see table 9.2)

	Steps to be Taken	Insolvency Act 1986	Insolvency Rules 1986	Cross reference to text
	Debtor's proposal and statement of affairs			
1.	Debtor discusses his financial affairs with intended nominee (insolvency practitioner or authorised person in relation to the voluntary arrangement) who is to act in the matter.	IA 1986, s 253(2)		Para 4.1

	Steps to be Taken	Insolvency Act 1986	Insolvency Rules 1986	Cross reference to text
2.	Debtor prepares for intended nominee (usually with the advice and assistance of nominee) a proposal on which to make his report to the court. The proposal must state why the debtor considers a voluntary arrangement desirable and give reasons why his creditors may be expected to concur. It must also state or otherwise deal with the matters set out in rule 5.3(2)[see appendix 2 above].	IA 1986, s 256 IA 1986, s 256A (where no application for interim order)	IR 1986, r 5.2 IR 1986, r 5.3(1) IR 1986, r 5.3(2)	Para 4.2 Para 4.4
	Amendment of proposal: this may be done with the agreement in writing of the nominee at any time up until the presentation of his report to the court.		IR 1986, r 5.3(3)	Para 4.3
3.	Debtor gives intended nominee written notice of his proposal, a copy of which accompanies the notice. Both documents are delivered either to the nominee or to a person authorised to take delivery of documents on his behalf.		IR 1986, r 5.4(1) IR 1986, r 5.4(2)	Para 4.3
4.	*If the intended nominee agrees to act* he indorses a copy of the notice with his agreement and the date of receipt. The copy is then returned forthwith to the debtor at the address specified in the notice.		IR 1986, r 5.4(3) IR 1986, r 5.4(4)	Para 4.3
5.	*Where the debtor is a bankrupt*, notice of the proposal is also given to the Official Receiver and (if any) the trustee. The notice must contain the name and address of the insolvency practitioner who has agreed to act as nominee.	IA 1986, s 253(4)	IR 1986, r 5.4(5)	Para 4.3

	Steps to be Taken	Insolvency Act 1986	Insolvency Rules 1986	Cross reference to text
6.	*If a statement of affairs has not already been filed in connection with a bankruptcy petition* debtor must deliver a statement of his affairs to the nominee.			Para 4.5
	Time: Within 7 days after the receipt of his proposal by the nominee. The nominee may extend the time for delivery.		IR 1986, r 5.5(1)	
	An undischarged bankrupt, who has filed a statement of affairs in his bankruptcy, need not deliver a further statement unless required by the nominee.		IR 1986, r 5.5(2)	
	The statement of affairs must show the debtor's assets and their estimated value, give a list with particulars of secured or partly secured creditors, preferential and unsecured creditors, any debts owed by or to the debtor to or by persons who are 'associates' and any other particulars required by the nominee.	IA 1986, s 435	IR 1986, r 5.5(3)	
	It will be made up to a date not earlier than 2 weeks before the date of the written notice of the proposal served on the nominee. The period of 2 weeks may be extended by the nominee to not earlier than 2 months before the date of the written notice. Where an extension is granted, the nominee should give his reasons in his report to the court.		IR 1986, r 5.5(4)	
	The statement of affairs is not verified by affidavit, the debtor certifies that it is correct to the best of his knowledge and belief[1].		IR 1986, r 5.5(5)	

	Steps to be Taken	Insolvency Act 1986	Insolvency Rules 1986	Cross reference to text
	Note: Material omissions or the inclusion of information that is false or misleading in any material particular, entitle the supervisor of or any person bound by a voluntary arrangement to present a bankruptcy petition against the debtor.	IA 1986, s 276(1)		
	Where application is made for an Interim Order			
7.	Debtor applies to the court for an interim order.		IR 1986, rr 7.3, 7.4 (1)	Para 2.2
	Court: except in the case of a bankrupt, an application to the court under Part VIII of the Act must be made to a court in which the debtor would be entitled to present his own petition in bankruptcy.		IR 1986, r 5.8(1)	
	The application must contain sufficient information to establish that it is brought in the proper court		IR 1986, r 5.8(2)	
	In the case of a bankrupt such an application must be made to the court having the conduct of his bankruptcy and will be filed with those bankruptcy proceedings		IR 1986, r 5.8(3)	
	Debtor files in court originating application and copy, together with other copies for each person to be served, and also a supporting affidavit or witness statement.		IR 1986, r 6.40 IR 1986, r 5.7(1) IR 1986, r 7.57	
	The supporting affidavit or witness statement will deal with the following:		IR 1986, r 5.7(1)	Para 2.3

	Steps to be Taken	Insolvency Act 1986	Insolvency Rules 1986	Cross reference to text
	(1) the reasons for making the application; (2) particulars of any execution or other legal process which to the debtor's knowledge has been commenced against him; (3) that he is an undischarged bankrupt or as the case may be that he is able to petition for his own bankruptcy; (4) that no previous application for an interim order has been made by or on behalf of the debtor in the period of 12 months ending with the date of the affidavit or witness statement; (5) that the nominee under the proposal (naming him) is a person who is qualified to act as an insolvency practitioner or authorised to act as nominee in relation to the voluntary arrangement, and is willing to act in relation to the proposal; (6) where the applicant intends to apply for a stay of any action, execution or legal process pending the hearing of the application for an interim order evidence in support of stay of proceedings; (7) the copy notice indorsed with the agreement of the intended nominee to act in relation to the proposal and a copy of the debtor's proposal to the nominee, must be exhibited to the affidavit or witness statement.	IA 1986, s 254	IR 1986, r 7.57 IR 1986, r 5.7(2)	

	Steps to be Taken	Insolvency Act 1986	Insolvency Rules 1986	Cross reference to text
	Where the debtor is an undischarged bankrupt the application may be made by the Official Receiver or the trustee as well as by the debtor[2].	IA 1986, s 253(3)		
8.	Court fixes venue for hearing.		IR 1986, r 5.7(3)	Para 2.3
9.	Applicant gives at least 2 days notice of the hearing as follows: (1) *where the debtor is bankrupt*, as relevant to the following: the bankrupt, the Official Receiver and the trustee (i.e. whoever is the applicant will give notice to the other two); (2) *where the debtor is not a bankrupt* to any creditor who (to the debtor's knowledge) has presented a bankruptcy petition against him and (3) *in either case* to the nominee. Where (1) and (2) do not apply and the nominee waives 2 days notice the application may be heard earlier provided a Bankruptcy Registrar or District Judge is available.		IR 1986, r 5.7(4) IR 1986, r 5.7(4)	Para 2.3
10.	Applicant applies for a stay of proceedings order pending the hearing of the application for an interim order. The application will specify the action, execution or legal process to be stayed. A separate supporting affidavit or witness statement will not be required where the necessary evidence has been included in the affidavit or witness statement filed in support of the main application.	IA 1986, s 254(1)	IR 1986, r 7.4, IR 1986, r 7.57	Para 2.5

	Steps to be Taken	Insolvency Act 1986	Insolvency Rules 1986	Cross reference to text
11.	Court hears application for stay. In the High Court the application will normally be heard on the day it is filed. The order will usually be drawn up by the Court.			Para 2.5
	Note: Any court in which proceedings are pending, on proof that an application for an interim order has been made, may stay the proceedings or allow them to continue on such terms as it thinks fit.	IA 1986, s 254(2)		
12.	Provided there is no bankruptcy order in existence and (so far as is known) no pending petition the court will be prepared to make a 14 day interim order with the application adjourned 14 days for consideration of the nominee's report, where the papers are in order and the nominee's signed consent to act includes a waiver of notice of the application or a consent by the nominee to a making of an interim order without the attendance of either party[3]. Otherwise the court hears application for interim order. Any of the persons served with notice in step 9 above may appear and the court must take into account any representations made by them, especially where the debtor is an undischarged bankrupt.	IA 1986, s 255(3), (4)	IR 1986, r 5.9(1) IR 1986, r 5.9(2)	Para 2.4
	The court may not make an order unless it is satisfied that the debtor intends to make a proposal, is in a position to do so, has not made a previous application within the past 12 months and that the nominee is an insolvency practitioner or person authorised to act in relation to the voluntary arrangement and is willing to act.	IA 1986, s 255(1)		

	Steps to be Taken	Insolvency Act 1986	Insolvency Rules 1986	Cross reference to text
	An interim order is effective for 14 days beginning with the day after the making of the order, unless extended by the court. It will provide:—	IA 1986, s 255(6) IA 1986, s 256(4)		Para 2.6
	(1) that during the period of the order, no bankruptcy petition may be filed or proceeded with and that no proceeding, execution or legal process may be commenced or continued against the debtor or his property without the leave of the court;	IA 1986, s 252(2)		
	(2) for the date by which the nominee's report is to be delivered and the date, time and place for consideration of the report;	IA 1986, s 256(1)	IR 1986, r 5.9(3) IR 1986, r 5.11(1)	
	(3) *where the debtor is an undischarged bankrupt* any necessary orders relating to the bankruptcy.	IA 1986, s 255(3)		
	The order may also provide for an extension of time for filing the nominee's report (at this stage only the nominee may apply) together with consequential amendments extending the effect of the order and the date for considering the report.	IA 1986, s 256(4)	IR 1986, r 5.9(4)	
	The order will be drawn by the court and at least 2 sealed copies will be sent to the applicant, who will serve 1 copy on the nominee. The applicant will also give notice of the order to all those persons served with notice of the hearing.		IR 1986, r 5.10(1) IR 1986, r 5.10(2) IR 1986, r 12.11 IR 1986, r 12.10 IR 1986, r 13.3	

	Steps to be Taken	Insolvency Act 1986	Insolvency Rules 1986	Cross reference to text
13.	Nominee prepares his report.			
	Information for the report:			Para 4.5
	If the nominee is unable to complete his report on the basis of the information contained in the proposal and statement of affairs, he may call on the debtor to supply him with:—			Para 4.6
	(a) further information as to why he is unable to pay his debts;			
	(b) particulars of any previous proposal for a voluntary arrangement under the Insolvency Act 1986;			
	(c) any other information which the nominee thinks is necessary.		IR 1986, r 5.6(1)	
	He may also ask the debtor whether at any time he has been concerned in the affairs of any insolvent company or has been adjudged bankrupt or entered into an arrangement with his creditors.		IR 1986, r 5.6(2)	
	In any event the debtor must give the nominee access to his accounts and records.		IR 1986, r 5.6(3)	
	Recommendation for creditors' meeting:			
	Where the nominee reports that, in his opinion, the debtor's proposal has a reasonable prospect of being approved and implemented, and that a meeting of creditors should be summoned to consider the debtor's proposal, he annexes to the report his comments on the	IA 1986, s 256(1)	IR 1986, r 5.11(3) IR 1986, r 5.17(1) IR 1986, r 5.18	Para 4.7 Para 4.8

	Steps to be Taken	Insolvency Act 1986	Insolvency Rules 1986	Cross reference to text
	proposal. He will also specify a date, time and place for the meeting, the proposed date will be not less than 14 days from when report filed, nor more than 28 days from the date the report is considered by the court. The time will be between 10.00 and 16.00 hours on a business day at a place convenient to the creditors.			
	Where the nominee reports that, in his opinion, a meeting of creditors should not be summoned, he must give his reasons for that opinion in his report.		IR 1986, r 5.11(3)	
14.	Nominee delivers report to the court together with:			Para 4.7
	(1) copy of debtor's proposal (including any amendments *see step 2 above*; and			
	(2) copy or summary of any statement of affairs provided by the debtor.		IR 1986, r 5.11(2)	
	Time: Not less than 2 days before the interim order ceases to have effect.		IR 1986, r 5.11(1)	
	Where the nominee as a result of asking for the above information, or otherwise, finds that more time is needed to complete the report, he may apply to the court to extend the period for which the order has effect. Where an extension is granted the time for filing the report will also be extended.	IA 1986, s 256(4)	IR 1986, r 5.9(4)	
	Notice of the extension, including the new hearing date should be given to all those persons served with notice of the original hearing date.		IR 1986, r 5.10(2)	

	Steps to be Taken	Insolvency Act 1986	Insolvency Rules 1986	Cross reference to text
15.	Court endorses nominee's report with date of filing in court.		IR 1986, r 5.11(4)	Para 4.7
16.	Nominee sends: (1) copy of his report, and comments *if any* accompanying it, (2) copy of debtor's proposal, and (3) copy or summary of debtor's statement of affairs, *if debtor is undischarged bankrupt* to Official Receiver and (if any) the trustee: *if debtor is not a bankrupt* to any person who has presented a bankruptcy petition against the debtor. *Note:* any creditor of the debtor is entitled to inspect the file at all reasonable times on any business day.		IR 1986, r 5.11(6) IR 1986, r 5.11(5)	Para 4.7
17.	*Where the nominee fails to file his report*, the debtor may apply for the court to direct that the nominee be replaced by another insolvency practitioner and for the continuance or renewal of the interim order. The debtor is required to give 7 day's notice of the application to the existing nominee. Unless the debtor has advance notice that the report will not be filed, time will be needed to enable the debtor to file his application and give notice to the nominee. 1. *In a proper case* the court adjourns the hearing for 14 days (or such period as it thinks appropriate) and	IA 1986, s 256(3)	IR 1986, r 5.12(1)	Para 4.9

	Steps to be Taken	Insolvency Act 1986	Insolvency Rules 1986	Cross reference to text
	continues the interim order to enable the debtor to proceed with the application.			
	2. *Order* The order of adjournment is drawn by the court and at least two sealed copies are sent to the applicant, who serves one sealed copy on the nominee. The applicant also gives notice of the order to all persons served with notice of the hearing, and to the proposed nominee.		IR 1986, r 5.10	
	3. *Application* Debtor forthwith lodges application to remove nominee together with supporting affidavit or witness statement exhibiting the consent of the new insolvency practitioner to act as nominee.		IR 1986, r 7.4, IR 1986, r 7.7, IR 1986, r 7.8	
	4. Court appoints application to be heard on same day as the adjourned hearing.			
	5. Debtor gives 7 days notice of his application to the nominee (and to the proposed new nominee) and encloses a copy of the supporting affidavit or witness statement.		IR 1986, r 5.12(1)	
	The Court may not appoint a replacement nominee unless a statement by the replacement nominee indicating his consent to act is filed in court		IR 1986, r 5.12(2)	
	The rule is silent as to service of written evidence (affidavit or written evidence).			
18.	Provided that there is no bankruptcy order in existence	IA 1986, s 256(1)	IR 1986, r 5.11(2), (3)	Para 4.10

	Steps to be Taken	Insolvency Act 1986	Insolvency Rules 1986	Cross reference to text
	and (so far as is known) no pending petition, the court will be prepared to make the following orders without the attendance of either party:			
	(1) a standard order on consideration of the nominee's report, extending the interim order to a date 7 weeks after the date of the proposed meeting directing the meeting to be summoned and adjourning to a date about 3 weeks after the meeting. Such an order may be made if the nominee's report has been delivered to the court and complies with the Act and the Rules and proposes a date for the meeting not less than 14 days from that on which the nominee's report is filed in court nor more than 28 days from that on which that report is considered by the court.		IR 1986, r 5.11(2), (3). IR 1986, r 5.13	
	(2) a 'concertina' order, combining a 14 day interim order and standard order under *sub paragraph (1) above*. Such an order may be made if the initial application for an interim order is accompanied by a report of the nominee and the other conditions for a 14-day interim order and standard order are satisfied[3].			
	Otherwise the court holds hearing to consider nominee's report.			
	Any of the persons served with notice of the hearing may appear or be represented. In the event of non-attendance, evidence of service will be required.		IR 1986, r 5.13(1)	

	Steps to be Taken	Insolvency Act 1986	Insolvency Rules 1986	Cross reference to text
19.	*Court orders* (1) Where the court is satisfied that a meeting of creditors should be summoned where there is a bankruptcy order it will extend the interim order to a date 49 days after the date fixed for the meeting. It will also adjourn the application to the same date for consideration of the chairman's report of the result of the meeting. The period of 49 days takes into account, adjournments of the meeting (r 5.24(2): 14 days maximum), time for filing chairman's report (r 5.27(3): 4 days), challenge of chairman's or meeting's decision (r 5.22(6) : 28 days) plus a margin of 3 days. In a case where there is <u>no</u> bankruptcy order the court will extend the interim order and adjourn the application for consideration of the chairman's report to a date 21 days after the date fixed for the meeting. The difference is because where there is a bankruptcy order it may only be annulled after a full 28 days has expired after the filing of the chairman's report and where there is no bankruptcy order either the meeting will have approved the scheme or not approved it and unless the debtor indicates that he is going to appeal it does not justify any further protection for him from his creditors. (2) *Where nominee requires more time to prepare his report* court may order that:	IA 1986, s 256(5)	IR 1986, r 5.24(2), (3) IR 1986, r 5.27(3) IR 1986, r 5.22(6)	Para 4.10

	Steps to be Taken	Insolvency Act 1986	Insolvency Rules 1986	Cross reference to text
	(i) period of time for which interim order has effect be extended to a further date;	IA 1986, s 256(4)		Para 2.6
	(ii) time for filing report be extended to not less than 2 business days before that date;		IR 1986, r 5.11(1)	
	(iii) the hearing of the application be adjourned to the same date.			
	(3) *Where nominee fails to file his report* court may order that:			
	(i) the period of time for which interim order has effect be extended for a specific period to enable the debtor to apply for the nominee to be replaced;	IA 1986, s 256(3)	IR 1986, r 5.12(1)	Para 4.9
	(ii) if the debtor has already given the present nominee 7 days notice of his intention to apply to the court to have him replaced (*as in step 17 above*) or the nominee has waived notice; the court may, subject to being satisfied that the proposed new nominee is an insolvency practitioner, order that the nominee be replaced.			
	Order will also incorporate the provisions of paragraph 2 above.			

	Steps to be Taken	Insolvency Act 1986	Insolvency Rules 1986	Cross reference to text
	(4) Where, on the application of the nominee, the court is satisfied that the debtor has failed to supply the nominee with all necessary information to enable him to complete his report or for any other reason it would be inappropriate to call a meeting of creditors, court may order that the interim order be discharged. Any order made under this paragraph will be drawn by the court and at least 2 sealed copies will be sent to the applicant, who will serve 1 copy on the nominee. The applicant will also give notice of the order to all those persons served with notice of the hearing.	IA 1986, s 256(6)	IR 1986, r 5.13(2)	Para 2.6
	Where no Interim Order is to be obtained			
20.	The nominee delivers 2 copies of his report to the court[4] within 14 days (or any longer period allowed by the court) after receiving both the debtor's proposal *see step 2 above* and the debtor's statement of affairs *see step 6 above* With his report the nominee must deliver a copy of the debtor's proposal, statement of affairs and written notice of proposal duly endorsed by nominee with the date of receipt The nominee also delivers 2 copies of Form 5.5 listing the above documents and containing a statement that no application is to be made for an interim order		IR 1986, r 5.14(2)	

	Steps to be Taken	Insolvency Act 1986	Insolvency Rules 1986	Cross reference to text
	Note: the court does not consider the report unless an application is made in relation to the debtor's proposal		IR 1986, r 5.14(1)	
	Recommendation for a creditor's meeting			
	Where the nominee makes known his opinion that the debtor's proposal has a reasonable prospect of being approved and implemented, and that a meeting of creditors should be summoned, the nominee's comments on the debtor's proposal must be annexed to his report.	IA 1986, s 257	IR 1986, r 5.14(3)	
	Where the nominee reports that, in his opinion, a meeting of creditors should not be summoned, he must give his reasons for that opinion in his report.			
	On receipt of the nominee's report and Form 5.5 the court files one copy and returns the second to the nominee endorsed with the date of its filing in court		IR 1986, r 5.14(4)	
	The nominee sends a copy of the debtor's proposal and statement of affairs and of the nominee's report and any comments accompanying it (a) to any person who has presented a bankruptcy petition against the debtor, or (b) (where the debtor is an undischarged bankrupt) to the official receiver and any trustee.		IR 1986, r 5.14(6)	
	Court: except in the case of bankrupt the nominee's report is to be filed in the court in which the debtor would be entitled to present his own bankruptcy petition.		IR 1986, r 5.15(1) IR 1986, r 6.40	

	Steps to be Taken	Insolvency Act 1986	Insolvency Rules 1986	Cross reference to text
	The report must contain sufficient information to establish that it is filed in the appropriate court.		IR 1986, r 5.15(2)	
	In the case of a bankrupt the report is filed in the court having the conduct of the bankruptcy and is filed with those bankruptcy proceedings		IR 1986, r 5.15(3)	
21.	*Applications to the Court*			
	Any application in relation to any matter relating to a proposal or a voluntary arrangement must be made to the court in which the nominee's report is filed.		IR 1986, r 5.16(1)	Para 2.8
	Should the debtor wish to apply to the court for the nominee to be replaced he must give the nominee at least 7 days' notice of the application.	IA 1986, s 256A (4)(a) or (b)	IR 1986, r 5.16(2)	
	Should the nominee wish to apply to the court for his replacement as nominee he must give the debtor at least 7 days' notice of the application.	IA 1986, s 256A (4)(b)	IR 1986, r 5.16(3)	
	The court must not appoint a replacement nominee unless a statement by the replacement nominee indicating his consent to act is filed in court.		IR 1986, r 5.16(4)	
	Creditors' Meeting			
22.	Nominee sends out notices calling creditors' meeting for the date stated in the application to all creditors named in the statement of affairs, and also to any creditors of whom he is otherwise aware.			Para 6.2

	Steps to be Taken	Insolvency Act 1986	Insolvency Rules 1986	Cross reference to text
	Time: At least 14 days before the date fixed for the meeting.		IR 1986, r 5.17(2)	
	Each notice will specify the court to which the nominee's report has been delivered and state the requisite majorities for particular resolutions.			
	Attached to the notice will be a copy of the proposal, the nominee's comments thereon, a copy of the statement of affairs or a summary (which includes a list of creditors and the amount of their debts) and a form of proxy.		IR 1986, r 5.17(3) IR 1986, r 5.18(3)	
23.	Conduct of the creditors' meeting.			
	(1) The nominee will be the chairman of the meeting. If he is unable to attend, he may nominate another insolvency practitioner or an employee who is experienced in insolvency matters to act as chairman.		IR 1986, r 5.19	Paras 6.6 – 6.10
	(2) The chairman's decision on entitlement to vote is subject to appeal to the court by any creditor or the debtor. An appeal shall not be made after the end of 28 days beginning with the day on which the chairman's report is filed in court. *For the appeals procedure see steps 26 and following below.*		IR 1986, r 5.22(3) IR 1986, r 5.22(6)	
	(3) Voting approval of the debtor's proposal or any modification requires a majority in excess of three quarters in value of the creditors present in person or by proxy and voting on the resolution. Even with a 75%		IR 1986, r 5.23(1) IR 1986, r 5.23(2) IR 1986, r 5.23(3)(4)	

	Steps to be Taken	Insolvency Act 1986	Insolvency Rules 1986	Cross reference to text
	majority the resolution is invalid if those voting against it include more than 50% in value of the creditors counting only those to whom notice of the meeting has been sent, are not to be left out of account because their claim is secured, and are not associates of the debtor. Any other resolution requires a majority in excess of one half.			
	(4) If at the meeting, a majority for approval has not been obtained, the chairman may, and shall if so resolved, adjourn the meeting for not more than 14 days. The meeting may be adjourned from time to time within the period of 14 days but the final adjournment must be to a day not later than 14 days after the first meeting. If the proposal is not approved at the final meeting, it is deemed rejected. Notice of any adjournments shall be given by the chairman forthwith to the court.		IR 1986, r 5.24(2) IR 1986, r 5.24(3) IR 1986, r 5.24(5) IR 1986, r 5.24(4)	
	(5) Where a proposal is approved which provides for 2 or more insolvency practitioners to act as supervisors, the creditors may resolve as to whether they are to act jointly or separately and allocate their duties.		IR 1986, r 5.25(1)	
	(6) If, at the meeting, it is proposed that a person other than the nominee be appointed as supervisor, there must be produced to the chairman written confirmation that the person is an insolvency practitioner and has consented to act. The consent may be given orally at the meeting.		IR 1986, r 5.25(2)	

	Steps to be Taken	Insolvency Act 1986	Insolvency Rules 1986	Cross reference to text
24.	Chairman prepares report of creditors' meeting. The report must:— (1) state whether the proposal was approved or rejected and, if approved, with what, if any, modifications; (2) set out the resolutions taken at the meeting and the decision on each one; (3) list the creditors (with their respective debts for voting purposes) who were present or represented and how they voted on each resolution; (4) state whether in the opinion of the supervisor the EC Regulation applies to the voluntary arrangement and if so whether the proceedings are main proceedings or territorial proceedings. (5) include such further information (if any) as the chairman thinks appropriate. *Time*: Within 4 days of the meeting. Time for appeal or applications to the court in respect of the decision of the chairman and decisions of creditors' meeting runs from this date[5], *see also step 26 below.* *Note:* where no interim order has been obtained the court does not consider the chairman's report unless an application is made to the court in relation to it.	IA 1986, s 262	IR 1986, r 5.27(1) IR 1986, r 5.27(2) IR 1986, r 5.27(3) IR 1986, r 5.22(6) IR 1986, r 5.23(7) IR 1986, r 5.27(5)	Para 6.15 Para 6.5

	Steps to be Taken	Insolvency Act 1986	Insolvency Rules 1986	Cross reference to text
25.	Immediately the report has been filed the chairman must:			
	1. send notice of the result of the meeting to all those persons who were given notice of the meeting, *see step 22 above* and where the debtor is an undischarged bankrupt to the Official Receiver and, if any, the Trustee.		IR 1986, r 5.27(4)	Para 6.15
	2. *if the proposal for a voluntary arrangement is approved*, report to the Secretary of State the following details of the arrangement:			
	(a) the name and address of the debtor and the date when the arrangement was approved;			
	(b) the name and address of the supervisor;			
	(c) the court in which the chairman's report has been filed.		IR 1986, r 5.29(1)	
	The information listed in *paragraph 2* will be entered in a register of individual voluntary arrangements maintained by the Secretary of State; the register is open to public inspection;		IR 1986, r 5.28	
	If debtor is undischarged bankrupt notice is given to the Official Receiver and the trustee (if any).		IR 1986, r 5.27(4)	
	Appeal to the Court			
26.	Appeal may be made by application to the court in respect of decisions of the chairman or of the meeting of creditors.	IA 1986, s 262	IR 1986, r 5.22(3) IR 1986, r 5.23(7)	Para 6.8 Para 7.1

	Steps to be Taken	Insolvency Act 1986	Insolvency Rules 1986	Cross reference to text
	Time: Before the end of period of 28 days from the date of filing in court of chairman's report of meeting.	IA 1986, s 262(3)	IR 1986, r 5.22(6)	Para 7.8
	Applicants:			Para 7.7
	(1) The debtor or any creditor may make application in respect of decisions of the chairman as to:			
	(a) entitlement to vote;			
	(b) whether a vote is to be left out of account;			
	(c) whether a person is an associate of the debtor.			
	(2) The debtor, any creditor entitled to vote at the meeting, the nominee or his replacement, and *if the debtor is an undischarged bankrupt* his trustee or the Official Receiver, may apply to challenge the decision of the meeting of creditors on one or both of the following grounds:			Paras 7.1, 7.10
	(a) that the arrangement approved by the meeting unfairly prejudices the interests of creditors,			
	(b) that there has been some material irregularity at or in relation to such a meeting.	IA 1986, s 262		
27.	Court hears application. *High Court* all applications are heard by the bankruptcy registrar or district judge who may refer matter to the judge.			Para 7.10

	Steps to be Taken	Insolvency Act 1986	Insolvency Rules 1986	Cross reference to text
	County Court applications under rules 5.22 and 5.23 of the Insolvency Rules 1986 (ie those in *paragraph 1 of step 26 above*) may be heard by the district judge or referred to the judge; applications under Section 262 of the Insolvency Act 1986 (i.e. those in *paragraph 2 of step 26 above*) will be heard by the judge.			
28.	Court makes order. 1. *Applications under rules 5.22 or 5.23 of Insolvency Rules 1986*. Court may only make an order if it considers that the matter is such as to give rise to unfair prejudice or material irregularity. *Where the order reverses or varies the chairman's decision or declares that a creditor's vote is invalid*, the court may order that another meeting of creditors be summoned or make such other order as it thinks just. No direct provision is made as to procedure for calling new meeting but it is assumed that *steps 22–25* above will apply. Similarly no direct provision is made for suspension or revocation of an order or for the continuance of the interim order where the court's decision eliminates the majority in favour. 2. *Applications under Section 262*. Where the court is satisfied as to either of the grounds set out in *paragraph 2 of step 26 above* it may		IR 1986, r 5.22, IR 1986, r 5.23(7) IR 1986, r 5.22(5) IR 1986, r 5.22(5)	Para 6.8 Paras 7.2 – 7.6

	Steps to be Taken	Insolvency Act 1986	Insolvency Rules 1986	Cross reference to text
	(a) revoke or suspend any approval given by the meeting and/or			Para 7.9
	(b) give a direction to any person for the summoning of a further meeting to consider any revised proposal by the debtor or where there has been some material irregularity at or in relation to the meeting, to reconsider the original proposal	IA 1986, s 262(4)		
	(c) give supplemental directions as it thinks fit, including directions in particular with respect to:			
	(1) things done since the meeting under any voluntary arrangement approved by the meeting, and			
	(2) such things done since the meeting as could not have been done if an interim order had been in force in relation to the debtor when they were done.	IA 1986, s 262(7)		
	It is assumed that such directions will include:—			
	(i) that the debtor *or where he is an undischarged bankrupt* the Official Receiver or his trustee do within 7 days after service of a copy of the order give notice to the court whether it is intended to make a revised proposal or to invite reconsideration of the original proposal, and that any revised proposal be submitted to the nominee within 7 days thereafter;			
	(ii) that in the event of notice of intention to make a revised proposal being given to the court, the nominee			

	Steps to be Taken	Insolvency Act 1986	Insolvency Rules 1986	Cross reference to text
	thereunder do file a copy of his report and comments on the revised proposal within 21 days of such notice; (iii) that the person charged with summoning the meeting (who may be the nominee) do summon such meeting for a date not less than 14 and not more than 21 days from the date of service of the notice of intention to invite reconsideration of the original proposal or from the date of filing of the nominee's report on the revised proposal; (iv) that the notice calling the further meeting of creditors be sent at least 14 days before the meeting to all persons who received notice of the original meeting and that where the debtor has submitted a revised proposal, a copy together with the nominee's comments shall be sent with the notice; (v) that rules as to adjournment of original meeting are to apply to the conduct of such meeting; (vi) that the application for an interim order be restored for hearing on a date 70 days (10 weeks) hence for consideration of the chairman's report of the meeting and that the interim order be continued or renewed to that date (the adjournment of 70 days is arrived at by adding together the maximum periods of time allowed under (i), (ii), (iii) and (iv) above plus 3 days).			

	Steps to be Taken	Insolvency Act 1986	Insolvency Rules 1986	Cross reference to text
29.	*Where court has revoked or suspended arrangement*: applicant			
	(1) serves sealed copies of the order on the debtor, the supervisor of the arrangement and *where the debtor is an undischarged bankrupt*, on the Official Receiver and the trustee.		IR 1986, r 5.30(2)	Para 7.9
	(2) *where the court directs that a further meeting be summoned*, gives notice of the order to the person directed to summon the meeting of creditors.		IR 1986, r 5.30(3)	
	(3) within 7 days gives notice of the order to the Secretary of State.		IR 1986, r 5.30(5)	
30.	Upon receipt of the order debtor or *where he is an undischarged bankrupt* the Official Receiver or the trustee:		IR 1986, r 5.30(4)	Para 7.10
	(1) gives notice of it, forthwith, to all persons who were sent notice of the creditors' meeting or appear to be affected by the order; and		IR 1986, r 5.30(4)(a)	
	(2) within 7 days (or such further time as the court may allow) gives notice to the court whether it is intended to make a revised proposal or to invite reconsideration of the original proposal.		IR 1986, r 5.30(4)(b)	
31.	Where the court has directed that a meeting of creditors be summoned to consider a revised proposal and it is satisfied that the debtor does not intend to submit such a proposal, it shall revoke the direction and revoke or suspend any approval given at the previous meeting.	IA 1986, s 262(5)		Para 7.9

	Steps to be Taken	Insolvency Act 1986	Insolvency Rules 1986	Cross reference to text
	The court may also give supplemental directions as it thinks fit including directions as to things done since the meeting approving the arrangement.	IA 1986, s 262(7)		
	Proceedings subsequent to approval of arrangement			
32.	Provided there is no bankruptcy order in existence and (so far as is known) no pending petition the court will normally be prepared to make the following order without the attendance of either party: a final order on consideration of the chairman's report. Such an order may be made if the chairman's report has been filed and complies with the rules. The order will record the effect of the chairman's report and discharge the interim order[6]. In other cases the court considers chairman's report of the creditors' meeting.		IR 1986, r 5.27(1)	
	At this stage the chairman will have notified the court of any adjournments of the meeting and reported as to whether the debtor's proposal had been approved or rejected. If the proposal has been approved, the supervisor should have obtained the specific penalty pursuant to regulation 12 (2) of the Insolvency Practitioners Regulations 1990[7].		IR 1986, r 5.24	
33.	Court makes order. **Either** (1) *where proposal approved*			Paras 7.9, 7.10

	Steps to be Taken	Insolvency Act 1986	Insolvency Rules 1986	Cross reference to text
	(i) *Where debtor is not an undischarged bankrupt*, the order will state that the proposal has been approved and make no further order.			
	If there is a pending petition against the debtor and the interim order is still in force at the date of the order, the petition is deemed, unless the court otherwise orders, to have been dismissed. The order will provide for the vacation of the land charges entry; 2 sealed copies of the order will be sent by the court to the debtor. Where there is a pending petition and the interim order has ceased to have effect at the date of the order, it will be necessary to apply in the petition proceedings for the petition to be dismissed and for the vacation of the land charges entry.	IA 1986, s 260(4), (5)	IR 1986, r 6.27	
	(ii) *Where the debtor is an undischarged bankrupt*, the order will recite that the proposal has been approved and may give directions as to the conduct of the bankruptcy and the bankrupt's estate as it thinks appropriate for implementing the proposal.	IA 1986, s 261		
	If 28 days have elapsed since the filing of the chairman's report the order may provide for the annulment of the bankruptcy.	IA 1986, s 261 (2)(a)		
	It will normally be more convenient to adjourn generally with liberty to restore when the proposal has taken effect.			

	Steps to be Taken	Insolvency Act 1986	Insolvency Rules 1986	Cross reference to text
	Note: when s 264 of the Enterprise Act 2002 takes effect an application to annul the bankruptcy order may be made by the official receiver if not made by the bankrupt within the prescribed period	IA 1986, s 261 (2)(b) (as amended by EA 2002)		
	(iii) When the chairman has failed to file his report, the court may be prepared to accept it at the hearing and order that the time for filing be extended; the remainder of the order will be as in (i) and (ii) above. If the report is not ready, the time for filing may be extended and the hearing adjourned to a later date.			
	(iv) Where the supervisor appointed at the creditors' meeting has failed to obtain the specific penalty pursuant to regulation 12 (2) of the Insolvency Practitioners Regulations 1990, (*see step 32 above*), it will be dealt with as in (iii) above.			
	(v) Where there is a pending application by way of appeal (*see step 26 above*) the court may adjourn the hearing to await the result of the application.			
	Or			
	(2) *where proposal not approved*:			
	(i) The order will recite that the proposal has been rejected and make no further order.			
	(ii) If the interim order is still in force, the court may discharge the order.	IA 1986, s 259(2)		

	Steps to be Taken	Insolvency Act 1986	Insolvency Rules 1986	Cross reference to text
	(iii) Where the chairman has failed to file his report, the court may be prepared to accept it at the hearing and order that the time for filing be extended; the remainder of the order will be as in (i) and (ii) above. If the report is not ready, the time for filing may be extended and the hearing adjourned to a later date.			
	(iv) Where there is a pending application by way of appeal (*see step 26 above*), the court may adjourn the hearing to await the result of the application.			
	Proceedings after approval of voluntary arrangement.			
34.	1. The debtor or where he is an undischarged bankrupt, the Official Receiver or the trustee puts the supervisor in possession of the assets included in the arrangement.		IR 1986, r 5.26(1)	Para 10.1
	2. The supervisor pays to the Official Receiver or the trustee monies due in respect of remuneration, fees, costs, charges and expenses, and advances made on behalf of the estate.		IR 1986, r 5.26(2)	
	Alternatively, he may give a written undertaking to pay these items out of the first realisation of assets.		IR 1986, r 5.26(3)	
	3. Supervisor:			Para 10.11
	(a) keeps accounts and records of his acts and dealings, including in particular, records of all receipts and payments of money;		IR 1986, r 5.31(1)	

	Steps to be Taken	Insolvency Act 1986	Insolvency Rules 1986	Cross reference to text
	(b) not less than once in each 12 months prepares an abstract of receipts and payments or a statement of no payments or receipts; sends copies together with his comments on the progress and efficacy of the arrangement to the court, the debtor and the creditors;		IR 1986, r 5.31(2)	
	Time: Not later than 2 months after the end of each 12 month period. The court may on the application of the supervisor, vary the dates for sending the abstract and comments;		IR 1986, r 5.31(3) IR 1986, r 5.31(5)	
	(c) when required by the Secretary of State, must produce for inspection, at the premises of the supervisor or elsewhere, his records, accounts and copies of the abstracts and comments (the records and accounts may be audited by the Secretary of State);		IR 1986, r 5.32	
	(d) may apply to the court for directions in relation to any particular matter arising under the voluntary arrangement.	IA 1986, s 263(4)		
35.	If the debtor, any of his creditors or any other person is dissatisfied with any act, omission or decision of the supervisor, they can apply to the court, who may:— (a) confirm, reverse or modify any act or decision, (b) give directions to the supervisor or (c) make such order as it thinks fit.	IA 1986, s 263(3)		Paras 10.4, 10.5

	Steps to be Taken	Insolvency Act 1986	Insolvency Rules 1986	Cross reference to text
36.	Replacement *or* appointment of additional supervisor.			Para 10.6
	(a) The court may order the appointment of another insolvency practitioner in place of the existing supervisor or to fill a vacancy. The order will only be made where it is expedient to appoint another supervisor and it is not possible for an appointment to be made without the assistance of the court.	IA 1986, s 263(5)		
	(b) When the arrangement only provides for one supervisor, the court may appoint a second supervisor. It is assumed that the court will direct whether acts to be done in connection with the arrangement, may be done by any one of them or must be done by both.	IA 1986, s 263(6)		
	Before making an appointment, the court will need to be satisfied that the person is an insolvency practitioner and has consented to act.			

1 The debtor commits an offence if he makes any false representation or commits any fraud in order to obtain the approval of his creditors to his proposal: Insolvency Act 1986, s 262B.

2 See CPR Practice Direction: Insolvency Proceedings, para 16.1(1), [see Appendix 6].

3 See CPR Practice Direction: Insolvency Proceedings, para 16.1(2), (3), [see Appendix 6].

4 The filing of the nominee's report in court constitutes an insolvency proceeding for the purposes of IR 1986, r 7.27 (court records) and r 7.30 (file of court proceedings), IR 1986, r 5.14(8).

5 Insolvency Act 1986, s 262. Notwithstanding that no application is made the bankruptcy registrar or district judge has an inherent jurisdiction, under subsection (7) of this section to discharge directions for convening a creditor's meeting made under Insolvency Act 1986 s 252, where he can foresee that such a meeting would be pointless: *Re Cove (a debtor)* [1990] 1 All ER 949, sub nom *Re a Debtor (No 83 of 1988)* [1990] 1 WLR 708.

6 See CPR Practice Direction: Insolvency Proceedings, para 16.1(4), [see Appendix 6].

7 Insolvency Practitioners Regulations 1990, SI 1990/439, reg 12(2)(as amended).

9.6 Procedural Table: Partnership Voluntary Arrangements (without moratorium)*

SUMMARY OF TABLE

Members' proposal and statement of affairs (Steps 1 – 6)

Nominee's report to the court (Steps 7 – 9)

Meetings of creditors and members (Steps 10 - 14)

Where voluntary arrangement is approved (Steps 15 – 17)

Appeal to the court (Steps 18 – 30)

Application to reverse or modify act, omission or decision of supervisor (Steps 31 – 35)

Application by supervisor for directions (Steps 36 – 40)

Conversion of voluntary arrangement into winding up (see Table 9.3 Steps 40 – 43)

Action following completion or termination of the arrangement (see Table 9.3 Steps 44 – 45)

* for procedure with moratorium see Table 9.4

	Steps to be Taken	Insolvency Act 1986 As applied and modified by IPO 2002 art 6	Insolvency Rules 1986 As applied and modified by IPO 1994 art 18	Cross-reference to text
1.	The members of the insolvent Partnership (the members) instruct insolvency practitioner (or other person authorised to act as nominee in relation to the voluntary arrangement) to act as nominee and give advice and assistance on preparation of proposal.			Para 4.1 Para 13.6
2.	The members or the Liquidator, Administrator or Article 11 Trustee ('Trustee') prepare proposal for nominee to enable him to report to the Court.	IA 1986, s 2(3)(a)	IR 1986, r 1.2	Para 4.2 Para 4.4, Para 13.5

	Steps to be Taken	Insolvency Act 1986 As applied and modified by IPO 2002 art 6	Insolvency Rules 1986 As applied and modified by IPO 1994 art 18	Cross-reference to text
	The proposal must include:			
	(1) the terms of the proposed arrangement;			
	(2) an explanation of why, in the opinion of the members a voluntary arrangement is desirable and why the creditors may be expected to concur with the arrangement; and		IR 1986, r 1.3(1)	
	(3) a statement dealing with the various matters set out in IR 1986, r 1.3(2):		IR 1986, r 1.3(2)(a)-(q)	
3.	*Where the proposal is made by the members* In the event that the nominee cannot properly prepare his report on the basis of the information in their proposal he may call upon them as members:			Para 4.5
	(1) to provide him with any further information with respect to the Partnership affairs which the nominee thinks necessary for his report; and		IR 1986, r 1.6(1)(a)–(c)	
	(2) to inform him of any person who is or, during the 2 years preceding the giving notice to the nominee of the proposal, has been a member of the Partnership, whether and in what circumstances that person has been concerned in the affairs of any other Partnership which has become insolvent or has himself been adjudged bankrupt or entered into an agreement with his creditors.		IR 1986, r 1.6 (2)(a)(b)	
	Where the proposal is made by an Administrator, Liquidator or Trustee who himself is to be nominee it must also specify such other matters as he considers appropriate to enable members and creditors to reach an informed decision on the proposal.		IR 1986, r 1.10(1)	

	Steps to be Taken	Insolvency Act 1986 As applied and modified by IPO 2002 art 6	Insolvency Rules 1986 As applied and modified by IPO 1994 art 18	Cross-reference to text
	Where the proposal is made by an Administrator, Liquidator or Trustee, where another insolvency practitioner is the nominee, the proposal is prepared in the same manner as for a proposal by the members of the Partnership.		IR 1986, r 1.12(1)–(4)	
4.	Where the proposal is made by the members, they must give the nominee written notice of their proposal. The notice accompanied by a copy of the proposal must be delivered either to the nominee himself or to a person authorised to accept documents on his behalf. Where the Partnership is being wound up by the Court and the Liquidator is to be the nominee, notice must also be given to the Official Receiver.		IR 1986, r 1.4(1) IR 1986 rr 1.4(2), 1.12 (2) IR 1986, r 1.10(2)	Para 4.3
5.	The nominee, if he agrees to act, endorses receipt of notice with date of receipt and returns same to members.		IR 1986, r 1.4(3), (4)	Para 4.3
6.	(1) Where the proposal is made by the members, they must deliver statement of the Partnership's affairs to nominee. *Time*: Within 7 days after delivery of proposal or such longer time as the nominee may allow. The statement must comprise the following particulars: (i) a list of the Partnership assets, divided into appropriate categories with estimated values assigned to each category; (ii) particulars of any secured claim on the Partnership property, including the amount of the claim and how and when the security was created;		IR 1986, r 1.5(1) IR 1986, r 1.5(1) IR 1986, r 1.5(2) IR 1986, r 1.5(2)(a) IR 1986, r 1.5(2)(b)	Para 4.5

	Steps to be Taken	Insolvency Act 1986 As applied and modified by IPO 2002 art 6	Insolvency Rules 1986 As applied and modified by IPO 1994 art 18	Cross-reference to text
	(iii) the names, addresses and amounts of the claims of preferential creditors;		IR 1986, r 1.5(2)(c)	
	(iv) the names, addresses and amounts of the claims of unsecured creditors;		IR 1986, r 1.5(2)(d)	
	(v) particulars of debts owed by or to the Partnership to or by persons connected with it;		IR 1986, r 1.5(2)(e)	
	(vi) the names and addresses of the members of the Partnership; and		IR 1986, r 1.5(2)(f)	
	(vii) such other particulars as the nominee may in writing require to enable him to make his report to the Court.		IR 1986, r 1.5(2)(g)	
	The statement of affairs must be made up to a date not earlier than 2 weeks before the date of the notice to the nominee (*see Step 4 above*) and must be certified as correct by 2 or more partners.		IR 1986, r 1.5(3), (4)	
	(2) Where the proposal is made by the Liquidator, Administrator or Trustee, where another insolvency practitioner is the nominee: they shall provide the nominee with a copy of the Partnership's statement of affairs at the same time as the proposal.		IR 1986, r 1.12(5)	
7.	Where the nominee is not the Administrator, Liquidator or Trustee, the nominee reports to Court as to:			Para 4.7
	whether, in his opinion,	IA 1986, s 2(2)		
	(a) the proposed voluntary arrangement has a reasonable prospect of being approved and implemented,	IA 1986, s 2 (2)(a)(b)(c)		

	Steps to be Taken	Insolvency Act 1986 As applied and modified by IPO 2002 art 6	Insolvency Rules 1986 As applied and modified by IPO 1994 art 18	Cross-reference to text
	(b) meetings should be summoned of the members of the Partnership and of its creditors to consider the proposal; and (c) if so, the date, time and place at which he proposes the meetings should be held			
	Time: Within 28 days, or such longer period as the Court may allow after being given notice of the proposal.	IA 1986, s 2(2)		
	A copy of the proposal and a copy or summary of the Partnership's statement of affairs must be delivered with the report.		IR 1986, r 1.7(1)	
	If the nominee is of opinion that meetings should be summoned, he must also annex his comments on the proposal and if his opinion is otherwise, he must give his reasons.		IR 1986, r 1.7(2)	
	Where the nominee has failed to submit the report, the Court may on the application of the person intending to make the proposal direct that the nominee be replaced as such by another insolvency practitioner qualified to act in relation to the Partnership.	IA 1986, s 2(4)		
8.	Court endorses the date of filing of the report and files it.		IR 1986, r 1.7(3)	Para 4.7
9.	Nominee sends copy of report and his comments to the Partnership.		IR 1986, r 1.7(4)	Para 4.7
10.	Where nominee reports that meetings should be summoned, then, unless the Court otherwise orders, the person making the reports summons meetings for the time, date and place proposed in the report.	IA 1986, s 3(1)		Para 6.3

	Steps to be Taken	Insolvency Act 1986 As applied and modified by IPO 2002 art 6	Insolvency Rules 1986 As applied and modified by IPO 1994 art 18	Cross-reference to text
	The date of the meetings must be not less than 14 nor more than 28 days from the date on which the nominee's report was filed (*see Step 8 above*).		IR 1986, r 1.9(1)	
	At least 14 days notice of the meetings must be given and the notice must state the effect of the Insolvency Rules 1986 Rule 1.19 (1), (3), (4) as to majorities and be accompanied by:		IR 1986, r 1.9(2)	
	(1) a copy of the proposal;		IR 1986, r 1.9(3)(a)	
	(2) a copy of the statement of affairs or, if the nominee thinks fit, a summary of it;		IR 1986, r 1.9(3)(b)	
	(3) the nominee's comments on the proposal; and		IR 1986, r 1.9(3)(c)	
	(4) forms of proxy.		IR 1986, r 1.13(4)	
	The meetings of the members of the Partnership and of the creditors may be held on the same day or on different days. If held on the same day the meetings must be held in the same place. In either case the creditors' meeting must be held in advance of the meeting of the members of the Partnership.			Para 6.3
	If the meetings are not held on the same day they must be held within 7 days of each other.			
	Any person who is or has been an officer or member of the partnership at any time in the immediately preceding two years may be required to attend either the creditors' meeting or the meeting of the members			Para 6.4
11.	Where the nominee is the Administrator, Liquidator or Trustee, he shall summon meetings of the members of the	IA 1986 s 3(2)		Para 5.3 Para 5.4

	Steps to be Taken	Insolvency Act 1986 As applied and modified by IPO 2002 art 6	Insolvency Rules 1986 As applied and modified by IPO 1994 art 18	Cross-reference to text
	Partnership and of the Partnership's creditors to consider the proposal for such a time, date and place as he thinks fit.			
12.	Creditors and members attend respective meetings and decide whether or not to approve the proposal (with or without modifications). *See also table 9.3 step 11 for fuller summary of conduct of meetings* At the creditors' meeting, a majority in excess of three-quarters (in value) of the creditors present in person or by proxy and voting is necessary to pass a resolution approving or modifying the proposal but for any other resolution proposed at the meeting a majority of one-half (in value) is sufficient. Even with a 75% or 50% majority a resolution is invalid if those voting against it include more than 50% in value of the creditors counting only those to whom notice of the meeting was sent, are not left out of account because their claim is secured, and are not connected with the partnership. At the meeting of the members of the Partnership, subject to any express provision made in the Partnership agreement or deed, a majority of more than one-half (in value) of the members present in person or by proxy and voting is necessary to pass any resolution. Value of members is determined by reference to the number of votes conferred on each member by the Partnership agreement or deed.	IA 1986, s 4(1)	IR 1986, r 1.19(1), (2) IR 1986, r 1.20(1)	Paras 6.7 – 6.11

	Steps to be Taken	Insolvency Act 1986 As applied and modified by IPO 2002 art 6	Insolvency Rules 1986 As applied and modified by IPO 1994 art 18	Cross-reference to text
13.	Approval of arrangement	IA 1986, s 4A(2)		Para 6.13
	The arrangement is approved if the decision to approve it has been taken, in accordance with the rules, by both creditors' and partnership meetings, or by the creditors' meeting alone.			
	If the decision taken by the creditors' meeting differs from that taken by the partnership meeting, a member of the partnership may apply to the court.	IA 1986, s 4A(3)		
	Such an application may not be made after the end of the period of 28 days beginning with (1) the day on which the decision was taken by the creditors' meeting or (2) the day, if later, on which the decision was taken by the partnership meeting.	IA 1986, s 4A(6)		
	Where an order is made the member of the partnership who applied for it must serve sealed copies of it on (a) the supervisor and (b) the members.		IR 1986, r 1.22A(2) IR 1986, r 1.22A(3)	
	The officers of the partnership or the supervisor must forthwith after receiving a copy of the court's order give notice of it to all persons who were sent notice of the creditors' or partnership meetings or any person who is affected by the order even if he did not receive notice of the meetings.		IR 1986, r 1.22A(4)	
14.	Chairman of meetings reports results of meetings to the Court and, immediately thereafter, gives notice of result of meetings to persons who were sent notice of meetings.	IA 1986, s 4(6)		Para 6.15

	Steps to be Taken	Insolvency Act 1986 As applied and modified by IPO 2002 art 6	Insolvency Rules 1986 As applied and modified by IPO 1994 art 18	Cross-reference to text
	Time: Within 4 days of the meetings being held.		IR 1986, r 1.24(3)	
	The report must:		IR 1986, r 1.24(2)	
	(1) state whether the proposal was approved or rejected and, if approved, with what, if any, modifications;		IR 1986, r 1.24(2)(a)	
	(2) set out the resolutions taken at each meeting and the decision on each;		IR 1986, r 1.24(2)(b)	
	(3) list the creditors and members (with their respective values) present or represented at the meetings and how they voted on each resolution; and		IR 1986, r 1.24(2)(c)	
	(4) include, such further information (if any) which the chairman thinks it appropriate to make known to the Court.		IR 1986, r 1.24(2)(d)	
	Where the voluntary arrangement is approved at the meetings:			
15.	Supervisor sends copy of Chairman's report to Registrar of Companies. *Time*: Forthwith.		IR 1986, r 1.24(5)	Para 6.15
16.	The members or, if the Partnership is in liquidation or is subject to an administration order or where a joint bankruptcy order[1] has been made and a person other than the Liquidator, the Administrator or the Trustee (as the case may be) is appointed to act as supervisor of the voluntary arrangement, the Liquidator, the Administrator or the Trustee does all that is required for putting the supervisor into possession of the assets included in the arrangement. *Time*: Forthwith.		IR 1986, r 1.23(1) IR 1986, r 1.23(1)	Para 10.1 Para 13.5

	Steps to be Taken	Insolvency Act 1986 As applied and modified by IPO 2002 art 6	Insolvency Rules 1986 As applied and modified by IPO 1994 art 18	Cross-reference to text
17.	Supervisor proceeds to put the voluntary arrangement into effect.			Paras 10.1 – 10.3
	If the Partnership is being wound up or an administration order or a joint bankruptcy order is in force the Court may, at any time after the period of 28 days beginning with the first day on which the Chairman's report (*see Step 14 above*) has been made, stay all proceedings in the winding up or under the joint bankruptcy order or discharge the administration order or, give such directions with respect to the conduct of the winding up or the administration or of the proceedings under the joint bankruptcy order as it thinks appropriate for facilitating the implementation of the approved voluntary arrangement. It may not, however, make such an order if an application challenging the decision taken at the meetings, is pending or is subject of an appeal.	IA 1986, s 5(3) IA 1986, s 5(4)		
	Application to the Court to challenge a decision taken at meetings of creditors and members of the Partnership to consider a proposal for a voluntary arrangement.	IA 1986, s 6		
18.	Applicant issues originating application to reverse a decision taken at meetings.		IR 1986, r 7.2(1), r 7.4 (1)	
	Time: Within 28 days after the filing of the Chairman's report as to the result of the meetings.	IA 1986, s 6(3)		Para 7.9
	The Applicant may be:			
	(i) a person entitled to vote at either of the meetings;	IA 1986, s 6(2)(a)		
	(ii) the nominee or any person who has replaced him as such; or	IA 1986, s 6(2)(b)		

	Steps to be Taken	Insolvency Act 1986 As applied and modified by IPO 2002 art 6	Insolvency Rules 1986 As applied and modified by IPO 1994 art 18	Cross-reference to text
	(iii) if the Partnership is being wound up, is the subject of an administration order or a joint bankruptcy order the Liquidator, the Administrator or the Trustee as appropriate. The grounds of the application will be that the voluntary arrangement unfairly prejudices the interests of a creditor or member of the Partnership and or that there has been some material irregularity at or in relation to either of the meetings. If the Applicant is the Liquidator, the Administrator or the Trustee the application will be without notice (*see Step 22 below*). If the Applicant is the nominee the application will be without notice unless the Partnership is in liquidation, is the subject of an administration order or a joint bankruptcy order when the Liquidator, the Administrator or Trustee will be the Respondent. If the Applicant is a person entitled to vote the nominee will be the Respondent.	IA 1986, s 6(2)(c) IA 1986, s 6(1)(a) (b)		
19.	Applicant serves sealed copy of the application upon Respondent (if any).		IR 1986, r 7(4)	Para 7.10
20.	Applicant files affidavit or witness statement in support and serves copy on any Respondent. *Time*: Not less than 14 days before the hearing.		IR 1986, r 7.7(1), r 7.8 (1)(a) IR 1986, r 7.8(1)(a)	
21.	Respondent files affidavit or witness statement in reply and serves copy on Applicant. *Time*: Not less than 7 days before the hearing.		IR 1986, r 7.8(1)(b) IR 1986, r 7.8(1)(b)	

	Steps to be Taken	Insolvency Act 1986 As applied and modified by IPO 2002 art 6	Insolvency Rules 1986 As applied and modified by IPO 1994 art 18	Cross-reference to text
22.	Parties attend hearing of application in Chambers before Bankruptcy Registrar or District Judge.			
	The Bankruptcy Registrar or District Judge may give such directions as he thinks fit including directing who should be the Respondent to the application and adjourn the matter to be heard by the Judge in Court.		IR 1986, r 7.10(1), (2)	
23.	The Applicant lodges in the Registrar's office or with the Court. (1) copy application; and (2) original exhibits for use of Judge.			
24.	Parties attend adjourned hearing of application in Court.			
	If the Court is satisfied as to either of the grounds of the application to challenge the decision of the meetings (*see Step 18 above*) it may:			Para 7.9
	(1) revoke or suspend the approvals given by the meetings or any approval given at a meeting at which there was some material irregularity and; or	IA 1986, s 6(4)(a)		
	(2) direct the summoning of further meetings to consider any revised proposal or a further meeting in place of that at which there was an irregularity to reconsider the original proposal.	IA 1986, s 6(4)(b)		
	If at any time after directing further meetings to consider a revised proposal the Court is satisfied that no revised proposal is to be submitted, it must revoke the direction and	IA 1986, s 6(5)		

	Steps to be Taken	Insolvency Act 1986 As applied and modified by IPO 2002 art 6	Insolvency Rules 1986 As applied and modified by IPO 1994 art 18	Cross-reference to text
	revoke or suspend any approval given at the previous meetings.			
25.	Where required, the Parties attend the Court Associate to lodge Counsels' briefs properly endorsed.			
26.	Court draws up order and sends copies when perfected to Applicant.			
27.	Applicant serves sealed copies of the order on: (1) the supervisor of the voluntary arrangement; and (2) on the members of the Partnership or the Administrator, the Liquidator or Trustee (depending upon who made the proposal for a voluntary arrangement). If the order contains a direction for further meetings notice must also be given by the Applicant to whoever is required by the order to summon the meetings.		IR 1986, r 1.25(2) IR 1986, r 1.25(2)(a) IR 1986, r 1.25(2)(b) IR 1986, r 1.25(3)	
28.	Members or Liquidator, Administrator or Trustee (as the case may be) give notice of the order to all persons who were given notice of the meetings and to any other persons who appear to be affected by the order. *Time*: Forthwith after receiving the copy of the order.		IR 1986, r 1.25(4)(a) IR 1986, r 1.25(4)(a)	
29.	Members or Liquidator, Administrator or Trustee (as the case may be) give notice to Court whether it is intended to make a revised proposal or to invite re-consideration of the original proposal.		IR 1986, r 1.25(4)(b)	

	Steps to be Taken	Insolvency Act 1986 As applied and modified by IPO 2002 art 6	Insolvency Rules 1986 As applied and modified by IPO 1994 art 18	Cross-reference to text
	Time: Within 7 days after receiving the copy of the order (or such longer period as the Court may allow).		IR 1986, r 1.25(4)(b)	
30.	Applicant delivers copy order to Registrar of Companies. *Time*: Within 7 days after the making of the order.		IR 1986, r 1.25(5) IR 1986, r 1.25(5)	
	Application to reverse or modify an act, omission or decision of a supervisor of a voluntary arrangement	IA 1986, s 7(3)		
31.	Applicant issues ordinary (or originating) application to reverse supervisor's decision. The Applicant may be a creditor or any other person dissatisfied by an act, omission or decision of the supervisor. The supervisor will be the Respondent to the application.	IA 1986, s 7(3)	IR 1986, r 7.2(1), r 7.4(1)	Paras 10.4, 10.5
32.	Applicant serves sealed copy of application upon supervisor.		IR 1986, r 7.4(3)	
33.	Applicant files affidavit or witness statement supporting application and serves copy on supervisor.		IR 1986, r 7.7(1), r 7.8(1)(a)	
34.	Follow Steps 21–24 above. The Court may: (1) confirm reverse or modify any act or decision of the supervisor; (2) give directions to the supervisor; or (3) make such other order as it thinks fit.	IA 1986, s 7(3)(a) IA 1986, s 7(3)(b) IA 1986, s 7(3)(c)		

	Steps to be Taken	Insolvency Act 1986 As applied and modified by IPO 2002 art 6	Insolvency Rules 1986 As applied and modified by IPO 1994 art 18	Cross-reference to text
35.	Court draws up order and sends copies when perfected to the Applicant.			
	Application for directions: the supervisor may apply to the Court for directions in relation to any matter arising under the voluntary arrangement	IA 1986, s 7(4)(a)		
36.	Applicant issues ordinary application. Unless there is an obvious Respondent the application must be made without notice (*see Step 22 above*).		IR 1986, r 7.2(1), r 7.4 (1)	Para 10.2
37.	Applicant serves sealed copy of application, on Respondent if any.		IR 1986, r 7.4(3)	
38.	Applicant files affidavit or witness statement supporting application, and serves copy on Respondent if any.		IR 1986, r 7.7(1), r 7.8 (1)(a)	
39.	Follow Steps 21–25 above.			
40.	Court draws up order and sends copy when perfected to the Applicant.			

1 Insolvent Partnerships Order 1994, art 11.

Appendix 10

Enterprise Act 2002

* * * *

251 Abolition of Crown preference

(1) The following paragraphs of Schedule 6 to the Insolvency Act 1986 (categories of preferential debts) shall cease to have effect—

(a) paragraphs 1 and 2 (debts due to Inland Revenue),
(b) paragraphs 3 to 5C (debts due to Customs and Excise), and
(c) paragraphs 6 and 7 (social security contributions).

(2) The following paragraphs of Schedule 3 to the Bankruptcy (Scotland) Act 1985 (c 66) (list of preferred debts) shall cease to have effect—

(a) paragraph 1 (debts due to Inland Revenue),
(b) paragraph 2 (debts due to Customs and Excise), and
(c) paragraph 3 (social security contributions).

(3) In section 386 of the Insolvency Act 1986 (categories of preferential debts) for the parenthetical words after "Schedule 6 to this Act" there shall be substituted "(contributions to occupational pension schemes; remuneration, &c. of employees; levies on coal and steel production)".

252 Unsecured creditors

The following shall be inserted after section 176 of the Insolvency Act 1986 (winding up: preferential debt)—

"Property subject to floating charge

176A Share of assets for unsecured creditors

(1) This section applies where a floating charge relates to property of a company—

(a) which has gone into liquidation,
(b) which is in administration,
(c) of which there is a provisional liquidator, or
(d) of which there is a receiver.

(2) The liquidator, administrator or receiver—

(a) shall make a prescribed part of the company's net property available for the satisfaction of unsecured debts, and

(b) shall not distribute that part to the proprietor of a floating charge except in so far as it exceeds the amount required for the satisfaction of unsecured debts.

(3) Subsection (2) shall not apply to a company if—
(a) the company's net property is less than the prescribed minimum, and
(b) the liquidator, administrator or receiver thinks that the cost of making a distribution to unsecured creditors would be disproportionate to the benefits.

(4) Subsection (2) shall also not apply to a company if or in so far as it is disapplied by—
(a) a voluntary arrangement in respect of the company, or
(b) a compromise or arrangement agreed under section 425 of the Companies Act (compromise with creditors and members).

(5) Subsection (2) shall also not apply to a company if—
(a) the liquidator, administrator or receiver applies to the court for an order under this subsection on the ground that the cost of making a distribution to unsecured creditors would be disproportionate to the benefits, and
(b) the court orders that subsection (2) shall not apply.

(6) In subsections (2) and (3) a company's net property is the amount of its property which would, but for this section, be available for satisfaction of claims of holders of debentures secured by, or holders of, any floating charge created by the company.

(7) An order under subsection (2) prescribing part of a company's net property may, in particular, provide for its calculation—
(a) as a percentage of the company's net property, or
(b) as an aggregate of different percentages of different parts of the company's net property.

(8) An order under this section—
(a) must be made by statutory instrument, and
(b) shall be subject to annulment pursuant to a resolution of either House of Parliament.

(9) In this section—

"floating charge" means a charge which is a floating charge on its creation and which is created after the first order under subsection (2)(a) comes into force, and

"prescribed" means prescribed by order by the Secretary of State.

(10) An order under this section may include transitional or incidental provision."

* * * *

254 Application of insolvency law to foreign company

(1) The Secretary of State may by order provide for a provision of the Insolvency Act 1986 to apply (with or without modification) in relation to a company incorporated outside Great Britain.

(2) An order under this section—
(a) may make provision generally or for a specified purpose only,
(b) may make different provision for different purposes, and

(c) may make transitional, consequential or incidental provision.

(3) An order under this section—
(a) must be made by statutory instrument, and
(b) shall be subject to annulment in pursuance of a resolution of either House of Parliament.

255 Application of law about company arrangement or administration to non-company

(1) The Treasury may with the concurrence of the Secretary of State by order provide for a company arrangement or administration provision to apply (with or without modification) in relation to—
(a) a society registered under the Industrial and Provident Societies Act 1965 (c 12),
(b) a society registered under section 7(1)(b), (c), (d), (e) or (f) of the Friendly Societies Act 1974 (c 46),
(c) a friendly society within the meaning of the Friendly Societies Act 1992 (c 40), or
(d) an unregistered friendly society.

(2) In subsection (1) "company arrangement or administration provision" means—
(a) a provision of Part I of the Insolvency Act 1986 (company voluntary arrangements),
(b) a provision of Part II of that Act (administration), and
(c) section 425 of the Companies Act 1985 (c 6) (compromise or arrangement with creditors).

(3) An order under this section may not provide for a company arrangement or administration provision to apply in relation to a society which is registered as a social landlord under Part I of the Housing Act 1996 (c 52) or under Part 3 of the Housing (Scotland) Act 2001 (asp 10).

(4) An order under this section—
(a) may make provision generally or for a specified purpose only,
(b) may make different provision for different purposes, and
(c) may make transitional, consequential or incidental provision.

(5) Provision by virtue of subsection (4)(c) may, in particular—
(a) apply an enactment (with or without modification);
(b) amend an enactment.

(6) An order under this section—
(a) must be made by statutory instrument, and
(b) shall be subject to annulment in pursuance of a resolution of either House of Parliament.

* * * *

264 Individual voluntary arrangement

(1) Schedule 22 (which makes provision about individual voluntary arrangements) shall have effect.

(2) The Secretary of State may by order amend the Insolvency Act 1986 so as to extend the provisions of sections 263B to 263G (which are inserted by Schedule 22 and provide a fast-track procedure for making an individual voluntary

arrangement) to some or all cases other than those specified in section 263A as inserted by Schedule 22.

(3) An order under subsection (2)—

(a) must be made by statutory instrument, and

(b) may not be made unless a draft has been laid before and approved by each House of Parliament.

(4) An order under subsection (2) may make—

(a) consequential provision (which may include provision amending the Insolvency Act 1986 or another enactment);

(b) transitional provision.

265 Disqualification from office: justice of the peace

Section 65 of the Justices of the Peace Act 1997 (c 25) (disqualification of bankrupt from appointment as justice of the peace) shall cease to have effect.

* * * *

271 Insolvency Services Account: interest

(1) The following shall be inserted after paragraph 16 of Schedule 8 to the Insolvency Act 1986 (company insolvency rules: money)—

"16A

Provision enabling the Secretary of State to set the rate of interest paid on sums which have been paid into the Insolvency Services Account."

(2) The following shall be inserted after paragraph 21 of Schedule 9 to the Insolvency Act 1986 (individual insolvency rules: money)—

"21A

Provision enabling the Secretary of State to set the rate of interest paid on sums which have been paid into the Insolvency Services Account."

272 Insolvency Services Accounts

(1) Section 405 of the Insolvency Act 1986 (operation of Investment Account) shall cease to have effect.

(2) The following shall be substituted for section 408 of that Act (recourse to Consolidated Fund)—

"408 Adjustment of balances

(1) The Treasury may direct the payment out of the Consolidated Fund of sums into—

(a) the Insolvency Services Account;

(b) the Investment Account.

(2) The Treasury shall certify to the House of Commons the reason for any payment under subsection (1).

(3) The Secretary of State may pay sums out of the Insolvency Services Account into the Consolidated Fund.

(4) The National Debt Commissioners may pay sums out of the Investment Account into the Consolidated Fund."

* * * *

SCHEDULE 22

INDIVIDUAL VOLUNTARY ARRANGEMENT

Section 264

Annulment of bankruptcy on making of voluntary arrangement

1

The following shall be substituted for section 261 of the Insolvency Act 1986 (effect of voluntary arrangement: undischarged bankrupt)—

"261 Additional effect on undischarged bankrupt

(1) This section applies where—
- (a) the creditors' meeting summoned under section 257 approves the proposed voluntary arrangement (with or without modifications), and
- (b) the debtor is an undischarged bankrupt.

(2) Where this section applies the court shall annul the bankruptcy order on an application made—
- (a) by the bankrupt, or
- (b) where the bankrupt has not made an application within the prescribed period, by the official receiver.

(3) An application under subsection (2) may not be made—
- (a) during the period specified in section 262(3)(a) during which the decision of the creditors' meeting can be challenged by application under section 262,
- (b) while an application under that section is pending, or
- (c) while an appeal in respect of an application under that section is pending or may be brought.

(4) Where this section applies the court may give such directions about the conduct of the bankruptcy and the administration of the bankrupt's estate as it thinks appropriate for facilitating the implementation of the approved voluntary arrangement."

Fast-track for making voluntary arrangement

2

The following shall be inserted after section 263 of that Act (implementation of voluntary arrangement)—

"Fast-track voluntary arrangement

263A Availability

Section 263B applies where an individual debtor intends to make a proposal to his creditors for a voluntary arrangement and—

(a) the debtor is an undischarged bankrupt,

(b) the official receiver is specified in the proposal as the nominee in relation to the voluntary arrangement, and

(c) no interim order is applied for under section 253.

263B Decision

(1) The debtor may submit to the official receiver—

(a) a document setting out the terms of the voluntary arrangement which the debtor is proposing, and

(b) a statement of his affairs containing such particulars as may be prescribed of his creditors, debts, other liabilities and assets and such other information as may be prescribed.

(2) If the official receiver thinks that the voluntary arrangement proposed has a reasonable prospect of being approved and implemented, he may make arrangements for inviting creditors to decide whether to approve it.

(3) For the purposes of subsection (2) a person is a "creditor" only if—

(a) he is a creditor of the debtor in respect of a bankruptcy debt, and

(b) the official receiver is aware of his claim and his address.

(4) Arrangements made under subsection (2)—

(a) must include the provision to each creditor of a copy of the proposed voluntary arrangement,

(b) must include the provision to each creditor of information about the criteria by reference to which the official receiver will determine whether the creditors approve or reject the proposed voluntary arrangement, and

(c) may not include an opportunity for modifications to the proposed voluntary arrangement to be suggested or made.

(5) Where a debtor submits documents to the official receiver under subsection (1) no application under section 253 for an interim order may be made in respect of the debtor until the official receiver has—

(a) made arrangements as described in subsection (2), or

(b) informed the debtor that he does not intend to make arrangements (whether because he does not think the voluntary arrangement has a reasonable prospect of being approved and implemented or because he declines to act).

263C Result

As soon as is reasonably practicable after the implementation of arrangements under section 263B(2) the official receiver shall report to the court whether the proposed voluntary arrangement has been approved or rejected.

263D Approval of voluntary arrangement

(1) This section applies where the official receiver reports to the court under section 263C that a proposed voluntary arrangement has been approved.

(2) The voluntary arrangement—
  (a) takes effect,
  (b) binds the debtor, and
  (c) binds every person who was entitled to participate in the arrangements made under section 263B(2).

(3) The court shall annul the bankruptcy order in respect of the debtor on an application made by the official receiver.

(4) An application under subsection (3) may not be made—
  (a) during the period specified in section 263F(3) during which the voluntary arrangement can be challenged by application under section 263F(2),
  (b) while an application under that section is pending, or
  (c) while an appeal in respect of an application under that section is pending or may be brought.

(5) The court may give such directions about the conduct of the bankruptcy and the administration of the bankrupt's estate as it thinks appropriate for facilitating the implementation of the approved voluntary arrangement.

(6) The Deeds of Arrangement Act 1914 (c 47) does not apply to the voluntary arrangement.

(7) A reference in this Act or another enactment to a voluntary arrangement approved under this Part includes a reference to a voluntary arrangement which has effect by virtue of this section.

263E Implementation

Section 263 shall apply to a voluntary arrangement which has effect by virtue of section 263D(2) as it applies to a voluntary arrangement approved by a creditors' meeting.

263F Revocation

(1) The court may make an order revoking a voluntary arrangement which has effect by virtue of section 263D(2) on the ground—
  (a) that it unfairly prejudices the interests of a creditor of the debtor, or
  (b) that a material irregularity occurred in relation to the arrangements made under section 263B(2).

(2) An order under subsection (1) may be made only on the application of—
  (a) the debtor,
  (b) a person who was entitled to participate in the arrangements made under section 263B(2),
  (c) the trustee of the bankrupt's estate, or
  (d) the official receiver.

(3) An application under subsection (2) may not be made after the end of the period of 28 days beginning with the date on which the official receiver makes his report to the court under section 263C.

(4) But a creditor who was not made aware of the arrangements under section 263B(2) at the time when they were made may make an application under subsection (2) during the period of 28 days beginning with the date on which he becomes aware of the voluntary arrangement.

263G Offences

(1) Section 262A shall have effect in relation to obtaining approval to a proposal for a voluntary arrangement under section 263D.

(2) Section 262B shall have effect in relation to a voluntary arrangement which has effect by virtue of section 263D(2) (for which purposes the words "by a creditors' meeting summoned under section 257" shall be disregarded)."

Role of official receiver

3

The following shall be inserted after section 389A of that Act (authorisation of nominees and supervisors)—

"389B Official receiver as nominee or supervisor

(1) The official receiver is authorised to act as nominee or supervisor in relation to a voluntary arrangement approved under Part VIII provided that the debtor is an undischarged bankrupt when the arrangement is proposed.

(2) The Secretary of State may by order repeal the proviso in subsection (1).

(3) An order under subsection (2)—
- (a) must be made by statutory instrument, and
- (b) shall be subject to annulment in pursuance of a resolution of either House of Parliament."

Index